EDWARD B. EASTWICK

THE
ANVÁR-I SUHAILÍ
OR
THE LIGHTS OF CANOPUS

Elibron Classics
www.elibron.com

Elibron Classics series.

© 2005 Adamant Media Corporation.

ISBN 1-4021-8619-3 (paperback)
ISBN 1-4212-9086-3 (hardcover)

This Elibron Classics Replica Edition is an unabridged facsimile
of the edition published in 1854 by Stephen Austin, Hertford.

ANVÁR-I SUHAILÍ;

or,

THE LIGHTS OF CANOPUS.

THE

ANVÁR-I SUHAILÍ;

OR,

THE LIGHTS OF CANOPUS;

BEING THE PERSIAN VERSION OF

THE FABLES OF PILPAY;

OR,

THE BOOK "KALÍLAH AND DAMNAH,"

RENDERED INTO PERSIAN BY HUSAIN VÁ'IZ U'L-KÁSHIFÍ:

LITERALLY TRANSLATED INTO PROSE AND VERSE,

BY

EDWARD B. EASTWICK, F.R.S., F.S.A., M.R.A.S.,

MEMBER OF THE ASIATIC SOCIETIES OF PARIS AND BOMBAY; HONORARY MEMBER OF THE MADRAS
LITERARY SOCIETY; ETC.; PROFESSOR OF ORIENTAL LANGUAGES, AND LIBRARIAN IN THE EAST-
INDIA COLLEGE, HAILEYBURY; AND TRANSLATOR OF THE "GULISTÁN" "BÁGH O BAHÁR," ETC.

Just as thou hearest now from Pahlaví,
' Kalílah ' donned the Arab garb we see:
Till Nasar's time, unchanged, it thus survived;
But when great Nasar in the world arrived,
Wise Abú'l Fazal, vazír of the State—
Storehouse of wit and peerless in debate—
Bade it appear clothed in the Persian tongue:
He gave the word, and lo! the task was done.
And thus transcribed, new wisdom breathed in it,
Its guiding precepts shone with added wit,
And its great Patron thus bequeathed to fame—
To sight and soul—the impress of his Name.
To Rúdakí the praises all belong;
The blind bard heard and clothed the tales in song;
'Twas he that ranged the words at random flung,
Pierced the fair pearls and them together strung.   FIRDAUSÍ.

HERTFORD:

PRINTED AND PUBLISHED BY STEPHEN AUSTIN,
BOOKSELLER TO THE EAST-INDIA COLLEGE.
—
M.DCCC.LIV.

HER MOST GRACIOUS MAJESTY,

QUEEN VICTORIA.

MADAM,

It is recorded that Núshírván, the most powerful monarch of his age, sent a high officer of state to procure a translation of the original of this work. It is further stated that when, after years of toil and difficulty, the translation was obtained, it was deposited in the cabinet of the king's most precious treasures, and was regarded as a model of wisdom and didactic philosophy.

The light of knowledge is now, however, so universally diffused, that, but for your Majesty's gracious condescension, the translation of the same book into English would be a work of too little merit or importance to deserve notice.

In one point of view, however, the gracious permission to dedicate this translation to your Majesty, may be regarded as likely to have important results, as it may lead other and more worthy laborers to open up to the English public a Literature, which delights and guides the immense population of your Majesty's Empire in the East, and which still remains to a great extent unknown and unexplored in Europe.

Every fresh proof, indeed, of the interest which your Majesty takes in matters relating to India, will undoubtedly be received by the inhabitants of that vast country with grateful feelings; and that such feelings may long be perpetuated and augmented, is the prayer of,

MADAM,

Your Majesty's most loyal and devoted

Servant and subject,

EDWARD B. EASTWICK.

PREFACE

TO THE PRESENT ENGLISH TRANSLATION.

In the year 1820, Major Stewart, Professor of Persian at the East India College, Haileybury, published a translation of the Seventh book of the 'Anvár-i Suhailí,' and dedicated it to the Junior Civil and Military Servants of the Hon. East India Company. In 1835, a literal translation of the First book of the same work was published by the Rev. H. G. Keene, Arabic and Persian Professor at Haileybury, and dedicated to the Students of the College. In a memorandum inserted by Mr. James Ross at the beginning of his translation of the 'Gulistán,' that gentleman announced his intention of publishing a translation of the first two books of the 'Anvár-i Suhailí,' in 1826: but this version never made its appearance, in consequence of the death of the translator, by which melancholy event the public were deprived of several other proposed additions to our knowledge of Persian Literature. Enough however, has been already said to prove that a Translation of the 'Anvár-i Suhailí,' has long been considered desirable by competent judges. The high encomiums, too, which have been passed upon the Work in all countries, and by the scholars of all nations; especially by those illustrious Orientalists, Sir William Jones and Baron Silvestre de Sacy, furnish another justification of this attempt to make it known to English readers. The opinion of the former of these distinguished men as to the merits of the work is couched in the following terms, 'The most excellent book in the language is, in my opinion, the collection of tales and fables called 'Anvár-i Suhailí,' by Ḥusain Vá'iz, surnamed Káshifí, who took the celebrated work of Bidpai or Pilpay for his text, and has comprised all the wisdom of the Eastern

nations, in fourteen beautiful chapters.' [1] In another place he says, [2] 'The
fables of Vishnu Sharman, whom we ridiculously call Pilpay, are the most
beautiful, if not the most ancient, apologues in the world : they were first
translated from the Sanskrit, in the sixth century, by order of Buzurjmihr,
or 'Bright as the Sun,' the chief physician, and afterwards the vazír [3] of the
great Núshírwán, and are extant under various names in more than
twenty languages.'   Baron DE SACY remarks, 'Hosaïn Vaïz s'est proposé
comme on le voit, de rendre la lecture du livre de Calila plus agréable
à tout le monde, en la rendant plus facile. Il ne s'est pas contenté de
supprimer ou de changer tout ce qui pouvoit arrêter un grand nombre
de lecteurs, il a encore ajouté au mérite primitif de l'ouvrage, en y insérant
un grand nombre de vers empruntés de divers poëtes, et en employant
constamment ce style mesuré et cadencé, ce parallélisme des idées et des
expressions, qui, joint à la rime, constitue la prose poétique des orientaux,
et qui, ajoutant un charme inexprimable aux pensées justes et solides,
diminue beaucoup ce que les idées—plus ingénieuses que vraies, les métaphors
outrées, les hyperboles extravagantes, trop fréquentes dans les écrits des
Persans—ont de rebutant et de ridicules pour le goût sévère et délicat des
Européens. Quoique le style de Hosaïn ne soit pas exempt de ces défauts,
on lit et on relit, avec un plaisir toujours nouveau, son ouvrage, comme le
Gulistan de Saadi.' [4]

The 'Anvár-i Suhailí' is the work which candidates for interpreterships
in India are required to read after the 'Gulistán.' The vast abundance
of words, and the great variety of style, reaching from that of ordinary
dialogue to the highest flights of poetry, render it incontestably the best
book in the language to be studied by one who desires to make rapid progress
in Persian. At the same time, however, as Major STEWART has very justly
remarked, 'It must be acknowledged that it is too difficult for the generality
of students without the assistance of a munshí or teacher;' and as good

---

[1] Preface to the 'Persian Grammar,' p. xvi., l. 11.

[2] Third Anniversary Discourse to the Royal Asiatic Society, February 2, 1786 : Works,
vol. i., p. 32.

[3] M. de Sacy shows this to be a mistake.

[4] Mémoire Historique, Calila et Dimna, p. 43, l. 23.

Persian munshís are not very easily procurable in India—in fact, in many provinces are altogether wanting—it is hoped that this Translation and the Notes appended to it will prove of service to those who desire to qualify themselves for examination in our Indian territories. To them the present Translation is offered with far more confidence than to the English public, for it is impossible not to perceive that those very characteristics of style, which form its chiefest beauties in the eye of Persian taste, will appear to the European reader as ridiculous blemishes. The undeviating equipoise of bi-propositional sentences, and oftentimes their length and intricacy; the hyperbole and sameness of metaphor, and the rudeness and unskilfulness of the plots of some of the stories, cannot but be wearisome and repulsive to the better and simpler judgment of the West. Kings always sit on thrones stable as the firmament, rub the stars with their heads, have all other kings to serve them, and are most just, wise, valiant, and beneficent. Ministers are invariably gifted with intellects which adorn the whole world, and are so sagacious that they can unravel all difficulties with a single thought. Mountains constantly race with the sun in height, all gardens are the envy of Paradise, and every constellation in Heaven is scared away in turn by some furious tiger or lion upon earth. These absurdities are so prominent that they would probably induce the generality of readers to close the book in disgust. Those, however, who have patience enough to proceed with the perusal will not fail to discover many beautiful thoughts, many striking and original ideas forcibly expressed; and though their first beauty cannot but have suffered very considerably in translation, still enough will remain to justify, in some degree, to all candid judges, the celebrity of the work.

It may be here desirable to direct attention to those parts of the Book which are generally considered the best. The whole work consists of an elaborate Preface and Introduction by Ḥusain Vá'iẓ, and of Fourteen Chapters or Books with a very brief Conclusion. The Preface may be dismissed from consideration at once, as being a turgid specimen of the obscure and repulsive preludes with which Persian writers think fit to commence their compositions. A few helpless infantine ideas struggle in the gigantic coils of an endless prolixity and verboseness, which it would require a Hercules to disentangle. Nevertheless, this Preface may be read by those who wish for a model of such compositions in Persian. The arrangement is the same in all. There is, first, an address to the One God; secondly, a lengthy eulogy of his Prophet, Muḥammad; thirdly, a panegyric on the High Personage to whom the work is dedicated, with a meagre explanation of the reasons which induced the Author to commence his undertaking. The whole is thickly larded with quotations from the Ḳur'án, and with difficult and unusual words; so that it would really seem as if a preface were intended, like a thorny hedge, to repel all intruders, and to preserve the fruit within from the prying eyes of readers.

In the Introduction, Ḥusain Vá'iẓ is at once simpler and more agreeable. The description of the Bees and their habits, is prettily given. The story of the Pigeon, who left his quiet home to travel; and of the old woman's Cat, who was discontented with his meagre fare and safe seclusion, are among the happiest in the whole work.

The First Two books form rather more than a fourth of the entire composition. The plot of them is borrowed from the First Chapter of the 'Pancha-tantra,' and of the 'Hitopadesha,' to which, indeed, the Second book of the 'Anvár-i Suhailí' is a very proper sequel. The First story of the First book of the 'Anvár-i Suhailí,'—that of 'the Merchant and his Sons,'—corresponds to the opening of the Second book of the 'Hitopadesha,' and of the First Chapter of the 'Pancha-tantra:' the Fifth story of the same, 'the Ape and the Wedge,' to the Second fable in both Sanskrit works; the Seventh story of the Persian, 'the Jackal and the Drum,' is the same as the Second in the 'Pancha-tantra,' but is not found in the 'Hitopadesha;' the Eighth Persian story, 'the Recluse who was plundered by a Pretended Disciple,' answers to the Fourth of the First book of the 'Pancha-tantra,' and to part of the Sixth fable of the Second book of the 'Hitopadesha;' the Eleventh Persian story, 'the Raven and the Snake,' agrees with the Eighth of the Second book of the 'Hitopadesha,' and the Sixth of the First book of the 'Pancha-tantra;'

the Twelfth Persian story, 'the Heron and the Crab,' corresponds to the Seventh of the First book of the 'Pancha-tantra,' and the Seventh of the Fourth book of the 'Hitopadesha;' the Fourteenth Persian story, 'the Lion and the Hare,' answers to the Ninth fable of the Second book of the 'Hitopadesha,' and the Eighth of the First book of the 'Pancha-tantra,'; the Fifteenth Persian story, that of 'the Three Fishes,' corresponds to the Third fable of the Fourth book of the 'Hitopadesha,' and the Fourteenth of the First book of the 'Pancha-tantra;' the Nineteenth Persian story, which has been extracted by Sir W. Jones into his 'Persian Grammar,' is exceedingly beautiful, and we owe it entirely to Persian taste, as no traces are found of it in Sanskrit; the Twenty-first Persian story, that of 'the Crow, the Wolf, the Jackal, and the Camel,' corresponds with the Eleventh fable of the Fourth book of the 'Hitopadesha,' and with the Eleventh of the First book of the 'Pancha-tantra;' the Twenty-second Persian story, that of 'the Ṭiṭawa and the Ocean,' is the Tenth of the Second book of the 'Hitopadesha,' and the Twelfth of the First book of the 'Pancha-tantra;' the Twenty-third Persian story, that of 'the Two Geese and the Tortoise,' is the Second of the Fourth book of the 'Hitopadesha,' and the Thirteenth of the First book of the 'Pancha-tantra;' the Twenty-fourth Persian story, that of the 'Monkeys and the Bird that gave them advice,' is the Second of the Third book of the 'Hitopadesha,' and the Eighteenth of the First book of the 'Pancha-tantra;" the Twenty-Fifth Persian story, that of 'Sharp-wit and Light-heart,' is the Nineteenth of the First book of the 'Pancha-tantra,' but is not found in the 'Hitopadesha;' the Twenty-eighth Persian story, is the Twenty-first of the First book of the 'Pancha-tantra.'

In the Second book, the story of Kalílah and Damnah is continued, but as this continuation is not found in the Sanskrit, so also none of the Persian stories it contains are to be found in that language. The apologue is for the most part laid aside, the First and Second stories being the only instances of it. On the whole it is not inferior to the First book.

The Third book is borrowed from the First of the 'Hitopadesha' and the Second of the 'Pancha-tantra.' The First Persian story corresponds to the opening of the above mentioned Sanskrit books, and contains also the Fifth of the First book of the 'Hitopadesha.' The Fourth Persian story, 'of the Woman who wished to barter husked Sesamum for unhusked,' is the Second of the Second book of the 'Pancha-tantra'; the Fifth Persian story, that of 'the Wolf and the Bowstring,' is the Seventh of the First book of the 'Hitopadesha,' and the Third of the Second book of the 'Pancha-tantra.'

The Fourth book is the Third and Fourth of the 'Hitopadesha' and the Third of the 'Pancha-tantra.' The First Persian story corresponds to the opening of the same books in Sanskrit; the Fourth Persian story, that of 'the Hare and the Elephants.' is the Fourth of the Third book of the 'Hitopadesha,' and the First of the Third book of the 'Pancha-tantra'; the Fifth Persian story, of 'the Pious Cat,' is the Second of the Third book of the 'Pancha-tantra'; the Seventh Persian story, of 'the Pious Man who was cheated out of a Sheep by confederate Rogues,' is the Third of the Third book of the 'Pancha-tantra,' and the Tenth of the Fourth book of the 'Hitopadesha'; the Eighth Persian story, that of 'the Merchant's Wife and the Thief,' is the Eighth of the Third book of the 'Pancha-tantra'; the Ninth Persian story, 'the Thief and the Demon who went to rob the Recluse,' is the Ninth of the 'Pancha-tantra'; the Tenth Persian story, 'the Carpenter and his artful Wife,' is the Eleventh of the Third book of the 'Pancha-tantra,' and the Seventh of the Third book of the 'Hitopadesha'; the Twelfth Persian story, 'the Mouse that was changed into a girl,' is the Twelfth of the Third book of the 'Pancha-tantra,' and the Sixth of the Fourth book of the 'Hitopadesha'; the Thirteenth Persian Story, 'the Snake and the Frogs,' is the Fifteenth of the Third book of the 'Pancha-tantra,' and the Twelfth of the Fourth book of the 'Hitopadesha.'

The Fifth book is borrowed from the Fourth of the 'Pancha-tantra.' The First Persian story corresponds to the opening of the same book in Sanskrit; the Third Persian story of 'the Ass without Heart and Ears,' is the Second of the Fourth book of the 'Pancha-tantra.' Though the general plot of this book is borrowed from the Sanskrit, it differs in all except outline, and is nowise inferior to it, but, on the whole, may be pronounced the very best of all the fourteen books into which the 'Anvár-i Suhailí' is divided.

The outline is simple, natural, and well preserved; and the stories are vigorous and amusing.

The Sixth book is borrowed from the Fifth book of the 'Pancha-tantra.' The First Persian story, of 'the Devotee and the Ichneumon,' corresponds to the Second story of the said Sanskrit book; the Second Persian story is the Ninth of the Fifth book of the 'Pancha-tantra,' and the Eighth of the Fourth book of the 'Hitopadesha.' This is also an excellent book, and decidedly among the best of the fourteen.

The Seventh book is said by Stewart to correspond to the Third book of the 'Pancha-tantra,' and I have inserted his remark; but on reference, I cannot find any agreement, and none of the stories are alike.

In the rest of the Books I can trace no connection with the Sanskrit. The Ninth and the Twelfth are decidedly the dullest and worst written, especially the latter, the plot of which is childish, ridiculous, and unnatural, and full of the most extravagant metaphors and conceits.

It will be seen, from the comparison which has been made, that the first Seven books, forming rather more than two-thirds of the whole work, have been in a greater or less degree borrowed from the Sanskrit, and chiefly from the 'Pancha-tantra.' It is also from the 'Pancha-tantra' that translations have been made into most of the vernacular dialects of India, such as Gujaráthí, Maráthí, Braj-Bháshá, Bengálí, etc. It may be here remarked that the 'Pancha-tantra' has been generally supposed to be of an age anterior to the 'Hitopadesha.' Of course the question does not admit of proof; but on perusing the former book immediately after the latter, it would seem that the 'Hitopadesha' is the older of the two, as well from the style as from the greater amplification of the subjects in the 'Pancha-tantra.' Be that, however, as it may, it is quite clear that the larger portion of the 'Anvár-i Suhailí' has been borrowed from one or other of these Sanskrit works, and it is unnecessary to proceed to isolated expressions or general reasons for establishing the identity. At the same time it must be acknowledged that many of the stories which are of purely Persian origin, though somewhat different in character, are in no degree inferior to those taken from the the Sanskrit. Thus the story of 'the Gardener and the Nightingale,' the

Nineteenth of the First book; that of 'the Painter and his Mistress,' the
Seventh of the Second book; of 'the Thief and the Monkey,' the Second of
the Fifth book; of 'the Farmer's Wife,' the Second of the Seventh book;
and of 'the Farmer and the Purse of Gold,' in the Fourteenth book, are
equal to any of the stories in the 'Hitopadesha' or 'Pancha-tantra.'

Having said thus much of the 'Anvár-i Suhailí' itself, and of its
Sanskrit originals, it remains that some notice be taken of the Translations
which have been made into other languages, and of which the Baron
DE SACY has given a full account in the 'Mémoire Historique' prefixed to his
edition of Calila et Dimna.' This profound scholar is of opinion, that,
after the physician Burzuyah had brought the works of which the 'Anvár-i
Suhailí' is an expansion, into Persia (see p. 6 of this translation) during
the reign of Núshírwán; they were immediately translated into Pahlaví,
under the same reign, that is, circa A.D. 570. This version perished,
no doubt, in the invasion of the Arabs. At least, no copy has yet been
discovered.

The Arabic translation of 'Abdu'lláh bin Al-Muḳaffʻa

was made by the person whose name it bears, under the second Khalíf
of the 'Abbásís, Manṣúr, (see p. 7 of this translation) between the years
136—158 of the Hijrah. This 'Abdu'lláh bin Al-Mukaff'a (wrongly
called by many, Al-Muḳann'a, as at p. 7 of this translation) was born
in Persia, and was, until converted, by religion, a Fire-worshiper. His
father, who was collector of taxes in 'Irák, under Hajjáj bin Yusúf, had
been guilty of extortion, and was, therefore, put to the torture, and his
hand remaining shrunken in consequence, he got the name of Al-Muḳaff'a,
i.e., 'he that has shriveled hands.' He was put to death by the Governor
of Baṣrah, in accordance with a secret order despatched to him by Manṣúr.

Of the Greek version of Simeon Seth.

This was made towards the close of the eleventh century, by order
of the Emperor Alexis Comnenes. It is chiefly remarkable for the
substitution of Greek proper names for the Oriental ones. Thus, a king

of the rats is called $T\rho\omega\gamma\lambda o\delta\acute{v}\tau\eta s$, and three rats, his counsellors, are termed $T\upsilon\rho o\phi\acute{a}\gamma o s$, $K\rho\epsilon o\beta\acute{o}\rho o s$, and $'O\theta o\nu o\phi\acute{a}\gamma o s$.

Of the Hebrew version attributed to the Rabbi Joël.

Nothing certain is known of the Translator. The version contains two additional Chapters, the Sixteenth and Seventeenth, the former of which, being the story of 'the Two Swans and the Duck,' was found by M. de Sacy in one Arabic MS. : the latter, or the story of 'the Dove and the Fox,' he was unable to discover in any Arabic version.

Omitting a Syriac version doubtfully mentioned by M. de Sacy, and of which nothing certain is known, we come next to

Rudaki's Persian Version

(See p. 7 of this translation). This poet, called also Ustád Abú'l Hasan, was born blind, and flourished at the court of Sultán Nasr bin Ahmad, the third prince of the Sámánides, who, it is said, presented him with 80,000 dirams for his metrical version, which, however, seems not to have survived to modern times.

Of the Persian version of Abú'l M'adli Nasru'lláh.

This was executed (see p. 8 of this translation) by command of Bahrám Sháh, thirteenth sultán of the Ghaznivites, who died A.D. 1151. It is filled with Arabic quotations, and difficult and obsolete words; and its reputation has been entirely lost sight of in the blaze of the more elegant version executed by Husain Vá'iz. As enough has already been said of the latter, we have only further to observe that it was made about the beginning of the 15th century, and proceed to notice

The more modern Persian version, called "Iyár-i Dánish.'

This was made by the celebrated Abú'l-Fazl, vazír of the renowned Akbar. His intention was to simplify the translation of Husain Vá'iz, and render it more intelligible. He further introduced two Chapters which Husain Vá'iz had retrenched. Of these the one is the Preface or Introduction of the Arabic translator, 'Abdu'lláh bin Al-Mukaff'a; and the other is the life

of Burzuyah before his journey to India to procure the Fables. Abú'l Faẓl
seems to have fallen into the error common to many others, of supposing that
Buzurjmihr, the Grand Vazír of Núshírwán, and not Burzuyah, was the
Pahlaví translator of the book. M. de Sacy has proved, however, that this is
not the case.

Mr. Colebrooke says of this version, 'The ''Iyár-i Dánish' comprises
sixteen chapters, ten of which, as Abú'l Fazl states in his preface, were
taken from the Hindí original, entitled ' Kartak and Damnak,' and six were
added by Buzurjmihr ; namely, the four last, containing stories recited by
the Bráhman Bídpáí in answer to the questions of King Dábishlím ; and
the two first, consisting of a preface by Buzurjmihr, with an introduction
by Burzuyah. Both these introductory chapters had been omitted by
Ḥusain Vá'iẓ, as foreign to the original work : but he substituted a different
beginning, and made other additions, some of which are indicated by him,
and the rest are pointed out by Abú'l Faẓl; who has, nevertheless,
retained them as appendages not devoid of use, and therefore admissible
in a composition intended solely to convey moral instruction. The whole
of the dramatic part, including all the dialogue between Dábishlím, King
of India, and Bídpáí, a Bráhman of Sarándíp, as well as the finding of
Húshang's legacy, appears to have been added by the translators, although
the appellations of the king and of the philosopher, are stated to be of
Indian origin. For Abú'l Fazl has inserted the story at the close of
the second chapter ; after expressly declaring, in one place, that the
substance of the work begins with the third ; and in another, that the
two first were added by the author of the Pahlaví translation.'

*Of the Urdú version, entitled K̲h̲irad-Afrúz, or, ' The Illuminator of the
Understanding.'*

This is a close Hindústání translation of the ''Iyár-i Dánish,' and was made
A.D. 1803, by Maulaví Ḥafiẓu'd-dín, for the use of the College of Fort
William, at the suggestion of Dr. Gilchrist. It is written in good plain
language, and is a very useful book for students. The editor was Captain
Thomas Roebuck, a scholar of extraordinary industry and ability, to whom

Urdú literature is much indebted. This translation obtained the highest pecuniary reward ever bestowed at the College.

Of the Turkish Version, called 'Humáyún Námah;' or, 'Imperial Book.'

This was made in the first half of the tenth century of the Hijrah, under the reign of the Emperor Sulaimán I., by 'Alí Chalabí bin Sálih, Professor at Adrianople, in the College founded by Murád II. It is a close translation of the 'Anvár-i Suhailí,' but when the Persian verses are obscure, they are often suppressed, and Turkish verses substituted.

There are some other Turkish versions, and amongst them a poetical one by Jamálí.

Of European versions.

The Hebrew version was translated into Latin by John of Capua, towards the close of the fifteenth century, and published under the title of 'Directorium Humanæ Vitæ, alias Parabole Antiquorum Sapientum;' and from it several Italian, Spanish, and German translations were made. An Italian imitation of the 'Directorium,' ascribed to Doni, was translated into English, and printed in 1570. A Greek version (perhaps that of Sethus) from the Arabic, was edited in 1697, with a Latin interpretation, by Starkius. In French, a part of the Fables appeared in 1644, under the title of 'Le Livre des Lumières (Anvár-i Suhailí) on la Conduite des Royes;' the translator is named David Said, of Isfahán. The work was, however, little known in Europe, till Galland, the French translator of the 'Arabian Nights' Entertainments,' undertook a version of the first four chapters from the Turkish of 'Alí Chalabí. The remaining ten chapters were afterwards supplied by Cardonne, Professor of the Persian Language at the Royal College of Paris, from the same original, as appears by the title 'Contes et Fables Indiennes de Bidpai et de Lokman, traduites d'Ali Tchelebi ben Saleh, auteur Turc.' The English work, 'Instructive and Entertaining Fables of Pilpay, an ancient Indian Philosopher,' of which a fifth edition was published in 1775, is said to have been taken from another French translation, which was made from the Persian and published in 1709.

b

It only remains that a few words be said of the present translation.[1] It is perhaps the only version of the whole of Husain Vá'iz's work which pretends to exact faithfulness. The Preface and the First book are much more literal than the remaining parts, and this greater scrupulousness at the beginning is intended for the benefit of students. No difficulty has been intentionally slurred over, and though it cannot be doubted that many mistakes will be found in so long a work, it is hoped that they will be indulgently viewed; and that the labor, at least, which has been expended upon the translation, more especially upon the Verses, which amount to between five and six thousand, will be appreciated. In fact a few words of approbation are the only encouragement that either the Translator or the Publisher can look for; as, so little suited are Oriental works in general to the European palate that, to use the words of Husain Vá'iz (in a somewhat different sense), they would make

'The market of Egyptian Joseph flat.'

EDWARD B. EASTWICK.

Haileybury, September 28th, 1854.

---

[1] In some words I have adopted Webster's system of spelling. Thus, in the words 'honor, color, favor, odor,' and their derivatives, I have uniformly rejected the 'u'; as also the second 'l' in such words as 'jeweler, traveler,' etc.; and in the past participles of verbs not having the accent on the final syllable, such as 'traveled.'

CONTENTS.

c

ERRATA.

Page	6	Line	1	*For*	cell	*Read*	shell.
,,	32	,,	29	,,	hands	,,	bands.
,,	33	Note	2	,,	*zarwah*	,,	*zarwah.*
,,	63	Line	31	,,	hell	,,	belt.
,,	141	,,	27	,,	resolved	,,	revolved.
,,	142	,,	3	,,	the moon	,,	a fish.
,,	160	Note	2	,,	Chadzko	,,	Chodzko.
,,	164	Line	25	,,	addressing	,,	adducing.
,,	169	Note	1	,,	his	,,	this.
,,	183	Line	27	,,	pillar	,,	pillow.
,,	197	,,	20	,,	the	,,	thy.
,,	203	,,	9	,,	draw	,,	bear.
,,	208	,,	34	,,	ushed	,,	hushed.
,,	234	,,	15	,,	now	,,	know.
,,	240	,,	35	,,	my	,,	any.
,,	255	,,	19	,,	hast drunk	,,	must drink.
,,	262	,,	14	,,	be cannot	,,	he cannot.
,,	295	,,	34	,,	plain. The	,,	plain. Thus saying, the
,,	327	,,	18	,,	fire	,,	flame.
,,	353	,,	20	,,	is beyond what were supposed	,,	were beyond what is supposed
,,	378	,,	18	,,	is	,,	are.
,,	400	,,	39	,,	assay	,,	essay.
,,	405	,,	33	,,	and lovers	,,	their lovers.
,,	,,	,,	34	,,	their from	,,	and from.
,,	413	,,	7	,,	is	,,	are.
,,	423	,,	3	,,	is	,,	are.
,,	459	,,	8	,,	light for reason	,,	light of reason.
,,	483	Note	1	,,	in the present	,,	in the presence.

Page 521	Line 12	*For*	then	*Read*	there.
,, 548	,, 37	,,	should acquire	,,	should not acquire.
,, ,,	Note 1	,,	*kafúf*	,,	*kafút.*
,, 576	,, 4	,,	*nakhshah*	,,	*nakhshab.*

With reference to Note 4, page 546, on re-perusing the lines to which they refer, I see that the literal translation will be, 'From the veritable to the imitator there are [great] differences : the former is like David and the latter is rust.' David is said to have been an armourer, as is mentioned in the Ḳur'án; See Sale, p. 248, l. 20. The sense here given to *ṣadd* is unusual.

The Note at page 600 is wrongly placed, and refers to the word 'raised,' in line 2 of page 601.

IN THE NAME OF THE MOST MERCIFUL AND COMPASSIONATE GOD!
O GOD! AID THIS WORK AND BRING IT TO A FORTUNATE CONCLUSION!

PREFACE.

THE Lord, the Absolutely Wise[1] [May his wisdom be glorified!] the glad tributes of whose praise and adoration flow on and circulate upon the tongues of all created beings, both high and low, according to the saying, '*And there is nothing which does not celebrate his praise;*'[2] and the benefits of the tables of whose infinite favours, in accordance with the enduring rule, '*And He bestowed on each thing creation, and then guidance,*'[3] pervade and extend through the collective parts of all creatures both in heaven and earth:

VERSE.

Secret-teacher of the reason that can measure subtleties!
Giver of perceptive powers to the spirits of the wise!
Gem-bestower, Thou! of knowledge too refined for grosser sight,
Gradual back to day Thou bringest the decreasing shades of night.

in His Word ancient and venerable, and in His Book deserving of precedence and reverence, addressed[1] the Lord—the Asylum of prophecy, the Sultán of the throne, '*I have with God,*'[4] the knower of mysteries, according to the words, '*And He taught thee that thou didst not know,*'[5] the lucidly eloquent, as it is said, '*I am the most eloquent of Arabs and Persians,*'[6]

DISTICHS.

From past eternity to th' unending future 'tis
Muḥammad's name that gilds whatever is.
Sole lamp is he, whence beams of radiance shine,
In him Creation's splendours all combine.

---

[1] Twelve lines in the Persian separate the verb *farmúdah,* 'addressed,' (l. 15), from its nominative *ḥaẓrat ḥakím,* 'the Lord, the Absolutely Wise,' (line 1).

[2] See Ḳur'án, Mar., ch. xvii. 44; Sale, p. 213, l. 19: 'The seven heavens praise Him, and the earth, and all who are therein: neither is there anything which doth not celebrate His praise.'

[3] Ḳur'án, Mar., ch. xx. 46; Sale, p. 237, l. 24: 'Pharaoh said, Who is your Lord, O Moses? He answered, Our Lord is he who hath created all things; he hath created them, and directeth them by his Providence.' There is a slight variation, it will be seen, in the reading of this as quoted above.

[4] This quotation is given more fully in the Gulistán, chapter ii. story 9, as follows, 'I have a season with God, in which neither ministering angel nor any prophet that has been sent, can vie with me.'

[5] This is a quotation from the Ḳur'án, Flügel, ch. iv. 113; Mar., 112; Sale, p. 69, l. 16. The passage is as follows, 'God hath sent down unto thee (the Prophet) the book of the Ḳur'án, and wisdom, and hath taught thee that which thou knewest not; for the favour of God hath been great to thee.'

[6] I conjecture this quotation to be a Ḥadís, as I am unable to find it in the Ḳur'án.

B

On him be the blessings and benedictions of God, and on his offspring, and on his immediate companions, and on his followers, and on those who trace up to him!—with reference to the guidance of those who study the subjects of discipleship,[1] and the protection of those who seek the objects of advantage[2] —in the manner following: and pointed out to that Teacher of wisdom (of whom it is said, ' *One mighty in power taught him*')[3] the path of instruction for the candidates of the school of manners, and the way of information and the method of improving the understanding of the students of the college of industry and research, after this fashion, ' *Invite to the path of thy Lord with discretion and with gracious exhortations.*'[4]   The meaning of these words of happy tendency is as follows:—' O Summoner of mankind to the tables of the benefits of wise counsel and salvation, and O Guide of men to the paths of welfare of the present existence and of the world to which all return![5] invite my servants to the right way discreetly, and direct my adorers with kind admonitions from the gulf[6] of sensual desire to the garden of God's favour; since it is not possible to discipline the headstrong appetites save by the lash of wisdom, nor can the sensual temperaments be brought to reason but by salutary admonition; according as it has been said, ' *Hadst thou been severe of heart, they would have been scattered.*'[7]

VERSE.

Each horse-tamer, who would vanquish the unbroken, fiery steed,
Must the young colt first with kindness, and with gentle measures lead:
Fury will but stir the courser to more headlong heat; and so,
From the rider's want of spirit, steeds will dull and sluggish grow.

Just as the taming of horses new to the bridle is, without observing the niceties of gentle management, impracticable; so, to reduce to submission the passions of the many—who, in consequence of brutish and ferine[8] violence having got the mastery over their natures, have fed without prohibition or

---

[1] Observe here a good specimen of the verbiage so admired by the Persians.
[2] The verb, *khitáb farmúdah* properly comes here, but I have been obliged to take it several lines earlier to connect the sense better.
[3] This is a quotation from the Ḳur'án, ch. liii. 15; Sale, p. 387, l. 15: ' By the star when it setteth, your companion Muhammad erreth not, nor is he led astray: neither doth he speak of his own will.   It is no other than a revelation, which hath been revealed unto him. One mighty in power, endued with understanding, taught it him; and he appeared in the highest part of the horizon.'
[4] Ḳur'án, Flügel, ch. xvi. 126; Mar., 125; Sale, p. 208, last line of text: ' Invite men unto the way of thy Lord by wisdom and mild exhortation; and dispute with them in the most condescending manner; for thy Lord well knoweth him who strayeth from his path, and he well knoweth those who are rightly directed.'
[5] Here seven words are used in translating *ma' ád.*
[6] At page 4, l. 3, in the edition of 1851, *háwiyah-i* should be read for *háḍiyah-i.*
[7] Ḳur'án, Fl., ch. iii. 153; Mar., 160; Sale, p. 30, l. 14: ' And as to the mercy granted unto the disobedient from God, thou, O Muhammad! hast been mild towards them, but if thou hadst been severe and hard-hearted they had surely separated themselves from about thee.'
[8] *Sabá' i* signifies ' belonging to a *savage* beast,' opposed to *bahímí,* ' of *any* animal.'

repulse in the pasture-ground, '*Leave them that they may eat and enjoy them-selves*,'[1] and who have not experienced the bridle of the check from forbidden things, and the lash of the commandment [to do] what is right—will, without the application of preliminary prudent measures, be in like manner impossible;

COUPLET.

Wisdom can solve things difficult, and bring   To the expectant heart each wished-for thing.

and [it is said] '*He who has received wisdom, verily he has received a great good.*'[2]

COUPLET.

Seek wisdom, study greatness, that men aye   May note thy morrow happier than to-day.[3]

The 'gracious exhortation' spoken of in the enjoined invitation is declared to be a discourse[4] of such a nature that the hearer is made aware[5] that it is purely wholesome counsel and essentially benign and clement, and they say that 'gracious exhortation' is speech of such a comprehensive description that each one of those who hear may derive benefit from it, in proportion to the degree of his capacity and aptitude. Such is the exhortation of the Ḳur'án, and the advice [contained in] the sacred book,[6] which comprehends both exoteric and esoteric kinds [of knowledge], and contains all mysteries religious and mundane, and from the words and meaning of which every one, whether reader or hearer, according to his degree, reaps advantage, and '*to it the speaker alludes.*'

COUPLET.

The young spring of its loveliness makes soul and spirit fresh;[7]
Its scent delights the pious, and its hue enchants the flesh.

And this kind of speech has been poured out and sent down on not even one of the greatest prophets, except our Prophet (May blessing and peace be upon him!); nay, it is the distinctive privilege of His Holiness, the seal of prophecy[8]; *as he (The blessing and peace of God be upon him!), indicated in this,* '*I have received the All-comprehensive Words*[9]:' and, inasmuch as sincerity of obedience is a cause of inheriting special intimacy with God, and productive of the verification of relationship to Him, assuredly the minds of a select number of His great people (who are characterised by the mark, '*Ye are the*

---

[1] Ḳur'án, Fl., ch. xv. 3; Mar., 4; Sale, p. 194, l. 13: 'The time may come when the unbelievers shall wish that they had been Muslims. Suffer them to eat and enjoy themselves in this world; and let hope entertain them . but they shall hereafter know their folly.'

[2] Ḳur'án, ch. ii. 270; Sale, p. 30, l. 28: 'He giveth wisdom unto whom he pleaseth; and he unto whom wisdom is given, hath received much good; but none will consider except the wise of heart.'

[3] The Bombay lithographed ed. reads *bih-gardad* for the *bih-nigarand* of the ed. of 1851.

[4] *Sukhant-rá gúyand* for *sukhan ast kih gúyand.*

[5] Lit., 'It does not remain concealed from the hearer.'

[6] *Furḳán*, a name given to the Ḳur'án as discriminating right from wrong, truth from falsehood.

[7] For *tázah* the lithographed edition reads *zindah.*

[8] This is a title of Muḥammad.   [9] *Jawám'iu-l-kalim,* a name for the Ḳur'án.

B 2

best nation that hath been raised up unto mankind' [1] *)*, have become the recipients
of the lights of the most resplendent rays of that universality [of knowledge]
the borrowing of which may be [affirmed to be] from the niche of the high
prophetical office of that holy person[2]; and hence they consider *that* to be
perfect discourse, in the survey of the beauty of the meaning of which, the
eye of the superficial observers derives benefit from the words, and is
irradiated by the expressions; while the nostril of the esoteric examiners is
perfumed by the sweet odours of the truths and niceties which are discoverable under its external sense; so that each individual, in proportion to his
capacity, has derived a share from its table of unlimited advantages.

HEMISTICH.

No seeker passes from it uncontent.

And, from the tenor of these premises, it is understood that the more the face
of each word is adorned with the soft down and mole[3] of knowledge, and the
more the cheek of each advice is embellished with the cosmetic of universal
wisdom, so much the more is the heart of true lovers inclined to survey its
adornments.[4]

COUPLET.

The more each one is lovely 'mid the fair,   The more the gaze of all is centred there.

And of the many treatises,[5] the foundations of whose composition are [laid] on
the questions of philosophy; and of the multitude of books, the rules of whose
arrangement are so grounded, and which comprise the auspicious things of
advice; the book of Kalílah and Damnah[6] is one which the philosophers of
Hind have composed in a peculiar style, and the methods of whose comprehensive knowledge the Bráhmans, who are adorned with the bright rays of
learning, have arranged in a special manner, and have combined with one
another philosophy and merriment and mirth; and, having disposed the form
of the narrative in tales, on account of the bias of most dispositions to them,
have recounted the stories and fables by the tongues of wild beasts and
animals and birds, and in the body of them have interwoven a variety of wise
rules and salutary counsels, so that the sage may peruse them with a view to
profit, and the ignorant person may read them for recreation and the [amuse-
ment of the] romance, and that the lecturing on them may be easy to the

---

[1] Kur'án, ch. iii. 110; Sale, p. 45, l. 18: 'Ye are the best nation that hath been raised
up unto mankind; ye command that which is just and ye forbid that which is unjust, and ye
believe in God.'

[2] That is, Muḥammad.

[3] This is a constant image with Persian poets. The mole on the face is as prized as it
was in England some eighty years ago, when it was represented by a black patch.

[4] *Julwahdí*, pl. of *julwat*, 'the adorning of a bride.'

[5] The lithographed edition reads *az jumlah-i kutub* for *az jumlah-i rasáíl*, and the former
where the latter occurs in the edition of 1851.

[6] The Persian Dictionary of Professor Johnson gives *Dimnah*, but I have always heard
the word called *Damnah*, and, from the fact of its being written *Damnak* in Maráthí, Gujráthí,
and other languages, I am inclined to think the latter pronunciation correct.

teacher and the recollection of them to the student: and, in point of fact, that enlightened book is an orchard, the branches of the hidden meanings of which are made bright with the flowers '*And therein shall they enjoy whatever their souls shall desire, and whatever their eyes shall delight in*,'[1] and the environs of the rose-garden of which are aromatised and perfumed with the gentle breezes of [the verse] '*What eye hath not seen nor ear heard*.'

DISTICHS.

Each maxim there a blossom is more bright—
More dazzling—than the insect lamp of night.[2]
Its words youth's gracefulness and freshness shew,
With meanings fraught which like life's waters flow.

And the gushing over of that fountain of truths and sage meanings is to this degree, that, from the beginning of the display [of creation] to this time, it has in every age conferred benefit on the students of the assembly of discipleship and the apt scholars of the convention of felicity, and the garment of the following beautiful verses is a graceful and becoming robe of honour on the lofty stature of this book:

VERSE.

Its form is fringe like to the robe of joy[3] and happiness,
Its sense the gem that decks the ring of fortune and success:
While from its verses' tinted cheek love's wiles and witchcrafts beam,
Its diction's labyrinthine curls like musky ringlets seem.

And that sage of luminous mind, the Bráhman Bídpáí, composed this book in the Hindí tongue, in the name of the world-adorning Hindú sovereign Dábishlím, who was the ruler of several countries of Hindústán; and, perhaps, in the commencement of the exordium some portion is on this account inserted by the pen of narration, and the said sage has founded his discourse on exhortations, in order that in the government of their subjects, and in the expansion of the carpet of justice, and in clemency, and in educating and maintaining the fathers of the state,[4] and in repelling and opposing the enemies of the realm, it might prove of service to rulers; and Dábishlím made this book the pole-star[5] of his wishes and the pillar of his designs, and with the key of the perusal of this [volume] he always opened[6] the doors of the solution of difficulties and unveiled knotty points, and in his time this precious jewel was hid from the sight of every one, like a peerless gem in the cabinet of its

---

[1] Ḳur'án, ch. xliv.; Sale, p. 364, l. 20: 'Enter ye into paradise, ye and your wives, with great joy. Dishes of gold shall be carried round unto them, and cups without handles: and therein shall they enjoy whatever their souls shall desire, and whatever their eyes shall delight in.'

[2] The firefly is called the *shab chirágh*, 'night-lamp,' but the same word may also mean 'a carbuncle,' or 'a glow-worm.'

[3] This is a good specimen of absurd and strained metaphor—'The form of the book is like the fringe of the robe of happiness.'

[4] That is, The nobles.   [5] Lit., The point to which the face is turned in prayer.

[6] Lit., Made the opening.

cell, and like a ruby of Badakhshán, shewed not its face from the recess of the mine save after a thousand toils;[1] and after him each one of his descendants and kinsmen who succeeded him on the imperial throne trod the same path and exerted himself to conceal it; and, notwithstanding all this excessive caution, the fragrant breath of the excellencies of this book had filled the regions of the world with odour, like the borders of a rose-garden; and the musk-scattering bag of its virtues caused the nostrils of the diligent inquirers[2] after the odours of history and tradition to be scented with ambergris.

VERSE.

Like musk is moral worth; from sight concealed,   'Tis by its odour to the sense revealed.
So the sun's face[3] is ne'er obscured with clay,   But still its rays diffuse a brighter day.

Till in the time of Kasra Núshírwán[4] this intelligence became universally diffused that ' Among the treasures of the kings of Hindústán there is a book which they have compiled from the speech of animals and brutes and birds and reptiles and savage beasts; and all that befits a king in the matter of government and vigilance, and is useful for princes in the observance of king-craft, is exhibited in the folds of its leaves, and men regard it as the stock of all advice and the medium of all advantage.' Núshírwán (by the rain of whose beneficence the trees of the river of justice were rendered verdant, and by the drops of the showers of whose favour the freshness of the rose-garden of equity was augmented,

COUPLET.

His justice added to the world fresh grace,   And swept oppression dust-like from its face),

felt the greatest eagerness and most unspeakable desire to peruse this book. The physician Burzuyah,[5] who was chief of his class in Párs,[6] at the request of Núshírwán proceeded to Hindústán, and was there during a long period;

---

[1] Lit., A thousand blood of the liver.

[2] The lithographed edition reads *mustanshikán*, 'snuffers-up,' which seems better as preserving the metaphor.

[3] The lithographed edition reads *chashmah-i* for *chihrah-i*, which I think preferable; since ' a fountain' may be said to be muddied, but a face can hardly be so.

[4] Núshírwán (*núshín*, 'sweet,' *rawán*, 'life' or 'soul'), the son of Kubád, surnamed *al-'adil*, 'the Just,' and called by the Arabs Kasra, and by the Persians Khusrau (our Chosroes), was the twentieth King of the fourth dynasty of Persia, viz., that of the Sassanides or Khusravians. He was cotemporary with Justin and Justinian—from the first of whom he took Edessa, Antioch, and Apamea, in Syria; and, from the second, Raca and Dara, in Mesopotamia, and Halab or Aleppo in Syria. He defeated the Khákán or ruler of Turkestán, and conquered Afghanistán and other Eastern provinces as far as the Indus. His own son, Núshízád, who, on account of professing Christianity, had been imprisoned by him, raised the standard of revolt against him, but was defeated and slain. Masrúk, King of Æthiopia, who had invaded Arabia, was overcome by him, and driven back to his own country. Finally, after a glorious reign of 48 years, he died, and was succeeded by his son Hurmuzd. Muhammad was born in the reign of Núshírwán, A.D. 578. [See D'Herbelot, *s.v.*]

[5] D'Herbelot gives no information respecting this worthy besides what is here furnished, except that some attribute the translation to Buzurg Mihr, the celebrated Vazír of Núshírwán, and preceptor of his son Hurmuzd. See D'Herbelot, vol. 1. p. 217.

[6] Párs, called by the Arabs, who have no *p* in their language, Fárs, is said to have been the name of a son of Shem, by whom Persia was colonized.

and, by a variety of artifices and devices, having secured[1] the book, got possession of it, and, having translated the Indian words into the Pahlaví[2] dialect, which was the language at that time spoken by the Sulṭáns of Írán,[3] submitted it to Núshírwán, and, being so fortunate as to have [his gift] accepted, was honoured with [the monarch's] approbation. [Hereupon] His Highness the Sháh's estimation of the book ascended the ladders of perfection; and the actions of Núshírwán, as might be traced in his development of justice, and in his beneficence, and his conquest of countries, and his [method of] soothing the hearts of his subjects, were based on the perusal of the book: and, after Núshírwán, the Persian kings also honoured it, and kept it out of sight with excessive care, until the time when the second Khaliph of the 'Abbásís, Abú J'afar Mansúr-bin-Muḥammad-bin-'Alí-bin-'Abdu' lláh-bin 'Abbás[4] (May God approve of them!) heard news of that book, and displayed the greatest eagerness[5] to obtain it, and, by some clever devices, having got possession of the Pahlaví copy, commanded Imám Abú'l-Ḥasan 'Abdu'lláh-bin-Muḳann'a,[6] who was the chief of the learned men of that age, so that he translated the whole of it from the Pahlaví into Arabic, and he (the Khaliph) kept it continually under perusal, and based his imperial ordinances and his regulations as regards justice and clemency, on those counsels and precepts. Next, Abú'l-Ḥasan Naṣr bin Aḥmad Sámání[7] commanded one of the learned men of the age, so that he translated the work from the Arabic language into Persian, and the poet Rúdakí,[8] by direction of the Sulṭán, arranged it in order of verse; and, again, Abú'l-Muzaffar Bahrám Sháh-bin-Sulṭán Masa'úd,[9]

---

[1] *Tamassuk namúdah*, lit., 'having clutched,' 'having struck the claws into.'

[2] Pahlaví, the ancient language of Persia, or that modification of it which intervened between the Zend and the language of Firdausí.

[3] Írán, a name of Persia given to it from Iraj, son of Farídún.

[4] This Khalifah succeeded his brother, Abú'l 'Abbás Ṣifá, A.H. 136. In consequence of a rebellion in his capital of Anbar, he determined to deprive it of the honour of being his chief city, and with this view laid the foundations of Baghdád A.H. 145. He died while on pilgrimage to Mukkah, A.H. 158, and was succeeded by his son Mahdí.

[5] This meaning of *shaghf* is omitted in Johnson's Persian Dictionary, but I venture to adopt it from the evident requirement of the context.

[6] D'Herbelot gives no additional particulars respecting this personage. Muḳann'a, the famous veiled prophet of Khurásán, lived in the reign of the son of Manṣúr, and was consequently nearly cotemporary with the above learned man.

[7] This was the the third prince of the family of Sámán, and to him M'utamad, fourteenth Khalífah of the house of 'Abbás, gave the government of Transoxiana, A.H. 261.

[8] Rúdakí, in the edition of 1851 improperly written Rúdagí, was the earliest of the Persian poets; and is said by his verses in praise of Bukhárá, to have induced Naṣr Sámání to return to that capital after he had deserted it for the attractions of Hírát. He received 80,000 dirhams for his version of Bídpáí's fables. See Elphinstone's India, vol. 1., p. 563, note †.

[9] Bahrám Sháh, son of Masa'úd, was the thirteenth Sulṭán of the race of the Ghaznivites. He rebelled successfully against his elder brother, Arslán Sháh, supported by the forces of Sulṭán Sanjár Saljukí. His son, Khusrau Sháh, was the last of the dynasty, and after him the house of Ghúr mounted the throne. Bahrám Sháh was a great patron of literary men. He died A.H. 567, A.D. 1151.

one of the descendants of Sultán Mahmúd-i Ghází of Ghazní, who is celebrated by the sage Sanáí,[1] issued a command, so that the most eloquent of
eloquent men and the most powerful of rhetoricians, Abú'l Ma'álí Naṣru'lláh-
bin-Muhammad-bin-Al-Ḥamíd (God rest his soul, and grant him increasing
triumph in the mansions of Paradise!) translated it from the copy of Ibn-i
Mukann'a, and this book, which has now become celebrated by [the name of]
Kalílah and Damnah, is the translation of the aforesaid learned man[2]; and,
in truth, its style in elegance resembles the sweetness of life; and in freshness
it is like many-hued coral; and its fascinating words are like the love-
allurements of honey-lipped mistresses, whose charms provoke dissension;
and its life-increasing meanings may be compared to the ringlets of tender
youths, who delight the heart.

VERSE.

Its words are like the ringlets of the beauties of Chigil;[3]
And in its every page new joys th' enraptured spirit fill,
Its meanings, [sparkling] underneath its letters' inky night,
Are brilliant as the sunny ray, or like the moon-beams bright.

To the blackness of its letters, which may be termed the collyrium of the jewels[4]
of meaning, a place might be given on the white page of the tablet of the
visual organ; and to the whiteness of its paper, which may be called the
dawn of the morning of joyousness, a location might be assigned on the dark
pupil of the world-viewing eye.

COUPLET.

On the white tablet of a Ḥúrí's eye 't were due,
That Eden's penman traced its letters' inky hue.

And, although those who sit on the throne of the court of style are unanimous
in praise of the magnificence of the words, and in applauding the eloquence
of its compounds,

HEMISTICH.

Truly the word is that which Ḥazdm[5] said;

nevertheless, through the introduction of strange words and by overstraining
the language with the beauties of Arabic expressions and hyperbole in metaphors and similes of various kinds, and exaggeration and prolixity in words
and obscurity of expression, the mind of the hearer is kept back from enjoyment of the meaning of the book, and from apprehending the pith of the

---

[1] Sanáí (or Sináí) was a celebrated Persian poet, often styled Khwájah or Ḥakím Sanáí.
His proper name was Muhammad-bin-Adam, and he was the author of a religious poem called
the Iláhí Námah, consisting of prayers and hymns, also of some odes, and of a religious poem
called the Ḥadíkah, or 'palm-plantation.' He flourished about 1180 A.D.

[2] Lit., Our Lord.

[3] A city (says the Dictionary) in Turkestán, famous for handsome men and expert archers.

[4] The Orientals to this day believe that if pearls, rubies, or other jewels are dissolved and
mixed with collyrium, they produce a most beneficial effect on the eyes.   From the same notion,
I have been advised to look constantly at a turquoise ring to refresh the weary sight.

[5] I am ashamed to say I can throw no light on this dictum of Ḥazám.   The lithographed
edition reads Ḥazám-i, and one MS. Ḥuzám.

subject; and the disposition of the reader also is unable to perform the task of connecting the beginnings of the story with the terminations, and of adjusting the commencements of the discourse with the conclusions; and this circumstance will undoubtedly be a cause of disrelish and a source of ennui both to the reader and the hearer, especially in this age, so characterized by fastidiousness, in which the minds of its children have become nice to such a degree that they expect[1] to perceive the meaning without its being decked out on the richly ornamented bridal-bed, as it were, of language; how much more when in some of the words they may require to employ a minute comparison of the dictionary, and to examine glossaries[2] with care. Hence, too, it all but came to pass that a book of such preciousness [as this is] was almost neglected and abandoned, and that the people of the world were deprived of its advantages and excluded from them. On this account, at the present time, His Highness the seal of sovereignty, whose luminously gifted nature comprehends all perfections, and whose sublimely characterized qualities have risen from the dawning-place of excellence and spirituality, the magnanimous Lord, who, notwithstanding his proximity to His Majesty the Sultán of the age and the Khákán[3] of the time, the spreader of the carpet of security and peace, the Diffuser of the marks of goodness and beneficence, the Sun of the zenith of the Khaláfats and empire, the Jupiter of the zodiac of dominion and principality,

COUPLET.

King! thou art balm to eyes of princes, ruler thou of east and west!
Abú 'l-Ghází Sultán Husain,[4] realm and doctrine on thee rest.

(May God perpetuate his kingdom and his power!) yea, notwithstanding the being looked on with favour by the glances of that high personage, endowed as they are with the properties of the philosopher's stone, [still] he has shaken free his magnanimous skirt from the dust of worldly pageants *('But the present life is only a deceitful provision')*[5] and has not permitted the page of his pure heart to be inscribed with

---

[1] One MS. reads *mí-dánand* for *mí-ddrand*, which is the reading of the lithographed edition and that of 1851.

[2] *Kashf-i ma'dní*, 'Manifestation of Meanings,' is the title of certain glossaries.

[3] A title of the ruler of Turkestán, see p. 6, note 4. It is applied generally to any monarch.

[4] Husain Mírzá, king of Khurásán, son of Mansúr, the son of Baikarah, the son of 'Umar Shekh, second son of Tímúr or Tamerlane, was surnamed Abú 'l Ghází, on account of his victories; for he defeated and put to death Jadighiar, the son of Muhammad Mírzá, the son of Baissancor, the son of Sháh Rukh, fourth son of Tamerlane, who had made himself master of Khurásán, and of the city of Hírát, his capital, in A.H. 875 = A.D. 1470. He also carried on many wars and obtained signal victories over the Uzbak Tátárs, who had chased Bábar from Transoxiana. He was a great patron of learned men; and Khondemir finished his history at his Court, A.H. 904. He died A.H. 911 = A.D. 1505. (See D'Herbelot, *s.v.*)

[5] Kur'án, Mar., ch. iii. 186; Sale, p. 53, l. 10: 'Every soul shall taste of death, and ye shall have your rewards on the day of resurrection; and he who shall be far removed from

COUPLET.

The magic of this five-day, fleeting dream—
Land and domains—which fools perpetual deem,

and has kept in full view, [as a guide] to his own affairs, this saying of
happy tendency—

COUPLET.

Fairer the mole of self-restraint upon the cheek of might;
The robe of charity appears upon the rich more bright,

and regards the promoting of the wishes of the oppressed and the disappointed,
and the furthering of the affairs of the bereft, as the means of acquiring
provision for the final state; nor has suffered himself to be stigmatized with
neglecting the meaning of this excellent memento,

COUPLET.

Fortune's ten-day fickle friendship is a false, bewildering spell:
Deem advantage lies in serving those, my friend! who love thee well.[1]

And he is the great Amír, the place where all excellencies and high qualities[2]
centre through the sublimity of his spirit, the favoured with the gifts of the
sole King, the Orderer of the state and of religion, the Amír Shekh Aḥmad,
celebrated by the title Suhailí,[3] *(may God bestow on him, as an especial distinc-*
tion, the peace of Salmán amd the perfection of Kumail,)[4] who, without
compliment, is the star Canopus, shining from the right hand of Yaman,
and a sun, diffusing radiance from the dawning-place of affection and fidelity.

COUPLET.

Where'er, Canopus! falls thy ray, and where   Thou risest, fortune's marks are surely there.

With a view to the universal diffusion of what is advantageous to mankind,
and the multiplying what is beneficial to high and low, he condescended to
favour me with an intimation of his high will that this humble individual,
devoid of ability, and this insignificant person of small capital, Ḥusain-bin
'Alí-u'l-Wá'iz, known by the name of Káshifí (*May God most High strengthen*
him with His hidden favours),[5] should be bold enough to clothe the said book
in a new dress, and bestow fresh adornment on the beauty of its tales of
esoteric meaning, which were veiled and concealed by the curtain of obscure

---

hell-fire, and shall be admitted into Paradise, shall be happy; but the present life is only a
deceitful possession.'

[1] These lines occur in the third ode of Ḥáfiz; Calcutta lithographed edition, p. 34, l. 7.

[2] It should be as in both the lithographed and MS. editions, *wa'l-ma'álí.* The printed
edition has dropped the *wa.*

[3] Of this worthy I know no more than that he was the Generalissimo of Sultán Ḥusain
above mentioned [see p. 9, note 4], that he was surnamed Suhailí, and that at his instiga-
tion, Káshifí completed his new translation of Bidpáí's Fables.

[4] This word Kumail signifies in Arabic 'accomplished,' and is the surname of several
illustrious persons. A king of this name reigned in Egypt, A.D. 1218, and was the nephew
of Saladin, and a great conqueror. See D'Herbelot, vol. i., page 246: for Salmún see
D'Herbelot, vol. ii., p. 802, but it is doubtful to whom the allusion applies.

[5] The lithographed edition reads *bi'l-lutfu'l khafí* for the *bi'l-lutfu 'l-ḥakkí* of the printed
edition.

words and the wimple of difficult expressions, by presenting them on the stages of lucid style and the upper chambers of becoming metaphors, after a fashion that the eye of every examiner, without a glance of penetration or penetration of vision, may enjoy a share of the loveliness of those beauties of the ornamented bridal-chamber of narrative, and the heart of every wise person, without the trouble of imagining or the imagining trouble,[1] may obtain the fruition of union with those delicately reared ones of the closet of the mind.

DISTICHS.

Thus spake the man of eloquence to me,
'O gardener of the garden of debate!
Thou in this garden, pure and heavenly,
So plant the trees of hidden meaning that
Whoe'er the taster of the fruits may be,
Shall thus address thee, "O thou fortunate!
Sweet are the fruits that this thy garden fill,
Each than the last seems fairer, lovelier still." '

And as there was no evading obedience to that peerless mandate, and the maxim ' *Wisdom is from Yaman,*' shewed itself from the dawning-place of the light of Canopus,

COUPLET.

Wisdom from Arabia come—so the Prince of Arabs [2] said;
Should we marvel if Canopus has then wisdom on us shed?

After prayer for the blessing of God, and asking leave, I entered on this undertaking; and, whatever has flowed from the tongue [1] of my pen and the pen of my tongue from the invisible world,—that has been written down: and [the reader] must know that the basis of the book Kalílah and Damnah is on practical wisdom,[3] and by practical wisdom is meant knowledge of the actions of the will and the practices natural to the human race, in a manner that may be conducive to the ordering of the affairs of the world to which we must return, and the present world of men, and may tend to arriving at perfection in those things at which men aim. And this kind of wisdom is first of all divided into two kinds, the one, that which may be referred to each person individually; the second, that which relates to a body of men viewed in association. The former of these, which is referable to each person individually, and in which the society of another is not supposable, they call 'refinement of morals;' and the other, which has reference to a collective body, admits of a second two-fold division,—the one, partnership in abode and

---

[1] These intolerable insipidities are considered beauties of style.

[2] That is, Muḥammad. Canopus, after which star Shehk Aḥmad was called, rose to the right of the heavens looking from Hîrât, and consequently in the direction of Arabia; and the Prophet said that wisdom came from Arabia, wherefore wisdom might be looked for under the auspices of this Canopus. Such is the meaning of this trifling.

[3] The *ḥikmat-i 'amalí* is φρόνησις opposed to '*ilm,* ἐπιστήμη and *dánish,* σοφία.

habitation, which they call domestic economy; and the other community in city and country, and, moreover, in clime and realm, which is named civic economy; and the said book comprehends the three kinds that have just been mentioned, and various advantages connected with the latter sorts, and that which has reference to 'refinement of morals,' is not treated of, save incidentally. Wherefore, although the means existed of adducing somewhat as to the excellencies of morals, we were loth to allow of a complete change in the arrangement of the book, and hence avoiding the hindrance of an increase to its chapters, we adhered to the same plan that had been adopted by the sage of Hind, and having dropped the first two chapters, in which no extraordinary advantage was discoverable, and which did not enter into the original design of the book, we wrote the other fourteen in a clear and easy style, and included in the composition the tales in the way of dialogue between the King and the Bráhman, after the manner mentioned in the beginning : and before introducing the opening chapters, we thought it necessary to commence with a story, which may serve as a source of the narrative ; and further, since the style adopted in the said book is to employ as a medium obscurity of expression, so, if in the composition of the said work the reins of narration have turned from the usual road in which authors write, and from the mode of composition of ordinary writers to the path of descent, the excuse will be plain.

COUPLET.

I that have strung these pearls of sense, indite
No word but that which others bade me write.

It is further to be noted that in the midst of the tales I have but briefly availed myself of the various sorts of Arabic expressions, by introducing certain verses from the Ḳur'án and sayings of the Prophet necessary to be mentioned, and traditions and well-known proverbs; and have not clogged the work by employing Arabic verses, but have adorned the page of the narrative with the jewels of Persian poetry, which is inlaid like blended gems and gold.

DISTICHS.

Let thy discourse be blent in skilful wise,
Now sink to prose, and now poetic rise.
Since now in this the changeful mind finds ease,
Now that delights, and this has ceased to please.

Moreover, in the place where the different chapters are written, wherever the introduction of a story or the recital of a maxim seemed pertinent, in accordance with the observation,

HEMISTICH.

'Tis fit that nosegays should with grass be bound.

I shall proceed with the steps of boldness on the road of self-discretion, and this poor person, though he sees that in attempting this work he is a mark for the shafts of censure, nevertheless submits with [1] the tongue of humility in the audience-hall of apology, and on the standing-ground of respectful representation, to the orators arrayed with eloquence, and the eloquent invested with [2] oratory, this apophthegm, ' *He that is commanded is excused* '; and in reply to the threatening sentence, ' *Whoever composes, makes himself a butt,*' he offers this rejoinder deserving of acceptance, ' *He who composes produces something new.*' [3]

VERSE.

When equity informs the sight we pass	As pearls, what are in truth but beads of glass.
I for my failure am with shame oppressed;	Do not with sarcasm wound anew my breast.
For none amid the ranks of pious men,	Reproach the fallen, or th' abased contemn :
No faults are seen by merit-searching eyes,	And we may well the blame of fools despise.

HEMISTICH.

To ev'ry fault the eye of favour's closed.

May God graciously guide us to that which He loves, and be pleased with and seal up our states and our hopes and our fates happily and fairly ; and this book, which is entitled the 'Anvár-i Suhailí,' has fourteen chapters after the manner that is herewith particularly detailed :

Chapter I. On avoiding the talk of slanderers and calumniators.

    ,,   II.   On the punishment of evil doers, and their disastrous end.

    ,,   III. On the agreement of friends, and the advantages of their mutually aiding one another.

    ,,   IV. On the subject of attentively regarding the circumstances of our enemies, and not being secure as to their stratagems and machinations.

    ,,   V. On the detriment of giving way to negligence, and of permitting the objects of desire to escape from one's hands.

    ,,   VI. On the calamitious results of precipitation, and the injuriousness of haste.

    ,,   VII. Of vigilance and deliberation, and of escaping from the injuries of foes.

    ,,   VIII. On avoiding the malevolent, and not relying on their professions of attachment.

    ,,   IX. Of the excellence of clemency, that it is the best attribute of kings, and the most pleasing quality of the mighty.

    ,,   X. On the subject of requiting actions by way of retribution.

---

[1] The lithographed edition and MSS. read *bar zabán*, while the edition of 1851 omits the *bar*.

[2] *Shi'ár* is an under garment, *disár* one worn above another.

[3] The printed edition has a different reading, *man ansafa*, 'Whoever deals justly.'

After the list of the chapters the story commences, which will form the source
of the narrative : and success is from the One God.

CHAPTER I.

ON AVOIDING THE TALK OF SLANDERERS AND CALUMNIATORS.

INTRODUCTION.

THE jewellers of the street of the bázár of meanings, and the money-changers of the mint of eloquence, and the portrait-painters of the marvels of narration, and the statuaries of the wonders of romance, have adorned the frontispiece of the volumes of history after this manner; and have decked and embellished the title-page of the scrolls of nocturnal conversations in this wise: to wit, that —In former times, in the remote limits of the empire of China, there was a king, the fame of whose wealth and successful fortune had passed through all quarters and directions of the world, and the tale of whose magnificence and regal dignity was manifest like the sun at noonday. Celebrated princes had drawn the ring of obedience to him through the ear of their soul, and kings of exalted rank had for him put on the shoulders of their hearts the saddle-cloth of allegiance,[1]

VERSE.

Like Farídún[2] in pomp was he, Jamshíd[3] in regal state,
Like Dárá[4] widely-sheltering, and like Sikandar[5] great:
Flame and water blent together by his justice and his might,
As moon-like beauties' cheeks, whereon commingle red and white,

On the border of the carpet of his daily-increasing fortune, world-subduing nobles and right-counselling Vazírs always belted on the cincture of obedience to the waist of their soul: and at the foot of his throne, stable as the firmament, venerable sages and men wise in counsel, sate ever in the chair of loyalty. His treasury was stored with jewels of various kinds, and coins of divers sorts; and his army, numerous and renowed, exceeded the limits of calculation and reckoning. His valour was combined with generosity, and his dominion was joined with due repression of crime.

DISTICHS.

He scarred the faces of the rebel horde,   And clove his foeman's forehead with the sword;
The bloody by his justice vanquished stand; Relieved, the helpless own his bounteous hand.

---

[1] The ring in the ear and the cloth on the shoulder are marks of servitude in the East.
[2] Farídún was the seventh king of Persia, of the first dynasty, famous for overthrowing the tyrant Zahhák, and for the justice and magnificence of his reign.
[3] Jamshíd was the fourth monarch of the first or Peshdádyan dynasty of Persia. He was dethroned by Zahhák. These comparisons are more trite in Persian poetry than Diana's bow or Phœbus' rays with us.
[4] Dárá is Darius Codomanus, whom Orientals make the cousin of Sikandar or Alexander.
[5] Alexander.

And they called that king Humáyún Fál,[1] since by his comprehensive justice the state of his subjects was fortunate, and by his perfect benignity, the condition of the indigent and poor was linked and conjunct with freedom from care and with tranquillity. If the officer of justice does not exert himself in controuling the condition of the subject, the thief of wickedness with the aid of oppression will bring ruin on the fortunes of high and low; and if the ray of the candle of equity does not illumine the dark hovel of the distressed, the shades of oppression will cast a gloom, like the heart of the tyrannical, over all regions and quarters of the state,

DISTICHS.

A monarch's fortunes in his justice lie;	God's favour is his best security.
Repents he of his justice; then, too late,	He'll see misrule his empire devastate.

And this King had a Vazír, a cherisher of his subjects and a diffuser of mercies, whose world-adorning intellect was wont to be the light of the dormitory of the state; and whose right-aiming purpose would, by a single deliberation, solve a thousand difficult knots. The weighty anchor of his benignity secured the ship of the ocean of sedition in that troublous whirlpool; and the rough blast of his chastisement tore up, root and branch, the skirt-detaining boughs of the thorn-thickets of injustice.

VERSE.

So well his soul its purpose could pursue,	A single scheme a hundred hosts o'er-threw:
Did he the ordering of the state begin,	A single letter could a kingdom win.

And forasmuch as the affairs of the empire derived perfect lustre from his auspicious counsels, they call him Khujistah Ráí;[2] and Humáyún Fál embarked in no undertaking without his advice, nor commenced any matter, small or great, without consulting him, nor belted the waist of war in the plain of battle without his permission, nor took his seat on the throne of mirth and enjoyment in the palace of festivity without a signal from him: and assuredly it behoves illustrious monarchs and fortunate princes, according to the injunction, '*And consult them in your business*,'[3] not to enter upon state deliberations without the aid of the counsels of sagacious and eminent men; and to direct the administration of their affairs and their mandates, according to the advice of consummate ministers and intelligent counsellors; so that, according to the purport [of the saying] '*A people consults not without God's guiding them to the most perfect matter*,' whatever proceeds from them is consistent with what is most advisable, and comprehends the security of the world and the welfare of the children of Adam.

---

[1] Humáyún Fál, *i.e.*, Fortunate presage.   [2] That is, Fortunate mind or opinion.
[3] See p. 2, note 7, where a portion of the same verse of the Kur'án is noticed. Fl. ch. iii., 153; Mar., 160; Sale, p. 30, l. 16: 'And as to the mercy granted unto the disobedient from God, thou, O Muḥammad! hast been mild towards them; but if thou hadst been severe and hard-hearted, they had surely separated themselves from about thee. Therefore forgive them, and ask pardon for them; and consult them in the affair of war.'

COUPLET.

In all things counsel should be taken ;—where 'Tis not, advantage will be wanting there.

It happened that one day Humáyún Fál went forth to the chase. Khujistah
Rái, like fortune, waited on the stirrup of Humáyún, and[1] the spacious extent
of the hunting-ground was a cause of envy to the sky above, on account of the
auspicious footsteps of the King ; and the celestial eagle, in the expectation
of becoming the prey of the royal falcon, turned towards the centre of the
earth. The hunting animals, having broken their bonds and having sprung
forth from their fetters and confinement, put themselves in motion in pursuit
of game. The hunting pard, covered with its leopard skin, became eyes all
over its body, to gaze the better on the beauty of the dark-eyed antelopes ;[2]
and the dog, with its lion-like claws, in the desire of capturing the hare,
learned a thousand kinds of vulpine artifices. The high-soaring hawk, like a
far-flying arrow from the thumb-stall of the archer, set his face towards the
zenith : and the food-providing[3] falcon with the wound of its blood-spilling
talons, tore out the arteries from the throat of the quarry.

DISTICHS.

Forth leapt the light-winged falcons, swift to soar,
Sharpening their talons in the quarry's gore ;
Now swept the hawk destructive through the sky,
Parrot nor francolin was left on high :
On every side the ambushed leopard strains,
No passage for the bounding deer remains ;
And by its coursings, fleet Arabia's hound,
Makes scant for flight the plain's extremest bound.

And when the King had finished the sport of the chase, and had emptied the
desert of beasts and the air of birds, his retinue obtained leave to depart, and
the King and his Vazír bent their steps towards the capital; but during that
time their caftans[4] of steel were rendered soft as wax by the heat of the sun ;
and from the warmth of the horse-armour, which boasted an equality with a
flame of fire, the swift-paced courser was burnt up on the spot,

DISTICHS.

Mine, then, and mountain to fire-temples grew,
The earth was baked, and scorched heaven's vault of blue :
The birds concealed amid the branches slept,
The beasts within their lurking-places crept.

---

[1] The printed edition omits *wa*.
[2] That is, The spots on the leopard are said to arise from his vehement desire to gaze on
the antelope, as some philosophers tell us that monkeys obtain prehensile tails from their
desire to hang on trees.
[3] This word may also mean 'captive-taking.'
[4] The dictionary renders *khaftán*, ' a vest worn under armour' ; but the addition of *faulád*
shows that this sense is inadmissible here.

C

Humáyún Fál, said to Khujistah Rái, 'In such a heated atmosphere it is not
wise to bestir ourselves, nor is it possible to escape the heat by taking shelter
in the shade of a pavilion. From the ardent warmth, the terrestrial globe is
heated like a smith's forge ; and the earth's centre, like the expanse of æther,
has become a quarry of fire. How dost thou advise—that for a time we
should rest in the shade, and when the 'Anká [1] of the sun inclines to its nest
in the west, we too may alight at our victorious abode ?'   Khujistah Rái
unloosed the tongue of praise and said,

COUPLET.

' Sun of this region! shade of the Most High!
Than phœnix-wings more blest thy canopy.

To thy subjects, who take refuge under the shadow of the phœnix, as under a
king's banner, there is no apprehension from the flame of the sun's world-
consuming torch,

COUPLET.

From the sun of changeful fortune, wherefore should we danger dread ?
When the shadow of thy favour o'er us is, protective, spread.

Nevertheless, it appears to be essentially beneficial that the sublimely-gifted
person of the King, the shadow of God, in the shade of whose fortune the
people are at rest, should take refuge from the heat of the atmosphere, whence
results a variety of annoyances and aches ;

HEMISTICH.

By thy security all climes are safe.

And I behold in the vicinity a mountain lofty as the magnanimity of the brave,
and exalted as the rank of the pious.   A short time ago, I went there : from
head to foot it was clothed in a green mantle, and a thousand fountains of
sweet water bubbled up from its pure breast. Its odoriferous herbs and flowers
shone like the stars of heaven, and its fountain-like rivulets glittered like the
brooks of the garden of Paradise. The advisable course is this, that the reins
of intention should be turned in that direction, that for a short time we may
be gladdened like verdure beneath the willow-shade ; and for a moment may
be refreshed and contented like the jasmine at the water's edge, and at the
boundary of the parterre,

COUPLET.

By the bank of the rivulet seated, watch the current of life flow past :
For this token may well suffice. us of a world's pageant which may not last.'

Humáyún Fál, agreeably to the advice of Khujistah Rái, turned his face in
that direction and in a short time, having passed over the distance, made

---

[1] The 'Anká is a fabulous bird which is said to be *m'alúm-u'l ism, majhúl-u'l jism,*
'known in name, unknown in body.'

with the dust of the hoof of his cream-coloured steed, magnificent as that of Rustam,[1] the skirt of the mountain, like the sleeve of those possessed of prosperous fortune, a kissing-place for the happy. He beheld a mountain which raised its lofty summit beyond the highest part of the sky and which brought the top of its green sword[2] near the gilded shield of the sun, or rather it was like a Shekh, who, according to the description, '*And* [*we made*] *the mountains as stakes*'[3] has brought the foot of constancy under the robe of dignity, while from his eyes the stream of tears flowing on has reached his skirt. The king having ascended the mountain,[4] and having girt his clothes around his waist as a cloud [girdles a hill], made a circuit round it on every side. On a sudden, an expanse appeared, in extent like the plain of hope; and a space was presented to his eyes, like the expansion of anticipation in excessive amplitude. In its verdure it resembled the flower-garden of heaven, and in its waters and air it equaled the verdant meads of Paradise; and in its area, the violet sprang up in vicinity to the rose, like the captivating tresses of the beautiful, and young hyacinths, with self-springing tulips, grew up delightful like the civet-diffusing ringlets of the sugar-lipped fair. The willow of Tabaristán was arrayed in its vermilion satin vest,[5] and the straight cypress had robed itself with its silken pistachio-coloured head-dress. The tongue of the perfume-loaded zephyr disclosed to the four quarters of the world the secrets of the sweet plants of the garden, and, from the discourse of the Nightingale, the story of the Rose's hue and fragrance reached the ears of the dwellers in the Mansions on High.

DISTICHS.

Delightful, heart-expanding, its water and its air,
A resting-place auspicious,—a gladsome spot and fair.
Upsprang, beside each brooklet, sweet flowers of many a hue,
With their faces and their limbs all sprinkled o'er with dew.
Trees reared aloft their stature like idols tall; and they,
Seemed each than its next neighbour more beauty to display.
And birds upon the branches poured forth full many a note;
Which like sounds of rich-toned organs through heaven seemed to float.

---

[1] *Rakhsh*, the name of Rustam's charger, and the only steed which could support the hero's χεῖρες βαρεῖαι as he leaned upon its loins. All other horses were crushed by the weight.

[2] In this ridiculous metaphor, the peak of a mountain is compared to a green sword, which rises so high as to strike the sun.

[3] Ḳur'án, Mar., lxxviii., 6; Sale, p. 433, l. 8: 'Have we not made the earth for a bed, and the mountains for stakes to fix the same.' The same idea occurs in the 16th and 31st chapters of the Ḳur'án.

[4] The lithographed edition reads *babáldi*, for the printed edition's *bah-báldi*. The metaphor is overstrained even beyond Persian comparison. Either the king moved round the mountain like a cloud, or he tucked up his garment like a cloud belting a hill—Risum teneatis!

[5] The lithographed edition reads *nímchah* for the printed edition's *nímah-i*.

c 2

> And there, the lovely cypress, surpassing Eden's, waved,
> On every leaflet shewing, 'Good! good [1] to them!' engraved.

And in the midst of that verdant plain was a lake, whose water, like that of life, strengthened the soul, and was like Salsabíl in Paradise, of exquisite delicacy and purity.

COUPLET.

Glanced in its waves fish of a silver hue,   Like the young moon in heaven's vault of blue.

The Vazír commanded that they should adorn the margin of the lake with a throne for the king; and Humáyún Fál seated himself on the cushion of ease. The attendants of his auspicious retinue disposed themselves to rest under the shade of trees on the bank of a rivulet, and regarding their Eden-like halting-place, after that fiery atmosphere, as a rare blessing, repeated with the tongue of ecstasy this couplet,

COUPLET.

I from the waste, O God! of toil and pain   Am freed—and sit on Irám's [2] flowery plain.

The King and the Vazír dismounted from their horses and elephants in a corner of the plain, and without playing [chess] through check to the queen on their vain imaginations, averted the countenance of their lofty spirits from the worthless trifles of this world, and bending their meditations on the wonders of God's creation, and the marvels of His infinite productions, performed the recital of the praise of that King Most High, the artist of whose fixed decree, with the pen of omnipotence, has engraven such beautiful pictures on the surface of the mountain's stony tablet; and the magic of whose power brings forth from the heart of the rock all these variegated plants. At one time they repeated a couplet from the Gulistán, [3]

> Not sole, the rose-couched Bulbul hymns His name;
> Each thorn's a tongue his marvels to proclaim.

At another they contemplated this picture from the Nigáristán, [4]

COUPLET.

> For the rose-leaf now He fashions a light chariot on the winds;
> Now a chain of limpid water [5] on the breezes' feet he binds.

---

[1] *Túba,* 'good,' is the name of a tree in Paradise.

[2] Irám is the name of fabulous gardens said to exist in Arabia Felix, and to be filled with all delights, so as to be a counterpart of Paradise. They are said to have been made by Shaddád-bin-Aad or Iram-bin-Omad.

[3] The lines occur in the Gulistán of S'adí, book ii., story 2. See my translation (p. 129) (Austin, Hertford, 1852). The version above I prefer as giving the force of the *nah.*

[4] There are three works of this name (which signifies 'A Gallery of Pictures.') The first was written by Ahmad-bin-Muhammad 'Abdu'l-Ghafáru'l-Kazwiní; the second by Mír-u 'd-dín u'l Isfaraini; and the third by Maula-bin-Sulaimán. The first contains anecdotes of each prince of the several Persian dynasties.

[5] The ripple on the water is compared to a chain which is said to be put upon the wind, in order to make an antithesis to the former sentence, where the air in its free course is compared to a car.

Now from the linked writing, which the omnipotent pen has inscribed on the page of the waters, they read these words, '*And we cause springs to gush forth in the same;*'[1] and from the green tablet of the grass, which was coloured by the pen of Creative power, they perused the verse, '*And we make therein gardens.*'[2] Meanwhile, the sight of Humáyún Fál fell on a tree, stripped of its clothing from the shedding of its leaves, as one which had experienced ⌊the effects of⌋ autumn, and which from age was without vegetation or growth, like helpless old men. The hatchet of the peasant, Time, had continued to cut off and mutilate its limbs, and the saw of the carpenter, Fortune, had sharpened its greedy teeth in making shreds of its weft and warp.[3]

COUPLET.

The young tree is the garden's pride and crown :
Grows it but old, the gardener cuts it down.

The centre of the tree, like the heart of careless darveshes, had become hollow, and a swarm of bees had taken refuge in that fortress, to store up provision for their support. When the King heard the buzzing of the bees, he inquired of his sage Vazír, 'What is the cause of the assembly of these light-winged insects[4] in this tree, and at whose command do these busy creatures resort to the heights and slopes of this meadow?

COUPLET.

What is the cause of their resorting here ?   And in this chamber whom do they revere?

Khujistah Ráí spake as follows, 'O fortunate Prince! they are a tribe doing much good and but little injury; and by reason of the cleanliness and neatness which is inherent in their natures, they have received the honour of God's inspiration, as set forth by the admirable saying, '*Thy Lord spake by inspiration unto the bee;*'[5] and have bound the belt of obedience round the waist of their soul by the communication of the favour of the royal command,

---

[1] Kur'án, Fl., ch. xxxvi. 34; Mar., 33; Sale, p. 332, l. 5: 'And we make therein gardens of palm-trees and vines; and we cause springs to gush forth in the same; that they may eat of the fruits thereof, and of the labour of their hands.' The text of Maracchi, and the MSS. I have inspected, give *minu'l-'uyún*, whereas the *minu* is omitted here both in the printed and the lithographed editions by an error.

[2] This is the same quotation from the Kur'án, which has been made a line or two above. See Sale, p. 332, l. 5.

[3] The *púd* is the 'weft,' that is, the cross-threads in weaving, and those which pass transversely to the *tár* or 'warp.'

[4] In the text 'birds;' as these Persians will not have a sentence—nay, not a word—without a comparison.

[5] Kur'án, Fl., ch. xvi., 70; Mar., 68; Sale, p. 202, l. 28: 'Verily here is a sign unto people who understand. Thy Lord spake by inspiration unto the bee, saying, 'Provide thee houses in the mountains, and in the trees, and of those materials wherewith men build hives for thee: then eat of every kind of fruit, and walk in the beaten paths of thy Lord.'

'*Provide thee houses in the mountains.*'[1]   They have a king, Y'asúb,[2] in bulk larger than they; and their nation have placed their heads on the line of obedience to his majesty and dignity, and he is seated on the square throne of wax which has been prepared for him, and has appointed to their several offices his vazír and chamberlain, and porter and guard, and spy and deputy. The ingenuity of his attendants is such, that each one prepares hexagonal chambers of wax, of such a fashion that there is no inequality in their partitions, and the most perfect geometricians would be unable to compass the like without compasses and a rule and other instruments.   And when the house approaches completion, by the king's command, they come forth from that abode, and a noble bee, in the language they possess, acquaints[3] them with the condition of office; that they are not to exchange their cleanliness for grossness,[4] nor to pollute the train of their purity with the contamination of uncleanness.   In fulfilment of their promise, they sit not but on the branch of the fragrant rose and the pure blossom, in order that what they eat from those delicate leaves may, in a short time, become concreted in their inside into the form of a fresh and sweet-tasted viscous humour, and a juice may be extracted from it such that the description, '*Wherein is a medicine for men,*'[5] may rightly apply to its quality; and when they return home, the warders try them by smelling whether they have kept to their troth, that is, whether they have avoided that which does not possess the requisite purity; after which, permission is given them to re-enter their hexagonal chambers and constructed apartments; and if (which God forbid!) they have transgressed the purport of this couplet,

COUPLET.

The hand of truthfulness in faith's girdle place,
Exert thyself to shun the faithless one's disgrace,

and there be found on them an odour which may be a cause of disgust and loathing, they immediately sever them in two; and if the warders, inclining to negligence, give them a passage, and the king should scent the unsavoury odour, he, having inquired into the state of the case, will conduct the unlucky

---

[1] See the preceding note. This Arabic sentence is the sequence of the one preceding. I take this opportunity, however, of correcting from the MSS. a reading in the lithographed and printed editions. These add, after the quotation, *rd* as belonging to *farmdn*, while it appears to me better to regard *farmán* as the gen. case dependent on '*indyat*, rather than as the dative after *kamr bastah*, though this construction is admissible.

[2] This word also signifies 'Prince.'

[3] *Firástddan*, in this sense, is not to be found in the Dictionary, though established by this passage.

[4] *Kasáfat.* This meaning is not to be found in the Dictionary, but is established by the above passage.

[5] Kur'án, Fl., ch. xvi. 71; Mar., 69; Sale, p. 203, l. 1: 'There proceedeth from their bellies a liquor of various colour: wherein is a medicine for men.' This alludes to a cure wrought by Muḥammad with honey: See Sale's note in line 32 of the same page.

bee to the place of punishment, and first give orders for the execution of the warders, and after that, put to death the disrespectful bee, that no other of their race should commit a similar ill-action: and in case that a stranger from another hive should wish to enter their dwelling, the warders forbid him, and should he not desist, they slay him: and it is recorded that Jamshíd, Emperor of the world, borrowed from them the regulations respecting warders and guards, and the appointment of chamberlains and doorkeepers, and the arrangement of thrones and regal cushions; and in course of time these customs were perfected.'

When Humáyún Fál heard these words, his noble mind felt an inclination to examine their institutions. He arose and went to the foot of the tree, and for a time amused himself with watching their court and palace, and their manner of coming and going, and the rules of their waiting and attendance. He beheld a multitude with their waists girded in obedience to the divine command, and like Sulaimán seated in the air,[1] having selected a pure diet and a clean dwelling, none of them interfering[2] with the other, and none of them suffering molestation or annoyance at the hands of his own species.

COUPLET.

Bravo! ye lofty ones of low estate;   Great little beings, humble, but elate.

He said, 'O Khujistah Ráí! wondrous is it that in spite of the taint of fierceness which is implanted in their nature, they are not intent upon injuring one another; and that although they possess a sting, they furnish nought but delicious honey; and notwithstanding the awe which attends their forms, they show nought but gentleness and softness. And among men we behold the reverse of this, a number of whom oppress their fellows, and aim at overthrowing the existence of those who resemble themselves.

COUPLET.

The inhumanity of mankind scan,   How man stands watching 'gainst his fellow-man!

The Vazír said 'These animals that you see are created with one sole disposition, and men are made of different temperaments; and inasmuch as in their composition, soul and body, and gross and fine, and light and darkness have been blent together; and the coin of material and angelic nature, and sublime and low feelings have been poured into their mould; a difference of temper and a peculiar bent is produced. According to the saying, '*And assuredly all men knew their respective drinking-place,*'[3] a share in angelic

---

[1] Muhammadans believe that Sulaimán or Solomon, as also Jamshíd, possessed a throne on which they could transport themselves through the air.

[2] Lit., 'To not one business with the advantage or injury of another.'

[3] Kur'án, Fl., ch. ii. 57; Mar., 59; Sale, p. 7, last line: 'And when Moses asked drink for the people, we said, strike the rock with thy rod; and there gushed thereout twelve fountains, according to the number of the tribes, and all men knew their respective drinking-place.' In Maracchi, the Latin verse is numbered wrong—60 for 59.

intelligence has been given to them,[1] and moreover, a portion of Satanic temper sent down upon them, so that every one should place the hand of compliance on the skirt of reason, and by the step of exaltation should be promoted to the rank of, '*And now have we honoured the children of Adam.*'[2] And all who place the head of obedience on the writing of the mandate of their sensual feelings, from excess of debasement[3] will remain on the descending grade of '*Nay! they are most in error as to the way,*' and it has well been said.

COUPLET.

Part of thy nature drags thee down, part lifts thee to the skies;
Quit thou thy fiendish portion then, and e'en o'er angels rise.

Aud the majority of mankind, by reason of their following the sensual inclinations which seek to enslave them, manifest censurable qualities, as greediness and avarice, and envy and rancour, and cruelty and pride, and hypocrisy and conceit, and slander and calumny, and false accusation and such like.

COUPLET.

How small self-knowledge is to dullards lent!
Vice they approve to virtue's detriment.
Like smoke which to the brain works out its way,
Or like light-quenching winds to lamps are they.'

The King said, 'According to thy statement, and the manner in which thou hast detailed the condition of the sensual, the most salutary course for mankind is that each should draw the foot of retirement under the robe of freedom from the world, and having closed on himself the gate of the society of others, should employ himself in self-purification; that salvation should arise from the cruel whirlpool of error, which is the source of blameable qualities.

HEMISTICH.

Herefrom 'tis better, if they can, to flee.

I have heard that ease is to be found in solitude, and liberty in retirement, and I have been convinced to-day that the society of the majority of persons is more hurtful than the poison of the viper, and association with them more full of difficulties than the peril of yielding up one's life; and with reference to the circumstance that many sages have passed long intervals in the corner of a cave, or the bottom of a pit, their views were directed to this,

---

[1] Lit., 'They have given to them.' In the following sentences *har kuddm*, is more than once used with a plural verb.

[2] Kur'án, Fl., ch. xvii. 72; Mar., 71; Sale, p. 215, l. 17: 'And now we honoured the children of Adam by sundry peculiar privileges and endowments; and we have given them conveniences of carriages by land and by sea, and have provided food for them of good things: and we have preferred them before many of our creatures which we have created, by granting them great prerogatives.'

[3] The printed and lithographed editions have here, by a typographical error, *razdlat* for *razdlat*, which would delay the student.

VERSE.

Why do the wise to the lone cavern fly?
'Tis that, alone, they find tranquillity.
Since darkness better is than man's dark deeds,
The wise man from the bustling mart recedes.

Moreover, perfect pure-hearted darveshes voluntarily subject themselves to solitude, and devote themselves to the concerns of others,

COUPLET.

I wish for solitude, that, if with whirlwind-force the wheel of destiny
Should smite this rubbish-bag of wordly things, the blow may fail to injure me.'

Khujistah Rái said, ' What has passed from the divinely-inspired tongue of his majesty the King, the asylum of the world, is the essence of truth and the perfection of right reasoning, since society is the cause of disquiet to the mind, and retirement the source of inward and outward contentment; according as they have said,

QUATRAIN.

Knowest thou to whom by night and day collected thoughts belong ?
That hermit who, when men collect, joins not the giddy throng.
Contentment, like a tender bud, in the heart's garden[1] grows ;
Amid the crowd it sheds its leaves as droops the gathered rose.

Nevertheless, several of the great leaders of the Faith, and chiefs of the true belief, have preferred, on the ground of advantage, the state of companionship and association to that of solitude ; and have said the society of a good companion is better than the being alone, but that when an amiable friend is not to be had, solitude is better than society.

COUPLET.

Thyself from others, not from friends, seclude :
Furs are not spring-wear, but for winter rude.

And in fact, society is the means of obtaining excellencies and advantages, and the bond of union between the great and the eminent.

COUPLET.

With the hand of seeking be the skirt of social converse sought ;
Sit not sole,—for lonely moments are with fear of madness fraught.

And from the purport of the tradition, ' There is no monachism in Islám,' [2] it is understood that the advantages of society are superior to the utilities of solitude ; and how can it be possible for man to set up for retirement, and not engage in society with those of his species, since the power of the triumphant omnipotence of God has imposed on mankind the obstacle of mutual necessity,

---

[1] One MS. reads dar bágh-i dil, which for the sense I much prefer to dar ghunchah-i dil, for how can a rose grow in a blossom ?   The number of syllables may be preserved by making ndzak an epithet of dil.

[2] This a saying of Muḥammad, which I have myself heard abundantly quoted by Sunnís.

and made them mutually necessary to each other, by reason of which they
have become social in disposition; that is to say, requiring to congregate,
which is called civic life : and the meaning of this word, civic life, is the
giving friendly aid and assistance to those of the same race reciprocally,
because neither the life of an individual nor the existence of the human
species is possible, save by aiding one another : as if, for example, an individual
should have to arrange for his food and raiment and abode, he must first
possess himself of the tools of a carpenter and smith, since without these
preparations, instruments for the culture of the fields and for harvest, and
whatever is dependent thereon, cannot be procured; and during this interval
life could not be supported, and after preparing these tools if he should spend
all his time in one avocation, he would be unable to engage in and perform
others, how much less could he succeed when he would have to occupy himself with the whole circle of employments.   Hence the necessity for a body of
persons mutually aiding one another, and for appointing each over a distinct
business[1] to the extent that may be sufficient for his support; and further to
give whatever may be beyond this to another, and that in proportion to their
own work they should make exchanges so as to remunerate themselves, so
that all transactions may be reduced to order by reason of this assembling;
and from these premises it is seen that men stand in need of one another's
assistance, and assistance without assembling together is impossible, wherefore
for the body of mankind to abide in solitude, belongs to the class of impossibilities, and in fact the proverb, ' *Assembling with others is a gift from God*,'
refers to this.

COUPLET.

> Seize the border thou of union, and thy business thus effect;
> For to compass aught unaided, is what thou canst ne'er expect.'

The King said, 'What the Vazír has spoken is the essence of wisdom, and
the choicest philosophy, but it occurs to me that consequent upon the
necessity of mankind for assembling together, the diversity of their temperaments will assuredly lead to disputes; because some will be stronger than
others, inasmuch as their bulk and strength will be greater; and a few others
will be superior to the rest in wealth and rank, and greediness and appetite
will prevail over others.   In those who excel the rest in strength and wealth,
the desire of conquest and tyranny will spring up, and undoubtedly it will
sway them to such an extent, that they will draw most men into the bonds
of obedience to them, and the greedy man will feel the lust of getting into
his grasp other men's gains; and these matters will lead to dissension and
will finally result in mischief.

---

[1] The best MS. I have consulted omits *ziyddah* after *ba-muhimmi*, and rightly, as it
appears to me.   The *ziyddah* which follows may have led to its erroneous insertion here.

COUPLET.

Dissension doth so fierce a flame upraise,   That all that is will perish in its blaze.'

The Vazír said, 'O king of kings, Asylum of wisdom! a plan has been ascertained for the removal of the dissension, which causing every one to be content with his own rightful share, retrenches the hand of his aggression from grasping the rights of others; and this plan they call 'coercion,' and the pivot of this is the rule of justice, the meaning of which is, the due regard of the mean, that is, the centre of the circle of excellence, which in accordance with the saying, *'The best things are means,'* comprehends the fact that extremes are worthless, as has been said,

VERSE.

Extremes of quality as separate are,   As the bright sun and the obscurest star : [1]
Wherefore to choose the midmost thing is best,   Since all 'the Golden mean' [2] as true attest.'

The king said, 'Whence can one know those means through the recognition of which the face of affairs assumes the appearance of a just equality?' The Vazír said, 'He who causes these things to appear is a perfect and completely excellent person, *aided by God,* who was sent by the divine Majesty to men, and sages call him Námús-i Akbar [3] and the wise in the faith term him 'messenger and prophet,' and assuredly his commands and prohibitions will be in unison with what is advisable for men in this world and that to which we return; and when that prophet *(May the blessing and peace of God be upon him !)* who is the Giver of the canons of law, bends his steps towards the other world, there is no alternative but to employ the coercion [4] of the ruler for preserving obedience to the laws of religion fixed by him. Since the majority of mankind are neglectful of their own interests, and the rule [5] of inclination and sense has the mastery over them, wherefore of necessity the existence of a powerful ruler is imperative, in order that—preserving the regulations of command and prohibition of the prophet, by which is meant law—he may cause the politico-economic regulations to be preserved, so that as well the most excellent sect may be exalted with the diadem of fortune, and also the robe of the state may be adorned with the embroidery of the exaltation of religion, for *State and Church are twins,*

COUPLET.

In reason's code, the prophet and the king,   Are but two jewels in the self-same ring.

And to the same effect they have said,

---

[1] In the text *suhd,* an obscure star in the Lesser Bear.

[2] Lit., 'By this proof, that the best of things are the means.' By 'means,' of course are meant the $\mu\epsilon\sigma\acute{o}\tau\eta\varsigma$ of Aristotle.

[3] A name of the Angel Gabriel, but here applied to Muhammad.

[4] The best MS. I have consulted reads *siydsatí,* which I prefer to *siydsi,* the reading of the printed and lithographed editions.

[5] Lit., 'And obedience to inclination and sense prevails over them.'

COUPLET.

The king's authority exalts the Law :   And by its sanction, kings inspire fresh awe.'

Humáyún Fál said, ' What ought to be the condition of this powerful ruler, the existence of whom among the people after the Prophet *(The blessing and peace of God be with him !)* [1] is requisite, and what ought to be his qualities in governing the affairs of the State and of the Faith ?' Khujistah Rái said, ' This ruler should be wise in the rules of judicial coercion and in the niceties of equity, for if he be not such, the State is on the road to decay, and its fortunes on the eve of departure,

COUPLET.

An empire is by justice rooted fast ;   And by thy justice will thy actions last.

And next it is necessary for him to understand the management of the Pillars of the State, and what body ought to be strengthened, and whom he ought to select to sit in counsel with, and what class he ought to bring down, and whose converse he ought to shun ; since of the attendants of the imperial court there are but a few who specially bind the girdle of fidelity to the king around the waist of sincere attachment, and who exert themselves for the earthly renown and heavenly recompense of the monarch : nay the generality of them choose the path of service with a view to obtain their own advantage, or to repel disagreeables from themselves.

COUPLET.

The braggart followers, thy pride and joy: The zealous labourers, whom thou dost employ.[2]

And since their principal business is based on covetousness, it is probable that they will entertain malice against a person whose favours they cannot requite, and that they will be envious of that other class, who may derive advantages from attending on the king superior to their own allowances ; and when rancour and envy have arisen in them, they will set on foot a variety of stratagems and state things which have not really occurred : and if the king be destitute of the covering of vigilance, and should listen to the discourse of interested persons with the hearing of acceptance, and should not condescend to inquire into and investigate the circumstances, a variety of injuries and mischiefs will arise therefrom, and divers evils will result.

VERSE.

Lend not thine ear to selfish men, for these   Bear envy in their bosom—fell disease !
They in a moment will embroil a world ;   A moment sees it to confusion hurled.

But when a vigilant and prudent monarch undertakes investigation of affairs,

---

[1] *Sal'am* is a mysterious word added to the name of Muḥammad, formed from the abbreviation of the following words, *ṣalla alláh 'alaihi wa sallam,* ' The blessing and peace of God be with him !'

[2] Lit., ' The boasters who are dearness to thee—the labourers who are for a thing to thee.' One MS. reads *shavad* for *shavand.*

and himself inquires into all matters collective and particular, he discriminates the brightness of truth from the shadows of falsehood, and both in this world the foundations of his empire remain free from disturbance, and in the world to come he attains the happiness of salvation and the exaltation of Paradise.

DISTICHS.

He that is just in this house of to-night, Improves his mansion of to-morrow's light;
Justice dominion's sole condition is, And gentleness secures eternal bliss.

And every wise king who, basing his acts on wisdom, makes the advice of sages his rule of conduct, his state will be prosperous and his people happy and joyful, like the great king of Hind, Dábishlím, who based the foundation of his empire on the rules delivered to him by the Bráhman Bídpáí, and having diligently inquired of him what would be advantageous for kings, in consequence reigned for a long time successfully: and after he migrated from this fleeting habitation to the pavilion of eternity, his good name and glorious tradition continues to this day on the page of time.

COUPLET.

Though all existing things in thought I scan, Good name appears the one true end of man.'

When Humáyún Fál heard mention of Dábishlím and Bídpáí, he became smiling and glad in the garden of joyousness, and on the plain of cheerfulness, like a fresh bud which in the morning-time unfolds its tender lip smilingly at the movement of the morning zephyr, and he said, ' O Khujistah Ráí! now for a long time the desire to hear the story of this King and Bráhman has been fixed in my inmost heart, and the idea of their discourses and interviews has occupied a place in the cabinet of my mind.

HEMISTICH.

For ages I for thy curled ringlets long.

Yet however much I have discharged the duties of search, and inquired of every one as to their narrative, I have obtained no portion[1] of this story nor has a letter of the record of their histories become known to me.

COUPLET.

With none I find a token of that heart-enslaving fair;
Or I am slow in finding, or no trace of her is there.

And I had always opened the ear of attention, considering from whose tongue their names would be heard by me, and ever kept the eye of expectancy on the high road of anticipation, pondering on the place whence the beauty of this matter would appear.

COUPLET.

My ear each sound attends, but where that lip's fair tidings, say ?
My gaze is on the road, but where that glorious vision's ray ?

---

[1] The MSS. I have consulted and the lithographed edition read *his ah as in kissah*, but the printed edition reads *hakkat*, or *hakkah* which appears to me not so intelligible, and which wants the jingle so pleasing to the Persian ear.

And now that I have learned that the Vazír is informed of their history I pay due thanks to God and say,

COUPLET.

At length I thus my heart's fond wish attain;   And what I sought of God at length I gain.

I hope that with all possible speed thou wilt favour me with the words of the King and the Bráhman, since in telling this history, to thee results the advantage of discharging the obligation due for my bounties, and to me by reason of hearing these admonitions a variety of advantages will be gained for my subjects ; and a narration—by the means of the recital of which, a debt of gratitude is discharged, and by the blessing of the hearing of which, advantage accrues to a whole people, high and low,—must be exceedingly auspicious.

STANZA.

The wise man's tongue, fraught with sagacity,	The key of wisdom's treasure-house will be.
Ope then the door, bring forth the coin and see,	For prudent counsel will the touchstone be.
So counsel those of regal dignity,	That the folks' happiness therein may be.[1]

BEGINNING OF THE STORY OF KING DÁBISHLÍM AND THE BRÁHMAN BÍDPÁÍ.

The clear-minded and wise-counselling Vazír unloosed the tongue of explanation, and in the delivery of his discourse fully discharged all that was due to eloquence, and said,—

COUPLET.

'O auspicious foot of Majesty! whose glorious influence lends,
To the stars of heaven the fortune that on their course attends.

I have heard from the sugar-ravishing parrots of eloquence, and the melli-fluous nightingales of the flower-garden of genius, that in one of the chief cities of Hind, which is the mole on the face of the empire, there was a king of wakeful fortune and prosperous days, and a monarch [2] world-adorning, subject-cherishing, tyrant-consuming. The royal throne derived lustre from his illimitable justice, and the imperial tribunal gained ornament from the beauty of his commands and prohibitions. The stain of oppression and injustice was erased from earth's page, and the countenance of justice was shewn to all worlds in the mirror of his beneficence.

COUPLET.

Justice! thy rays all earth irradiate,   Yea! justice gilds the counsels of the State.

And they called this monarch King Dábishlím, and the meaning of this word in their language is, 'Great King.' From the excess of his greatness, he cast

---

[1] Every line in the Persian rhymes with the verb signifying ' will be.' I have, therefore, imitated this.

[2] Instead of *wa bah rdí*, the reading of the lithographed and printed editions, and out of which I am unable to make sense, I would propose to read *wa rdí*, which is also the reading of all the MSS. I have consulted.

not the loop of the noose of his lofty spirit save on the niched battlement of the citadel of heaven; and by reason of his independence,[1] he looked not save on the sublimest actions and the most exalted matters. Ten thousand[2] furious elephants were among his forces, and the number of his soldiers, skilled and valiant in war, would not enter into the area of computation. He possessed full treasuries and flourishing dominions.

HEMISTICH.

Thou sole possessest all, all monarchs have.

And notwithstanding all this magnificence, he was wont to weigh the affairs of his subjects, and to investigate himself every dispute between those who sought justice.

COUPLET.

Who serve thee, thou, O king! preserve, and shew   A kind and lowly bearing to the low.[3]

When he had strengthened his own dominion by a strict administration of justice, and had cleared the extent of his empire from aspirants, he was wont, with untroubled mind, to adorn the banquet of pleasure, and to gather the wish of his heart from fortune in its various degrees of happiness; and in his assembly councillors clothed in wisdom, and sages robed in excellence, were wont to be present, and adorned the assembly by elegant expressions and praise of noble qualities. One day he had taken his seat on the cushion of pleasure, and had set forth a royal banquet.

COUPLET.

With all things meet he had adorned the banquet-chamber bright,
And opened wide the portal of rejoicing and delight.

After the gratification of listening to the strains of mellifluously chaunting minstrels, he shewed an inclination to hear a tale of wisdom improving the intellect; and after the spectacle of the cheeks of moon-faced Venus-fronted beauties, he evinced a desire for gazing on the bridal-display of words of beneficial tendency; and having made inquiries of philosophers and counsellors of excellent qualities and admirable endowments, he bestowed on the ear of his sense, the adornment of the jewels of their discourses, which resembled royal pearls.

HEMISTICH.

Speech is a pearl befits the ear of kings.

Then each one of them celebrated some glorious quality and some laudable attribute, until the steed of discourse reached in its career the plain of

---

[1] The word *istighná* = the Greek αὐτάρκεια, 'sufficiency in oneself,' somewhat stronger than our 'independence.'

[2] I have not translated the word *ḳiláddah-i*, which is a word added to 'elephants,' as we say 'so many *head* of cattle.' In the same manner *rás*, 'head' is added to 'horses,' and *zanjír*, 'chain,' also to 'elephants,' and *nafar* to 'men.'

[3] I have translated these lines very freely, making a vain attempt to preserve the play upon words of the original.

generosity and beneficence. All the sages were unanimous as to this, that
generosity is the most noble of qualities, and the most perfect of attributes,
and therefore they have related it as a tradition from the First Teacher,[1] that
the best quality of those which are ascribed to God Most High, is beneficence,
because His beneficence permeates through all creatures, and His bounty
reaches all created things, and the Lord of the great Prophecy (May the
blessings of God be upon him!) said that generosity is a plant which springs
up in Paradise, and which grows on the borders of the stream Kausar;[2] for,
Generosity is a tree in Paradise.[3]

VERSE.

The liberal brings God's favour on himself ;	True treasure lies in the forsaking pelf.
Wouldst thou the trace of ceaseless treasure[4] find ;	'T is only in an ever-bounteous mind.

After the king had understood this question, his natural spirit of generosity
bestirred itself, and he commanded so that they opened the door of a vast
treasure, and proclaimed a distribution to high and low; and they made both
strangers and citizens content with a full portion, and by general largesse
raised both high and low to an independence of fortune above their brethren.

COUPLET.

From his palm, as from the rain-cloud, forth his bounty's drops appear ;
So he washed want's writing from the tablet of misfortune here.

All the day, like the radiant sun, he was employed in showering down gold,
and like fresh fortune, in gratifying the desires of others, until the time when
the golden-pinioned Símurgh[5] of the sun turned to its nest in the west, and
the black-visaged raven of the night,[6] spread the wings of darkness over the
regions of the world.

VERSE.

When day its mysteries had coverèd,	And mantling night her shadows had outspread.
The Súfí[7] sun sate down in lonely nook.	And heaven the Pleiads' rosary[8] uptook.

The king placed the head of leisure on the pillow of repose, and the hands of

---

[1] A name of Gabriel.

[2] For a description of this river, see D'Herbelot *s.v.*, Cautser; and Sale's Preliminary
Discourse, p. 68, 1. 42 : 'It is whiter than milk or silver, and more odoriferous than musk,
with as many cups set around it as there are stars in the firmament ; of which water
whoever drinks will thirst no more for ever.' It properly signifies 'abundance,' and is the
title of the 108th chapter of the Ḳur'án.

[3] This sentence I presume to be a Ḥadís, for I cannot find it in the Ḳur'án.

[4] The word *rawán* signifies also 'soul,' so that the expression may also mean 'a treasure
of the soul.'

[5] The Símurgh, or 'Anḳá, is a fabulous bird, said to reside in the mountain Ḳáf, or
Caucasus, and to be of prodigious size. The idea has probably been derived from a tradition
of the Jews about a huge bird, called Yukhush, mentioned in the Talmud.

[6] For *siyáh chihrah-i* in the printed and lithographed editions, should be read *siyáh
chihrah*, as this adjective is dependent on *ghuráb*.

[7] The Súfís are a renowned order of mystics, higher than the Ḳalandar or Matamati, in
that they do not acknowledge a spiritual head.

[8] The Pleiades are compared to a rosary of white beads in the hand of a devotee.

sleep overspread the vestibule of the area of the brain. Then the limner of fancy depicted to him a serene-visaged old man, on whose countenance the traces of wise counsel were visible, and on whose front the marks of super-human power were discernible, who advanced and saluted the king, and said: 'To-day thou hast expended a treasure in the way of God, and hast offered up a vast sum to obtain the favour of the divine Majesty. In the morning, place the foot of intention in the stirrup of success, and betake thyself towards the east of the capital; for a treasure worthy of kings, and a supply of money gratuitously given, is delivered to thee; and by the finding of such a stone thou wilt place the foot of glorious superiority above the stars,[1] and wilt raise the head of haughtiness beyond the pinnacle[2] of the highest heavens.' When the king heard these good tidings, he awoke from sleep; and gladdened by the thought of the treasure, and the joyful intelligence of the sage old man, performed the duties of ablution, and stood up to fulfil the prescribed devotions of his faith, until the time when the treasurer of omnipotent power opened the door of the horizon, and the gold-sprinkling hand of the sun drew under the garment of its rays the jewels of the stars from the cabinet of the sky.

COUPLET.

At early dawn when morning, with bright silver sprinkled o'er,
Had removed the golden padlock from heaven's palace-door.

The king commanded so that they adorned a swift wind-paced courser with a saddle of gold and a gem-studded bridle, and having mounted with fortunate omens and auspicious destiny, he turned his face towards the east.

COUPLET.

Stirrup to stirrup [3] on with him went fortune and success;
Rein touching rein, high triumph and support his progress bless.

And when he had passed beyond the limits of habitation into the expanse of the desert, he cast his glance on every side, and sought traces of his object. In the midst of this his eyes fell on a mountain, lofty as the magnanimity of the beneficent lords of piety, and fixed as the fortunes of equitable kings. At the foot of the mountain a dark cavern appeared, and a man of serene heart was seated at its door, liberated, like the Companion in the cave,[4] from the trouble of rivals.

COUPLET.

He nothing heeds, yet nought escapes his ken :
Sides with—is severed from—all living men.[5]

---

[1] Lit., 'The twin stars near the pole of the Lesser Bear.'

[2] I have to correct a mistake in the printed edition. It should be *zarwah* for *zarwah*.

[3] Lit., 'Stirrup within stirrup.' *Daulat wa ikbál-rd* is governed by some such verb as *dásht*, understood as preceding.

[4] Abúbakr, who lay hid with Muḥammad in his celebrated Hijrah or flight from Makkah, in a cave of the mountain named Ṭúr.

[5] Lit., 'Burned, and yet performing with.' I have endeavoured to keep the play on words in *súkhtah wa sákhtah*.

When the sight of the king fell on that holy sage, his heart became inclined
to his society, and his desire bent towards his company. The old man having
read the wish of the king from the illuminated page of his mind, unloosed
the tongue of humble address,

COUPLET.

'O Thou! to whom is given by God this world-wide sovereignty,
Thy place is on our head and eyes, alight and welcomed be!

O king! although the sorrowful[1] hovel of the wretched, in comparison with
the gilded palace, may appear contemptible, and the store of the cell of the
distressed in juxta-position to the gem-adorned dwelling of the great, is of no
account; nevertheless,

HEMISTICH.

It is an ancient custom and established rite

for kings to survey with a look of pity the condition of faḳírs, and to honour
hermits with their address and visits, and to regard this as the complement of
the perfection of good manners and of high qualities.

VERSE.

To condescend to holy men adds greatness to the great;
King Sulaimán would not o'erlook an insect's low estate.'

Dábishlím conducted the speech of the Darvesh to the place of acceptance, and
dismounted from his steed: and having with his auspicious words opened an
acquaintance with him,[2] asked the aid of his spirit.

VERSE.

With whom the blessings of the pious go,
He learns the secrets of the heart to know;
Whoe'er have fathomed wisdom's mysteries,
Have learned them through the teaching of the wise.

And after the king showed an intention to depart, the Darvesh unloosed the
tongue of apology.

COUPLET.

'To kings so great, due hospitality   Cannot be shown by one so poor as I.

Nevertheless, in simple unstudied guise[3] I would offer to the king a thing of
worth which I possess, and which descended to me as a patrimony, and that
is the account of a treasure, the purport of which is, that in a corner of this
cave is a vast treasure, wherein are coins and jewels of inestimable value;
and I, since I have obtained possession of the treasure of contentment—for
'Contentment is a treasure without decay'[4]—busied not myself in searching for

---

[1] The printed edition, by a typographical error, reads *ajzdn* for *aḥzdn*.   One MS. reads
kulbah-i tárík.

[2] The expression is rather obscure, *istínds* signifies 'being intimate.'

[3] *Má-ḥaẓar*, ' whatever is prepared in haste' (especially victuals).

[4] This I presume to be a proverb.   I do not find it in the Ḳur'án.

any other, and for my interest in this life also made it my capital; since in the bázár of reliance on God, there is no coin more current than it.

COUPLET.

Who trust in God has ne'er beheld, has ne'er discovered aught:
Contentment's store who ne'er has found, his findings are but nought.

I hope that the Khusrau,[1] conqueror of kingdoms, will cast the glance of attention upon it, and command his servants to engage in search for it; and having caused it to be conveyed to the public treasury, expend it fittingly;—It is not far off.' Dábishlím, on hearing this speech, communicated to the Darvesh the incident of the night, and informed the Companion of the cave of the circumstances of this adventure. The Darvesh said, 'Although this trifle is insignificant with reference to the lofty spirit of the king, still, since it has been consigned to you from the invisible world, you must bestow on it the honour of acceptance.

HEMISTICH.

What th' Unseen sends us cannot have defect.[2]

The king commanded, so that all engaged in excavating the cave in every part and in all directions; and in a short space of time, having recovered the clue to the treasure, they brought the heaps into the presence of Humáyún.

VERSE.

Rare ornaments of priceless gems were there,
Many a ring, bracelet, and ear-ring fair.
Many a casket and box with lock of gold,
Which the pearl and the ruby and sapphire hold.
Many a tool of gold, and silver cup,
Things costly and rare filled them brimming up.

The king commanded, so that they removed the locks from the chests and caskets, and he gazed upon precious gems and wondrous rarities. In the midst of all, he saw a box adorned with jewels and with bands tightly fastened round it on all sides and in all directions, and locked with a padlock of Turkish workmanship, made of steel inlaid with gold. The firmness of that lock was such, that the tooth of no key could unloose its wards, nor the skill of any solver of difficulties find the way to the solution of its knot. However much they searched, no trace of its key nor hint of the means of opening it appeared. The king felt an intense wish to open that lock, and an unbounded curiosity to examine its contents. He said to himself, 'It would seem that they have deposited in this box a rarity more precious than gems of price;

---

[1] The general title of the Sassanides or third dynasty of Persia, who reigned 431 years, commencing 229 A.D. The most celebrated kings of this dynasty were Bahrám-Gúr, Núshírwán and Parwíz.

[2] I found it impossible to introduce into English the play on *'aib*, 'fault,' and *ghaib*, 'future.'

otherwise, what can be the cause of all this careful security?' He then gave orders, so that skilful nimble-handed smiths prepared to break open the lock; and when the lid of the chest had been opened, a casket was taken out of it studded with gems like the zodiac, and within that casket was deposited a small box, like the orb of the moon in exceeding brightness. The king commanded, so that they brought the small box before him. He opened its lid with his royal hand, and beheld a piece of white silk, on which were written some words in the Syriac character. He marvelled as to what this might be: some said it was the name of the owner of the treasure, and others argued that it might be a talisman which had been written for the security of the treasure; and as the words of the Pillars of the State on the subject waxed long, Dábishlím said that until this should be read, the doubt would not be removed, and that as no one of those present was acquainted with the rules of the character, they should hasten in search of some one by whom the object might be effected. At last they heard of a sage who had perfect skill in decyphering and writing strange characters, and by the imperial command they in a short time brought him to the foot of the sublime throne. Dábishlím after shewing him due respect, said, 'O sage! the cause of troubling you is this, that you should explain in clear language the purport of this writing, and unfold truly and exactly, the circumstances of these lines.

HEMISTICH.

From this it may be I may have my wish.'

The sage took the writing, and brought the words letter by letter under the survey of inquiry. After a long reflection, he said, ' This writing contains a variety of beneficial things, and this, and no other, is, in very truth, the written treasure. The purport is, in brief, that—'I, King Húshang,[1] have deposited treasure for a great king and a mighty monarch, whom they call Dábishlím, and by means of divine revelation I have learned that this treasure will fall to his lot; and I have placed this testament amongst the gold and jewels, in order that when he removes this treasure and reads this will, he may be on his guard, since to be infatuated with gold and silver is not the part of wise men, because these are but borrowed stuff which every day may be handled by a new person and will prove faithful to none.

VERSE.

Who would wish for this world's riches, a vain and fleeting shew?
To whom have they proved faithful, that to me they should be so?
These bones the marrow of true faith and abiding virtue lack;
The odour of fidelity comes not from this vain rubbish-sack.

But this testament is a manual of practice, which cannot be put aside by

---

[1] Second king of the Píshdádyan, or first dynasty of Persia. (The word signifies 'sage.') For his history see D'Herbelot s.v. Huschank.

kings; wherefore that prudent monarch will find fortune his friend, who acts in accordance with these precepts, believing that every prince that exists, who does not choose to rely on these fourteen rules that I set forth, will find the foundation of his fortunes disturbed, and the basis of his empire insecure.

The first precept is, that with reference to any one of his attendants to whom the king may give exaltation in his immediate presence, he should not honour with acceptance the words of another, with a view to his over-throwal; for whoever is admitted to intimacy with a king, a number of persons will assuredly feel envy of him, and when they see the foundations of the king's favour firm with respect to him, by clever stratagems they will strive to ruin and subvert him, and pretending loyalty and good advice, will speak cunning and deceitful words, until the king's mind may become changed towards him, and in this state of affairs their desire may be accomplished.

COUPLET.

Listen not to all men's speeches, but to mine give heed;
Base men for their purpose specious reasons never need.

Precept the second, to wit:—Let the prince not admit the sycophant and calumniator into his assembly, for they are mischievous and contentious and their end is very disastrous; moreover, when the king observes this quality in any one, let him, with all speed, quench the fire of his calumny with the scymitar of punishment, that the smoke of it may not darken the world's surface.

COUPLET.

To quench the spark is thy sole course to end
A flame which would o'er heaven and earth extend.

Precept the third, to wit:—He should observe to all his nobles and Pillars of his state, the way of cordiality and kindness; for all affairs are set in movement by the alliance of unanimous friends, and by the aid of comrades of one accord.

HEMISTICH.

By unison the world may be acquired.

Precept the fourth, to wit:—Through the kind bearing of an enemy and his flattery, let him not be elated; and although he fawn and humble himself, let him not turn from caution to confidence, since true friendship will in no wise spring from an enemy.

VERSE.

Shrink from a smiling enemy   As you'd keep fire from fuel dry:
Should he in open battle fail,   By fraud he'll struggle to prevail.

Precept the fifth, to wit:—When the jewel of his wish has come into his grasp, let him not incline to sloth in preserving it, nor ruin it by neglect, since another expedient may be impracticable, and however much he may repent, regret will be unavailing.

COUPLET.

Leapt from the string no shaft returns again ;   Bite thy back-hand [1] regretful—'tis in vain.

Precept the sixth, to wit:—Let him not shew levity and precipitation in business, but let him affect circumspection and deliberation; for the harm of too much haste is great, and the advantage of patience and steadiness is immense.

DISTICHS.

> Be thou precipitate in no affair,
> Nor turn thy reins from thoughtfulness and care:
> What is not done, thou may'st with quickness do,
> But when 'tis done 'tis then in vain to rue.

Precept the seventh, to wit:—Let him on no account suffer the reins of deliberation to slip from his hand. If a body of enemies attack him in confederation, and he sees an advantage in this, viz., in endeavouring to win over one of them, supposing that escape from the rest is likely to ensue from such a course, let him at once take steps to effect this object, and in accordance with *'War is wile,'* let him hew down the basis of their intrigues with the axe of stratagem, since the wise have said,

COUPLET.

> From the snare of thy foe's guile, thou mayst scape by wiles, I ween ;
> *'Tis truly said that keen things are best answered with the keen.*

Precept the eighth, to wit:—Let him beware of the rancorous and envious, and not be deceived by their flattering words; since when the plant of envy has been rooted in the ground of the breast, no fruit from it can be expected but mischief and injury.

VERSE.

> When envious passions to the breast belong,
> The heart is set on injury and wrong.
> The envious, being present, thee cajole,
> But, absent, mischief only fills their soul.

Precept the ninth, to wit:—Let him make clemency his under and outer garment, and not for a slight fault bring his attendants into the place of exposure to invective and rebuke, for the great have always washed out, with the water of forgiveness and clemency, the stain of misdeeds from the records of the actions of the lowly, and have absolvingly covered their disrespect and boldness with the skirt of indulgence.

COUPLET.

> From Adam's time to thine, O king! 'tis still the same ;
> The great extend forgiveness, and the lowly are to blame.

And when some of his attendants have acted criminally and disloyally, and

---

[1] I trust I may be pardoned this compound for 'back of the hand.'

have been holpen by the forgiveness of the king, let him again irrigate them with the water of his favours, that they may not wander bewildered and distressed in the wilderness of dejection.

COUPLET.

Those who, by thee upraised, have favour found,
Encourage, nor dash sudden to the ground.

Precept the tenth, to wit :—Let him not employ himself in injuring any one, that in the way of retribution, according to '*And the retaliation of evil ought to be an evil proportionate thereto,*'[1] evil may not result to him, but let him shower down on the heads of men the rain of kind deeds, that in the garden of '*If ye do well, ye will do well to your own souls*'[2] the flowers of his wish may bear fruit.

STANZA.

If thou dost good, to thee too, good they'll do ;
If ill, they will repay thee, and worse too.
Art thou of good and ill now ignorant ?
There comes a day that they'll supply this want.

Precept the eleventh, to wit :—Let him not indulge an inclination for a thing which is not in accordance with his condition nor suited to his state, for many a person, having left his own business, has attempted something which did not befit him, and having failed in effecting his purpose, has been deprived of his own employment also.

COUPLET.

A crow the mountain-partridge-gait in vain
Would try, but failed, nor could its own regain.

Precept the twelfth, to wit :—Let him adorn his position with the ornaments of mildness and constancy, for the heart of the mild is lovely and the profound saying, 'The meek man is all but a prophet,' is a true tradition.

COUPLET.

Mildness than steel a greater sharpness boasts,
Yea, 'tis more conquering than a hundred hosts.

Precept the thirteenth, to wit :—Having acquired faithful and trustworthy servants, let him avoid sycophants and perfidious men; for when the sweepers

---

[1] Ḳu'rán, Fl., ch. xlii. 38; Mar., 39; Sale, p. 360, l. 47: 'Whatever things are given you, they are the provision of this present life; but the reward, which is with God, is better and more durable for those who believe and put their trust in their Lord; and who avoid heinous and filthy crimes; and when they are angry, forgive; and who hearken unto their Lord and are constant at prayer; and whose affairs are directed by consultation among themselves, and who give alms out of what we have bestowed on them; and who, when an injury is done them, avenge themselves (and the retaliation of an evil ought to be an evil proportionate thereto): but he who forgiveth and is reconciled unto his enemy, shall receive his reward from God; for he loveth not the unjust doers." Maracci has omitted the second *aḥsanatum*.
[2] Ḳur'án, Ch. xvii. 7; Sale, p. 210, l. 11: 'If ye do well, ye will do well to your own souls ; and if ye do evil ye will do it unto the same.'

of the court of empire are endued with the quality of fidelity, both the secrets of the state remained concealed, and men live in safety from any wrong on their part; and if, which God forfend! the face of their condition be blackened with the mole of perfidy, and their words be dignified with confidence by the king, it may chance that they may cast the innocent into the place of destruction, and that bad results may ensue thereupon, both for time and eternity.

VERSE.

Faithful should be the servant of the king,
That in the realm fresh glories may upspring.
But if to perfidy he turn aside,
What woes, through him, that hapless state betide!

Precept the fourteenth, to wit:—He must not permit the dust of dejection from ill-fortune and the vicissitudes of life, to settle on the garment of his spirit, because the wise man is ever involved in the bonds of calamity, while the careless man passes his life in delights and ease.

VERSE.

The chain is on the lion's neck, while the jackal, all night long,
With thoughtless freedom ranges the ruined wastes [1] among.
The wise man fears to venture forth from the lowly cell of care,
The careless wantons, unrestrained, in the garden and parterre.

And let him know assuredly, that without the display of Eternal grace, and the bounty which is exposed to no decay, the shaft of happiness cannot strike the target of his wish, and no excellence nor skill, however great, can accomplish anything without the aid of the Divine decree and omnipotent power.

COUPLET.

Greatness comes not from science or from skill,
But from the mandates of the Eternal will.

And to each of these fourteen precepts which have been mentioned, there is a certain tale attached, and a story which can be relied upon; and if the king desire to obtain information regarding the detail of these stories and tales, he must direct his steps to that mountain in Sarándíp,[2] which was the alighting-place of the Father of Mankind, for his difficulty will be there solved, and all his wish will present itself to him in that garden of desires, '*And God is the aider to the acquirement of the wish and of wished-for objects.*'" When the sage had offered to the royal ear this genuine statement, and had presented to the loftiness of the King's spirit, this casket of jewels, in

---

[1] One MS. explains on the margin *aṭlál* as *makán-i khrdb*, and *damn* as *sargín*; but another, and a better one, reads *aṭráf* for *aṭlál*.

[2] Ceylon, where is the mountain called Adam's Peak, on which he is said to have fallen when expelled from Paradise.

which were enclosed the pearls of spiritual meaning; Dábishlím honourably saluted him, and with the utmost reverence, kissed the scroll and placed it, as an amulet, on his princely arm, and said, 'The treasure of which they told me, is a treasure of secrets, not a purse of dirhams and dínárs.[1] It is a store of wisdom, not of gems and pearls. Praise be to God! I have such an amount of worldly goods that I have no need of this superfluity, and through loftiness of spirit, I regard this small finding as unfound. It is fitting that in gratitude for this book of advice, which alone may be looked upon as a real treasure, they should distribute this hoard, by way of alms, among the deserving, that the offering of this good action may accrue to the victorious spirit of King Húshang; and we too, in accordance with the saying, '*He who points to a good action is like him that does it*,' may share in the blessing of the reward.' The ministers of his majesty the King, by the royal direction, bestowed the whole of that hoard of coins and gems, in the way of the divine approval, on the deserving.

COUPLET.

Money was given for deeds of charity, Lo! now how money chimes with almonry![2]

And when he had discharged this duty, the king turned towards the capital, and adorned the cushion of empíre with the imperial dignity, and passed the livelong night in pondering on a journey to Sarándíp, that his desire might be accomplished and his wish attained, and that having acquired perfect knowledge of the several precepts, he might make them the prop of his government and the pillar of his empire and rule. The next day, when the bright sun like a pomegranate-coloured ruby, showed its face from the corner of the mountain of Sarándíp, and the diamond-hued heaven showered down sparks of brightest ruby on the earth,

COUPLET.

The sun poured down his rays of golden hue,
The stars those pearly lamps of night withdrew,[3]

Dábishlím commanded, so that they made present at the foot of the high throne, two persons from among the confidential servants of his majesty, who for sincerity of counsel were referred to as advisers, and for excellence of advice and aid in explanation[4] were the pivot [of the royal affairs], and after distinguishing them by the imperial favour, the King disclosed to them the circumstances of his midnight meditation, and said, 'The desire of journeying

---

[1] A dirham is from the twentieth to the twenty-fifth part of a dínár, as standards vary, and this latter is equal to a ducat or sequin, (*zecchino*) about nine shillings.

[2] In the original, *diram*, the name of a coin, rhymes with *karam*, 'liberality.' I have made a feeble effort to preserve the play upon words. 'Almonry,' I use, of course, as the place where 'alms' are distributed.

[3] By a typographical error in the printed edition, *kam shud* is written for *gum shud*.

[4] In one MS. opposite *muvdzarat* is written on the margin, *ydrí dddan mín kashf-u'l-lughát*.

to Sarándíp has fixed itself in my mind, and the purpose of proceeding and setting forward in that direction has snatched the reins of choice from the grasp of power. What do you think advisable in this matter, and how do you regard the expediency of this step? And for a long time I have unloosed the knot of my difficulties with the finger of your counsel, and have based on your opinion of happy tendency, the foundation of the affairs of my government and my fortunes. To day, also, bring to the place of representation whatever may be the scope of your prudent thoughts, and that which your penetrating judgment approves, in order that I also may try it in its various bearings, and make that plan, which obtains the writing of unanimity, the principle[1] of action.'

COUPLET.

On due deliberation base each deed,   For unmatured no plan can e'er succeed.

The vazírs said, 'It is not fitting to answer this question impromptu ; and in the purposes of kings and their affairs, due deliberation is required, since an unconsidered word is like gold unweighed.

HEMISTICH.

First weigh thy words, and then prepare to speak.

We will deliberate on this matter to-day and to-night, and will apply the coin of each cogitation to the touchstone of trial, and that which among our thoughts turns out to be full weight, we will to-morrow have the honour to represent.' Dábishlím consented to this. The next day at early dawn they presented themselves before his Majesty the King, and each having stationed himself in the place that belonged to him, they opened the ear of sense to hearken to the command of the King, and after permission to speak, the superior vazír, having come forward and knelt respectfully, performed the due blessings and eulogies, and said as follows,

COUPLET.

'World-taker! world-bestower! Thou to whom is given
Eternal empire, by the unchanging will of Heaven!

It has thus entered the mind of thy slave, that although but little advantage is to be calculated upon from this journey, nevertheless, much labour must be undergone, and being entirely excluded from pleasure and ease, and repose and delight, the heart must be placed on toil and abstinence ; and it is not concealed from the luminous and world-conquering mind of the King, that according to '*The spark of travel is*[2] *a fragment of hell*,' journeying is a breast-consuming flame and a heart-rending arrow, and according to the saying, '*Expatriation is the greatest of calamities*,' the leaving one's country is a liver-piercing dart; men of experience have come to the conclusion that

---

[1] The word *aṣl-u'l-báb*, a common enough form, is omitted in the Dictionary.

[2] In the printed edition, *mí-u's-saḳr*, is written by a mistake for *min-u's-saḳr*.

they should not step beyond the corner of their house, and the drops of tears are therefore trampled on because they could not repose in the nook of their own dwelling.

COUPLET.

> In travel, toil and contumely and deep abasement meet,.
> If happiness and joy exist, at home they are most sweet.

It behoves a wise man not to exchange ease for toil, nor to give, from the palm of his hand, the ready-money of enjoyment for the goods of contingency; nor, from choice, select the misery of travel in preference to the dignity of repose,[1] that that may not befal him which befel that Pigeon.' The King asked, How was that?

STORY I.

The vazír said, 'I have heard that two Pigeons consorted together in one nest, and dwelt in amity with one another in one abode, neither were their minds disturbed by rivals nor their hearts panged by misfortune. They contented themselves with water and grain, and like solitarily dwelling hermits, consigned themselves to reliance on the Divine will. One was named Bázindah,[2] and the other Nawázindah. And both of them, evening and morning, were wont to sing, in unison, harmonious strains, and at all times, with soul-enlivening melodies, to utter various cooings.

COUPLET.

> In memory of that idol's face, our solitude we prize,
> That love has freed us from the world, and snapped all other ties.

Fortune was envious of the agreement of those sympathising friends, and the malevolent eyes of time threw their baleful influence on those two happy companions.

COUPLET.

> This seems the task by which Fate's occupied,
> To sever love, and friends from friends divide.

The desire of travel developed itself in Bázindah, and he said to his friend, 'How long shall we continue in one nest and spend our time in one abode? I feel a desire of wandering through different parts of the world for two or three days, and putting in practice the high command, ' *Say, go through the*

---

[1] As the text stands in the lithographed and printed editions, it seems to me, no sense can be elicited from it. The vazir is arguing against travel; he could not therefore say, that it behoved a wise man, '*izz-i akdmat-rá bar gull-i ghurbat na guzínad,* 'not to choose the dignity of repose, in preference to the degradation of travel.' The right reading, that of some MSS., is, clearly, *gull-i ghurbat-rá bar 'izz-i akdmat.* The printed edition has here, in four different places, *koshah* for *goshah.*

[2] *Bázindah,* 'playful,' said in the dictionary to be 'a kind of pigeon!' *Nawázindah,* in the dictionary, *nawdzandah,* 'caressing.'

earth' [1] since in travel many marvellous things are seen and many experiences are gained, and the venerable have said, ' *Travel is the means of triumph.*' Until the scymitar comes forth from the scabbard on the battle-field of the brave, honor is not gained; and until the pen moves in the path of perambulation from its point,[2] the painting of beautiful styles is not manifested on the page of existence. The sky which is ever journeying, is the highest of all things; and the earth which is ever quiescent, is trampled down and kicked by all beings both high and low.

VERSE.

View the earth's sphere and the revolving skies ;
This sinks by rest, and those by motion rise.
Travel man's tutor is, and glory's gate,
On travel treasure and instruction wait.
From place to place had trees the power to move,
Nor saw nor axe would wrong the stately grove.'

Nawázindah said, ' O my heart's friend ! thou hast not undergone the toils of travel, nor experienced the hardship of absence from friends, nor has the maxim, ' *Travel is travail,*' reached thy soul's ear, nor has the stormy blast, ' *Parting is burning,*' blown on the garden of thy heart. Travel is a tree which brings forth no fruit but that of separation, and absence is a cloud which lets fall no drops but the rain of disgrace.

COUPLET.

Poor and friendless sits the wanderer alone at evening prayer ;
His resting-place the road-side, his heart broken with despair.'

Bázindah said, ' Although the trouble of travel is wearing to the mind, still it enlivens by visiting new countries and seeing the wonders of the world ; and, moreover, when the disposition has become accustomed to the inconveniences of the journey, it is no longer harassed by them, and the toil of the road ceases to make the same impression on the spirits, in consequence of the interest taken in the wonders of the strange country.

COUPLET.

What matter though in travel's path the thorn of trouble grows ;
Since from this thorn we gather, every moment, pleasure's rose.'

Nawázindah said, ' O beloved friend ! the recreation of seeing various parts of the world and viewing the gardens of Iram, delights us if in the society of true companions and intimate friends ; and when one has been separated from the happiness of seeing those with whom one is accustomed to be, it

---

[1] Kur'án, ch. vi, 11 ; Fl., and Mar. ; Sale, p. 82, l. 29 : ' Say, go through the earth, and behold what hath been the end of those who accused our prophets of imposture. Say, unto whom belongeth whatsoever is in heaven and in earth ? Say, unto God. He hath prescribed unto himself mercy.'

[2] I do not think the *az sar* makes good sense. It is probably only inserted to make a jingle with *sair*, which precedes.

follows[1] that one's grief finds no solace from that amusement, nor is one's sorrow to any extent alleviated by those spectacles; and I am of opinion, that the pain of separation from friends and the grief of parting from those we love, is the hardest of all pains and the most cruel of all griefs.

COUPLET.

'Tis sure a shadowing forth of hell from friends to separate;
Forgive me, heaven! for my error—hell is but its entrance-gate.

Now that, Praise be to God Most High! we have a corner and supply of food, draw the foot of freedom from care under the garment of welfare, and yield not the collar of sense to the grasp of lust.

COUPLET.

Seize thou contentment's skirt, and be at rest;
For travel's stone holds trouble[2] in its vest.'

Bázindah said, 'O friend and consort! speak not another word of parting and separation, for sympathising friends are not wanting in the world, and he who parts from his friend, suffers no grief when he has met with another. If here I fail to encounter my friend, I shall in a short time bring myself into the society of a new soother of the heart, and thyself hast heard this saying which they have uttered,

COUPLET.

Fix not thy heart on any place, nor yet on comrades any,
For land and sea are wide enough, and mankind, too, are many.

I expect that after this, thou will not rehearse to me the volume of the toils of travel, for the flame of the labour of travel makes a man ripe,[3] and no person of raw mind and reared in repose, can put to its speed the horse of expectation in the plain of hope.

HEMISTICH.

Much travel's needful ere the raw turns ripe.'

Nawázindah said, 'Dear friend, at this time that thou removest thy heart from the society of thy friends, thou hast severed the string of ancient amity. Thou mayest unite with new comrades, and the precept of the wise man, that

COUPLET.

'Do not an old and well-tried friend forego   For new allies, for this may end in woe.'[4]

thou mayst transgress. What impression then will my word have on thee? Nevertheless,

---

[1] Lit., 'It arises that what amount of relief does his grief receive from that amusement.'
[2] Troubles, or lit. 'revolutions, vicissitudes.'
[3] In Persian, *pukhtah* means 'cooked,' and also 'shrewd;' in vulgar language 'wide-awake.' The pun cannot be preserved in English.
[4] Some MSS. read *bdshand*, which would refer to the 'new friends,' who could be said to be 'not good.'

COUPLET.

He shall his foeman's fondest wish fulfil,   Who to well-wishing friends bends not his will.'

Having here cut short their dialogue, they took leave of each other, and Bázindah tearing his heart from the society of his companion, issued forth on the wing.

HEMISTICH.

Like prisoned bird, forth from his cage he flew.

With real curiosity and perfect gratification he traversed the expanse of air, and passed over lofty mountains and Eden-like gardens. All of a sudden at the skirt of a mountain—which boasted equality with the elevation of the highest heaven, and from greatness regarded the whole terrestrial globe as a mere hillock beneath its foot,—he saw a meadow. Its emerald surface was more heart-expanding than the garden of heaven, and the northern[1] breeze, as it passed over loaded with perfume, was more fragrant than a bag of Tátárian musk.

VERSE.

There countless roses their pavilions kept;[2]
The grass moved wakeful, while the waters slept.
The roses, painted with a thousand hues,
Their heavenly fragrance each a league diffuse.

Bázindah was pleased with that delightful spot and heart-expanding tract, and as day was closing, he in that very place unloosed the baggage of travel. As yet he had not rested from the toils of the way, nor breathed a moment in ease and comfort, when suddenly, the swift-stepping carpet-spreader, the wind, raised up the canopy of the clouds in the court of the air, and made the tranquil earth a pattern of the tumult of the Resurrection, through the uproar of the heart-terrifying thunder, and the dread of the bosom-rending lightning. The fire of the thunderbolts on one side consumed the heart of the spotted tulips, and on the other, the shaft of the hail nailed the eye of the wakeful narcissus to the target of the earth.

COUPLET.

In pieces was the mountain's breast by the lightning's arrows riven,
And earth to its foundations shook at the thundering voice of Heaven.

In such a time as this Bázindah had no shelter to secure him from the arrows of the thunder-cloud, nor corner where he could rest in safety from the violence of the intensely cold wind. At one moment he hid himself under a branch and at another time he sought to shield himself in the leaves of the trees, and every moment the affliction of the hail and rain increased, and every instant the terrors of the thunderbolts and the lightning waxed greater.

---

[1] The *Dictionary* renders *nasím-i shimál* 'Boreas,' but here it evidently means 'a cool breeze,' a zephyr probably as coming from the cold northern hills.

[2] Freely rendered, metri causâ. Lit., 'Hundreds of thousands of roses blossomed in it.'

COUPLET.

Night, gloomy night—heaven's awful voice—a tempest-shower so fierce as this,
What care the gay in banquet-halls ? our perils do not mar their bliss.

In brief, with a thousand sufferings he passed the night until day, and having no remedy, he endured that ill-timed calamity, and every moment his thoughts recurred to the quiet corner of his nest, and the society of his prudent friend, and he heaved a cold sigh of regret and pain from his inflamed heart.

STANZA.

Had I but known from thee to sever,
Would kindle griefs nought can allay,
I would have parted from thee never,
Nor left thy side a single day.

But when the vanguard of approaching day had made an impression, that instant the writing of the gloom of the thunder-cloud was obliterated from the page of time, and by the warmth of the world-irradiating sun, the expanse of the earth, and the surface of the world, received brightness.

COUPLET.

From the east outdrew the sun his golden poniard bright,
And through earth's peopled quarters spread a flood of yellow light.

Bázindah again rose on the wing, hesitating whether he should return to his home, or, whether since he had formed the resolution, he should upon the whole wander for two or three days through the regions of the world. In the meantime, a swift-winged, hard-taloned royal white falcon, which descends to the earth on the head of its quarry swifter than the rays of the sun, and when soaring on high reaches heaven quicker than the sight ;

COUPLET.

Attacking now it left heaven's bolt behind,
Now soared more swiftly than the fiery[1] wind.

marked out Bázindah. When the poor Pigeon beheld the pitiless falcon, its heart began to flutter, and all strength and power of motion which existed in its limbs and members inclined to the regions of non-existence.

COUPLET.

When on the dove the rapid falcon stoops   The helpless quarry unresisting droops.

When Bázindah saw himself again entangled in calamity, he remembered the advice of his faithful friend, and clearly understood the crudeness of his own project, and the unreasonableness of his thoughts.

HEMISTICH.

Offerings he vowed and many a promise made,

---

[1] *Atish-nishán* 'fiery,' seems a strange epithet for the wind, unless it should be taken as referring to the Samúm. I confess I cannot see its applicability. The wind might indeed be compared to fire in its rapidity, and the epithet may here be introduced to correspond to *átish.*

that if he should escape from that dangerous place in safety, and emerge from that terrible position into tranquillity, he would not allow his mind to entertain another thought of travel, and he would regard as an invaluable prize the society of his cordial friend, which now seemed to him as impossible to realize, as the philosopher's stone,[1] and for the remainder of his life would not so much as pronounce with his tongue, the name of travel.

COUPLET.

If I once more obtain my hold on the skirt of meeting thee,
While my life remains none from my grasp thyself shall ever free.

By the blessing of that excellence of intention, which includes an increase of security, an opening of the door [of release] was obtained. In the very moment that the claw of the falcon was about bringing him into the grasp of possession, from another quarter a hungry eagle—from the injury of whose talons the sign Aquila was not safe in the nest of the sky, and who, when hungry, carried off from the meadow of heaven, the signs Aries and Capricorn,

COUPLET.

Aries itself through fear of him would graze not on the sky,
Save that Bahrám,[2] the blood-drinker, each day stood watchful by,

—had mounted on the wing in search of food. When it beheld the state of the falcon and Pigeon, it said to itself, 'Although this Pigeon is but a small mouthful, and a trifling morsel, nevertheless, upon the whole, one may break one's fast upon it, and somewhat allay one's impatient appetite.' It made an effort to carry off the Pigeon before the falcon. Although the animal vigour which is implanted in the nature of the falcon cannot be placed in the balance with that of the eagle, still, the former did not weigh its approach, but engaged with it in the place of strife and contest, having taken its seat in the balance with it.

COUPLET.

The feathered rivals then to strive began,   The quarry, dodging, from between them ran.[3]

The two were occupied in fighting with one another, and Bázindah eagerly catching at the opportunity, threw himself under a stone and made room for himself in a hole into which it would have been impossible for a sparrow to enter, though it had been at pains to try; and therefore passed another night distressfully. When in the morning the white-pinioned dove of the dawn began to fly from the nest of heaven, and the dark-coloured raven of night began, like the 'Anká, to be hid from sight,[4] and when

---

[1] Lit., 'Which—like the philosopher's stone—seemed to admit of being pointed out only in the sphere of non-existence.'

[2] The planet Mars.

[3] Lit., 'He, by a hundred tricks, escaped from between them.'

[4] The fabulous 'Anká, as not existing, is said to be hid from sight.

The peacock-sun with glorious augury,   Walked proudly in the garden of the sky.

Bázindah, though from hunger he had not power to fly, began by some means or other to flutter and move his wings. Fearful and affrighted, he looked to left and right, and observed the utmost caution before and behind. On a sudden he beheld a pigeon, with a little grain scattered in front of it, and a thousand other devices and stratagems of the same kind employed. With Bázindah the host of appetite prevailed over the region of the body; when he beheld his own species, without reflection he went forward, and the grain had not yet reached his craw when his foot was entangled in calamity.

COUPLET.

Satan's the net, the world the grain, our lusts the enticements are,
Our hearts the fowl which greediness soon lures within the snare.

Bázindah began to reproach that pigeon, saying, ' O brother! we are of the same species, and this accident has befallen me by reason of my homogeneousness with thee. Wherefore didst thou not acquaint me with these circumstances, nor fulfil the duties of courtesy and hospitality in order that I might have practised caution, and not thus fallen into the snare?' The pigeon replied, ' Leave off these words, for caution is unavailing against destiny, nor is it of any use to struggle against fate.

COUPLET.

When from fate's string its arrow once has hied,
Expedient's shield can ne'er it turn aside.'

Bázindah said, ' Art thou at all able to point out to me the way of escape from this calamitous strait? and then thou wouldst cast on my neck, till the day of resurrection, the chain of obligation.' The pigeon replied, ' O simple of heart! had I known a stratagem for escaping, I would have liberated myself from the snare, nor would I have become in the manner thou hast seen, the cruel cause[1] of the capture of birds; and thy state is exactly like that of the young camel, which after going a long way, grew tired and said, with lamentation and entreaty, to its mother, ' O unkind; stop just so long that I may recover myself and rest a moment from my weariness.' The mother replied, ' O thou without sight! dost thou not see that the end of the nose-string is in the hand of another. Had I, in brief, the power to choose, I would release my back from the load and thy foot from the journey.'

DISTICHS.

The camel's young one thus its dam addressed—
' After this march at least a moment's rest.'
She answered,—' Were the nose-string given to me,
None should me in this file thus loaded see.'

---

[1] *Mazlimat dár*, the word in the printed and lithographed editions, is not in the Dictionary. One MS. reads *mazlimah dári*, and explains it by *khodrí*, I must confess I would rather read *mazlimah kár*, did the manuscripts allow it.

E

When Bázindah was thus rendered desperate, he began to tremble, and with his utmost efforts endeavoured to fly. As the string of his impulse was strong, the cord of the net, which in the lapse of time had become worn, was broken, and Bázindah finding his throat clear of the throttle of the net, flew pleased away, and turned his face in the direction of his native place. From joy at having obtained a light delivery from that weighty bond, his heart forgot the pangs of hunger, and in the midst of his flight, he arrived at a deserted village, and rested on the corner of a wall which was near a field of corn. A village boy who was watching the field, in his customary beat, passed near that deserted place. When his eye fell on the pigeon, the burning desire of roast meat emitted its smoke from his heart. From the palm of his hand [1] he slipped a shell into his bow and drew up the string.[2] Bázindah was not on the alert against that trick, and was turning towards the field and the open space and meadow, when suddenly, from the juggling of the deceitful heavens, the impression of the blow of that shell reached the feathers of that discomfited one. From excess of fear and terror, he fell head downwards to the bottom of a well which was at the foot of that same wall, which was a well such that, from its exceeding depth, the circle of the heavens appeared like a wheel at the top, and had they woven together the black and white thread of day and night, it would not have reached its bottom.

STANZA.

No well was that—a cavern so profound,
It reached the seventh climate's farthest bound.
If heaven [3] should try its utmost depths to know,
'Twould fail, and must its measurement forego.[4]

When the young rustic saw that what he wished for was at the bottom of the well, and that the cord of counsel was too short to reach there, he went away disappointed, and left that half-killed one in his painful imprisonment. In short, Bázindah, for another night and day, passed his time with broken heart and ruffled feathers, at the bottom of the well, and in despairing accents according with his state,[5] his thoughts recurring to Nawázindah, he made mention of his feelings, of his hapless and outcast condition, and described his weakness and helplessness, and said,

---

[1] *Rúi-dast* in the Dictionary is said to mean 'back of the hand,' a sense here clearly impossible.

[2] *Paiwast.* I suppose the weapon in which the shell was placed to have been a cross-bow. *Paiwastan* would then mean, 'to draw the string up, and place it in the notch ready for discharging the bow.'

[3] One MS. reads *khirad*, which is perhaps better than *falak*.

[4] Lit., 'Would not go round the measurement.'

[5] *Zabán-i hál* is said in the Dictionary to be 'language expressed by one's condition, in contra-distinction to language of the tongue.' I hardly know whether the words can bear this meaning. It is evident that Bázindah actually uttered words, and did not merely gesticulate his grief.

ODE.

O I recall the time when near thy dwelling was my stay; [1]
Would now my eyes were brightened by the dust of thy doorway!
My heart's wish was that I, my friend! from thee, should never part :
What can I do? my toil is vain, and vainly throbs my heart.

Bázindah, the next day, by trying every way possible and all the devices he knew, brought himself to the top of the well, and weeping and bemoaning himself, at the mid-hour between sunrise and noon,[2] arrived near his own nest. Nawázindah heard the sound of the wings of her friend, and flying forth to meet him from the nest, said,

COUPLET.

'Tis I whose eyes expand, my friend to find,
How shall I thank thee—thou so true and kind![3]

And when she had embraced Bázindah, she found him excessively weak and thin. She said, 'O beloved friend! where hast thou been? and what is the state of thy circumstances?' Bázindah said,

COUPLET.

'Ask me not what woes of love, what pangs have been my lot,
All the griefs that parting brings, I've tasted—ask me not.

As for the toil and travail and affliction, which have passed over me,

COUPLET.

I need the quiet night-time and the pleasant moon as well,
That to thee I may the story of all my sorrows tell.

The sum of the matter is this, that I had heard that in travel, much experience is obtained; at length I have gained thus much experience, that so long as I live I will not make another journey, and, until I am compelled, I will not go forth from the corner of my nest, and by my own choice I will not exchange the happiness of beholding my friends for the pain of the struggles of exile.

COUPLET.

For travel's conflict I'll not lust again,   In sight of friends perpetual pleasures reign.'

And I have introduced this apologue that his majesty, the ruler of the world, may not exchange the dignity of a settled abode for the degradation of travel, and not voluntarily choose separation from friends and country, which has no other fruit but wretched bewailing and tearful eyes."

COUPLET.

When thoughts of friends and country fill my soul,
Tears from my eyes in melting torrents roll.[4]

---

[1] *Sar-i kúi* signifies 'end of the street.'
[2] I have thought it better thus to translate *cháshtgáh*, as breakfast-time may vary through the twelve hours.
[3] Lit., 'Helpful and cherishing.'
[4] Lit.. 'My dwellings are brimful of thy tears.'

Dábishlím said, 'O wise vazír! although the labour of travel is great, its advantages, too, are beyond computation. When any one has fallen, in traveling, into the whirlpool of hardship, he becomes improved and polished, and experiences are acquired by him, from which, throughout his life, he may derive advantage; and indubitably complete advancement appears in travel, both external and internal. Seest thou not that the pawn by traveling six stages, owing to the knowledge it thus acquires, obtains the rank of a queen; and the light-speeding moon by a journey of fourteen nights, progresses from the place of a thin crescent to the dignity of the full orb.

COUPLET.

To Pharaoh's[1] state by travel mounts the low.
When would the moon, untraveled, fairer[1] grow?

And if a person subside into the corner of his wretchedness, and step not beyond his miserable home, he remains deprived of seeing the marvels of various countries, and devoid of the honour of waiting on the great amongst mankind. The falcon secures a place on the wrist of kings, because it crouches not in its nest; and the owl, because it cannot turn its inclinations from solitude, remains behind the wall of disgrace.

COUPLET.

Swoop like falcon forth, to distant regions fly.
Owl-like how long will thou behind the ruin lie?

And one of the great sages inspired the whole body of his disciples with the desire of travel, by this,

QUATRAIN.

Each one who travels pleases aye the more,
All eyes approve him and all hearts adore.[2]
How pure the waves that our embraces woo,
Confine them and you make them fetid too.[3]

And if that hawking-falcon, which grew up with the young of a kite, had remained in their nest, and had not winged its flight through the air in travel, it would not have attained the honour of the notice of a king.' The vazír besought, saying, 'How were the circumstances of that affair?'

STORY II.

King Dábishlím said, "I have heard tell that once on a time two hawks, swift of wing, consorted together, and their nest was on the crest of a mountain, such that the celestial eagle could not, by the power of its wing, approach it, and the constellation Aquila, in spite of soaring so high, could not reach its vicinity.

---

[1] There is a very good equivoque in the Persian between *Kai-khusrau* 'Chosroes,' and *kai khúshrú* 'when fair?' In order to preserve it I have changed Chosroes into Pharaoh, who serves equally well for the illustration.

[2] Lit., ' In the fullness of excellence he becomes the light of every eye.'

[3] Lit., 'There is not a thing purer than water, if it abides in one place, it becomes fetid.'

COUPLET.

No mountain that—which on earth's surface lies—
A heaven you'd call it, placed above the skies.

And they passed their time happily in that nest, and lived delighted and content in beholding each other.

COUPLET.

O nightingale! that with the rose dost sit,　　　Thy state is blissful, therefore value it.

After a time, God Most High vouchsafed them a young one. By reason of the innate affection[1] which they felt at the sight of their son, both of them went in search of food, and brought viands of every description for their hearts' treasure, and in a short time his strength began to increase. One day, having left him alone—each had gone somewhither, and a delay took place in their return,—the young hawk felt the cravings of hunger. He began to search [for food], and turning himself on every side, came to the edge of the nest. Suddenly he fell thence, prone towards the bottom of the mountain. It chanced that in that spot a kite had issued from its nest in quest of food, which it sought for its young, and as it sate, expectant, on the side of the mountain, its sight fell on that young hawk, which was descending from the top of the mountain to the bottom; it entered its imagination that it was a mouse which had escaped from the talons of a kite.

HEMISTICH.

Still,[2] in the jar—one thought—I view thy face.

Without reflection, it made haste, and before it could touch the ground, seized it in mid-air, and carried it to its own nest, and on carefully examining it, by the character of its claws and beak, perceived that it belonged to the kind of hunting-birds, and through homogeneousness, pity sprang up in its heart, and it thought to itself: 'The mercy of God is visible in this matter, and has made me the instrument of its preservation; and had I not been present in that spot, and this young bird had fallen from the top of the mountain on the ground, undoubtedly all its limbs and members had been parted from one another, and its bones would have been pulverised by dashing against the stone of misfortune, and would have been scattered like dust on the wind of annihilation; and since the divine decree has so required that I should be the means of its preservation, it is most right that it should participate in education with my sons, nay, that I should bring it up as a son, and that it should be ranged in the series of my other children.' Then the kite, through pity, undertook the rearing of the young hawk, and treated it in the very same way as that in which it behaved

---

[1] One MS. reads *shafkati* for *shaghfi*, and I am inclined to prefer it. The Dictionary gives no suitable meaning for the latter.

[2] The lithographed edition and MSS. read *hamán khiydl* for the *hamah khiydl* of the printed edition.

towards its own young, until it grew up; and the original instincts which
were innate in it, according to the saying '*Mankind are mines like mines of
gold and silver,*' began to develope and reveal themselves. Although it
imagined that it was one of the sons of that kite, yet it saw that its aspect
and courage, and the terror it inspired, was different from theirs. Often it
wondered, saying, 'If I do not belong to them, why am I in this nest? and
if I am of this family, why am I opposed to them in form and qualities?

QUATRAIN.

| I think not I to this same band belong | Nor count myself excluded from the throng, |
| Included and excluded thus 'tis best, | To live contented and neglect the rest.' |

One day the kite said to the hawk, 'O son, dear to my heart! I see that
thou art very sad, and the cause of thy dejection is hid from me. If thou
hast any wish in thy heart, disclose it to me that I may occupy myself in
obtaining it; and if any desire passes through thy mind, make it known
unhesitatingly, that to the extent of my power I may exert myself in
accomplishing it.' The hawk replied, 'I, too, find in myself a feeling of
dejection, and I do not know the cause of it, and if I know it I cannot
tell it.

COUPLET.

Behold this wondrous flower, which has blossomed here for me.
Its hue cannot be tokened, nor its odour hidden be.

I now see it to be advisable that thou shouldest favour me with the honor
of leave, that I may journey in various parts of the world for two or three
days. Perchance, by the fortunate influence of movement, the dust of grief
may be effaced from the page of my heart, and when my mind is occupied
with the wonders and marvels of great cities and districts, it is possible that
the form of cheerfulness may be manifested in the mirror of my mind.'
When the kite heard the mention of parting, anguish arose in his heart,[1] and
he said,

COUPLET.

'Thou speak'st of bitter parting—sad thy tone,
Do what thou wilt—leave that at least undone.'

Then complaining, he added, 'O son! what plan is this thou hast formed?
and what thought is this thou hast entertained? speak not of travel, for it is
a man-devouring sea, and a dragon which carries off human beings.

COUPLET.

| Travel's the present hell of human kind, | Hence travel—travail[2] like in form we find. |

The cause, in general, why men make choice of traveling, is to procure the
means of subsistence, or because they find it difficult to remain in their own

---

[1] Lit., 'Smoke arose from his heart.'
[2] Lit., 'The form of travel and hell,' there being an equivoque on *safar* 'travel,' and
sakar 'hell.' To keep the play on words I have translated the second word, ' travail.'

country; and neither of these two things has happened to thee. Thanks be to God that our abode is a corner free from care, and that there is food procurable, sufficient for us to live upon, and thou hast exaltation above my other sons, and all those older[1] than thee bow before thee. Notwithstanding all this, to choose to travel and abandon the pleasure of a settled abode, appears to be far from the path of good sense; and long ago they have said,

HEMÍSTICH.

'Tis ever wisdom to let well alone.'[2]

The hawk said, 'What thou hast been pleased to say, is kindly and tenderly spoken; but whenever I meditate with myself, this corner and this food appear unworthy of my condition, and things pass through my mind which I am unable to express.' The kite perceiving that the saying '*Everything turns back to its original nature,*' was here made evident, stepped beyond the limits of this argument, and said, 'That which I say is on the ground of contentment, and what thou sayest proceeds from greediness, and the greedy person is always disappointed; and as long as one is not contented, he finds no repose, and as thou art not thankful for the blessings of contentment, and knowest not the value of freedom from ease, I fear that that will befall thee which befell that greedy cat.' The hawk asked ' How was that?'

STORY III.

The kite said, 'In former times there was an old woman in a state of extreme debility. She possessed a cot more narrow than the heart of the ignorant, and darker than the miser's grave; and a cat was her companion, which had never seen even in the mirror of imagination, the face of a loaf, nor had heard from friend or stranger the name of meat. It was content if occasionally it smelt the odour of a mouse from its hole, or saw the print of the foot of one on the surface of a board, and if, on some rare occasion, by the aid of good-fortune and the assistance of happy destiny, one fell into its claws,

HEMISTICH.

Like a poor wretch who finds out buried gold,

its cheek lighted up with joy, and it consumed its past sorrow with the flame of its natural heat, and a whole week, more or less, it subsisted on that amount of food, and used to say,

COUPLET.

In slumber see I this, my God! or with my waking eyes?
Myself in plenty[3] such as this, after such agonies?

---

[1] One MS. reads *hamah buzurgán* for *hamah buzurgí.*

[2] Lit. : ' It is not the act of wise men to abandon good days.'

[3] There is a mistake in the printed edition here, *bas* for *pas.*

And inasmuch as the house of the old woman was the famine-year of that cat, it was always miserable and thin, and from a distance appeared like an idea. One day, through excessive weakness, it had, with the utmost difficulty, mounted on the top of the roof; thence it beheld a cat which walked proudly on the wall of a neighbouring house, and after the fashion of a destroying lion, advanced with measured steps, and from excessive fat, lifted its feet slowly. When the cat of the old woman, saw one of its own species in that state of freshness and fat, it was astonished, and cried out, saying,

HEMISTICH.

'Truly with pride thou advancest, then wilt thou not tell me from whence?

Thou, whose state is thus pleasant, whence art thou? and since it appears that thou comest from the banquet-chamber of the Khán of Khatá,[1] whence is this sleekness of thine, and from what cause this thy grandeur and strength?' The neighbour-cat replied, 'I am the crumb-eater of the tray of the sultán. Every morning I attend on the court of the king, and when they spread the tray of invitation, I display boldness and daring, and in general I snatch off some morsels of fat meats, and of loaves made of the finest flour; and I pass my time happy and satisfied till the next day.' The cat of the old woman, inquired 'What sort of a thing may fat meat be? and what kind of relish has bread, made of fine flour? I, during my whole life, have never seen nor tasted aught save the old woman's broths, and mouse's flesh.' The neighbour-cat laughed, and said, 'Therefore it is, that one cannot distinguish thee from a spider, and this form and appearance that thou hast, is a reproach to our whole race; and the shape and character which thou hast brought from the house to the desert, is an eternal[2] disgrace.

COUPLET.

Cat, by thy tail and ears, one might thee deem,
Yet, in all else, a spider thou wouldst seem.

And if thou shouldst see the court of the sultán, and smell the odour of those delicious viands and agreeable meats, it is probable that the mystery, ' *Who shall restore bones to life when they are rotten*,'[3] may come forth from the curtain of what is hidden, to the plain of manifestation, and thou mayst acquire a fresh form.'

---

[1] *Khatá*, Northern China, the Cathay of Milton. This word has been omitted in the new edition of Johnson's Persian Dictionary.

[2] The MSS. and lithographed edition read *bar dawdm* for the *bar dáram* of the printed edition, which I conclude to be a typographical error.

[3] Kur'án, ch. xxxvi., 78; Sale, p. 333, last line, 'He saith, who shall restore bones to life when they are rotten? Answer,—He shall restore them to life who produced them the first time; for He is skilled in every kind of creation; who giveth you fire out of the green tree, and behold ye kindle your fuel from thence.' See also Sale, p. 198, note *e*: 'Obba Ebn Khalf came to Muhammad with a rotten bone, and asked him whether it were possible for God to restore it to life.'

COUPLET.

The scent of the beloved one passed o'er the lovers' grave,[1]
What marvel if to those dry bones the breath of life it gave.

The cat of the old woman, said, most beseechingly, 'O brother! thou art bound to me by the rights of neighbourship and the link of homogeneousness, why not perform what is due to courtesy and fraternity, and this time, when thou goest, take me with thee; perchance, by thy good fortune, I may obtain food, and by the blessing of thy society, I may acquire a place.

COUPLET.

From pious company withdraw thou not, Nor those unclasp who share a prosperous lot.'[2]

The heart of the neighbour-cat melted at his lamentable position, and he resolved that he would not attend the feast without him. The cat of the old woman, from the happy tidings of this promise, felt new life, and descending from the roof, stated the case to her. The old dame began to advise the cat, saying, 'O kind companion, be not deceived by the words of worldly people, and abandon not the corner of content, for the vessel of covetousness is not filled save with the dust of the grave; and the eye of lust is not stitched but with the needle of annihilation and the thread of death.'

VERSE.

Contentment makes man wealthy—Tell it then
To the unsatisfied and world-o'er-wandering men,—
They ne'er knew God, nor paid Him worship due,
Since with their lot they no contentment knew.

The cat had not taken into its head a longing for the table of the delicacies of the sultán, to such an extent only as that the medicine of advice could be profitable to it.

COUPLET.

'Tis but to cage the wind advice to give   To lovers, 'tis but water in a sieve.

In short the next day, along with its neighbour, the old woman's cat, with tottering steps conveyed itself to the court of the sultán, and before that helpless one could arrive[3] there, ill-fortune had poured the water of disappointment on the fire of its crude wish, and the reason was as follows:—The day before, the cats had made a general onslaught on the table, and raised a clamour and uproar beyond bounds, and had annoyed, to the last degree, the guests and their host. Wherefore, on this day, the sultán had commanded that a band of archers, with swiftly impelling notches, standing in ambush,[4]

---

[1] I have put the verb in the past tense, *metri causâ*. Literally, it is: 'If the scent should pass.'

[2] Lit.: 'Take not thy hand from the waist of the prosperous, (or) of those approaching.' I should prefer the latter sense of *mukbil*, since the old woman's cat could hardly be said to be prosperous, but perhaps that epithet refers to her neighbour.

[3] In the printed edition, the words *ba-rasad* and *nass* are run together so closely as to make them look like one word, which might occasion difficulty to the student.

[4] One MS. reads *dar goshah*, which I much prefer to the unmeaning (unmeaning even for a Persian epithet) *goshah ṭayyár* or *goshah ṭiyár*.

should watch, so that for every cat, who holding before its face the buckler of impudence, should enter the plain of audacity, the very first morsel that it ate, should be a liver-piercing shaft. The old woman's cat, ignorant of this circumstance, as soon as it smelt the odour of the viands, without the power of checking itself, turned its face like a falcon, to the hunting-ground of the table, and the scale of the balance of appetite had not yet been weighted by heavy mouthfuls, when the heart-piercing arrow quivered in its breast.

VERSE.

From the bone trickling flowed the sanguine tide,
In terror of its life it fled and cried:
' Could I escape this archer's hand, I'd dwell
Content with mice and the old woman's cell.
Dear friend ! the honey pays not for the sting,
Content with syrup is a better thing.'

' And I have introduced this apologue, that thou, too, mayest regard the secluded corner of my nest as a blessing, and mayest understand the value of the food and morsels, which reach thee, untoiled for by thee; and showing thyself contented with a little, mayest not seek for more, lest, God forbid! thou arrive not at the condition thou seekest, and this place, too, depart from thy hand.' The hawk said, 'What thou hast been pleased to say, is the essence of good advice and kindness, nevertheless, to stoop to trifles is the business of the mean, and to show content with mere eating and drinking, is the disposition of brutes. Every one who would sit on the throne of greatness must rise up in pursuit of high things, and he who wishes to put on his head the crown of exaltation, must belt himself with the girdle of search. A lofty spirit is not satisfied with low things, and a noble intellect approves not of base positions.

VERSE.

None ever found the way on high to rise,
Till he obtained the step of high emprise.
Seek rank, that to the moon thou mayest mount,
None drink cloud-water from a well's low fount.'

The kite said, ' This idea that thou hast taken into thy head, will not be realised by mere imagining; and this cauldron of desire, will not reach the boiling point by vain longing. No affair makes progress, unless the means are ready; and no result manifests itself, unless men first take order for the pre-requisites.

COUPLET.

Boasts will not pillow thee where great men sit,
Wouldst thou have greatness, greatly strive for it.'

The hawk said, ' The strength of my claws is the best means of procuring the blessings of fortune, and the power of my beak the best way of obtaining the grades of high rank. But, perhaps, thou hast not heard the story of that swordsman who sought kingship and rule by the help of the arm of courage, and, finally, the robe of his noble spirit was adorned with the fringe of sovereignty?' The kite inquired 'How was this matter?'

STORY IV.

The hawk said, ' In ancient times there was a poor mechanic at his wit's end to maintain his family, and who, from extreme distress, had never read a single letter from the page of pleasure, and the gains of whose craft sufficed not for more than the expenses of his family, and the emoluments of whose profession went not beyond providing bread and raiment. The favour of God, (May his glory be magnified!) bestowed on him a dear son, on whose front the tokens of greatness were manifest; and on whose countenance the signs of high fortune were apparent.

COUPLET.

Of happy fortune and high augury, The fairest plant in joy's parterre was he.

By the blessing of his footsteps, the state of his father became one of cheerfulness,[1] and, by his happy auspices, the income from his craft began to exceed his expenses. The father, regarding his footsteps as auspicious, caused him, to the extent of his power at the time, to be educated; and the boy, in his childhood, was wont to speak of nothing but archery, and continually played with shield and sabre. When they conveyed him to school, he would suddenly make off and appear in the midst of the plain; and whenever they instructed him in writing, his thoughts darted away to the straight spear.[2] He was always reading the inscription of conquest from the lines of the sabre, and ever perusing, from the ornaments of the shield,[3] the sketch of ennoblement.

VERSE.

When his instructor writes down 'Há' and 'Mim,'
These to his fancy shield and helmet seem.
Will he of ' Alif,' ' Be'—his notions shew,
'Alif' the shaft resembles, 'Be' the bow.[4]

When from the stage of childhood he arrived at the boundaries of puberty, his father said, ' O son, my mind is entirely bent on thy state, and the period of manhood has no relation to the season of boyhood. The marks of audacity and hardihood are very manifest on the pages of thy condition. I wish that before evil dispositions cast thee into the perils of lust, I may make

---

[1] One MS. reads *shádmáni* which I prefer to *sdmani*. Other MSS. omit the *hál* before *pidar*.

[2] There is an equivoque which I have been unable to retain in English. *Khatt* signifies ' writing' and *naizah-i khatti* 'a straight spear.'

[3] *Nirang* signifies 'spell,' as well as 'sketch.' Eligat lector.

[4] In ' Be' the boy found the shape of a bow, in 'Alif' that of an arrow. There is more difficulty in tracing the resemblance between ' Há' and a shield, and between ' Mím' and a casque.

the strong fortress, '*Whoever marries, verily he perfects half his religion,*'[1] thy mansion; and now I have arranged the hand of promise, fitting thy condition, in order that I may draw into the bands of marriage with thee, a lady from a tribe which may be equal to ours. What dost thou think adviseable herein?' The son said, 'O father! I have already given the hand of promise to the high person on whom my heart is set, and have deposited in cash for her, the marriage portion due in case of divorce. I will not trouble you in this affair, nor do I expect aid or assistance therein.' The father said, 'O son! I have perfect cognizance of all thy affairs. Thou hast not sufficient means of assistance that thou couldest rightly perform thy betrothal. What thou sayest thou hast prepared, whence is it? and what sort of bride is it that thou wooest?' The son went into the house, and brought out a sword a hundred times more sanguinary than the glance of the beautiful, and a thousand degrees more lustrous than the teeth of the carne-lian-lipped fair. Then he said, 'O father! know that I will plight my troth to the bride of empire, and will unite myself, in the nuptial knot, with the chaste virgin of sovereignty; and for her there is no better plighted troth than a sharp sword, and no fairer portion than a blood-shedding poniard.'

COUPLET.

On him whom fortune favours none make war,   Empire's best dowry is the scymitar.

And since the spirit of that young man was restricted to [the acquisition of] empire, in a short space of time he took possession of an extensive kingdom, and by the stroke of the world-subduing blade, he conquered various countries of the world : and hence they have said,

COUPLET.

Only to him will empire plight her word,   Who pays her bridal portion with the sword.

'And I have introduced this story in order that thou mayest know, that, whatever can be mentioned as belonging to fortune, I already possess, and the Divine providence has opened the gates of happiness before the face of my condition, and I, too, am in hopes that I shall shortly arrive at my desire, and reach the hand of my desire to the neck of its object. And now by no charming of any one, will I give up this condition or abandon this idea.

HEMISTICH.

Reproaches shall not drive us from this door.'

The kite perceived that that high-spirited bird would not be brought into the net by the string of wiliness, nor be caught by the grain of deceit and

---

[1] This is a tradition handed down by Anas-bin Málik, who was the last of the Sahabah, or companons of Muḥammad, and who died at Basrah, A.H. 91, aged 103. See the *Mishkdtu-'l-Maṣdbíh* translated by Matthews, Calc. edition, 1810, p. 79. 'When a servant marries, verily he perfects half his religion; then let him practise abstinence before God, for the remaining half.'

artifice. It was, therefore, compelled to suffer it to travel, and applied to its own wounded breast, the cautery of separation. The hawk, having taken leave of the kite and its young ones, flew from the nest and soared on high; and after it was tired, descended on the top of a mountain, and opened the eye of observation in every direction. All at once, it saw a mountain-partridge, which had begun to walk proudly along in perfect beauty, while the sound of its jocund cry reverberated through all parts of the mountain. The hawk found in its nature an eager desire to hunt the partridge, and in one pounce, filled its crop with the flesh of its breast, which was agreeable to its appetite. It found the flesh of such a sort that the deliciousness of its flavour, equalled the water of life, and the delicacy of its taste boasted an equality with the relish of the most surpassing dainties, [according to the saying] '*And the flesh of birds of the kind which they shall desire,*'[1] and as during the whole period of his life it had never tasted flesh of such delicacy, it exclaimed,

COUPLET.

'From head to foot thy nature pleases mine,   Sure for me only they did thee design!'

It then reflected, 'This, of itself, among the advantages of travel, suffices me, that thus early I have escaped from coarse food, and have obtained the flavour of viands which are agreeable to my mind, and have been elevated from a dark and narrow nest and low and mean-spirited companions, to exalted places and lofty situations.

HEMISTICH.

Of dazzling great adventures—this, the first.

[Let us wait to see] what happy fortune will next advance from the corner of the unknown future to the area of visibility.'

HEMISTICH.

What fate itself brings from the curtain forth.

Then the hawk, swift of flight, passed some days in flying about at pleasure, and merrily chased the partridge and quail, till one day it was perched on the top of a mountain, at the skirt of which it beheld a number of horsemen who had formed line in hunting, while their falcons swooped in pursuit of the quarries.

VERSE.

Then at the signal of the hunting-drum[2]
Forth on the wing the swooping falcons come,

---

[1] Ḳu'rán, Fl., ch. lvi, 21; Mar., lvi, 23, Sale, p. 395, l. 2: 'These are they who shall approach near unto God. . . . Youths which shall continue in their bloom for ever, shall go round about to attend them, with goblets and beakers, and a cup of flowing wine: their heads shall not ache by drinking the same, neither shall their reason be disturbed; and with fruits of the sorts which they shall choose, and the flesh of birds of the kind which they shall desire.'

[2] I am not aware that hawks are flown at a signal given by a drum, as would appear from this passage, *Tabl-báz*, or, *Tablak-báz* is said to be a little drum hung from the saddle; or the player of such a drum.

> The rapid gos-hawks[1] here their pinions ply
> And in the quarry's blood their talons dye,[2]
> There the white falcon—from his hapless prey,
> The quail and pheasant—tears life's coin away.

Now this was the king of the country who had come out with his attendants for his accustomed sport of hawking, and the place where the game fed
happened to be the skirt of that mountain.   Meanwhile the hawk which was
on the King's wrist flew and made a stoop at a quarry, and this high-
couraged hawk also stooping at the same prey, presently carried it off before
the other.   When the King's glance fell on its swiftness of flight, and rapid
seizure, his heart was set upon it, and the high mandate went forth, so
that dexterous fowlers, by ingenious stratagems, cast a snare round its neck,
and by the guidance of fortune, it attained the honor of serving the monarch.
The gracious regard of the King became confirmed with reference to its
natural aptitude and innate merit, and after a short time its post was fixed
by the favouring aid of fortune, on the wrist of the Prince, and by means of
its lofty spirit it rose from the abyss of degradation and abasement, to the
pinnacle of honor and prosperity, and if it had been content with the society
of crows and kites, in the same spot where it first abode, and for the sake of
travel, had not measured the regions of the desert and the tract of the wilderness, its attaining this rank, and its promotion to this dignity, would have
been of the number of impossibilities, and I have cited this apologue that it
may be understood, that in travel the most complete exaltation is attained,
and that it conducts a man from the most utter meanness of baseness and
obscurity, to the loftiest place of approval and splendour.'

STANZA.

> Travel 's the spring-time of the soul, for then
> Their wishes, flower-like, bloom attained by men,
> Travel ! that thou may'st aye successful be:
> '*Walk through earth's regions*'[3] is God's own decree.

And when the discourse of Dábishlím was ended, the other vazír advanced
and performed the customary ceremonies of prayerful salutation, and said,
'That which his imperial Majesty, the shadow of God, has been pleased to
say in explanation of travel and its advantages, does not belong to such a
class of things that the suspicion of doubt can approach it, nevertheless it
occurs to the mind of your slave, that for the angelically-gifted[4] person of the

---

[1] The Dictionary does not distinguish the hawks scientifically.   The *jurrah* is said to be a
male falcon.

[2] Lit.: 'Whets its claws?'

[3] Ḳur'án, ch. lxvii, 15; Sale, p. 416, l. 28.   'It is He who hath leveled the earth
for you, therefore walk through the region thereof, and eat of his provision; unto Him shall
be the resurrection.'

[4] The lithographed edition reads *ṣifát* for *malakát*.

King, on whose safety the happiness of the world is dependent, to voluntarily undertake the toil of travel, and to migrate from the exhilarating garden of pleasure into the heart-afflicting desert of sorrow and labour, appears distant from the ways of wisdom.' Dábishlím said, 'The undertaking toil is the part of men of courage, and the business of the lions of the forest of war; and indubitably until the skirt of the pleasant life of kings is impinged on the thorn of trouble, the flower of tranquillity does not blossom for their weak subjects in the garden of freedom from care, and so long as the foot of high-spirit of monarchs has not traversed the wilderness of calamity, the head of the indigent poor does not touch the pillow of repose.'

COUPLET.

None in thy realm will peace or comfort find,
While thoughts of selfish ease engross thy mind.

And know that there are two classes of mankind, one, kings, to whom has been given the dignity of ruling over states, and imperial sway : and the other, subjects, on whom is bestowed the favour of security and repose. These two kinds do not admit of combination, but it is necessary either to choose ease and abandon the reigns of dominion, or to be contented with the honor of kingly power, and draw back the hand from delight and leisure.

STANZA.

He who on comfort tramples, and delight;
Fortune will give him rule and kingly might.
Thus by the rose the garden's crown is worn,
Because, though soft, it couches on a thorn.

And the wise have said, ' *Labour is the way to wealth,*' and exertion elevates the seeker on the post of success, and to traverse the wastes of struggling with the step of constancy, brings the beauty of the desired object under the gaze of inspection. The acquirement of things wished for depends on attempting things perilous.

COUPLET.

Let him not try the hell of royal state,   Who thinks in ease to live effeminate.

Every one who raises the banner of exertion in the plain of courage, and puts away the qualities of indulgence and listlessness in undertaking toils, has taken the shortest path to his object, and has looked on the countenance of his wish with the eye of hope, like that Tiger who entertained a desire to rule over the joy-expanding wilderness, and by the blessing of toil and exertion which he employed, and by the auspicious influence of patient endurance of severe sufferings and disagreeables which he displayed, in a short time the veil of hindrance fell off from the face of his wish, and he advanced the hand of hope to the skirt of his object.' The vazír inquired ' In what manner was this affair?'

STORY V.

King Dábishlím said, 'In the environs of Baṣrah[1] there was an island of an excessively pleasant climate, and a desert of surpassing beauty and freshness, where limpid waters flow on every side, and a life-bestowing zephyr breathes around.

VERSE.

> Trees flourished thickly interwoven there,
> Whereon grew fruits, sweet-flavoured, fresh and rare.
> Their boughs, than Túba's[2] more delightsome, shade
> Grass, than the lily finer in its blade.

And from its excessive exquisiteness they called it the 'Joy-expanding Wilderness,' and a Tiger bore sway there, such that from dread of him fierce lions could not set foot in that retreat, and from awe of him the wild beasts and savage animals could not allow the thought of that solitude to encircle their minds.

VERSE.

> When with his tail he furious lashed the rock,
> Heaven's lion dropped his talons at the shock.
> And where he but for one short instant paused,
> A long year's stoppage to that road he caused.

He had lived much time in that wild, according to his wish, and had never seen the form of disappointment in the mirror of existence. He had a young one whose countenance made the world seem bright to him, and in meeting which lustre of his eyes, his vision was enlightened. His intention was that when that young one came to years, and stained his teeth and claws in the gore of wild beasts, he would commit that solitude to his charge, and pass the rest of his life at ease in the corner of retirement. The blossom of his wish had not yet expanded on the stem of desire, when the autumn of death gave the fruit of the garden of his existence to the wind of destruction.

HEMISTICH.

> How many a hope has crumbled into dust.

---

[1] Baṣrah, a city on the Tigris, about one and a half day's journey from where the river enters the Persian Gulf. It was built by command of the Khalífah 'Umar, A.H. 15, A.D., 636. It is situated in a sandy soil, but has a small stream flowing near it, which is said to make of the valleys it waters a terrestial Paradise.

[2] The tree of Paradise, See Sale's Prel. Disc., p. 69, l. 11 : ' Concerning this tree, they fable that it stands in the palace of Muḥammad, though a branch of it will reach to the house of every true believer ; that it will be laden with pomegranates, grapes, dates, and other fruits of surprising bigness, and of tastes unknown to mortals. So that if a man desire to eat of any particular kind of fruit, it will immediately be presented him ; or if he choose flesh, birds ready-dressed, will be set before him according to his wish. They add that the boughs of this tree will spontaneously bend down to the hand of the person who would gather of its fruits ; and that it will supply the blessed not only with food, but also with silken garments, and beasts to ride on ready saddled and bridled, and adorned with rich trappings, which will burst forth from its fruits ; and that this tree is so large, that any person mounted on the fleetest horse, would not be able to gallop from one end of its shade to the other in a hundred years.' See page 20, line 2.

And when this Tiger was seized by the claw of the lion, Death, several wild
beasts who for a long time entertained a desire for that wilderness, made a
unanimous movement, and set about appropriating it. The young tiger saw
that he possessed not the strength to resist. He went voluntarily into exile,
and amongst the wild beasts a huge contest arose. A blood-spilling, tumult-
causing lion, overcame all the others, and brought by conquest that joy-
expanding wilderness which resembled Paradise, into the area of his own
possession, and the young Tiger having for some time endured distress in the
mountains and wastes, conveyed himself to another haunt, and disclosed the
affliction of his heart to the wild beasts of that district, and asked their aid to
remedy this interruption [of his happiness]. They, having received intelligence of the victory of the predaceous lion and of the overpowering might
of that martial king of beasts, rejected with aversion [the request for] help
and assistance, and said, ' O unfortunate! thy place is now in the possession
of a lion such that from terror of him the birds will not fly over that wilderness, and from fear of him the elephant will not approach that desert. 'We
have not strength to fight with him, nor to sustain his teeth and claws, and
thou too art not able to enter with him the arena of strife and encounter.
Our opinion demands that thou shouldst betake thyself to his court, and with
perfect loyalty enter his service.'

VERSE.

Forbear 'gainst him the flag of war t' unfurl,
Whom from his fixèd seat thou canst not hurl.[1]
'Tis best that thou submissive accents use,
Be humble to him, and thyself excuse.

These words seemed reasonable to the young Tiger, and he looked upon his
best course to be this, that he should voluntarily enter the service of the lion,
and to the extent of his ability, offer the duties of attendance. He, therefore,
put in practice the maxim '*Returning is best*,' and through the intervention
of one of the nobles, he obtained the honor of waiting on the lion, and
having become the object of the imperial regard, was appointed to an office
suited to his spirit. The tiger having tightly fastened the belt of obedience
on the waist of affection, displayed the marks of prudence and dutiful service
in such a manner as every moment to cause an increase of nearness to the
king's presence, and an augmentation of the royal favour to such an extent,
that he became an object of envy to the nobles and ministers of his majesty;
in spite of which every instant his painstaking and zeal in the service
waxed greater, and he incessantly displayed increased exertion, in the affairs
of the state.

COUPLET.

They who excel in zeal, in toil precede,　　　Must of all others fairly take the lead.

---

[1] Lit.: ' With a person that thou canst not move from his place, thou shouldst not
plant thy foot in strife.' I have transposed the lines for the English order.

F

Once upon a time an important and necessary affair arose which called the lion away to a distant jungle; and at that time the heat of the oven of the sky, was unmitigated,[1] and the expanse of waste and mountain, like a furnace of glass, fiercely inflamed. From the excessive heat of the air, the brain of animals was boiled in their cranium, and the crabs in the water were fried like fish in the frying-pan.

VERSE.

> Had sudden clouds collected then—so burned
> The air—their drops to fiery sparks had turned.
> Birds in their passage through the liquid air,
> Moth-like, consumed, had lost their feathers there.
> The sun so fiercely through the æther shone,
> It melted e'en the heart of the hard stone.

The lion reflected, 'At such a time, when the shell at the bottom of the deep, like a fowl on a spit, is roasting; and the ocean, from fear of the sun's heat, steps not in the midst[2] of the fire to the shore, an affair of this importance has occurred. Who may there be among my attendants, who would not be affected by the labour? and who, undeterred by the heat of the atmosphere, would approach this undertaking?' In the midst of this reflection, the Tiger came in with the line of attendants, and observed that the king was thoughtful. On the ground of his abundant affection and complete tact, he advanced near the throne of royalty, and was emboldened to ask the causes of that thoughtfulness, and having learned how the case stood, he took upon himself to accomplish the matter, and having been honored with permission, he set off with a body of attendants, and arriving at that place at noon, he betook himself to the accomplishment of the affair, and the instant that the business was settled to his satisfaction, he changed his reins to return. The officers and counsellors, who had been appointed to attend upon him, unanimously represented as follows: 'In such heat as this, all this distance has been traversed by the steps of completion, and now that the affair has been settled and that there is not the slightest cause for uneasiness; and the confidence placed in you by his high majesty, has been demonstrated to the extent that it has, it will certainly not be removed from advisability, if you should repose a short time under the shade of a tree, and allay the fiery tongue of thirst by drinking cool water.'

COUPLET.

> Rest! and the load of toil support no more;
> Repose![3] for earthly troubles have no shore.

The Tiger smiled and said, 'My intimacy and rank with his majesty the

---

[1] In the margin of one MS. *asír* is explained by *khális*, 'pure,' 'unadulterated.'
[2] *Az miyán* here seems to be used for *dar miyán*.
[3] Lit.: 'Ungird thyself.'

king, is a banner that I have by toil and effort set up. It would not be well to level it with the ground by indulgence and sloth. Without supporting trouble it is impossible to arrive at the carrying off treasure, and unaccompanied by the heart-afflicting thorn, we cannot reap the enjoyment of surveying the rose-garden.

STANZA.

He may embrace his wishes' neck, who will,   Shield-like, confront the darts of coming ill;
This will not from mere longing hopes arise,   'Tis won by efforts stern, and tearful eyes.'

The informers furnished intelligence of this to the lion, and recited the book of this affair, from the preface to[1] the conclusion. The lion nodded the head of approval, and said, 'Such a person is fit for sway and chieftainship, who can raise up his head from the collar of toil;[2] and the people may be at peace in the just reign of that ruler who does not place his head on the pillow of repose.'

VERSE.

That monarch's reign will peace and rest ensure,
Who can himself the loss of rest endure.
Happy the sovereign who submits his mind
To hardships, that his subjects rest may find.

He then sent for the Tiger, and having distinguished him with special honors, committed that jungle to him, and having bestowed on him the place of his sire, conferred on him, in addition, the dignity of being his heir. And the use of this apologue is, that thou mayest learn that to no one does the sun of his wish rise from the eastern quarter of hope, without the diligent use of great exertion; nor, without complete and searching labour, does the preamble of hope yield the issue of the acquirement of the desired object.

COUPLET.

Who bears not toil, will ne'er the treasure gain;
His is the guerdon, brother! whose the pain.

And since in this journey the object is the quest of knowledge, I have formed a firm resolution, and have placed the foot of endeavour in the stirrup of intention. From the mere thought of the labour which may accrue in going[3] and returning, the page of my purpose shall not receive the inscription of abrogation, and the cavalier of lofty spirit, will not turn back from this path, ' *This is a matter that is absolutely determined.*'[4]

---

[1] The printed edition by a typographical error omits *tá* before *khátimah.*

[2] This sentence and the following one appear to me rather obscure: I suppose *sar az giríbán-í mushakkat bar dwardan* means ' To put on toil like a garment, drawing the head through the collar.' The employment of *sar-afrází* by itself, for ' an exalted person' is very unusual.

[3] *Zaháb wa iyáb,* two not very common words, explained in the margin of one MS. by *kúshish* and *báz gashtan.*

[4] Kur'án, Fl. ch. iii. 187; Mar. iii. 183; Sale, p. 53, l. 14: " Ye shall be proved in your possessions and in your persons; and ye shall hear from those unto whom the Scripture was delivered before you, and from the idolaters, much hurt; but if ye be patient and fear God, this is a matter that is absolutely determined.'

F 2

COUPLET.

When his foot a monarch places in the stirrup, firm of will,
Is it strange if fortune ceases then the reins to manage still !

When the vazírs perceived that the prohibitions of advice could not prevent
the king's purpose, they conformed to his opinion, and employed themselves
in preparing the necessary articles for the march; and having paid the
congratulations usual on commencing a journey, repeating this couplet, they
sent up shouts to the revolving vault of heaven :

COUPLET.

Since thou wilt go, may God's grace thee attend!
And all Saints' spirit guide thee and befriend!

Then the King Dábishlím committed the reins of public affairs to the hand
of the good sense of one of the pillars of the state in whom he reposed
confidence, and repeated in the ear of his intelligence, with reference to the
tender treatment of his subjects and protection of his people, certain words
of advice which might serve as the fringe of the robe of kingly power : and
among them the following,

VERSE.

' Thy kingdom will Sikandar's mirror[1] be,
Wherein thou mayst thy own appearance see;
It will not shew thy features fairly traced,
Unless oppression's stain be thence erased.
Let, like the morn, thy beams delight the eye,
And dread thy sorrowing subjects' morning-sigh;
A hundred archers' slaughtering shafts do less
Than one crone's sigh—one sigh of helplessness.'

And when his mind was relieved from the cares of state, he turned his face
with a retinue of chosen attendants and servants, towards Sarándíp, and, like
the moon, advanced stage by stage, and, like the sun, proceeded from city[2] to
city,[2] and at every halting-place he made the acquisition of new experiences,
and from every caravan he gained fresh advantages, until after traversing the
stages of land and sea, and enduring the hardships of cold and heat, the shores
of Sarándíp appeared to him, and the fragrant breezes of that country reached
the nostrils of the king.

COUPLET.

Who scents thy fragrance on the morning gales,
News from his loved one—happy news—inhales.

And after he had rested from the fatigues of his journey for two or three
days in the city of Sarándíp, and had left his superfluous baggage there, he
turned his face with two or three of his confidential attendants towards the

---

[1] Alexander the Great is said to have had a glass which shewed him the whole world and
all things done in it.
[2] *Shahr* may also mean mean 'month' as well as 'city,' and an equivoque is of course
intended here, alluding to the sun's progress.

mountain, and when he had ascended its heights, he beheld an elevation which cast the shadow of its skirt on the sun, and the glitter of whose peak[1] threw its radiance on the beams of the planet Mars.

VERSE.

In height it matched heaven's crystal sphere, and made
There, with its rocks, alternate light and shade;
Matched with the swift white courser of the sky,[2]
Its summit passed it in the contest by:
The heaven beneath its peak of iron hue,
Seemed like the grass which on its skirt up-grew.

On every side were meadows adorned with a variety of fragrant herbs, and in all directions flower-gardens, which resembled the abundant delights of Paradise.

STANZA.

Its meadows' borders emerald fruits unfold,
Its heights are girdled with bright belts of gold;
Beside its waters flourish Túba-bowers,
And Eden draws fresh fragrance from its flowers.

Dábishlím perambulated it on every side, and made the devotional circuit of its holy places. In the midst of this going to and fro, his eyes fell on a cave, the darkness of which matched the light of the eye,[3] and the mysterious saying, '*Light in darkness*,' was illuminated by its gloom. By searching inquiry of those who lived near those places, he learned that it was the abode of a sage whom they called Bídpáí, that is to say, 'the kind physician,'[4] and that from certain of the great men of Hind, it had been heard that his name was Pílpáí, which, in Hindí they call Hastí-pát, and that he was a man who had ascended the steps of learning, and had adorned, with the ornaments of excellent qualities, the jewel of reason : and at that period had abandoned the society of men, and contenting himself with a small pittance, had sewed up his eyes from things connected with the world, and consumed with the flame of the fire of abstinence, the rubbish of unholy dispositions. The eye of his wakefulness, from the excess of his vigils, beheld not the countenance of sleep, and the ear of his senses, from the extent of his abstinence, heard nought but the summons, ' *God inviteth unto the dwelling of peace.*'[5]

---

[1] *Tígh*, 'peak,' signifies also and more usually 'sword,' and *khanjar* which here means 'ray,' commonly signifies 'dagger.'

[2] *Khing-i falak*, 'the sun.' It is barely possible to exceed the extravagance of this metaphor, in which the mountain is said to race in height with the sun, and to win by a neck.

[3] Light exists in the black pupil of the eye, hence the saying 'Light in darkness.'

[4] The dictionary explains *Bídpáí* as a corruption of *Vidyá-priyá* or *Veda-priya*, 'dear to science,' or 'a lover of the Veda.' But here the derivation seems to be from *vaidyah priyah*, 'dear physician.'

[5] Kur'án, ch. x. 26; Sale, p. 156, l. 34: 'God inviteth unto the dwelling of peace, and directeth whom he pleaseth into the right way.' The 'dwelling of peace' is, Sale tells us in his note, 'Paradise' as is shewn by ch. ii. 221 of the Kur'án, where the same expression is used with *jannat*, 'Paradise' for *dáru-s salám* 'dwelling of peace.'

VERSE.

His breath a treasure, sifting verities;   His face the sun of those who early rise.[1]
In each thing he—purse-holder to the sky—   In all the confidant of destiny.

Dábishlím, in the desire of meeting him, stood some time without the cave, and, by the language of gesture, asked of the inward [soul] of that perfect saint, permission to come as a pilgrim to him. The clear-minded sage—by secret inspiration and intelligence, free from doubt—obtained information of the meaning of the world-conquering king, and uttered the cry, '*Enter ye therein in peace and security.*'[2]

DISTICHS.

That wisdom-teaching[3] cave, the monarch high
Entered; and made it China's gallery.[4]
In service of that sage, he girt his waist,
The belt of homage on his soul he placed.

He looked and beheld a Bráhman, who had stepped with the foot of abrogation into the world of retirement, and had unfurled the pennon[5] of truth in the plain of subtlety. Angelic mind revealed itself in his human countenance, and the cleanliness of his body was a manifest demonstration of the purity of his spirit. The king sagaciously discerned that he should obtain from him his wish, and by the auspicious influence of his spirit, would arrive at his object. With all respect he advanced towards him, and when he drew near the Bráhman, he performed due salutation and fulfilled the requisite homage. The Bráhman after receiving and replying to the salute, and performing the conventional compliments, signed [to the king] to sit; and having inquired of him as to the fatigues of the road, asked the reason of his taking on himself the trouble of the journey and abandoning the pleasure of a fixed residence. Dábishlím repeated, from beginning to end, the story of his dream, and of the treasure and the testament, and the consignment of its completion to Sarándíp. The Bráhman smiled and said, 'Honor to the high spirit of the king! that in the pursuit of wisdom he takes upon himself all this toil, and, on account of the repose of his oppressed subjects and the peace of the poor among his people, accepts various kinds of labour and trial.

VERSE.

O thou who by true wisdom lov'st to reign!
Thou in this way thy empire mayst maintain;

---

[1] Votaries who rise early to perform their devotions. The expression is also used of thieves who rise up with the dawn to rob honest sleepers.

[2] Ḳur'án, ch. xv. 46; Sale, p. 176, l. 6: 'But those who fear God shall dwell in gardens amidst fountains. The angels shall say unto them, 'Enter ye therein in peace and security.'

[3] *Ḥikmat-dyín* cannot here mean 'Mirror of wisdom,' the only signification given in the Dictionary.

[4] He adorned the cave by his presence, and made it like that of Mání, who is said to have filled a cave in Chinese Tartary with strange and beautiful paintings. Mání was the founder of the sect of the Manicheans, and was burnt by order of Bahrám.

[5] *Shukḳah-i'alam* 'strip'—or 'long shred'—'of a banner.'

The plant thou waterest now with tender care,
Must on its boughs the fairest[1] produce bear.

Then the Bráhman having opened the lid of the casket of secret knowledge, filled the shell of the king's ear with the jewels of wisdom, and putting aside his own avocations for some days, employed himself in instructing the monarch, and in the midst of their converse, mention was made of the testament of Húshang. The king recounted to the sage, the precepts, one by one; and the Bráhman addressed the great monarch on the subject: and Dábishlím indited his words, with the pen of understanding, on the tablet of memory; and the book 'Kalílah and Damnah,' is composed of the questions and answers of the King and Bráhman; and we have arranged it in fourteen chapters, after the manner set forth in the catalogue of the book, and, '*Aid is from God from whom help is supplicated; He is sufficient for us, and in Him is our trust.*'

The great king Dábishlím said to the Bráhman Pílpáí, 'The purport of the first precept was, that when one is exalted by being honored with the confidence of kings, he will assuredly be envied by his peers, and those who envy him, endeavouring to destroy the pedestal of his honor, will, by deceitful words, work a change in the king's disposition towards him. Wherefore it behoves a king to ponder well on the speech of interested persons; and, on discovering that it is not devoid of an admixture of falsehood and corruption, not to conduct it to the confines of acceptance.

DISTICHS.

Admit not interested men, for they
With honey too the poisoned sting convey.
Thy honey-bringing friend, to outward eye—
Both stings and wrongs thee, in reality.

And I make my request to the Bráhman, that he may be pleased to relate a story suitable to this case, and may detail the history of some one who was the intimate counsellor of a king, and the basis of whose dignity was injured by the interested words of an envious person, and with whom friendship terminated in enmity, and concord in contention.' The Bráhman said, ' The centre of the basis of dominion, rests on this precept, and if a king does not deter interested persons from mischief and injurious acts, they will bring the majority of the nobles, to misery and disgrace; and hence complete disorder will find its way into the empire, and spread even to the prince; and when a mischief-maker has found the means of coming between two

---

[1] There is an equivoque intended in the use of the word بيهى, which cannot be preserved in English. بيهى *bihí* is a 'guava,' a fruit of an exquisite flavour; and بهى *bahíy* means 'beautiful,' 'excellent.'

friends, the conclusion of their affairs will assuredly draw towards a terrible and disastrous catastrophe, as befell between the Lion and the Ox.' The king asked, 'How was that?'

STORY I.

The Bráhman said, 'They have related, that there was a trader who had compassed land and sea, and traversed the regions of east and west, and experienced the chills and heats of fortune, and tested the sweets and bitters of many [1] days.

COUPLET.

Prudent and faithful and expert was he,   By much experience taught sagacity.

When the van of Death's array—for so the infirmity of age is termed—began to make inroads into the realm of his constitution, and the advanced guard of fate, by which white hairs are implied, took possession of the outworks of the fortress of his existence,

VERSE.

When the changing watch of age, strikes the drum of deep distress,[2]
The heart grows cold to joyous things, to mirth and happiness.
The white hair comes, its message gives from fate and terror's king,
And the crooked back and stooping form death's salutation bring.

The merchant knew that every moment they were about to beat the drum of departure, and would demand back the stock of life which they had deposited in the tabernacle of the body. He assembled his sons, three youths, intelligent and learned, but who, from the pride of riches, and the inpetuosity of youth, had overstepped the path of moderation, and extended the hand of expenditure to the property of their father; and having averted their faces from business and professional employment, passed their precious time in vanity and sloth. Their kind father, from excess of that affection and tenderness which fits the character of the paternal relation, began to admonish them, and opened to them the gates of disinterested advice, which comprehended all the topics of fear and hope: and said, 'O youths! if ye understand not the value of the property, in the acquisition of which ye have suffered no toil, ye are excusable in the judgment of men of wisdom, but ye ought to know that wealth may be made the source of happiness in this world and in that which is to come, and whatever men seek of every degree in the two worlds may be secured by means of wealth, and all people seek for one of three conditions. The first is abundance of worldly goods and an

---

[1] *Bisyár* may very well be taken with *chashídah*. I have made it depend on *ayyám*, because that construction is not so common, and because, taken by itself, *chashídah* corresponds better to *paimúdah* and *ṭayy kardah*, which are used simply, without an adverb.

[2] Keene makes *kús-i durd* the nominative to *zanad*, which it may very well be. Old age is compared to a watch which is relieving guard and beats a drum, or, as Keene takes it, the drum of pain beats the signal for old age to relieve guard.

ample supply of effects and chattels, and this is desired by the class whose mind is limited to drinking and dress, and labouring for the fulfilment of sensual gratifications. The second condition is exalted rank and elevation in dignity, and the class whose object this is, is that of the nobility and men of office; and it is impossible to attain these two conditions save by wealth. The third condition is the obtaining the reward of a future state, and the arriving at the grades of religious excellence; and the class who look to this object are the people of salvation and pious eminence; and the acquisition of this dignity may be through lawful wealth, [according to the saying,] ' *Good is pure wealth to the man that is pure,*' [1] and the Great Doctor of Mysticism has said in his Poem.[2]

COUPLET.

If for the Faith thou bear'st thy wealth, 'It then,'
The Prophet says, 'is pure to righteous men.'

Wherefore it is plain that by the blessing of wealth, most objects of pursuit are attained, and to get wealth without a profession, and the due quest of it, appears impossible, and if a person, as is rarely the case, obtains it without toil, inasmuch as he has not undergone labour in acquiring it, he will assuredly, through not knowing its worth and value, quickly pass it from his hands. Therefore, having averted your faces from sloth, incline towards the acquisition of money, and employ yourselves in the same profession of traffic in which ye have for many years seen me engaged.' The eldest son said, ' O Father! thou enjoinest us to acquire money, and this is repugnant to dependence on God, and I feel assured that whatever is predestined to me by fate will accrue to me although I employ no labour or exertion for it, and as to that which is not my destiny, however much I may exert myself in pursuit of it, it will be all in vain.

VERSE.

Whate'er my fate, will surely be my lot.
And that unfated will, as sure, be not.
Why then for that which I can ne'er obtain,
Use fruitless efforts and exertions vain.

And I have heard that a sage has said, ' That which was my destiny, though I have fled from it, has adhered to me; and that which was not fated for me, however much I have stuck to it, has fled from me.' Wherefore, whether we undertake a profession or not, it is all the same.

HEMISTICH.

Eternal fate can ne'er be overthrown.

---

[1] I have not found this in the Ḥadís, but there is something like it in the Mishkátu-'l-Maṣábíh, vol. 2, p. 2, l. 3.

[2] This couplet is from the Maṣnavi, or poem of Jalálu'ddín Muḥammadu-'l-Balkhí, or 'l-Konoví, more commonly called Maulaví Rúmí, who composed about A. H. 600. He founded a celebrated sect of darveshes at Cogni in Natolia, and his work is regarded by them as of equal authority with the Ḳur'án.

Accordingly, the story of those Two Princes is a proof of this, since one of them gained the treasure of his father without toil, and the other—in the hope of that treasure—lost his country and the sovereignty.' The father asked, 'How was that?'

STORY II.

The son said, 'In the country of Ḥalab,[1] there was a king of prosperous fortune, and a sovereign of extensive sway, who had experienced many vicissitudes, and seen many revolutions of night and day: and he had two sons who were immersed in the whirlpool of the vanity of youth, and intoxicated with the inebriation of the wine of prosperity, inclined to gaiety and mirth, and employed in pleasure and amusement, while they listened to the melody of this song from the voice of harp and bell.[2]

COUPLET.

Be gay, for in the twinkling of an eye
Autumn will come, and life's young spring pass by.

The king was a wise and experienced man; and he possessed an abundant supply of jewels, and immense treasures in money. After considering the habits of his sons, he feared, lest, after he was gone, they should cast those hoards that he had acquired into the place of dissipation, and give them, on the occasion of their requirement, to the wind of destruction. And in the neighbourhood of that city, there was a holy man, who had turned his back on worldly things, and was looking to prepare a store for the final state.

COUPLET.

Inflamed with those all-glorious rays that spring
From Godhead; and enamoured of heaven's king.

The monarch had a strong attachment to him, and reposed exceeding confidence in him. He commanded all his treasures to be collected, (and in such a way that no one heard of it), buried them in the abode of the holy man, and left this parting injunction to the saint, that, when fickle fortune and unstable rank, should avert their faces from his sons, and the fount of prosperity, which, like the mirage, possesses nought but a semblance of reality, should be filled up with the mire of adversity, and his sons should become poor and necessitous, he should inform them of that treasure; since, perchance, after seeing ill-fortune and experiencing trouble, they might be schooled, and expend it in a right way; and having turned from profusion and dissipation, might observe the path of moderation. The holy man accepted the king's bequest; and the latter with a view to his present object,

---

[1] Aleppo.
[2] The *chaghánah*, says the Dictionary, is a little staff with bells, which, when moved, rings out an accompaniment to other instruments.

prepared a deep pit in one of his palaces, and made it appear as though he was burying his treasures there, and caused his sons to be informed, that when necessity shewed itself, a sufficient store, which would amply supply their wants, was there treasured, and after these circumstances, in a short time, both the king and the holy man accepted the divine invitation, and became insensible from the cup of '*Every soul shall taste of death.*'[1]

COUPLET.

From fate's cup needs must every child of clay
Drink of the wine '*All earthly things decay.*'[2]

And that hoard which was buried in the cell of the devotee, remained hidden and concealed; nor did any one obtain information of it. The brothers, after the death of their father, fell to strife and contention, with regard to the division of his dominions and treasure, and the elder brother, by strength and valour, having got the mastery, took possession of all the effects, and left his younger brother afflicted and destitute. The hapless [prince] deprived of all share in the office of government, and of all part of his patrimony, thought to himself that as the sun of good fortune and power had set its face towards the western region of decline, and Heaven, exercising cruelty, had displayed the quality of insincerity and alienation; to turn the face a second time in search of worldly things, and to attempt again the once-attempted could effect no useful result.

VERSE.

Or old, or new, so transient is this earth 　'Tis not in all one grain of barley worth.
Prepare a better kingdom then than this, 　Forsake this cell and ope the door to bliss.

'There is nothing better,' thought he, 'than that, as the collar of fortune has escaped from the grasp of choice, I should take hold of the skirt of reliance on God and contentment, and not let go the dignity of the Darvesh, which is a sovereignty without decay.

COUPLET.

The Darvesh in whose peaceful cell, thy rays, Contentment! beam,[3]
Is poor in mind, but reigns in truth, a sovereign lord supreme.'

With this resolution he issued from the city, and said to himself, 'Such a one, the devotee, was the friend of my father; my advisable course is to turn my face towards his cell, and at his feet commit the conduct of my devotions to the direction of abstinence.' When he reached the abode of the holy man,

---

[1] Ku'rán, Fl., ch. iii. 182; Mar. 186; Sale p. 53, l. 8 : 'Every soul shall taste of death, and ye shall have your reward on the day of resurrection ; and he who shall be far removed from hell-fire, and shall be admitted into Paradise, shall be happy ; but the present life is only a deceitful provision.' Death is, in the text, compared to a banquet, as, in the Parables of the New Testament, the future world is compared to a feast ; Matthew xxii. 10.

[2] Ķur'án, lv. 26 ; Sale, p. 392, l. 23 : 'Every creature which liveth on the earth is subject to decay ; but the glorious and honourable countenance of thy Lord shall remain for ever.' The lines are, lit. : ' Every one that is born, to him it is necessary without remedy to drink, from the cup of fate, the wine, ' Every soul shall taste of death.'

[3] Lit. : 'The darvesh who has the corner of contentment secured to him.' Keene reads *ganj* for *kunj*.

he found that the parrot of his soul had taken flight from the cage of the body, towards the Paradise of '*In a lofty garden,*'[1] and that the cell of that luminous mind remained empty. For a time grief and dejection at the circumstance overcame him. At length he chose that very spot for his abode, and by way of discipleship he became the occupant and attendant[2] of that cell, and near the hermitage was a water-course, and they had dug a well outside the edifice, and made a way from it to the water-course, whence water flowed continually into the well, and the people of the hermitage[3] made use of it, and bathed and performed their ablutions with it. One day the prince let down a bucket into the well. There was no sound of water, and on his examining it carefully, there was no water at the bottom of the well. He reflected, saying, 'Alas! what accident has happened that no water comes into this well, and if a complete stoppage has found its way to the well, and the water-course, and it is altogether worn out, it will be impossible to continue longer in this abode.' Then in order to learn the certainty of the matter, he descended into the well, and minutely inspected the sides and all parts of it, and the channel by which the water came.[4] All of a sudden an excavation met his view, from which a portion [of masonry] had fallen into the channel of the water and prevented it from flowing into the well. He reflected, 'Ah! whither does this excavation go? And where does this cavity issue?' He then made the cavity larger, and he no sooner stepped into it than he came upon the treasure of his father. When the Prince beheld that wealth and immense sum of money, he prostrated himself in thanks to God, and said, 'Although this wealth is vast, and these gems beyond calculation, still I must not swerve from the path of reliance on God, and the highway of contentment, and I must limit my expenses to my wants.

HEMISTICH.

Till, what the unknown future shows, we see.

On the other side, the elder brother being firmly established in his dominions took no thought for his subjects, and his army, and in hope of the imaginary treasure which he fancied to be in the palace of his father, expended all that he could lay his hands upon, and from excess of haughtiness and pride, made no enquiries after his brother, and was ashamed of showing attachment to

---

[1] Ḳur'án, ch. lxix, 22; Sale p. 420, l. 22: 'On that day ye shall be presented before the judgment-seat of God; and none of your secret actions shall be hidden. And he who shall have his book delivered into his right hand shall say, 'Take ye, read this my book; verily I thought that I should be brought to this my account: he shall lead a pleasing life in a lofty garden, the fruits whereof shall be near to gather.'

[2] I do not know a word that exactly translates *mujáwir*. It signifies 'the religious attendant of a shrine.' Keene translates *az sar-i irddat*, 'in the warmth of his attachment.'

[3] A hermitage can hardly be inhabited by more than one person; we might therefore translate *ṣaum'aah* 'monastery,' but Keene renders it 'hermitage' and justly, for *ahl* no doubt refers to a number of hermits who had successively occupied the cell.

[4] As there was *no* water we must take *áb wa ráh-rá* for the figure hendiadys.

him. Suddenly an enemy arose against him, and with a numerous and warlike army advanced into his country. The Prince found his treasury empty, and his army unprovided and distressed. He went to the place where his father had pointed out the treasury, in order that with that abundant wealth he might prepare a numerous host, [according to the saying,], '*There is no king without men, and no men without money.*' The more he exerted himself the less could he find any trace of the treasure, and the more he toiled and laboured the farther was he excluded from obtaining his object.

COUPLET.

Wouldst thou keep thyself from sorrow, then this counsel hear of me,
Seek'st thou that to thee unfated, all thy toil will fruitless be.

And when he had altogether lost all hope of finding the treasure by a variety of devices, after issuing bonds,[1] he contrived to get together a force, and directing his course to repel the enemy, issued from the city. After the lines of battle had been drawn up on both sides, and the fire of slaughter had been kindled, an arrow from the ranks of the enemy's force struck the elder Prince in a mortal place, and he fell dead on the spot; and from this side also, they discharged a shaft, and the strange king too was slain, and both armies were left disordered and leaderless. It almost came to pass that the fire of revolt blazed up, and that the people of both kingdoms had been consumed by the flame of confusion. At last the chiefs of both armies assembled and made search, with mutual consent, from the royal families and the imperial stock, for a king of beneficent disposition and good qualities, in order that they might consign to him the duties of the empire and the conduct of state affairs. The general opinion agreed in this conclusion, that the fortunate chief the head of whose auspiciousness would be worthy of a diadem of exaltation, and the finger of whose happiness would befit the signet-ring of dominion, was that same devout Prince. The officers of state went to the door of his cell, and with all possible respect and reverence brought him from the corner of obscurity to the court of acceptance, and from the nook of retirement to the high-place of the throne of fortune; and by the blessings of reliance on the divine favour, he obtained the treasures of his father and was established in his kingdom. And I have introduced this example in order to prove that the attainment of fortune is not dependent on exertion and labour, and that it is better to place trust in reliance on God, than to pillow oneself on one's own efforts.

VERSE.

The best of all professions is to lean   On Providence—Can aught be lovelier seen
Than faith? Trust then in God and struggle not :   Thou to thyself less true art than thy lot.
Wert thou but patient, what thy fate must be   Will come and cling all lover-like to thee.

---

[1] So I have ventured to render *tamassuk namúdah*, but it perhaps implies 'scraping forces together.'

When the son had concluded this story, the father said, 'What thou hast uttered is pure truth and justice, but this world is a world of means and causes, and the divine command has been issued accordingly, that, on causes, the happening of events in general in this world should depend; and the profit of working for a livelihood is greater than the reliance on Providence, because the advantage of such reliance accrues to him that so relies, and no more; and the benefit of working circulates to others from the worker, and to convey benefit to others is a proof of goodness, for, '*The best of men is he who benefits mankind,*' and when any one has the ability to benefit others, it is a shame if he chooses to be idle and receive benefits from them: but perhaps thou hast never heard the story of that man who after witnessing what befell the Hawk and the Raven, neglected causation, and hence the divine wrath fell upon him. The son asked 'How was that?'

STORY III.

The father said, 'They relate that a darvesh was passing through a waste, and was meditating on the tokens of [God's] mercy, and on the instances of divine power, when suddenly he beheld a swift royal falcon, which, holding a piece of flesh in its claw, was hovering round a tree, and in the most extreme agitation circled near a nest. The man was astonished at this circumstance, and stood for a time gazing at it. He saw a Raven without feathers and unfledged lying in the nest, and the Hawk divided the flesh piece by piece, and in proportion to what the callow raven could swallow, placed the pieces in its mouth. The man exclaimed, ' Glory to God! behold His kingly favor and infinite compassion, that in the corner of this nest a raven unfledged and that has neither power to fly, nor vigor to attack, is not left by Him without support.

VERSE.

Earth's surface is His general table spread,   There friend or foe is nought distinguishèd.
And thence each day His bounties are so wide,   In Ḳaf the Símurgh finds its wants supplied.

Wherefore it must assuredly be from weakness of faith and dulness of belief, that I, ever occupied in quest of daily subsistence, remain afoot and unseated, and having plunged into the wilderness of greediness, by every sort of artifice procure my daily bread.

VERSE.

The All-Provider will ensure me food,   Why, like the base, then, stir in fretful mood?
I with contented cheerful heart respire,   I have my lot, 'tis all that I desire.

The best course is for me henceforth to place the head of freedom from care on the knee of retirement, and draw the line of abrogation on the page of employment and business.

HEMISTICH.

Food is from God Most Blessed and Most High.

He then washed his hands of worldly concerns and sate down in a corner, and fixed his heart sincerely on the gratuitous[1] beneficence of the Causer of Causes.

HEMISTICH.

Ponder not causes and the Causer slight.

For three days and nights he remained quiet in the corner of retirement, but no gratuitous supply reached him from any channel, and every moment he became more attenuated and weak. At last his infirmities[2] came strongly[2] upon him and the recluse became mighty feeble, and was unable to perform the usual duties of worship and devotion. Then God Most High sent to him the prophet of that age, and gave him a message, severely rebuking him, saying, ' O creature of mine ! I have placed the pivot of the world on causes and means, and, though my omnipotent power can perform a thing without a cause, nevertheless my wisdom has made this requisite, that things in general should be effected and brought about by causes, and hence the rule of an interchange of benefits is established. Wherefore if thou canst be the means of imparting advantage to another, it is better than to be obliged to be succoured by others.

COUPLET.

Be like the hawk—the quarry chase, and food to others give;
Not like the raven's callow brood, a remnant-eater, live.'

And I have introduced this story in order that thou mayest know that it is not practicable for every one to put aside the veil of secondary causes, and that commendable reliance on God is that which, with a due regard to means, maintains a firm faith, so as to participate in that gracious promise, ' *The industrious man is the friend of God*,'[3] and a great authority has said, ' Work lest thou become sick ; and own that thy food is from God, lest thou be an infidel.'

VERSE.

Do not—to slothfulness—on God depend,
The saying hear, ' *Who labours is God friend.*'[3]
With labour be combined thy confidence,
And, whilst thou toilest, trust Omnipotence.

The next son then began to say, ' O Father ! we have not power to rely implicitly on God, wherefore there is no alternative but to practice a profession ; and when we engage in a profession, and God Most High, from the treasure of his bounties, provides us with wealth and property,[4] what

---

[1] Keene translates *bi-'illat* 'faultless,' but I am convinced that a play upon words is intended, and that the meaning is ' the causeless (gratuitous) beneficence of the Causer of causes.'

[2] There is here an oxymoron in *ṣuf rúi ba-ḳuwat* and in *ḳawiy ṣaif*, which is lost in Keene's translation.

[3] From this Arabic proverb probably is derived the old monkish one ' Laborare est orare,' and our clever rendering thereof ' Work is worship.'

[4] For *mandí* the only meanings given in the Dictionary are ' Mode, manner, way, disposition.' The word is probably chosen here to chime with *mál*, but it must mean 'wealth, opulence.'

must we do with it?' The father said, 'To amass wealth is easy, but to keep it and derive advantage from it, is difficult, and when any one acquires wealth, he must know two necessary things: the one, to take care of it in such a manner that it may be safe from inroads and consumption, and that the hand of the thief and the robber and the cut-purse, may be kept back from it, since gold has many friends and the possessor of it many a foe.

COUPLET.

Heaven does not strike the poor and needy crowd,
It strikes the pompous gathering of the proud.

The second thing is, that he should reap the benefit of the profits, but not squander the principal, for if men spend everything from their capital, and are not contented with the interest, in a short time the dust of annihilation will rise up from it.

VERSE.

| A sea to which no waters flow, | Dry to the footstep soon would grow. |
| Dig from a hill and nought return, | Thou soon that hill wouldst overturn. |

Whoever is without income, and continually expends money, or whose expenses are greater than his income, will eventually fall into the vortex of want, and it is probable that his affairs will terminate in destruction, like that wasteful Rat which destroyed itself from grief.' The son asked 'How was that?'

STORY IV.

The father said, 'They have related that a farmer had placed in a barn a quantity of corn for a store, and had closed up the doors of expenditure there, in order that in the day when excessive want and extreme necessity should arrive,[1] he might be able to derive advantage from it. By chance, a Rat—who from exceeding greediness, desired to steal grain from the granary of the moon,[2] and to snatch, with the claw of rapacity, the cluster of the Pleiades from the corn-field of the sky—had its abode in the vicinity of that spot, and its nest in the neighbourhood of that barn. He was continually burrowing under-ground in every direction, and with his stone-rending teeth he every-where made excavations. All at once, his mining operations terminated in the midst of the grain, and from the roof of his house, grains of wheat, like bright-falling stars from the sky, came pouring down. The rat saw that the promise, '*Your sustenance is in the heaven,*'[3] was fulfilled; and that

---

[1] Lit. 'When want should reach excess, and need, extremity.'

[2] *Khirman-i máh* 'the halo round the moon,' but *khirman* by itself means 'harvest, granary.' An equivoque is therefore intended here, and continued in *khúshah,* which means 'ear of corn,' 'cluster of fruit,' as well as 'cluster of stars.' It is impossible to preserve the pun in English.

[3] Kur'án, ch. li. 22; Sale p. 384, l. 15: 'There are signs of the divine power and goodness in the earth to men of sound understanding, and also in your ownselves: will ye not also consider? 'Your true sustenance is in the heaven,' and also that which ye are promised.'

the dark saying, '*Seek ye your food in the recesses of the earth,*' was cleared up. He then performed the duties of thanksgiving for the display of those blessings, and, by the acquisition of those precious jewels, having obtained great opulence, he began to assume the proud demeanour of Ḳárún[1] and the arrogant pretensions of Pharaoh; and in a short space of time the rats in that quarter became acquainted with the circumstances, and girt the waist of service in attendance upon him.

COUPLET.

The treacherous friends thou seeest here   Are flies that round the sweets appear.

Friends of the trencher and companions of the cup assembled near him, and—as their custom is—adopting a course of flattery, uttered not a word, save such as would suit his inclination and gratify his humor; nor loosed their tongue except in his eulogy and praise, and in thanking and blessing him. He too, like one demented, opened his mouth in boasting and vain-glorious talk, and his hand in ruinous expenditure; in the idea that the grain of that building would not come to an end, and that wheat would continuously be showered down and descend from that orifice. Every day he expended a large portion of it on his companions, and having no regard to the final issue, turned not from the thought of to-day, to the anxious care for the morrow.

HEMISTICH.

To day, cup-bearer! wine we'll drink; 'to-morrow,' who has seen?

And at the season that the rats were engrossed with pleasure in that retired corner, the cold hand of famine and dearth had cast down the people, and the fire of hunger was kindled in the breast of the afflicted poor. On every side they offered a loved object for bread, and no one listened to them, and in all directions they desired to sell their household goods for a dish of meat, and no one would buy.

VERSE.

All longed a round of bread to see, but they
Nought could behold but the round orb of day.[2]
The world was straitened in that stern distress,
The hungry wailed—the full were pitiless.

The arrogant Rat having spread out the carpet of luxurious delight, had no intelligence of the famine, nor was acquainted with the scarcity of the season, When some days had passed, the occasion became one of life and death to the farmer, and the knife reached the bone. He opened the door of the building and saw that extensive damage had accrued to the grain. Then heaving a cold sigh from his heart inflamed [with grief], and, suffering much sorrow for

---

[1] Korah, who, as the Muḥammadans say, was the cousin of Moses, and quarreled with him on being advised to consecrate a portion of his immense riches to God. Keene renders the word *Ḳárún* 'Crœsus'!

[2] There is here a very sorry but not uncommon attempt at a witticism. A round loaf of bread is compared to the round orb of the sun.

that loss, he said to himself, 'It is not the proceeding of a wise man to lament in a matter the remedy of which is beyond the limits of possibility. Now it appears best to collect the remaining grain that is left in this building, and to convey it to another place. Then the farmer busied himself with carrying out the small portion that remained; and in that place the Rat, who imagined himself the owner of the house and lord of the edifice, was asleep; and the other rats, from their excessive greediness and cupidity, did not hear the sound of the farmer's feet, and the noise of the coming and going, above their heads. But one among them, an acute rat, having guessed how matters stood, ascended the roof to ascertain [what was going on] and, from a crevice, observed the real state of the case. He came down forthwith, and having told his friends the substance of the story, flung out of the hole, and they too went out, each to a corner, and left their patron alone.

VERSE.

Thy friends are all on parings set,	Each loves thee for what he can get:
As thy wealth fails thee, love grows less,	For their own ends, thy fall they'd bless.
From such a band of false allies,	To part, nor call them friends, were wise.

The next day when the Rat lifted his head from the pillow of repose, however much he looked to the left and right, he saw none of his friends, and the more he scrutinised, both before and behind, the less he discovered any traces of his companions. He began to bewail himself, and said,

COUPLET.

What has become of those, my friends that were, I do not know.
Alas! what can the matter be, that they have left me so?'

When, in order to ascertain what they were about, he—after a long interval, during which he had chosen to live retired—issued from the corner of his dwelling, and got intelligence of the calamitous dearth and the miserable distress and scarcity—in the utmost perturbation, he hastened home that he might exert himself to the utmost in taking care of the store he possessed. When he reached his house, he saw not a trace of the grain, and he then mounted through that hole into the granary, and there was not as much there for him to eat, as would suffice for one night's food. Thereupon his endurance being folded up,[1] he began to rend the collar of his life with the hand of affliction, and struck the head of insanity so often on the ground, that his brains were scattered, and by the ill-fortune of his wasteful living, he fell into the vortex of destruction and ruin. And the moral of this story is, that a man's expenses ought to be in proportion to his income, and he should enjoy himself with the interest of the principal he possesses, and should be careful of it in such a manner that no detriment may accrue to his capital stock.

---

[1] *Táḳ* is here used for the jingle with *ṭaḳat*; *tâk shudan*, according to the Dictionary, signifies 'to be folded.' So his patience resembled clothes folded up, and ready to be put away.

COUPLET.

Ever thy income and expense survey,   Contract expenses as thy means decay.'

And when the father had concluded this tale, the younger son arose and adorned the preamble of his discourse with benedictions and praise of his father, and said, ' O father! after one has taken care of his property according to rule, and has obtained full interest from it, how should he expend that interest?' The father said, 'The mean in everything is to be commended, especially as regards the mode of living. Wherefore it behoves the possessor of wealth, after obtaining his profit, to pay regard to two other rules. First, let him shun incongruous expenses and outlays, lest these bring forth repentance, and he loose the tongue of sarcasm against him; and, in point of fact, the squandering one's resources, and profuse expenditure are a temptation of the devil [as it is said,] ' *For the profuse are brethren of the devils.*'[1]

VERSE.

Men of a noble nature, less eschew   The parsimonious, than the profligate.
The liberal please all hearts in all they do;   But that most pleases which is moderate.

Secondly : It is necessary that he should avoid the disgrace of stinginess, and the stigma of miserly conduct, since the miser has an ill name, both in spiritual and worldly things, and a worldly avaricious man is at all times the object of reproach and as wretched as his foes could wish;[2] and the hoards of the miser become, in the end, the butt of the shaft of ruinous expenditure and waste. Thus, for example, when water is continually flowing into a large reservoir from sundry channels, and has not an outlet proportioned to the influx, it of necessity seeks a passage in every direction, and bursts out from every corner. So the walls of the reservoir are cracked, and in the end it is ruined and destroyed, and the waters are dispersed abroad on all sides and in all directions. ' *Warn the miser of a casualty or an heir,*'[3]

STANZA.

The wealth the miser nought enjoyed is cast,
By the rude hand of spoilers, to the wind;
Or has to some ungrateful heir now passed,
Who but with loathing calls his name to mind.'

When the sons had heard the admonitions of their father, and had fully

---

[1] Kur'án, ch. xvii. 29; Sale, p. 212, l. 16 : 'And waste not thy substance profusely, for the profuse are brethren of the devils ; and the devil was ungrateful to his Lord.'

[2] Keene reads *dushman-i kám*, and translates 'the enemy of joy.'

[3] I have taken the reading of the lithographed edition, which is *bashshiri 'l-bakhíla bi hddigin au wdrigin*. The printed edition reads *nashir mdl*, which I take to be a typographical error, but if not, it must be *nushara mdlu*, 'The wealth of the miser is scattered,' etc. One MS. reads *bashshiri mdlu*, and another, بِشر مال البخيل كاوث اوارث which is evidently corrupt.

recognised the advantages of his words, each made choice of a profession, and engaged in business; and the oldest of them[1] betook himself to commerce, and embarked on a distant journey; and he had with him two baggage oxen, such that the bull of heaven did not possess the power of contending with them in strength; and the celestial lion from their fierceness and the awe they inspired, hid, like a cat keeping a fast, the claw of terror in the paw of helplessness.

COUPLET.

Elephantine in body and lions in fight,   In their motion majestic, and matchless in might.

The name of one was Shanzabah,[2] and of the other, Mandabah; and the worthy merchant always managed them and attended to their condition himself.   As, however, the time of the journey waxed long and they traversed great distances, debility made inroads into their condition, and the mark of weakness was displayed on the aspect of their state.   By chance, in the midst of the way a vast slough intervened, and Shanzabah stuck therein. The merchant commanded, so that by every device they brought him out, and as he had not power to move, [his owner] hired a man and appointed him to the charge of the ox; and it was fixed that as soon as he gained strength he should bring him to the caravan.   The hireling abode one or two days in the jungle, and became dispirited by being alone, and abandoning Shanzabah, carried the news of his death to the merchant; and in that stage, Mandabah, from excess of fatigue and through parting from Shanzabah, died.   But Shanzabah, in a short space of time, having regained his strength, wandered in every direction in search of a meadow for grazing, until he reached a mead adorned with a variety of fragrant herbs, and clothed with plants of different kinds.   Paradise, from envy of that garden, bit the finger of jealousy; and heaven opened the eye of admiration in surveying it.

COUPLET.

In flowers and verdure fresh upsprung, and waters flowing there;—
(Avaunt, ill glances![3]) you might it with Paradise compare.

Shanzabah was pleased with that spot, and deposited the furniture of residence in the expanse of that meadow; and when he had for a time grazed in that pasture, without any bond of constraint or troublesome fetter,[4] and had lived, according to the wish of his heart, in that exhilarating air and heart-expanding plain, he became excessively robust and stout.   The delight

---

[1] Here the story for the first time coincides with the Hitopadesha. The tale of Shanzabah corresponds with the story of Sanjivaka, Hitopadesha, book 2. ('The separation of Friends.')

[2] All the MSS. I have seen, and the lithographed edition, read 'Shatrabah,' but the Dictionary explains 'Shatrabah' as being a corrupted form of Shanzabah.   I have therefore retained the latter.

[3] Orientals fancy that the evil eye affects everything beautiful, so the poet would repel its influence from the Paradise he is describing.

[4] Lit. : 'Fetter of annoyance.'

of ease and enjoyment of repose, carried him so far, that from the abundance of his gaiety, he uttered loud bellowings. And in the neighbourhood of that meadow lived a Lion, who inspired great awe from his savage and ferocious nature. Many wild animals [1] had girded themselves in his service, and countless beasts of prey had placed the head of obedience on the line [2] of his commandment, and the Lion from the pride of youth and the arrogance of dominion and success and the multitude of his servants and the number of his retinue, fancied no one superior to himself; and despised the swift-charging tiger and the huge-bodied elephant; but he had never seen an ox nor heard the voice of one. When the bellowing of Shanzabah reached him, he was much dismayed, and from fear that the beasts should discover that alarm had found the way to him, he moved nowhere, and remained quiet in one spot. And in his train were two subtle jackals, one named Kalílah, and the other Damnah, and both of them were famed for sagacity and acuteness. Damnah, however, was the cleverer, and more eager in pursuit of rank and fame. He, by his quickness of perception, discovered that fear had over-come the lion, and that he was intent on something which was passing through his mind. He said to Kalílah, 'What sayest thou as to the state of the king, in that he has abandoned the pleasureableness of exercise, and has fixed himself in one place?

COUPLET.

The signs of sorrow on his brow   Tell that his heart is pensive now.'

Kalílah replied, 'What business hast thou with this question? and what is thy concern with the uttering of this speech?

HEMISTICH.

Where thou! and where discourse of state affairs! [3]

And we in the court of this King obtain our food and pass our time tranquilly under the shade of his fortunes. Be satisfied with this and refrain from inquisitiveness into the secrets of kings, and scanning too narrowly their affairs, for we are not of the degree to be honored with the confidence of monarchs, or that with princes there should be room for attention to our words; wherefore it is idle and superfluous to talk of them, and whoever superfluously meddles with what does not befit him, meets with what the Ape met with.' Damnah inquired, 'How was that?'

---

[1] Keene translates *wuḥúsh* ' gentle animals,' but I am ignorant of any authority for such a meaning to the word.

[2] I am inclined to think *khaṭṭ* here means 'line' in the sense of 'writing' rather than in that of 'edge;' as it is usual to express reverence for a command contained in a letter, by raising the paper to the head.

[3] This form of expression is a common mode of indicating discrepancy between two things. So in Hindústání, ' Where Rájá Bhoj! and where the oilman Gangá!'

STORY V.

Kalílah said, ' They have related that a Monkey saw a Carpenter sitting upon a piece of timber, which he was cutting, and he had two wedges, one of which he hammered into the cleft of the wood, so that the cutting was facilitated, and the passage for the going and returning of the saw was widened, and when the fissure passed a certain limit he knocked in the other wedge and drew out the former one, and in this manner he continued working. The Monkey amused himself with looking on : suddenly the Carpenter, in the middle of his work, on some urgent occasion, got up and went away, and when the Monkey saw the coast clear he immediately seated himself in the piece of wood, and in that portion where it was cut asunder, the lower parts of his body went down into the cleft. The Ape drew out of the cleft of the timber the wedge that was in front, before hammering in the other, and as soon as it was extracted the two divisions of the wood closed and the hinder parts of the monkey were firmly fixed in the midst of the log. The wretched Ape, agonized by the pain, screamed out and said,

COUPLET.

' Each one on earth his own affairs should do.
Who does not thus, does vastly ill, 'tis true.

My business is to pluck fruit, not to handle a saw, and my profession is to look about me in the jungle, not to chop with hatchet and adze.

HEMISTICH.

To one so acting it will happen thus.'

The Ape was thus soliloquizing, when the carpenter returned and handled him as he deserved ; and the affairs of the Monkey terminated through that officiousness in his destruction, and hence they have said,

HEMISTICH.

Sure carpenters' is not a monkey's work.

And I have introduced this example that thou mayest know that every one should do his own business, and not step beyond his due limits, and ' *For every business there are men.*' And how finely have they said,

COUPLET.

This proverb of a friend I would recall,   ' All have their work and there is work for all.'

Give up this affair which is no business of thine, and regard the small provision and food which reaches us, as a piece of good fortune.' Damnah said, ' Every one who seeks to be about the persons of kings, ought not to do so for the sake of food and provision, since the stomach is filled in all places and with all things. But the advantage of attendance on princes is the obtaining of high office, in order that in that position one may, by favor, gratify his friends and deal rigorously with his enemies. And every one, whose spirit can stoop to the consideration of mere food, is to be reckoned with brutes, like a hungry dog who is pleased with a bone, and a mean-spirited cat that is content with a crumb of bread; and I have observed, that if a lion is chasing a hare, should he see a wild ass, he discontinues [chasing his first quarry] and turns to pursue the wild ass.

COUPLET.

Be ever lofty-souled, for as may be   Thy spirit, God and man will value thee.

And whoever has attained a lofty station, though his life should be short as that of a flower, still, on account of his fair fame, the wise attribute to him long life; and he who bows the head to servility and meanness of soul, though he may abide for a long time like the leaf of the pine, yet, in the opinion of men of eminence, he finds no esteem, and they make no account of him.'

COUPLET.

He that is famous, S'adí, never dies;   But he is truly dead whom men despise.

Kalílah said, 'The pursuit of dignities and high offices beseems that class, who by the nobleness of their descent and the grace of their manners and high birth, possess a fitness and capacity for such things; and we are not of this order so as to be suited to lofty stations, or that we should advance the step of exertion in pursuit of them.

COUPLET.

My dreamings are as boundless as the illimitable sea;
Alas! can such vain longings in this atom's scheming be?'

Damnah said, 'The source of greatness is intellect and accomplishments, not race and descent. Every one who possesses a clear understanding and a perfect judgment, raises himself from a low origin to an exalted rank; and whoever has a weak mind and a mean intellect, brings himself down from a lofty position to a low rank.

STANZA.

By aid of lofty sense and prudence high,   Man casts the noose of seizure on the sky.[1]
If the soul's vision ope not by emprise,   The sight to lofty things can never rise.

And the ancients have said that elevation to exalted rank is attainable only by great trouble; and descent from an honorable station is brought about with little pains; as one can lift on one's shoulder from the ground a heavy stone only with great exertion, and must by the slightest movement, drop it to the earth; and hence it is that no one is able to relish the pursuit of lofty things, save a man of high spirit who possesses the ability of undergoing labour.

COUPLET.

Love, O my soul! beseems not those in delicacy bred,
The much-enduring brave alone can in this tumult tread.

Every one who seeks the indulgence, ' *Obscurity is ease,*' having washed his

---

[1] That is—attains the highest dignities.

hands of honor, will, to all time, remain a recluse in the corner of abasement and unfulfilment of his wishes, and he who dreads not the thorny ground of ' *Notoriety is a misfortune,*' will in a short time pluck the rose of his wish, and sit in the flower-garden of honor on the cushion of pleasure.

STANZA.

> None will be honored till they suffer grief, and toil, and pain,
> The ruby must effuse its heart's blood,[1] ere it value gain.
> Ne'er did the traveler trace out in the scroll of happiness,
> Clear from blot of toil and trouble, the handwriting of success.

But perhaps thou hast never heard the story of those two companions, one of whom by the endurance of toil and hardship, reached the pinnacle of regal dignity, and the other, through indolence and self-indulgence, remained in the abyss of want and distress.'   Kalílah said ' How was that ?'

STORY VI.

Damnah said, 'Two friends, one of whom was named Sálim, and the other Ghánim,[2] were journeying on a road, and, in company with one another, traversed the halting-places and stages.   It happened that they passed along the skirt of a mountain, whose peak kept rein-and-rein with the bay courser of the sky, and whose waist was girt so as to keep stirrup-to-stirrup with the surface of the celestial girdle ;[3] and at the foot of the mountain there was a fountain of water, in clearness like the cheek of fresh-faced, rosy-cheeked [beauties], and in sweetness like the speech of sugar-lipped, sweet-spoken [fair ones].   In front of this fountain a large reservoir had been made, and around it umbrageous trees interlaced their tops.

VERSE.

> Here branches of sweet shrubs their odours gave,
> And here tall trees (their graceful) foliage wave.
> The hyacinth the cypress-foot attends,
> The violet before the lily bends.

In short those two comrades arrived from the terrible wilderness at that termination of their day's journey, and seeing it to be a pleasant spot, and an exhilarating resting-place, stopped there for their accustomed repose ; and after resting themselves, passed along in every direction on all sides of

---

[1] The Orientals have a notion that a stone gradually hardens into, and assumes the hue of a ruby. So Sa'dí, Gulistán (page 286 of the author's translation).
> 'Tis years before the pebble can put on
> The ruby's nature. Wilt thou on a stone,
> In one short moment mar what time has done ?

[2] Sálim, *i.e.*, 'safe.' Ghánim, *i.e.*, ' loaded with spoil.'

[3] Keene's version of this passage seems scarcely intelligible : ' Whose waist might bind the vault, whose girdle is the zodiac, stirrup to stirrup.' There is, as is too often the case in high-flown Persian, a confusion of metaphors. The mountain is said to be girt with the zodiac and to race with it on such equal terms as to keep stirrup to stirrup. I take *kamarash* as the nominative to *basti*, and supply, *khúd-rd.*

the reservoir and fountain and looked about them on every side. All at once they saw—on the margin of the reservoir, on the side whence the water came—a white stone, and on it written, in emerald characters—such that, save with the pen of omnipotence and on the page of wisdom characters like them could not be traced—these words, ' O traveler! who[1] hast honored this spot by alighting here, know that we have provided entertainment for our guests after the best manner, and prepared the tables of advantage in the most excellent fashion; but the condition is that thou shouldst plunge over-head into this fountain, and without dread of the danger of the eddy, or of the terrors of the vortex, get to shore as best thou canst; and at the foot of the mountain we have placed a lion carved out of stone, which thou must raise on thy shoulder, and without hesitation or delay, must convey thyself in one run to the top of the mountain, nor desist from thy undertaking from fear of the ravenous beasts that may cross thy path, nor of the sharpness of the heart-transfixing thorns which may lay hold of thy skirt; for when the course is finished the tree of desire will bear fruit.'

QUATRAIN.

No halt is reached until the journey 's done.
Through mortal agonies our will we gain.
And though the universal world attain
The splendours of success ; e'en then not one
Beam would him gild, who gives himself no pain.

After acquainting himself with the purport of this inscription, Ghánim turned to Sálim with these words, ' O brother! come on, in order that we may traverse this arena of danger with the steps of toil, and may display every endeavour that is possible to learn the particulars[2] of this talisman.'

COUPLET.

Either, successful, on high heaven to tread;
Or, with a valiant aim, lay down our head.

Sálim said, ' O friend beloved, from a mere legend, whose writer is unknown, and of the truth of which we are ignorant, to embark in a prodigious peril; and on the idea of an imaginary advantage and a supposed benefit, to precipitate oneself into a great danger is a proof of fatuity. No sensible man takes certain poison along with a questionable antidote, nor does any reasonable person willingly undergo ready-money labour for pleasure on credit.

COUPLET.

A wise man thinks a moment's pain outweighs
An age of ease and countless happy days.'[3]

---

[1] The printed and lithographed editions omit the *kih*, which, as the MSS. shew, should precede *in maznil-rd*. The former has a typographical error directly after, *musarraf* for *musharraf*.

[2] *Kamá hiyd,* ' as things are,' ' as the affair stands.' Perhaps a play upon words is intended with *kumáhah,* which signifies ' binding an amulet on the arm.'

[3] Lit. : ' A thousand years of enjoyment.'

Ghánim replied, 'O kind friend! the love of ease is the forerunner of ignominy and disgrace, and the undertaking of danger the token of fortune and honor.

STANZA.

Those easy souls, who venture nought,
Ne'er their hearts gladden with success.
Who fear the revel's after-thought,—
With vinous aches and throbbings fraught—
Ne'er drain the bowl of happiness.

The will of the high-spirited man stoops not to a corner and an allowance of food, nor, till he obtains a lofty situation, does he desist from the pursuit. One cannot gather the rose of pleasure without the thorn of toil, nor open the door of one's wish without the key of labour, and as for me, resolution will seize the reins and carry me to the top of the mountain, and I shall have no dread of the whirlpool of calamity, nor of the endurance of the load of hardship.

COUPLET.

Should toil in the search befall us, well it may be so,
When we long for Makka's temple, gladly through the wastes we go.'

Sálim rejoined, 'Granted that for the perfume of the spring of good-fortune one may put up with the disorder of the autumn of adversity, nevertheless to advance in a path which has no end, and to float on in an ocean whose shore is not visible, is far removed from the path of discretion; and it behoves every one who commences an undertaking, to examine its issue as well as he knows its beginning; and, casting his glance from the commencement of the affair to the end, to weigh the loss and gain of it, in order that he may not undergo vain toil, and not give to the wind of annihilation the ready money of his precious life.

VERSE.

Till thou hast first made sure thy stepping-place,
Step thou not onward in pursuit of aught.
And in each matter that thou dost embrace,
Be first a crevice for escapement sought.

It may be that they have written this inscription for a joke, and inscribed these characters for mockery and sport, and this fountain may be a whirlpool, such that it is impossible to reach the bank by swimming; and, if escape from it be attained, it is probable that the weight of the stone lion may be so great that one cannot lift it on one's shoulder, and were that, too, effected, it is possible that one could not reach the top of the mountain in a single run, and if all this be accomplished, it is quite unknown what the result may be. In fine, I go not along with thee in this business, and, moreover, dissuade thee from advancing farther in the matter.' Ghánim said, 'Cease these words, since I will not turn back from my intention for any man's words, nor will break the resolution I have formed, for all the doubts that the 'imps of men or genii' can suggest; and I know that thou hast not the strength to accompany me, and will not agree to bear me company. Well, then, look on at the spectacle, and aid with thy prayers and good wishes.

COUPLET.

No power hast thou to drain the cup, I ween;
Come, view at least the gay carousing scene.'

Sálim perceived that he was a man of an unchangeable impulse in his undertakings, and said, 'O brother! I see that thou wilt not be restrained by my advice, and that thou wilt not abandon this thing which ought not to be done; and I cannot bear to look on at this affair, nor can I find amusement in a thing which does not suit my feelings and is not approved by my heart.   I see my best course to be this—

HEMISTICH.

I from this whirlpool must my things remove. [1]

He then placed the baggage he had, on his beast, and bade his friend farewell, and set forward on his journey.   Ghánim, having washed his heart of his life, came to the brink of the fountain, and said,

COUPLET.

, I'll dive down into this wide-flowing sea,   Or there to sink, or bring back pearls with me.'

Then binding firmly round his waist the skirt of resolution, he stepped into the fountain.

COUPLET.

No fountain that—but there an ocean flowed
That the false semblance of a fountain shewed.

Ghánim saw that that fountain was a dangerous whirlpool, but keeping a stout heart, by swimming boldly, reached the shore of delivery; and having come to the edge of the water and recovered himself, he by strength and might, lifted the stone lion on his back, and voluntarily submitting to a thousand kinds of labour, brought himself in one run to the top of the mountain, and on that side of the mountain he saw a great city with an agreeable climate and a heart-expanding country.

COUPLET.

In goodness it with Eden might compare,   And was like Iram's garden—fresh and fair.

Ghánim having halted on the summit of the mountain, was looking towards the city, when suddenly, from that lion of stone, a terrible sound issued, such that the mountain and plain shook, and that noise having reached the city, many persons came out from the right and left, and turning their faces towards the mountain, advanced towards Ghánim.   Ghánim looked on with a wondering gaze, and was astonished at the multitudes of people, when, all

---

[1] Keene renders this line, 'That I should carry forth my own baggage from this pathless wilderness.'   I cannot think that *wartah* can refer to anything but the whirlpool, here.

of a sudden, a company of grandees and nobles came and performed the ceremonies of salutation, and offered the praises due to him, and having seated him, with the greatest respect, on a fleet courser, conveyed him towards the city, and after washing his head and body with rose-water and camphor, arrayed him in royal robes, and, with all honor and reverence, delivered into his able hands the rein of the sovereignty of that country. Upon Ghánim's inquiring into the nature of these circumstances, he was answered in the following manner, 'In the fountain that thou sawest, wise men have framed a talisman and fashioned that stone lion with every kind of care and consideration with regard to the rising of the degrees and the aspects of the fixed stars and planets, and whensoever a respected person resolves to cross the fountain, and lift up the lion and ascend to the summit of the mountain, this circumstance will undoubtedly coincide with the decease of the monarch of this city. Thereupon the lion utters a sound, and the noise thereof having reached the city, the people come forth, and having raised this man to the sovereignty, pass their lives tranquilly under the shelter of his justice until the time when his turn, too, arrives.

HEMISTICH.

When one departs another takes his place.

And when, by command of God, the sun of the existence of the ruler of this country sets in the horizon of death, simultaneously therewith, the star of the grandeur of that fortunate person exhibits its ascension from the summit of this mountain: and long ages have passed since this rule has been established after this same custom that has been mentioned; and thou art to-day the king of this city and the ruler of this age.

HEMISTICH.

The realm is thine—command whate'er thou wilt.

Ghánim perceived that the endurance of all those toils was through the requirement of fortune.

COUPLET.

When fortune comes to lend her willing aid,
She makes all issue as it should be made.

And I have introduced this example in order that thou mayest know that the draught of delight and enjoyment is not without the sting of annoyance and trouble; and to whomsoever the desire of exaltation arises, he will not be trampled down by any base person, nor be content with a low rank or a mean station; and I, until I obtain the dignity of the Lion's confidence, and am admitted into the number of those who stand nearest to his presence, will not lay my head on the pillow of repose, nor stretch out my feet on the couch of relaxation.' Kalílah said, 'Whence hast thou been able to grasp the key of this door? and how hast thou conceived the idea of entering into this affair?' Damnah said, 'At this crisis, when alarm and uncertainty has found way to the Lion, I mean to put myself in his way, and it is probable that, by imbibing the cordial of my advice, he may recover his cheerfulness, and by this means my propinquity and rank in his presence will be increased.' Kalílah said, 'How will thou obtain propinquity and access to the Lion? and even should it be so, thou hast not been used to the services of kings, and knowest not the customs and ceremonies [to be observed] in their attendance. In a short time, therefore, thou wilt lose what thou hast acquired, and thou wilt not again be able to apply any remedy for this.' Damnah rejoined, 'When a man is wise and able, the undertaking matters of importance has nothing injurious for him, and any one who has confidence in his own abilities, will acquit himself satisfactorily of every business upon which he enters. And another thing is this, if fortune manifests herself, she will shew the way to all that is required: as it has come down to us in history that the sum of the prosperity of a tradesman having been exalted, he obtained the royal dignity, and his renown and fame spread throughout the world. One of the ancient kings wrote him a letter to this effect, 'Thy craft was carpentry, and thou knowest the business of a carpenter well—from whom hast thou learned government and judgment in the transaction of affairs?' He wrote for answer, 'He who bestowed fortune upon me, has not omitted a single particle of instruction in the management of the world.'

VERSE.

When I from wisdom's opened scroll am taught,
I, thus instructed, do the thing I ought.
The man whose taper fortune deigns to light,
Gathers all fit materials to do right.

Kalílah said, 'Kings do not distinguish all men of merit by their favours, but mark by their especial and royal notice their own near connections who have obtained propinquity in their service by inheritance or desert, and since thou hast neither hereditary claims upon the lion, nor self-acquired pretentions, it is probable that thou wilt remain excluded from his notice, and it may be the cause of something that will accord with the wishes of thy foes.' Damnah said, 'Every one who has obtained a lofty rank in the service of the king has done so by degrees, and that station has not shewed itself without their toil and exertion and the influence of the King's favorable notice; and I too seek the same thing, and go about for the same end, and have reconciled to myself the endurance of many fatigues, and the tasting of many unpalatable draughts, and I know that whoever attends the court of princes must choose five things. First, he must quench the flame of anger with the water of mildness. Secondly, he must cautiously avoid the suggestions of the tempter, lust. Thirdly, he must not allow deceitful greediness, and mischief-exciting covetousness, to get the better of the guide, reason. Fourthly, he must base his actions on truth and moderation. Fifthly, the accidents and contingencies that may occur, these he must encounter with gentleness and courteous bearing : and whoever is endowed with these qualities, undoubtedly his wish will be accomplished most successfully.' Kalílah replied, 'Supposing that thou gainest access to the King; by what means art thou to obtain his approbation? and by what art will thou arrive at rank and promotion?' Damnah said, 'If close intercourse with his majesty be attained, I will adopt five qualities. First, I will perform his service in perfect sincerity. Secondly, I will shape my spirit in conformity to him. Thirdly, I will represent all his actions and words to advantage. Fourthly, when he commences an affair, which is allied to good policy, and in which I discover the weal of the realm, I will exhibit it to his eyes and feelings in the most attractive light, and bring under his observation its utilities and advantages, that his exultation at the goodness of his judgment, and the soundness of his plans, may be increased. Fifthly, if he should embark in a matter which might have a disastrous issue, and an unpleasant termination, so that injurious consequences may result to the kingdom, I will unfold to him, in eloquent language, and with great gentleness, the mischief of it, and make him aware of the evils that will issue from it, and as soon as the king perceives my merits, he will distinguish me by his approbation and favor, and will be ever inclined to my society, and eager for my advice, since no talent can be hid, and no man of talent will fail to participate in the marks of encouragement of support.

VERSE.

> Talent, like musk, can hidden ne'er remain ;
> Its scent will sudden spread the world around.
> Go, study then accomplishments to gain ·
> That from thy excellence the wide domain
> Of earth may with discourse of thee resound.

Kalílah said, 'Since it appears that thy mind is bent on this, and that thy resolution with regard to the accomplishment of this matter is firmly fixed, be well on thy guard, for attendance on kings is a thing full of danger, and an affair replete with difficulties: and the wise have said that there are three things on which none would venture save a blockhead who has never inhaled the fragrance of reason. First, the service of a king; secondly, the tasting [what may be] poison with doubt[1] [as to the result]; thirdly, the divulging one's secrets to women. And sages have compared kings to a lofty mountain; since, although mines of precious jewels are there, still there also is the abode of tigers and snakes and other noxious animals, and both the ascent is difficult, and the abiding there arduous; and they have also said that the society of a monarch resembles the sea, and the trader who chooses to travel by sea, either acquires much gain, or is overtaken in the whirlpool of destruction.'

---

[1] Keene translates *zihr ba-gumán*, 'poison upon an uncertainty.' The words may either mean that it is uncertain whether it be poison; or it being certainly poison, it is uncertain whether it could be counteracted. I incline to the latter meaning.

COUPLET.

Upon the sea, 'tis true, is boundless gain;
Wouldst thou be safe, upon the shore remain.[1]

Damnah said, 'All that thou hast said has been well-intentioned, and I know that a king is like a consuming fire; the danger of a person increases in proportion to his proximity to it.

COUPLET.

Withdraw thyself from a king's company,   As thou wouldst keep, from fire, fuel dry.

However, whoso dreads danger will not arrive at a high station.

COUPLET.

From danger greatness springs—the merchant ne'er
Gains forty for his ten[2]—whom risks deter.

And there are three things which no one without high spirit can undertake—the public service of a king; a voyage by sea; and the encountering foes; and I do not find myself to be mean-spirited, why then should I dread the king's service?'

VERSE.

Since such the powerful arm of my emprise;
In my own sleeve, all that I wish for, lies.
Wouldst thou rank high amid the noblest men?
Strive with the spirit thou possessest, then,
In short, all that thou wouldest lay hands upon,
Hast thou a lofty spirit, may be won.

Kalîlah said, 'Although I am opposed to this project, and deprecate this intention, nevertheless, since thy judgment is so decided in this matter, and thy mind so set on this scheme—may it be fortunate!

HEMISTICH.

Behold thy path! go happily in peace!

Damnah departed and made his salutation to the Lion. The Lion inquired, 'What person is this?' They replied, 'The son of such an one, who for a long time was an attendant at the royal court.' The Lion exclaimed, 'Aye! I recollect him.' He then called him before him and said, 'Where dost thou live?' Damnah answered, 'After the custom of my father, I have now become an attendant in the heaven-resembling court, and have made it the shrine of my wants, and the K'abah[3] of my wishes, and am in waiting that if an affair of importance should occur, and the august order should be issued,

---

[1] In the Gulistán, ch. i., story xvi., p. 63 of my translation, these lines occur.

[2] *Ṣad yak* is one per cent. and *dah chihal* of course 400 per cent, or forty for ten.

[3] The K'abah is the square temple at Makkah, built, as the Muhammadans pretend, by Abraham and his son Ishmael, on the site of a still more ancient temple, erected by Seth, and destroyed at the Deluge. It is termed *bait-u 'lláh*, 'the House of God,' and *al-ḥaram*, 'the sacred,' as that at Medinah is styled *musjid-u'n-nabí*, 'the mosque of the Prophet.' The two together were termed *ḥaramain*, 'the two sacred edifices,' and they are both the objects of pilgrimage, a mere sight of the K'abah being reckoned as meritorious as a year's devotion in any other temple.

I may satisfactorily accomplish it by my sagacity, and may engage in it with clear discernment. And as in the management of various matters of weight, there is occasion for the Pillars of the state, and the ministers of his Majesty, so it is probable that at the courts of princes an event may occur, which may be brought to a close by the aid of those of inferior degree.

HEMISTICH.

The fly too, like the peacock, here may aid.

In a matter which may be effected by the weak needle, the proud[1] javelin may prove inefficacious, and an affair which a poor penknife may accomplish, in that, the highly-tempered scymitar may prove at a loss. And no servant, though he may be of little estimation and mean position, is devoid of use for removing detriment and eliciting good, since even the dry stick which lies despised in the road, may possibly, some day, become serviceable; and though it be good for nothing else, yet it may chance that they may make a tooth-pick of it, or by means of it, may cleanse the ear of wax.'

COUPLET.

If from me thou a nose-gay canst not make,
As fuel for the pot thou may'st me take.

When the Lion heard the speech of Damnah, he was astonished at his eloquence and fluency of speech, and turning to his courtiers, said, 'Though a wise man should be of small reputation, yet his understanding and wisdom will, involuntarily, make his talents known to the nation, like the flame of fire, which, though he that kindles it may wish should burn downwards, will, to a certainty, raise its head aloft.

COUPLET.

If one sincerely loves, the sign   Of true love on his face will shine.'

Damnah was pleased at these words, and perceived that his fascinations had made an impression on the Lion, and that his artifice was completely successful. He loosed the tongue of advice, and said, 'It is incumbent on all the royal attendants and household, according to their understanding and knowledge, to ponder well every matter which may befall the king, and to represent whatever may occur to the mind of each, nor ever abandon the path of good advice, in order that the sovereign may thoroughly know his followers and dependants, and having become acquainted with the extent of the judgment and prudence and sincerity and discretion of each, may both derive advantage from their respective services, and may also reward each in proportion to his deserts; for so long as the grain lies hidden by the curtain of the earth, no one takes trouble in cultivating it, and when it draws back the veil of mould from its face, and raises its head in its gay robe of green, from the collar of the ground, and is perceived to be a fruit-bearing tree and a

---

[1] *Sar-afráz*, lit., 'head-exalting.'

useful plant; then assuredly [men] will foster it and profit by its fruits: and in all matters, the source [of advancement] is the encouragement of kings. Whomsoever, among men of merit, they distinguish by their favorable notice, from him they will derive benefit in proportion to the encouragement they bestow.

COUPLET.

I'm like the thorn, like earth am I—tulip and rose shall grow
From me, if thou, my cloud and sun, will only favor shew.'

The Lion asked, 'How must men of understanding be encouraged? and by what means can one reap fruit from them?' Damnah replied, 'The main point in this matter is that the king should look to worth, not birth; and if a party of incapables should allege the services of their ancestors and progenitors, that he should pay no regard to them, for a man should make good his pedigree by his abilities, not by his father.

VERSE.

Let thy own worth elate thee—do not base
Pretensions on thy long-descended race;
Do not, O shallow one! by dead men live,
But, by thine own renown, the dead revive:
The empty vaunt of buried sires disown;
O youth! rejoice not, dog-like, in a bone.

Though a rat be a partner in the same abode with men, yet by reason of the annoyance and injury which results from it, they think it right to exert themselves for its destruction; while the hawk, which is wild and strange—since advantage may be anticipated from it—they allure with every sort of kindness, and bring him up on the wrist of favor, indulgently and proudly.[1] Wherefore it behoves a king not to distinguish between friends and strangers, but to seek out men of ability and learning, and not to suffer precedence to be given to men who are remiss in business and wanting in talent, over persons of eminence and merit; since to bestow the office of wise men on fools, is like fastening ornaments for the head on the feet, and placing that which ought to deck the feet on the head; and wherever men of talent are depressed and ignorant, and fatuous persons get possession of the reins of power, the utmost confusion will find its way into the affairs of that country, and the disgrace of that circumstance will attach to the fortune of the king and his subjects.

COUPLET.

Tell the Phœnix its bright shadow o'er that country ne'er to throw
Where the raven has the ascendant, and the parrot sinks below.'

---

[1] The MSS. I have consulted, omit the sentence after *mi-árand*, which is found in the printed and lithographed editions. Keene translates *ba-ihtizáz* 'to exercise.' It may bear that sense, or mean, 'with exultation.' The word is no doubt chosen on account of its ambiguity, which is such a source of delight to the Persian author, and of despair to the translator.

When Damnah had finished speaking, the Lion showed him the utmost favor, and admitted him into the number of his particular favorites, and having taken a liking to his conversation, based his most important actions upon his counsel and advice. Damnah, too, taking the path of good sense, and intelligence and understanding and sagacity, became, in a short time, the confidante of the royal cabinet, and the man relied upon and referred to for advice and suggestions of improvement in the affairs of state. One day, having found a fortunate occasion and a convenient time, he asked for a private audience, and said, 'A long time has now passed during which the king has remained stationary in one place, and has relinquished the gratification of exercise and the pleasures of the chace. I wish to know the cause of this and to speak on this matter to the best of my ability.' The Lion wished to conceal from him the alarm he felt, when, meantime, Shanzabah bellowed aloud, and his voice agitated the Lion so much, that the reins of self-possession passed from his grasp. He was compelled to disclose his secret to Damnah, and said, 'The cause of my fear is this sound that thou hearest, and I know not whose voice it is, but I suspect that his strength and build is in proportion to his voice. If his form be such,[1] it is no good for me to remain in this place.' Damnah replied, 'Has the king any other thing upon his mind besides this voice?'—'No!' said the Lion. 'Then,' rejoined Damnah, 'it is not right, for such a trifle, to expatriate yourself and to depart from your own familiar residence. What dependence is there [to be placed] in a voice? and what weight [ought to be attached] to a cry that any one should remove for that? and it beseems a king to be firmly planted like a rock, so as not to be shaken by every wind nor to be dislodged by every outcry.

HEMISTICH.

That no tempest may dislodge thee, plant thy foot firm, like a rock![2]

And the ancients have said that regard should not be paid to every loud noise and powerful body; for not every external form furnishes sure information of the internal meaning, nor is every outward semblance a token of what lies within. A reed, though it be thick, is broken with a slender stick, and a heron, though of large stature, is overcome by the talons of a hawk of comparatively slim build; and whoever makes account of largeness of bulk, meets with what that Fox met with. The Lion asked; 'How was that?'

STORY VII.

Damnah said, 'They have related that a Fox was prowling over a moor, and was roaming in every direction in hopes of scenting food. Presently he came

---

[1] Keene translates *agar chunin șirati bdshad* by 'if such should be the fact,' but I think this would be rather *agar chunin bdshad*.
[2] Lit.: 'Draw thy feet under thy skirt.'

to the foot of a tree, at the side of which they had suspended a drum, and whenever a gust of wind came, a branch of the tree was put in motion, and struck the surface of the drum, and a terrible noise arose from it. The Fox, seeing a domestic fowl under the tree who was pecking the ground with her beak, and searching for food, planted himself in ambush, and wished to make her his prey, when all of a sudden the sound of the drum reached his ear. He looked and saw a very fat form, and a prodigious sound from it reached his hearing. The appetite of the Fox was excited, and he thought to himself 'Assuredly its flesh and skin will be proportioned to its voice.' He issued from his-lurking place, and turned towards the tree. The fowl, being put on its guard by that circumstance, fled, and the fox, by a hundred exertions ascended the tree. Much did he labour till he had torn the drum, and then he found nought save a skin and a piece of wood. The fire of regret descended into his heart, and the water of contrition began to run from his eyes, and he said, 'Alas! that by reason of this huge bulk which is all wind, that lawful prey has escaped from my hand, and from this empty form no advantage has resulted to me.'

VERSE.

Loudly ever sounds the tabor,
But in vain—within is nought:
Art thou wise, for substance labor,
Semblance will avail thee nought.[1]

And I have adduced this example in order that the King may not relinquish the pleasures of the chase, and his personal exercise, for a frightful noise and a huge form. If he will carefully observe, nothing will result from that voice and figure, and if the King will issue his command, I will approach him, and will acquaint the King with the state of the case, and the real truth of the matter. The Lion was pleased with the words of Damnah, and the latter, in accordance with the orders of the Lion, set off in the direction of that sound. As soon however as he got out of sight of the Lion, the latter began to reflect, and regretted that he had despatched Damnah, and said to himself, 'I have committed a great fault, and an ill-weighed action has proceeded from me: and the ancients, have said, that it behoves a King in the disclosure of his secrets, to have no reliance on ten classes of persons, and not to reveal to them the secret nature of any of his private affairs which he is extremely anxious to conceal. The first is, whoever has experienced oppression and vexation at his court, and for a long time endured trouble and distress without fault or crime on his part. The second is, he whose property and honor have gone to the winds in attendance on the King, and whose means have been straitened. The third is, he who has been degraded from his office, and has no hope of recovering it again. The fourth is a

---

[1] Lit. : ' Be not elated by the form, for in that is nothing.'

H 2

wicked, mischievous person, who is on the look out for mischief, and is disinclined to peace and repose. The fifth is the criminal, whose comrades have tasted the sweets of pardon, while he has experienced the bitterness of punishment. The sixth is the offender, whose fellows have been reproved, while a greater and extreme degree of severity has been shewn towards him. The seventh, is he who, while doing acceptable services, remains disappointed; while others, without the antecedents of service, receive greater encouragement than he. The eighth, is he whose station an enemy has sought, and has got the lead of him, and has reached that rank, and the prince has taken part with him. The ninth, he who conceives his own advantage to be associated with the injury of the king. The tenth is he who has met with no favor at the King's court, and who can make himself acceptable to the king's enemy. Kings ought not to entrust their secrets to these ten classes, and the first principle is this, that until they have repeatedly made trial of the religious principles, and good faith, and kindness, and worth of a man, they should not put him in possession of their secrets.

COUPLET.

> Not to each one thy secrets tell—for earth's wide space upon,
> Much we have wandered, yet have found in whom to trust not one.

Therefore in accordance with these promises, before making trial of Damnah, it was improper to be precipitate, and to send him to an enemy was far from a prudent and far-sighted line of conduct, and this Damnah appears to be a shrewd person, and he remained for a long time at my court distressed and disappointed. If, which God forbid![1] the thorn of vexation is rankling in his heart, he may, on this occasion, contrive perfidy, and stir up mischief; or it may be that he may find the enemy superior to me in strength and majesty; and, becoming eager to enter his service may acquaint him with what he knows of my secrets; and undoubtedly the remedy of that would exceed the measure of my counsels. Why did I not apply the purport of the saying, ' *Caution is suspicion,*' to my conduct? and why have the directions of the wise couplet

COUPLET.

> ' Intend not ill, but evil still suspect,   And from deceit and harm thyself protect '

been transgressed by me? If calamity arise from this embassy, I am deserving of a hundred times as much.' In this anxious meditation, the Lion, through excessive agitation, continued getting up and anon reseating himself, and kept the eyes of expectation fixed on the road, when all at once, Damnah appeared. The Lion was somewhat tranquillized, and remained quiet in the same spot, while Damnah, after performing the customary obeisance, said,

---

[1] Lit. : 'By flying for refuge to God.'

VERSE.
'Long as the spheres revolving circle, may our king continue still!
And may the sun of his high fortune gild the subjects of his will!

O world-possessing prince! he whose voice reached the august ear is an Ox, engaged in grazing in the environs of this forest, and, save feeding and sleeping, other business he has none, and his ambition does not travel beyond his throat and his belly.' The Lion asked, 'What is the extent of his might?' Damnah replied, 'I observed no pomp or grandeur about him, that I could thence infer his power; and I did not discover, in my own mind, any awe in him, whence I should suppose any extraordinary respect due to him.' The Lion said, 'Weakness is not therefore to be imputed to him, nor is one to be thereby deceived, for the strong wind, though it does not overthrow the weak herbage, nevertheless, tears up the strong trees by the root; and so long as the great and mighty do not encounter a foeman worthy of them, no display of their might and prowess is manifested.

COUPLET.
When in pursuit of puny finches will the noble goshawk go?
'Gainst the gnat the royal falcons ne'er their claws of terror show.'

Damnah said, 'The king ought not to think so gravely of him, nor make so much account of the proceedings, for I have acuteness enough to discern the extent of his power,[1] and I have informed myself of the exact state of his circumstances; and if the lofty judgment [of your majesty] require it, and the august command honors me by being issued, I will bring him, so that, having placed the hand of willingness on the line of obedience, he may cast the saddle-cloth of servitude on the shoulder of attachment.' The Lion was pleased with these words, and signed to bring him. Damnah went to Shanzabah, and, with a stout heart, without hesitation or backwardness, entered into discourse with him.

HEMISTICH.
And first he addressed him with, 'Whence art thou?

And how didst thou come here? and what may be the cause of thy coming to this place? and of thy commencing to abide here?' Shanzabah began to recount with truth the state of the matter, and Damnah, having learned his story, said, 'A Lion who is the king of the wild beasts and the ruler of these regions, gave me orders and sent me to bring thee to him, and instructed me that, shouldest thou use despatch, he will forgive the crime which has taken place in his service up to this point, but if thou shouldest delay, I am to return with haste and report the circumstances.' Shanzabah when he heard the name of the Lion and wild beasts, feared, and said, 'If

---

[1] Keene translates this, 'For I, with great penetration, have found out his business.' I incline to make *nihdyat* a substantive, thus *nihdyat-i kár*, 'the extent of his business.' The MSS. omit the *ba-firásat nihdyat*, and rightly as it appears to me.

thou wilt make me stout-hearted and secure me from his chastisement, I will come with thee, and by means of thy companionship obtain the honor of his service.' Damnah swore an oath to him, and gave him a promise and compact so as to tranquillize his mind, and both set off together to the Lion. Damnah went before and acquainted the Lion with his coming; and a short time after, the Ox arrived and performed the homage due. The Lion made warm inquiries [after his welfare], and said, 'When didst thou arrive in this neighbourhood? and what may be the cause of thy coming?' The Ox made a full recital of his story. The Lion then said, 'Abide here still that thou mayest reap a full portion of kindness and honor and compassion and bounty from us; for we have opened the gates of favor on the faces of the votaries[1] of our districts, and have spread the overflowing table of encouragement for the attendants of our court.

VERSE.

> Wide through this realm thy wandering steps may stray,
>   Yet none thou wilt complaining see.
> In all that we attempt, we first display
>   Care for our folks' prosperity.

The Ox, having paid the dues of blessing and praise, bound the girdle of obedience on his loins with willingness and zeal: and the Lion, too, having brought him nearer to his person, and shewed excessive and lavish honors and respect to him,[2] and, under cover thereof, employed himself in examining his character and investigating his conduct, and learned the measure of his judgment and understanding and the extent of his discernment and experience. He found him to be a person distinguished by perfect sagacity and endowed with intellect and penetration: the more he tested his qualities, the more his reliance on the abundance of his wisdom increased.

VERSE.

> Kindly he found him, and of judgment clear,
>   Weighing his words—one who could estimate
> The worth of men—whom travel far and near
>   In wisdom had instructed—made sedate
> By much experience—who, with practised ease,
>   In social converse knew the art to please.[3]

The Lion, after reflection and deliberation and anxious thought and prayer for guidance, made the Ox the confidante of his secrets; and every hour his place in the royal favor and his good fortune rose higher; and his

---

[1] *Mujáwirán* has two senses, 'neighbours,' and ' the attendants at a shrine.' Either sense will suit this passage. I have chosen the latter.

[2] Keene translates *mubálaghah wa iṭnáb* 'great force and length of speech.' There is not however here, I imagine, any reference to words but to deeds.

[3] I have translated these lines somewhat freely and diffusely.

elevation in the exercise of authority and in command became more exalted, until he outstripped all the pillars of the state and the ministers of the king. When Damnah perceived that the Lion carried his respect for the Ox to the last verge of excess, and that, having pushed his profuseness in rewarding and honoring him beyond the limits of moderation, he neither carried into effect his (Damnah's) advice, nor applied to him for counsel in any matter— the hand of envy drew the collyrium of aversion over the eyes of his heart, and the fire of anger cast the torch of jealousy into the cell of his brain.

COUPLET.

Wherever envy doth its torch illume,
The envious there themselves 't will first consume.

Sleep and rest departed from him, and peace and repose removed their gear from the area of his breast. He went with his complaint to Kalílah, and said, ' O brother ! behold the weakness of my judgment and the slackness of my prudence, that I have expended all my energies in freeing the Lion from anxiety,[1] and have introduced the Ox into his service, so that having obtained close access [to the king] and high place with him, he has got precedence over all the courtiers, while I have fallen from my station and position.'   Kalílah replied,

HEMISTICH.

' Thou didst it thine ownself, my life ! for self-done acts, what cure is there ?

This axe thou hast thyself struck on thine own foot, and this dust of mischief thou hast thyself stirred up in thine own path, and the same thing has befallen thee which befell the Devotee.   Damnah inquired, ' How was that ? '

STORY VIII.

Kalílah said, ' They have related that a king bestowed splendid apparel and a costly robe on a Devotee.   A thief having got intelligence of the circumstance, coveted it, and going to the Devotee pretended a wish to become his disciple, and voluntarily entered his service, and displayed diligence in learning the manners of that religious persuasion, until in this way he was admitted into the confidence [of the Devotee], and one night, having found an opportunity, he carried away the dress and made off.   The next day the recluse did not see the dress, and finding that that new disciple was missing, he knew that he had purloined it.   He started in pursuit of him, in the direction of the city, and on the road observed two he-goats[2] who were fighting with one another and wounding each other's heads; and during the time that these two fierce[2] adversaries, like savage lions, were engaged

---

[1] Keene translates this sentence. 'I had built all my projects on the carelessness of the Lion,' where he seems to me to have missed the sense, and to have assigned a wrong meaning to *fardghat*, which I believe never means 'carelessness,' but 'freedom from care,' *i.e.*, 'leisure.'

[2] Keene translates *nakhchír* ' wild beasts,' into which rendering he was led, I doubt not,

in battle with one another and the blood was dripping from their limbs and members, a fox had come up and was devouring their blood. All at once in the midst of their encounter, the fox happened to get between them, and on each side their heads came with violence against his ribs, and he was overtaken with the noose of death. The recluse, having gained from these circumstances another piece of experience, passed on, and at night, when he reached the city, the gate was closed. He walked about in all directions and was seeking for a place to halt in. It happened that a woman was looking from the terrace of her house into the street, and understood by the perplexity of the devotee, that he was a stranger. She invited him to her house, and the holy man, accepting her invitation, untied his sandals in her lodgings, and occupied himself in a corner of the hut with his devotions. Now that woman was notorious for vice and profligacy, and kept several damsels ready for purposes of debauchery, and one of them—the winning glance of whose beauty might have taught blandishment to the brides of Paradise, and at the glow of whose cheeks, the sun, which warms the world, was consumed with the fire of jealousy; whose languishing eye, with the arrow of its glance, pierced the target of the bosom, and whose life-giving lips, with the sugar of her mouth, bestowed sweetness on the soul like a package of sugar,

DISTICHS.

She, moon-like, moves, or like the cypress tall.
Two twisting curls in musky mazes fall
Down her white neck; her chin so silvery fair
Supports a chain of dimples fastened there.[1]

—had become attached to a youth—of beautiful countenance and musky ringlets, witty, and of graceful stature like the cypress, whose face resembled the moon, sweet-voiced and slender-waisted so that the proud beauties of Cathay[2]—from the curl of his locks—were, like the hyacinth, writhing with envy,[3] and the

---

by the epithet *tíz-chang* 'sharp-clawed,' which follows *nakhchír* in the printed and lithographed editions, and also in some MSS. It is quite clear, however, from the tenor of the story, that the *nakhchír* were butting animals. Moreover, in the Pancha-Tantra, (where the same story occurs, p. 35, l. 1. Kosegarten's edition) the word *huduh* 'ram' is used. In the corresponding place (in the Mitra-lábha) of the Hitopadesha, this story is omitted, I find, however, in one MS. the following reading, *kih án dú khasm-i tíz chang chun shírán-i darindah-i tíz chang*, where it must be evident to every one that the first *tíz chang* should be *tíz jang*, the three dots having, from the carelessness of the transcriber, been omitted beneath the *ch* in *chún*, and improperly introduced under the *j* of the preceding word, thus making *chang* of the word *jang*. I have no hesitation therefore in recommending the above reading with the said trifling correction, and translating it as I have done.

[1] I have been obliged to render freely this most unmanageable line. Is it not enough that the Persians should have the bad taste to admire a fat double chin in the fair sex, without comparing it to a bull with a pendulous necklace of waving flesh, and consummating their bad taste by giving this latter the hideous cacophonic name of *ghabghab*! I desire to be literal, but I cannot perpetuate such offences against the Nine as this.

[2] *Khatá*, 'Northern China.' The 'Cathay' of Milton, See note i. page 56.

[3] Keene translates (by a typographical error no doubt) *dar pich o táb* 'full of *writing* and disorder.' Literally it is, 'in twists and turns.'

honey-lipped fair ones of Samarkand,[1] from the desire of his mischief-exciting
sweetness, were panged like the hearts of lovers :

COUPLET.

His face! Ah! what a face ! a sun-like face was it.
His locks! What locks ! each curl with troublous transports knit.

—and ever together, like sun and moon, they lived conjoined in one mansion,
and like Venus and Mercury were united in one sign of the zodiac, and this
youth from the jealousy of love would positively never allow that his other
rivals should taste a draught from the cup of union with that damsel, or that
those athirst in the desert of pursuit, should, after a thousand toils, arrive at
that limpid fountain.

COUPLET.

My jealousy of thee is such that, could it granted be,
I'd choose that none beside should, e'en in fancy, think of thee.

The profligate woman being embarrassed by the behaviour of the damsel, and
impatient at the loss of income, could not put up with a girl who had cast
aside the veil of decorum, and had given up her whole soul to the affection
for her lover.[2] She was driven to aim at the destruction of that youth. On
the night that the recluse came to her house she had prepared a plan and
not neglected an opportunity for the deed, and, having measured out copious[3]
draughts of wine to the lover and beloved one, as soon as the people of the
house had gone to rest, she pounded a little deadly poison, and having placed
it in a pipe and brought it before the fair youth, took one end of the tube in
her mouth, and placed the other end in his nostrils, and was about to give a
puff and convey the influence of the poison to the brain of the youth, when
suddenly he sneezed, and from the force of the vapour which issued from his
brain all the poison entered the throat and neck of that woman, and she fell
lifeless on the spot.

HEMISTICH.

Thyself in compassing thy thought shalt fall.

When the recluse beheld that circumstance, and had with a hundred
anxieties passed through that night—which in length equalled the day of
resurrection—until the time when the devotee of the dawn, having obtained
release from the cell of the darkness of night, spread the prayer-carpet of

---

[1] The capital of Sogdiana, in 89 deg. 30 min. East long., 40 deg. North lat., said to have
founded by Kishasp, fifth king of the Kaianides, the second dynasty of Persia. It was pillaged
by Changíz Khán, but re-established by Timúr Lang, who made it the capital of his dominions.
Afterwards the Usbaks got possession of it, and still retain it.   The women are said to be
very beautiful.

[2] Keene translates, 'and thus exposed the very life of the affection of lovers.' With
regard to the expression 'cast aside the veil of decorum,' it only means that the girl had
abandoned herself to the passion for her lover.   Certainly, *hayd* seems a term ill applied to
such a person.

[3] Lit.: ' heavy.'

worship before the altar of the horizon, and the purport of this text of sublime meaning '*And shall lead them out of darkness into light*'[1] was manifest unto men ;

COUPLET.

The mirror-vaulted heavens brightness gain,
And China's glass was cleansed from rust and stain.[2]

The recluse having extricated himself from the dark abode of debauchery and crime of that band, went in search of another lodging. A shoemaker, who reckoned himself among his disciples, took the holy man to his house, by way of obtaining a blessing [for that good act] and enjoined his family to wait upon him, and he himself went to an entertainment given by some of his friends. Now his lady had a friend of an agreeable temper, of handsome face, and curling locks,

COUPLET.

Facetious and gallant, whose merry eyes in mischief roll,
Handsome—so that such as he bring mischief to the soul.

The messenger between them was the wife of a barber, who, by her witchery, could blend together fire and water, and by her oily tongue could make the hard stone melt like wax.

VERSE.

A mischief-maker, who some fraudful verse reciting,
Could the mosquito with the Símurgh wed ;
With crystal rosary, men's trust in her inviting,
The string was made of unbelievers' thread.[3]
Her lip in prayer—her prayer all spells and guile ;
In simple guise without—within all wile.

The shoemaker's wife, when she found the house empty, sent some one to the go-between saying, ' Inform my beloved that to-night there is honey without the buzzing of the bee, and intercourse without the hue-and-cry of the superintendent of police and the patrol.'

HEMISTICH.

Arise! and come hither, as I know and thou.

Her lover having come to the house by night, was expecting '*the opening of the door*,' when, all of a sudden, the shoemaker, like a sudden calamity, arrived and saw this man at the door of his house. Now the fact was, that before this he had had a little suspicion, and some doubt had arisen:—when

---

[1] Ḳur'án, ch. v. 18 ; Sale, p. 78, l. 18: 'Now is light, and a perspicuous book of revelations come unto you from God. Thereby will God direct him who shall follow His good pleasure, into the paths of peace; and shall lead them out of darkness into light by His will, and shall direct them in the right way.'

[2] I am unable to understand this line, and would greatly prefer the reading of one of the MSS., *raft bírún za dínah zang rang ; zang rang* meaning ' the hue of night,' as *zang* frequently means ' darkness.'

[3] *Zunnár*, a cord worn round the middle by eastern Christians and Jews, also the Brahmanical thread, which is the badge of the three twice-born classes in India. However much I may have failed to catch the spirit of these verses, they are worthy of admiration in the original. The description is Spenserian.

he found him in his house the side of conviction prevailed. He entered the house, and, in most violent wrath, began to beat his wife, and after he had chastised her thoroughly, he bound her fast to a post, and then placed his own head on the couch of repose. The recluse was thinking thus, 'To beat this woman without any apparent reason and clear offence, was far from the course of kind and manly feeling. I ought to have interceded for her, and not to have acquiesced in this folly;' when suddenly the barber's wife came in and said, 'O sister! why dost thou keep this young man so long waiting? quickly come forth and look upon the opportunity for love as a blessing.'

COUPLET.

Does the loved one, then, think of asking for the lover sick of pain?
Say, in peace come! for the breathings of existence yet remain.

The shoemaker's wife, with a melancholy voice, called to her and said,

VERSE.

How canst thou, O tranquil-hearted! the sad heart's affliction know?
The pangs of lovers, grief-devouring, all their sufferings and woe?
Spread thy pinions, dove! and soaring, o'er the lofty cypress go:
How canst thou the heart's affliction of the prisoned warblers know?

O kind friend! listen[1] to my piteous complaint, and learn my wretched condition. This cruel and merciless husband had seen, perhaps, my lover at the door, for he entered this house like a madman, and after he had beaten me much, tied me, with the utmost violence, to this pillar. If thou hast any compassionate feeling towards me, and art disposed[2] to pity my lover, release me with all despatch, and give me leave[3] to bind thee to this pillar in place of myself, and I, having quickly made my apology to my friend, will return and release thee, and by this act thou wilt both place me under an obligation to thee, and wilt also oblige my friend.' The barber's wife, from exceeding kindness, having consented to the other's release and the binding of herself, sent her out. The recluse, by hearing this dialogue, was put in possession of the clue to the quarrel of the husband and wife; and meanwhile the shoemaker awoke and called to his wife. The barber's wife, in terror lest he should[4] recognise her voice and so become aware of what was going on, had not courage to answer. However much the shoemaker shouted, not a breath issued from the barber's wife. The fire of his wrath blazed up, and he seized a cobbler's knife, and came before the pillar, and cutting off the nose of the barber's wife, placed it in her hand, saying,

---

[1] I doubt the reading *mi shanau*, and *mi kun* which is that of the lithographed and printed editions, and I am glad that the MSS., by omitting *mi* confirm my belief that this particle is not used with the imperative.

[2] Lit., 'Art in the place of pity,' a somewhat unusual expression, but which in fact nearly corresponds to the phrase I have adopted to translate it.

[3] Observe a rather rare use of the word *dastúrí*, which more generally means 'perquisite.'

[4] In the original 'that he should not recognise,' in the same manner as the Latin *vereor ne*.

'Lo! a present that thou mayest send to thy lover.' The barber's wife, from
fear, uttered not a sigh, but mentally ejaculated,

HEMISTICH.

'One takes the pleasure and another bears the pain.'

When the shoemaker's wife returned and beheld her adopted sister with her
nose cut off, she was excessively grieved, and, repeatedly begging her pardon,
released her and fastened herself to the pillar, and the barber's wife set off
homeward, nose in hand.

HEMISTICH.

Anon she laughed, bewildered—and anon she wailed.

The recluse beheld and heard all these proceedings, and surprise was added
to surprise at these strange incidents which manifested themselves from the
curtain of the unknown future. However the shoemaker's wife kept quiet
for a little, and then spreading the hand of cunning and deceit in prayer, she
said, 'O Lord and King! Thou knowest that my husband has inflicted cruel
injustice upon me, and has bound on my neck, by false and slanderous accusation, a crime which I have not committed. Of thine own goodness shew
mercy to me and give back to me my nose—the ornament of the page of
beauty!' The husband was awake while the wife was thus praying, and
heard that hypocritical complaint and perfidious prayer of hers. He shouted
out, 'O wicked and corrupt woman! what prayer is this that thou dost
make? and what supplication is this that thou employest? The prayer of
the unchaste is not regarded in this court, and the requirement of the vicious
obtains not the quality of currency on this road.

COUPLET.

Hopest thou the unseen world will succour thee?
Then pure thy tongue and pure thy heart must be.'

All at once the wife cried out, 'O tyrant! tormentor! get up that thou mayest
behold the power and infinite goodness of God, that, as my garment was pure
from the stain of this false charge, God Most High has restored to me my
nose that was mutilated, and has saved me from reproach and disgrace
amongst men.' The simple-minded man arose, and having lighted a lamp,
came up to her, and beheld his wife safe, and her nose in its right place, and
he nowhere perceived any trace of the wound or injury. Instantly he confessed his fault, and betook himself to entreaties for forgiveness, and with
the utmost tenderness asking pardon for his offence,[1] he removed the bonds
from her hands and feet, and made a vow not to proceed to similar lengths
before the display of positive proof, and the manifestation of a good cause,
nor at the suggestion of every mischievous tale-bearer to torment his chaste

---

[1] One MS. inserts before *bihili* the word *'aibash*. The word *bihili* is a strange one,
if of Persian origin, as the Dictionaries would shew, with the *hd-i hutti*. Can it be an Arabic
word compounded of *bah* and *hall* 'loosing?'

wife and virtuous spouse; and that for the rest of his life he would be guided by this woman, veiled in purity of conduct, whose prayers were assuredly free from any interposing curtain.

On the other side, the barber's wife carrying her severed nose in her hand came home, and was overcome with bewilderment as to what artifice she should think of, and in what manner she could disclose what had happened to her husband, and what excuse she should make to her friends and neighbours on the subject, and how reply to the questions of her kinsfolk and acquaintances? In this interval the barber awoke from sleep, and called to his wife, saying, 'Give me my tools,[1] for I am going to such a gentleman's house.' His wife was very long in answering, and dawdled in giving the instruments too, and at last put the razor alone into the barber's hand, The latter in a passion flung the razor in the darkness of the night towards his wife, and began to utter abusive words. His wife threw herself down, and screamed out, 'My nose! my nose!' The barber was amazed, and their friends and neighbours, coming in, saw the woman with her dress stained with blood, and her nose cut off. Hereupon they began to loose the tongue of reproval against the barber, and that unfortunate fellow remained astonished, neither having the face to confess, nor the tongue to deny it. However, when the world-illuminating dawn removed the curtain of darkness, and the universe-displaying mirror of the sun began to shine like the goblet of Jamshíd,[2]

COUPLET.

The leader of the Eastern host upreared his flag on high,
The Western king sank down amid a sea of sanguine dye:

the relations of the wife assembled and carried the barber before the Ḳází. By chance the recluse too, having come forth from the house of the shoemaker, by reason of a bond of friendship which existed between him and the Ḳází, was present at the tribunal. After they had gone through the customary interrogatories, and the friends of the barber's wife had stated their case the Ḳází demanded, 'Master barber! without any apparent crime, and without legal cause, why didst thou think fit to mutilate this woman?' The barber, being bewildered, was unable to state any reason, and the Ḳází, according to

---

[1] The MSS. and the printed and lithographed editions agree in writing this word *dast-afráz,* as before—at p. 88, l. 6, of the printed edition we find *páí afráz* for a 'shoe' or 'sandal.' The Burhán-i Ḳát'i, however, ignores both words. as also *afráz* itself, in this sense; and I am inclined to think that the reading in both cases should be *afzár,* which is another form of *awzár,* and signifies 'a shoe,' and also 'tools.'

[2] Jamshíd (the word *shíd* signifies 'sun') was the first king of the Píshdádayan, or first dynasty of Persia. He reigned over seven kingdoms of Asia till, affecting divine honours, he was dethroned by Zahhák general of the forces of the Arabian monarch, Shadád, son of Ad, and driven into exile. His son Farídún slew Zahhák, and recovered the throne. Jamshíd founded Istakhr, Hamadán, and Tús. He possessed a divining cup which mirrored to him future events, and to which allusion is here made.

the clear mandate, ' *Wounds shall be punished by retaliation,*'[1] gave commandment that retaliation should be exacted, and that he should be tortured.
Then the recluse rose up and said, 'O Ḳáẓí! in this matter there is need of
deliberation, and the eye of sagacity must be opened, because the Thief did
not carry off my dress, and the Goats did not kill the Fox, nor did the poison
destroy the profligate woman, nor did the Shoemaker cut off the nose of
the Barber's Wife, but we have all drawn upon ourselves these calamities.'
The Ḳáẓí let the barber go, and turning to the recluse, said, 'Please to
favor us with an interpretation of this compendium, and an explanation of
the import of this!' The recluse recited from beginning to end what he had
heard and seen, and said, ' If I had not had a desire to take a pupil, and had
not been fascinated by the pleasant talk of the thief, that deceitful impostor
could not have found an opportunity, and would not have carried off my
dress; and if the Fox had not displayed excessive greediness and gluttony,
and had abstained from blood-thirstiness, the fatal concussion of the he-goats
would not have reached him; and if the profligate woman had not schemed
the destruction of the young man, she would not have given to the winds her
dear life; and if the Barber's Wife had not rendered assistance in that unlawful
act, she would not have been mutilated nor disgraced. Whoever does evil
must not look for good, and he who requires sugar-cane must not sow
colocynth.

COUPLET.

Thus spake the sage—by long experience tried—
' Do not thou ill, lest ill should thee betide.'

And I have adduced this story that thou mayst know that thou hast shewn
this troublous way to thyself, and hast opened upon thyself this gate of
pain and difficulty.'

HEMISTICH.

Of whom complain then, since our woe 's self-made!

Damnah said, ' Thou speakest truly, and I have done this deed, yet, nevertheless, what plan dost thou advise for my escape, and of what contrivance dost
thou think for untying this knot?' Kalílah said, 'From the commencement
I disagreed with thee as to this business, and did not coincide with thee in
consenting to undertake this matter, and now too I find myself [justified in
keeping] aloof in this affair, and see no reason for meddling with it. But
perhaps thou wilt thyself excogitate somewhat for thyself, for they have said:

HEMISTICH.

'Each one best knows what is for his own good.'

Damnah said, 'I have been thinking that I will set about this business

---

[1] Ḳur'án, Fl. v. 49, Mar. v. 53; Sale, p. 82, l, 9: 'We have therein commanded them
that they should give life for life and eye for eye, and nose for nose, and ear for ear, and tooth
for tooth; and that wounds also shall be punished by retaliation; but whoever should remit it
as alms, it should be accepted as an atonement for him.' Compare Exodus, xxi. 23.

with the most delicate finesse, and will exert myself in every possible way, until I overthrow the Ox from this position, nay, until I drive him out of this country, for I cannot admit of procrastination and neglect in the duty of self-preservation, and should I choose to be remiss, I should not be excusable in the opinion of men of prudence and spirit. Nor do I seek any new dignity, nor claim more than belongs to my office : and the wise have said, ' Men of sense are justified in laboring for five things :—First, in pursuit of the rank and station, which they have held before. Secondly, in avoiding harm of which they have already had experience. Thirdly, in protecting advantages which they possess. Fourthly, in extricating themselves from the whirlpool of calamity which may have come upon them. Fifthly, in watching the attainment of advantage and the averting of evil in time to come. And I exert myself for this that I may get back to my own office, and that the lustre of my condition may be renewed. And the method is as follows,—to pursue the Ox with artifices until he bid farewell to earth's surface,[1] or pack up his chattels from this place; and I am not inferior to that weak Sparrow who obtained his revenge on the Falcon.' Kalílah inquired, ' How was that.'

STORY IX.

Damnah said, ' I have heard that two Sparrows had fixed their nest on the branch of a tree; and of worldly gear, water and grain sufficed them; and on the summit of a mountain, beneath which that tree lay, a Falcon had its abode, which, at the time of stooping on its quarry, issued from its lurking-place like lightning, and like heaven's bolt, clean consumed the harvest of life of the feebler birds.

COUPLET.

When he against the hapless birds his talons would display
Though there were fifty[2] gathered there, he'd bear them all away.

Whenever the sparrows produced young, and the time was near at hand for them to fly, that falcon, rushing forth from its ambush, used to carry them off and make them food for its own young. Now to those sparrows—in accordance with the saying, ' *The love of home is a part of faith*'—to migrate from that place was impossible, and yet from the cruelty of the tyrannous hawk it was difficult to be enabled to reside there.

HEMISTICH.

Nor mode of travel nor yet mind to stay.

On one occasion, their young ones, having gained strength and put forth

---

[1] Observe the uncommon phrase *pusht-i zamin* for 'earth's surface'; *lit.* 'back of the earth.'

[2] Here is a play on words beyond my skill to imitate. *Panjah* is ' a claw,' and *panjáh* ' fifty.'   The equivoque then is that he showed *panjah*, and bore away *panjáh*.

feathers and wings, were able to move; and the father and mother, pleased
with the sight of their offspring, testified their joy at their attempt to fly.
Suddenly the thought of the falcon passed through their minds, and, all
at once, having folded up the carpet of delight, they began to wail and
lament from distress and anxiety.   One of their children—in whose countenance the signs of discretion and ripe intellect were visible—having inquired
into the circumstances of that state [of emotion] and the reason of their
change from hilarity to despondency ; they replied, ' O son !

COUPLET.

Ask not of us how fierce the flame that now consumes our breast,
But ask the tears that fill our eyes, for they'll interpret best.'

They then recounted the history of the falcon's oppression and of its carrying
off their young, with all the particulars.   The son said, ' To draw back the
neck from the command of fate and the mandate of destiny, is not the way
for creatures, yet ' *The Causer of causes*' has appointed a remedy for every pain,
and has sent a cure for every sorrow.   It is probable that if ye exert yourselves
in repelling this misfortune, and take steps to untie this knot, both this
calamity will be averted from our heads, and this burden, too, will be
removed from your heart.'   These words pleased the sparrows; and while
one of them stopped to attend to the condition of the young ones, the other
flew forth in search of relief.   When it had flown a little way, it began to
reflect, saying, ' Alas ! whither shall I go ? and to whom shall I tell the
affliction of my heart?

COUPLET.

Grief on my heart has seized, and oh ! no medicine for that grief I know,
A medicine for the mind diseased—for inward grief—is hard, I trow.'

At last he resolved in his mind, that he would tell his story to whatsoever
animal his eyes first fell upon, and ask a remedy for his heart's distress from
it.   It happened that a Salamander having come forth from a mine of fire,
was wandering in the spreading plain of the desert.   When the glance of the
sparrow lighted upon him, and that strange form and extraordinary appearance came into his view; he said to himself, ' *I have fallen upon good*;' come
on, I will disclose the grief of my heart to this marvelous bird ; perhaps he
may undo the knot of my affairs and may shew me the way to a remedy.
Then with the utmost respect, he advanced to the Salamander, and after the
requisite ceremonies and salutation,[1] he paid the conventional compliments of
offering service.   The Salamander, too, in a kind and encouraging tone,
expressed the due courtesy required towards travelers, and said, ' The traces
of weariness are discernible in thy countenance.   If this arises from the fatigue

---

[1] One MS. inserts *wa* before *mardsim*, but it is evidently better to make this the accusa-
tive after *ri'dyat kardan*.

of journeying, be pleased to halt some days in this neighbourhood, that [this fatigue] may be exchanged for repose : and if the case be aught else, explain it, that to the extent of my power I may exert myself to remedy it. The sparrow loosed his tongue, and represented to the salamander his piteous condition, after a fashion, that had he told it to a rock it would have been rent in pieces by his distress.

COUPLET.

To whomsoe'er the story I of my sad grief impart,
I fresh inflict a dozen wounds upon his helpless heart.

After hearing this tale, the salamander, too, felt the fire of compassion kindled, and he said, 'Grieve not! for I will this night take such measures as to consume his abode and nest and all that therein is.   Do thou point out to me thy dwelling, and go to thy offspring until the time I come to thee. The sparrow indicated his dwelling in such a way as not to leave a doubt in the mind of the salamander; and with a glad heart and a mind freed from the load of grief, turned towards his own nest.   When the night came on, the salamander, with a number of its own kind, each carrying a quantity of naphtha and brimstone, set off in the direction of that spot, and under the guidance of that sparrow, conveyed themselves to the vicinity of the falcon's nest.   The latter unaware of that [impending] misfortune, had, with its young, eaten plentifully, and fallen asleep.   The salamanders cast upon their nest all the naphtha and brimstone that they had brought with them, and turned back: and the blast of divine justice having blown the flame of vengeance, fell upon those oppressors.   They rose up from the sleep of negligence, at a time when the hand of prevention was unequal to the quenching of that flame; and all of them, with their abode and nest, were at once consumed to ashes.

COUPLET.

Oppression's flame, lit with the tyrant's breath,
When it burst forth consumed him first to death.

And I have given this instance that thou mayest know that every one who labors to repel an enemy, though he may be small and weak, and his foe great and strong, may yet hope for victory and triumph.   Kalílah said, 'Now that the Lion has distinguished him above the rest, and has exalted the banner of his fortune ; to expel the lion's attachment to him from his heart, and to alter the Lion's feelings towards him, appears very difficult; and kings, when they shew favor to any one do not disgrace him without full cause, nor cast from their sight any one whom they have exalted, unless on the occurrence of some extraordinary act.'

COUPLET.

Water engulfs not wood—and wherefore so ?   It swallows not that which itself made grow.

Damnah said, ' What cause can be fuller than this, that the King has gone

I

to excess in favoring him, and has indulged in contempt for his other ministers, till, as a necessary consequence, they have become disgusted with his service, and the advantage of their services and benefit of their advice has been cut off from him; and from this state of things great calamities are to be expected: and sages have said, danger arises to a King, and misfortune to a country, from one of six things. First, disappointment, that is to say, making his loyal subjects destitute of hope in him, and abandoning people of judgment and experience, to disgrace. Secondly, mischievous embroilment, and this may be characterised as causeless war, and the occurrence of ill-digested undertakings, and provoking hostile parties to unsheath their swords. Thirdly, sensuality, which is being passionately fond of women, and being too addicted to the chase, and engaging in drinking, and shewing an inclination for idle amusements. Fourthly, adverse fortune, being such accidents as time produces, as plague, famine, earthquakes, conflagrations and inundations, and the like. Fifthly, violence of temper, which is carrying anger to great lengths, and being excessive in tortures and punishments. Sixthly, ignorance, which is such that in a crisis that calls for peace the king has recourse to war, and at the moment for war he inclines to peace, and when he should use gentle measures he adopts roughness, and when he ought to close up the barriers of severity he opens the door of kindness.'

COUPLET.

Inopportunely war or peace comes ill,
Let flowers or thorns the place that suits them fill.

Kalílah said, 'I saw that thou hadst girded thyself for revenge, and wast lying in wait for Shanzabah; and thou wishest that some evil may befall him by what proceeds from thee; and I know that to inflict injury has no good result, and that by way of retribution, every one's mischief recoils on himself.

COUPLET.

All who do ill—no end but ill attain;   Swift on them back the ill recoils again.

And whoever will open the eye of experience, and observe the retribution of good and bad, there is no doubt that he will incline to goodness and gentleness, and will keep his hand and tongue from annoyance and injury, as the just King said.' Damnah asked, 'How was that?'

STORY X.

Kalílah said, 'I have heard that in former times there was a King, who had opened the hand of despotic power and oppression, and had set the foot of obstinate wickedness beyond the beaten path of justice and beneficence.

COUPLET.

World-burning, merciless, and prone to blood,
Earth was embittered by his bitter mood.

The people night and day had lifted up their hands in prayer against his injustice, and had loosed the tongue of detestation. One day this King went to the chase, and when he returned, he ordered a proclamation, saying, 'O people! the eye of my heart has to this day been covered with a veil from beholding the aspect of rectitude, and the hand of my transgression has drawn the scymitar of tyranny against the countenances of the despairing oppressed, and the unhappy objects of persecution. Now I have become sincerely disposed to cherish my subjects, and steadfast in the office of administration of justice. My hope is that after to-day the hand of an oppressor will not strike the ring of vexation on the door of any peasant, nor the foot of a persecutor reach the court of the dwelling of any poor man.'

COUPLET.

Expect not ease that realm or clime among,
Where the folks' heart is by the monarch wrung.

The people felt new life at these tidings, and to the poor, the rose of desire blossomed in the garden of hope.

COUPLET.

When this glad news its sudden influence shed,
Transport the heart, and joy the soul, o'erspread.

In short the felicitous influence of his justice reached such a point, that the lambs drank milk from the dugs of the savage lioness, and the pheasant sported in communion with the hawk, and on this account they bestowed on him the title of 'The Justice-dispensing King.'

COUPLET.

So firm the basis, he to justice set,   Sulphur and flame as guard and guarded met.

One of the confidential ministers of the cabinet of state, took an opportunity to ask the state of the case, and inquired into the change of the bitterness of oppression and tyranny for the sweetness of mercy and good faith. The King said, 'That day that I went to hunt, I was galloping on every side, when suddenly I observed a dog pursue a fox, and bite through the bone of his leg with his teeth :—the hapless fox escaped into a hole with a maimed leg, and the dog came back. Presently a footman threw a stone and broke the leg of that dog, and had not yet gone on a few steps, when a horse kicked the footman, and his leg was fractured, and the horse too had advanced no distance, when his foot went down in a hole and snapped.' I came to myself and said, 'Sawest thou what they did, and what they experienced? Whoever does what he ought not, suffers what he would not.'

VERSE.

Seek to do good, shun evil, and take heed :
For as thou actest, so too shalt thou speed.
Ever in good dost thou incline to tread ?
Thou shalt then aye behold upraised thy head.
But if in vice thou walkest, thou shalt see,
Thyself down trampled by adversity.

And I have hit off this example with this view, that thou mayest dread retribution, and abandon a malevolent disposition, lest disastrous results should reach thee, and the meaning [of the saying] '*Whoever dug a pit for his brother assuredly fell into it himself,*' be manifested in thy case; and a sage has said, 'Do not evil, that thou mayest keep back evil;[1] dig not a pit, lest thou fall therein thyself.' Damnah said, 'In this matter I am the oppressed—not the oppressor, and I am he that suffers cruelty—not he that inflicts it; and if the oppressed should be occupied with the design of revenging himself upon his oppressor, what retribution can there be for that? and if injury should result from him to the injurer, what harm can therein ensue to him?' Kalílah said, 'Granted that by this proceeding no obstruction occurs to thy fortunes, but in what manner wilt thou exert thyself for the destruction of the Ox? since his power surpasses thine, and his friends and allies are more numerous than those who befriend and support thee.' Damnah said, 'One must not base one's proceedings on the greatness of one's strength, and the infinite number of one's allies; but prudence and counsel must be esteemed as superior to these, since it is probable that what can be effected by skill and stratagem, is unattainable by violence and force; and has it never reached thee how a Raven destroyed a Serpent by stratagem?' Kalílah said, 'How was that?'

STORY XI.

Damnah[2] said, 'They have related that a Raven had taken up its abode on the side of a mountain, and had made its nest in the fissure of a rock, and in the vicinity of it was the hole of a Snake, the water of whose mouth was deadly poison and the locality of death, and the venom of the roots of whose teeth was destructive to the constitution of existence and life. Whenever the Raven had young, the Serpent devoured them, and consumed the liver of the Raven with the brand of the loss of her offspring. When the cruelty of the Serpent had passed all bounds, the Raven, reduced to despair, made complaint of her plight to a jackal who was her friend, and said, 'I am thinking how I can deliver myself from the calamity of this Snake and the affliction of this life-pursuing tyrant.' The jackal asked, 'What steps wilt thou take in this emergency? and by what artifice wilt thou get rid of his annoyance?' The Raven said, 'I intend, when the Snake is asleep, to peck out with my blood-drinking beak the eyes with which he surveys the

---

[1] I read with the best MS. I have *bad makun kih bad áftí*, taking *áft* to be the verbal noun of *afat*, and to signify 'keeping back,' so as not to conclude both sentences with *uftí*, 'thou mayest fall,' according to the erroneous (as I think) reading of the lithographed and printed editions, and according to Keene's translation, which gives for the English, 'lest thou fall into evil.'

[2] The word *Damnah* is, by a typographical error, omitted in the printed edition, at the beginning of the story, and also in the Index.

world, that he may not be again able to attack those that are the lustre of my eyes; and that my offspring, the light of my vision, may remain secure from the wickedness of that malignant one.' The jackal said, 'This plan swerves from the right course, for wise men ought to attack their enemy in such a manner that there may be no peril of losing their life by it. Take care that thou abandonest this thought, that thou mayest not destroy thyself like the Heron who exerted himself for the destruction of the Crab, and gave his own dear life to the winds.' The Raven asked, 'How was that?'

STORY XII.

The jackal said, 'There was a Heron which had made its home on the margin of a piece of water, and had turned the countenance of his heart from all other objects to the pursuit of fish. In proportion to his wants he used to catch fish, and pass his life in comfort. When the infirmity of old age found its way to him, and his bodily faculties inclined to decay, he was unequal to the pursuit of fish, and being overtaken with the noose of grief, said to himself,

COUPLET.

Alas! the caravan of years so traceless disappear [1]
That no! not e'en their dust has reached my country's atmosphere.

Alas! that I have wasted in sport my precious life, and that I have not stored up anything which could afford me assistance [2] in the season of old age, or be a support to me; and at this day my vigour has failed, yet I cannot do without victuals. My best course is to base my proceedings on artifice, and spread the snare of deceit and pretended abstinence ;

HEMISTICH.

By this pretext I may, perhaps, live on.

He then seated himself at the brink of the water, lamenting and sighing and weeping. A Crab beheld him from a distance and, advancing, accosted him familiarly, and said, 'Friend! I observe thee sorrowful, what is the reason of this?' He replied, 'How can I not be grieved, for thou knowest that the material of my sustenance and the support of my life was the one or two fishes which I daily used to catch and by which I obtained enough to keep in the breath of life, and food sufficient to prevent me from dying. No extraordinary detriment accrued to the fishes therefrom, and my days, too, were decked with the ornament of contentment and happiness. To-day two fishermen passed by this spot, and were saying, 'In this lake there is an abundance of fish—we must settle them.' One said, 'In such a lake there

---

[1] 'Caravan' is made a noun of multitude in the text, with a plural verb; and I have accordingly given it a plural verb in English.
[2] Keene translates *páí mardí*, 'traces of manhood,' which is indeed the etymological meaning of the word, but the Dictionary furnishes a more apt secondary signification, of which I have availed myself.

are more fish than in this. First let us manage their business, and then let us turn this way.' Now, if events are to take this course, I must detach my heart from sweet life, and must fix it on the bitterness of death.' As soon as the Crab heard these tidings, it went back with all haste, and going to the fish, recounted to them this dismal news just as it had heard it. Hereupon, a commotion ensuing among them, they, in company with the Crab, betook themselves to the Heron, and said, 'Such and such intelligence has reached us from thee, and has wrested the reins of counsel from our hands;

COUPLET.

The more that we from head to foot this matter still survey,
The more from weakness, compass-like, we wander far astray.[1]

Now we would consult with you[2] for '*He who is consulted is trustworthy.*' It behoves a wise man, even when enemies apply to him for advice, not to slight the obligation of counseling rightly, especially in a matter where the advantage may revert to himself, and thou thyself sayest that the continuation of thy existence is bound up in us, and that thy life is dependent on our continuing to be. Therefore what dost thou consider advisable in our affair ?' The Heron replied, 'I have myself heard this speech from the tongue of the fishermen, and there is no possibility of opposing them, and I can think of nothing but this device,—I know a pool in the neigbourhood of this, the water of which, in purity, boasts of rivaling the real dawn,[3] and surpasses the world-displaying mirror in showing the images of forms. The grains of sand may be counted at the bottom of it, and the eggs of the fish may be seen in its basin, and yet with all this, neither can the diver of the understanding reach to its bottom, nor the traveller of the fancy see its shore, and the net of no fisherman has fallen in that lake, and the fish of that water have experienced no captivity but the chain of water.[4]

COUPLET.

A lake it is which like an ocean flows—
A sea which neither source nor limit knows.

If you could migrate thither, you might pass the remainder of your life in security and contentment, and delight and ease.' They replied, 'The thought is good, but without thy aid and friendly assistance, our departure thither is impossible.' The Heron answered, 'I will not withhold from you whatever strength and power I possess : but time presses ; every moment the fisher-

---

[1] *Sar gashtah* here signifies ' wandering from its head,' which the points of the compasses do when they are used. I have found it impossible to carry out the play on words in English.

[2] The MSS. and the lithographed edition read *kunam*, but since the plural is used in the preceding verses, I think it would be better to read *kunim*.

[3] According to the Orientals there are two dawns, the *subh-i kázib* ' false dawn,' and the *subh-i sádik*, or ' true dawn.'

[4] The ripple of the water is compared to a chain.

men may come, and the opportunity will be lost.' The fishes besought him, and after much entreaty, it was determined that every day he should remove some fish and convey them to that lake. The Heron, then, every morning carried some fish, and on the top of a hillock, which was near, devoured them, and when it returned, the others hasted to remove and emigrate, and sought for precedence and priority over one another; and wisdom wept with a warning eye over their folly and unwariness, and time, with its thousand eyes, shed tears over their lamentable condition. And undoubtedly any one who is beguiled by the flattery of an enemy and thinks fit to place confidence in a mean person of innate wickedness, this is his punishment. When many days had passed, the desire of (going to) this lake entered into the head of a Crab also. He wished to remove, and informed the Heron of that idea. The Heron reflected, 'There is not a more thorough enemy of mine than this. My best plan is to convey him to his friends.' He then advanced, and having taken the Crab on his neck, turned his face towards the resting-place of the fishes. The Crab, who saw the bones of the fish from a distance, perceived how the matter stood. He reflected that a wise man, when he sees an enemy intent on his life, is exerting himself for his own destruction if he neglects to struggle; and that, should he exert himself, his condition will not fail to be one of two things. If he comes off victorious, he leaves a reputation for courage upon the page of time; and if he fails, he at least escapes being reproached for want of courage and spirit in defending himself.

STANZA.

Should a foeman thee attack, to repel his injury
Struggle with thy utmost might, if for wisdom famed thou be.
Art thou successful, thou hast then thy wished-for object won.
But shouldst thou fail, thou art excused, thou hast thy duty done.

The Crab then threw himself on the neck of the heron and began to squeeze his throat tightly. The Heron was old and weak, and with a little throttling became insensible, and falling down from the air was leveled with the dust. The Crab, having descended from his neck, went his way, and having stepped along the road, came to the remaining fishes, and mingling lamentations for lost friends with congratulations on the life of the survivors, informed them how matters stood. All of them rejoiced, and reckoned the death of the Heron as a renewal of existence and a life without limit.

VERSE.

One breath of life that we should draw when such a foe is gone,
Transcends, I deem, a hundred years that circle idly on.
It is not for us to glory o'er our foeman's fallen day;
Yet from our foe one free-drawn breath excels all thou canst say.

And I have introduced this story with this object, that thou mayest know that many a one perishes by his own stratagems and deceit and the mischievous effects of his perfidiousness, according to the text, '*but the contrivance of evil shall only encompass the authors thereof,*' [1] recoil upon himself, nevertheless I will point out a way to thee, in accordance with which, if thou shouldest act, it may be the cause of thy preservation, and of the destruction of thy enemy. The Raven said, 'One must not slight the suggestions of friends, nor act in opposition to the wise.'

COUPLET.

> To the wine-house, thou, cupbearer! beckonest me to take my way;
> 'Twere not friendship's course resistance to thy counsels to display.

The jackal said, 'The advisable course is this, that thou shouldest soar aloft in air and cast thine eyes on the terraces of the houses and plains, and wherever thou beholdest an ornament which it is possible to carry, there stoop and snatch it up, and fly through the air in such a way as to be visible to men's eyes, and there is no doubt that some persons will follow thee to recover the ornament. When thou drawest near to the Serpent cast the ornament upon it, so that when the eyes of those men light upon him they may release him from the bonds of life, and then recover the ornament. And thy heart will be freed from care without any exertions on thy own part.' The Raven, in accordance with the suggestion of the jackal, turned towards an inhabited place. Presently it saw a woman who had put down an ornament on the corner of a terrace, and was herself occupied with her ablutions. The Raven carried off the ornament, and in the same manner as the jackal had said, threw it on the Serpent. The men who had come in pursuit of the Raven forthwith crushed the Serpent's head, and the Raven was set free [from its foe].'

HEMISTICH.

> The foe departed, with him went our tears.[2]

Damnah said, 'I have coined this fable that thou mayest know that things which may be accomplished by artifice, are impossible by mere force.' Kalílah replied, 'The Ox possesses strength and fierceness and understanding and prudence, all these things—and over such a person it is not possible to prevail by stratagem, since on every side that thou by deceit preparest a trench, he by forethought will repair it, and perhaps before thou canst make a supper off him, he may breakfast upon thee. But perhaps the story of that Hare never reached thy ears, who formed the design of entrapping the fox, and got caught itself?' Damnah asked, 'How was that?'

---

[1] Kur'án, Fl., ch. xxxi, 43; Mar. xxxv. 42; Sale p. 329, l, 33: 'The Koreish swore by God, with a most solemn oath, that if a preacher had come unto them, they would surely have been more willingly directed than any nation; but now a preacher is come unto them, it hath only increased in them their aversion from the truth, their arrogance in the earth, and their contriving of evil; but the contrivance of evil shall only encompass the authors thereof.'

[2] There is a play on words in this line which I have been unable to retain in English. 'The foe departed from the midst (or from the waist), and at the same time the tear from our bosom.'

STORY XIII.

Kalîlah said, 'I have heard that a hungry wolf was running along a plain on the scent of a meal, when he beheld a Hare asleep under the shade of a bush, and whose limbs the slumber of negligence had occupied. The wolf, accounting it a rare prize, began to steal gently towards it. The Hare being put on the alert by the terror of his breath, at the alarm of his step, started up, and was about to fly. The wolf, obstructing the road, exclaimed,

COUPLET.

'Approach! approach! for I from thee this distance cannot bear;
Depart not, ah! depart not! for thy parting brings despair!'

The Hare, from fear of him, was fixed motionless to the spot, and beginning to supplicate, rubbed the face of humble entreaty on the ground, and said, 'I know that the fire of the hunger of the prince of beasts is burning fiercely, and that his appetite is raging in quest of food, and I with this weak body and slender form, am no more than a mouthful to the king. What is the good of me, and what will be effected[1] by eating me? In this neighbourhood there is a fox, who is unable to move from excessive fatness, and from his quantity of flesh finds it impossible to stir. I imagine that his flesh by its succulence, resembles the water of life, and his blood from its sweetness and freshness is comparable to sharbat made with the finest sugar. If my lord will deign to take the trouble of stepping with me, I, by any stratagem that I find practicable, will make him a prisoner, and my lord may break his fast upon him. If this gratification is obtained, why so much the better; if otherwise I myself am still your prisoner and captive.

HEMISTICH.

Go! lasso others, we are already thine.

The wolf, deceived by his plausible speeches, took the way to the abode of the fox. Now in that vicinity there was a fox who in cunning might have lectured Satan, and in wily devices and trickery, have given lessons to fancy and imagination.

VERSE.

A sharp young fox he! who by craft made gain;
No! rather tax-collector of that plain.
He played his tricks through field and hamlet still,
And from all beasts bore off the prize of skill.
Outcries he raised amid the beasts that prowl
Along the waste; caused village dogs to howl.
And with a bound deceived the watchful eye;
Sweeping with bushy tail the courtyard of the sky.

---

[1] Lit.: 'What will be bound or what loosed from eating me?'

The Hare had an old quarrel with him, and on the present occasion, having obtained an opportunity, he determined on revenge, and having left the wolf at the entrance of the hole, he went into the abode of the fox and performed the customary salutations and benedictions. The fox, too, with the utmost deference, returned his salutations, and said,

COUPLET.

'Welcome art thou ! whence hast thou come ? enter, and seated be !
Come in ! and sit, on my two eyes a seat I'll give to thee.'

The Hare replied, 'It is a long time that I have continued still in the desire of being exalted by a meeting, and by reason of the obstacles of deceitful fortune, and the accidents of faithless and inconstant time, I remain excluded from that happiness. At this time a holy man[1] who has been exalted to kingly dignity in the Egypt of divine favor, and in the region of saintship is a sage indulgent to his disciples, has honored us by coming from the sacred shrine to this country, and having heard the fame of the monastic seclusion and retirement of your highness, has made this humble slave the medium of introduction, in order that he may irradiate the eye of his heart with your world-adorning beauties, and perfume the nostrils of his soul with the sweet scents of your musk-resembling thoughts. If there be permission for a visit, it is well and good, but if the occasion does not admit of it, another time may serve.

COUPLET.

Or let him from this door go back, like an unexpected woe,
Or stop like answered prayer to which the heavens acceptance show.'

The fox read from the page of this discourse the writing of fraud, and beheld in the mirror of these words, the delineation of the form of deceit. He said to himself, 'My advisable course is this, that I should act to them in accordance with their own conduct, and pour too part of their own mixture into their own throat.

HEMISTICH.

Those who cast clods are answered with a stone.'

The fox then made use of sundry complimentary expressions, and said, 'We have on this account girded our loins in the service of travelers, and have for this reason opened the door of our cell in the face of holy men, that we may benefit by the beauty of their enraptured state and the perfection of their sentiments. And especially to such a saint as thou representest, and to a perfectly holy man of the kind thou describest, how can I fail in hospitality, or what particle of service could I omit ? for '*the guest when he alights, alights to his own appointed food,*' and the ancients have said,

---

[1] '*Azíz*, besides signifying 'a holy man,' is also a special title of the kings of Egypt. It is therefore well chosen here in relation to *misr*, 'Egypt,' which follows.

STANZA.

Each one on earth thou seest, doth his own
Allotted food consume, whether his bread
Upon thy table or on his be spread.
Wherefore thou shouldst the favor not disown
Which guests on thee confer, in that they eat
As bounty, at thy table, their own meat.

Nevertheless I entertain the hope that thou wilt delay thus long, until I sweep out the corner of my cell and spread for my guest of fortunate footstep, a carpet which may befit the occasion.' The Hare imagined that he had succeeded in cajoling the fox,[1] and that the latter would soon do himself the honor of waiting on the wolf. He [therefore] replied, 'The guest is a man without ceremony, and of the simplicity of character suited to a darvesh; and is indifferent to decoration in place or dress; but since your noble mind desires to observe some ceremony, there is no harm, too, in that.' With these words the Hare went out and detailed all that had occurred to the wolf, and imparted to him the pleasing tidings of the fox having been deceived, and began again to renew—for, ' in everything new there is pleasure' —his encomium of the flesh and fat, and juiciness and freshness of the fox; and the wolf, having whetted the teeth of appetite, was licking his lips[2] at the anticipated relish of the fox's flesh, and the Hare flattered himself,[3] on account of the service, with the idea of release. The fox, however, through prudence and foresight, had, a very long time previously, dug a deep pit in his abode and had gradually carried out the earth from it and covered the top of it with a little rubbish and straw, and he had also a secret passage by which, on emergency, he could make his way out. When he had sent the Hare away,[4] he came to the mouth of the pit and disposed the rubbish in such a manner that it would give way on the slightest movement. He then came to the mouth of the secret way and called out, saying, ' Respected guests, be pleased to take the trouble of stepping forward!' and simultaneously with their ingress he went forth from that hole. The Hare with prodigious alacrity, and the wolf with the utmost greediness, entered that dark cell, and their stepping on the rubbish was simultaneous with their falling to the bottom of the pit. The wolf imagined that that stratagem, also, was of the Hare's doing and he tore him to pieces in an instant, and delivered the world from the reproach of his existence. And I have adduced this story in order that thou mayest know that artifices do not succeed against the wise, and one who possesses a share of caution and foresight, does not suffer

---

[1] Lit. : 'that his breath had taken in the fox.
[2] Lit. : 'was making his mouth sweet.'
[3] Lit. : 'bound with himself the thought of release.'
[4] The printed edition has, by a typographical error, a 'k' for a 'g' in the word gusil, 'dismission,' 'farewell.'

himself to be infatuated by the deceitful arts of any one.' Damnah said, 'It
is as thou sayest, but the Ox is conceited of himself, and is not on his guard
against my hostility; and through this supineness I may overthrow him; for
the arrow of perfidy which they discharge from the ambush of friendship,
penetrates the more deeply; and perhaps thou hast not heard in what way the
treachery of that Hare became effectual against the young Lion, and as he
was not on the alert against his treachery, he fell, in spite of his good sense
and sagacity, into the whirlpool of destruction.' Kalílah inquired 'How
was that?'

STORY XIV.

Damnah said, 'They have related that in the environs of Baghdád there
was a meadow, the breeze of which might have imparted fresh perfume to
the fragrance of Paradise, and the bright reflection of whose sweet herbs
might have added lustre to the eye of heaven. From every branch of its
flowery borders a thousand stars were shining, and at the beauty of each of
those stars the nine heavens were amazed.[1]

VERSE.

> There water 'mid the juicy verdure glides,
>   As in a mould of lapis lazuli
> Mercurial globules—on the streamlet's sides
>   Upspring sweet herbs; the dawn smells wooingly,
>   And perfume-raining zephyrs wanton by.

And in that verdant plain were many wild beasts,[2] and in consequence of the
excellent air and exhilarating country, and the abundance of water, and
ample supply of food, they passed their time in pleasure and enjoyment. But
in that neighbourhood lived a fierce and cruel Lion, who every day displayed
his ill-omened visage. to those helpless animals, and embittered their
happiness and existence. One day they, with one accord, went to the
Lion, and after declaring their loyalty and submissive obedience, said, 'O
king! we are thy subjects and followers, and thou, each day, after much
trouble and infinite exertion, art able to hunt down one of us or not, and we,
through dread of thee, are always distracted with distress, and thou, too, in
troublous inquietude in pursuit of us. We have now thought of a plan
which may be a source of comfort to thee, and to us the cause of security
and rest. If thou wilt discontinue molesting us as heretofore, and wilt not
daily distract us, we will send a quarry at breakfast-time as a daily supply
for the royal kitchen, and will not allow of any failure in the performance of

---

[1] *Sar garddn*, ' amazed,' or ' revolving,' The ambiguity is intentional.
[2] Keene again translates *wuḥush* 'harmless animals'; but, as before said (p. 85, n. 1), I
cannot think that this meaning can ever be attached to the word. It signifies rather an
animal of the desert—fierce, strong, and untamed—from *waḥsh* 'desolate.'

this.' The Lion assented and they used daily to cast lots, and on which-ever beast's name the lot fell, him they used to send as a portion to the Lion; till in this manner some time had elapsed. One day the lot fell on a Hare, and fortune made him a target for the arrow of calamity. He said to his friends, 'If ye will show me a little forbearance in despatching me, I will deliver you from the oppression of this tyrant.' They replied, 'There is no difficulty about this.' The Hare delayed for an hour, till the time of breakfast had passed, and the ferocious nature of the Lion being excited, he ground his teeth together from anger and fury. The Hare went very gently towards him and found him excessively vexed. The fire of hunger had seated him on the winds,[1] and the glare of anger was evident in all his movements and postures.

COUPLET.

To heat the stomach's oven more and more,
Will be disastrous when our food is o'er.

The Hare saw that the Lion, from excess of fury, was lashing the ground vengefully with his tail, and wishing in his heart to infringe the treaty. He advanced slowly and saluted him. The Lion asked, 'Whence comest thou? and what are the beasts about?' He replied, 'They, according to established custom, sent a Hare in company with me, and we set out together to wait on your highness. A Lion met us in the way and carried off the other Hare, and in spite of our vehement protestations that, this is the food of the king of beasts and the allowance provided for their monarch, he heeded not my words, and said, 'This is my hunting-ground and the game here belongs to me.'

HEMISTICH.

Perhaps thou hast not heard this proverb, 'Every lion has his wood!'

O king! he made use of such boasts and enlarged so on his own might and prowess, that I lost all patience, and running from his presence, hastened hither that I might represent to your enlightened mind the state of the case.' A blind sense of honor was stirred in the Lion [by these words], and he exclaimed,

VERSE.

'I am he who in dealing the thrust[2] and the blow,
Will teach lions the art of encountering the foe:
Who then is the lion who will dare to make prey
Of a quarry where I, and I only, bear sway?

He then added, 'O Hare! canst thou show him to me that I may wrest from him the justice thy heart requires, and may also wreak on him my own

---

[1] 'Caused him to be restless,' is, I suppose, the plain English of this extraordinary expression.

[2] The *ta'n* is evidently here opposed to the *zarb*, which is 'the cut' of a weapon—*ta'n* is 'the thrust,' not, I think, as Keene translates it, 'taunts,' which, in fact, are worse than useless in battle.

revenge?' The Hare replied, 'Why should I not be able, when he has spoken many disrespectful things of the king? and had I had the power, I should have made his skull a cup [1] for the beasts of the desert.

COUPLET.

But I, in God, am hopeful him to see,
To my heart's triumph, clutched, cast down by thee.'

Saying this he led the way, and the simple-hearted Lion, ensnared by his wiles, went on after him. The Hare brought the Lion to the mouth of a large well, the water of which, from its clearness, like a Chinese mirror, reflected objects distinctly, and could faultlessly represent, to the lookers in, the external shape and countenance of every one.

COUPLET.

None gazed therein but, on the tablet bright
Of its pure contents, read his form aright.

[The Hare said], 'O King! thy worthless foe is in this well and I am afraid of his terrors : if the King will take me up in his arms I will shew him his enemy.' The Lion lifted him up and looked down into the well. He beheld his own shape and that of the hare in the water. He imagined that it was that very lion and hare that had been his own allotted food which he held in his hug. He put down the Hare and plunged into the well, and after sinking twice or thrice consigned his bloodthirsty spirit to the flames of hell : and the Hare returning in safety, announced to the beasts the circumstances of the adventure, and performing due thanksgiving to God, fed at pleasure in the gardens of security and peace, and continued to recite this couplet,

COUPLET.

One draught of water, quit of wicked men,[2]
Transcends a life of threescore years and ten.

And by the citation of this example it may be discerned that however powerful an enemy may be, it is possible to get the better of him in a moment of supineness.' Kalílah said, 'If thou destroy the Ox, in such a manner as not to afflict the lion, it might have a shew of reason, and one might excuse it, but if his ruin is not to be effected without hurt to the lion, take care that thou dost not meddle in this matter, since no sensible person willingly disturbs his master to secure his own comfort.' With these words the conversation came to an end, and Damnah having retired from attendance [on the lion], betook himself to the corner of retirement, until one day having found an opportunity he thrust himself in private upon the lion, and stood like one

---

[1] This meaning of *áb khúrd* is not given in the Dictionary, nor is that of 'moist, juicy,' or 'fed with moisture,' which it evidently bears at p. 105, l. 7, of the printed edition. See p. 124, l. 18, of this translation.

[2] I take the sentiment intended by *az pas-i bad sigál* to be the same as that expressed at p. 119, l. 37. Keene translates 'after sad thoughts.'

grieved and pensive, heart-sore and hanging down his head. The Lion said, 'It is some days since I have seen thee, is all well?' He replied, 'Please God it may turn out well!' The Lion was startled[1] and said, 'Has anything happened?' 'Indeed, yes!' replied he. 'Relate it,' said the Lion. Damnah answered, 'For that a private audience and leisure are necessary.' 'This moment is the time,' said the Lion, 'explain it with all despatch, for a matter of importance admits not of delay, and if the business of to-day be put off till to-morrow a thousand calamities result.

COUPLET.

Do not procrastinate—begin to do!   For in delay are many evils, too.

Damnah said, 'No statement, the hearing of which may cause aversion in the hearer, should be rashly delivered, nor should it be uttered without thorough consideration and much thought, unless there be perfect confidence in the good sense and discretion of the hearer, and the latter too should consider the circumstances of the speaker, as to whether he is in a position to give faithful advice or not, and when he knows that the speaker can have no object but the discharge of the debt which he owes for past favours, he ought to listen to his word with the ear of attention, particularly when the advantages and benefits thereof will revert to himself.' The Lion said, 'Thou knowest that I am an exception to kings through the excellence of my judgment and the superabundance of my understanding, and that in listening to the words of every one I propose to myself, for observance, the discrimination that becomes a monarch; say therefore, without ceremony, whatever thou wishest, and unhesitatingly reveal whatever has come into thy mind.' Damnah said, 'I too have found permission to be thus bold, in that my confidence in the understanding and wisdom of the king is excessive, and it is moreover palpable that I speak from pure affection and the most genuine honesty, and stain not my words with doubt and suspicion and interested and corrupt motives; and, save the touchstone of the imperial mind, there is no standard for assaying language.

COUPLET.

Praise be to God! in the imperial mind,   A touchstone of pure coin and base we find.'

The Lion said, 'The abundance of thy honesty is manifest and the traces of it are evident on the visage of thy affairs, and thy words are altogether pregnant with good feeling and excellent advice, and doubt and suspicion find no possibility of entering into the precincts thereof.' Damnah said, 'The existence of all the beasts is bound up in the continuance of the king's life. Wherefore it behoves every subject who is characterised and impressed with

---

[1] Lit.: 'was from his place.' I note these idiomatical expressions as valuable to the student.

the marks of sincerity and royalty,[1] that he withhold nothing from the king of the right discharge of his duties, and the representation of faithful counsel: for the wise have decreed that, 'Whosoever conceals the truth from the king, keeps back an ailment from the physician, and does not see fit to disclose his poverty and hunger to his friends, may be regarded as a traitor to himself.' The Lion responded, 'Thy loyalty and singleness of mind, have long ago been apparent to me and I have long since known thy uprightness and good faith. Now speak! what event has happened? in order that, after acquaintance with the circumstances of the case, we may occupy ourselves with deliberation.' Damnah, when he had ensnared the Lion by his artful words, loosed his tongue, and said,

COUPLET.

'May wisdom guide thee, king! and victory
Thee follow, and thy foemen vanquished be!

Shanzabah has held private meetings with the leaders of the army, and has entered into conversation with the Pillars of the state, and said, 'I have tried the Lion, and fathomed the extent of his strength and might and judgment and sagacity, and in each have clearly discerned many defects and infinite weakness.

COUPLET.

Not he the hero that my fancy drew;
He is not such—my thought was all untrue.

And I am in amazement—that while the king has shewn all this profuseness in honoring that faithless ingrate and has made him the 'alter ego'[2] in the government and administration of the empire—in return for these favors, this procedure should have been developed by him, and in requital of such benefits such a pretension should have been set up by him: and assuredly in accordance with the saying, ' *Verily man becometh insolent because he seeth himself to abound in riches,*[3] one who beholds his hand unrestrained in command and prohibition, and finds the reins for slackening or compressing state affairs in the grasp of his own power, will have eggs deposited in the nest of the brain by the imp of mischief, and the tempest of rebellion will break forth from the blackness of his heart.

VERSE.

Whom fortune raises from profound distress,
Exalts, lifts to the summit of success.
'Twere strange if he should kingly aims forego,
Nor cast his lasso o'er the struggling foe.

---

[1] Lit.: 'pure disposition and legitimacy.'

[2] Lit.: 'The one of two.' I know of no English equivalent to *ṣání iṣnain*.

[3] Ḳur'án, ch. xcvi. 6; Sale, p. 448, l. 10: 'Read, by thy most beneficent Lord, who taught the use of the pen; who teacheth man that which he knoweth not. Assuredly. Verily man becometh insolent because he seeth himself abound in riches. Verily unto thy hand shall be the return of all.' In this quotation Abú Jahl is referred to, as all commentators agree.

The Lion said, 'O Damnah! ponder well what words these are which thou speakest. Whence hast thou learnt these circumstances? and if it be as thy words import, what measures can be adopted in relation to this affair?' Damnah replied, 'The loftiness of his rank, and the elevation of his position, is well known to the king, and when a sovereign beholds one of his servants vieing with himself in rank, dignity, wealth and pomp, he should speedily away with him, otherwise the affair will become impracticable, and the king will be overthrown, and as to a remedy for this matter, in such-wise as the enlightened soul of the king requires, how can our dull mind, and deficient intelligence arrive at it? But I know this much, that preventive measures should be promptly adopted in the case of the Ox, and that if your majesty deliberates, it is possible the affair may come to that point, that the step of counsel will be unequal to the extent of its measurement.

STANZA.

Thy foe was but an ant, a serpent now is he!
Then on this snake-turned ant take vengeance now.
For soon this serpent will a mighty dragon be,
If thou delay, and him to live allow.

And they have said that men are of two classes, the man of caution, and the weak man. The weak man is he who, at the time of the occurrence of an event, and the event of an occurrence, is confounded and distracted, and irresolute and perplexed; and the man of caution is he who, making use of foresight, considers the issues of affairs; and the man of caution is also of two kinds. The first is he who, before the appearance of danger has already thoroughly appreciated its character, and who, in the beginning of an affair, by the eye of understanding, discerns what others discover at the termination, and who consults for the issue of things at their commencement.

HEMISTICH.

Deliberation first and action last.

And such a person, before falling into the whirlpool of calamity, will be able to convey himself to the shore of safety, and him they call 'most cautious.' And the other is he, who, when calamity arrives, maintains an unshaken heart, and does not allow himself to be penetrated by dismay and terror, and doubtless from such a person the right road and advisable course will not remain concealed, and him they call 'cautious.' And with reference to the state of these three persons, of whom one is wise, and the second half-wise, and the third ignorant—the story of those Three Fishes is applicable, who chanced to be together in a pond.' The Lion asked, 'How befell that?'

K

STORY XV.

Damnah said, 'They have related that there was a pool of water at a distance from the highway, and hidden from the notice of travelers, and its retired waters were pure like the faith of the spiritual, and its appearance such as to suffice those who were in search of the water of life, and this lake communicated with a running stream. In it abode three large fishes, such that the celestial fish,[1] through envy of them, was broiled on the frying-pan of jealousy, like Aries by the heat of the sun. And one of those three fishes was Very Cautious, and the second Cautious, and the other Helpless. Suddenly, in the season of spring, when the world, from the adornment of its flower-gardens, was like the garden of paradise, and all parts of earth's surface, from its bright and sweet-scented plants, resembled the azure vault full of stars; when the chamberlain, the morning breeze, had adorned earth's floor with many-hued carpets, and the peerless gardener of creation had ornamented the world with flowers of divers colors,

VERSE.

Morn's[2] musk-diffusing breeze the garden fanned :
White as the loved one's cheek, the jasmine pale
Hung graceful—and like mistress, smiling bland,
Bending propitious to the lover's tale—
To the young breeze roses their hues unveil.

All at once, two or three fishermen happened to pass by that water, and by the will of God they discovered the circumstances of the abode of those three fishes in that lake, exactly as things really were. Having agreed therefore on a rendezvous with one another, they hastened to bring their nets, and the fishes, having gained intelligence of that circumstance, immersed as they were in water were, nevertheless, made to consort with the fire of anguish. When night drew on, the fish that was perfectly wise and possessed extreme caution, inasmuch as he had often witnessed the violence of oppressive fortune, and the petulance of the faithless heavens, and as his foot was planted firmly on the carpet of experience, began to reflect on the means of escape from the net of the fishermen, and to ponder on deliverance from their bonds.

VERSE.

Own him as prudent and as throughly wise,
Who founds his actions on a base secure.
But in whose caution aught defective lies,
His ground of action is most weak, be sure.

He therefore adopted expeditious measures, and before even consulting with

---

[1] Alias the sign Pisces.
[2] I have slightly amplified these verses. In Keene's translation, doubtless from a typographical error, we read : 'The garden was loaded with musk by the breeze of the *moon!*'

his friends, made his exit on the side adjacent to the flowing stream. In the morning the fishermen came and firmly secured both sides of the lake. Then the half-wise fish, who was adorned with the ornament of good sense, but who possessed no share of the stores of experience, when he beheld this state of things, felt much contrition, and said, ' I have chosen to be negligent, and the termination of the affairs of the supine is like the present. It behoved me, like that other fish, before the descent of calamity, to have taken thought for myself, and previous to the assault of misfortune to have pondered the way to escape.

COUPLET.

> Think of the cure before the thing occurs,
> He grieves in vain who till 'tis past defers.

Now since the opportunity of flight is gone, it is the time for stratagem and artifice, and although they have said that deliberation during the time of disaster yields but little advantage, and but small fruition is derivable from the produce of good sense in the period of calamity; still, notwith-standing all this, it behoves a wise man in no way to despair of the benefits of wisdom, nor to allow of delay or tardiness in repelling the devices of an enemy. He then made himself appear dead, and went floating on the surface of the water. One of the fishermen picked him up, and fancying him to be dead, threw him on the ground; and he, craftily flinging himself into a rivulet, preserved his life.

COUPLET.

> Die, friend! if thou enfranchisement wouldst gain,
> Undying, thou canst not thy friend obtain.

And the other fish in whose proceedings supineness prevailed, and in whose actions imbecility was apparent, darted about right and left, astounded and bewildered and fatuous, and, trying to escape, rushed to the surface and to the bottom,[1] until at last he was captured. And by considering this story, the prince may be convinced that measures should be speedily taken with reference to Shanzabah; and before opportunity and power expire, he should strike the fire of regret into the soul of that miscreant, with a high-tempered sword; and having given the harvest of his life to the winds of destruction, raise up the smoke of affliction[2] from his family to the sky.

COUPLET.

> Hast thou the mastery o'er thy treacherous foe,
> His brains then shatter with the stone of woe.'

The Lion said, ' I understand what thou hast spoken, but I have no suspicion that Shanzabah meditates any treason, and will allow himself to

---

[1] Keene seems to have had a different reading, as he translates, ' and kept looking to the surface and to the bottom.'

[2] *Dúd* signifies the ' breath of anguish,' as well as ' smoke.'

requite past favors by subsequent ingratitude, for up to this period I have indulged in nothing but goodness and kindness towards him.' Damnah responded, 'Exactly so, but by these bounties of the King he has reached his present elevation.

COUPLET.

At thy free will to smite, select the spot,
Since thou wilt salve the wound—it matters not.

A worthless fellow naturally bad, will be a sincere and loyal adviser so long as he has not reached the station which he hopes to gain, but when his wish is accomplished, ambition to obtain further advancement—which befits him not —will shew itself from the store-house of his thoughts: and the wise have said [1] that the service of the mean and ignoble is based on the canon of fear and hope. When once he is secure from the intrusions of. fear, he darkens the fountain of his loyalty, and when he has been rendered independent by the attainment of his object, he kindles the fire of ingratitude and mischief.' The Lion said, 'How then ought we to treat servants of a base disposition and sordid mind, in order that the traces of their ingratitude may not be evinced?' Damnah replied, 'You ought not to exclude them from your favors to such a degree that they should suddenly despond, and, abandoning your service, affect the side of your enemies; nor ought you so to bestow on them favors and wealth, that, having reached the zenith of. success, extravagant fancies may develop themselves in them. But rather they ought to pass their life always between hope and fear, and their course of action should be perpetually governed by promises and threats, and dread and expectation; since opulence and immunity make them self-sufficient, and that becomes a cause of rebellion and guilt; and [on the other hand] despair and destitution render menials bold, and hence arises injury to the royal power.

COUPLET.

Despair makes man audacious—insolent:
O friend! my desperation then prevent.'

The Lion said, 'To my mind it seems that the mirror of Shanzabah's condition, is pure from the stain of this deceit, and the page of his heart clear and unsullied by the character of these thoughts; and I have always been in the position of benefactor towards him, and have continuously associated his career with indulgence, and after an undeviating course of kindness and favor to him from me, how could he devise evil and mischief in return?

COUPLET.

My heart affection's flag for him displays,
Why should he then a hostile banner raise?'

---

[1] I have generally translated *buzurgán* 'the wise,' and Keene still more invariably renders 'the ancients.' The word may, I think, have either meaning.

Damnah said, ' The king must understand that straightforward conduct never proceeds from a crooked nature, and that one of an evil disposition and a bad stock, neither by the efforts of others nor self-exertion, will become of a praiseworthy character or pure, for ' *Every vessel allows that to percolate which is in it.*'

HEMISTICH.

That from the jar exudes which is within.

But perhaps the story of the Scorpion and the Tortoise may not have reached the august hearing of your majesty ? ' The Lion asked, ' How was that ? '

STORY XVI.

Damnah said, ' A Tortoise had a friendship with a Scorpion, and they always reciprocated the breathings of attachment, and practised unanimity.

COUPLET.

From morn till eve allies, associates they;

Companions, friends—till night gave place to day.

Once on a time it so happened that in obedience to an exigency, they were compelled to migrate from their country, and in companionship with one another, sought a more secure abode. By chance their way lay across a mighty stream, and a vast river intercepted their passage, and as it was impossible for the Scorpion to cross water, he remained aghast. The Tortoise said, ' Dear friend! what has come to thee that thou hast given the collar of the robe of life into the hand of grief, and snatched the skirt of thy heart from gladness and mirth ? ' The Scorpion replied, ' O brother! anxiety how to pass this water hast cast me into the whirlpool of dismay. It is neither possible to cross the water, nor can the separation from my friend be endured.

COUPLET.

Thou goest on, and I alone all sorrowful am left :

Strange that I tarry and survive at all of thee bereft!

The Tortoise said, ' Do not distress thyself, for I will convey thee without inconvenience across the water and bring thee to the shore; and making a vessel of my back will shield thee from calamity with my breast, for it would be a pity to gain a friend with difficulty, and let him slip with indifference.'

COUPLET.

Go! and with all thou hast a friend secure,

And let not aught to sell him thee allure.

Then the Tortoise having taken the Scorpion on his back, breasted the water, and set off. In the middle of the swim a sound reached the ear of the Tortoise and he perceived a tapping made by the Scorpion.[1] He asked, ' What

---

[1] With deference to Káshifí, this is impossible. The scorpion's sting is so placed that it can sting nothing below itself.

noise is this that I hear? and what operation is this in which thou art
employing thyself?' The Scorpion replied, 'I am trying the sharp point of
my sting against the armour of thy body.'[1] The Tortoise was thunder-struck,
and exclaimed, 'O unfeeling wretch! I, for thy sake, have cast my life into
the whirlpool of danger, and by the aid of the barque of my back thou art
crossing this water; if thou dost not feel obliged for the favor, and allowest
no weight to our old companionship, what at least is the reason for stinging,
when moreover it is positively certain that no injury will reach me from this
action, and that thy heart-lacerating sting will have no effect upon my
marble-like back?

COUPLET.

'Tis like that he his hands and heart will pang,
Who in blind anger strives a wall to bang.'

The Scorpion answered, 'God forbid that sentiments like these should
approach my mind in the whole course of my life or should have ever done
so! It is nothing more than this, that my nature instigates me to sting,
whether I wound the back of a friend or the breast of a foe.

STANZA.

He that becomes inured to doing ill,	His bent will show itself against his will.
The scorpion powerless against a stone,	Will make e'en there his stinging habit known.'

The tortoise reflected thus, 'Truly have the sages said that to cherish a base
character is to give one's own honor to the wind, and to involve one's own
self in embarrassment.[2]

COUPLET.

We may not grudge perhaps to strew the mire with gems and gold,
But from the base our kindness we and favour should withhold.

It is a saying of the ancients, that hope has no portion in the man who has
no nobility in his descent, since it would be inadmissible for the scion of a
corrupt stock to leave the world without requiting with evil the parties who
have benefited him.

STANZA.

How can one base by nature be instructed? Why
Foster a serpent in one's house? No pains nor care
Will the cane's flavour to harsh colocynth supply:
Who sows the thorn will not reap roses there.

And by citing this story, it will have crossed the enlightened mind of the
king, that Shanzabah's lack of noble descent, and the baseness of his nature,
ought to cause him apprehension, and that he ought to listen with the ear of
attention to the advice of his attached dependants. Whoever gives no heed to
the words of councillors, though they be harsh and undeferential, the issue of
his transactions, and the termination of his affairs, will not be devoid of

---

[1] Keene reads for *jaushan-i wujúd-i tú* 'the armour of thy body,' *jaushan wa khúd-i tú,*
'on thy armour and helmet,' which is also a good reading.

[2] Lit.: 'to lose the clue of one's own affairs.'

regret and reproach: as when an invalid looks contemptuously on the directions of the physician, and eats and drinks according to his inclination, most certainly weakness and debility will every moment prevail more and more over him.

COUPLET.

What harm, though stern and rough thy Mentor's tongue;
To bitter patience[1] sweetest fruits belong.

And it must be understood that the weakest of princes is he who is careless of the issues of affairs, and who despises the concerns of the kingdom, and, whenever an event of importance occurs, lays aside caution and circumspection, and after opportunity has expired, and the enemy has got the mastery, casts suspicion on those about him, and imputes[2] to them indiscriminately the then state of things.

QUATRAIN.

Why to another's care consign
Schemes that thine own exertions claim ?
And when thou hast been thus supine,
Why on another hang the blame ?'

The Lion said, 'Right roughly hast thou spoken and hast overstepped the limits of respect, yet the words of a councillor should not be rejected because they are harsh. On the supposition that Shanzabah be my enemy, the extent of his power is clear enough, and in point of fact, he is my food, and his material energies[3] derive their existence from herbs, while the support of my strength is drawn from flesh, and vegetable natures are always subdued by animal, and I do not make such account of him as to suppose that the thought of encountering me would pass through his mind, or that the insane idea of slaying me should find place in his heart's core.'[4]

COUPLET.

When shall a foeman boast of waging war with one like me ?
Shall fierce elephants matched in contest with weak midges be ?

And if Shanzabah should pretend, like the moon, to rival the sun of my splendour, which shines from the horizon of the divine favor, he will wane and fail; and if, like the sun, he array[5] himself against the crescent on my august and phœnix-like canopy, which is a symbol of that of heaven, he will in the end sink.'

---

[1] There is a favourite pun here on the word *sabr*, which means 'patience,' and also 'bitter aloes.'

[2] I fear this sense can hardly be given to *hawálah kunad*, but were it possible, it would suit what precedes better than 'delegates the matter to any one of them,' as that were hardly practicable after the foe had got the mastery.

[3] *Harakat* means also 'motion,' conduct.'

[4] *Suwaidá* is the diminutive of '*saudá* and signifies, 'coriander seed,' 'any little black seed or pip,'—hence, as it were 'the seed of the heart,' or ' the heart's core.'

[5] I have made a weak attempt to preserve the equivoque here. *Tígh* signifies 'ray,' as well as 'sword.' The word *máhíchah*, the diminutive of 'moon,' has been omitted from the Persian Dictionary, but *máhchah* is given.

VERSE.

The empty-handed, who would imitate
The rich, is like a limping palfrey, whose
Pace affects an amble. I made him great,
And I, too, can soon o'er him cast the noose.[1]

Damnah said, 'The king should not be misled by what he says as to
Shanzabah's being his food, or that he is able to overcome him, since, although,
in his own person, he may not have power for the encounter, he may by the
aid of a number of his allies advance towards his object, or by dissimulation
and fraud, and lying tales, and perfidy, excite mischievous delusions;[2] and
I fear lest when he has implanted in the beasts a zeal of opposition to the
king, they may act in unison with him, and a single person, however strong-
bodied and powerful he may be, cannot make head against many.

STANZA.

Gnats will an elephant o'ercome, if they
Unite against their foe so huge and grim.
And ants collected in one dense array,
Though fierce the lion be, will vanquish him.[3]

The Lion said, 'Thy words have made an impression on my heart, and I
perceive the sincerity of thy advice, but nevertheless this person is [in the
sacred character of] a suppliant[4] to me, for I have raised him up, and it is I
who have set up the banner of his power and advancement, and have
uttered encomiums of him in assemblies and meetings, and have poured from
my tongue statements of his intelligence, and loyalty, and sincerity, and
uprightness. If then I allow myself to declare the contrary of this, I shall be
charged with breaking my word, and personal levity, and weakness of
judgment, and all hearts will hold my words in reprobation, and all minds
disregard my promises.'

COUPLET.

The head thou didst with glory crown,   Whilst thou art able cast not down.

Damnah replied, 'Right judgment and prudence lies in withdrawing one's
business and plucking the skirt of friendship and companionship from a
friend the instant he shews signs of enmity, and from a servant as soon as he
displays the airs of a prince, and before an enemy can find opportunity for
breakfast, to have his supper ready for him; and though a tooth be man's old

---

[1] Lit.: 'I made that quarry proudly raise the head; I can again cast the lasso on his
neck.'

[2] Lit.: 'May raise up figures.' The phrase *nakshhá bar angíkhtan* deserves an explanation in the Dictionary.

[3] This stanza occurs in the third book of the Gulistán, p. 187 of my translation and
p. 124 of the Persian text, where for *mardí*, lit. 'manliness,' we find the much better
reading *tundí*, 'fury,' and for *ba dar drand* the inaccurate *ba-ddrand*, which with *púst* is
rendered 'vanquish,' but is rather 'flay.'

[4] Lit.: 'Skirt-holder.' Keene's version is, 'but then this idea clings to me, that I have
raised him.' But *súrat*, I imagine, is better rendered 'person' than 'idea.'

comrade, and a source of various benefits and advantages to him, when it begins to ache he can find no cure for the torment of it, save by extraction; and food which supplies the waste[1] [of our corporeal frame], and is the support of the material of life, after it has become corrupt in the belly, must be expelled in order that one may be quit of its injurious effects.

COUPLET.

He who to thy afflicted heart no gladness now supplies,
Forsake him, though thou, as thy life, didst him once love and prize.'

The insidious whispers of Damnah having made an impression on the Lion, he said, 'I am disgusted with the society of Shanzabah, and for me to meet him again is of the number of impossibilities. The best way is to send some one to him and declare to him how matters stand, and give him permission to go where he likes.' Damnah was afraid that if these words should reach Shanzabah, he would presently make known to the Lion his letters of indemnity,[2] and that his (Damnah's) deceit and artifice would come from the hidden chamber of concealment into the expanse of manifestation. He said [therefore], 'O king! this method is far from prudent, and so long as a word has not been spoken there is room for option left, but after declaration, the remedy has gone beyond the confines of ability.

COUPLET.

Thou canst the unsaid or say, or else abstain,   Once spoken no concealment will remain.

The word which has issued from the mouth, and the arrow from the bow, return not, either the one to the option,[3] or the other to the string;[4] and it has passed into a proverb, that whatever comes to the lip may prove a slip,[5] and, a sage has said, 'The tongue is the interpreter of the heart, and the heart the ruler of the dominion of the body, and speech is the displayer of the jewels of existence.' As long as the door of the casket of speech is fastened with the bolt of silence, and the seal of taciturnity is placed on the lid of the repertory of discourse, all the sweet herbs in the garden of life grow safely, and the young tree of existence yields all the fruit of security and enjoyment; but, when the rose-bud of eloquence unfolds its smiles, and the nightingale of oratory begins to warble, one cannot be safe, for the perfume of the rose-garden of language will be the source of gladness to the heart, and invigoration to the brain, or the cause of the display of the material[6] of the defluxion

---

[1] *Má yataḥallal*, 'that which is loosened or dissolved,' aorist of *taḥallul*, 5th conj. of *ḥall*.

[2] Keene translates 'he would instantly make his innocence and gratitude clear,' whence I suspect his reading must have been a different one from that in the text—*bardt-i ẓimmat-i khúd bar shir rúshan sdzad.*

[3] Lit.: 'To the hand.'

[4] Lit.: 'Thumb-stall.' Keene renders the word *shast* 'aiming-point.'

[5] There is an equivoque here, which I have tried to retain in English; it is 'Whatever comes to the *(zabán)* 'tongue,' comes to *(ziyán)* 'loss.'

[6] This verbiage goes beyond the limits of even Persian endurance. One MS. omits '*illat* but I would rather dispense with *ẓuhúr*, or *máddah* or both.

of the brain and the occasion of megrims; for tongues which had been bound, have by one approved and clever speech solved many difficult knots; and mischievous words have by a single inopportune allusion, bound the neck of the speaker with heavy chains.

STANZA.

If language with the eye of sense you scan,
Its stuff combines a blessing and a ban:
Yes! for the meed of wit unspoke before,
May make an outcast or to life restore; [1]
And oft the utterance of a word—though slight—
Has crushed the speaker in eternal night.' [2]

O king! if these words should reach Shanzabah, and he should discover the nature of his situation and ascertain his disgrace, it is possible that he may attempt to resist, and begin to fight or excite rebellion: and masters of prudence have not thought secret punishment suitable for a public offence, nor assigned public punishment to secret crimes. The advisable course is to meet his concealed offence with a hidden retribution.' The Lion said, 'To banish and remove my intimates on mere suspicion, and, without a palpable certainty, to endeavour to ignore all their claims, is with one's own hand to strike an axe against one's own foot, and to turn suddenly aside from the path of generous conduct and the road of good faith.

STANZA.

Nor law, nor reason, could to this agree,
That without proof, kings should their judgment give;
For their high mandate, like heaven's own decree,
Now snatches life away—now grants to live.'

Damnah replied, 'There is no evidence that rulers can have better than their own discernment. When this perfidious traitor approaches, let the king cast a scrutinizing glance upon him, and the foulness of his principles will be exhibited in his graceless visage, and the deformity of his purpose in his repulsive appearance, and the crookedness of his heart will be shewn by his changing color,[3] and his emotion as he advances, and by his looking to the left and right, and before and behind him, and by his being prepared for a struggle and collected for an encounter.' The Lion said, 'Thou hast well said, and if any of these signs be observable, of course the dust of doubt will be removed from the path of certainty, and the anxiety of suspicion will be changed for a state of absolute conviction.' When Damnah perceived that

---

[1] Keene translates, 'and the proof to be given is this, that a witty thing, not said before, may distress a man by vexation of heart, or give him life.' In the next sentence he renders *kamín* 'the ambush,' but I take it as an adjective agreeing with *lafzi*.

[2] Lit.: 'Gives the speaker to the wind, the instant that he utters it.'

[3] 'Changing colour' is certainly very inapplicable to an ox. This is the absurdity of an apologue, which, after all, seems to me a most unnatural and unnecessary invention.

by his mischief-exciting insinuations, the fire of calamity had begun to blaze on that side, he wished to see the Ox, and on his part, too, to kindle the flame of disastrous results.

COUPLET.

Like fire is strife betwixt two enemies,   The luckless mischief-maker wood supplies.[1]

He bethought himself that his interview with Shanzabah ought also to spring from the Lion's suggestion and advice, that he might avoid suspicion. He said [therefore], 'O king! if the high command obtains the honor of being issued, I will see Shanzabah, and having ascertained somewhat of the secrets of his mind and of his hoarded intentions, I will respectfully state it.' The Lion gave his permission, and Damnah approached Shanzabah like one grief-stricken and visited by calamity, and performed the required salutations and compliments. Shanzabah, after shewing him suitable respect, thus, with courtesy and affection, addressed him; 'O Damnah!

HEMISTICH.

Bethink thee ever thou forgettest me!

It is many days since thou hast enlightened the eyes of thy intimates with the rays of thy beauty, or converted the cottage of thy friends into a rose-garden with the flowers of the plants of social and kindly intercourse.

COUPLET.

Through ages thou—one moment e'en—thy friend recallest not,
Yet not one moment is by him the thought of thee forgot.'

Damnah said, 'Though personally I have been excluded from the honor of an interview, yet in thought and spirit I have constantly kept company with the idea of thy heart-enlivening beauty, and have unceasingly sown the seed of friendship and affection in the ground of the heart.

COUPLET.

To thee my soul! I from my heart have secret windows made,
Unknown to thee, and yet with thee, full oft in love I've played.

And in the cell of retirement and the corner of solitude, I have been engaged in the daily duties of prayer and praise, which may be to thee the cause of increasing fortune; and I shall continue so occupied.' The Ox said, 'What is the cause of this retirement?' Damnah replied, 'When a person cannot be master of his own will, and is captive to the authority of another, and draws not a single breath without fear and danger, and does not pass a moment without dread and trembling for his life and body, and when he cannot utter a word without terror and alarm, wherefore not choose the corner of his cot and close the door in retirement against both stranger and acquaintance?

---

[1] These lines occur in the eighth chapter of the Gulistán, p. 267, l. 15 cf my translation.

QUATRAIN.

From the mischief of this troublous [false and fickle] world [of pain],
Up, [my friend!] and some asylum—where thou canst it find—obtain ;
But if thou no foot to flee hast, then at least thy hand extend!
Grasp the skirt of safe retirement [and there let thy sorrow end].'

The Ox answered, 'O Damnah! develope thy statement more clearly,
and explain, in detail, the matter to which thou hast briefly alluded, in order
that the advantage of thy counsels may be more general, and the benefit of
thy discourse more complete.' Damnah responded, 'Six things in this world
are impossible without six things, viz. :—worldly wealth without pride, and[1]
the pursuit of the objects of desire without difficulty, and to sit with women
without calamity, and to expect[2] aught from the sordid without disgrace,
and association with the wicked without regret, and attendance on kings
without misfortune. To no one do they give a draught from the wine-cellar
of the world, but he becomes intoxicated and presumptuous, and raises up the
head of rebellion from the collar of contumacy and pride. And no one
moves a step in pursuit of lust that he does not fall into a state of ruin ; and
no man sits with women but he becomes calamitously involved in a variety
of mischievous results ; and no person enters into friendship with wicked
and depraved men, but eventually loads himself with remorse ; and no one
applies to mean and low people who does not become contemptible and
dishonored ; and not an individual chooses to attend on princes without
finding it impossible to escape from that cruel vortex.

VERSE.

Wouldst thou judge right of princes' company?
Then view it as a vast and shoreless sea.
To such an ocean full of risk and fear,
Most wretched aye the man that is most near.

And on the same subject they have said,

COUPLET.

Upon the sea 'tis true is boundless gain
Wouldst thou be safe?—upon the shore remain.'[3]

Shanzabah said, 'Thy words indicate that thou hast met with something
offensive from the Lion, and that thou art overcome with dread and alarm of
his terrors.' Damnah replied, 'I do not speak these words with reference to
my own person, nor am I distressed on my own account, but I am thinking
more of my friends than of myself in this matter, and this grief and chagrin

---

[1] Keene appears to have taken *mutdba'at* out of its proper place. He renders the passage
'worldly wealth without pride and subserviency,' but this makes but indifferent sense, and
destroys the equality of the sentences which are demarcated by the *wa*. I read *wa
mutdba'at-i hawd* as one sentence.

[2] Keene translates *tam'a ba laimán*, 'a desire for indulgence,' or perhaps he read the
passage differently, for *laim* signifies 'sordid,' 'base,'

[3] Those lines occur in the Gulistán, ch. i., story xvi., p. 63, of my translation.

which has overwhelmed me is for thy sake, and thou knowest how the antecedents of friendship and early ties of attachment have existed between us, and the promises and compacts which we formed at the first, and which during this interval have been mainly fulfilled with good faith; and I have no alternative but to convey to thee information of whatever may have occurred, whether good or bad, beneficial or injurious.' Shanzabah quaked inwardly, and rejoined, ' O kind comrade and sympathising friend! acquaint me, with all speed, as to the true state of the case, and fail in no particular of the minutiæ of kind feeling and attachment.' Damnah answered, ' I have heard from an authentic source, that the Lion has spoken with his august tongue to this effect, 'Shanzabah has become excessively fat, and he is not wanted at this court, and it is no matter whether he be absent or present. I shall give an entertainment to the beasts with his flesh, and I will make of his body, one day, the royal repast and a banquet for the public.' I, when I heard this speech—being aware of his violence and injustice—came hither, that, having warned thee, I might establish the goodness of my faith by a clear proof, and might fulfil what is incumbent on me by the law of honor and the rules of right feeling and generosity.

COUPLET.

I tell thee all that he who sent me bade,
Whether my words thee warn or make thee sad.

At present it appears to me that thy advisable course is to devise a plan, and with the utmost expedition to turn thy attention to the preparation of some expedient, and the encountering this crisis; if peradventure, a means of escape from this vortex should appear, and by some ingenious device salvation from this peril be attainable.' When Shanzabah had heard the words of Damnah, and resolved in his mind the promises and covenants of the Lion, he said, ' O Damnah! It is impossible that the Lion should play me false, and now moreover I have displayed no perfidy, and my firm step has not slipped from the path of true service, and again I have a belief of the sincerity of thy words, and an opinion of thy good intentions. The conclusion is therefore that [some parties] have concocted falsehoods against me, and by imposture and deceit have moved the Lion to wrath, and in his service there is a faction of worthless persons all profound masters of slander, and bold and audacious in treason and violence, and them he has oft proved, and has observed a variety of treacherous acts and foul deeds, and of course whatever they say, on that head, of others he believes and judges accordingly, and assuredly through the evil influence of the society of the wicked, evil suspicions arise with regard to the good, and by these groundless doubts the right course becomes concealed, and the story of the Goose and his false impressions from experience, is a proof of what I have said quite sufficient, and bears ample testimony to this state of things.' Damnah inquired, ' How was that?'

STORY XVII.

Shanzabah said, 'A Goose saw the brightness of the moon in the water, and, thinking that it was the moon, tried to lay hold of it, but got nothing. Several times it made a similar effort, and when it saw that all it got by the chace was what the man athirst gets by gazing on the mirage, or what the deluded destitute obtains by searching through ruined habitations [for treasures], it altogether abandoned the pursuit of fish, and all at once discontinued its occupation. The next night, whenever it saw a fish, it fancied it was the glitter of the moon, and made no effort after it, and gave no heed whatever to it, and exclaimed,

HEMISTICH.

Who tries the tried—on him will fall regret.[1]

So the fruit of his experience was this, that he continued hungry and passed his time fasting and foodless.

And if they have made the Lion listen to anything about me, and, in accordance with the saying, '*he who listens is alienated*,' a feeling of aversion has arisen in his heart, and he has given credit to what has been said, the cause of all this has been that same experience which he has had of others; and yet in point of reality, there is as much difference between me and the rest, as between bright day and dark night, and the vault of heaven and earth's centre.

DISTICHS.

Think not the virtuous and thyself the same;
Shír has two meanings with a single name.[2]
In the same meadow feed two wasp-like things,
Yet one gives honey, and the other stings.
Together graze two deer, from one proceeds
Pure fragrant musk, the other simply bleeds.'

Damnah said, 'Perhaps the aversion of the lion may not spring from this cause, but on account of its being a custom with kings to promote a person to high rank, undeserved on his part, while without any apparent reason they make another, who is a man of worth, the object of ruinous spoliation.'

---

[1] That is,—' Who attempts to do a thing after decided failures, will only meet with disappointment.'

[2] *Shír* signifies 'milk' and 'lion,' and is pronounced, as is evident by this line, in both cases, identically, and not, as some pretend, with the *m'arúf* sound of the vowel in the former case, and the *majhúl* in the latter.

VERSE.

Hurmúz,[1] thy king unsung on me unseen rich gifts[2] bestowed!
While Yazd's[3] proud chief though seen and sung gave not the guerdon owed.
Such is the wont of kings! but thou, O Ḥáfiẓ![4] murmur not,
All-giving God! thy favouring grace and aid be still their[5] lot.

Shanzabah said, 'If this aversion on the part of the Lion, which thou hast reported to me, is without cause, then no submission will enable me to step securely into the path[6] of safety: and it is impossible for the eye of hope to behold the face of the desired object, for if there be a reason for wrath it may be dispelled by attempts to please and by apologies; but if, which God avert![7] there be no reason for it, or if they have affected a change in his mind by deceit and calumny, the hand of remedy will be too short for it, and the thought of compassing its cure will be hopeless; since there is no visible measure to falsehood and slander, and no fixed limit to deceit and artifice. Now in what has passed between me and the Lion, I do not perceive any fault on my part, save that occasionally, and that too for his own good, I have opposed his opinion and plans, and that now and then, as exigency required, I have spoken with reference to the arrangements and furtherance of important matters, not in accordance with what he wished. This, perhaps, he may have imputed to boldness and disrespect, and have reckoned it akin to audacity and imprudence; yet not one of those things which I have originated has been immaterial with reference to the public weal; and with all this I have preserved the respect due to his exalted rank and majesty, without, through the whole course of my career, shewing presumption; but have to the utmost degree possible displayed the reverence and veneration due to him;

---

[1] Hurmúz, or, according to European pronunciation, Ormúz, was a city in the Persian Gulf, the capital of Kermán, and of great antiquity. It was ruined by the Seljuks, and a new town of the same name built on an island in the Persian Gulf, which was held some time by the Portuguese.

[2] Lit. : 'A hundred favors or kindnesses.'

[3] Yazd is the most eastern city of the province of Fárs, or Persia Proper, as Hamadán is the most western. It lies in 89 deg. E. Lon., and 32 deg. N. Lat. It is the chief residence of the Fire-worshipers who still remain in Persia.

[4] Muḥammad Shams-u'd-dín, surnamed Ḥáfiẓ, is the Anacreon of Persia, though a divine mysticism is claimed for him by many who assert that, in his poems, wine and love are the symbols of holy ecstacies. Ḥáfiẓ was born at Shíráz, in the reign of the Muzaffirian dynasty, and died A.H. 797. It is said that Tímúrlang, who had conquered Persia, reproached him with the slighting way in which he had spoken of his capital Samarkand; as in the celebrated Ode :

> Maid of Shíráz! if thou wouldst take
> My heart, nor on the offering frown;
> I'd give up, for thy dark mole's sake,
> Búkhárá and its royal town.

And that Ḥáfiẓ replied so wittily as to disarm the monarch's anger.

[5] I prefer taking shán, as referring to those kings for whom Ḥáfiẓ says he will pray, whether liberal or illiberal, rather than to suppose with Keene that the prayer is for all to whom God is rúzí rasán.

[6] Lit: 'By no offerings will the foot of stability be able to measure the path of uprightness.'. The dast aváizi signifies, 'the offering of presents to a superior by an inferior.'

[7] Lit.: 'By flying for refuge to God.'

so how can it possibly be supposed that loyal advice could be viewed as a cause for distrust, and faithful service as a ground for enmity?

COUPLET.

> Canst thou hope that where the medicine brings a fresh access of pain,
> There the illness will grow lighter, and the sick revive again?

And if this too be not the case, it is possible that the pride of royalty and the haughtiness of empire, may cause him to be offended with me, for it is a necessary condition of dominion, and a requisite of greatness, to be naturally ungrateful to those who give advice, and to bestow confidence and distinguished notice on sycophants and flatterers; and hence it is that the wise have said that it is more safe to dive to the bottom of a river with a crocodile, and to suck the poisonous drops from the lip of a serpent, whose tail has been struck off, than to attend upon kings, and that it is better and more conducive to security and freedom from anxiety, than to be in close proximity to princes: and I was aware that the perils of serving princes, were numerous, and the harm of superintending their affairs immense.   Some philosophers also have compared kings to fire, since, although, the beams of their favor illuminate the dark cell of the hopeful, nevertheless the flame[1] of their severity too consumes the harvest of the former claims of their servants; and sound reason avers that whoever is nearest the fire suffers most; but parties, who, admiring the brightness of the fire at a distance, are ignorant of its power to burn, hold an idea of some intense gratification in having access to princes, and suppose it to be beneficial; while in point of fact, it is not so, for if they were to get a taste of the rigor of kings, and of the terror and awe a monarch inspires, it would be clear to them that a thousand years of favor are not equivalent to one hour of torture, and the story of the dispute of the Hawk with the Domestic Fowl verifies this.   Damnah inquired, 'How was that?'

STORY XVIII.

Shanzabah said, 'Once on a time a Hunting Falcon engaged in a dispute with a Domestic Fowl, and, beginning to wrangle with it, said, 'Thou art a most false and faithless bird! and yet fidelity is the frontispiece of the page of commendable qualities, and moreover, in accordance with the import of this saying, ' *Verily, fidelity is a part of faith,*' fidelity is a perfect proof of right religious feeling and generosity; and honor, too, demands that none stigmatize the pages of his career with the character of unfaithfulness.

COUPLET.

A dog is thankful for his morsel—then   A dog is better than unthankful men.'

The Domestic Fowl replied, 'What ingratitude hast though seen in me?

As *pddshdhán* has preceded, *mí-sázad* in the singular appears objectionable.   I therefore greatly prefer the reading of one MS. *va sh'ulah-i siydsat,* instead of *valí bi-sh'ulah ;* according to which ' the flame' becomes the nominative.

and what unfaithfulness hast thou observed on my part?' The Hawk replied: 'The sign of thy ingratitude is this, that notwithstanding men shew so much kindness towards thee, and without any inconvenience or trouble on thy part, prepare for thee water and grain, from which the vital energy derives support, and looking after thee day and night, are constant in protecting and guarding thee, and that thou owest to them thy food and lodging; still, whenever they want to catch thee, thou runnest before and behind them, and fliest from roof to roof, and hurriest from corner to corner.

COUPLET.

Thou dost of salt the sacred sanction slight,   And shun'st thy patron in ungrateful flight.

And I, although I am a wild bird, and associate with men but for two or three days, and eat from their hands [for so short a time],[1] still keep in view what I owe to them, and hunt and give them the quarry : and however far I may have gone, at the slightest call that I hear, I come flying back.'

COUPLET.

Far though the well-trained bird one launches, still
He back with joyous pinion hastes at will.

The Hen answered, 'Thou sayest the truth. Thy returning and my flight is owing to this, that thou hast never seen a hawk roasted on a spit, and I have seen many domestic fowls frying in a frying-pan. Hadst thou been accustomed to see this spectacle thou wouldst never flutter about with them, and if I fly from roof to roof, thou wouldst fly from mountain to mountain.' And I have introduced this story in order that thou mayst know that the class who seek the company of princes have no knowledge of their severity, for whoever has experienced the effect of their rigor has no acquaintance with repose, nor any feeling of rest.

COUPLET.

Propinquity the greater terror brings: The near know best the cruelty of kings.'

Damnah said, 'It cannot surely be that the Lion entertains these thoughts with regard to thee on account of the grandeur of his imperial sway and the pride of success, for thou possessest many accomplishments and numberless excellencies, and princes are never independent of persons of talent.' Shanzabah replied, 'It may be that my talents may have caused his aversion, for the merit of a fleet horse proves his bane, and a fruit-bearing tree gets its topmost branches broken by reason of its fruit. The nightingale is imprisoned in a cage on account of its very talent, and the peacock is plucked and shamed, owing to its beauty and showy appearance.

---

[1] Keene translates 'if I form an attachment,' but the hawk is putting a general case. I prefer therefore to make the *agarchih* refer to the *dú sih rúzí*, 'but for two or three days.'

STANZA.

My suffering to my knowledge all is due :
The foxes', peacocks', to their fur and hue.
My virtues prove my fault, or on my head
Not dust would be, but gems their light would shed.

And of a truth, as the undeserving are more numerous than men of merit, and an inherent animosity exists between them; by means of their number they overwhelm the meritorious, and so violently distort their acts as to array their actions in the garb of guilt, and make their good faith put on the guise of perfidy, and their honesty look like foul conduct, and thus they turn that very virtue, which is the source of good-fortune and the means of happiness, into the material of distress and an auxiliary of woe.

COUPLET.

The eye of malice, may it out plucked be!   Makes us in vice's semblance virtue see.

And a sage has said, with reference to this,

COUPLET.

'If any virtue here its head should shew,
Some worthless fellow on it deals a blow :
To ruin they the virtuous man would bring,
And foul reproach upon his virtues fling.'

And again in describing the injustice of the censorious, they have said,

VERSE.

'Not visionless the eye of justice, when
Glass beads seem pearl-like to its searching ken.
The great shew equity in all they do,
While base men torture and are tortured too.
And they whose hearts no kindly thoughts admit,
Cry silk is woollen when you shew them it.

Damnah said, 'It is possible that the malevolent may have made this attempt. On that supposition; what would be the issue of the affair?' Shanzabah said, 'Unless destiny second their endeavours, no injury will thence result; but if the divine decree and God's predestination assist their artifice and treachery, it will be impossible to avert the consequences by any device.

HEMISTICH.

When fate precedes, what boots it to consult?'

Damnah rejoined, 'It behoves a man of understanding, whatever the position of his affairs may be, to make far-sighted prudence the guide of his actions, since no one ever based his proceedings on prudence but obtained triumphant success as regards the object of his wishes.' Shanzabah replied, 'Prudence is then serviceable when fate has not issued its decree against it, and stratagem then yields advantage when the ordinance of destiny is not promulgated in opposition to it: but against the requirements of fate, neither is any shift serviceable nor any stratagem of use; for that any can escape from the bonds of destiny and the shackles of fate—by artifice or counsel—is not to be thought of.

COUPLET.

Since when fate's hand the mighty flame has lit,
All thought, all counsel, is consumed in it.

And when the Creator, the Most High God—may He be sanctified!—causes His decree to issue, He clouds and darkens the eye of the vision of the clear-sighted with the anointing needle [1] of negligence, so that the way of escape from that mandate, becomes hidden to them, for, ' *When fate comes, the sight is blinded.*' [2]

When heaven's decree and fate's commands are sped,
The wise are blinded and their ears grow dead.

But perhaps thou hast not heard the story of the Villager and the Nightingale, [3] and hast not listened to their dispute?'   Damnah said, How was that?'

STORY XIX.

Shanzabah said, ' They have related that a villager possessed a sweet and pleasant orchard, and a garden more fresh than the bower of Iram.   The air of it gave mildness to the gales of spring, and the scent of its herbs, refreshing the spirits, conveyed perfume to the very soul.

VERSE.

That garden glittered with youth's radiant hue,
Life's waters seemed to steep its flowers in dew.
The sweet-voiced nightingale there gladsome sung,
And rapture in its perfumed breezes hung.

And in one corner of his garden there was a rose-bush, fresher than the shrub of successful desire, and more lofty than the branch of the tree of delight. Every morning on the top of the rose-bush the roses blossomed, colored like the cheek of heart-alluring damsels with gentle minds, and the face of silver-bosomed maids, scented like jessamine.   The gardener began to shew an exceeding fondness for these excellent roses, and said,

---

[1] The *mil* is not, as Keene renders it, ' a probe,' but a thick round bodkin, or rather metal rod, about six inches long, and as thick as a slender quill, which is dipped into the collyrium or powder for the eye, and then drawn between the eyelids, which are tightly closed on it, and on which it leaves a dark rim of the powder.   The use of this is highly beneficial, and protective to the eye against the glare of the ground in hot climates.   I adopted the practice in Sindh, and my example was soon followed by many officers, who derived great benefit from it.

[2] Exactly the Latin ' Quem Deus vult perdere prius dementat.'

[3] This story has been translated by Sir W. Jones in his Persian Grammar, and I have made but few alterations in his elegant version, and have ventured on them solely with a view to being more literal.

COUPLET.

> What the rose murmurs, know I not, again,
> To wake the hapless Bulbul's tender strain.

One day the gardener, according to his established custom, came to view the roses; he saw a plaintive Nightingale who was rubbing his face on the leaves and tearing asunder, with his sharp bill, the gold-besprinkled binding of that volume.

COUPLET.

> The nightingale that views the rose, grows blind,
> And straight lets go the reins that rule the mind.

The gardener, beholding the scattered condition of the rose-leaves, tore, with the hand of confusion, the collar of patience, and pierced the mantle of his heart with the soul-transfixing thorn of uneasiness. The next day he found the same action repeated, and the flames of wrath, occasioned by the loss of his roses,

> Wounded afresh the scar he had before.

The third day by the passes of the Nightingale's bill,

> The rose was ruined, thorns alone were left.

Then the resentment caused by the Nightingale broke out in the breast of the gardener; he set a deceitful springe in his way, and having caught him with the bait of treachery, confined him in the prison of a cage. The disheartened Nightingale opened his mouth, like a parrot, and said, 'O Sir! for what cause hast thou imprisoned me? and for what reason hast thou resolved to distress me? If thou hast thus acted through desire of hearing my songs, my own nest is in thy garden, where in the morning thy bower shall be the house of my music; but if thou hast another idea, inform me, O venerable sir![1] of what thou hast in mind' The gardener said,

COUPLET.

> How long O God! wilt thou me pang? O rival, mayest thou not abide,
> O God! how long conceal her cheek! cease, envious veil, her form to hide![2]

Dost thou not know how thou hast spoiled my fortune, and how often thou hast distressed me with the loss of my favourite rose? it is right that thy action should be requited, and that thou, being separated from thy friends and country, and secluded from all joy and diversions, should'st mourn in the corner of a prison; whilst I, afflicted with the anguish of separation from my darling flowers, weep in the cottage of care.

COUPLET.

> Would'st be my friend, O Nightingale! then mourn along with me,
> For we are two sad lovers and our business grief should be.'[3]

---

[1] The *pír* may be taken with *dihḳán*, and rendered 'the aged villager;' but it seems strange to introduce this epithet for the first time in the middle of the story. I have taken it as the vocative. Both Sir W. Jones and Keene elude the difficulty by not translating this word.

[2] This difficult, and not very pleasing, couplet is omitted by Sir W. Jones.

[3] This couplet is quoted from Háfiz.

The Nightingale said, 'Quit this resolve, and consider that if I am imprisoned for such an offence as tearing a rose, what will be thy punishment if thou tearest a heart asunder?'

VERSE.

He who by wisdom guides the spheres aright,
Will good and evil actions too requite.
He who does good will, justly, good ensue,
And evil-doers will receive their due.'

This discourse, taking effect upon the heart of the gardener, he set the Nightingale at liberty. The bird tuned his voice in his free state, and said, 'Since thou hast done me this service, assuredly, according to the sentence, '*Shall the reward of good works be any other than good?*'[1] it is necessary to reward thee first. Know that under the tree where thou standest there is a vessel[2] full of gold; take it, and spend it to supply thy wants.' The villager searched the spot and found the words of the Nightingale to be true. He said 'O nightingale! what a wonder it is that thou couldst see the vessel [of gold] beneath the earth, and not discover the springe above ground!' The Nightingale replied, 'Dost thou not know that, '*when fate descends caution is vain.*''

HEMISTICH.

No one can war with the decrees of fate.

When the mandate of the Divine will has been issued, no light remains to the eye of understanding, and neither prudence nor wisdom bring any advantage.

VERSE.

Strive not to grapple with the grasp of fate;
Canst thou with feebleness success combine?
All vain, 'gainst destiny, thy watchful state;
Go, then, and to its force thyself resign.[3]

And I have invented this story in order that thou mayest perceive that I am not an opponent of the hand of destiny and omnipotent power, and have no alternative but to bow my head reverently on the writing of the Divine decree.'

COUPLET.

By my Lord's threshold—His—my friend's—
My aims are bounded still.
For all that passes o'er me comprehends
But the expression of His will.

---

[1] Ḳu'rân, ch. lv., 60; Sale p. 393, l. 30: 'Shall the reward of good works be any other than good? Which, therefore, of your Lord's benefits will ye ungratefully deny?'
[2] Sir W. Jones renders it 'coffer,' and Keene 'dish,' neither adhering to the literal meaning of *dftâbah*, which is 'ewer.'
[3] Rhyme compels me to be unliteral. Keene more closely translates thus: 'Thy hand has no force for anything; caution is of no avail against destiny; whatever proceeds from fate approve of that.'

Damnah rejoined 'O Shanzabah! what I am positively sure of, and know of a certainty,[1] is this, that what the lion meditates with respect to thee is neither owing to the slanders of thy enemies, nor the success of thy merit, nor the peevishness of kings; but it is rather consummate ingratitude and treachery which impels him to it: for he is a successful tyrant, a morose and perfidious person, and a deceiver. The beginnings of intercourse with him impart[2] the sweetness of life, but the issue of his services has the bitterness of death. We must regard him as a poisonous painted serpent: his outside adorned with various colors, but filled within with deadly venom, against which no antidote avails.

COUPLET.

> All guile and cunning, fraud and wiles, are there;
> Nought truthful, patient, generous or fair.'

Shanzabah replied, 'I have tasted the food of the honey of favor, it is now the time for the wound of the sting of oppression; and I have passed a long interval in mirth and ease, now is the season for the assault of adversity and war.

COUPLET.

> Yes! for a while thou hast, my heart! felt union's fleeting gladness;
> Now thou must taste of absence too, to part with all its sadness.

It was, in truth, death which grasped my collar and brought me into this wilderness, otherwise how was I fitted to associate with a lion? One who feeds upon me, and to whom I am food, he ought not to have been able to drag me to him even with a thousand cords, nor to plunge me by a hundred thousand stratagems or sleights into the snare of his friendship.

COUPLET.

> To join my fate with him, could I then hope for this?
> On him from far to gaze were, sure, enough of bliss.

But the Divine decree, and thy too flattering words, O Damnah! plunged me into this vortex of destruction; and now the hand of counsel falls short of the skirt of remedy, and the course of events, by reason of my having neglected caution and forethought, is not in accordance with my wishes; and I, through my vain longings and unreasonable desires, have kindled such a fire as this for myself, so that, even ere the smoke has reached me, I am consumed by the heat of my grief and the flame of my disappointment.

HEMISTICH.

> What can I do? the act was mine—for self-done acts what cure?

And the sages have said, 'Whoever is not content with a sufficiency of worldly gear, but pursues a superfluity, is like a person who arrives at a hill

---

[1] 'Ala 'l-ḳaṭa, literally 'on cutting,' i.e., after the abscission of all other cases coming to this one.

[2] Did the MSS. allow it, I should prefer to read bakhshad here rather than bakhshíd.

of diamonds, and every moment his sight falls on a larger piece, and, engaged with the thought of its greater value, he proceeds onward until he reaches the spot where he obtains the desired object, but his return becomes impracticable, because the fragments of the diamonds have cut and wounded his feet ; but that heedless person, absorbed in his covetous fancies, is insensible to his situation, and, consequently, perishing most lamentably on that hill, is lodged in the craw of birds.'

COUPLET.

Thy state grows worse by aiming far too high,
Then for a moderate but real profit try.

Damnah said, 'Admirable are these words which thou hast uttered, for the source of every calamity which befalls a man will prove to be avarice and desire.

COUPLET.

Quit that pernicious lust of gain, for them
Whom it afflicts, all, everywhere contemn.

The neck that is bound by the chain of covetousness is at last severed by the sword of regret, and the head in which the madness of desire has fixed itself will in the end be rubbed in the dust of disgrace. Many a one, from excess of covetousness and greed, has been led, by the hope of wealth, into the vortex of calamity ; and has been involved, by the scent of gain, in ruinous disaster : just as that Hunter greedily desired to catch the fox, and the claws of the leopard tore the breath out of his body.' Shanzabah said, 'How was that?'

STORY XX.

Damnah said, 'One day a Hunter, passing through a waste, saw a fox excessively brisk and active, who was roaming about in the expanse of that wilderness, and showed himself gamboling in every direction. The Hunter was pleased with his fur, and formed the idea of selling him at a great price ; and the violence of his longing led him to pursue the fox until he found out his hole, and near it he dug a pit and covered it over with rubbish, and upon it he laid some carrion, and seating himself in ambush waited to catch the fox. Presently it happened that the fox came out of his hole, and the smell of that carcase drew him on gradually till it brought him to the brink of that pit. He here reflected, 'Although the brain of longing is perfumed by the aroma of this dead animal, nevertheless the smell of danger too reaches the nostril of caution; and the wise never meddle with a business which is fraught with peril, nor do the prudent commence an affair in which the possibility of mischief is discernible.

COUPLET.

Wherever they the perilous define,
Strive thou to keep thyself without the line.

And though it is possible that some dead animal may be here, it is also possible that they may have arranged beneath it a snare, and in every case caution is best.

STANZA.

> When two affairs present themselves to thee,
>   And of the twain thou know'st not which to do;
> That in which dread of danger there may be
>   Is what thou shouldst assuredly eschew.
>   But where no eye can lurking peril see,
>   In that step forward fearlessly and free.

Pondering thus, the fox relinquished the thought of that carcase, and took the path of safety. Meanwhile a hungry leopard came down from the top of a mountain, and, from the smell of the carcase, sprang into the pit. The Hunter, when he heard the noise of the snare, and the sound of the animal's fall into the pit, thought it was the fox, and, through excessive greediness, cast himself unreflectingly upon it; and the leopard, imagining that he would prevent him from eating the dead animal, leapt up and tore open his belly. Thus the greedy huntsman, through the ill luck that attended his cupidity, was caught in the snare of destruction, and the contented fox, by retrenching his desires, escaped from the whirlpool of adversity; and the moral of this story is, that the calamitous results of greediness, and the evil of excessive concupiscence will make a slave of a free man and hurl a slave headlong [to destruction.]'

COUPLET.

> Couldst thou a crown too large for thee obtain,[1]
> By earth where saints have trodden!—'twere but pain.

Shanzabah said, 'I did wrong to choose the service of the Lion at the first, and I was ignorant of his want of appreciation of merit: and they have said, that to associate with one who does not understand the value of your society, and the waiting on one who does not recognize the worth of your attendance, is like a man's scattering seed on salt ground in hopes of a crop, or whispering into the ear of one born deaf one's griefs and joys, or writing fresh [2] verses on the face of a stream, or to sport with the ornamental figures in a bath in the hope of begetting offspring, or to expect drops of rain from a furious whirlwind.[3]

----

[1] Keene must have read this passage differently, as he translates: 'If thou couldst give one lock of hair beyond what belongs to thy head;' which, with reference to what follows, 'by the dust of the feet of the holy it would give a head-ache,' hardly makes sense. *Kullah,* however, which is found in the lithographed and printed editions, and in the MSS. I have consulted, must mean 'cap,' 'crown,' 'tiara.' As to the phrase, 'By earth, where saints have trodden;' or, as Keene renders it, 'By the dust of the feet of the holy,' Orientals consider as sacred the ground over which holy men have passed, and commonly talk of it as 'collyrium for the eyes,' etc., and as in this case swear by it.

[2] *Tar* signifies also 'moist,' and is, therefore, introduced with reference to the *áb-i rawán,* 'running water,' though otherwise the epithet is inapt enough, for the freshness of a verse could not make it more or less permanent on water.

[3] Every one who has been in hot climates knows that these whirlwinds arise under a

STANZA.

To hope that kings will true and grateful be
Is, from the cypress-branch, to look for fruit.
The cane-juice grows not on the willow-tree,
No—though a thousand times thou give to it
The [sparkling] waters of eternity.'

Damnah said, 'Cease these sayings and take thought for thine own matters.' Shanzabah replied, 'What plan can I set up, and what stratagem can I adopt? And as for the qualities of the Lion, I know them well, and my sagacity admonishes me that the Lion has no wish with reference to me but what is good and kind, but those who are about him strive for my death, and exert themselves for my ruin; and if it be so, the inclination of the tongue of the balance of my life is rather toward the scale of destruction than that of continuance; for when crafty and cruel persons, and perfidious oppressors combine,[1] and join hand to hand, and set themselves unanimously against any one, they are sure to triumph over him, and overthrow him, as the Wolf, and the Crow, and the Jackal, made a set against the Camel, and by uniting, prevailed against him, and obtained their object and desire.' Damnah asked, 'How was that?'

STORY XXI.

Shanzabah said, 'They have related that a black-eyed Crow, and a Wolf with sharp claws, and a crafty Jackal, were in the service of a lion, accustomed to hunt his prey, and their forest lay near the highway. A merchant's camel was left behind in those parts, and recovering his strength, after a time, wandered about in every direction in quest of provender. He happened to pass through that wild spot, and when he approached the lion he saw no alternative but to do him service, and shew him respect. The lion, too, spoke him fair, and inquired into the state of his affairs, and after acquainting himself with them asked him as to his story and movements. The Camel replied,

COUPLET.

Though before this I could myself in my own acts command,
When thee I saw the reins of choice departed from my hand.

Whatever the king commands will doubtless comprehend all that is salutary for his subjects.

HEMISTICH.

Thou know'st our welfare better than ourselves.'

The lion replied, 'If thou desirest it, remain in our company—tranquil

---

cloudless sky, and, in fact, are produced by excessive heat, and, instead of giving forth refreshing rain, are charged with sand, as in the terrible desert of Arabia; nay, though they should be accompanied with thunder and lightning, they bring no rain, as I have myself witnessed.

[1] Lit. · 'Having set back to back.'

and secure.' The Camel was pleased, and remained in that forest until a
long interval had elapsed and he had become extremely fat. One day the
lion had gone in pursuit of a quarry, and a furious elephant had encountered
him, and between them a mighty battle and a huge conflict had arisen, and
the lion having received several wounds, came back to the forest and lay
down in a corner groaning and wounded. The Wolf, the Crow, and the Jackal,
who were the favorites that fed from the table of his liberality, were left
without food, and from the lion's innate generosity, and the pure
beneficence which kings feel towards their servants and attendants—when he
saw them in that state he was, affected, and said, ' Your sufferings are more
difficult for me [to bear] than my own. If hereabouts ye can find any game
I will come out, and having done the business for you, will return.' They,
quitting their places, in attendance on the lion, came out and went into a
corner, and beginning to consult with one another,¹ said, ' What is the use to
us of the Camel's being in this forest? Neither does the king derive any
advantage from him, nor have we any friendship with him ; now we must
induce the lion to tear him to pieces, and thus for two or three days the
king will be put at his ease from the pursuit of food, and we, too, shall be
proportionably benefited.' The Jackal said, ' Do not coquette with this fancy,
for the lion has given him a safe-conduct and introduced him into his
service ; and whoever instigates the king to act perfidiously, and emboldens
him to break his word, will commit treason ; and the traitor is universally
reprobated, and both God and man are displeased with him.

VERSE.

> In whomsoever treachery finds place,
>   His faith to God is false and spiritless.
> Truth on the human coin her stamp must trace,
>   For Nature's alloy is perfidiousness.'

The Crow said, ' We might devise some stratagem in this matter, and
extricate the lion from the obligation of this promise, and do you mind and
stay here and I will go and return.' He then went to the lion and stood
still. The lion inquired, ' Have you marked down any quarry and brought
intelligence of any game ? ' The Crow said, ' O king! the eyes of every one
of us fail through hunger, and we are bereft, too, of the power of motion. A
method, however, has come into our minds, by which, if the king assents, we
shall gain perfect ease and abundant blessings.' The lion said, ' Inform me
of thy meaning that I may distinctly apprehend it.' The Crow answered,
' This Camel is a stranger among us, and we cannot contemplate any
advantage from associating with him. For a hurried makeshift, here is a
quarry come to hand and game caught in the net.' The lion was wroth,

---

¹ Lit.: ' Introducing the path of consultation between them.'

and exclaimed, ' Dust on the head of the helpers of this age, who have no habit but that of hypocrisy nor any feeling but that of perfidy, and who altogether abandon the part of courtesy and liberality, and manly and generous sentiment.

VERSE.

Faith does not company with worldly men.
From those whose habit is injustice, then,
Expect not truth—a dog is better far
Than those dumb cats who full of cunning are ;
And round the cloth a plundering warfare wage—
The only chase in which they dare engage.[1]

In what sect is it lawful to break faith ? and by what creed is an attack sanctioned upon one to whom thou thyself hast given protection ?

COUPLET.

Break not the branch thyself didst elevate,
In breaking that thou injurest thine own state.'

The Crow said, ' I know these principles; but the wise have said that an individual may be sacrificed for all the inmates of a house, and the people of a house for a tribe, and a tribe for a city, and the inhabitants of a city for the august person of a monarch who is in danger because his safety might benefit the people of a whole region. And, besides, an evasion may be found, so that he who made the promise of neglect may be clear, and his person secured from the pain of fasting[2] and the dread of starvation.' The lion hung down his head, and the Crow returned and said to his friends, ' I have laid the case before the lion. At first he was refractory, but at last he became tractable. Now our plan is to go all together to the Camel and recount the story of the lion's hunger and of the distress that he is suffering, and say that we have passed our lives happily under the protection of the fortunes and beneath the shade of the majesty of this fortunate king. To-day, that this event has occurred, honor demands that we should lay down our lives and breath for him, otherwise we shall be stigmatized for ingratitude, and shall be deprived of the character of generosity and manliness. Our right course is to go, all of us, to the lion and reiterate to him thanks for his gifts and bounties, and acknowledge that we have no power to make any return save in offering up our lives and breath for him. Whereupon let each of us say, " To-day let the king break his fast upon me," and let the others make some objection; and thus, probably, death will be the doom of the Camel.' They then came together to the Camel and repeated all these particulars to him ; and he, in consequence of the simplicity of his heart, was

---

[1] Keene translates more literally : ' A dog is better than those dumb cats, who, with their stratagems, hunt after nothing but around the dinner table.'

[2] Keene's translation exhibits, through a curious error in typography, ' the pains of a sting,' instead of ' the pains of fasting.'

deluded by them; and so having settled matters as has been described, they went to the lion, and when they had acquitted themselves of the duty of setting forth their thankfulness and his praise, and offering eulogies and prayers for his welfare, the Crow loosed his tongue and said,

COUPLET.

'King! in this world success attend on thee!
And, at mirth's banquet, joy thy portion be!

Our tranquillity depends on the king's personal health; and now that an exigency has occurred, and my flesh may suffice to eke out the king's existence, he must condescend to kill me and turn me to account.' The others exclaimed, 'What good will eating thee do? and what satisfaction would thy flesh give?'

HEMISTICH.

Who then art thou, that one should reck of thee?

When the Crow heard these words he hung down his head, and the Jackal began to speak, and said,

COUPLET.

'King! from whose paw precursive destiny
Takes, in wrath's day, the roll of those to die.

A long interval has elapsed during which we have lived safe from the fierceness of the sun of vicissitude under the shade of thy daily increasing fortunes.   To-day, when the moon of the splendor of your majesty is involved in the eclipse of distress, I desire that the star of success may rise from the horizon of my condition; and that the king having made me his food, should be freed from the care of thinking about how to break his fast.' The rest replied, 'What thou hast said proceeds from an excess of affection and a proper sense of obligation, but thy flesh smells rank, and is coarse and unwholesome. Heaven forefend that by eating it the king's indisposition should be increased!' The Jackal was silent, and the Wolf came forward and loosed his tongue, saying,

COUPLET.

'King! may heaven's monarch be thy friend and stay!
And, in the battle field, thy foes thy prey!

I, too, am desirous of sacrificing myself for the king, and hope that he will smilingly assign a place to my limbs in his gums.' His comrades said, 'Thou hast spoken these words from pure attachment and thorough faithfulness, but then thy flesh would make one choke,[1] and, in ill effects, it is the next thing[2] to deadly poison.'   The Wolf stepped back again, and the

---

[1] _Khindk_ is literally 'a strangling cord;' _khumdk_ 'the quinsy.'
[2] Lit.: 'Substitute,' or 'representative,' 'locum tenens.'

Camel, extending its long neck on high,[1] broke the rein, ' *Every tall person is a fool,*'[2] and began to speak, and, after the due recital of blessings, said,

COUPLET.
'King! at whose threshold the bright azure sky
Has opened doors of hope and victory.

I have been brought up in this presence, and have been educated at this court; if I am fit for the royal kitchen, or may serve for the supply of thy table, I grudge not my life.'

COUPLET.
While breath remains I will not from thy dwelling-place[3] arise;
And, should it come to life itself, that e'en I'll sacrifice.

On this, the others with one voice exclaimed, 'This speech proceeds from excess of kind feeling and from true fidelity, and, in very truth, thy flesh is digestible, and suits the king's constitution. Blessings on thy magnanimity, that thou hast not grudged thy life for thy benefactor; and by dealing thus thou hast left a good name for a remembrance.

COUPLET.
The brave man's worth uncounted[4] gold, for he
Will in the deadly crisis helpful be.'

Hereupon they all made a unanimous assault on the Camel, and before the poor creature could draw breath, they tore his limbs to pieces. And I have adduced this story that thou mayest know that the artifices of interested persons, especially when they combine with one another, will not fail of effect.' Damnah said, 'What defence dost thou think of?' Shanzabah replied, 'I can think of nothing now but what deviates from the path of wholesome procedure, nor do I know of any remedy save war and conflict, and strife and slaughter: for every one who is slain for the protection of his own life is admitted into the circle of martyrs, and participates in the benefit of the saying, ' *Whoever is slain in defence of his life is a martyr.*' Moreover, if my death is fixed by the hand of the Lion, and predestinated; at least, then, let me be slain honorably, and let me perish gallantly and with spirit.

COUPLET.
'Tis well if I with glory yield my breath,
I want but fame—the body is for death.'

---

[1] I have ventured to take *bálá* with *gusíkhtah*, though it would be more naturally coupled with *mahár*, in which case it would signify 'high,' *i.e.*, 'sublime,' as referring to the saying of the prophet. The sentence cannot, I think, bear the meaning Keene assigns to it— 'tossing up the long rein of 'every tall man is a fool.''

[2] This is a saying of the prophet, and was spoken by him facetiously with reference to his two most intimate companions, 'Umar and 'Alí, of whom the former was tall and the latter short.

[3] Lit.: 'The end of thy street.'

[4] Lit.: 'A hundred thousand dirhams.'

Damnah said, 'A wise man is not precipitate in war, nor does he allow himself to anticipate matters at the time of battle, for ' *The aggressor is the most in the wrong.*' And by one's own choice to engage in great dangers is no proof of cleverness; nay, men of understanding handle the affairs of an adversary with civility and courtesy, and consider it best to avert a quarrel by gentleness.

VERSE.

> Sweet guile is better than unpleasant ire,
> 'Tis best to sprinkle water upon fire.
> When thou by gentle means thy wish canst gain,
> Why towards anger give, unchecked, the rein?

And, moreover, it is not right to hold even a weak enemy cheap, for even if he be wanting in strength, he will not be so helpless as regards artifice and stratagem, and he will by perfidious and false measures kindle the fire of mischief to the extent that its flame will not be quenched by the water of counsel; and thyself hast learnt to know the power of the Lion, and his might stands not in need of commentary or amplification; wherefore do not undervalue his hostility, but be on thy guard against the impetuosity of his attack, for every one that contemns his foe and disregards the issue of a conflict, will rue it as did the Genius[1] of the Sea owing to despising the Sand-piper.'[2] Shanzabah inquired 'How was that?'

STORY XXII.

Damnah said, 'They have related that on the shore of the Indian Ocean there is a kind of bird which they call *Títawa* or 'Sand-piper.' A pair of these had their nest on the sea-shore, and had fixed their abode at the brink of the water. When the time for depositing their eggs had come, the female said, 'We must seek a place to lay our eggs where we may live in peace.' The male replied, 'Here is a pleasant place and agreeable spot, and to migrate from hence appears impossible. The eggs must be laid.' The female rejoined, 'Here is the place for deliberation, for if the sea roll up its waves and carry off our young, and all our life's labor should be wasted,

---

[1] The original has *vakíl-i daryá*, and Keene has literally translated it; 'Envoy of the ocean;' but, as it seems to be intended merely for a personification of the ocean, the Sanskrit having only *samudrah*, 'the ocean,' I have rendered it as above.

[2] What kind of bird the *títú* is seems difficult to discover from the Dictionaries. The Persian Dictionary gives *Títú*, (P) 'a kind of water fowl,' and directly afterwards *Títawa*, (A) 'a species of the *katá*;' and on reference to the latter word, it will be found to be 'a bird of the Tetraonidæ or grouse family, which makes a noise like *katá, katá!* In the Hitopadesha the word is *Tittibhih*, whichProfessor Johnson, in his Vocabulary, renders 'wagtail,' and in his Translation 'lapwing.' Shakespear omits the word *títú* altogether, but gives a much more probable rendering for *Tittibhih*, under the word *titihrí* (to which he refers from *taitawí*), and which he translates 'sandpiper,' 'Tringa Goensis.' The Sanskrit Dictionary gives Parra Jacana, or Goensis, for *Tittibhih*. It would be well if lexicographers would endeavour to agree as to the scientific nomenclature of animals, trees, etc. But here the compilers of dictionaries seem to plunge at once into Oriental supineness.

how shall we remedy that?' Her mate answered, 'I do not suspect that the Genius of the Sea would show this hardihood, or put such a slight upon us;[1] and admitting that he should imagine such a disrespect and allow our offspring to be drowned, he may be forced to do us justice.

COUPLET.

Is my will thwarted, then I'll wreak my vengeance on the sky;
I am not one that e'en from heaven will bear indignity.'

The female replied, 'To step without the limits of one's own rank, and to boast of what exceeds our power, is unsuitable to persons of discretion. What strength hast thou that thou shouldest threaten the Genius of the Sea with thy vengeance, and what terrors are thine to enable thee to rise to the dignity of a conflict and feud with him?

COUPLET.

To thine own ruin thou a spoiler art;
A sparrow thou and playest the falcon's part.

Abandon this idea, and choose for our eggs a place of security and a safe spot, and turn not away thy head from my advice; for whoever hearkens not to the words of those who give him counsel, and does not act upon the advice of friends who wish him well, meets with what befell the Tortoise.' The male Sandpiper inquired, 'How was that?'

STORY XXIII.

The female said, 'They have related that in a pool whose water from the pureness of its nature reflected every image like a clear mirror, and by its sweetness and excellence gave a foretaste of the spring of life and of the fountain of Salsabíl,[2] resided two geese and a Tortoise, and in consequence of their being neighbours, the thread of their circumstances had been drawn out into sincere friendship, and vicinity had ended in cohabitation, and, being pleased with the sight of each other, they passed their lives contentedly.

COUPLET.

Sweet, life's season gliding on in the presence of our friends,
Sweet, each moment to which friendship her enchanting radiance lends.

Suddenly the hand of perfidious fortune began to lacerate the cheek of their condition with the nails of vicissitude, and the glass-coloured sky began to display in the mirror of their life the form of separation.

HEMISTICH.

What joy is there which fortune darkens not?

---

[1] *Jánib farú guzdshtan,* observe the phrase.

[2] Paradise is watered by a great number of springs and fountains, whose pebbles are rubies and emeralds, their earth of camphire, their beds of musk, and their sides of saffron; the most remarkable among them being Salsabil and Tasn'ím. See Sale's 'Preliminary Discourse,' p. 69.

VERSE.

From the goblet of union with loved ones how sweet is the wine that is quaffed,
But the headache of parting soon follows, soon mars the delight of the draught.
At this table none can chew even so much as a morsel in truth,
But a pebble will come intervening 'twixt the bread and the luckless one's tooth.[1]

In that water which was the source of their life and the support of their existence, a complete failure manifested itself, and a glaring alteration was evident. When the geese perceived that state of things they withdrew their hearts from the home to which they were accustomed and determined on emigrating.

VERSE.

Travel is better for the man whose breast
By various cares and troubles is oppressed.
For though 'tis pain indeed abroad to roam,
'Tis better than adversity at home.

Therefore with hearts full of sorrow and eyes full of tears, they approached the Tortoise, and introducing the subject of parting, said,

COUPLET.

Time's evil eye disparts our destinies :   How can I say what ills from it arise !

The Tortoise wept at the pang of parting, and in the utmost sorrow piteously exclaimed, ' What words are these? and how can I expect to live without you ? or how can existence be supported without sympathising friends ? '

VERSE.

Life without thee, we may unlawful call.
Or reft of thee is it then life at all ?
All life without thee is alas! the same—
Death, living death—and life alone in name.

And since that I have not power even to take leave, how can I endure the load of separation ?

COUPLET.

From thee unparted I'm the cypress free,   I shake at parting like the aspen tree.'

The Geese replied, ' Our hearts too are wounded by the sharp points of separation, and our breasts consumed overmuch by the fierceness of the flame of the fire of parting: but the distress of being without water is on the point of giving the mould of our existence to the wind of annihilation, and therefore of necessity we are about to forsake our friend and country, and to make choice of the anguish of exile.

COUPLET.

Ne'er did sad lover willing quit his love,   And none from Paradise of choice remove[2]

---

[1] This homely comparison affords a good example of how the Persian poets descend ' per saltum' from the turgid and inflated to the mean.
[2] M. Quatrèmere, in his review of M. Alexandre Chadzko's ' Grammaire Persane,' in the

The Tortoise rejoined, 'O friends! ye know that the distress of the want of water affects me more, and that without water I cannot support myself. At this crisis the rights of ancient companionship demand that ye should take me with you, and not leave me alone in the sorrowful abode of separation.'

COUPLET.

Thou art my life and wouldst depart, but when
Life goes, what can the lifeless trunk do then?

The Geese answered, 'O friend unique, comrade esteemed! the pang of parting from thee is more poignant than that of exile, and the grief of leaving thee a greater cause of despondency and depression, and wherever we go, though we should be in the happiest circumstances, and should pass our time in the utmost comfort, yet, deprived of seeing thee, the eye of our rejoicing would be darkened, and the vision of our fortune obscured; and we too have but one wish, and that is thy society and companionship; but for us to proceed on the earth's surface and so to traverse a great and long distance is impossible, and for thee too to fly through the expanse of air and accompany us is impracticable; and such being the case, how can we travel together? or in what manner can we keep company?' The Tortoise answered, 'Your sagacity will be able to devise a remedy for this matter too, and the contrivance of this affair will be attained by your discernment, and what plan can I excogitate while my spirit is broken by the thought of separation, and my heart crushed with the load of parting?

COUPLET.

A heart is needed first in everything:
From a torn heart no rightful counsels spring.

The Geese replied, 'O friend! during this period [of our friendship] we have observed in thee somewhat of levity and precipitancy and rashness: perhaps thou wilt not act upon what we say, nor keep firm to thy promise after thou hast made it?' The Tortoise rejoined, 'How can it be, that ye should speak with a view to my advantage, and I act in opposition, or fail to perform a compact which is for my own good?

COUPLET.

I pledged my faith that from my faith I ne'er would deviate;
I gave my troth that that my troth should rest inviolate.'

Said the Geese, 'The condition is that when we take thee up and fly through the air thou wilt not utter a single syllable, for any one who may happen

---

'Journal des Savants,' October, 1853, translates the phrase '*áshikán-i bí dil*, 'les amants à qui leur passion a fait perdre la raison,' and he gives as his reason, '*dil* exprime souvent l'intelligence, la raison.' I think, however, that, though his rendering is very admissible the words may also be translated 'despairing lovers,' as in these lines the epithet 'sad' or 'despairing' would be more appropriate. The lover, although slighted or desponding, refuses to quit the street of his beloved one. Were he Majnún, as M. Quatrèmere would make him, he would, like Majnún, wander through the deserts at random.

M

to see us will be sure to throw in a word, and say something in reference to us directly or indirectly.[1] Now how many soever addresses or allusions thou mayest hear, or whatever manœuvres thou mayest observe, thou must close the path of reply, and, good or bad [whate'er betide] not loose thy tongue.' The Tortoise answered, ' I am obedient to your commands, and I will positively place the seal of silence on my lips, so that I shall not be even disposed to answer any creature.'

STANZA.

In far-off Greece I met an ancient sage,
And said, ' O thou! ripe with the love of age!
What suits man best in every state?' Said he,
'Wouldst hear the truth, 'tis taciturnity!'

The Geese then brought a stick, and the Tortoise laid hold of the middle of it firmly with his teeth, and they lifting the two ends of the stick, bore him up. When they got to a height in the air, they happened to pass over a village, and the people of the village having discovered them, were astonished at their proceedings, and came out to look at the sight, and raised a shout from left and right, ' Look! how [two] geese are carrying a tortoise.' And as in those days the like of it had never been witnessed by that people, their cries and exclamations increased every moment. The Tortoise held his peace for a time, but at length the cauldron of his self-esteem began to boil, and his patience being exhausted, he exclaimed,

HEMISTICH.

' May blindness seize on those that cannot see!'[2]

No sooner had he opened his lips but he fell from on high. The Geese exclaimed, ' *The duty of a messenger is but to convey his message.*'[3] It is the part of friends to give advice and of the fortunate and well-disposed[4] to listen to it.'

STANZA.

Well-wishers give advice—but only they
Who are well-tempered list to what they say.
I wish thee well, but if thou cross-grained be,
When will my counsel take effect on thee?

And the moral of this story is, that whoever listens not to the admonition of

---

[1] Such is the distinction, I believe, between *t'ariz* and *kindyat*, and the parallel terms follow directly after—'*ibdrat* and *ishdrat*.

[2] I suppose this not very lucid observation of the tortoise to imply, ' You who are shouting to others to look at what is plain enough to everyone, hold your peace: and may he, who cannot see what is straight before his eyes, become blind!'

[3] This very common expression occurs, slightly modified, in ten or eleven passages in the Kur'án. The exact words will be found in Mar., ch. xxiv., 55; Fl. xxiv., 53; Sale p. 269, last line but three. Sale slightly alters the meaning to suit corresponding passages. Keene's version is inaccurate, ' Nothing belongs to a messenger but to arrive.'

[4] *Nīk-bakht* seems to me, as Keene rightly renders it, to include both fortunate and well-disposed.

friends with the hearing of acceptance, will have hastened his own destruction and torn away the veil [1] of disgrace from the face of his own ignominy.

COUPLET.

Who lists not to the counsel of his friends,   Shall gnaw remorsefully his fingers' ends.'

The male Sand-piper said, ' I have heard this apologue that thou hast recited, and have become acquainted with its import; nevertheless, fear thou not and keep where thou art, for the faint-hearted and fearful never attain their wish; and I keep to what I have said, that the Genius of the Sea will see fit to be tender of us.' The female laid her eggs, and when the young—rending the white vest of the shell—raised their heads from the collar of life, the sea, rolling onwards in waves, snatched them under the skirt of destruction. The female on witnessing the catastrophe, became agitated, and exclaimed, ' O wretch! I well knew that there was no striving [2] with the waters. Now that thou hast destroyed our young and set my spirit on fire, at least devise some plan by which my lacerated feeling may be salved.' The male replied, ' Speak respectfully, for I keep to the promise thou dost wot of, and I will acquit myself of the vow I have made and wrest justice from the Genius of the Sea.' He immediately went to the other birds, and having convened in one place all the leaders and chiefs of each class, he explained his case to them, and having requested their assistance and aid, began, in a voice of supplication, this song.

COUPLET.

' Endless were the sad recital of my heart's distress and woe,
It is now the time to aid me and your sympathy to shew.

Unless all my friends act in concert and unison in this matter, and by a combined effort extort justice for me from the Genius of the Sea, his boldness will increase and he will afterwards attack the young of other birds: and when this custom has become established, and this habit been confirmed, we must tear away our hearts from our children and bid adieu to our country and our homes.

COUPLET.

Or with a hundred woes bear with the thorns of this distress, [3]
Or step into the drear abode of utter nothingness.'

The birds, sad and dejected at what had happened, serried their pinions and hastened to present themselves at the court of the Símurgh, and caused the statement of what had occurred, to arrive at the place of representation, and

---

[1] Keene translates this expression ' veil of advice,' whence it is evident he must have have read *niḳdb-i naṣiḥat* for the reading of the edition, *niḳdb-i faṣiḥat*.

[2] The word *bází*, (lit.: ' playing,') seems to me to be used here in order to make a (very obscure) pun, as *db-bází*, like *jalakrídá*, signifies ' swimming about sportively,' or ' gamboling in the water.'

[3] Keene translates, ' We must either, by a hundred insults, work his sorrow with disgrace;' but *sáḳhtan bá* is, I believe, always used in the sense of putting up with a thing.

L 2

said, 'If thou feelest commiseration for thy subjects, thou mayest fitly be their king; but if thou hast no care for the distresses of the oppressed, and dost not sympathize with the injured, efface the writing of the sovereignty of the birds from the page of thy fortunes, and the title to be their guardian shall be made over to another.'

COUPLET.

The sufferings of the weak commiserate: Take heed—or dread the tyranny of fate.[1]

The Símurgh consoled them and set off from his metropolis with his servants and retinue, to repel that unfair attack, and the birds, encouraged by his aid and protection, turned their faces towards the shore of the Indian Ocean; and when the Símurgh with an army—the limits of whose ranks[2] could not be contained in the capacity of the computation of any accountant, and the number of whose lines and classes could not be weighed in the scales of surmise and possibility—

STANZA.

All warlike, fierce and brave, blood-drinkers they;
All gallant veterans eager for the fray.
With feathery hauberks they their breasts defend;
And beak and claw like lance and knife protend.

arrived near the sea, the morning breeze, which agitates the line of billows, conveyed that news to the Genius of the Sea, who not finding in his resources ability to contend with the Símurgh and the army of the birds, was compelled to put himself in the posture of supplication and restore the young of the Sand-piper.

Now my object in addressing this tale, is to shew that one ought not to despise any enemy though he may be very contemptible, for a diminutive needle may effect that to which the lofty spear is incompetent, and a burning stick from the fire, though it seem small to view, will consume whatever comes in contact with it; and the sages have said, 'the friendship of a thousand persons will not countervail the hostility of one.'

COUPLET.

A thousand e'en too few for friendship are;
But one for enmity too much by far.

Shanzabah said, 'I will not commence the battle, that I may not be stigmatized with the infamy of ingratitude, but when the Lion attacks me I shall consider self-preservation and defence of my own person a duty. Damnah said, 'When thou approachest the Lion, and seest that, having raised himself up, he is lashing the ground with his tail, and the flame of his wrath

---

[1] It is impossible to retain the play on words in the original between *zír dastán* and *zabar dastí*.
[2] The lithographed edition and one MS. read *ḥadd va ḥaṣr*, and Keene translates accordingly, 'extent and limits;' but I prefer the reading of the printed edition, *ḥadd-i ḥuṣur*, 'the limits of whose ranks,' making *ḥuṣur* correspond to *ṣafúf* in the parallel sentence which follows.

appears kindled like the fire of his eyes, know that he is about to attack thee.' Shanzabah said, 'Should anything of this sort be observable, undoubtedly the veil of suspicion will be removed from the cheek of certainty, and information will be afforded on the point of the perfidious intentions of the Lion.' Damnah then, mirthful and inspirited, betook himself to Kalîlah.

COUPLET.

From the blind fool who can behold with joy another's smart,
Expect not faith nor truth from him—he stands from all apart.

Kalîlah inquired, 'How have affairs progressed? and what is the upshot of the matter?' Damnah made answer,

HEMISTICH.

'I thank my fortune and the times as well.

Praise be to God! the most complete solution of the matter has been effected, and this so difficult affair has been well and easily accomplished.' Thus spake Damnah, while fate, with the tongue of retribution, was whispering the import of this couplet in the ear of the wise men of the assembly of discernment.

COUPLET.

Glad seized the guests the ringlets of the boy,[1]
Would heaven but grant them tenure of their joy.

Then both set off to the Lion, and by chance the Ox arrived immediately on their traces. The Lion caught sight of the Ox, and the insinuations of Damnah produced the desired effect, and the Lion, beginning to roar, lashed the ground with the tail of fury, and ground his teeth together through excess of wrath. Shanzabah felt certain that the Lion meant to attack him, and said to himself, 'The service of kings in terror and dread, and attendance on princes in fear and alarm, resemble being in the same house with a serpent, and lying under the same shelter with a lion. Although the snake may be asleep and the lion slumbering, in the end one will raise his head and the other open his jaws.'

COUPLET.

Do not at royal courts on kings attend;
I fear 't will like the stone and pitcher end.

He thus reflected and then prepared for battle. Each side beheld the signs that the shameless Damnah had pointed out to them, and commencing the conflict, spread their shoutings and cries through the extent of earth and the expanse of heaven.

---

[1] Lit.: 'Cup-bearer.' The meaning of this somewhat enigmatical couplet is simply that earthly pleasures are transient, and Damnah's exultation would be but fleeting.

STANZA.

Their tumult made the deer and beasts of prey,[1]
Through that wild waste and desert shrink away.
These in the cavern of the mountain-side,
Those in thick bushy coverts cower and hide.

Kalílah, beholding this spectacle, turned to Damnah, and said,

QUATRAIN.

With guileful art[2] a hundred wiles hast thou
Together blent—then from the issue fled.
Two hundred years may rain, nor settle now
This troublous dust thou hast occasioned.

O unwise! seest thou or not the evil results of what thou hast done? and perceivest thou or not the disgraceful issue of thy proceedings?' Damnah said, 'What is the evil result?' Kalílah answered, 'In this act which thou hast perpetrated seven hurtful consequences are apparent. One is, that thou hast unnecessarily plunged thy benefactor into difficulty, and hast brought mighty trouble on the person of the Lion. The second is, that thou hast stirred up thy master so to act as to incur the stigma of a breach of promise and faithlessness, and has consented to this his dishonor. The third is, that thou hast considerably exerted thyself for the slaughter of the Ox, and hast submerged him in the whirlpool of destruction. The fourth is, that thou hast taken upon thine own neck the murder of that innocent creature who will be slain through thy efforts. The fifth is, that thou hast made a large number suspicious of the king, and it is probable that through fear of him they will abandon their country and betake themselves to some other place, and, wandering from their families, will sink under the woes of expatriation and the calamities of exile. The sixth is, thou hast exposed the generalissimo of the armies of the wild beasts to the possibility of destruction, and consequently the knot of their union may hereafter be left disordered. The seventh is, thou hast made thy own weakness and imbecility palpable, and hast not fulfilled that boast of thine, that thou wouldest manage this business with courtesy and kindness; and he is the most doltish of mankind[3] who rouses slumbering mischief, and desires to carry on by conflict and ferocity, an affair which admits of being arranged peacefully and with gentleness.' Damnah replied, 'Perhaps thou hast not heard what they have said,

COUPLET.

If wholesome reason fail in an affair,   We then must use insaner measures there.'

---

[1] *Wuhúsh* means any beast of prey that flies from man ; but *sab'a* implies also 'savage,' 'ravenous.' As the English language supplies but one word for both these significations, I have chosen 'deer' to stand for the former class in general.

[2] Lit.: 'With color and smell.'

[3] *Mardum.* This word comes in mal-à-propos when a beast is speaking. This is one instance out of many of the difficulty of preserving the character of an apologue through so long a book as the 'Anvár-i Suhailí.' In fact, the apologue may be well enough for a short and pithy statement, but for a work of many pages it is altogether inapt.

Kalílah said, ' In this affair, what point hast thou settled by the canon of reason? or how hast thou disposed thy plans by the aid of the architect of counsel, which not succeeding there was occasion to resort to violence and roughness? After all, dost thou not know that sound judgement and correct thought take the lead of courage and valor?

HEMISTICH.

Judgment excels the bravery of the bold.

COUPLET.

The fully wise can in a word attain
Things that a hundred hosts [1] attempt in vain.

And thy infatuation and conceit of thine own opinion, and the manner in which thou art deluded by the pomp of this deceitful world—which, like the attractions of the mirage, possesses nought but mere semblance—were always known; but I hesitated to lay them open to thee, thinking that thou mightest take warning and awake and rouse thyself from the sleep of pride and negligence, and intoxication from the liquor of conceit and ignorance; but since thou hast passed all bounds, and every moment becomest more dizzy and distracted in the wilderness of error and the abyss of self-deception, it is time that I should recount some little of thy complete ignorance and darkness and excessive boldness and blind obstinacy, and reckon up—though it be but a drop from the ocean, and an atom from a mountain—a few of thy faulty speeches and foul acts.

VERSE.

That thou mayst know the things that thou hast done—
Thou hast been treacherous—failed, too, of success!
All have some value, thou art nought alone.
All have their being, thou but nothingness.'

Damnah said, ' I believe, brother! that from the beginning of my life to this period, an unfitting word or improper action has never proceeded from me; yet if thou hast observed any fault in me, thou oughtest, assuredly, to represent it to me.' Kalílah rejoined, ' Thou hast numerous faults, and the first is, that thou imaginest thyself faultless; and next, that thy talk exceeds thy deeds: and they have said that there is no greater danger to a king than this, that the words of his minister should outstrip his actions. Now the people of this world are divisible into four classes as regards their words and actions. First, there is the man who says and does not, and this is the custom of hypocrites and misers. Secondly, there is he who does not speak but act, and this is the habit of gallant [2] men. The third is he who says and

---

[1] I have omitted, metri causâ, to translate *jarrár*, ' numerous.'

[2] The reading of the editions, '*ddat-i ddamíyán va jawán-mardán*, appears to me absolute nonsense. On consulting the MSS. I find that *va* is omitted, and *ddamíyán* inserted only in the margin. I would expunge it altogether, or, if it must be read, prefix to it some adjective as *nik*, and read, '*ddat-i nik ddamíyán va jawán-mardán;* but it would be better entirely suppressed.

does, and this is the characteristic of men who know[1] how to pass through life. The fourth is he who neither says nor does, and this is the quality of the mean and sordid. And thou belongest to that class who say and do not invest their words with the ornament of action; and I have always found thy talk to outrun thy capacity; and the Lion, deluded by thy sayings, has been exposed to so perilous an affair as this, and if (which God prevent!) a calamity should befal him, anarchy and confusion would prevail in this region and the disorders and disquiet of the people would exceed all bounds, and the lives and property of all would incur the risk of plunder and spoilation, and the guilt of all this misery would be on thy neck.

STANZA.

The man who acts or thinks unworthily,
Shall not the face of goodness ever see.
And he who makes the tree of wrong take root,
Whence should he gather beneficial fruit?

Damnah replied, 'I have always been a faithful minister to the king, and have planted nought in the orchard of his affairs save the shrub of wholesome advice.' Kalílah rejoined, 'A plant whose fruit is this proceeding which we now witness, were better plucked up by the root; and advice which produces such a result as this we now behold, ought rather never to have been spoken nor heard; and how can any advantage be looked for in thy discourse, when, in point of fact, it is not adorned with the ornament of deeds? Learning, without practice—like wax without honey—is devoid of all flavour; and talking without doing—like a tree without leaves and fruit—is only fit to be burned.

VERSE.

Knowledge, that leaves no trace of acts behind,
Is like mere body, destitute of mind.
Knowledge the stem and acts the fruit will be,
'Tis simply for the fruitage grows the tree.
The barren branches do but shock the eye,
And can but fuel to the cook supply.

And men of eminence, have, with the pen of condescension, deigned to inscribe on the pages of their records, this writing, that there are six things from which it is impossible to derive advantage. The first is, talk without action: the second, wealth without prudence: the third, friendship without experience: the fourth, knowledge without virtue: the fifth, alms without pious intentions: the sixth, life without health.[2] And though a king be, in his own person, just and inoppressive, yet one ill-disposed and of foul character, will cut off from his subjects the benefits of their monarch's

---

[1] *Ma'ásh dán* I presume to be nearly equivalent to *kár ázmúdah*. I have not met with the word, to the best of my remembrance, elsewhere.

[2] Keene must have read *suhbat* for *sihhat*, for he translates 'life without society.'

justice and clemency, and from dread of his opposition the afflicting tale of the oppressed will never gain the honor of representation to the king, like water, sweet and limpid—in which the form of a crocodile is visible—wherein no swimmer, though athirst and even exceedingly parched, dare strike out with his arms or with his feet.'

COUPLET.

Athirst I've reached the clear pure fountain's brink;
Yet to what end? I'm powerless to drink!

Damnah replied, 'My object in this transaction was simply to attain the honor of the king's service.' Kalílah answered, 'Efficient servants and active attendants and experienced ministers, are the ornament and grace of the court of kings; but thou desirest that all others should be discharged from waiting on the Lion and that thou shouldst be the confidant and counsellor, and that intimate access to his majesty should be restricted to thyself alone; and this notion proceeds from complete ignorance and excessive want of understanding, for princes cannot be confined to any one thing or any single person, and kingly rank is like the possession of loveliness and beauty; for just as a charmer seeks the more to display her attractions, the more men are in love with her; so a king, too, the more numerous his attendants and the larger his retinue, is the more desirous of increasing his train and multiplying those about him. And this vain longing that thou entertainest, is a clear proof of excessive stupidity; as the sages have said, 'Five things are marks of folly: first, to seek one's own advantage by injuring others: secondly, to look for the rewards of the future life without mortifying the flesh,[1] and piety : thirdly, to make love to women with rough language and ill-temper: fourthly, to expect to learn the niceties of science in slothful indulgence and ease: fifthly, to expect friendship from men without being faithful, and observing the duties of a friend.' And it is from excess of the kindly feeling that I entertain for thee, that I say these things; but it is as clear as the sun that the dark night of thy depravity will not be illuminated by the torch of my preaching. The gloom of ignorance and foulness of envy, which is interwoven in thy nature, will not be dispelled by the lustre of my counsels.

COUPLET.

Not Zamzam's[2] well could bleach, nor Kausar's[2] tide
His fortune's woof[3] that fate has darkly dyed.

---

[1] *Riydzat-i 'ibddat*, 'the discipline of devotion,' appears to me to be a questionable reading. I would therefore read *riydzat va ' ibddat*, though I cannot find his suggestion supported by the MSS.

[2] Zamzam is the famous well at Makkah, otherwise called Hagar's well. The water is considered holy, and is much used in the ceremonies of the Hajj. For Kausar, see Sale's 'Preliminary Discourse,' p. 68.

[3] *Gilim*. Lit. : 'blanket,' or rough cloth used to sleep on.

And my case, in relation to thee, is like what the man[1] said to that bird, namely, 'Take not useless trouble nor waste thy words upon a set who are not inclined to listen to thee.' It would not however give heed and was punished in the end.' Damnah inquired, 'How was that?'

STORY XXIV.

Kalílah said, 'They have related that a troop of monkeys had their abode in a mountain, and lived upon the fruits and herbage there. It befell that on a night more dark than the hearts of the guilty, and gloomier than the souls of men of ruined fortunes, the frost of winter began to assail them, and from the gust of a boisterous wind of icy chillness the blood in their bodies began to congeal.

VERSE.

Such was the cold, the lion of the sky,
　Wished he his [shaggy] skin inverted had.[2]
The garden birds for heat so restlessly
　Longed, that to have been spitted they'd been glad.[3]

The poor creatures, distressed by the cold, were seeking shelter, and having briskly girded themselves in search of it, were running about in every direction. On a sudden, beside the road, they beheld a piece of sugar-cane lying shining,[4] and, under the idea that it was fire, collected sticks and laid them about it, and commenced blowing, and a bird on a tree over against them called out 'That is not fire,' but they paid no attention, nor desisted from their unprofitable task. Meanwhile it happened that a man[5] came there and said to the bird, 'Trouble not thyself, for by thy speaking they will not be deterred, and thou wilt meet with vexation.

---

[1] Keene has the following note:—' From the story it appears that it was not a man, but another bird, who said this to the bird. There is some mistake.' The editions do indeed faultily read *mardí* in one place, and *murgh-i digar* in the subsequent passage; but, on referring to the MSS., I find it should be *mardí* in both places. In the next line the printed edition has *nishínad* for *na shuníd.*

[2] The peasants in Italy, and the Afghán mountaineers, wear a cloak of skins, the plain side of which they turn inwards in warm weather, and reverse it in winter, so as to have the warm fur next their bodies. This custom may have given rise to this most strange expression. For a note on *wájhún*, see M. Quatremère's review of M. Chodzko's Grammar, 'Journal des Savants,' October, 1853.

[3] The literal translation of this impracticable line is: 'The birds in the gardens had the horse-shoes in the fire, that it would be pleasant to be at the spit at the fire.' With such impossible idioms has the hapless translator to deal. 'To have the horse-shoes in the fire' signifies 'to be ready;' and the Burhán-i Kát'i explains that in order to get a sort of magic influence over a person, it is a custom to write his name on a horse-shoe and put it in the fire, and it is supposed he and the shoe will become malleable together.

[4] Keene has, 'they saw a bright lump of quicksilver;' but *nai párah* can mean nothing but 'a piece of reed,' or 'cane.' *Párá*, indeed, means 'quicksilver,' but it is a word of Sanscrit origin.

[5] Here the editions have, by a mistake, *murgh-i digar* for *mardí.* See note 1, above.

COUPLET.

He that is joined to evil fortune, leave him to his fate;[1]
For he will not, by all thy efforts, prove more fortunate.

And to exert oneself in correcting and amending such persons is like trying a sword upon a stone, or to seek from deadly poison the properties of a sovereign antidote.

STANZA.

Expect no trace of goodness in the man,
Who, from the outset, is by nature bad.
For by no efforts of thy making can
A white hawk from a dingy crow be had.'

When the bird saw that they did not attend to his words, from excess of kindness he came down from the tree in order that he might make them hear distinctly his advice, and admonish them against the futile toil they were undergoing. The monkeys collected round the bird, and separated his head from his body, and my dealings with thee have just the same character, and I do but waste my time and speak vain words, and besides that no advantage will accrue to thee, I am in danger too of being damaged.'

STANZA.

Thy hearer to thy counsel gives no heed;
Then why vain burthens on thy soft heart lay?
Thou saidst, 'Mount as on Burák,[2] on the steed
Of Happiness, and thus thyself convey
To the wished halting-place, from trouble freed.
He hears not, but his path will aye proceed,
Then leave him fatuous lagging on his way.

Damnah said, 'O brother! the great have always fulfilled their duty faithfully towards their inferiors as regards advice and admonition, and have shunned partiality and dissimulation; and it is incumbent on men of real eminence to persevere in the due practice of counsel and exhortation, whether any one attends to them or not.'

STANZA.

Withhold from none thy warnings, but say on,
Although the hearer may thy words neglect.
The clouds shower down their rain the hills upon,
Though in their stony breasts they nought effect.

Kalílah said, 'I do not close the gate of advice against thee, but I am afraid that thou hast based thy affairs on perfidy and deceit, and hast

---

[1] I have been obliged to omit the words *az dghdz-i kúr*, 'from the commencement of the affair,' which Keene joins with *tawdm gashtah*, but which I should prefer to connect with *ṭark girid.*

[2] Burák was the winged animal, smaller than a mule and bigger than an ass, upon which Muhammad performed his journey 'by night, from the sacred temple of Makkah to the further temple of Jerusalem,' and thence through the seven heavens to the presence of God. See Ku'rán, ch. xvii.; Sale p. 209 ; and Prideaux's Life of Mahomet, p. 43.

adopted as thy practice, conceit and egotism: '*The worst of qualifications is obstinacy.*' And when thy repentance comes, it will be unavailing, and however much thou mayest gnaw the back of thy hand and lacerate the surface of thy breast, it will be to no purpose, and a proceeding which is based on deceit and treachery will terminate in disgrace and conclude in dishonor. So it happened to the cunning partner; and the perniciousness of his stratagem turned out the noose of the snare of calamity, and closed on his own neck; while his careless associate, by the blessing of his uprightness and honest simplicity, attained his wish.' Damnah said, 'How was that?'

STORY XXV.

Kalílah said, 'They have related that there were two associates, one of whom was shrewd and the other careless. The former, by his extreme acuteness and cunning, could cast a thousand spells upon the water, and him they called Sharp-Wit. The latter, from his excessive stupidity and dullness, could not discern between things profitable and injurious, and him they called Light-Heart. These two formed the intention [1] of trading, and set out upon their travels in company with each other, and went on traversing many a stage and march. It chanced that they found a purse of gold in the way and viewing it as an unlooked-for piece of good-fortune, halted. The clever partner said, 'O brother! there is in this world plenty of profit that is never realized. Now it appears to be best to be content with this purse of gold and to finish our lives in the nook of our cottages in unfettered ease.'

VERSE.

How long, gold-seeking, round the earth wilt go?
As grows thy treasure so thy care will grow.
Nought will the eye-cup of the greedy fill, [2]
Pearls brim the shell, but not until 't is still.

They then retraced their steps, and, entering the city, alighted at a lodging. The careless partner said, 'O brother! come on, let us divide this gold, and freeing ourselves from anxiety, spend our several portions according to our several inclinations.' The clever one replied, 'It is not advisable to divide at present. Our judicious course would be to take such sums as we require for our immediate expenditure, and place the rest very carefully in deposit somewhere, and every certain number of days come and take from thence as much as we require, and preserve the remainder in the very

---

[1] Keene renders *ishán-rá dá'iyah-i bázárgání shud*—'They had a claim upon a certain merchant.' I think, however, that the words may bear the sense I have given to them, which would suit the general story better, for it is not likely they would have given up their claim, which they would more easily have realized with the aid of their newly-acquired funds.

[2] *Kásah-i chashm* signifies, I imagine, 'the socket of the eye,' or is it used metaphorically? 'the eye of the greedy, like a cup which can never be filled.'

same manner, which will be less perilous and more safe.'   The stupid
partner was deluded by this specious talk, and met his plausible proposal
with approval, and taking out cash enough to meet his present[1] wants, in
the manner aforesaid, the rest they, in conjunction, buried under a tree;
and directing their course towards the city, went and stopped, each in his
own quarters.

COUPLET.

Next day when the sly juggling sky   Undid the box of subtlety,

The partner who affected to be astute went to the foot of the tree, and
having dug out from the earth the gold, carried it off; and his careless
associate, unaware of what had been done, was engaged in spending the cash
he had, till nothing was left.   He then came to the clever one, and said,
'Come now, in order that we may take up something from that deposit, for I
have become very much in want.'   The sharp fellow dissembling his
knowledge of what had happened, said, 'Very good.'   Then both came
together to the foot of the tree, and the more they sought the less they found.
Sharp-Wit then seized Light-Heart by the collar, saying, 'Thou hast made
away with this gold without any one's knowing about it.'   The poor man
swore and protested and bemoaned himself, but all in vain.   In short, the
matter came from wrangling to a summons before a judge, and from disputing to an appeal to the law.   The cunning partner took the careless one to
the house of the Ḳáẓí, accused him, and recounted to the Ḳáẓí the particulars
of the case and the tenor of the dispute, and after Light-Heart had denied it,
the Ḳáẓí demanded of Sharp-Wit, proof in support of his charge.   Whereupon Sharp-Wit replied, '*Ḳáẓí! may God most high preserve thee!*

COUPLET.

Take the fruition of thy life, for from the throne of fate,
The mandate is confirmed which does thy course perpetuate.

I hope that the Glorious and Almighty God through His perfect power will
give that tree the power of speech, in order that it may furnish testimony of
the theft of this unjust and treacherous person who has carried off the whole
amount of the gold, and deprived me of my share.   The Ḳáẓí was astonished
at these words, and after much discussion and long debate they came to this
agreement, that the next day the Ḳáẓí should present himself at the foot of
the tree, and call upon the tree to bear witness; and if its evidence should
corroborate the charge, he should issue his commands in accordance with its
testimony.   The sharp partner went to his house, and having told the whole
story to his father, withdrew the veil from the business and said, 'O father!

---

[1] The MSS. differ here.   *Naḳdí sarah* signifies current coin, opposed to *nabahrah*.   One
MS. reads شر وجه which I do not understand.   Another reads *bar in wajah kih mazkúr
shud naḳdí kamtar*, 'in the manner above-mentioned, a little money,' which seems simplest
and best.

it was in reliance on thee that I formed the idea of the tree's evidence, and in confidence of thy support that I planted this tree of artifice in the court of the judge, and the whole affair depends on thy kindness. If thou wilt agree to it we will carry off that gold, and get as much more[1] and pass the remainder of our lives in comfort and ease.' The father asked, 'What can it be, which depends upon me in this matter?' The son answered 'The centre of that tree is hollow to such an extent that if two persons were concealed in it they could not be seen. Thou must go to-night and stop in the tree until to-morrow when the Ḳází comes and calls for testimony, then thou must give thy evidence in the usual manner.' The father said, 'O son! Give up the thought of deceit and trickery, for though they mayest deceive thy fellow-creatures, thou canst not deceive the Creator.'

QUATRAIN.

Heaven's Sovereign Lord knows all thy mystery,
He can thy every hair and vein descry.
Granted thy wiles may blind thy fellow-man,
Can they cheat him who does all nature scan?

Oh! many are the artifices that prove a source of ruin to their author, and the just recompense of which recoils on him, so that he is left disgraced and exposed to ignominy, and I fear lest thy deceit should turn out like the artifice of the Frog. The son inquired, 'How was that?'

STORY XXVI.

The Father said, 'They have related that a Frog had taken up its abode beside a Snake, and fixed its dwelling hard by that cruel tyrant. As often as the Frog had young ones the Snake used to devour them, and pang her heart with the burning regret for the loss of her children. Now this Frog had a friendship with a Crab. One day she went to him and said, 'O kind friend! excogitate for me some suitable device, for I have a powerful enemy and a mighty foe, against whom resistance is not to be thought of, and from whom it is not possible to remove or migrate,[2] for the spot where I have fixed my residence is an exceedingly pleasant place and heart-delighting abode. It is a meadow, the verdant environs of which are as exhilarating as the garden of heaven, and whose delicious breeze diffuses odour like the ringlets of the fair.

VERSE.

A hundred thousand flowers there are beaming,
The verdure smiling and the hushed waves dreaming.

---

[1] In what manner? Does the *án zar* refer to his own share, and the *chandán-i dígar* to his partner's? or had he some other rascality in view? or is it a mere careless unmeaning expression of the author? I incline to the latter opinion.

[2] Keene renders this, 'nor is any tale or allegory of vengeance within my reach,' which makes but indifferent sense. He seems to have overlooked the very common meaning of *naḳl*, 'migration' which it obviously bears in this passage.

Each flower is still a brighter hue assuming,
Each a far league the love-sick air perfuming.
The rose her book of hundred leaves [1] unfolding,
The tulip's hand a cup of red wine holding.
The northern zephyr ambergris round spreading,
Still through its limits varied scents is shedding.

And no one would of his free choice abandon such a spot, nor withdraw his heart from this exemplar of the Paradise above.

COUPLET.

My home is in the Magians' street, how fair a spot is it!
No man of sense in all the world would such a dwelling quit.'

The Crab said, 'Do not distress thyself, for one can pinion a strong enemy with the lasso of deceit, and precipitate a powerful foe into the snare of stratagem.

COUPLET.

If one the grains of craft around him fling,
Sly birds enow he'll to his snare soon bring.'

The Frog said, 'What problem from a book of stratagems hast thou solved with reference to this? And what remedy hast thou secured to repel the assault of this malevolent foe?' The Crab replied, 'In such and such a place there is an ichneumon, contentious and mettlesome. Catch some fish and kill them, and drop them from in front of his hole to the abode of the snake, in order that the ichneumon may devour them one by one, and keep going on in quest of another. It is quite certain that when he comes to the Snake's hole, he will carry him off too, and liberate thee from his wicked injuries.' [2] The Frog by this plan, which was in conformity with the decree of fate, slew the Snake, and when after this occurrence two or three days had passed, the ichneumon felt an inclination to bestir himself in quest of fish to eat, [3] and repeat what he had now become accustomed to. He again set out in search of fish by the same road that he had previously measured with the foot of desire, and as he found no fish he devoured the Frog with all its young.

COUPLET.

Thou didst me from the wolf's claws free; but now
I do at last perceive a wolf art thou.

And I have adduced this story to thee that the conclusion of deceit is embarrassment and the end of fraud and treachery is repentance and humiliation.

COUPLET.

Do not into the vale of guile and fraud thy footsteps bend,
For thou wilt fall into the snare of sorrow in the end.'

---

[1] *Ṣad waraḳ* is also the name of a kind of rose.
[2] Lit.: 'From his wickedness and injuries.'
[3] Lit.: 'In quest of eating of fish.'

The son said, 'O father! curtail these speeches and suspend these remote and far-off anxieties, for this matter offers but little trouble and much advantage.' The desire of gain and fondness for his son led the poor old man from the alighting-place of uprightness and religious principle into the wilderness of injustice and perfidy; and the recondite saying, ' *Verily your wives and your children are a temptation to you,*'[1] was made patent. Having abandoned, then, the path of honorable feeling with neglect, and having entirely folded up the carpet of magnanimity, he thought fit to undertake a proceeding which is prohibited and forbidden both by law and custom, and in that dark night he placed himself in the tree, with a heart gloomy and foul. In the morning—when that judge of clear intelligence, the sun, showed himself in the tribunal of the sky, and the perfidy of black-visaged night became clear as day to mankind—the Ḳáẓí with a number of the notables, presented himself at the foot of the tree, and a crowd of people formed in lines to view the sight. The Ḳáẓí then turned his face towards the tree, and after stating the charge of the plaintiff and the denial of the defendant called upon him to explain the state of the case. Thereupon a voice issued from the tree, saying ' Light-Heart has taken away the money and acted injuriously to Sharp-Wit, his partner.' The Ḳáẓí was astonished, and sagaciously discerned that some one was concealed in the tree, and that some adroit contrivance would be required to capture him.

COUPLET.

Each secret plan from reason's eye concealed,
Can but by counsel's mirror be revealed.

He then gave orders for them to collect a quantity of firewood, and deposit it round the tree, after which they set fire to it, so that they extorted a cry of anguish[2] from that imprudent and vain schemer. The covetous old man for some time bore with it, but when he saw that his life was in peril, he called for quarter, and the Ḳáẓí, having brought him out and comforted him, inquired how matters stood. The half-burned old man gave a true narration of what had occurred, and the Ḳáẓí, being informed of the circumstances, related to the people the honest disposition and forbearance of Light-Heart, and the perfidy and villainy of Sharp-Wit, and simultaneously with this, the fraudulent old man removed the furniture of life from this transitory world to the mansion of eternity, and in the heat of his burning worldly passions

---

[1] Ḳur'án, Fl. lxiv., 15, Mar, lxiv., 16 ; Sale, p. 411, l. 2 : ' O true believers! verily of your wives and children you have an enemy ; wherefore beware of them.' I have translated the verse a little differently from Sale, whose note is, ' For these are apt to distract a man from his duty, especially in time of distress ; a married man caring for the things that are of this world, while the unmarried careth for the things that belong to the Lord.' See also 1 Cor. vii, 25.

[2] *Dúd* is, properly, 'smoke,' but signifies also ' a sigh,' for the Persians have a most forced but favourite simile, in which the sighing of the distressed is compared to smoke issuing from a chimney. In Keene's translation this passage is a good specimen of the disadvantage of being too literal, ' Till they brought smoke out of the family (or breath out of the body) of that unfinished man, raw business.'

arrived in the flames of the next world's penal fire. The son, too, after suffering the severest punishment and roughest usage, had to put the corpse of his father on his shoulders, and so betake himself to the city: while Light-Heart, through the blessing of his truth and honesty, and integrity and good parts, received back his gold and proceeded to occupy himself with his own matters.

And the moral to be drawn from the relation of this story is, that people may know that the final result of deceit is distasteful, and the conclusion of treachery is misfortune and contempt.

VERSE.

Who in the narrow pass of fraud dares tread,
Will at the last bring ruin on his head.
Fraud, like a snake bicephalous, uprears
A double danger and alternate fears:
That head may wound the enemy 'tis true,
But this darts mischief on its fosterer, too.'

Damnah said, 'Thou hast fixed on prudence the name of deceit, and given to counsel the title of fraud and perfidy. I have managed this affair with sound judgment and effected this important matter with just discernment.' Kalílah replied, 'Thou art at such a point in imbecility of judgment and weakness of counsel that the tongue fails in describing it, and such is thy position as to baseness of mind and overpowering greediness of place that explanation is helpless in narrating it. To thy master and benefactor, the advantages of thy craft and deceit are such as thou seest, so that in the end, what will be the punishment and torture which will overtake thee! for the infamy of thy double-face and double-tongue, will yield an evil result.' Damnah rejoined, 'What harm is there in having a double face? for the delicate rose by being double-faced, forms the ornament of the garden; and what fear from being double-tongued? for the pen of the minister with its two tongues, is the safeguard of property and land. The sword which has but one face—its office is to drink blood; while the comb, which has two faces, rests on the place where the hair is parted—on the forehead of the lovely.

STANZA.

He, like the sword, drinks blood, this world[1] among,
Who from close nature[2] has one face—one tongue:
But he, bilingual, two-faced, like the comb,
Will on men's foreheads, chief-like, find his home.'

Kalílah answered, 'O Damnah! cease this rhetoric, for thou art not that

---

[1] *Daur* signifies 'an age,' 'revolution of time,' 'the world,' and also 'the circulation of the cup,' which in connection with *mi khurad*, supplies an equivoque.
[2] *Pák gauhar* 'purity of nature,' but also 'singleness of essence' which is the meaning here.

N

double rose that the eye should be refreshed by gazing on thy beauty, but rather the heart-afflicting thorn from which nought but injury results to men; nor art thou that two-tongued pen that thou shouldest furnish information of the secrets of state and of the empire: nay, thou art the forked-tongued serpent, the wound of whose fang is nought but fatal poison. Moreover, the serpent, even, is better and more excellent than thou, for from one of his tongues comes poison, and from the other the antidote, while venom rains from both thy tongues, and neither has the vestige or trace of an antidote: and it is proper that from a man's tongue all that is salutary should be produced for his friends, though if poison be brought forth for his foes, it is right enough; according as a sage has said,

COUPLET.

Poison and antidote my tongue supplies,
This for my friends—that for my enemies.'

Damnah said, 'Leave off rebuking me, for, perhaps, a reconciliation will spring up between the Lion and Shanzabah, and the foundation of friendship and concord may be again laid.' Kalílah replied, 'This speech again belongs to the class of sayings which are fraught with impossibility; but thou, perhaps, hast not learned that three things are stable before the occurrence of three things, but, after that, their stability enters into the category of impossibilities, and their abiding into the class of things that cannot be. First, the water of a fountain and conduit is sweet so long as it has not reached the sea, but when it has joined the ocean, thenceforward purity and sweetness are not to be expected from it. Secondly, unanimity amongst relations continues so long as malevolent and wicked men have not intruded between them: but after the interference of evil and ill-disposed persons, harmony and concord in the circle of relatives and kinsmen are not to be looked for. Thirdly, the reservoir of companionship and friendship will continue clear so long as they allow tale-bearers and mischief-makers no opportunity of speaking; but when double-faced and double-tongued persons find the means of introducing their calumnies between two affectionate friends, no confidence can after that be placed in their friendship; and hereafter, if the Ox should escape from the claws of the Lion, it is not possible that he should be moved by his courtesies or kind speeches, or should show any eagerness for reconciliation and a renewal of confidence, and, even on the supposition that the gates of amity could remain open, each would be apprehensive of the other.'

COUPLET.

The broken cord may yet be joined again,   But in the midst a knot will aye remain.

Damnah said, 'If I relinquish my attendance on the Lion, and keep assiduously to the border of my cot, and, seizing with the hand of eager purpose the skirt of the advantages of thy society, should place the head of seclusion in the collar of retirement, what then?' Kalílah replied, 'Heaven forbid that I should associate with thee longer, or incline again to thy society, and I have all along been kept in terror by intimacy with thee, and in my heart have unceasingly repudiated thy alliance. For the learned have said, 'One should abstain from the society of the ignorant and depraved, and embrace the service of the sensible and good, since union with vicious and profligate persons is like fostering a snake. However great pains the snake-catcher may take in looking after the serpent, in the end it will give him a taste of poison from its gums; [1] and attendance on men of understanding and virtue resembles the tray of the perfumer, of which, though one may not get any of the contents, the sweet odour of its extract of roses will yet eventually fill his nostrils with fragrance.

VERSE.

Be like the perfume-sellers, for thy dress
Near them will share the odors they possess.
How long wilt thou, like to the blacksmith's forge,
Thick smoke and sparks on all sides round disgorge?

O Damnah! how can one hope for faithfulness and kindness from thee?— thou who hast thought fit to practice such behaviour towards a king; and ignore the favors of him who has made thee his friend and honored [minister], his confidential adviser, and illustrious to such a degree, that, under the shadow of his fortunes, thou mountest elevated like the sun; and by means of attending on whose heaven-resembling threshold, thou dost place the foot of boasting on the forehead of the twin polar stars.

COUPLET.

In thee no gratitude, no shame, is left,   Thou art of manly honour all bereft.

And from such a person, should I choose to remove myself a thousand leagues, a lofty understanding would hold me excused, and if I abandon the society of so worthless a person, reason will affirm that I have been rightly guided. [2]

STANZA.

From fellowship of seeming friends 't were better far to part:
   Absence is better than, with one thou lovest not, to stay.
A comrade whose society delighteth not thy heart,
   'T were best from him a hundred leagues to be removed away.

And just as the companionship of the good and pious possesses immense advantages, so association with base and wicked persons produces infinite mischief, and the society of the bad is rapid in its effects, and its injurious results manifest themselves in a very brief period; wherefore

---

[1] Keene takes *búí* as the reading, and translates ' After all, the flavour of venom will give out a smell from his gums.' Should any one prefer this sense I have nothing to say against it.

[2] According to Keene, ' Reason, our guide, will connect me with rectitude.'

it behoves him that is thoroughly wise to form friendship with men of wisdom and of praiseworthy conduct and veracious and amiable manners, and to avoid false, slanderous, unamiable and profligate companions.

VERSE.

> Since on mankind thy door thou canst not close,[1]
> Nor in thy lonely closet sole repose,
> Bestow thy friendship on the good, for it
> Is not for each dark-hearted miscreant fit.
> This saying of a sage recurs to me—
> (God's mercy on his saintly spirit be!)
> 'He who of foolish men becomes the friend.
> Will find their friendship troublous in the end.'

And whoever chooses an unworthy friend or leans upon the aid of an ignorant person, will meet with what that Gardener met with.' Damnah inquired, 'How was that?'

STORY XXVII.

Kalílah said, 'They have related there was a Gardener who for a long time had been occupied with various kind of tillage, and had spent his fair life in the culture of gardens and pleasure-grounds. He possessed a garden whose Eden-typifying parterres, by the delightfulness of their shrubs, threw the dust of envy into the eyes of the gardener of Iram; and, by the freshness of their flowers and streamlets, infixed a scar on the breast of the flower-garden of Khawarnak.[2] A peacock-like splendour shone on its many-coloured trees, and the radiance of the diadem of Káús[3] gleamed on its gold-bespangled flowers. The surface of its ground was bright like the cheek of a gem-covered beauty, and the breath of its zephyr was fragrant as the dwelling of an ambergris-selling artist. Its trees, youthful in promise, were, by the abundance of their fruits, back-bent like men of age; and its luscious[4] fruits, like the sweetmeats of Paradise, were fully ripened without the heat of fire. The hues of its vernal and autumnal fruitage reached the utmost verge of freshness and delicacy; and its apples, unfraught with evil,[5] like the chins of

---

[1] Keene translates, 'as long as it is possible to close' etc., and separates the two first verses in sense from the two following. They appear to me to be so connected as that the two former are the reason of the two latter.

[2] Khawarnak was a celebrated palace built by Sinimmár, the architect, at the command of N'umán-bin-Munzir, 10th king of Hírat, for King Bahrám Gúr, in Babylonia; and is said to have been one of the wonders of the world. The stones of which it was composed assumed various tints at different hours of the day, and were all based on one stone in such wise that were that one to have been removed, all would have fallen in ruins. Dreading the betrayal of this keystone, or fearing lest Sinimmár should erect a palace, still more beautiful, for his enemies, N'umán commanded the architect to be hurled from the topmost tower.

[3] Kai Káús, second king of the Kaianian or second dynasty of Persia, and son of Kai Kubád.

[4] I read, with the MSS., miwah-i ḥaldwat ámizash for the ḥaldwat dwízash of the printed and lithographed editions.

[5] Síb is 'an apple,' dsíb 'calamity,' and for the sake of the equivoque síb-i bí dsíb 'the uninjurious' or 'wholesome' 'apple' is a favourite phrase in Persian.

heart-ravishing silver-bodied beauties, made prey of hearts; and, by their lovely colour and exhilarating odour, brought a whole world into their fetters.

STANZA.

To a friend's chin the apple they compare,
Pink-hued, and mid the garden shewing fair.[1]
'T is like a lamp that glitters from a tree,
Who, in bright day, a lamp there e'er would see?

The pear suspended from each bough flagons of the water of life, with cups full of the sharbat of the sugar-cane, and, by the public proffer of an unartificial comfit,[2] stimulated the inclinations of the indolent devoid of capital and interest.

VERSE.

How shall I sing its praises? for, sweet in taste, the pear
Is a flask of many sugar-canes suspended in the air.

And the quince, clothed in wool, like vigil-keeping Ṣúfís,[3] thrust forth its head with its yellow cheeks from the bars of the monastery of creation, while its dust-discoloured countenance acquainted the grief-soiled hearts of lovers with the affection[4] of their moon-resembling mistresses.

COUPLET.

I—from my love—am yellow, and the quince—from moon and sun,
It from sun and moon—and I, from doting on my moon-faced one.

The golden ball of the orange, amid the verdant foliage, was like the globe of the most bright sun shining in the azure[5] sky, and the gilded censer of the citron, with its heart-delighting odour and exhilarating perfume, was flashing in the court of the garden.

VERSE.

Like the lips of smiling beauty, the pomegranate's [cool] hue
Made the mouths of lovers water,[6] delightful to the view.
There, heaven, like a goldsmith, who might their worth appraise,
Had cast rich ruby jewels in the assay-fire's blaze.[7]

---

[1] Lit., as Keene translates, 'its colour grew red, and the whole face was lighted up in the garden.'

[2] In plain English 'you could gather the pear without paying for it, and it was one of nature's sweetmeats.' I take *bi-dúd* (literally 'without smoke') to refer to *bi ḥardrat-i átish rasídah*, 'ripened without the heat of fire,' which occurs twelve lines above.

[3] The Ṣúfís are a religious order, who lead a stricter and more contemplative life than the common Darveshes. The word signifies, originally, 'one clothed in wool and who refrains from wearing silk.' Or more probably it is a corruption of σοφός 'wise.' The former etymology is the one here selected, for the sake of the equivoque.

[4] Here is an equivoque impossible to follow in English, *mihr* signifying 'the sun' and also 'love' 'affection.'

[5] Lit.: 'green,' an epithet constantly given by Persians to the sky, however unsuitable it may appear to us.

[6] *Ab-i dandán*, literally 'water of the teeth.' In the Dictionary we find *ḥaríf-i áb ú dandán*, 'whatever is agreeable to one's disposition.'

[7] Here is another equivoque—*nár* signifies 'fire' in Arabic, and 'a pomegranate' in Persian. The seeds of this fruit are compared to rubies which have been placed in its red pulp as in the fire—to test them.

When my voice would sing the praises of the peach, 't is surely fit,
That my words should borrow freshness, and gain lusciousness, from it.
Ere our lip, like lip of lover, on its tender lip is glued,
The juices of its beauty and deliciousness exude.

On one side was the incomparable fig, the description of whose excellence has
been placed by the hand of Omnipotence on the leaf of [the verse] ' *By the
fig,*'[1] and in which the same hand has mingled a sweet confection from the
poppy and sugar-candy,[2] and on the other side grew the pellucid grape, the
recital of whose perfections has been described by the pen of infinite wisdom
on the illustrious page, '*And we cause corn to spring forth therein, and grapes,*'[3]—
like a moist blister that has started up on the palm of the green leaf; and, on
the edges of the parterres, the gold-striped circular melons, with tender down
and fair[4] cheeks, showed themselves, like the full moon, which appears on the
horizon of the cerulean sky.

VERSE.

The melon balls[5] that grew in that green field
From Eden's fruitage bore the ball away.
Musk they and wine—no musk such scent can yield—
Soft-downed—in their soft down no hair have they.

And the old peasant was so much attached to each tree, that he felt
neither paternal[6] cares nor solicitude for offspring; and passed his time in
that garden in solitude. But, to be brief, he at last became oppressed by
the horror of loneliness, and much dejected by the dread his solitary and
separate life inspired.

HEMISTICH.

The rose, the violet is here—in vain, without a friend.

In short, heart-sore from the grief of being alone, he came forth to wander in
the plain, and, at the skirt of the mountain, which stretched out limitless as
the area of the expanse of hope, he was walking onward, when, by chance, a

---

[1] Kur'án, ch. xcv, 1; Sale p. 447, l. 17: 'By the fig and the olive; and by Mount
Sinai and this territory of security; verily we created man of a most excellent fabric.'   Sale
adds in a note, 'God swears by these two fruits because of their great uses and virtues; for
the fig is wholesome and of easy digestion, and physically good to carry off phlegm, etc.'

[2] I conjecture the meaning to be that the fig tastes like opium and sugar, which, indeed
in my judgment, it does. Keene translates, 'and had composed a rare sweetness out of
fragrant herbs and fine sugar.'

[3] Kur'án, ch. lxxx. 28; Sale p. 435, l. 32: 'We pour down water by showers; afterwards
we cleave the earth in clefts, and we cause corn to spring forth therein, and grapes, and
clover, and the olive, and the palm, and gardens planted thick with trees, and fruits, and
grass, for the use of yourselves and of your cattle.'

[4] *Turfah* signifies, according to the Dictionary, 'anything new, agreeable, wonderful.'

[5] In the game of Chaugán, the victor strikes the ball away from his antagonist. Hence,
one who gets the mastery is said to carry off the ball, as we should say a man carries off the palm.
Keene's translation is here hardly intelligible—'with a freshness of ringlets, in the form of
its hair never was.'

[6] I use 'paternal' in the sense of 'with reference to a father,' not in the common sense
of fatherly towards children. The whole sentence, however, means no more than that the
gardener had no family to care for.

Bear, too, of uncouth manners and ungainly form, of unpleasant aspect and foul nature, had, by reason of feeling lonely, turned its face from the top of the mountain downward. The moment they met, on both sides, through the similarity of their nature,[1] the chain of kindly feeling was put in motion, and the heart of the peasant became inclined to the society and companionship of the Bear.

DISTICHS.

Each atom in this earth and heaven, we find,
Resembles straw and amber[2] to its kind.
Things igneous with fiery essences unite,
And bodies luminous seek things of light.
Pure natures wishfully pursue things pure,
And gloom attracts the sorrowful and dure.
How are the vain seized on by vanities,[3]
And to wise men how pleasing are the wise!
The foolish fools to follow them compel,
And others, others like them please as well.

The inexperienced Bear, observing the civility of the peasant, became completely attached to his society, and at a slight signal, placed his head at his feet and entered that Paradise-resembling garden, and by the peasant's presenting and honoring him with those delicious fruits, the friendship between them was cemented and the root of the plant of amity became firmly implanted in the ground of each of their hearts.

VERSE.

And some time in that garden's corner, yet   They linger—well contented to have met.

And whenever the Gardener, from excessive fatigue, placed the head of tranquillity in the shade of repose on the pillar of rest; the Bear, from motives of love and affection, sate beside his pillow and drove away the flies from his face.

HEMISTICH.

I would not e'en a fly should darken that dear lip.

One day the Gardener had reclined and gone to sleep in his accustomed manner, and a number of flies collected on his face. The Bear was occupied in driving them off, but, however often he dislodged them, they presently returned, and when he repelled them on this side they made an onslaught on the other. The Bear waxed wroth, and lifting up a stone of twenty mans' weight[4]—inwardly resolving to kill the flies—dashed it down on the face of

---

[1] This is surely a slander upon horticulturists. The care of flowers would dispose us, one would think, to gentle feelings, not to bearish ones—yet the first tiller of the ground was a fratricide.

[2] In Persian, amber is styled *kahrubá* 'the straw-attractor.'

[3] Keene translates, ' what is it that carries away vain persons? some vanity.'

[4] If the *man* be reckoned at 40 lbs. weight, this stone would weigh 800 lbs. or about half a ton.

the hapless peasant. The flies suffered no harm from the terrible blow of that stone, but the old Gardener was reduced to dust: and hence the sages have said that a wise enemy is every way better than an ignorant friend.

COUPLET.

Foes that embitter life are better far,   Than they who ignorant but friendly are.

And I have related this story with this object, to show that friendship with thee presents the same result as if one's head should be exposed to destruction and one's breast be the target for the shafts of calamity.

COUPLET.

Fools' company like to an empty pot,   Is black without, and aught within is not.'

Damnah said, 'I am not so imbecile as not to distinguish that which is for my friend's advantage from what is injurious to him, or not to discriminate between what is good and evil with respect to him.' Kalílah replied, 'I acknowledge that thou hast not reached this degree of folly, but the dust of selfishness makes the eyes of the heart dark and blinded. It is to be expected that from some interested motive, thou wilt neglect thy friend and get ready a thousand incongruous evasions to excuse thyself, just as in the matter of the Lion and Shanzabah, thou hast stirred up all this treason and still layest claim to innocence and goodness, and the case of thee with thy friends is like the case of that Merchant, who said, 'In a city where a mouse devours a hundred mans of iron, what wonder if a sparrow-hawk should carry off a lad?' 'Damnah inquired, 'How was that?'

STORY XXVIII.

Kalílah said, 'They have related that a Merchant of small means was going on a journey; with prudent forethought he placed a hundred mans of iron in deposit in the house of a friend, in order that if an emergency should arise he might make that his capital, and thus support the thread of his existence. When the Merchant had brought his journey to an end, and had again reached his destination, he found himself in want of the iron, but the friend who had taken it in trust had sold the iron and expended what he got for it. One day the Merchant went to him to demand the iron. The trustee brought him into the house, and said, 'O sir! I had laid by that iron in deposit in a corner, and felt quite secure, not having observed a mouse's hole there, and, before I found it out, the mouse had taken advantage of the opportunity and had eaten up the whole of the iron.' The Merchant replied, 'Thou speakest the truth, for mice have a great fondness for iron, and their teeth have great power over such a juicy and tender morsel.

COUPLET.

Morsels of iron truly are, to mice,   Like macaroni to the gullet, nice.'

The trustworthy and veracious man was delighted at hearing these words, and said to himself, 'This silly Merchant has been deceived by my speech, and has given up all thoughts of the iron. I can do nothing better than give him an entertainment, and in his reception observe all the ceremonious requirements that are usual, so as to settle the affair.' He then invited the Merchant to a feast, and said,

COUPLET.

'If thou wilt as an honored guest my humble cottage grace,
Thou wilt oblige me, and thy feet upon my eyelids place.'

The Merchant replied, ' To-day a matter of importance has occurred, but I promise that I will return early nextmorning. He then left the [fraudulent trustee's] house and carried away a son of his, and having concealed him in his own dwelling, presented himself in the morning at his entertainer's door. The host, in great distress, loosed the tongue of apology, saying, 'O worthy guest! hold me excused, for ever since yesterday a son of mine has been lost, and I have two or three times had him cried in the city and environs, and have gained no tidings of the missing one.

COUPLET.

Like Jacob, grieving, I exclaim, 'Alas!   Who of my long-lost Joseph tidings has?'

The Merchant answered, ' Yesterday when I came forth from thy house I saw a lad of the description you give carried off by a hawk, which, flying, bore him though the air.' The trustee screamed out, ' O devoid of understanding! why dost thou utter that which is impossible? and why expose thyself to the charge of lying so enormously? A hawk, whose whole body does not weigh half a man,[1] how could it lift and bear through the air a lad weighing ten mans?' The Merchant laughed and said, 'Be not surprised at this!—in the city where a mouse can devour a hundred mans of iron, a mousing hawk too can fly off in the air with a lad of ten mans' weight. The fiduciary perceived how matters stood and said, 'Be not troubled, for the mouse has not eaten the iron.' 'Be not distressed,' rejoined the other, ' for the hawk has not carried away thy son. Return the iron and take back thy son.'

And I have adduced this story that thou mayest know that among a set, where treason to one's benefactor is admissible, it is clear enough what they would think permissible towards others; and since thou hast allowed thyself to act thus towards the king, others can have no hope left of finding thee faithful, nor any expectation of thy fulfilling thy duties. And I see clearly that it is necessary to keep aloof from the darkness of thy evil

---

[1] According to this passage, the *man* would be six or eight pounds, for a hawk would hardly weigh more than four pounds, and a lad of ten or twelve years old would weigh about seventy or eighty.

deeds, and that it is incumbent on me to avoid the blackness of thy
deceit and treachery.

COUPLET.

> To part from thee—fortune is linked in this,
> And not to see thee is the source of bliss.'

When the conversation of Kalílah and Damnah had reached this point, the
Lion had finished the business of the Ox, and had laid him prostrate in dirt
and gore. As soon, however, as the Lion had made an end of Shanzabah with
the claws of chastisement and had delivered the expanse of the forest from his
presence, and when the violence of his rage had diminished and the fury of
his wrath was allayed, he fell a-thinking and said to himself, 'Alas! for
Shanzabah, with all his goodness, and understanding, and judgment, and
talents. I know not whether I have acted in this matter rightly or made a
false step, nor whether in what they have reported to me of him they have
discharged their duty faithfully or trodden the path of treachery. I at least
by allowing myself to be urged on to this, have involved myself in a misfortune, and with my own hand have made my faithful friend drink of the
potion of death.

COUPLET.

> Would any friend thus act towards his comrade and ally?
> Nay! would an infidel act thus?—an infidel am I.'

The Lion hung down his head remorsefully, and loosing the tongue of
reproach, inveighed against his own folly and rash haste; and the spectre of
Shanzabah seemed, by his piteous plight, as with words,[1] to convey to the ears
of the Lion the purport of this quatrain.

QUATRAIN.

> Friend! without cause does one a comrade kill?
> Aye! but if faithful would he slay him still?
> Talk not of friendship, call thyself my foe,
> Lives there who could his foeman slaughter so?

The perpetual smile of the Lion was changed from grief at this event into
weeping, and his constitutional heat was doubled by the violent burning of
this occurrence.

COUPLET.

> The fingers of thy loss have planted in my breast the thorn of pain;
> And on this thorn of sorrow for thee, say, what rose shall bloom again?

Damnah, who beheld from a distance the traces of regret manifest on the
countenance of the Lion, and marked the tokens of repentance upon his front,
broke off his dialogue with Kalílah, and going before the Lion, said,

---

[1] It is hardly possible to translate, concisely, the phrase *lisán-u'l-hál*, the meaning of
which is, that a man's condition—his circumstances, as it were—speak: thus, pallor and
trembling tell of having witnessed something dreadful. It is opposed to *lisán-i kál*
'actual words.'

VERSE.

'O King! may fortune's throne thy station be,
And heaven's couch a resting place for thee!
Be thy head joyfully upraised on high,
And thy foe's forehead 'neath thy footsteps lie!

What is the cause of thy pensiveness and what the reason of thy meditation? Where is a time happier and a day more auspicious than this when the king moves proudly to the post of triumph and victory, and the enemy is groveling in the dust of disgrace and the gore of defeat?'

COUPLET.

Behold hope's morn her conquering beams[1] display
The foe's sun, foiled, in darkness sinks away.

The Lion said, 'As oft as I recal the respectful service, the various converse, the proofs of wisdom, and[2] the many abilities of Shanzabah, I am overcome with pity and grief, and distress overwhelms me: and, in truth, he was the prop and support of the army, and my retainers, by his aid, rapidly increased in prowess.'

COUPLET.

He who upheld the world has passed away,
He who of princes was the hope and stay.

Damnah replied, 'There is no ground for the king to pity that ungrateful traitor, but rather to offer the thanksgivings due to God for this triumph which has been attained, and to unclose the gates of gladness and rejoicing in the court of the heart for this victory which has presented itself.

COUPLET.

The morn of triumph from hope's East is shed,   The schemer's night of vain desire is sped.

We must regard this auspicious blazonry of conquest with which the register of successful fortune is adorned, and this august heralding of victory, with which the chronicle of happiness is ornamented, as a high preface and sublime opening to the pages of time.

STANZA.

Good-fortune brings to us glad news to-day,
Wakes many a warbling in hope's measure gay.
With thousand longings for this day I burned,
With thousand wishes to this crisis turned.

O monarch! asylum of the world! to pardon one from whom our life is insecure is a fault, and it is the act of wise men to confine a state-enemy in the prison of the grave. The finger which is the ornament of the hand and the instru-

---

[1] Here again the two-fold meaning of *tígh* supplies an equivoque. It may mean 'a sword' as well as 'ray,' 'sunbeam.' So *tígh kashídah* would be 'having drawn the sword.'

[2] The reading of the printed editions appears to me quite incorrect. Instead of *va atwdr va dạdr-i dánish-i ṣuḥbat*—which seems to me absolute nonsense—I read, from the MSS., *va atwdr-i-ṣuḥbat va dạdr-i dánish.*

ment of grasping and retaining, should a serpent inflict a wound upon it, is
cut off; and men regard the pain of this operation as the very spring of comfort.

COUPLET.

Why should thy foeman's memory make thee sad? [1]
For his death rather let thy heart be glad.'

The Lion was somewhat soothed by these words, but time exacted just
retribution for the Ox, and in the end the career of Damnah closed igno-
miniously and with disgrace, and the plant of his evil deeds and the seed of
his false words coming up, he was slain in vengeance for the Ox, and the
results of perfidy and deceit have ever been uncommendable, and the consequences of fraud and malevolence to be deprecated and inauspicious.

VERSE.

In their plots ever perish wicked men,
As scorpions come not to their homes again.
If thou dost ill, look not for good; since ne'er
Will the sour colocynth grape-clusters bear.
Thou who didst barley in the autumn sow,
Expect not wheat in harvest-time to mow.
This maxim by the sage was uttered—'Do
No ill, lest thou from time ill-treatment rue.
He in both worlds a good reward will find,
Who lives—a benefactor to mankind.

---

[1] Lit. : 'What can the enemy do to any one? that thou shouldst remember him!' I read
chih kird for *chih kari*, which is to me unintelligible.

CHAPTER II.

ON THE PUNISHMENT OF EVIL-DOERS AND THEIR DISASTROUS END.

INTRODUCTION.

The King said, 'I have heard the story of the calumniator and traducer, who, with consummate craft, clothed the beauty of truth with the guise of suspicion, and having caused his benefactor to swerve from the path of generous feeling, led him to incur the stigma of ingratitude and bad faith; and, after his words, mingled with guile, had made an impression, induced the Lion to exert himself to ruin the pillar of his state and crush the support of his own imperial sway. At the present time, should the eloquent sage see it to be advisable, let him recount the termination of Damnah's career, and set forth in what manner the Lion, when, after the occurrence of that event, he had returned to his senses and become suspicious with regard to Damnah, sought to remedy what had happened, and how he obtained information of the circumstances of his perfidy, and by what shifts Damnah contrived to hold on,[1] and what stratagem his friend devised, and what was the issue of his affairs at last. The sage said,

COUPLET.

'O king! be thou of fate and realm the stay!
And wisdom's lamp illuminate thy way!

In truth, prudence and foresight require that kings should not stir the instant they hear anything, nor despatch a mandate with reference thereto, until they have been informed of the certainty of the affair by clear proof and lucid demonstration.

COUPLET.

Not thou to interested folk give heed,　　　　Lest if thou act thou shouldst repent thy deed.

But after that the words of designing persons have chanced to persuade, and an unpraiseworthy action or speech which cannot be commended has actually gone forth, the remedy and amends would be to punish the calumniating sycophant in such wise as might serve for a warning to others; and, from dread of that chastisement, no one would pursue the same conduct in future, and thus it would be a duty to warn all to abstain from the like behaviour.

VERSE.

The plant that yields but thorns uproot,　　Conserve the tree that gives the fruit.
The lamp of an incendiary　　　　　　　　Is better quenched. That one should die
And fiery torments undergo,　　　　　　　Is better than all mankind's woe.

---

[1] *Tamassuk namúdan*, a rare phrase.

And the story of the Lion and Damnah verifies this dictum, for when the former got intelligence of the perfidy of the latter, and was apprised of his deceit and wickedness, he inflicted on him such a punishment that the eye of heedfulness in the others was enlightened, so that they made the verse, *Wherefore take example from them, O ye who have eyes!* [1] the continual task of recitation of their tongue. And the manner of this event was in this wise: when the Lion had finished the business of the Ox, he repented of the precipitancy he had shown in that affair, and bit the finger of contrition with the tooth of reproach, and laid the head of regret on the knee of amazement.

COUPLET.

Cold sighs of sorrow and remorse he drew,
Deeds such as mine did ever mortal do?

He was ever musing, pensively saying, 'Why did I act precipitately in this matter,' and continually reflected, 'Wherefore did I not manage this affair with caution and deliberation?'

STANZA.

The reins of will to passion's grasp I threw,
Sinned against reason and discretion too.
What 'vails it now that 'I have known or know,'
What use repeating 'Wherefore did I so?'

The Lion passed a long time in this manner in grief and chagrin, and in consequence of his dejection of mind and distracted feelings, the enjoyment of the beasts was suspended and the state of his subjects became one of distress, and the deep saying, '*People follow the faith of their kings,*' diffused its influence through the inhabitants of that forest, so that all of them became melancholy and sad.

COUPLET.

My heart is like a tulip scorched; and by my sighing's flame
In all thou seest their hearts too are scorched and scarred the same.

And he was incessantly recalling to mind the meritorious services, aid and former devotion of Shanzabah; and as his sorrow grew, confusion and distress overpowered him, and he was wont to find consolation in talking of his sayings or acts, or in hearing him spoken of.

COUPLET.

I'm not one moment negligent of thee,   Thy name is ever said or heard by me.

He continually gave private audiences to each one of the beasts, and required them to narrate.   One day he was conversing with a leopard on this subject, and was describing his heart-burnings and the disquietude of his soul.   The

---

[1] Ḳur'án, ch. lix. 2, Sale p. 402, l. 13: 'But the chastisement of God came upon them, from whence they did not expect; and he cast terror into their hearts. They pulled down their houses with their own hands, and the hands of the true believers. Wherefore take example from them, O ye who have eyes.!' This refers to the Jews, who were expelled by Muhammad from Madínah.

leopard said, ' O, King! to brood much over a business in which the hand of counsel falls short of the skirt of remedy, leads to madness, and to seek a cure for a matter which is inscribed in the circle of impossibilities, lies not in the centre of reason and understanding ; and sages have said,

COUPLET.

Back to thy hand no power can bring   The shaft that once has left the string.

And whoever exerts himself in searching for a thing which it is impossible to gain, may possibly, without obtaining what he is in quest of, let slip that too which he already has ; just as the fox desired to get possession of the fowl, and lost the piece of skin of which he had boasted.' The Lion inquired, ' How was that ? '

STORY I.

The leopard said, ' They have related that a hungry Fox had come forth from his hole in quest of food, and was roaming about in every direction and was measuring the forest sides with the step of greediness and avidity in search of a morsel. Suddenly an odor which invigorated his soul reached his nostrils. Turning on the scent of it he saw a fresh piece of skin, the flesh of which had been eaten by some wild beast that had left the hide. When the eyes of the Fox lit upon that piece of skin they brightened up, and the greatest vigor was diffused through his limbs at viewing that quantity of food.

COUPLET.

The fragrance of my much-loved friend came to me e'en in death,
And to my body back returned life's then departed breath.

The Fox, having got that piece of skin into the claw of possession, turned his face towards his own abode.

HEMISTICH.

Hast gained a friend ? then privacy is best.

In the midst of the way he happened to pass beside a village, where he beheld fat fowls busy feeding in the wide plain, while a slave named Zírak[1] had girt the loins of guardianship in watching them. The Fox's appetite for the flesh of the fowls was excited, and the delightful idea of the brains of their heads made him forget the piece of skin. In the midst of this state of things a Jackal chanced to pass by that hamlet.   He inquired, saying, ' O brother! I observe that thou art very thoughtful.   What event has occurred and what occurrence has taken place ? '   The Fox replied, ' O friend! Thou seest those fowls, the tongue of whose individual condition continues to repeat the meaning of [the verse], ' *And the flesh of birds of the kind which they shall*

---

[1] That is, ' Subtle.'

desire,[1] and the mysterious meaning of [the verse], '*Therein shall ye have that which your souls shall desire,*'[2] pervades them from head to foot.

COUPLET.

From head to foot incarnate soul is there,   A soul so delicate and pure is rare.[3]

And after a long interval during which I have suffered from the pains of want and the torments of hunger, the treasurer of the stores of God's bounties bestowed on me this piece of skin, and now the craving of appetite requires to get one of these fowls into its grasp, and cloy the palate of desire with the sweetness of its flesh, which possesses the deliciousness of life.

COUPLET.

My joy is soured, but if she from her honeyed lips bestow
Sharbat on me, my heart's palate will straightway sweeter grow.

The Jackal said, 'Alack! alack! a long time has passed over me, during which I have been in ambush for these fowls, and on the watch to make a prey of one of them, but that slave Zírak, who is their guide, keeps his eye on the path of protection after such a fashion, that the huntsman of imagination, from dread of his guardianship, cannot bring their forms under the net of his scheming; and the painter of the mind, from fear of his defensive care, is unable to draw their lineaments on the tablet of fancy; and I pass my life in this longing, and live from day to night and from night to day on a mere idea. Thou that hast found a fresh piece of skin, regard it as a piece of good-fortune, and relinquish this vain pretension.

COUPLET.

To thine own mistress be thy heart inclined,
And shut thine eyelids upon all mankind.'

The Fox said, 'O brother! till we can elevate ourselves according to our heart's wish upon the higher apsis of desire, to sit down disappointed in the lower apsis of mortification and abasement would be a great pity; and until we can gaze on the rose of enjoyment in the parterre of repose, to direct our steps into the thorny wake of adversity and suffering would be a glaring fault.

---

[1] Kur'án, Fl. lvi. 21; Mar. lvi. 23; Sale p. 394, l. 24: 'These are they who shall approach near unto God, they shall dwell in gardens of delight; (there shall be many of the former religions, and few of the last.) Reposing on couches adorned with gold and precious stones, sitting opposite to one another thereon, youths, which shall continue in their bloom for ever, shall go round about to attend them with goblets and beakers, and a cup of flowing wine: their heads shall not ache by drinking the same, neither shall their reason be disturbed: and with fruits of the sort they shall choose, and the flesh of birds of the kind which they shall desire. And there shall accompany them fair damsels, having large black eyes, resembling pearls hidden in their shells, as a reward for that which they shall have wrought.'

[2] Kur'án, ch. xli. 31; Sale, p. 356, l. 18: 'As for those who say our Lord is God, and who behave uprightly, the angels shall descend unto them and shall say, 'Fear not, neither be ye grieved: but rejoice in the hopes of Paradise which ye have been promised. We are your friends in this life, and in that which is to come: therein shall ye have that which your souls shall desire, and therein shall ye obtain whatever ye shall ask for; as a gift from a gracious and merciful God.'

[3] The *rúh* here I presume to mean 'esprit,' for which word we have no exact English equivalent. The lines are literally translated, but do not appear very apposite.

COUPLET.

On honor's cushion till our foot we place
Why in the dust sit down of foul disgrace?

And high spirit does not suffer me to cower over an insipid piece of skin, and give up the thought of the delicious flavour of fat flesh.' The Jackal replied, 'O thou of vain longings! to reprehensible greediness thou hast given the name of high spirit, and on culpable cupidity thou hast imposed the title of the preamble[1] of greatness, and art insensible to the maxim that greatness is in the poverty of the darvesh, and happiness in contentment.

COUPLET.

If in this market there be gain, 'tis what the poor contented know.
On me the blessings of content, O God! and poverty bestow.

Thou hast no better course than to be content with the portion which they have assigned to thee from the court of ' *Our daily bread is allotted by fate,*' and not tamper with vain and unsuitable aims, to which the result, ' *Whoever seeks what does not concern him, verily he relinquishes what does concern him,*' is attached.

COUPLET.

Our daily food is destined, and the time, too, they allot,
Aught more or aught before this, by our struggles we win not.

And I fear that through this impertinent scheming thou wilt lose that piece of skin also, and wilt thyself be overthrown, and there is a close resemblance between thy story and the case of that Ass who sought a tail and lost his ears also.' The Fox inquired, 'How was that?'

STORY II.

The Jackal said,

' An ass existed once, who tail[2] had not,
His grief grew daily for his tail-less lot:
Then off he started of a tail in quest,
A tail he sought for and he took no rest.
But suddenly—without design—his way
He took, where a ripe corn-field lay;
There from a corner him the peasant spied,—
Jumped up, and, cruel, docked his ears beside.
Thus the poor donkey a new tail would find,
And failing, left his ears, too, both behind!
They who, by like transgressions, may offend,
Will find a like requital in the end.'

---

[1] I suspect the word *dibájah* has been foisted in here, but all the MSS. agree in giving it, though it would be much better omitted.

[2] The merit of these lines, such as it is, consists in a series of puns on *dum* 'tail,' *dam* breath,' and *kadam* 'step,' and these equivoques are lost in English.

The Fox, from excessive greediness and avidity, frowned and said,

COUPLET.

'My thoughts are on my friend, and do any dream that I
Could cease of him to think, their thought were phantasy.'

Do thou survey the spectacle how I, by adroit stratagems, will get possession of a fat fowl, and behold with what artifice I will draw a comely prey into the net of possession.' He said this, and turning towards the fowls, he left the skin in that same spot. The Jackal, when he saw that his advice made no impression on the obstinate mind of the Fox, turned his face away from him, and made off to his own abode. Meanwhile, a kite that was hovering there, chanced to observe that piece of skin, and imagining it to be a dead animal, brought it, with the utmost speed, into the area of its own possession, and soared up into the sky. In the other direction, the Fox had not as yet got near the fowls, when Zírak jumped out from his hiding-place and threw a walking-stick at him. As soon as the stroke of it came upon the fore-foot of the Fox, the poor animal, in fear of his life, tore away his thoughts from the fowl, and in the utmost hurry, stumbling along,[1] made for that piece of skin. When he reached the destined spot, not a trace of the skin did he see. He then turned his face towards the point of prayer, and was about to make a piteous detail of his misfortunes, when just as he was weeping over his hard case, he beheld the kite carrying the piece of skin in its claws, as it exclaimed,

COUPLET.

'Thine was the luck and thine the stroke to try,
Who can do aught if thou hast played awry?'

The Fox, from grief at missing the fowl and regret at losing the skin, beat his head against the ground till his brains were dashed out. And the reason of inventing this story is, that the king has destroyed with his own hand one of the Pillars of the state, and gives no heed to the edification of the remaining nobles, and neglects to encourage the hearts of his courtiers and to show favor to his chiefs and the leaders of his army. Shanzabah has been slain and nothing will bring him back, but the other ancient ministers remain aloof from the service.

The Lion, after much reflection, said, 'This speech is the essence of good counsel and loyalty, but with regard to Shanzabah I have committed a great fault, and the chief part of my distress is to compensate for it.'

The leopard said, 'The remedy and compensation for it is not obtainable by grieving but will be procured by right counsel and just judgment.

---

[1] Lit. 'falling and rising,' a common phrase to express distressed movements.

COUPLET.

Has an ant fallen in a shining [1] cup,—
It needs no force, but one to take it up.

The advisable course is that the king of beasts should cease from lamenting and mental discomposure, and base his actions on deliberation, and proceed in the affair of Shanzabah and in the investigation of what befell him in such a manner that the right and wrong of it may be clearly manifested to his sagacious mind; and if that which they brought to the ears of the king respecting Shanzabah be really true, he, by his own act, arrived at the punishment of his own perfidy and the retribution of his treason. But if they have uttered calumnies regarding him and have made false statements, then must the slanderers and sycophants be made a target for the arrow of vengeance.

HEMISTICH.

'Tis good the evil-doer to remove.'

The Lion said, ' Thou art the vazir of the kingdom, and I have long been proud of thy judicious procedure, and have made thy foresight my guide and example in securing advantages and repelling misfortunes. Take up this matter in whatever way clear reason and lucid intelligence may require and extricate me from the whirlpool of distress.' The leopard engaged that he would, in a short time, present to the bright notice of the king the real state of this affair, and not leave under the veil of concealment or the curtain of delay one particle of the minutest points of its full ascertainment.

COUPLET.

With judgment clear I will it state,   As hair from leaven extricate.

The Lion was comforted by this promise, and, as it was late, the leopard demanded his congé, and betook himself to the fulfilment of his promise. It chanced that he passed by the abode of Kalílah and Damnah, and he observed that a dispute was going on between them, and that loud words were spoken by both parties. Now the leopard had from the first been suspicious of Damnah. At this time, when the sound of talking and expostulation reached his ears from their dwelling, his doubts were augmented. He advanced and and standing behind the wall, opened the ear of attention to their words. Kalílah said, ' O Damnah! thou hast done a great deed and embarked in a mighty affair, and having led the king to a breach of faith, thou hast caused him to be associated with utter perfidy, and thou hast kindled the flame of mischief and disorder among the beasts and wild animals, and I do not feel secure that the punishment thereof may not each moment come upon thee, and that thou mayest not be overtaken by the trouble and exposure consequent thereupon.

---

[1] For *rakhshindah*, 'shining,' the lithographed edition reads *laghzindah*, 'tripping,' which is perhaps better as applied to the ant. In the next line but one, in the printed edition, *wakkad* is, by a mistake, written *wa kdd* which might mislead the student.

COUPLET.

Whoever dares unsheath the tyrant's sword,
Blood will for that from heaven on him be poured.

And I know that when the inhabitants of this wild become acquainted with thy act, no one will hold thee excused nor lend their aid to rescue thee; nay, all will be unanimous in voting for slaying thee and putting thee to the torture, and it is not advisable for me after this to dwell with thee; for they have said,

STANZA.

Sit not with bad men, for their company—
Though thou be pure—will cast a stain on thee.
The sun with all its gloriousness of light,
Is by a cloudy atom hid from sight.

Get up and unite thyself in friendship with some other comrade, and hereafter refrain from converse or intercourse with me, for thou wilt get no more friendship or companionship from me.'   Damnah said, 'Dear friend!

COUPLET.

Should I tear my love from thee and remove my heart away,
Where should I my love bestow? whither then my heart convey?

Lay not the beginnings of separation and exclude me not from thy society, nor reproach me any more in the matter of Shanzabah, for to recall a thing which is past does but cause chagrin, and to deliberate on a matter which comes not into the area of remedy, belongs to the class of impossibilities. Put from thy thoughts this vain regret, and turn them towards mirthfulness and freedom from care, since one foe has set out for the world of nonentity, and the atmosphere of desire has been cleared from the dust of doubt, and the cupbearer of the wish has poured the draught of tranquillity into the goblet of joy, and the portals of hope have been opened wide to the face of success, and the bud of expectation has bloomed in the bed of happy tidings.'

COUPLET.

Cup-bearer! give the wine about, and as to friend or foe, be gay,
For our friend has come to glad our hearts and our foe has passed away.

Kalílah said, 'Notwithstanding that thou hast deviated from the path of generous conduct, and hast overthrown the pedestal of magnanimity with the axe of perfidy, thou still expectest to be free from anxieties, and hopest that thy time will pass in safety and happiness.

HEMISTICH.

Thou hast nurtured vain desire, framed a thought that cannot be.'

Damnah said, 'It is not that I was unaware of the shame of perfidious conduct, or the retributive consequences of deceit and fraud, or that the villany of slander and the odiousness of selfish machinations was concealed from me. But the love of place and the greediness of wealth, and the irresistible influence of envy incited me to such conduct, and as things are now situated, I know no remedy for this business, nor am I able to devise any cure for it.

HEMISTICH.

What can I? this to cure exceeds my power.'

The leopard, having heard this segment of their discourse, and having learned the true state of the case, went to the Lion's mother and said, ' I will communicate a secret on condition that the queen will be pleased to promise that without urgent cause she will not suffer it to be disclosed.' Then after many oaths and promises and injunctions [to secresy,] he fully recounted all that had passed between Kalílah and Damnah, and minutely repeated the reproaches of Kalílah and Damnah's confession. The Lion's mother was astonished at the details of this adventure, and next day came, according to her usual custom, to see the Lion. She found him excessively sad and pensive, and inquired saying, ' O son! what is the cause of thy trouble and perturbation ?

VERSE.

Why wanes thy moon, of its full glories shorn?
Why has the cypress dwindled to a thorn? [1]
Wherefore this trouble that thy looks express?
And from whose wrath these outcries of distress?

The Lion said, ' The slaughter of Shanzabah and the remembrance of his qualities and excellent gifts, is the sole cause of my grief, and however much I try, the recollection of him will not depart from my mind nor will my heart forget his memory.

VERSE.

By thy dear life! I cannot thee one moment e'en forget,
And could I once, what shall I do, for now it may not be!
Then not in jest thy Khusrau bid live, thee forgetting; yet,
Could I, I would—what shall I now? I still must think of thee.

As often as deliberation is held on affairs of state, and I feel the want of an attached well-wisher and kind counsellor, and a faithful friend, and a minister on whom I can rely, the phantom of Shanzabah comes before me and says,

COUPLET.

In mode of service—in fidelity,
Thou mayst seek long, nor find one such as I.'

The mother of the Lion said, ' In aiding the light of certainty to overpower the gloom of doubt and conjecture there is no evidence like the testimony of a pure heart, and the king's language leads one to understand that his heart bears witness to the innocence of Shanzabah, and assuredly

---

[1] _Khilál_ 'a tooth-pick' or 'skewer.'

since he was not put to death on lucid evidence and convincing testimony, and since the interested informer, under the form of advice, set forth his condition in a way opposite to the truth; hence every moment fresh regret springs up and unbounded remorse is occasioned, and if what they conveyed to the king had been pondered over and the courser of ire had been curbed with the bridle of patience, and thou hadst removed the darkness of that doubt with the light of clear intellect, at this moment[1] thou wouldest not have fallen into the snare of repentance nor wouldest thou have placed the volume of gladness and cheerfulness upon the shelf of non-existence.

VERSE.

Be thou sedate in what thou hast to do,
For fiery haste will prove abortive, too.
Did not the lamp so hot itself illume,
'T would not its substance and the moth consume.
Patience supplies to every ward its key,
One ne'er did patient men regretful see.'

The Lion said, 'O mother! as thou hast said, in this affair my passion got the better of my reason, and the fire of wrath burned up the foundation of mildness, and now there is no remedy for a matter which is included in the category of impossibilities, save to waive the thought of it. That, however, may be regarded as the worst of states in which my subjects have made me the target of the arrow of reproach, and have cast upon my name the lot[2] of unfaithfulness and cruelty, and however diligently I strive to bring home to the Ox a plain case of treason, and to prove against him the commission of a crime, in order that I may be absolved by others for slaying him, and may remove myself from the opprobrious remarks of those who know me and the sarcasms of strangers, it is no wise attainable or assured to me. The unfortunate Shanzabah had both a clear mind and pleasing manners, and with all these qualities it is not possible to charge him with what envy slanderously imputes to him, and such a person cannot be of the class that foul desires or vain longings should find a lodgment in his brain, so that he could have revolved my death or thought of warring with me. And, moreover, with regard to him, there has been no neglect of various kind offices or forms of favor, which might have become a link to hostility and aversion and the means of enmity and contention; and my wish is to use extreme efforts in investigating this matter, and to conduct the inquiry into these reports to the very limits of excess, and though this regret is unavailing, and that misfortune will not find a cure by this suit, still it may be that my mind may be consoled by it and the mischievous slanderer may be chastised, and my

---

[1] Here again is an equivoque on *dam* 'moment,' *dám* 'snare,' *nadam* 'repentance,' which cannot be retained in English.
[2] *Kur'ah* is the lot cast by the Arabs with arrows.

excuse may be admitted by men.[1]   And if thou hast known anything on this
or heard any tidings, favor me with the information and advice.'   The Lion's
mother said,

COUPLET.

'My heart is full of gems of mystery,
But on my tongue bands too and fastenings lie.

I have heard a thing, but the disclosure of it is not admissible, and I have
discovered a delicate matter, but to reveal it is not allowable.   For certain of
thy ministers have charged me to conceal it, and have been urgent with me
beyond measure to hide it, *'The hearts of the noble are the sepulchres of secrets.'*

COUPLET.

I asked of the old tavern-keeper, which is, then, salvation's way?
He called straight for the wine-cup, and quoth he, 'No secrets to betray."

And the king knows that to publish a secret is utterly wrong, and to reveal
what men would hide is inexpressibly mischievous; and were it not that the
wise have enjoined us to avoid that quality, I would have detailed the whole,
and would have swept away the dust of grief from the court of the heart of my
beloved and fortunate son ? '   The Lion said, ' The glosses of the wise and
the sayings of philosophers, are numerous.   If one party of them have been
commanded to abstain from disclosing secrets they had in view, the welfare
and safety of the speaker and others, too, have enjoined the revelation of
them for the public advantage, where the common weal may be conceived to
be therein.   And if any one has unjustly aimed at the life of one of the
faithful, and confides this secret to another, and imparts it to him with great
and strict oaths, and displays excessive earnestness in enjoining its concealment, and that confidant—for the preservation of the life of that Muslim,
—reveals the secret and acquaints the person [whose life is in danger] with
that information, in order that he may look to his affairs; he will,
undoubtedly, not be censurable by the law, nor will he be exposed to the
rebuke of God; and to keep back a secret in circumstances like these, shews
an agreement with the base, and it is possible that the conveyer of this
intelligence, by disclosing this secret desired to clear himself[2] and make over
the care of it to the surety of thy keeping, or he may have been afraid of me,
and made use of thee as the medium of communication.   I hope that thou
wilt acquaint me with it and act as befits thy counsel and affection.

COUPLET.

Impart to us the secret, for we may trusted be,
And cease these airs, this coyness, for true of heart are we.'

---

[1] Surely the use of the word *mardum* 'men, is out of place here; it should be 'animals;'
but into such inconsistencies the absurd notion of ascribing to irrational beings rational
thoughts will be sure to lead.

[2] Lit. : 'To draw out his own foot from the midst.'

The mother of the lion said, 'This intimation which thou hast given is worthy of the highest praise, and the purport of what thou hast set forth is worthy of much commendation ; but the disclosure of secrets has two palpable and absolute faults. The first of these is, the enmity of that person who, in reliance on another, has made him the confidant of his secrets : the second is, the suspicion of others ; for when a person has become notorious for rending veils and revealing the secrets of men, after that no one will impart anything to him, nor account him fit to be a confidant : he becomes both banished from the eyes of his friends, and overtaken, too, by the gibes of his enemies.

COUPLET.

However much my heart burns sore, my secret to reveal,
The fear of those who hate me sets upon my lips a seal.

And I have seen in the sayings of the wise that, ' *He whose secret does not slumber, his mischief will not slumber,*'—whoever does not conceal, in the casket of non-existence, the gem of his secret, that secret will assuredly set up a flag against his life. And it has become proverbial, that whoever lets his secret go out of his hands, gives his head in exchange for it.

HEMISTICH.

Wouldst thou keep fast thy head—thy secret keep.

But perhaps thou hast not heard the story of that Equerry who ventured to tell the king's secret, and in the end gave up his head for it,' The Lion said, ' How was that ? '

STORY III.

The lioness said, ' In times gone by there was a king, by the ornament of whose justice the throne of empire was adorned and ennobled, and the splendor of whose unstinted bounties shone over all the provinces of his realm.

COUPLET.

In pomp Farídún, and Jamshíd in state,   Like Dárá watchful, like Sikandar great.

One day he had gone out to hunt, and at a time when the hunting-ground [1] was close at hand, and every one was engaged in conducting the business which belonged to his post, he said to his Equerry, ' I wish to race my horse with thine, for I have for a long time desired to know whether the speed of this black, on which I am mounted, is greater than that of the pie-bald which thou art riding.' The Equerry, in accordance with the command of his prince, began to put his horse to its speed, and the king gave the rein to his fleet courser. As soon as they had got to a distance from the chase, the king pressed down his stirrups and reined in his horse,

---

[1] I read, with the MSS., *nakhchírgáh*, which corresponds to *shikárgáh* five lines below, and is evidently preferable to the *khargáh* of the editions.

11111111111111111

and said, 'O Equerry! my intention in coming this distance, is, that at this moment a thing has entered my mind, and an anxiety has overpowered my heart, and of all the special attendants of our presence, no one is fit to be the confidant of this secret, wherefore I wished to retire to this privacy, and—in such way that none should suspect—tell this secret to thee.' The Equerry made the obeisance due, and said,

COUPLET.

'O Khusrau! may heaven's sun thy servant be,   And happy fortune shine serene on thee! Although this despicable atom perceives not himself to be meet for this, but as the brilliancy of the hue of the royal favor has condescended to bestow on me the shade of fortune, I hope that the morning zephyr, which is the confidant of the secrets of the truths of spring, will not scent a portion of the fragrance of this parterre; and the heart, notwithstanding that it is the treasury of this coin, will not be able to advance to the limits of this intelligence.

COUPLET.

Just as the soul lies hid within the frame,   Thy secret in my soul shall lurk the same.'

The King commended him, and said, 'I am exceedingly in dread of my brother, and I have this day read, from the page of his movements, the writing of injurious designs,[1] and I have clearly observed that he has girt up the loins of malice for my destruction, and I have determined[2] that, before he can do mischief, I will remove the stone of his existence from my road, and clear the garden of the realm from the affliction of his thorn.

COUPLET.

The feeble fox, whose dog is he?   To do the lion injury.

Thou must keep a constant watch on his actions, and perform all that vigilance requires for my safeguard and protection.' The Equerry bowed, and having taken upon himself the business of guarding and concealing the matter, confirmed this by many assurances, and he had as yet not reached his place, when he inscribed the writing of faithlessness on the volume of his transactions, and turning aside from the path of loyalty and confidence, set his foot in the wilderness of perfidy and ingratitude.

STANZA.

Give thy heart little to the love of friends;
   For in this world's flower-grounds,
The scent that faith and friendship lends,
   Is in no comrade found.
I told the secret which my heart had nursed,
   Full sore it made me weep:
Would that my simple heart had known, at first,
   None can a secret keep.

---

[1] Hendiadys. In the text 'design and injury.'
[2] I omit, with the MSS., the *man ham bar dnam* of the editions.

The Equerry, having sought an opportunity, threw himself at the feet of the sultán's brother, and exposed to his gaze the story in the way that he had heard it.   The king's brother received this favor from him with prompt payment, and with many promises and innumerable gifts, bestowed on him advancements, and, by judicious counsel, secured himself from injury from his brother.   In a short time, as is the wonted vicissitude of fortune and the uncertainty of position, the spring of the fortunes of that brother to the king changed to the autumn of ruin, and the bud of his prosperity on the plant of his life shed its leaves.

STANZA.

What breeze of spring e'er blew beneath the sky,
    Unfollowed by the autumn of mishap?
Hope not from mother fortune for a constancy,
    That she will nurse thee gently on her lap;
There, the true scent of kindness does not lie.

And when the royal cushion and imperial throne was emptied of the adornment of the regal splendour of the elder brother, the younger set his foot on the step of the throne of sovereignty, and exalted the crown of royalty by placing it on the head of success.

COUPLET.

In the land of fortune's garden bloomed the bud of happiness,
And new beauties every sapling in dominion's orchard dress.

The first order that passed the lips of the king, and the earliest mandate for the delivery of which the imperial signal was given, was for the death of that Equerry.   The unfortunate wretch loosed the tongue of supplication, saying,

COUPLET.

'Great king! auspicious rule be thine!   And may thy star serenely shine!

What is my crime save that of affection and loyalty to thee?'

HEMISTICH.

The meed due to my actions is not this.'

The king pronounced this fiat, 'The worst of crimes is to divulge secrets, and that crime has been committed by thee, and after that thou hast failed to keep the secret of my brother, who selected thee for his confidant from all his attendants, what reliance can I have in thee?

HEMISTICH.

Better to part with an unfaithful friend.

However much the Equerry bemoaned himself, it was unavailing, and he was overtaken by the regal chastisement, and forfeited his head for the betrayal of the secret.[1]

---

[1] Throughout this story there is a play on *sirr* 'secret,' and *sar* 'head.'

COUPLET.

Is thy tongue ever to its secret true ?   What has the sabre with thy head to do ?

And the moral for the king to draw from the invention of this story is, that the divulging secrets has a bad result, and to disclose men's secret matters yields not the fruit of happiness.' The Lion said, 'Kind mother! he who betrays his own secret, intends that it should go abroad, otherwise he ought to be his own confidant; and after he has made known to another what was hidden in his mind, he should not be hurt if that other should disclose it to a third; for when one cannot draw one's own load, it is no wonder if another also cannot support the burthen.

COUPLET.

To thine own secret thou art unfaithful,—then   Canst thou expect more faith in other men ?

And, moreover, when a person by disclosing a secret makes known what it is right should be known; in that case, though they may account the disclosure a fault, still the revealing what ought to be known may serve to cover that fault. I trust that thou wilt oblige me by stating what it is right to state and thus remove the load of grief from my heart; and if thou canst not tell it openly, thou wilt let me understand its nature by hints, and though thou wilt not detail it in plain language, thou wilt at least not withhold it from me by signs.' The lion's mother replied, ' On condition that thou wilt bring to punishment that evil-doer who has stirred up the dust of this mischief, and that thou wilt conceal the beauty of forgiveness from his audacious eye, which is blinded to the path of truthfulness and rectitude. And although the learned in the faith and those versed in the knowledge of the true God, have used the strongest expressions as to the excellence of mercy and the pre-eminence of beneficence, and have stimulated and urged men to the adoption of that habit, still, in the case of crimes whose effect may extend to the mischief of the world, and the detriment of which may be diffused through the natures of mankind, punishment is better than mercy. And in requital of this offence—the injury of which has fallen on the king's mind, and has stained the skirt of his purity and good faith with the defilement of perfidy and treachery—should no vengeance be taken, it would serve to embolden other incendiaries, and the pretence[1] of the tyrannical would be confirmed, and everyone would regard it as a license to be relied on, and a pattern on which dependence could be placed for cruelty and wicked acts. Wherefore, in this place, pardon and connivance must not be allowed scope and in accordance with the irrefragable mandate, ' *And in this law of retaliation ye have life*,'[2] the remedy must be regarded as one of things requisite.

---

[1] For *hujjat* we find in the Dictionary 'argument, proof, pretext;' I would rather therefore—did the MSS. allow it—read some one word signifying 'acts,' 'proceedings.'

[2] Ḳur'án, Fl. ii., 175; Mar. ii., 180; Sale, p. 19, l. 27 : ' O true believers! the law of retaliation is ordained you for the slain, the free shall die for the free, and the servant for the servant, and a woman for a woman : but he whom his brother shall forgive, may be

COUPLET.

Whoever bids thee vex thy subjects, them   As public enemies to death condemn.

The drift of this preamble is that the perfidious Damnah, who persuaded the king of the world to this deed, is a sycophant and a slanderer, and wicked, and a villain.' The Lion said, 'I understand; thou must return, in order that I may deliberate on his punishment.' The lioness returned to her own abode, and the Lion, after long deliberation, gave command to summon his army; and having sent for his nobles and Pillars of the state, and ministers, and chief officers into his presence, besought the attendance of his mother, and after the assembling of all the nobles and people, delivered his royal order, so that they brought Damnah to the foot of the imperial throne, and the king, turning his back upon him, plunged into a long reverie. Damnah looked round, and found the door of calamity open, and the way of escape closed. He turned to one of the king's intimates, and said softly to him, 'What is the cause of this assemblage, and what has happened, that the king has fallen into meditation and reflection?' The lion's mother overheard, and said aloud, 'It is thy life on which the king deliberates, and since thy treason has become known and the villany of thy harmful acts manifest, and the falsehood which thou didst utter in relation to his attached friend, is patent,[1] and the curtain has been removed from the face of thy machinations and artifices; it is not fit that the king should leave thee one instant alive, or keep such a manifester of depravity in the expanse of ' *Existence, which is the chief good.*' Damnah said, 'The wise of past ages have left no particle of wisdom unsaid, and, for the convenience of those to come after them, have prepared clear ways, and one of their sagacious sayings is this, that whoever is unceasingly zealous in the service of the king, quickly reaches the rank of admission to his favour, and whoever has become the intimate of the sultán, all the friends and foes of the monarch become his enemies; the friends, through envy of his post and dignity; and the foes, by reason of his advising the king sincerely in matters of state and religion.

COUPLET.

The greater nearness to the king,   Will aye the greater danger bring.

And those who are intimate are in great peril, and hence it is that men of true piety have set their backs against the wall of security and rest, and have turned their faces from the fleeting, faithless, untrustworthy world, and have chosen the worship of the Creator in preference to the service of the creature, for with the glorious Lord[2] neither error nor neglect are admissible,

---

prosecuted and obliged to make satisfaction according to what is just, and a fine shall be set on him with humanity. This is indulgence from your Lord, and mercy. And he who shall transgress after this, by killing the murderer, shall suffer a grievous punishment. And in this law of retaliation ye have life: O ye of understanding, that peradventure ye may fear.'

[1] *Bd ṭarḥ uftddan,* a rare phrase.

[2] *Ḥaẓrat 'izzat :*—Observe the phrase.

nor are cruelty or tyranny allowed. To requite good with evil and to recompence obedience with punishment, is what cannot occur, and there can be no swerving from the path of justice in the commands of the king of kings.

QUATRAIN.

> God's justice moves in uniform career,
> All others' tenderness [1] is cruelty.
> There is no wrongful dealing, such as here
> Is found, nor man's mistakings there can be.

In general the actions of creatures, in contrast to the character of the Creator, are stained with a variety of contradictions and inconsistencies, and in deviation from an exact observance of what is due, men at one time bestow on offenders deserving of chastisement, the reward meet for the conduct of friends; and, at another time, visit upright councillors, who deserve encouragement, with the punishment which befits the sins of traitors. For vain desires have the mastery over their actions, and error is evident in what they do. In their words they display self-interest, and in their deeds their hypocrisy is palpable. Good and evil are to them alike, and gain and loss in their sight are equal. One man may hand over to the treasurer of the king all the treasures upon earth's surface, and he will not feel a grain of gratitude towards him, but will exalt the head of another who abuses him to the pinnacle of honor.

COUPLET.

> Behold their proud ingratitude, and their thankless coldness see!
> They care not whether minstrel or mourner thou mayst be.

I ought not, from the first, to have hovered round the royal service, nor to have stepped out of the cell of retirement, and beyond the corner of privacy, nor to have accepted the duty of attendance on the king, which resembles consuming fire; for whoever does not appreciate freedom from care, and prefers the service of the creature to that of the Creator, meets with what befell the solitary Devotee.' The lioness asked, 'How was that?'

STORY IV.

Damnah said, 'They have related that a Devotee had renounced the concerns of the world and had made choice of the corner of retirement; and satisfied the requirements of food and raiment with barley-bread and coarse woollen garments.[2]

---

[1] A very obscure line. *Rizd* signifies 'endeavouring to please.' It seems to me to mean that, 'even that which man intends to be equitable is harsh and unjust, whereas God's justice is pure.'

[2] If you supply '*irás kardah* before *as takallufát*, the meaning might be ' turning from the luxuries of eating and dress,' since *takalluf* signifies also ' costliness.'

The draggings of distress had made him sad,
On a hill's skirt his lone abode he had.
Ease he forsook his frame to macerate,
And could with simple herbs his hunger sate.[1]

The rumour of the devotion and upright character of that saintly man spread in a short time through the districts and environs of that country, and people began to come from far and near for the purpose of securing good-fortune and a blessing: and when they beheld the effect of the luminousness of divine worship clear and evident upon his bright forehead, waxing warmer in the matters of faith, they displayed still greater zeal. Now in that country there was a king, just and liberal, and the friend of darveshes; who used to give to the pursuit of divine favor precedence over compliance with those desires that affect a king, and who imitated nothing but the character of prophets and the morals of holy men.

COUPLET.

Pure morals, kindly manners, and to deal with all aright,
Are pleasing in the poor recluse, but in the prince more bright.

When the tidings of the devout hermit reached him, he put in practice the wise saying, ' *Happy is the prince and happy the fakir,*' and waited on the saintly man, and having besought the aid of his blessed spirit, requested some piece of advice which might prove useful to kings. The pious recluse said, ' O king! God has two pavilions, one transitory, which they call the world, and the other enduring, which they call the life to come. Magnanimity requires that thou shouldest not rest satisfied with this transitory abode, but transfer thy views to the empire of the enduring world.

VERSE.

Seek then the world to come, for joys are there!
Not with its smallest portion could compare
A hundred worlds; then strive, where now thou art,
To win of that more happy world a part.'

The king said, ' By what plan can that kingdom be subjugated ? ' The Devotee replied, ' By aiding the oppressed and attending to the complaints of the destitute; and every king who desires repose hereafter must labour for the case of his subjects.

VERSE.

He peaceful slumbers underneath the clay,
Whose people sleep in peace beneath his sway.
And they will fruit from youth and fortune find,
Who show themselves to those below them kind.

---

[1] I have found it impossible to translate literally these impracticable lines. The literal rendering would be, ' He was weary at the pullings of his collar by grief, and fastened his own skirt to the skirt of the mountain. He placed his body from voluptuousness under cruelty and set his heart from contentment with grass ! '

Kings who religion cherish, will succeed
In winning at faith's game the ball, their meed.' [1]

When the recluse had finished his advice, and had filled the treasury of the king's heart with the jewels of admonition, the counsels and exhortation of the pure-minded and saintly man made an impression on the king, and he laid the hand of discipleship on the skirt of his spirit, and was continuously in the habit of presenting himself in his company, and by the blessing of obedience to his persuasive words, turned away his head from following lust and vanity. One day the king was waiting on the darvesh, and they were discoursing on every subject, when suddenly a party of petitioners for justice raised their clamours and outcries [2] to the etherial ball. The Devotee called them to him and inquired into the case of each, separately, and instructed his highness the king, in the orders fit and proper for each of their suits. The king was excessively grateful for this, and besought that he might occasionally hold a court of requests under his fortunate superior tendence. The holy man, in order that the suits of the distressed might be speedily and satisfactory settled, and that he himself, by directing these matters, might obtain the advantage of an eternal recompense, consented; and in any affair, as the occasion required, the recluse delivered his decree, and the king, with willingness and eagerness, gave heed to him, until things came to that pass that most of the affairs of that realm were united to the skirt of the management of that lofty and saintly man, and he was daily more and more employed in the affairs of the state and of the revenue. The bewitching love of place deposited its furniture in the environs [3] of the saint's heart, and made a breach in his religious duties and seasons of prayer, and the desire of pomp and state having raised the head of the darvesh from the pillow of repose, made him aim at the diadem of pride.

COUPLET.

Whom does not this witching sorceress from the one true path beguile ?
Who drinks not the draught of error from the goblet of her wile ?

The world is a deceitful woman, which has brought many a lion-like man under the noose of her love, and a perfidious dame [4] that has thrown many famous warriors like the hero Rustam, into the pit of calamity.

---

[1] Religion is compared to the game of *chaugán*, in which the pious carry off the ball of happiness.

[2] *Nafír* in Persian is 'a fife,' in Arabic ' a crowd of fugitives.'

[3] With the MSS. I read *khwush khwush hubb-i jáh*, instead of the *khwush hhwush sauddí hubb-í* of the editions.

[4] There is an equivoque here which cannot be retained in English. *Zál* signifies, ' the father of Rustam,' as well as ' old woman.' *Taham-tan*, 'strong-bodied,' is an epithet of Rustam, who, according to some accounts, was enticed into a pit and slain.

VERSE.

Its Rustam a false treacherous dame [1] enslaves;
   Its hero buried in the pit of woe;
Its Egypt swept by Wrong's Nilotic waves;
   Its Joseph in torn clothes with blood which flow.
Its meetings hard by separation are;
   Its promise on the hill-top of deceit;
Its sea of blood from each Asfandiyár, [2]
   And of each monarch's crown its royal seat.

And when the recluse had tasted, in place of the brackish water of abstinence, the pleasant flavour of sensual desire and the delicious sharbat of worldly lust, the delight of worshipping God was effaced from his mind, and he inserted in his ear the ring of ' *Love of the world is the head of all sin.*'

COUPLET.

When the recluse gave ear to fortune's bell,
He lost all pleasure in his lonely cell.

The king too, when he saw that the abilities of the Devotee, and that his counsels were beneficial to the state, at once placed the reins of full power in the hand of his able management. Before, the darvesh had to take thought for bread; now he had the cares of the world upon him, and he exchanged his former anxiety how to procure a blanket, for the scheme of subjugating an empire.

COUPLET.

No longer in the bed thou sawest are the flowers gay;
Autumn came; and spring's verdure all, alas! has passed away.

One day a darvesh, who, from time to time, used to come into the presence of the recluse, and used to pass whole nights with him in prayer and supplication, paid a visit of devotion to him, and beheld his state and circumstances. The flame of regret was kindled in the area of his heart.

COUPLET.

Dark have grown life's [fairy] waters, where is holy Khizr? say!
From the rose-bough blood is dropping: where do spring's soft breezes stray?

When the night had come, and the hum of men was for the most part hushed, he said to the recluse, 'O Shekh! what is this state of things that I behold, and the change of condition that I observe?

COUPLET.

Thy course did one bright day of hope appear;
Where is that hope? and where that bright career?

---

[1] Here again is an equivoque on *zál*, which may be either a woman, or the father of Rustam.

[2] Asfandiyár called *rúin-tan*, 'brazen-bodied,' was a celebrated Persian hero, slain by Rustam, after a combat of two days' duration. He was the son of Gushtásp, of the first dynasty of Persian kings.

However much the holy man endeavoured to excuse himself, he was unable to utter a word which could completely stand the test of the touchstone of wisdom.[1] 'These speeches,' said his guest, 'are mere sensual pretexts. The purport of these prolix orations, and the pith of the whole discourse is that the mind of your Holiness is bent upon worldly things, and that your exalted spirit is in bondage to ambition and avarice.

COUPLET.

Can a phœnix[2] such as thou art condescend to carrion?
Fie! that such a glorious shadow o'er a carcase should be thrown.

Come and shake the skirt of thy solitary devotions free from the dust of rival pursuits, and draw the head of retirement under the collar of reliance on God, and bring not to the palate of desire the envenomed dainties of the world.

COUPLET.

O'er the table of the world's feast do not thou hope's hand extend;
For they with this dainty morsel venom too and poison blend.'

The recluse answered, 'O kind friend! from discourse with my fellow-creatures and intercourse with mankind, so great an alteration has not found its way into my condition; and, in my heart, I am mindful of that very thing thou talkest of.' The guest rejoined, 'Thou hast now lost the sense of perception, because sensual inclinations have veiled thy sight, and when thou comest to thy senses, repentance will be unavailing.

COUPLET.

Thus hast thou done, and, when thy time is spent,
It will be fruitless though thou shouldst repent.

And thy case is like that of the blind man, who mistook a snake for the thong of a whip, and hence fell into the whirlpool of destruction.' The recluse inquired, 'How was that?'

STORY V.

He that had come from the journey said, 'Once on a time a blind man, and one that saw, halted at a place in some wild tract of country. When the time of their starting in the grey of the morning[3] arrived, they were about to set out. The blind man was searching for his whip, and as it chanced that a snake lay there frozen by the cold, he imagined that it was his whip and took it up. When he touched it with his hand he found it softer and nicer than his whip, at which he was pleased, and mounted his

---

[1] *M'arifat* signifies here, and very frequently elsewhere, 'knowledge of holy things.'
[2] The Humá is a bird which the Persians say, flies without ever touching the ground. Yet it is said to feed on bones.
[3] *Shabgír* I take to be ' starting on a journey between midnight and dawn.'

P

horse, and forgot the whip he had lost. However, when the day had dawned, his companion, who could see, looked and saw a snake in the hand of the blind man. Hereupon he shouted out, 'Comrade! what thou tookest for a whip is a poisonous snake. Fling it away before it makes a wound on thy hand.' The blind man fancied that his companion coveted the whip, and replied, 'O friend!

HEMISTICH.

What can I do? 'Tis owing to my luck.

I lost my whip and God has given me a better one. Thou too, if fortune befriend thee, will find a nice whip. But I am not one of those who would allow my whip to be wheedled out of my hand by imaginary tales.' He that could see laughed and said, 'O brother! my duty as thy companion demands that I should acquaint thee with this danger. Listen to what I say, and throw down that snake.' The blind man frowned and said,

COUPLET.

'Why, O suitor! thus excessive and beyond all limits plead?
Hear this saying:—Each day's fortunes are by destiny decreed.

Thou hast taken a longing for my whip and thou pressest me beyond all bounds to throw it away, in the greedy hope that when I throw it down, thou mayest pick it up. Do not indulge a vain idea, and give up a desire which is nought, for this is a whip which has come into my hands from the unseen world.

HEMISTICH.

One must not by a foe's deceit be led.'

However much the man that could see urged his point, and confirmed what he said by oaths loud and strong, it was of no use whatever, and the blind man gave no heed to him. So when the air became warm and the snake's body got rid of its chill, it wound itself back, and in its progress[1] wounded the blind man in the hand and killed him.

And I have adduced this story that thou too may not trust in the world, nor be fascinated by its appearance, which is painted like the body of a snake; nor be fond of its softness and delicacy, for its wound is deadly and its poison fatal.

VERSE.

Think not sweet sharbat from the world to drink;
Honey with poison is commingled there.
That which thou fondly dost sweet honey think,
Is but the deadly potion of despair.'

The recluse having listened to this discourse, called to mind the times of

---

[1] *Ḥarakat* may apply to the snake or to the movements of the blind man. I have chosen the former application with much doubt as to its accuracy.

his solitude and abstraction from the world, and beheld the stain of worldly interests, which had not suffered the skirt of his heart to remain in its original purity. He felt that what his friend had said was out of pure kindness and friendship. Thus he began to let fall the tears of repentance from his eyes, and to heave burning sighs from his breast, which was consumed by the fire of regret.

COUPLET.

I have a heart worn down with grief, then why not weep and sigh ? [1]
I have a weary [2] fortune too, then why not wail and cry?

All night long, like a lighted taper, he wept, while his heart was consuming ; and, like a moth longing for the flame, he fluttered in eager desire after the divine excellence ; [3] until the time when the white-robed votary of the true morn [4] spread the prayer-carpet of the sun before the shrine, '*And when the morn breathed forth,*' and the black-appareled ascetic of the night lodged itself in the private closet of '*When the night draws in.*'

COUPLET.

While o'er heaven's breast morn drew her robe of light,
Earth did her face unveil from gloomy night.

Again men pressed in crowds to the cell of the recluse, and the gales of pride beginning to blow, gave the corn of his nightly repentance to the wind of indifference.

COUPLET.

Each night I say, ' To-morrow I these wishes will forego;'
But every morn again I feel fresh longings for them grow.

In short, the recluse, having taken up the affairs of the state, deposed the nobles and ministers from their offices, and began, too, to indulge in a deviation from the path of equity in the adjudication of matters. One day he gave orders to put to death one of the people, whose death was not permitted by the law, and after the punishment was over, he turned in quest of a remedy and amends. The heirs of the man that had been executed demanded justice of the king against the recluse. The nature of the complaint was made known, and their case was referred to the tribunal of the law. The decree of the judge was forthwith issued to the effect that, by way of retaliation, they should put the recluse to death, and although he got persons to intercede for him, and promised money and valuables, he failed of his object, and, as a disastrous consequence of sacrificing the worship of the Creator for the

---

[1] Here, with what will appear to us considerable bad taste, *dh dh* is made to rhyme with *zdr zdr*.

[2] Lit.: 'drowsy,' *khwáb alúdah.*

[3] I make *shauḳ-i-jamál* refer to the Deity, as in the case of the moth, it does to the brightness of the taper.

[4] The *ṣubḥ-i ṣádiḳ* is 'the true dawn,' opposed to *ṣubḥ-i kázib* 'the twilight,' but the epithet is chosen here with reference to *záhid.*

service of the creature, he was overtaken in the whirlpool of destruction. Thus he lost[1] the pleasures of the world and failed to gain the happiness of the world to come.

And I have framed this story to show that as I, too, turned away my face from the shrine of God's worship, and hurried to the imperial court, and withdrew my head from the line of obedience to the All-Provider, and placed it on the threshold of the prince's service,

HEMISTICH.

I merit all imaginable woe.'

When Damnah had finished this discourse, the attendants of the royal throne were astonished at his eloquence, and the Lion, with his head bent, as before, in meditation, could not think how to enter upon the affair or how to reply to Damnah. A lynx who, of all the courtiers, was honored with the nearest access to the king, when he observed the amazement of those who were present in the assembly, turned his face to Damnah and said, ' All these reproaches that thou hast heaped on the service of kings, whose head, reaching to the polar star, is crowned with the diadem, ' *A just king is God's shadow upon earth*,' befit thee not.[2] But hast thou not heard that a single hour of a king's life which is passed in the dispensation of justice and in taking care of his people, is taken to be an equivalent for sixty years of piety and devotion; and many of the worshipers[3] at the shrine of devotion and the priestly office, and of the crowned heads of the kingdom of spiritual enlightenment and miraculous gifts, have voluntarily chosen the service of kings, according to the saying, ' *The service of kings is half the road* [*to heaven*]' with a view to assisting the oppressed and lightening the burthens of the distressed : and among the number of such cases, the story of the Saint of radiant mind, testifies to the justice of this matter.' Damnah asked, ' How was that ? '

STORY VI.

The lynx said, ' They have related that in a city of Fárs there was a venerable old man who had carried off the reed of superiority from the horse-men of the circus of sanctity,[4] while the peak of his crown of abnegation of worldly pleasures touched the summit of the celestial sphere.

---

[1] *Bar dmadan* is here idiomatically used to signify ' emerging from,' in the sense of 'letting slip,' 'losing.'

[2] *Nah hadd-i tú bavad* ' is not in thy limits,' i.e., is unsuited to thee. A common phrase at the end of letters is *ziyddah hadd-i adab*, ' more would be beyond the bounds of respect.' So *adab* might be understood here with *hadd*.

[3] Lit. : ' the sitters on the carpet of prayer.'

[4] I take *wildyat* here as used equivocally, signifying both ' a country ' and also ' the state of a *walí* or saint ' ; so too in the first line of the verses following, *kaṣabu's-sabḳ* I imagine to be ' the *jarid* of superiority' ;—as horsemen catch the *jarid*, and thus outdo others, so this saint snatched away from others the superiority.

VERSE.

In saintship's realm imperial state had he,
He crowned himself, while he abandoned all.
The circus of his steed—eternity:
And with the Infinite he played at ball.[1]

They used to call him the Saint of radiant mind. The echoing rumour of his miraculous gifts pervaded the provinces of Rúm and the countries of the west, and the hubbub[2] of his séances reached the inhabitants of Egypt and Syria and Arabia Petræa and Felix. The wise men of 'Irák, as well as the refined of Khurásán, placed their heads on the line of attachment to him; and the pious people of Turkistán, as well as those transported with divine love in Hindústán, laid the hands of sincerity on the skirt of discipleship to him. One day a darvesh from Transoxiana, resolved on going as a pilgrim to the holy shrine of that Saint, and, with many toils, conveyed himself from the environs of Samarkand to the capital of Fárs: and truly until one has wounded the foot of search in the thorny brake of trouble, the hand of attainment will not reach the collar of the rose of desire.

COUPLET.

The nightingale, that cannot bear the woes
Of the sharp thorn, must speak not of the rose.

The darvesh who had thus traveled, after crossing the waste of despond,[3] alighted at the K'abah of peace and safety, and having made the dust of the threshold of the Saint a kissing-place for the lips of respect, put in motion the knocker of eagerness. The attendant of the monastery, after inquiring into his case and informing himself of the circumstances of his fatiguing journey, pronounced these words, 'O darvesh! rest a little, for his highness the shekh has gone to wait on the reigning monarch, and the hour for his return is by-and-bye.' When the darvesh heard talk of waiting on the king, he exclaimed, 'Fie on the toilsome journey and the wasting of my time! A shekh who goes to wait on a king and finds pleasure in visiting and discoursing with him, what can he do to aid me? or how point out to me the right way?

---

[1] The literal translation of these exceedingly difficult lines, is 'He in the country [or in the state of a walí] has become a sultán in majesty. He made a tiara from the abandonment of the two worlds. He galloped his Rakhsh from eternity without beginning, and played at ball in the horse-tennis of eternity without end.' Here note that sultán pandh is a phrase similar to dárá panáh in p. 12, l. 18 of the Persian text, and that Rakhsh was the name of Rustam's celebrated steed. These lines may be taken as a specimen of what the translator of Persian verses has to encounter. The late well-known Persian scholar, Mr. Swinton, wrote to recommend that I should inquire the meaning of some phrases here of the Persian ambassador, so difficult did he consider them.

[2] I have chosen this uncouth word as corresponding, in sound as well as sense, to دبدبه dabdabah.

[3] I have no doubt that an allusion to the Hajj is intended here as حرمان may be vowel-pointed so as to be hirmán 'disappointment,' or haramáni 'the two sacred cities of Makkah and Madinah.'

COUBLET.

Dog-like, to perish at his feet was once my wish, my trust:
Alas! those hopes all suddenly have crumbled into dust.'

He then came forth from the monastery, and took his way to the bázár, and through the impurity of his deceitful heart, which had not been tempered in the furnace of austerity, he impressed on the coin of the she<u>kh</u>'s career the stamp of short measure; and ignorant of his true condition, gave vent to unreasonable censures.

COUPLET.

Boaster! thou walkest by the water's brink,
How canst thou know the state of us who sink!

Suddenly the police-magistrate of the city caught sight of him, and it happened that a thief, who resembled him in appearance, had, on the previous night, escaped from prison, and the king had severely reprimanded the magistrate and the watch, and had given the strictest injunctions to catch the thief and to cut off his hands. The magistrate saw the darvesh, and imagining him to be the runaway thief, had him straightway conveyed to the place of punishment. In vain the darvesh showed his safe-conduct[1] and gave a true account of himself, he gained nothing thereby, and there was nothing at hand for him but to have his hand[2] cut off. At the instant that the pitiless executioner had placed a sharp knife on the hand of the darvesh, and was about to sever it, there arose the shouts of the retinue of the Saint of radiant mind, as they called out to clear the way; and the she<u>kh</u> with a grand cavalcade,[3] arrived where that crowd was assembled, and having inquired into the circumstances, was informed of the position in which the darvesh was placed. He told the magistrate, 'This is one of the darveshes belonging to my place, and the suspicion thrown upon him is contrary to the facts—release him.' The magistrate kissed the she<u>kh</u>'s horse's hoof, and expressed himself under a vital obligation; he then apologized to the darvesh and went about his business. The poor darvesh finding himself set free from the snare of destruction and from the merciless hands of the executioner, proceeded with the she<u>kh</u>'s retinue as one of his attendants, and as they were going, the she<u>kh</u> laid his hand on the shoulder of the darvesh and whispered to him, 'Brother! to forswear fellowship with darveshes is not right, for did we not wait upon the king, ill-used persons like thyself would find no escape from the hands of their oppressors.' The darvesh perceived that his repudiation of the she<u>kh</u> had sprung from ignorance and folly, and that whatever is done

---

[1] *Barát-i ẓimmat*—our 'passport.'

[2] I have designedly used this phrase to represent the play upon words in the text.

[3] *Maukib* I take to be 'a cavalcade,' *markab*, which occurs two lines further on, 'a horse, or whatever serves as vehicle to a man.' Yet if this be right, I would rather read *bá* than *dar* with the former word.

by the thoroughly righteous is sure not to be wrong; because the intentions of a perfect saint melt into unison with those of God himself, wherefore not a single action will spring from him which will not be in accordance with the divine will, nor will anything he does, though apparently unreasonable and improper, be in reality unadvisable.

DISTICHS.

The child whose throat is cut by Ḵẖiẓr's knife,[1]
A people could not render back to life.
And should his ship be wrecked in open sea,
A hundred hopes in Ḵẖiẓr's wreck will be.
Be sure that where his healing hands restore
The breach, it will be there perceived no more.
And should he one decapitate, e'en then
He'd give a hundred thousand heads again.
Earth that the true saint touches turns to gold,
And this to ashes in the trifler's hold.

And the moral of this story is that eminently holy men have voluntarily taken upon themselves the service of kings and have thought it no harm to frequent royal courts.

HEMISTICH.

Who then art thou, to be accounted of?'

Damnah said, 'With regard to what thou hast said, that the excellent have sought eminence in the service of kings, it is true they have done so, but with a view to an advantage of the highest consequence, and they have not entered upon this measure without divine inspiration, nor have they suffered the smallest worldly or carnal motive to blend itself therewith; and whoever has such a bent as this, whatever he may do or say, none may be so bold as to blame him; but when will the like of us reach this dignity? or how can we justify our pretension to a rank so high? And as to what thou hast further said, that a king is the shadow of God, I admit that too; but it is the temper of true kings to make their actions run parallel to the right way and keep them far removed from the path of wrong; not to patronise one for a temporary selfish motive, and, then, without just occasion, order him to be punished: and the most praiseworthy of all royal qualities is to hold dear those of their servants who exhibit commendable dispositions, and to degrade their faithless and perfidious ministers.

---

[1] I have taken some liberties with these most unpoetical and tiresome verses. There is no word for knife in the first line, and the second is, literally ' the common people will not find his head.' In the fourth line I have translated *durustī* freely, by ' hopes;' and *nāḵis* in the last line means 'imperfect' rather than 'trifler.' One MS., very properly I think, omits the seventh and eight lines, which, if retained, should follow the second. For *zamān* I would gladly read *ẓimn* and translate it ' guarantee.' On the whole a more wretched attempt at poetry is not to be found in the ' Anvār-i Suhailī ' than this.

STANZA.

The rose-plant of the righteous man's estate,
With mercy's rain he does invigorate.
The wicked, like the wound-inflicting thorn,
Are by his terror from the roots uptorn.'

The lioness said, 'What thou sayest is true, but thy case appears the
very opposite of this, since the collective voice of this assembly pronounces
that Shanzabah was a worthy minister of the king, and of an amiable temper,
and the common report is, that the harvest of his promise was consumed by
the fire of thy calumny, and that the pedestal of the king's faith was overturned by the disastrous influence of thy mischievous meddling.

COUPLET.

Thy envy has a conflagration lit,   And a whole universe consumes in it.'

Damnah said, 'It is not concealed from the irradiated mind of the king,
and all who are present know, that between me and the ox none of the
materials of contention and enmity existed, how then can hostility as anciently
entertained by us, be thought of? And he too, although he had the power
to attack me, and the opportunity of injuring me, and strength to get rid of
me, nevertheless observed towards me only the path of kindness and benevolence; and I too was not contemptible and unimportant in the king's sight,
that I should exert myself to get rid of the ox through envy and hatred, but
I gave the king a piece of advice and disinterestedly conveyed to his ears
a speech that I had heard and the traces of which I had observed; and it
was my duty to be grateful for the king's kindness, and to exhibit with
truthfulness the apparent treachery and dangerous intentions of the ox; and
as to what I said, the king too, himself, made investigation, and discovered
that which verified my words and confirmed the charge I brought, and, at the
call of his own judgment, carried out the measure; and now there are many
persons, who were in league with Shanzabah, and partners of his perfidy and
hostile intentions, who are afraid of me since I have adopted the habit of
telling the truth. It is a true and just saying, that '*Truth is bitter.*'

COUPLET.

All to whom I truth have spoken have become my enemies.
Since the truth may not be said, the best course in silence lies.

And, assuredly, a party of hypocrites will exert themselves to get me put to
death, and I did not suspect that the recompense of my advice and the result
of my service would be this, that my continuing to live should be a cause of
anxiety and disturbance to the king.' When Damnah had spoken thus far
and the day had waned, the Lion said, 'He must be delivered over to the
judges, in order that they may inquire into his case, since in penal sentences
and judicial proceedings, without adducing clear evidence and conviction on
certain proof,

HEMISTICH.

It is not right commands to execute.'

Damnah said, ' What judge is more righteous than the reason of the prince, and what magistrate more equitable than the fair justice of the fortunate king? and, praise be to God! the luminous mind of the sultán is a clear mirror, or rather a world-displaying goblet, and the condition of every one of his attendants is therein clearly displayed.

COUPLET.

Be, and it was ![1] thy wisdom said to the mysterious scroll;
And at thy word e'en fate's decrees their destinies unroll.

And I know of a certainty that in removing the veil of doubt, and undoing the wimple of uncertainty and surmise, nought equals the sagacity of the king and his discernment, and, assuredly, when the mirror of his command is purified from the rust of self-interest and bias, I am convinced that if proper investigation is made my immunity[2] will in all respects be established, and the honesty of my mind, like the dawning of the light of the real morning, will shine luminously to all.[3]

HEMISTICH.

No secret 's hidden 'neath thy wisdom's light.'

The Lion said, ' O Damnah! this matter shall be investigated to the utmost possible extent, and this affair shall be inquired into with all imaginable care.

STANZA.

In sifting this affair I'll labour so,
That forth I'll drag it as a hair from dough.
Thyself dost know that every hidden thing
Of heaven itself, my mind's light forth can bring?

Damnah said, 'I am the more anxious for this excessive strictness[4] by reason of my innocence, for I know that in this scrutiny my loyalty will be more abundantly evident, and had I been guilty in this affair, I should not have continued in attendance at the king's court, nor sat tamely waiting for misfortune; but I should have repeated to myself the purport [of this injunction] ' *Go through the earth*,'[5] and have gone to another region.

---

[1] This expression, intimating God's omnipotence, like the 'Let there be light and there was light' of Scripture, occurs with a shade of variation in the Ḳur'án, as at ch. xvi. 40; Sale p. 200, l. 39 : ' Verily our speech unto anything, when we will the same, is, that we only say unto it, ' Be,' and it is.'

[2] *Barát-i zimmat* in a somewhat different sense from that in p. 180 of the Persian text, last line but three.

[3] *'Alamiyán* ' men,' ' mankind.'

[4] Lit. ' in excess and straining to the utmost.'

[5] Ḳur'án, Fl. ch. xvi. 38; Mar. 36; Sale p. 200, l. 29 : ' Wherefore go through the earth, O tribe of Koreish! and see what hath been the end of those who accused their apostles of imposture ;" and, Ḳur'án, Fl. ii. 131, Mar. 137; Sale p. 47, l. 25 : ' There have already been before you examples of punishment of infidels, therefore go through the earth, and behold what hath been the end of those who accuse God's apostles of imposture.'

HEMISTICH.
For wide and ample is the plain of earth.'

The lioness said, 'O Damnah! thy vehement desire for inquiry appears
to be not devoid of mental alarm, but thou hopest by cunning to bring
thyself out innocent; but to look for escape from this strait without thy case
being investigated is an impossible thought and a vain desire.' Damnah
replied, 'I have many enemies, and those who bear malice towards me are
infinitely numerous. What I look for is that my case may be entrusted to a
judge who may be clear from interested feelings and from suspicion, and who
will truthfully convey to the royal ears whatever is said or heard; and that
the king will refer this to his world-adorning judgment, which is the mirror
of victory and triumph, so that I may not be put to death on a mere
suspicion and that in the day of retribution no blame may accrue on account
of that innocent blood.

COUPLET.
I fear not death,—but may it never be:
My blood [accusing] should entangle thee.[1]

The Lion said, 'I have never in any command deviated from the path of
justice, and, save in the way of equity, is is impossible for me to tread; and
if this perfidious act has proceeded from thee, thou shalt meet the punishment
which is thy due.

HEMISTICH.
What in life's field thou sowest, thou shalt reap?'

Damnah replied, 'Why should I imagine such treason? and by what
means suffer the desire of high affairs and the longing for offices of dignity to
pass through my mind? and for my part I know well the king's justice, and
have surveyed the tokens of his righteous dealing, and I feel certain that he
will not prevent my participating in his world-adorning justice, nor cut off
from me the hope of the blessings of the due which he dispenses to all.

COUPLET.
For justice God did thee create, O king!
From a just Lord, no unjust act can spring.'

One of the by-standers said, 'What Damnah says is not intended in honor
of the king, but by these words he hopes to avert calamity from himself.'
Damnah rejoined, 'Who is more tender of me than I myself am, and who my
truer friend than myself? and whoever permits himself to remain in a
difficulty, and takes no thought for his own preservation, what hope can
others place in him?

COUPLET.
Since thou neglectest e'en thine own affair,
How canst thou for another's business care?

---

[1] Lit.: 'Should seize thy skirt.'

Thy speech is a proof of a want of understanding and judgment, and of an abundance of ignorance and error; and think not that this circumstance will remain hid from the king's sagacity, [not so!] but after due reflection he will distinguish between thy reproach and salutary advice, since his luminous mind can deliberate in a single night on the affairs of a whole life, and subdue vast armies by a thought.

COUPLET.

In one short breath his thought—far-sighted, world-subduing too—
Can things effect, which none beside could in a life-time do?'

The lynx said, 'I am not so much astonished at thy former tricks and perfidiousness, as at thy declamation in thy present condition, and thy display of maxims, and quaint sayings, and saws.' Damnah rejoined, 'Aye! it is the place for admonition if it alights in the spot of acceptance, and it is the season for uttering maxims if they gain a hearing from the ear of under-standing.' The lioness said, 'O traitor! art thou still in hopes of escaping by thy juggles and deceit?' Damnah answered, 'If one return evil for good, and think injury a just recompence for benefit, [I am, then, indeed, without hope]. Yet I, at least, have fully discharged my engagements as a servant, and have been faithful to my duty as a counsellor. The king well knows that no false accuser would dare to utter his calumnies before him, and if he think fit to deal cruelly with me, the infamy thereof will recoil on himself, and if he act precipitately with regard to me, and neglect the advantages of deliberation and the blessings of proof and patient investigation, he will repent in the end; as they have said,

COUPLET.

They who in action too great rashness show,
Will their own reason's structure overthrow.

And whoever deprives himself of the excellent quality of patience by acting precipitately, meets with what that woman met with, who, displaying over-haste in her proceedings, could not discriminate between her friend and the slave.' The Lion, who was listening to what Damnah said, when he heard this shrewd remark, asked, 'How was that?'

STORY VII.

Damnah said, 'They have related that in the city of Kashmír there was a merchant possessed of great wealth and opulence, and many servants, and a great establishment. He had a wife of moon-like face and musky ringlets, such that heaven's eye had never beheld a luminary like her, nor had so fair a figure ever come into the hand of Time. Her cheek was bright and radiant like the day when lovers meet, and her tresses dark, and long as the day of separation.

VERSE.

Her beauty like the mid-day glorious sun,
     Like the narcissus, half in sleep, her eye.
Her cheek the rose and rose-juice, blent in one,
     Her waist was slender and her bosom high.
Sweeter than honey or rose-conserves taste,
Softer than budding roses when embraced.

And in close vicinity lived a painter, who, by his expertness, had acquired a world-wide notoriety,[1] and was admired by all for his pictures. The souls of the painters of China wandered distracted in the desert of jealousy at the brush of his portraiture, and the heart of the artists of Cathay were bewildered in the waste of envy at the skill of his delineation.

VERSE.

That skilful master could, with science rare,
     His paintings, like the wind,[2] on water trace.
And when the cheeks and tresses of the fair—
     The heart consuming with their magic grace—
He showed; it seemed as though he did pourtray
The hue of night upon the board of day.[3]
When he his reed upon the tablet drew,
Reason, like pictured things, insensate grew.

In short there arose between him and the wife of the merchant a mutual attachment, and the painter began to feel a blind and uncontrollable love for that graceful form, and the monarch, Love, overcame the territory of his heart, the metropolis of the affections; and the forces of desire commenced their ravages over the seven regions of his body.

HEMISTICH.

King Love his heart, his faith's domain, subdued.

The visual organs of the young lover, like the heart of the pious, became watchful, and the eyes of his vigils, like April clouds, began to rain down tears.

COUPLET.

Taper-like with inward burning, nightly where my love doth sleep,
Now from scorching pain I suffer, now from sorrow sadly weep.

The merchant's wife, too, had beheld the youth and surrendered her heart to him, and had placed the volume of patience and forbearance in the niche of oblivion.

COUPLET.

My heart is gone, my bosom, too, of life is void and leer,
Patience, away! for now for thee no place continues here.

---

[1] Lit.: ' Pointed at by the finger of the world.'
[2] The wind as it curls the waters is said to delineate figures upon them.
[3] The black hair on the white cheek looked like night painted on day !

The attraction of love exerting its influence on both sides, they found the means of meeting without the intervention of a go-between, and the path of intercourse between them was clear from the dust of rivals. The woman said to her lover, 'Thou art ever [1] favoring me with thy presence and adorning and shedding light upon my humble dwelling, and no doubt delay takes place until thou callest out and castest a pebble. If by thy skill in painting—in which thou art the phœnix of the age and the leader of the time—thou wouldest take thought and paint something, and make a thing which might be a token between me and thee, it would not be unwise, and rather conformable to judicious counsel.'

The young artist replied, 'I will make a mantle of two colors, which shall be white on one side, like a star shining in the water; and black on the other, like an Æthiop's hair gleaming on the lobe of the ear of a fair beauty. When thou beholdest that signal, come out quickly.' While they were making this agreement, a slave of that painter was standing behind the wall, and overheard them.

COUPLET.

Ope not thy lips, if thou hast joys in hand,
For many a listener near the wall may stand.

Several days passed and the mantle was finished and the visits agreed upon took place. One day the painter had gone out on important business, and stopped away late. The slave borrowed that mantle of the painter's daughter, on pretence of studying the manner in which the colors were mixed, and having put it on, came to the house of the lady. She, without reflection, from the excessive transports of joy which she felt at her lover's visit, did not distinguish between her paramour and his rival, nor observed the difference between her friend and this stranger.

COUPLET.

Her body to his clasp she gave, and did love's writing trace,
The slave beheld the fair and shared her kisses and embrace.

The slave, by means of this robe obtained his wish; and after he had done with it, gave back the mantle. It happened that at the very same time, the painter returned, and having rent the garment of patience, from desire to behold his mistress, he threw the mantle over his shoulders and went towards the merchant's house, and the lady running forth to him, again said, with many endearments, 'Is it well with thee, my friend, that thou hast in this same instant come back again?' The young man saw how matters stood, and having made some excuse for coming, returned forthwith,

---

[1] I omit *kih* after *wakt* as do the MSS. Either that or the *va* before *ld shak* must evidently be dispensed with.

and finding out the whole affair, chastised the slave and his daughter severely, burnt the mantle, and gave up the connection with the lady: and if she had not acted precipitately, she would not have been contaminated by the foul embraces of the slave, nor have been deprived of the visits of her darling lover and the conversation of a friend dear to her as her life.

COUPLET.

When thou the tree of haste hast planted, know,
That on it the sad fruit of grief will grow.

And I have brought forward this example that the king may perceive that he ought not to act precipitately with reference to me; and the real fact is, that I do not utter these words from fear of torture, and terror of his majesty; for although death is a sleep not to be coveted, and a rest little to be desired, nevertheless, come it will, and many mighty ones, driven to extremity at its hands, have learned that it is impossible for any one to evade the circle of annihilation and extinction. Whoever sets foot in the world of existence, must needs quaff the potion of death and clothe himself in the vestments of decay.

STANZA.

Ne'er did heaven place one in the sunny ray
Of safety, but at the last it made
Him, like the twilight of false morn, decay.
And when the sempstress, Fortune, has o'erlaid
One's stature with the coat of being, she
Uncloaks [1] him in the end, assuredly.

And had I a thousand lives, and knew that in expending them I should benefit the king, I would surrender them all in an instant, and regard that as equivalent to perfect happiness in both worlds.

COUPLET.

Life is dear, but were it asked by one dearer far, like thee,
Who would grudge his life, since love more precious than his life would be!

But it is the bounden duty of the king to look to the end of this matter, for he cannot preserve his dominions without the swords [of his officers], and he must not assail the lives of his useful servants on a vain surmise.

HEMISTICH.

Thou wilt be sole, if many friends thou slay.

And it is not possible to find at all times a servant who will show himself equal to the administration of affairs, nor to lay hands upon a minister worthy of one's confidence and deserving of promotion.

---

[1] Here is an equivoque—*ḳabā kardan* is 'to make a cloak,' and also 'to rend a garment by tearing open the bosom.'

COUPLET.

The sun must gild it many a year, ere that which first has been a stone
A ruby turns, in Bada<u>kh</u>shán—in Yaman, a carnelion.

When the lioness observed that the speeches of Damnah were honored
by attention from the ear of acceptance, she was overcome with alarm lest
the Lion should give his belief to these gold-washed, counterfeit coins, and
specious truth-resembling pretences and insinuating falsehoods of his; and
lest the grace of his language and oily talk should cause the Lion to neglect
the investigation of this history. She, therefore, turned towards the Lion,
and said, 'Thy silence would indicate that what Damnah says is true, and
what the rest say is false, and I did not think that thou, notwithstanding
thy sagacity and acuteness and understanding and intellect, wouldest be deaf
to the language of truth, and be deceived and shaken by vain and delusive
prating.

COUPLET.

How can the Bulbul sweet to thee appear?
Thou who to babbling birds dost lend thine ear.'

She then rose in wrath and went to her own abode. The Lion commanded
them to keep Damnah bound in prison, till the judges should investigate his
case, and declare what was right to be done with him. The court of inquiry[1]
broke up, and the lioness came to the lion and said, 'O son! I have long
heard of the marvelous cleverness of Damnah, and now I know to demonstration that he is the wonder of the age and the phœnix of the time. How,
I pray, could he utter all these false sentiments apparently so magnanimous,
and how arrange those rare excuses and honeyed sayings? So fine are the ex-
tenuations which he chooses, that if the king should give him an opportunity
to speak, he would, by a single word, extricate himself from this calamity;
and, at the present moment, both the king and the army, in a body, would
rejoice exceedingly at his being put to death, and, therefore, the best way is
to relieve thy mind at once with regard to him, and not to give him opportunity to speak nor the chance of a reply.

HEMISTICH.

Haste is not good save in a good affair.'

The Lion said, 'The business of those who surround monarchs is envy and
variance, and the employment of the high officers of state, malevolence[2] and
strife. Day and night they pursue each other and search out one another's
merits and demerits, and whoever has most of the former, they assail him
the more vehemently, and the deserving are the greatest objects of envy and

---

[1] So I venture to translate *majlis-i mazdlim.*
[2] The editions have *darúgh giram,* of which I can make no sense. I read with a MS.
darúgh karam.

malice; and they never feel jealous of one who has no merit, and Damnah is adorned with many accomplishments, and possesses my most intimate favour. It is possible that the envious have combined and wish to get rid of him by treachery.' The lioness replied, 'How can envy be carried so far as to cast one into the place of destruction?'[1] The Lion answered, 'Envy is a fire which, once kindled, burns up the green and the dry, and when carried to excess, it impels a man not to desire good even to himself, as was the case in the matter of those three envious persons.' The lioness asked, 'How was that?'

STORY VIII.

The Lion said, 'They have related that three persons were fellow travelers, and having become companions, entered on their journey together. The oldest of them said to the other two, 'Why have you left your city, and how? and what is the cause of your expatriating yourselves, so that ye have chosen the toil of travel in preference to the ease of residing with your neighbours?' One of them said, 'Because that in the town in which I dwelt, things occurred that I could not endure the sight of, and envy overpowered me, and I was continually consumed by the flame of jealousy. I, therefore, thought to myself that I would leave my home for a day or two, and thus, perchance, avoid the sight of what I did not wish to see.' The other companion said, 'I, too, was embarrassed with the same painful feeling, and have, therefore, chosen to leave my country.' The oldest said, 'Both of you are partners in suffering with me, and I too have set out for the desert, owing to the same indignant feeling.

COUPLET.

To tell the truth, that sight I cannot see,   That others eat, and I spectator be.

On finding that all three were envious, with a feeling of pleasure at their homogeneousness, they set out. One day there lay a purse of gold in their road, and the three ran simultaneously to the spot and exclaimed, 'Come! let us divide this gold, and returning hence to our own homes, pass some time pleasantly.' Each, however, felt his envious passions excited, so that, being unwilling that the others should get a share, they remained mute. They neither had the courage to leave the gold lying in the road, nor could they endure to divide it with one another. They passed a whole day and night hungry and thirsty in the desert, and denying themselves food and sleep, quarreled together, without finding any solution of their strife.

---

[1] A most inapt speech of the lioness, who had before her the example of Damnah's destroying Shanzabah through envy; but the remark is made merely as a peg to hang the next story upon.

STANZA.

The world's affairs in which no order lies,
Are like to an unfathomable sea.
Hence men of abject mind and mean emprise
Succumb to pains which have no remedy.

The next morning, the king of that territory, who had come forth to hunt, passed, with a number of his retinue, by that spot, and beheld those three persons seated in the desert. On his inquiring into their circumstances, they stated the facts as they really were, and said, ' We all three are endued with the quality of envy, and for this reason we have left our country and our homes, and wander in an unsettled state. Here, too, the same feeling has evinced itself, and has ended in our trouble and distress. We want a judge to issue his command for the division of this gold among us.

HEMISTICH.

Thank God! that which we sought is now obtained.'

The king said, ' Do you each set forth the nature of his own envious feeling, that I may perceive the extent of the deserts of each, and may in accordance therewith divide the gold among you!' One said, ' My envy is so great that I never wish to benefit any one, nor choose to be kind to any, lest that person should become happy or prosperous.' The next said, 'Thou wert born a good man and hast no spice of envy. The degree of my envy is such that I cannot bear to see any one do a benefit to another or bestow his property on him.' The third said, ' Both of you have no part in this matter, and your pretensions are vain. I, in fine, am such that I never wish any one to bestow a favour on me, or show kindness even to myself, judge then what my feelings are towards another!' [1] The king bit the finger of astonishment with the tooth of reflection, and marveled at the words of these wretches, on the tablet of whose qualities was displayed the writing indicative of malignity, ' *Do they envy other men ?*' [2] He said, ' By your own words this gold is a forbidden thing for you, and each deserves a punishment suited to his crime. He who is unwilling that he himself should do good to others, his recompense is none other than that he should fail to participate in the happiness of a reward, and in both worlds be bankrupt and destitute. And as for him who cannot endure that any man should benefit another, the best course is to release him with all speed from the prison of existence, and to remove the weight of this suffering from the surface of his soul. And as for the third, who envies even himself, and who does not wish to have himself even benefited, he deserves to be punished by a variety of tortures and ignominious

---

[1] Lit: ' What will arrive to another?'
[2] Kur'án, Fl. iv. 57; Mar. iv. 52; Sale p. 62, l. 15 : ' These are the men whom God hath cursed, and unto him whom God shall curse, thou shalt surely find no helpers. Shall they have a part of the kingdom, since even then they would not bestow the smallest matter on men? Do they envy other men that which God, of his bounty, hath given them?'

sufferings, and, suspended for a long period in the grasp of chastisement and reprobation, to taste the flavor of torment, till the time when the bird of his spirit is caught in the snare, ' *Say, the angel of death who is set over you* [*shall cause you to die*].'[1] He then commanded that they should let the first person go into the desert, naked from head to foot, and without food or provisions, and all that he had they took from him, the king saying,

STANZA.

'Who wishes good to no man, why,
    We must not wish aught good for him.
And trees that do no fruit supply;
    We with the axe must sharply trim.'

And with respect to the second envious person, he gave orders for his decapitation with the pitiless scymitar, which having been done, they released him from the pangs of envy: while on the third they rubbed pitch, and left him in the sun, so that he perished after cruel and protracted sufferings. Thus the king conveyed the disgraceful envy of those three persons to its just recompense: and the perfectly wise have said,

QUATRAIN.

Where envy's cruel tortures are, no remedy is there;
It is a hateful feeling which wild beasts and devils share.
They say the envious person is the enemy of man,
For he is his own enemy if well his thoughts you scan.

There is no pain greater than that of envy, because the envious man is always in grief at the joy of others, and in travail at their delight.

COUPLET.

In this distress the wretched sufferer dies;
Do what he will, there, too this torment lies.[2]

And this story is for this purpose—that it may be shown that envy may be carried to such a length, that a man may not wish well even to himself, and hence we may infer how he will stand with reference to another; and I suspect that the tale about Damnah may have been set afloat by envious persons.' The lioness said, 'I have not observed in the ministers of this court the habit of envying, nor have I the slightest suspicion that any one of them is tainted with this blameable quality; and the probability is that the unanimous vote of all for his execution is with a view to the king's advantage, and if not, these circumstances are not required to get rid of

---

[1] Ḳur'án, Fl. xxxii. 11; Mar. xxxii. 12; Sale p. 310, l. 12 : ' And they say, when we shall lie hidden in the earth, shall we be raised thence a new creature ? Yea! they deny the meeting of their Lord at the resurrection. Say, the angel of death, who is set over you shall cause you to die; then shall ye be brought back unto your Lord.' Flügel reads يتوفاكم for the يتوفيكم of Maracci and the ' Anvár-i.'

[2] The only sense I can extract from this difficult couplet.

him.' The Lion replied, 'I entertain doubts in this matter, and in order
that they may be removed I will not act, as regards Damnah, precipitately,
lest it should turn out that I bring loss on myself in seeking the advantage
of others, and, in pleasing the creature, anger the Creator. Until I have
most narrowly scrutinised the affair, I shall not think it allowable for me to
put him to death, since I have been compelled to endure all these regrets
from acting with too great haste in the matter of Shanzabah. The right
plan is not to sacrifice the meritorious and able on a mere suspicion, and
not to carry out any mandate till the beauty of certainty shews its
countenance from behind the curtain of doubt; nor transgress the purport of
this saying, which has issued from the exalted mind, and sprung from the
pure intellect of one of the greatest sages :

VERSE.

When a transgression may have met thine eye,
Pause long ere thou the punishment apply.
With ease thou may'st Badakhshán's ruby break,
Once crushed, again a gem thou canst not make.
They who in headlong fury draw the steel,
Shall sharp regrets and vain contrition feel.[1]

Here the dialogue between the Lion and his mother ended, and they departed
to their respective couches. When, however, they had conveyed Damnah to
prison, and had placed heavy fetters on his feet and neck, fraternal tenderness
and friendly sympathy led Kalílah to go and see him. As soon as he entered
the dungeon and his eyes fell on Damnah, he began to shower down the
rain of his tears from the clouds of his eye, and said, 'O brother ! how can I
behold thee in this calamity and trouble, and what pleasure can I henceforth
feel in life ?

VERSE.

Reft of thee, my spirit's solace! can thy lover longer live?
Art thou from my bosom banished, what can joy or comfort give?
' Live without me!' couldst thou say it? 'nor let parting cloud thy brow!'
I have swayed a kingly sceptre, can I play the herdsman now?'

Damnah, too, began to weep, and exclaimed,

COUPLET.

From my much-loved friends to part,
Pangs my breast and breaks my heart.

And all this travail and affliction, and the grief of my prison and my heavy
fetters is not so distressful to me as to be compelled to submit to part from
thee and to be consumed in the fire of separation.

---

[1] Lit. : 'Shall gnaw the back of his hand with the tooth of regret.'

STANZA.

There's not a night, but parted from the taper of thy cheek,
  My heart, consuming o'er the flame of grief, is wasted not:
Nor moment, but ensanguined tears my pallid visage streak,
  While, torn from thee, I melt away, and weep my hapless lot.'

Kalílah replied, 'O Damnah! since affairs have reached this point and matters have culminated in this, I might well address thee in severe language, for from the beginning of this adventure I foresaw it all, and used the most strenuous admonitions, but thou didst not give heed to them, but leant upon thy own weak judgment and erring counsel, and at the last the very thing has happened which I foretold:

COUPLET.

I bade thee, heart! not thither go, lest thou shouldst be made captive there,
Thou went'st at length and there befell thee that of which I made thee 'ware.

And had I failed to advise thee at the commencement of this business and had chosen to be supine in dissuading thee, I should this day have been the partner of thy perfidy, and I could not have addressed to thee such language as I do. O careless one! did I not tell thee what the wise implied when they said, that 'The slanderer dies before his predestined time?' The meaning of this is, not the being cut off from life or the annihilation of the delights of existence, but that a grief arises which makes life hateful and makes death every moment wished for, as has happened to thee. Assuredly death is pleasanter than this life.

COUPLET.

A thousand times 'twere better not to be,
Than bear the rankling [1] cares which harass thee.'

Damnah said, 'O brother! thou didst ever speak the truth and fulfil all the duties of a monitor, but sensual desire and covetousness and ambition impaired my judgment, and deprived thy admonitions of their due weight in my mind; and although I knew that the mischief of this proceeding was infinite, and the danger of it unbounded, I nevertheless entered upon it with the utmost energy—like a sick man who is overpowered by the desire of eating—though he knows the injurious consequences, he heeds them not—and a person of this character, who cannot refrain from obeying his appetite, must submit to all the calamity and suffering which is sure to occur to him, and if he reproaches any one, it must be himself.

COUPLET.

I must not 'gainst others murmur for the grief that rends my heart,
I have caused my own affliction, 'tis a self-inflicted smart.'

Kalílah replied, 'He is a prudent man, who in the beginning of every

---

[1] There is a misprint here in the edition of 1851, which might cause trouble to the student. For *dilat rázi* it should be *dilat-rá zi*. In the next line read *naṣíḥat* for *baṣíḥat*.

affair casts his eyes to the conclusion, and before he plants the shrub considers its fruit, that he may not repent of the deed when it is done, nor regret the speech when it is spoken, since such repentance and such regrets yield nothing but exultation to one's enemies and despondency to one's friends.

HEMISTICH.
Of what avail thy final sorrow when thou didst go wrong at first ?

Damnah responded, ' O brother! to have no enemies is the characteristic of a mean spirit, and to live safe and secure is the condition of every mean wretch and simpleton. Wherever there is a man of high spirit, he cannot be quit of sharp troubles and vast dangers.

COUPLET.
When wilt thou win the ball of hope with bat of fierce desire ?
First stake thy head, and then to this high contest-ground aspire.'

Kalílah answered, ' Fleeting riches and uncertain office are not worth all this care and trouble.

COUPLET.
Look thou not in riches' orchard for the fruit of happiness,
Change is all the fruit it beareth, therefore thy fond hopes repress.

Thou oughtest not to have cast the ray of thy regard on worldly wealth and station, and thou wouldest not have fallen into the pit of trouble and difficulty; nor shouldest thou have sown the plant of rancor and envy, and to-day thou wouldest not have gathered the fruit of calamity and disgrace.'

Damnah said, ' I know that I have scattered the seeds of this woe, and whoever sows anything will assuredly reap the same.

COUPLET.
Good genders good, from evils, evils grow :
As wheat-seeds, wheat; and barley, barley show.

And I have sown poisonous herbs and cannot therefore look for rose-comfits, and now the affair is beyond my control and my hand is unable to grasp it. The finger-tips of counsel cannot loose the knot of destiny, nor does the countenance of successful deliberation shew itself in the mirror of thought. I have erred wittingly, and sinned with my eyes open, and in spite of knowing that the royal gem was not worth the peril of the whirlpool of trouble.

COUPLET.
Light at first the toil of ocean seemed in hope of future gain ;
I did mistake, a hundred jewels are not worth one hurricane.'

Kalílah said, ' Now in what manner hast thou devised thy release, and by what passage hast thou conceived a way to escape ?' Damnah replied,

COUPLET.
' A way to flee thy love were hard to find,
No loop-hole for debate is left behind.

It appears that the vessel of life will be submerged in this whirlpool of destruction, and that the sun of existence will set in the western region of annihilation and extinction. Yet will I in no wise give way to weakness, nor will I spare any devices or stratagems that can be made available for my release. But my grief is increased by the apprehension that thou mayest be suspected with me; and, owing to the companionship between us, which had reached the bounds of complete accord, thou too mayest fall into the whirlpool of destruction, and if—which God forbid!—they should inflict pain upon thee to make thee utter what thou knowest of my secrets, my distress will then be doubled. In one aspect there will be thy personal sufferings, and the shame that thou shouldest have fallen into trouble on my account: in another, no hope of escape will be left to me, inasmuch as the truth of thy word is known to all, and there can be no opposing truthful evidence from one like thee, who hast based thy conduct on sincerity and uprightness; and supposing this to be the case, we shall see one another again only at the day of resurrection, and we cannot hope to meet save at the time of the last judgment.' Kalílah replied, 'I have heard what thou hast said, and thou knowest that I cannot endure the torture, nor sustain the pangs of the rack and the agony of punishment; nor conceal what I know; nor, to flatter any one, can I speak that which is false and contrary to fact; and even before they put the question I shall state what has occurred. Thy advisable course is to confess thy crime and to avow what thou hast done, and thus, by penitence and contrition, save thyself from suffering in the final state. Since thou knowest of a certainty that thy end in the present case will be destruction; at least, let not the punishment of this world be combined with the disgrace and chastisement of the next; and if thou must endure the pangs of punishment in this transitory state, at least thou mayest avoid tasting the bitter waters of torment in the city of eternal existence.' Damnah said, 'I will consider of these matters,, and advise with thee on the course I may decide upon.' Kalílah, pained and full of grief, retired, and indulging his heart in a variety of distresses and anguish, laid himself down on the bed of despondency and writhed through the night, and as morning rose, his spirit sank.

HEMISTICH.

It passed, and mingled all these hopes with dust.

However, at the time that these words were exchanged by Damnah and Kalílah, a thief, who was confined in the same prison, and who lay sleeping near them, was awakened by their conversation, and having heard all that they said, kept it in mind, and preserved the recollection of it that he might make use of it when occasion offered.

HEMISTICH.

Each speech its time, each saying has its place.

The next day, when the golden-clawed lion of the sun put himself in motion in the azure-colored waste of the sky, and the dark-visaged black-scrolled jackal of the night was hidden in the corner of the prison of concealment;

COUPLET.

Day's justice o'er the universe outspread its golden hue,
And night, that gives injustice sway, her robes around her drew.

Again the court of grievances was formed and embodied. The lioness renewed the disquisition as to Damnah, and said, ' To leave tyrants alive is the same as killing the just, and to treat evil-disposed persons well, is like acting ill to the good.

COUPLET.

Who benefits on evil men confer,   Upon the good no less heap injuries.[1]

And he who, although he has full power over him, suffers the profligate to live, or assists the oppressor, is the accomplice of their debauchery and injustice ; and the threat ' *Whoso aids the tyrant, God will give that tyrant absolute power over him,*' comes to pass in his case.

COUPLET.

Sin not, nor take with evil-doers part.   Nor suffer evil men to please thy heart.'

The Lion enjoined the judges to use despatch in transacting the affair of Damnah, and to report daily what transpired as to his treason or the reverse. Wherefore the judges, and nobles, and notables, and ministers, and high and low, met in the court of the grandees and general assembly, and the representative of the ḳáẓí turned his face towards those present, and said, ' The king displays the utmost urgency as to the inquiry into the affair of Damnah, and investigating that which is laid to his charge; and has given command that until the face of his affair is cleansed from the dust of doubt, the judges shall not occupy themselves with any other matter, and enjoins that the sentence which is passed with regard to him shall not be inconsistent with the requirements of justice, nor swerve from the path of right towards oppression or injustice. It behoves each of you to declare what he knows, for such declaration comprises three advantages of high importance. The first is that to aid the right, and to raise the banner of truth and justice is of great weight in the law of God, and of ineffable value in the code of courtesy and creed of magnanimity. The second is, that to destroy the foundation of injustice, and lay waste the basis of tyranny, and to rebuke the perfidious, is in accordance with the will of the Creator, and approved by mankind in general. The third is, that to escape from the deceitful and mischievous, and to obtain security from perfidious and wicked men, is absolute gain, and relief in which all partake.' When the speech was

---

[1] These lines occur in the fourth story of the first Book of the Gulistán. See my translation, p. 44, l. 8.

ended, all those who were present kept silence, and from no quarter was any answer returned, for they had no certainty as to the affair of Damnah, and they did not wish to say anything on mere suspicion, lest a command should be issued upon what they affirmed, and blood should be spilled at their word, though they might deliver sentiments not in agreement with the facts. When Damnah observed this state of things, his heart was refreshed and rejoiced, like the garden of Iram by the breeze of spring. He contracted his features, however, like one in grief, and said, ' O leaders of the faith and of the state! and O counsellors of the realm and nation ! were I guilty, I should be glad to keep silence, but I am innocent, and no one can lay hands on him who is clear of guilt, and he is excusable if he exert himself in his own affair to the extent of his ability; and I desire that every one who is acquainted with aught that affects my case, will state it truthfully, and observe what is due to justice therein.   For hereafter every speech will have its reward, and it behoves every one—whose word is equivalent to a command in setting forth the right, or in putting an individual to death—to deliver his testimony without admixture of suspicion or conjecture, and moreover with sincerity and firm conviction, and whoever on mere suspicion or doubt plunges me into destruction will meet with what befell that physician, who was destitute of science and experience.' The judges inquired, 'How was that?'

STORY IX.

Damnah said, ' They have related that a man without any stock of understanding and without the adornment of experience, was laying claim to be a physician. He had neither sufficient science nor perfect judgment. So ignorant was he in discriminating drugs that he could not tell a cocoa-nut from Turkish wormwood,[1] and he was so unskilful in the prognosis of diseases, that he could not discern between ophthalmia and gout, and he gave no heed to the qualities and quantities of medicine in judging as to compounds, and in writing his prescriptions, he attended not to the kind or amount of food and drink.

COUPLET.

A sorry leech ! whoe'er his visage eyed,   Ne'er life's fair lineaments again descried.

And in the city in which this person had opened the shop of ignorance, and proclaimed his notification for the destruction of men, there was another doctor celebrated for his perfect skill, and whose visits[2] were renowned for remedies and success. His breath was like the breath of Ís'a,[3] revivifying; and his step, like that of Khizr, restoring life.

---

[1] Or hyssop.

[2] Lit.: ' step.'

[3] Or Jesus. The cures of our Saviour are as renowned among the Muhammadans as among Christians.

STANZA.

The circling, changeful vault of heaven—did he the wish express—
Were from its dizziness at once set free:
And did his fortune-bringing feet the blooming garden bless,
The aspen of its tremors cured would be.

Inasmuch, however, as it is the custom of perfidious fortune that men of merit ever obtain from the tray of its harshness only the morsel of toil, and the undeserving bear away from the tables of its benefits the viands of abundant honor and distinction,

COUPLET.

These times refuse to purchase merit, therefore breaks my heart;
For gear then so unvalued, where shall I go seek a mart?

the affairs of this most learned man of the age and phenomenon of the time were on the decline, and the star of the light of his vision was overtaken with the eclipse of debility. By degrees the light of the world-surveying eye of that dear person—by which the vision of the wise was enlightened, and the survey of the garden of whose beauty was more agreeable to the pupil of the eye of those gifted with sight than to gaze on gardens of flowers—grew dim, until the time when no vestige of illumination was left in it. The hapless man took his retired seat in the corner of his humble dwelling, and that public impostor[1] began to set up his deceitful pretensions out of all reason.

COUPLET.

The fairy veils her visage, the fiend's all coquetry,
Reason consumes with wonder things so unthought to see.

In a short space of time he was regarded as a physician certain to heal, and the fame of his cures was spread by lying rumour from tongue to tongue. The king of that city had a daughter, such, that from the horizon of beauty no luminary like her had risen, nor had the perfumer of the morning displayed any musk to equal that which was scattered from her curling tresses.

COUPLET.

Moon-visaged, musk-diffusing, hearts' delight;
Life-giving, heart-enchanting, heavenly bright.

Her he had bestowed on his brother's son, and the ceremonies which accompany the marriage-knot and the bridal night, had been performed in a manner befitting royalty and with a lustre becoming kings.

COUPLET.

The moon as guest was welcomed by the sun,
And Venus joined with Mercury in one.

And from the conjunction of those two fortunate luminaries a royal gem was formed in the shell of her womb. It happened, however, that at the time of

---

[1] A peculiar phrase, *jalil-i 'dm.*

parturition an accident occurred, and the princess was seized with severe pain. They summoned the wise physician to the presence and informed him of the nature of the illness. The skilful leech, having learned the true state of the case, made the prognosis of the disease and said, ' The cure of this disease is obtainable by a medicine which they call Mihrán. Let them take a fourth part of a dram of that medicine, and pound and sift it, and mix it up with a little pure musk and cinnamon, and sweeten it with sugar-candy, and give it to the patient, and her sufferings will be instantly removed.' They replied, ' O physician ! where may that medicine be ? and whom are we to ask for it ? He answered, ' I have seen in the medicine-repository of the palace a little of this medicine, deposited in a casket of virgin silver, on which was set a padlock of pure gold, but now, owing to my want of sight, I am unable to find it.' In the midst of this colloquy, the pretended physician came up and said, ' I take upon me to discover that medicine, and I well now how to compound that mixture.' The king called him before him, and commanded him to go to the repository of medicine, and having brought out the required drug, to prepare the drink which the physician had ordered. Hereupon the ignorant doctor entered the repository, and looked for a casket of the description which the true physician had mentioned, but as there were numerous caskets of the same character, he failed to discover the said medicine, and without discriminating between them, he took up one and brought it out. It happened not to be the drug they called Mihrán, but a small quantity of deadly poison, which having been deposited there for state purposes, was kept in that casket. This he opened and mixed the poison with the other ingredients, and having made it into a drink, gave it to the princess. No sooner did she taste it than she expired. When the king beheld that event, consumed with regret for the loss of his daughter, he raised to the etherial sky the torch of his sighs, and he commanded them to give the remaining portion to that ignorant physician, so that he too fell lifeless on the spot, and the recompense of that unseemly deed reached him immediately.

COUPLET.

This is a wholesome moral, all who evil do,
Not only injure others but harm themselves too.

And I have introduced this story that it may be known that every action that men do through ignorance has a disastrous result, and every affair that they transact in doubt and on mere conjecture, is fraught with most intense danger.' One of those present said, ' O Damnah ! thou art of the number of those, the foulness of whose mind is evident to the higher ranks, and the impurity of whose morals is manifest to those below, and the perverseness of thy disposition accords with thy shape and form and appearance.'

The ḳáẓí asked, ' Whence does thou utter this speech ? and what proof hast thou of this remark? Thou must recount the proofs of it and declare the arguments in support of thy observation.' He replied, 'Sages skilled in physiognomy have pronounced that every one with wide eyebrows, whose right eye is smaller than his left, and who is subject to a perpetual throbbing of the eye, and whose nose inclines to the left, and whose glance is ever cast down to the ground, his ill-omened nature will be filled with mischief and deceit, and be replete with profligacy and perfidiousness, and these signs are to be found in him.' Damnah answered, 'In the commands of God partiality and deception are impossible, and in the actions of that holy Being, error and neglect, and mistakes and faults, are not to be supposed.

COUPLET.

Mistakes and faults may spring from me and thee,
In earth's Creator error cannot be.

If these tokens which thou hast mentioned were really a true proof and genuine demonstration, and truth could thus be distinguished from falsehood, and error from correctness, and right from wrong; mankind would then be quit of evidence and oaths; and judges might rest from pleadings and citations, and henceforward it would not be well to praise any one for his good deeds or to reproach him for his ill-actions, since no created being could divest himself of those marks which, at the time of the creation of his nature, would be made to accompany him. Wherefore, in accordance with the directions which thou hast given, the reward of the good and the punishment of the bad, would be obliterated from the pages of the ordinances of the law and of justice, and had I done this thing—which they say I have—(*Let us take refuge with God from it!*) it was owing to these marks having impelled me to it, and since it was impossible to put them away, it is not fitting that I should be overtaken with punishment for them.

COUPLET.

Rebuke us not that we grow wildly here,
For as they rear us, such we do appear.

Wherefore by thy sentence I am set free from this calamitous imprisonment, and thou hast given a convincing proof of thy ignorance and spurious pretensions to be a judge, and hast shewn by an unfounded speech and a baseless semblance, and an unluminous charge and a declaration not listened to, that thou hast made an incongruous entrance into the assembly of the wise.

COUPLET.

By thy discourse the old and wise now know,
How far the branchings of thy folly go.'

When Damnah had delivered this reply, all those who were present, placed the seal of silence on the casket of speech, and none was able to utter a word more. The kází commanded him to be conveyed back to prison, and they made a detailed representation to the Lion of what had occurred. When Damnah, however, had re-entered the prison, a friend of Kalílah, whom they called Rúzbih, passed by. Damnah called him, and said, 'Since yesterday I have no tidings of Kalílah, and at this crisis I am most anxious for his visits.

COUPLET.

True friend is he who comes thy hand to press
In time of trouble and of deep distress.

What news hast thou of him? and what excuse hast thou brought for his not coming?' As soon as Rúzbih heard Kalílah named, he drew a hot sigh from his burning heart, and showering tears of blood from the clouds of his eyes, said,

COUPLET.

My heart is gone, then how shall I my loved one seek?
Tongue-bound, to whom shall I my sorrows speak?'

Damnah was impatient at the distress of Rúzbih, and said, 'Declare the facts with all speed.' Rúzbih replied, 'O Damnah! how shall I tell them?

VERSE.

To leave my love consumes my inmost heart,
    My breast is wounded and no salve have I:
Like taper burns life's thread with hidden smart,
    And my soul's anguish stifles e'en a sigh.

O Damnah! that dear friend has migrated from this transitory abode to the enduring city, and has impressed on the hearts of his friends and companions the wound of separation.

COUPLET.

Comrades, alas! that of our friend bereft,   Captive to parting sorrows we are left.'

When Damnah heard the intelligence of Kalílah's death, he swooned, and when, after a long interval, he recovered his senses, he uttered loud laments, and in deepest grief, with streaming eyes, exclaimed,

STANZA.

'Alas! the root of joy's fair plant is severed now in twain,
And of the fruitful branch of mirth no tokens now remain:
Sigh then, my heart! my soul's repose is all now swept away,
Eyes rain down blood for him—now gone—who was your visual ray.'

When Damnah had carried his lamentations beyond bounds, and had rent the garment of patience with the hand of complaint, while each moment he rubbed his face in the dust, and wept in a manner to which none could endure to listen, Rúzbih began to exhort him, and said, 'O Damnah! thou thyself knowest that the kingly and eternal writer [1] has written the name of continuous existence on the paper of the life of no created thing, and the pourtrayer of the forms of creation has not engraved the figure of

---

[1] The *Tughránavís* is the person who appends the imperial titles, signature, etc., to a paper.

life on the pages of possibility, save with the pen of ' *Everything shall perish except Himself*,' [1] nor has the tailor [2] of the establishment of eternity sewed the garment of the existence of any living being without the fringe of annihilation, nor has the carpet-spreader of the pavilion of omnipotence lighted the taper of entertainment [3] without the violent wind of calamity.

STANZA.

Since heaven has built this structure without the thorn of woe,
None ever in life's garden did the rose of pleasure know:
Life's flower-garden none in Time's meadow e'er could find
In all its vernal beauty, safe from autumn's chilling wind.

This is a draught which all must taste, and a burthen which all must bear. There is no salve for this wound but patience—no remedy for this disease but compulsory endurance.

COUPLET.

Patience is needful: for this mental pain,
Save patience, all medicaments are vain.'

By these words Damnah was in some degree consoled, and said, 'O Rúzbih! right is on my side in this lament, for Kalílah was to me an attached friend and a right-counselling brother, with whom I found refuge in time of trouble, and from whose judgment and consideration and tenderness and advice, I could in emergencies derive succour. His head was a treasury, and all the coin of secrets therein deposited remained concealed from the world, and the spy of Time remained in despair of becoming acquainted with them. Alas! that that kind friend has removed his auspicious company from my head, and has left me in the corner of the world's tenement without comrade, or associate, or friend, or confidant.

COUPLET.

To whom shall I my secrets tell, since I can in none confide?
And how shall I, of friends bereft, for my future course provide?

Hereafter what pleasure can I find in life? or what advantage will the stock of existence supply? And were it not that at this crisis various suspicions [of my motives] might arise in the minds of men, I could kill myself with lamentation,[4] and free myself from the pain of solitude and the sufferings of my friendless condition, since in this abyss into which I have fallen, no appearance of escape is visible, without the aid of a friend and the help of sympathisers.

---

[1] Kur'án, Fl. xxviii. 88, Mar. xxvii. 87 : Sale p. 297, l. 9 : 'And be not thou an idolater; neither invoke any other god together with the true God; there is no God but He. Everything shall perish except Himself; unto Him belongeth judgment; and before him shall ye be assembled at the last day.'

[2] With such execrable taste do the Persians ride their metaphors into the lowest bathos.

[3] One MS. omits *saráfati*, which in fact is inserted only to rhyme with *dfati*. The same MS. omits the text from the Kur'án after *kalam*, and reads *mamát* ' death,' instead.

[4] Or ' in a piteous manner.' This passage, particularly the *dnastí*, is obscure.

COUPLET.

From hope's city I must wander forth, alone and friendlessly,
Now despair alone is left us, shorn of every remedy.

Rúzbih said, 'If Kalílah has fallen from the garden of life into the thorny brake of extinction and annihilation, the plant of the affection of other friends is refreshed and rendered verdant by the drops of true love.

COUPLET.

Grieve thou not, though in this garden branches of the rose are dead,
Still the hyacinth curls its tresses, still the Nasrín[1] lifts its head.

Damnah said, 'Thou speakest the truth, thy existence is a remedy for my trouble, and thy life the alleviation of every disaster, and to-day thou art to me the very same friend and brother that Kalílah was before. Give me thy hand and accept me as a brother.' Ruzbíh advanced with the greatest alacrity and said, 'By this favor thou hast bound me to thee, and hast set up the banner of my exaltation on the pinnacle of the highest places. How can my faithful heart discharge its gratitude for this kindness? and how can my tongue, though lavish in praise, express its thankfulness for this blessing?' They then took each other's hands and tied the knot of brotherhood, and concluded the ties of companionship and agreement as is the custom of such covenants. Damnah then said, 'In such a place there is a hoard, belonging to me and Kalílah. If thou wilt take the trouble to bring it here, thy labour will not be unrewarded.' Rúzbih, by the direction which Damnah furnished, brought the deposit. Damnah separated his own share, and gave to Rúzbih what belonged to Kalílah, and besought Rúzbih ever to be in attendance at court, and to learn whatever passed with reference to him.

HEMISTICH.

Duty directs a promise be fulfilled.

The next day, early in the morning, the lioness came and inquired what had passed at the late assembly. The Lion repeated the particulars of the proceedings in the manner that the judges had reported to him. The lioness, having learned the nature of the report, was vexed, and said, 'If I speak bluntly, it may displease the king, and if I connive at this I shall be acting supinely with relation to my duty as an adviser and a friend.' The Lion replied, 'Forbearance and too great tenderness are not right in stating the heads of salutary counsel, and thy words are certainly clear from all mixture of doubt. It will meet with speedy approbation—offer what thou hast to say.' The lioness said, 'The king does not discriminate between truth and falsehood, and discerns not his own advantage from what would be

---

[2] The Dictionary says *nasrín* is the 'name of a flower,' but adds no more.

injurious to him; and Damnah, having obtained the opportunity, will raise some mischief, such that the clearest intellects will fail to remedy it and the sharpest scymitars prove ineffectual against it." The Lion responded, 'Do, thou not go away to-day; the affair of Damnah may perhaps be concluded.' The high command was then issued that the judges should assemble again, and should re-open the case of Damnah in a general meeting. In accordance with this mandate, high and low came together, and the ḳáẓí's deputy repeated the same discourse which has been before cited, and demanded evidence with respect to Damnah from those present. No one uttered a word regarding him, and not a particle of information was adduced with reference to him, either good or ill. The principal judge turned to Damnah and said, 'Though the audience befriends thee by its silence, yet the hearts of all are unanimously convinced of thy treason, and inwardly agree as to thy death; such being the case, what advantage will it be to thee to live among this people? it would be more suitable to thy condition and be better for the issue of thy affairs, that thou shouldest confess thy crime, and, by repentance and contrition, deliver thyself from the punishments of a future state; and by dying thou wilt secure one of two delights, either that thou wilt emancipate others or thyself.

STANZA.

The wise declare, in death some pleasure lies,
And kindly thus the explanation give:
One of two natures must be his who dies.
Or bad, whence others less agreeably live,
Or inoffensive, of kind sympathies.
So men him love, and in their bosoms hive.
If good, he from this troublous world gets free!
If bad, men from his troubling freed will be.

O Damnah! if thou wilt confess thy guilt, thou wilt secure two excellent things, the remembrance of which will be perpetuated on the surface of time. One is, the acknowledgment of thy crime so as to secure salvation in the world to come, and the choosing the realms of eternity and happiness rather than the abode of fleeting existence and affliction. The other is, that the renown of thy eloquence and oratory, and the power of thy rhetoric and speaking, in these fascinating answers that thou hast given, and these specious excuses which thou hast offered, will be spread by the tongues of high and low, and thy ability and boldness are known to all thy contemporaries, and all will testify to thy eminent gifts and understanding. Do thou take counsel with thy sagacity, and be wise according to the truth of this saying, that 'death with honor is better than life with disgrace.'

COUPLET.

Better to make one's exit well and die,
Than live dishonored and with infamy.'

Damnah replied, 'The ḳáẓí ought not to pronounce sentence according to his own suspicion and the conjectures of others, without plain proof and clear evidence, nor should he transgress the tenor of that saying, ' *Verily a half-opinion is a sin*,'[1] and even if you have this doubt, and though your minds should be convinced as to my guilt, I know my own affairs better, and to hide one's own certainty because of another's doubt, is not right in judgment nor approved by the laws of religion. And notwithstanding that you, on bare suspicion that I may perhaps have exerted myself to procure the death of Shanzabah, have spoken and speak all this, and have thus marred my credit, yet should I causelessly aid in my own destruction, and unjustly accede to my own execution ; on what explanation of the matter should I be excuseable, and how should I exonerate myself from the old monition, '*And throw not yourselves with your own hands into perdition?*'[2] I am fully convinced, too, that no one has the same claims on me that I have on myself, and therefore that which I would not allow with respect to my inferior, and out of generous spirit not permit with regard to him, how can I consent to it in my own case?[3]

COUPLET.

My own self to precipitate I'm free,   But what have other men to do with me?

O ḳáẓí! cease to speak thus; if it is intended for advice, better is wanted ; and if it be reproach, it is better that a ḳáẓí should not utter it, for the words of judges are orders, and it is requisite for them to avoid mistake and error, and jesting and light talk ; and very strange is it that thou wast always truthful and just, and yet, owing to my ill-fortune and calamity, thou hast in this matter laid caution aside, and on thy own suspicions and those of interested persons, hast afflicted the eye of truth with the opthalmia of neglect,

STANZA.

Each heart, a glad pavilion, is plenishèd by thee,
To my expectant heart, then canst thou a torture be ?
In this world's vernal season, thou bloomest like a rose,
And wilt thou to me nothing but thorn on thorn oppose?

The judges of the tribunal of wisdom, by the signet of whose mandates the bond of the nurture of merit is sealed, have pronounced the following decision :—That the coin of my testimony, which is not adorned with the

---

[1] This Arabic proverb is faultily given in both editions. The printed edition has *dṣim*, 'a sinner.' The lithographed edition has *uṣimuṇ*, which is no word at all. The proper reading is *iṣmuṇ* 'a sin.'

[2] Ḳur'án, Fl. ii. 191; Mar. ii. 196; Sale p. 21, l. 17 : 'Contribute out of your substance towards the defence of the religion of God, and throw not yourselves with your own hands into perdition ; and do good, for God loveth those who do good.' On which passage Sale has the following note ; 'Be not accessory to your own destruction, by neglecting your contribution towards the wars against infidels, and thereby suffering them to gather strength.'

[3] I read *dáram* for the *dárad* of the printed edition, on the authority of the lithographed edition and MSS.

seal of certainty, is not admitted or recognised as of full weight in the mint of acceptance, and whosoever gives evidence in a matter with which he is not acquainted, will meet with what that Falconer met with.' The ḳáẓí inquired, 'How was that?'

STORY X.

Damnah said, 'They have related that there was a lord of the marches, renowned for his eminent qualities, and famed and celebrated for his excellent nature and admirable gifts.

COUPLET.
His manners please, his words the heart delight,
His sense unbounded and skill infinite.

And this lord of the marches had a wife, who, by her beauty, was a calamity to the soul; and by her grace, a source of mischief to the world. Her lip was more invigorating than the waters of life, and her mouth more sweet than a bundle[1] of sugar.

VERSE.
Her face like fire, her cheek like water, bright,
Than sun and moon more dazzling in its light :
Her brow the bow, its shaft she made a look,
And thus a hundred hearts she captive took.

She combined with perfect beauty and fascination, the grace of chastity and continence, and she adorned her mischief-exciting cheek with the mole of devotion and abstinence.

VERSE.
To worldly matters she had closed her eye,
Sate curtained by the veil of chastity ;
Ee'n to the glass her form would not display,
And from her shadow shrank, alarmed, away.

And this lord of the marches had a slave from Balkh,[2] excessively bold and audacious, who forbade not the pupil of his eye to gaze on that which it was unlawful to see, nor cleansed the desires of his breast from the dust of debauchery and mischief. Now this slave was allotted the office of Falconer in the service of the lord-marcher, and was appointed to capture fowls. One day he caught sight of that chaste lady, and the fowl of his heart was taken captive by the snare of her love.

COUPLET.
The falcon of this sorrowing heart amid thy snares is captive ta'en,
Ah ! many is the noble bird that by thy glance's dart is slain.

---

[1] Lit., 'ass-load.'
[2] *Balkhi* may also mean 'proud, arrogant.'

R

However much the slave who had lost his heart shook the chain of union, she was not drawn into a meeting, and, in spite of all his wishes, she became not his captive.

COUPLET.

All my blandishments are vain with my fair but scornful friend,
Happy they whom with the fair, fortune's favoring smiles attend.

The Falconer having girt the waist of hope in the desire of capturing that peacock of the garden of beauty, let fly the hawk of contrivance in the air of the desire of meeting, but however much he did so, it found not the way to the wished-for nest.

COUPLET.

Go! for some other bird these arts apply,
The 'Anḳá has its lofty nest too high.

When he despaired of success, as is the wont of evil men, he determined to assail her reputation and employ a stratagem to secure her disgrace; he then purchased two parrots from a fowler, and taught one of them in the language of Balkh to say, ' I saw the porter in the house sleeping with my mistress:' and the other to repeat, ' I for my part say nothing.' In the space of a week, they had learned these two words. One day the lord of the marches had prepared a wine-party, and was sitting at his ease on the cushion of pleasure, when the Falconer entered, and, by way of an offering, presented the birds. The sweet-spoken parrots began their mellifluous discourse, and, in accordance with their custom, repeated the same two sentences. The lord of the marches was ignorant of the language of Balkh, but was pleased at their merry prattle and the similarity of their words [to those of men], and taking a liking to those bewitching sounds, which excited joy, he delivered the birds to his wife, in order that she should attend to them and exert herself to cherish them. The hapless lady, too, was ignorant of the language the birds spoke. She took care of them and caressed her enemies under the guise of friends.

COUPLET.

I fed my lusts, they proved my overthrow,
I knew not I was cherishing my foe.

In short the lord of the marches became so accustomed to the parrots that he would never sit at the wine-feast without their sweet notes and their unrivaled modulations; and to listen to their exhilarating trills he closed his ears to the touching sounds of the lute, and the exciting murmurs of the harp. One day a party of people from Balkh, came as guests to the lord of the marches, who caused the parrots to be brought into the assembly which he prepared for his visitors. The birds began, in their accustomed manner, to sing the same two sentences. When the guests heard that, they looked at one another, and at last holding down their heads, ashamed, remained astonished at the circumstance. The lord of the marches observed that the flame of his companions' mirth was quenched and that the pleasurable excitement of his guests was exchanged for amazement and reflection. He asked for an explanation of this state of things, and pressed them for it beyond measure, and however much his guests excused themselves, he would not admit of a refusal. One of them, who had more boldness than the rest, said, 'Perhaps, O lord of the marches! thou art ignorant of what these birds say?' He replied, 'I do not understand their words, but I feel a gratification and pleasure in my heart at their delightful tones. Do ye acquaint me with the meaning of what they say.

COUPLET.

The night of Sulaimán ne'er met my eyes,[1]
That I should understand birds' colloquies.'

They then told the lord of the marches the meaning of the words of the parrots, and made him understand the purport of their discourse. Hereupon he desisted from drinking, and said, 'My friends! excuse me. I was ignorant of this matter, and now that I have learned the true state of the case, no other excuse is needed. In our city it is not the custom to entertain in a house where there is a profligate and unchaste wife.' In the midst of this colloquy, the slave who acted as Falconer, cried out, 'I have seen it repeatedly, and I bear witness to it.' The lord-marcher started up, and gave orders to put his wife to death. The lady sent a person to him with this message, 'O fortunate lord!

COUPLET.

Wilt thou we live, or takest thou life away,
Thy will is law—a law that all obey.

Nevertheless reflect in this affair, and act not precipitately.

HEMISTICH.

Haste not to slay me, for I am in thy power.

The wise think deliberation requisite in all affairs, especially in shedding blood, since if it be necessary to take life, the opportunity of doing so is left; and if—which God forbid!—they should, through precipitation, put an innocent person to death, and it should afterwards be known that he did not deserve to be slain, the remedy would be beyond the circle of possibility, and the punishment thereof would hang to all eternity on the neck of the guilty party.

---

[1] I am ignorant of the allusion here. Sulaimán understood the language of birds, but I do not know what night is here referred to.

Give not too hastily thine anger vent,   Lest in the end it cause thee to repent.'

The lord of the marches commanded that they should bring the lady to the party and place her behind a curtain, and he told her the state of the case, and said, 'Parrots are not of the same nature as men, that what they say should be tainted with interested motives. They speak what they have seen, and the Falconer too adds his testimony to corroborate their charge, and this is not a matter that any eloquence can render excusable.

HEMISTICH.

There is no absolution for this sin.'

The lady replied, 'It is a religious duty to take the proper steps in my case, and whenever the circumstances of it are rightly known, if I be worthy of death, thou mayest in one instant set thy mind at rest on that head.' The lord of the marches answered, 'How can this affair be investigated?' His wife replied, 'Inquire of the men of Balkh whether the birds know aught else in the language of Balkh, save these two sentences. And when it is discovered that, except these two phrases, they utter nothing, it will occur to thee that that base and shameless person, whose wish I did not grant, and whose vain desire and profligate intentions did not terminate in success, has taught them these two speeches. But if they can speak anything else in that language, it becomes lawful for thee to shed my blood, and life is to me a thing prohibited.' The lord of the marches proceeded with due circumspection, and for three days the guests examined into the matter. They heard nothing, however, from the tongue of the parrots except those two sentences, and as soon as the innocence of the lady was established, her husband abandoned his intention of putting her to death, and commanded them to bring in the Falconer. He entered with the utmost eagerness, saying to himself that he should, perhaps, obtain promotion. The lady asked him, 'O cruel and treacherous man! didst thou behold me do anything in violation of God's law.' He replied, 'Yes; I saw thee.' The instant that he pronounced these words, a hawk, which he had in his hands, attacked his face and struck its beak into his eye, and tore it out. The lady exclaimed, 'Verily, the punishment of the eye which pretends to have seen what it has not seen, is no other than this, ' *And the retaliation of evil ought to be an evil proportionate thereto.*'[1]

---

[1] Kur'án, Fl. xlii. 38, Mar. xlii. 39; Sale, p. 360, l. 27: 'Whatever things are given you, they are the provision of this present life; but the reward which is with God is better and more durable for those who believe, and put their trust in their Lord : and who avoid heinous and filthy crimes; and, when they are angry, forgive; and who hearken unto their Lord, and are constant at prayer; and whose affairs are directed by consultation among themselves, and who give alms out of what we have bestowed on them; and who, when an injury is done them, avenge themselves: (and the retaliation of an evil ought to be an evil proportionate thereto:) but he who forgiveth and is reconciled unto his enemy, shall receive his reward from God; for he loveth not the unjust doers.'

COUPLET.

To pluck the eye malignant out were best,
For all must him who pries for ill detest.'

And I have introduced this story to the end that ye may know that to be bold in calumniating, and to bear witness to what has not been seen, is the cause of shame in this world and of disgrace in the next.'

When Damnah's speech was finished, they wrote it all down on the spot, and transmitted it to the Lion, and he showed what had passed to his mother. The lioness, having informed herself of it said, ' O king! all my efforts in this matter have been no further beneficial than to cast suspicion on this execrable wretch, and hereafter his deceitful artifices will be occupied with compassing [1] the king's destruction, and he will throw the affairs of both king and people into confusion, and he will accomplish more with respect to all the Pillars of the state than he ventured on with regard to Shanzabah, who was a sincere, attached, and loyal minister ; for from a bad heart will spring nothing but bad actions, and from an infirm nature arises nought but mischief and audacity.

STANZA.

Hope not the Humá's blessings from the owl
Ill-starred; nor that the sparrow hawk-like deeds
Will do. Soon as the feet of miscreant foul
Are raised on high, is't strange if he proceeds
To scatter all around him mischief's seeds.[2]

This speech made a great impression[3] on the heart of the lion, and he was oppressed with long and anxious reflections. At last he said, ' O mother! tell me from whom thou hast heard the tale of Damnah, that I may have a pretext for killing him ?' She replied, 'O king ! to divulge the secret of one who has placed confidence in me, is forbidden by the laws of honor, and a secret which they have committed to me as a deposit, I am necessitated by high feeling to preserve. I can go so far, I will ask that person's permission, and if he concede it, I will then tell it plainly.' To this the Lion assented, and the lioness coming out from his presence, honored her own court by proceeding thither, and sending for the leopard, gratified him by a variety of honorable attentions, and said,

COUPLET.

O thou whose wrath destructive is as time ;
Whose fame like sun-light spreads through every clime!

thou knowest the honors which the king of beasts vouchsafes to thee, and the marks of the royal favor and support towards thee are written in the

---

[1] *Makṣúr shudan* is here idiomatically used in the sense of ' being restricted solely to one purpose.' I have translated it somewhat freely.

[2] Lit., ' if he extend on every side the hand of mischief.'

[3] The phrase is somewhat n͟n͟n͟n͟n͟

volume of manifestation, and for this reason it is incumbent on thee to shew thy gratitude, in order that, according to the promise, '*If ye be thankful, I will surely increase my favours towards you,*'[1]—the bounty of the king may be duly enlarged.' The leopard replied, 'O queen! the imperial favour and kingly bounty which the ruler of this age has lavished and still lavishes on his humble servant cannot be sufficiently acknowledged by me, whatever I might call in to aid me in the task; nor have I the power to evince my thanks for a thousandth part of his kindness, nor for a particle of their amplitude.

COUPLET.

Grant that the lily's tongues all met in me,   Ne'er from the praises due should I get free.

And I have oft traversed the plain of loyalty with the step of praise, and now too, in whatever the empress of the time may be pleased to indicate, she will observe nought but submission and devotion.' The lioness said,

COUPLET.

'Thy work is founded with a manly soul,
Be generous now and thus complete the whole.

HEMISTICH.

A favor is no favor till complete.

The Lion at the first communicated to thee the state of his thoughts, and thou didst undertake the duty of endeavoring, to the utmost extent of thy power, to exact from his perfidious foe vengeance for Shanzabah.

HEMISTICH.

To-day thou must this covenant fulfil.

The advisable course is that thou shouldest proceed to the Lion, and truthfully recount what thou hast seen and heard; otherwise the artifices of Damnah have reached that height that the Lion will forego the intention of putting him to death, and in that case no one will be safe from his malice at the Lion's court, and in a short space he will, by his wily machinations bring destruction on the nobles and officers, and will contrive, by his calumnies and misrepresentations, the ruin of everyone concerned in his case and who strove to secure his death.' The leopard replied, 'O queen! I take upon me the carrying through of this matter.[2] And I hitherto kept back my evidence and withheld this true testimony, in order that the king might get a specimen of Damnah's nature, and become acquainted with his

---

[1] Ḳur'án, Fl. xiv., 7; Mar. xiv., 8; Sale, p. 190, l. 11: 'And when your Lord declared, by the mouth of Moses, saying, If ye be thankful, I will surely increase my favours towards you; but if ye be ungrateful, verily my punishment shall be severe.'

[2] The text appears to me corrupt here, in both the printed and lith. editions. One MS. inserts *va* after *barad*, and I translate accordingly, though I would rather suppress the *kih* after *gháyat*, did the MSS. allow it, or make the first sentence end at *tá gháyat*, and substitute *va* for *kih*, which would be better still.

subtle artifices and fraud, and had I, previous to this, plunged into the matter and meddled in the management of it, (as the king was unacquainted with the tricks of Damnah and the baseness of his nature, and the wickedness of his disposition,) it is probable that he would have imputed my words to selfish motives, and entertained evil suspicions of me. But now that the affair has reached this point, I will not neglect the public weal, and if I had a thousand lives, and could devote them to secure the king a moment's ease of mind, I should still be unable to discharge one of all the duties of thankfulness, which I owe him for his favours, and should still regard myself as falling short of what loyalty imposes on me.

COUPLET.

Both worlds for his one hair I'd give, but yet,
Must in both worlds still blushing own my debt.'

The lioness then went to the Lion, and recounted what had passed between Kalílah and Damnah, as she had heard it, and delivered this testimony in the assembly of the beasts. These tidings being bruited abroad, the thief also,[1] who had overheard their colloquy, sent some one to say that he, too, had evidence to give. The Lion issued his orders that he should attend; and he duly bore witness to what had passed between them in the prison. They asked him why he had not made a representation of it on the first day. He replied, 'No sentence is pronounced on the evidence of only one person, and I thought it not right to bring punishment, uselessly, on an animal.'[2] The Lion approved of what he said; and on the evidence of these two, it became incumbent to sentence Damnah to be punished, and the signatures of the judges having been affixed, all the beasts agreed in pronouncing for his execution in retaliation for that of the Ox.

COUPLET.

Each fool who sows the seed of others' pain,
Will, for his harvest, punishment obtain.

The Lion commanded that they should find and keep him carefully in ward, and that they should withhold his food and torture him with various severities and threats, so that he at last expired of hunger and thirst in the prison, and the retributive disgrace of his fraud and perfidy reaching him, he passed from the hell of imprisonment to the incarceration of hell [according to the saying] '*And the utmost part of the people, which had acted wickedly,*

---

[1] See p. 195, l. 2, of the printed edition of the Persian text, whence it is evident that the reading of the editions here and of some MSS. is a gross mistake, and that for *dú digar* we should read *duzd digar*, as the best MSS. have it, or, were the word admissible, *duzdigar*, 'thief,' which would seem justified by *karigar* and similar forms.

[2] The sense seems obscure here. If no sentence would be pronounced, how could the punishment be inflicted?

was cut off; praise be unto God, the Lord of all creatures,[1] in order that it might be known that such is the end of deceivers and the termination of traitors.

DISTICHS.

Whoever places in man's path a snare,
Himself will, in the sequel, stumble there.
Joy's fruit upon the branch of kindness grows:
Who sows the bramble will not pluck the rose.
Since loss or gain are to our acts assigned,
Do good, for 'tis far better good to find.

---

[1] Ḳur'án, Fl. vi. 45; Mar. vi., 44; Sale, p. 95, l. 25: 'And when they had forgotten that concerning which they had been admonished, we opened unto them the gates of all things; until while they were rejoicing for that which had been given them, we suddenly laid hold on them; and behold, they were seized with despair; and the utmost part of the people, which had acted wickedly, was cut off, praise be unto God, the Lord of all creatures!'

CHAPTER III.

ON THE AGREEMENT OF FRIENDS AND THE ADVANTAGES OF THEIR MUTUALLY AIDING ONE ANOTHER.

INTRODUCTION.

The King said to the Bráhman, 'I have heard the story of friends whose relations, owing to the endeavors of mischievous calumniators, terminated in enmity, and thus the innocent party was put to death, and how God Most High brought on that perfidious disturber the retribution due. Now, if the time calls for it, be pleased to explain the state of friends, one in heart and of one accord, and the way in which they enjoy fruit from the plant of friendship and amity, and their placing back to back and standing face to face in repulsing their foes, and their giving each other's inclination precedence over their own.' The Bráhman replied,

STANZA.

O Khusrau of the age! whose throne is set
    By justice on the azure arched sky,
Heaven's piebald courser [1] does, for thee, forget
    His rage: since, tokens of thy victory,
    Scars on the sun and moon inflicted lie.

Know that in the opinion of the perfectly wise and of people of merit and approved qualities, there is no coin more valuable than the existence of sincere friends, and no rank more lofty than the attainment of attached companions.

COUPLET.

For young and old, far as earth's climes extend,
Must in some exigence require a friend.

And assuredly those persons, the coin of whose friendship has been adorned with the stamp of sincerity in the mint of attachment; and the shrub of whose amity has been watered in the garden of speciality by the drops of unanimity and obligingness, are a delight to the soul and the means of abundance and success; and the advantage of friends is great, and their benefits incalculable. And in the number of them is to be included, that in prosperous times they increase the amount of pleasure and happy converse, and in disasters they tread the path of assistance and are accompanied by companionship and support.

---

[1] *Bád* signifies both ' the wind,' and ' a steed,' hence the equivoque in the original, which I have been unable to preserve.

STANZA.

Get thee a friend—he truly stands alone,
Who in this worldly pageant friend has none:
Of goods that on man in this life attend,
Not one can equal an enduring friend.

And among the number of the stories which they have written on the pages of narration concerning attached companions and united friends, the story of the Crow and the Mouse, and the Pigeon, and the Tortoise, and the Stag, is a lucid narrative and sweet tale.' The King inquired, 'How was that?'

STORY I.

The Bráhman said, 'They have related that in the country of Kashmír there was a delightful spot and an incomparable mead, the surface of whose ground—from the profusion of its flowers—was adorned like the expanse of heaven, and by the reflection of its perfume-shedding plants, the wings of a crow showed like a peacock's tail.

VERSE.

Founts like life's waters there on all sides spring,
  The tulip kindles, too, its lamp of light;
Upstarts the violet with enameling
  Of grass; and morn's young breath reveals to sight
The rose's bosom; and there wind-flowers shine
Like emerald branches holding cups of wine.[1]

And inasmuch as there was much game in that green plain, huntsmen visited it the more frequently and everywhere set their snares for the capture of animals and the imprisonment of birds; and in the vicinity of that plain, a Crow had made its nest on a large tree, and read from the pages of its leaves the maxim, '*Love of country is a part of religion.*' One day, seated on the top of the tree, it was looking down and up and to the right and left, when, on a sudden, it beheld a fowler, who, with a net on his neck, a pouch at his back, and a stick in his hand, was coming towards the tree. The Crow was alarmed, and said to itself,

STANZA.

O God! what can the occurrence be,
  Him hither in such haste to lead?
Nought know I of the cause why he
  Comes this way, hurrying with such speed.

And it is probable that he may have girded himself to attack me and have placed the arrow of deliberation in the bow of stratagem to make me his prey; hence caution requires that I keep my place and watch,

---

[1] The original has 'standing on one leg' as an epithet of the anemone or wind-flower in this verse, but as the idea is simply ludicrous to our taste, I have omitted it.

Till from the curtain what proceeds I see.

The Crow, hidden by the leaves of the tree, employed the eye of expectancy; and the fowler coming to the foot of the tree spread his net and having scattered some grain over it, seated himself in ambush. After some time had elapsed, a flock of pigeons arrived, whose chief was called Ring-dove, of clear intellect and the utmost sagacity, and perfect intelligence and strong judgment; and these pigeons agreed in submitting to him, and gloried in obeying and ministering to him, and spent not their time save in his service, which was to them the service of safety and the adornment of their successful and happy state. As soon as the eyes of the pigeons fell upon the grain, the fire of hunger began to blaze and the reins of choice dropped from the hands of power. Ring-dove, according to the tenderness which is due from superiors to inferiors, endeavoured to induce them to reflect and pause, saying,

COUPLET.
Not to the grain, through greed, impetuous fly.
Beware! for snares beneath each seed may lie.'

They replied, 'Prince! matters with us have reached the pitch of urgency, and our affairs have issued in extreme distress. When our crops are empty of grain, and our hearts are full of anxiety, we have not the power to listen to advice, nor time to watch the consequences; and the wise have said,

COUPLET.
Hunger meets peril hardily,   The sate of life dread not to die.'

Ring-dove perceived that he could not restrain with the noose of counsel those greedy grain-seekers, nor draw them out with the rope of reproach from the pit of incaution and ignorance.

COUPLET.
He who becomes enslaved by greed,   Can hardly from those bonds be freed.

He wished to withdraw from them and to escape on one side, but the power[1] of the divine decree bound his neck with the chain of fate, and dragged him towards the snare.

HEMISTICH.
I blindly follow, as he draws the hook.

In short the whole flock of pigeons, at once laying aside caution, alighted. The instant that they began to pick up the grain they were caught in the fowler's net. Ring-dove exclaimed, 'Did I not tell you that the consequences of precipitation are not commendable, and that to enter upon affairs without reflection, is not to be approved?

---

[1] In the original *ḳáïd*, 'leader.'

COUPLET.

The path of love is full, my heart! of terror and dismay;
He stumbles who, too hastily, would hurry on this way.

The pigeons were quite overcome with shame and alarm, and the fowler, issuing from his place of concealment, was running with the utmost delight towards them, in order that, having seized and secured them, he might return home. As soon as the pigeons beheld the fowler they were distracted with fear, and each flapped its wings and struggled to free itself. Ring-dove exclaimed, 'O comrades! you are exerting yourselves each for his own release, while you are all careless of your companions' safety,

HEMISTICH.

And acts like these ill suit fraternity.

Among friends, it has been declared that they ought to think of their companions' safety before their own, as once on a time two comrades were sitting in a vessel, when, suddenly, near the shore, the vessel foundered, and both fell into the water. A boatman on the shore plunged into the water, and tried to save one of them, but whichever he wanted to rescue, called out,

COUPLET.

In this dread troublous vortex, O my friend!
Leave me, and first to him thy arm extend.'

And if you have not sufficient firmness to prefer your comrade's life to your own, and to esteem his safety more precious than yours, at least, let all of you, with mutual consent and co-operation, put out your strength, so that, perhaps, by the fortunate influence of this unanimity and agreement, the net may be raised from its place and we may all obtain deliverance.' The pigeons did as they were directed and all made a common effort, and by this manœuvre, tore up the net and made off. The fowler, notwithstanding this circumstance, followed on their traces, and hoping that they would at last get weary and fall, went on with his eyes fixed in the air. The crow thought to himself. 'It will take a vast interval of time before a similar strange occurrence comes from the womb of nonentity into the expanse of existence, and I, myself, am not safe from an accident of this nature. It will be better to follow them with speed that I may learn how their affair terminates, and storing up that experience for my future life, make use of it in the time of need.

COUPLET.

Share of experience do not then refuse,   That thou in time of trouble may it use.

The Crow flew after them, and Ring-dove with his flock flew on, bearing the net, and the greedy and audacious fowler, fixing his eyes upon them traveled onward. When Ring-dove observed that the fowler still followed them and that his appetite being stimulated urged him not to rest until he had laid hands upon them, he turned to his companions and said, 'This hostile person has prepared with the utmost diligence to pursue us and is bent upon killing us, and until we disappear from his sight he will not give us up. Our best course is to make for inhabited places and to fly towards orchards and trees, that his view of us may be intercepted and that he may turn back in despair and ashamed.' The pigeons, in accordance with his direction, sped on and hastened from the wild waste and desert towards buildings. When the fowler lost sight of them, he turned back with extreme regret, and the Crow flew on as before, in order to learn the circumstances of the pigeons' release, and treasure them up as a means of averting a similar danger, and as a remedy for an occurrence of the same nature, in accordance with the maxim, ' *Happy is he who is taught by the lesson of others.*'

STANZA.

The wise is he who, testing loss and gain,
Attentive shares the lessons of his friend,
Takes that from which his comrades good obtain,
Shuns what to them proves hurtful in the end.

The pigeons, freed from the terror of the fowler, referred to Ring-dove as to the means of liberating themselves from the net, and that wise and prudent bird, after long reflection and consideration, replied, ' I am constrained to think that there is no escape from this perilous position without the help of a faithful friend :

HEMISTICH.

None unattended can this road conclude.

In this neighbourhood there is a mouse, Zírak by name, distinguished among my friends by his superior faithfulness, and pre-eminent among all my comrades and those who have a regard for me in the code of friendship.

COUPLET.

A true companion and a friend sincere,
Love in his acts and faith alone appear.

It is probable that by his aid some means of escape from these fetters will be found and a plan offer itself for our release.' They then alighted at a ruin where the mouse dwelt, and, approaching his hole, rapped with the knocker of the door of eagerness. When the voice of Ring-dove reached the ear of Zírak, he came out, and when he beheld his friend bound in the fetters of calamity, he caused tears of blood from the fountain of his eyes to flood the expanse of his cheek, and raised to heaven sighs of grief from his consuming heart, and said,

VERSE.

' What state is this I see, what state is it?
In such a state I cannot patient be:
How can I, comrades, here inactive sit,
When a dear friend imprisoned thus I see?

O beloved friend! and O companion suited to my mind! by what stratagem didst thou fall into this net, and from what cause wast thou overtaken in this distress?' Ring-dove replied, 'A variety of good and ill, and divers gains and losses, have been bound up with the decrees of fate. Whatever the writer of the supreme will inscribes with the pen of predestination in the tribunal of eternity on the pages of the affairs of created things will assuredly come forward into the field of existence, and to endeavour to avoid or shun it is altogether unavailing.

COUPLET.

> Bitter and sweet the pen has traced, my son!
> What does fate reck, though thou look sourly on?

And the divine will and God's decree have plunged me into this vortex of destruction, and displayed to me and my companions the grain, and although I dissuaded them from acting with levity and precipitation, and rebuked them for their haste and neglect of caution, the hand of destiny drew down before the eye of my vision also the curtain of carelessness; and clear-sighted reason, and far-seeing prudence kept me behind the dark screen of ignorance and folly, and thus the whole of us were all at once overtaken with the hand of trouble and the claw of calamity.' The Mouse replied, 'Oh strange! that one like thee, with all this shrewdness and sagacity, could not resist the disastrous influence of fate, nor avert with the shield of stratagem and counsel the shaft of destiny.' Ring-dove answered, 'O Zírak! cease these words, for those who, in strength and power, and reason and foresight, are superior to me; and in dignity and wealth, and excellence and perfection are before me; cannot contend with the eternal decrees nor withdraw their heads from the mandate of Him who has no decline, '*There is none who can avert His decree, and there is none to reverse his judgment.*'[1] When the ruler whose commands all obey, moves the chain of His purpose, he transports the fish from the bottom of the ocean into the expanse of air, and the bird from its aerial height, he brings down into the centre of the earth; and there is no resource for any creature in the decrees of destiny and providence but to acquiesce and be resigned.

DISTICHS.

> Though all earth's atoms struggled to be free,
> They could do nothing against God's decree.
> When fate's dark features from the mantle[2] rise,
> Of sight and hearing both they rob the wise.

---

[1] Ḳur'án, Fl. xiii., 41; Mar. 43; Sale, p. 189, l. 13: 'Do they not see that we come into their land, and straiten the borders thereof, by the conquest of the true believers? When God judgeth, there is none to reverse His judgment; and He will be swi t in taking an account.' I have been unable, however, to find the first half of the saying in the Ḳu'rán; it is probably therefore proverbial.

[2] *Charkh* has several very different meanings. It may signify 'the sky,' or 'the collar of a coat.' This latter sense, I think, it bears in the present passage; though I have translated it 'mantle,' as being somewhat more poetical.

Fish on the shore from ocean's breast are tost,
And soaring birds in earth-set snares are lost.
Fate like an angry tempest is; mankind
The feeble straw swept headlong by the wind.

And thou must know that in the matter of the issue of the mandate of fate, the wise and the fool are alike, and in the whirlpool of destiny the poor peasant and the world-conquering king are on the same footing.

COUPLET.

Thou mayst have gold or mayst be strong, thou canst not change fate's mandates therefore.
Nor is it fit to God's decree to answer with a ' Why?' or ' Wherefore ?'

Zírak replied, ' O Ring-dove! be of good cheer, for every garment that the habit-maker of the Divine Will prepares for the person of any individual attendant of the court of God's worship, whether its collar be adorned with the button of wealth, or its skirt worked with the border of distress, is indubitably a pure favor and absolute beneficence. And the climax of this bounty is that the creature remains ignorant of its nature, nor sees the recondite mercy involved in it,[1] and with reference to this they have said,

COUPLET.

Lees or pure, to thee 'tis nothing, thou hast drunk the beverage up,[2] '
All the Filler gives is kindness, with whate'er He fill the cup.

And if thou dost well consider it, what has befallen thee was for thy good ; and the wise have said, ' The pure honey is not found without the cruel sting, nor does the rose of joy grow up without the thorn of trouble.'

HEMISTICH.

Full many a wish in disappointment lies.'

And when Zírak had finished this discourse and began to busy himself in severing the meshes which confined Ring-dove, the latter exclaimed, ' Kind friend! first undo the fetters of my companions, and after thou hast satisfied thyself of their release, come to me.' The mouse, paying no attention to these words, went on with his work. Ring-dove said again, and with greater emphasis, ' O Zírak! if thou desirest to please me and act true to thy obligations as a friend, it is requisite for thee first to release my friends, and by this favour, thou wilt place the chain of obligation on my neck.' The Mouse answered, ' Thou hast reiterated this remark, and hast laid excessive stress upon it. But carest thou not for thine own life? and dost thou not admit the duty of self-preservation or neglectest thou the maxim, ' *Begin with thine own self.*'[3] Ring-dove replied, ' Thou shouldest not reproach me, for they have written out for my name the diploma of the chieftainship of these

[1] The hiding from man his future (which, be it what it may, is for the best) is the greatest of mercies.
[2] The MSS. and the editions vary much in this line. The lithographed edition reads *dam dar kash* ' keep silence,' for the *khwush dar kash* ' drink pleasantly' of the printed edition.
[3] A proverb similar to our ' Charity begins at home.'

pigeons, and I have made myself responsible for superintending their affairs. Inasmuch as they are my subjects, they have just claims upon me, and I too have claims upon them, because I am their prince, and now that they have faithfully discharged their duty to me, and that by their aid and assistance I have escaped from the hands of the fowler, I too ought to acquit myself of the duties which belong to me, and perform the functions of a leader; and every king who seeks his own ease, and leaves his people entangled in the bonds of trouble, it will not be long before the draught of his happiness is discolored, and the eye of his fortune darkened.

COUPLET.

In thy dominions will be rest for none,
If thou should'st seek for thine own ease alone.'

The Mouse answered, 'The king is to his people what life is to the frame, or the heart to the body; wherefore, the first thing will be to take care of his condition, since, if the heart is whole, there cannot result so much detriment from the ill-state of the members, but if—which God forbid!—the heart be injured, the safety of the limbs is of no use whatever.

COUPLET.

What harm though servants be diminishèd,
If a hair fall not from the monarch's head.'

Ring-dove rejoined, 'I fear lest, if thou shouldst begin to remove my bonds, thou mightest become weary, and some of my companions might be left imprisoned; while, as long as I am bound, though thou be utterly tired, thou wilt not forsake me, nor will thy feelings suffer thee to neglect to set me free, and, moreover, we have been partners in calamity, and honor demands that our release and freedom too should be simultaneous.

VERSE.

Dost boast of friends? then boast his friendship, who
Acts like a friend in joy and sorrow too.
They who in joy alone their friendship shew,
Speak not of them, they but augment thy woe.'

The Mouse answered, 'This is the custom of the magnanimous and the fundamental principle of the generous; and by this laudable disposition and amiable temperament, the confidence of people in thy friendship becomes more unclouded, and the reliance of thy subjects on thy beneficence and high-mindedness is increased.

COUPLET.

Thy hopes of friendship on the man devolve,
Who can things adverse and entangled solve.'

Then Zírak, with the utmost energy and ineffable zeal, severed the meshes of Ring-dove's companions, and, last of all, released the neck of Ring-dove himself from the chain of calamity. The pigeons bade him farewell, and, safe and secure, returned to their own nests, and the Mouse retreated into his hole. When the Crow beheld the Mouse's assistance, and how he undid the meshes, he longed to secure his friendship and alliance, and viewing his fidelity and fraternity as a rare blessing, said to himself, 'I can never be secure from the adventure which befel the pigeons, and, consequently, I can never be indifferent to the friendship of such a person as this, who renders help in adversity.

VERSE.

> Of mere companions both the east and west
> Are full; but those one really wants, are few.
> Many hang round thee from self-interest,
> To those who help, the name of 'friend' is due.

The crow then flew lightly down to the door of the mouse's hole, and called out. The Mouse asked, 'Who art thou?' The Crow replied, 'It is I, the Crow, and I have urgent business with thee. Zírak was a mouse of prudence, who had experienced many vicissitudes and seen both good and ill fortune, and he had in that place prepared many holes for places of refuge, and had cut passages from one to the other, and he was in the habit of making ready for emergencies before they occurred, and of providing for all things wisely and prudently. When he heard the Crow's voice, he recoiled, and said, 'What hast thou to do with me or what connection have I with thee?' The Crow recounted the case from beginning to end, and informed him of his acquaintance with his fidelity and excessive truthfulness in the matter of the pigeons, and said, 'I have discovered thy perfect honor and loyalty, and goodly generosity and discharge of duty, and know how those pigeons reaped the fruits of thy friendship, and the consequences of thy amity; and how they obtained deliverance from that whirlpool of destruction by the blessing of thy constancy and attachment. I have bent all my energies to secure thy friendship, and am here to go through the preliminaries for commencing our intimacy.

COUPLET.

> To thee our hearts expectant look. Lo! now
> Our wish is told, the arbiter art thou.'

The Mouse replied, 'The path of companionship between me and thee is closed, and the road of intercourse shut.

COUPLET.

> No profit in the mart with thee, but deadly peril meets my eyes,
> For in our friendship's path a gulf, than east and west more distant, lies.

Go! cease attempting to weld iron that has not been heated, nor take steps in pursuit of a thing, the attainment of which is every way surrounded with difficulties; for the pursuit of that which comes not within the range of possibility, is like trying to impel a ship on dry ground or to gallop a horse on the surface f the sea; and whoever labors in scarch of impossibilities makes himself an object of ridicule, and does but display his own ignorance to the wise.

COUPLET.

Remove thy net and other game pursue,
Thy noose is vain for that thou hast in view.'

The Crow replied, 'Forbear to speak thus, for the generous leave not the needy unsatisfied, nor do the rich strike the back of their hands on the supplicating foreheads of those—whoever they may be—who seek their portals; and I have taken refuge, at this threshold, from the vicissitudes of fortune, and have made these doors my asylum and retreat from the chances of revolving time.

COUPLET.

Thy sheltering door alone I safe can tread,
And at thy threshold only rest my head.

Now that I have made the dust of this thoroughfare the place of my attendance, and consider my honor pledged to the service of this sanctuary, no ill-treatment will make me turn back, nor any contumely drive me elsewhere.

COUPLET.

Smite me with thy vengeful sabre, sovereign power rests with thee,
Or I bow in willing service, if this honor thou decree.'

The Mouse rejoined, 'O Crow! desist from those artifices, nor scatter the grain of deceit before the net of dissimulation, for I well know the disposition of those of thy race, and since our natures are different, I shrink from thy society.

HEMISTICH.

'Tis anguish to the spirit with a different race to dwell.

Nothing can now make me secure with thee, and whoever chooses the companionship of one with whom he can never be secure, will meet with what the Partridge met with.' The Crow asked, 'How was that?'

STORY II.

The Mouse replied, 'They have related that on the skirt of a mountain a Partridge[1] was proudly walking, and the echoing sound of its merry cry pealed through the vault of heaven. It happened that a bird of prey, a hawk, was flying there. When its sight fell on the graceful movements of the Partridge, and the sound of its glee caught its ear, it longed in heart to associate with it, and began to inscribe on the tablet of its imagination the traces of its

---

[1] The *kabk-i dari* is said, in the dictionary, to be 'a beautiful sort of partridge.' Hence, and, because its note is described as so pleasing, I take it to be 'the black partridge,' which is not only a very beautiful bird, but has the most joyous enticing cry imaginable.

friendship. It reflected that in this world every creature stands in need of a suitable companion, and cannot do without an agreeable friend and kind associate, and that it has passed into a proverb that 'where friends are failing there is ever ailing :'[1]

COUPLET.

He whose delights no friendly comrade shares,
His tree of joy on earth no produce bears.

and that this Partridge would be a friend of comely countenance and smiling aspect, light-hearted and graceful, and that in the society of such a companion, the mind would be refreshed and gratified, and the bosom cheered and soothed by the friendship of such an ally.

QUATRAIN.

I want a friend, say who that friend should be ?
One who my progress from all knots will free,
No dust of pain will on the glass remain
Of my clear spirit, when his form I see.'

He then softly inclined towards the Partridge, who, when it saw him, cautiously ensconced itself in the fissure of a rock. The hawk, descending from the air, alighted in front of that cleft, and stated what had occurred, saying, 'O Partridge! hitherto I have been blind to thy perfections, and thy excellence and transcendant merit have been hid from me. To-day thy mirthful cry has occasioned such joyous emotions in my heart, and thy bewitching movements have so captivated me, as to make me trust that thou wilt not henceforth stand in dread or awe of me, and that thou wilt be disposed to become my friend and associate, since where friendship precedes, happy results follow, and the tree of amity bears for its fruit the object of one's wishes.

COUPLET.

Such fruit grows on the tree of amity,
The more we pluck, the more its boughs supply.

The Partridge replied, ' O conquering hero! suffer this helpless afflicted one to escape, and be pleased to devour some other partridge, and deem

COUPLET.

That I on thee should tranquil look, alas ! this were but idle scheming,
That union grow 'twixt thee and me, forgive me, God ! 'tis nought but dreaming.

Whenever water and fire consent to blend together, then one may conceive that friendship might arise between thee and me, and when sun and shade can be associated, it will be supposable that we can become companions.

HEMISTICH.

Cease from this fancy, which can ne'er take place.'

---

[1] I have made a feeble attempt to retain the play on words in the original, where *bi yár* 'friendless' chimes with *bímár* 'sick.'

The hawk replied, 'O friend! reflect that it can be nothing but friendship which could lead me to speak kindly to one like thee. My claws are not grown weak, that I should fail in making prey of such as thou art, nor has my beak become powerless or debilitated that I should fail to secure any food. There is no more in it than this, that the desire of fellowship and fraternity with thee, and the wish for propinquity and attachment to thee, induces me to agitate the chain of friendship; and thou mayest anticipate many advantages from associating with me. And among these the first will be that when birds of the same species with myself observe that I foster thee under the shadow of the wings of my protection, they will withdraw the hand of violence from thy skirt and will survey thee with respect; and thou, with mind at ease, mayest wander over mountain and plain. Another advantage will be that I will convey thee to my own nest, so that thou wilt be elevated to a superior station and a lofty abode, and wilt be advanced in dignity above thy fellows. Moreover, I will bring thee a partner of thy own kind, gentle and beautiful, whom thou mayest in real truth desire to espouse, so that embracing her with the hands of enjoyment thou mayest pass thy time to the wish of thy heart.

COUPLET.

Time shall not wrong, nor heaven distress thee more,
Thy hopes all won, thy joy-cup brimming o'er.'

The Partridge answered, 'Thou art the ruler of the birds and the reins of dominion over them are in the grasp of thy option, and I am one of thy subjects and of those who pay thee tribute, and the like of me are not devoid of weaknesses and infirmities, and at the time when I am aided by thy favor and hope for thy support, it is possible that I may do something which may displease thy august mind, and the talons of my lord's anger may destroy me. It cannot but be best that I should content myself with retirement and not lift up the banner of service in thy command, which is fraught with danger to me.

COUPLET.

To gaze upon the sun's bright face I in myself no fitness see,
Better that, like the shadow, meek behind the wall I prostrate be.'

The hawk replied, 'O brother! hast thou not heard and learned that the eye of friendship is blind in discovering faults, and that everything that proceeds from a friend, though it be the greatest of blemishes, seems the chiefest of beauties.

COUPLET.

Poison from thee thy friend would sugar deem, And of his praises make thy faults the theme.

And since I survey thy actions with the eye of friendship, and inscribe the writing of thy words and adventures on the volume of attachment, how could I trace the character of error in thy discourse? or how interpret amiss aught that thou couldst say or do?

HEMISTICH.

The eye of friendship ne'er can see a fault.'

Although the Partridge repeated many excuses worthy of being approved, the hawk rejoined to them with satisfactory answers, and at last, by promises and a solemn covenant, he drew the Partridge out of the hole, and they then embraced one another, and ratified their agreement by oaths; and the hawk, taking him up, conveyed him to his own nest, and mutually pleased with each other, they passed their time in amusement and mirth. When two or three days had passed in this manner, and the Partridge felt safe with the hawk, he began to adopt an insolent tone, to speak with too great freedom, and without any reason, burst into laughter in the midst of conversation; while the hawk magnanimously appeared not to hear it, and forbore to punish it. Nevertheless, resentment found room in his breast, until one day he suddenly became slightly indisposed, so that he was unable to stir in search of food. He passed the whole day in his nest, and when night came and his crop was emptied of the food it contained, the fire of hunger blazed up and set his savage nature in motion, and the feelings of irritation against the Partridge, which he had stored up in the course of time, made him furious. In vain the monitor reason presented to his eyes his promise and compact, he did not glance at it with the eye of consent, and was seeking for a pretence to break his agreement and devour the Partridge. The latter observed the signs of wrath in his countenance, and with the sight of his eyes perceived that his destruction was at hand. Drawing a cold sigh from his afflicted heart, he said,

COUPLET.

'Like lover blessed, I cried, rejoicing, 'I have won my wishes' pearl,'
But little knew what giant surges this deceitful sea could hurl.

Alas! that at the beginning of this adventure, I did not cast my eyes to the conclusion, but associated with one of a different race, and forgot the precept of the wise.

HEMISTICH.

A comrade of a different race avoid.

Consequently, this day the vessel of my life has fallen into a whirlpool, such that the mariner of deliberation is unable to set me free; and the cord of my existence is broken in such wise, that the finger-tip of thought is baffled in attempting to unite it.

COUPLET.

My friend unfaithful and my life despair,
Heaven grants no tidings, nor fate hears my prayer.'

Thus was he soliliquizing, and meantime the hawk was unfolding his cruel talons and whetting his blood-shedding beak with the venom of tyranny, and as his first measure, sought a pretext[1] against the Partridge. The latter, cautiously observant, took care to be thoroughly respectful, so that the hawk found no excuse for attacking him. At length, losing patience, he called out angrily to the Partridge, 'Is it fitting that I should be in the sun and thou pass thy time in the shade?' The Partridge replied, 'O world-subduing prince! now it is night, and the shades of darkness have enveloped the whole world. By the heat of what sun are you distressed? and what thing is it that affords me the convenience of shade?' The hawk replied, 'O thou insolent one! dost thou make me out a liar, and deny my assertion? I will give thee thy punishment.' He had no sooner uttered these words, than he tore the Partridge in pieces.

And I have adduced this story that thou mayest know, that whoever associates with those of a different race, and passes his time with one from whose injuries he cannot be safe, his life, like that of the mountain-partridge, is sacrificed to his companionship,[2] and lost. In the same manner I am thy food, and I can never live secure from thy appetite. Wherefore, how can the road of amity between me and thee be opened? or in what manner can the requisites for an alliance be procurable?' The Crow answered, 'O Zírak! refer the matter to the decision of thy own judgment, and perpend it well, and reflect; What advantage could I gain by injuring thee, and were I to devour thee, how far would it satisfy[3] me? while, in thy personal existence and the acquisition of thy friendship, there are a thousand advantages, and a hundred thousand benefits discernable. Besides it is not seemly that I should have traversed a long and distant journey to seek thee, and thou avert thy face from me, and smite the breast of my hope with the hand of discouragement; nor is it fitting that thou, possessed of the kindly disposition and serene mind that thou hast, should slight my claims as a stranger, or that the poor should retire from thy threshold discomfited.

COUPLET.

> Praise by the care of poorer men is earned,
> Why has your city not this canon learned?

And from the excellent qualities that I have observed in thee, I do not suppose that thou wilt altogether refuse to suffer me to partake of thy beneficence, and to perfume with the exhilarating odor of thy courtesy, the nostrils of my expectation.

HEMISTICH.

> Thyself art poor, then when wilt thou to poor men favour show?'

---

[1] Lit.: 'Made the seeking pretences his van-measure.'

[2] I feel considerable doubt as to this passage. I take the *kardah* in the sense of *fidá kardah*.

[3] Hence I conclude that *músh* in this story signifies 'a mouse,' and not a rat, which could hardly be considered a small repast for a crow. It is strange that there is not a distinct word for each animal in Persian.

The Mouse answered, 'There is no kind of enmity so grave in its effects as that implanted by nature. For if an accidental hostility should arise between two persons, slight measures may suffice to remove it, and a trifling cause may dispel it. But if enmity has sprung up in the original nature, and its consequences have implanted themselves in the minds of both parties, and if to that hereditary hostility be added new reasons for hate, and former dislike be combined with subsequent quarrels, the removal thereof can in no wise enter the circle of possibility, and the getting rid of it is altogether beyond the limits of human power, and its extinction involves the annihilation of both parties.

HEMISTICH.

Till the head goes, that thought the head leaves not.

And the wise have said, 'Natural enmity is of two kinds. The first is when the injury resulting from it is not confined to one of the two parties. Now the one is vexed by the other. and now the injury is reversed, as in the case of the elephant and the lion, who cannot meet without a contest. Yet it does not follow that the victory is always on one side, and that the other will as constantly be put to flight. But on some occasions the raging lion is triumphant, and on others the furious elephant is the conqueror. Now this kind of enmity is not so intense that its wounds cannot be salved, because the party with which the victory remains, his heart will undoubtedly be pacified. The other kind is where the injury is always on one side, and the advantage on the other, like that of the mouse and the cat, and of the wolf and the sheep; and where the pain is restricted to one party, and the pleasure to the other; and this enmity is so powerful that not the revolution of the sky can change it, nor the vicissitudes of time undo its knot: and where it is known that one party aims at the life of the other, without there having been a previous attempt in time past from that other party, or the possibility of injury from him in the future, how can a reconcilliation take place there? or, how can intercourse there be carried on?

VERSE.

When day and night together meet,
And shade with sunshine blends,
Then I with thee will take my seat;
Yet, even then,
Discerning men
Would ridicule such friends.'

The Crow replied, 'Praise be to God! no hostility from me to thee was mixed up in my original composition, and if in those of my race a fortuitous enmity has sprung up to thee, the mirror of *my* heart, at least, is free from the dust of malignity, and the glass of my mind is prepared to receive the refraction of the rays of love and affection; and assuredly as the maxim, *From heart to heart there is a window,*' is true, I am in hopes that the sincere heart of that dear friend will testify to the truth of my friendship.

Think not thy loved one cannot read thy heart?'

The Mouse answered, 'Thou art beyond measure importunate, and troublest me by thus pressing on me thy friendship; and should I accept it and thou, too, stand to thy purpose, it is probable that on some trifling cause thou wilt break the chain of amity and return to thy former original habits and natural hostility—like water, which though it be kept long in one place so as to alter its smell and taste, yet retains its primitive properties, and if they pour it on fire, does not fail to quench it. And to consort with an enemy is like mixing with snakes and vipers, which is not safe; and friendship with foes resembles associating with tigers of sharp claws, which deserves not to be tried: and the wise have said, 'We must not be beguiled by the assurances of our enemies, although they pretend to be friendly, nor must we confide in their words though they prepare the way to an agreement most assiduously.

COUPLET.

To hope new [1] friends will spring from ancient foes,
Is from a furnace [2] to expect a rose.

And whoever, relying on an enemy, is elated by his civilities and listens to his cajolements with the ear of approval, will meet with what befell that Camel-rider.' The Crow inquired, 'How was that?'

STORY III.

The Mouse said, 'They have related that a Camel-rider, as he was journeying, arrived at a place where the people of a caravan had made a fire, and after their departure the fan of the wind stirred it and set it in a blaze, and the sparks leaping forth from it, fell among the wood in all parts, and in every corner of the desert a dreadful conflagration [3] arose, and in the midst of those flames a large snake—a huge venomous serpent was left, and being intercepted could not find a way to escape in any direction, nor any path to get free. He was on the point of being fried like a fish in a frying-pan, and like a roasted partridge on the fire, his blood was about to drop from his poison-scattering eyes—when he beheld that rider, and calling for help, exclaimed,

COUPLET.

'What if thou should'st take pity on my lot,
And of these difficulties solve the knot?'

The Camel-rider was a merciful and kind man. When he heard the snake's supplication and beheld its distress and trouble, he thought to

---

[1] The editions here have a misprint, *tú* for *nau* 'new.'
[2] This line loses all its point in English. In the original there is an equivoque on *gul* 'a rose,' and *gulkhan*, 'a furnace for heating baths.'
[3] Lit., 'a tulip-bed,' the brilliant colour of which flower resembles that of a conflagration.

himself, 'It is true that snakes are the enemies of men, but he is now helpless and dismayed. My best course is to take pity on him and sow in the soil of action the seed of kindness, which can bear no other fruit than happiness in this world and exaltation in that to come.' He then fixed the huntsman's-bag [1] that he had with him to the point of a spear and reached it thither. The snake, too happy to avail himself of it, crept into the bag, and the rider thinking it a good act drew him out from the midst of the fire. He then opened the mouth of the bag and said to the snake, 'Go whithersoever thou wilt, and in gratitude for thy escape from this calamity, withdraw into solitude nor hereafter put thyself into a position to injure man; for he that injures God's creatures, is disgraced in this world and miserable [2] in that to come.

COUPLET.

Fear God, nor any living thing distress,
This is the one sole road to happiness.'

The snake replied, 'Cease from these words, young man! for I will not depart till I have bitten thee and thy camel.' The rider answered, 'Have I not done thee a kindness and brought thee out of the fire? is this my recompense, and such the reward I am to receive?

COUPLET.

On my part is the kindly deed,   From thee shall cruel acts proceed?'

The snake rejoined, 'True! thou hast done a kind action, but it was shown to an undeserving object; and thou hast been clement, but thy clemency was mis-placed. Thou knowest that I am a vehicle of mischief and that no benefit to men can be anticipated from me. Wherefore when thou didst exert thyself to release me and showedst kindness to one with whom thou oughtedst to have dealt roughly; of course it is necessary, in requital, to cause thee distress, for showing kindness to the bad is equivalent to injuring the good.

VERSE.

The canons of the law and prudence too,
Bid us not harm the good and pure.
And so we should not kindly actions do
To those from whom men wrongs endure.

And moreover in accordance with that verse of the Ḳur'án, ' *The one of you shall be an enemy unto the other,* ' [3] an ancient enmity exists between us and you, and prudence requires that we should bruise the head of an enemy, and

---

[1] *Túbrah* may be either 'a huntsman's bag,' or 'a nosebag for a horse.'
[2] The epithet *dushman-i kám* 'miserable,' is worth remarking. It properly signifies 'foe's wish,' *i.e.,* miserable as even one's enemies could desire.
[3] Ḳur'án, Ch. xx. 121; Sale p. 242, l. 17: 'And thus Adam became disobedient unto his Lord and was seduced. Afterwards his Lord accepted him on his repentance, and was turned unto him and directed him. And God said, 'Get ye down hence all of you; the one of you shall be an enemy unto the other.'

agreeably to the command, '*Kill ye the two black things*,'[1] you ought to get rid of us, and while it is decreed that man should not permit us to go unscathed, thou hast in this matter abandoned the lawful and prudent course and chosen to be merciful, and I will assuredly inflict a wound on thee for a warning to others.' The rider said, 'O snake! let justice be appealed to, for in what creed is it deemed right to requite good with evil? and in what sect is it admissible to give the foulness of wrong in exchange for the purity of advantage?' The snake replied, 'Such is the custom of you men, and I, too, do but practice what you pronounce; and I sell to you what I have bought from you in the mart of recompense.

HEMISTICH.

Buy for one instant what whole years you sell.'

In vain the man protested, the snake exclaimed, 'Decide with all speed whether I shall wound thee first, or commence with the camel.' The young man replied, 'Desist from this idea, for it is not fortunate to requite good with evil.' The snake answered, 'This is the custom of men, and I do but act in the same manner as they.' The rider denied this accusation, and said, 'If thou canst prove this by clear testimony, and wilt bring evidence to establish thy charge that men are wont to requite actions in this manner, I will purchase thy wound with my life, and will acquiesce in my own destruction.' The snake looked about him and saw at a distance a buffalo, which was feeding in the plain. 'Come,' he said, 'let us ask the truth of my assertion from this buffalo.' The man and the snake then approached the buffalo, and the snake addressed it saying, 'O buffalo! what is the reward of good?' The buffalo replied, 'If thou inquirest what it is among men, [I answer] the reward of good is evil. Lo! I was for a long time with one of them, and every year I brought forth a young one, and filled his house with milk and butter, and supplied the means on which his marriage and his subsistence were based. When I grew old, and became unable to bear young, he gave up attending to me, and turning me out of his house set me loose in the plain. After that I grazed for a long time here, and passed my time without work, according to my own wish. I began to grow somewhat fat, and yesterday my master came by here, and thought I looked fat. Hereupon he brought a butcher, and sold me to him; and to-day they are going to take me to the slaughter-house, and mean to kill me. Behold! such is the reward of all the good that I have recounted.

HEMISTICH.

Such, friends, my state! to whom can I it tell?'

The snake replied 'Lo! thou hast heard. Prepare thyself quickly for the

---

[1] What the two black things referred to in the maxim may be, I know not; probably the scorpion and the snake.

wound.' The Camel-rider replied, 'In legal trials they do not pronounce sentence upon the evidence of one witness. Bring another, and do what thou wilt.' The snake looked about him, and seeing a tree said, 'Come, and I will ask this tree.' They then came together to the foot of the tree, and the snake inquired of it, 'What is the reward of good?' It replied, 'Among men the reward of good is evil, and the return for benefit, injury; and the proof is this: I am a tree that have sprung up in this wilderness, and I stand on one leg in the service of every comer and goer. When a child of Adam comes here oppressed with heat, and weary from the desert, he rests for an hour under my shade, and for a time indulges in repose. When he opens his eyes he says, 'Such a bough will do for the handle of an axe, and such a bit is fit and proper for a spade. One might cut some good planks out of its trunk, and of them make some fine doors;' and if they had saws or hatchets they would cut out of my branches and trunk whatever they fancied, and in spite of the enjoyment derived from me, would think fit to inflict all this suffering on me.

COUPLET.

I thinking how he best might shaded be,
He pondering how to mar and uproot me.'

The snake said, 'Lo! two witnesses have been brought; yield up thy body, that I may wound it.' The man replied, 'Life is very dear, and it is difficult to tear away the heart from the things of life, as long as it is possible to retain it. If one other person testifies in this matter, I will, without scruple, yield my body to this calamity, and acquiesce in God's decree.' Now, through a strange coincidence, a fox was standing by, observing their proceedings, and listening to their words with the ear of attention. The snake exclaimed, 'See there! Ask this fox what answer he would give.' Before the rider could put the question to him, the fox bawled out to the man, 'Dost thou not know that the return for good is evil? What good hast thou done to this snake, that has made thee worthy of being punished in requital?' The young man recounted the particulars; whereupon the fox said, 'Thou appearest to be a sensible man, how is it that thou speakest what is contrary to the truth?

COUPLET.

When will a man of sense himself to speak untruths permit?
For wise men to belie the fact, in truth, can ne'er be fit.'

The snake said, 'He speaks the truth, and behold! here, hanging to the saddle-strap, is the bag in which he brought me out of the fire!' The fox expressed his surprise, saying, 'How can one believe this story, that a snake of this size could be contained in a bag so small?' The snake answered, 'If thou dost not credit it, I will go again into the bag, that thou mayst see it with thine own eyes.' The fox rejoined, 'If I behold the thing, and have ocular demonstration of it, and find that these words are true, I will pronounce sentence between you in such wise as not to infringe justice, and to be wholly void of fraud and self-interest.'   The man opened the mouth of the bag, and the snake, confiding in what the fox had said, entered the bag. The fox then cried out, 'O young man! when thou hast got thy enemy fast, shew him no mercy.

COUPLET.

Is thy foe captive and o'ercome by thee?
Reason commands thou shouldst not set him free.'

The man tied the mouth of the bag and dashed it against the ground till the snake was killed and the malice of his evil nature was extinguished, so that creation was emancipated from his power of injury.

HEMISTICH.

One who so badly lives is better slain.

And the moral of this story is, that it behoves a wise man not to abandon the path of caution nor to rely on the humble words of an enemy, and never to be led to trust in him, so as not to be overwhelmed by his attack.

QUATRAIN.

Whoe'er upon a foeman's word relies,
  The lamp of sense with him has lost its light.
Then will true friends from former foes arise,
  When darkness separating leaves the night.'

The Crow replied, 'These words which thou with perfect wisdom hast uttered, I have heard, and I have irradiated my mental vision with these bright gems which thou hast brought forth from the mines of sense, and it would be more in accordance with thy beneficence and generosity, and magnanimity and courtesy, to forego these excessive scruples, and, believing my words, throw open the path of friendship. And the wise have said, 'Fly to the beneficent and shun the niggardly, for the beneficent is willing, upon the acquaintance of an hour, to impart a variety of kindnesses and good offices, and putting off the coldness of a stranger, to assume, with the utmost cordiality, the part of a friend and a companion. While the niggard, forgetting the obligations of ancient communion, will efface from his memory, in the twinkling of an eye, the friendship of a hundred years. And hence it is that the pious who have shaken themselves free from the world, are prone to friendship and slow to enmity—like a vessel of gold, which it takes long to break and but a short time to mend; while the base are slow to become friends and their friendship is soon overturned—like a vessel of earth, which is easily broken and can never be mended; and how finely have they said,

VERSE.

Seek such a friendship for thyself to gain,
  As may through endless years endure.
Houses of unbaked bricks, a few days rain
  Will level with the earth; be sure.

And I am of the number of those whose friendship may be depended upon and moreover, I am in want of thy companionship, and now that I have planted myself in waiting at this court, I will go back to no other door, and I will assuredly not taste food nor take rest until thou admit me as a friend into thy intimacy.

COUPLET.

From the skirt of one so fair as thou I'll ne'er consent to part,
For with many a flood of tears thou hast been purchased by this heart.

The Mouse responded, 'I am willing to purchase with my life thy affection and regard, and all this denial is simply that I may be excusable in the sight of reason, shouldest thou intend perfidy; and that thou mayest not say, that thou hast obtained a dull and facile[1] friendship; else from the beginning of our discourse I have found my heart pre-disposed to intimacy with thee, and my mind intensely inclined to communion with thee.

VERSE.

Since friendship's love-light in this heart has beamed,
Know that that heart too is with friendship fraught.
For lover ne'er, unsought, for union schemed,
But by his loved one's seeking love was taught.'

He then came forth and stood before his hole. The Crow said, 'What prevents thee from advancing still further, and in my presence seeking to become intimate with me? but thou still feelest a trembling in thy soul.' The Mouse replied, 'Whenever one grudges not his own life for his friend, and devotes his own dear self for his comrade, he may be called a true friend and a brother to one's mind. And if one displays the same cordiality in worldly matters and does not neglect to aid his friend with the wealth he possesses, he is a mediocre friend inclining to the mean [between warmth and indifference]. And they have said, 'He who is pledged[2] to his friend on account of his temporary requirements as to money and station, is like a fowler who scatters grain to benefit himself not to feed the birds;' and since this friendship is mixed up with interested motives, it is probable it will terminate in enmity.

COUPLET.

When selfish motives lead to friendship's tie,
That friend will soon become an enemy.

But he who in the path of amity withholds not his life and is ready to sacrifice his own existence, is an incomparable friend; and the rank of a friend who bestows his life is far higher than that of him who expends only his wealth.

---

[1] Lit. : 'Slow-reined and soft in the withers,' <i>i.e.</i>, soft-paced.
[2] I have ventured so to translate <i>dar miyán</i>, but the passage is altogether very difficult and obscure.

Life-generous[1] *is most generous of all.*

COUPLET.

Those, who are generous with coin, are rife.
'Tis hard to find the liberal of life.

And let it not be concealed that in accepting thy overtures of friendship and in opening the way to our meeting, I risk my life, and notwithstanding that in the path of amity this point has been reached, that,

HEMISTICH.

Though life be risked I would e'en life resign.

And had I entertained suspicion, I should never have shown this eagerness nor have come forth from the corner of my humble dwelling, but I confide in thy friendship and the sincerity of thy desire to be my companion has passed the limits of doubt and distrust; and on my side, also, regard and attachment has been produced to a two-fold and multifold extent. Thou hast, however, friends who differ from thee in being hostile to me, and do not accord with thee in thy kindly feeling towards me. I fear lest one of these should see me and attack me.' The Crow answered, 'I have a compact with my friends that they shall be the friends of my friend and the foes of my foe.' The Mouse rejoined, 'Undoubtedly, whoever contracts alliance with the friend of one's enemy, or unites himself with the enemy of one's friend, is most fitly enumerated among one's foes.

COUPLET.

From these two ranks the heart aside should wend,
Who love our foes, and those who hate our friend.

And hence it is that the wise have said, 'Friends are of three kinds : genuine friends, friends of our friend, and foes of our foe. And enemies too are of three sorts : avowed enemies, enemies of our friend, and friends of our enemy.'

COUPLET.

Of my own foe my fears are not so great,
As of foes' friends and those who my friends hate.'

The Crow replied, 'I understand the drift of thy discourse, and, praise be to God! the ground of friendship and rules of amity have this day been so disposed between me and thee, and have been so ratified, that I shall regard as my friend whoever is friendly to thee, and esteem as my ally all who endeavour to conciliate thee, and whoever unites himself with thee, it is right that I too should unite with him, though he should be altogether hostile to me; and whoever separates from thee it behoves me to part from him, though he were altogether akin to me.

---

[3] I have been obliged to coin the word 'life-generous,' *i.e.* 'one who grudges not his life for his friend.'

COUPLET.

He on whose check there is no mark of servitude to thee,
Were he my sire, yet still would seem my foe and enemy.

And my eager desire for sincere amity and my resolve to prove a faithful friend is such, that should I find any opposition to thee even in my eyes and tongue, which are the sentinels of the body and the interpreters of the heart, I would, with an instantaneous motion, hurl both from the shore of existence into the whirlpool of destruction.

COUPLET.

Should of thy limbs a single one be leaguing with thy foe,
Then think him doubled, draw two swords and strike a double blow.' [1]

The Mouse, emboldened by these words, advanced, and cordially accosted the Crow, and after embracing one another, they spread out the carpet of rejoicing.

HEMISTICH.

For pleasant converse now prepare, thy friend in thy embrace is fast.

After some days had passed in this manner, and the Mouse, to the extent of his power, had performed the rites of entertainment and the duties of hospitality, he said, ' O brother ! if thou wouldst prepare to reside here and transport thy wife and children to this place it would be an extreme favour, and the obligation which I feel in my soul for the blessing of meeting with thee would be doubled, for this region in which my dwelling is, is a cheerful spot and an exhilarating abode.' The Crow replied, ' There is no question as to the excellence of this place, the extent of its plain, and the refreshing air. It is, however, near the highway, and close to the public road. There is ever reason to expect some calamity from the coming and going of passengers, and to anticipate something odious from the attacks of travelers. Now, in such a place there is a meadow, from its exceeding brightness, full of light as the garden of Paradise ; and from the clearness of its atmosphere, a place of delight and goodness, like the orchard of Iram.

VERSE.

Fresh grass upsprang the streamlet's bank beside,
The morning breeze brought odors from each bower.
And hyacinths the captive violets tied,
And lassoed with their locks each humbler flower.

There a Tortoise, who is one of my friends, has his home, and in that neighborhood food is procurable for me in abundance, and little mischief is to be apprehended. If thou art inclined, I will go there with thee, and pass the rest of my life in ease and enjoyment.

COUPLET.

Till round me buried they the shroud shall fold,
Think not that of thy skirt I'll loose my hold.

---

[1] That is, ' Kill your foe, and cut off the limb that sides with him.'

I know no wish equal to the honor of having thee for a neighbor, nor any hope brighter than the happiness of being with thee. Wherever thou advancest, like the sun I follow thee shadow-like, and through whatever land thou passest, shedding thy favors,[1] I hang at thy feet like a skirt, and so long as the collar of life does not fall into the grasp [of death] the destroyer of delights, I will not draw back my hand from the hem of thy society.

COUPLET.

> The border of unchanging fortune and the collar too of hope,
> 'Twere shame indeed if I should seize them, and again should let them drop.

And this region where I am now abiding is not my original fatherland, but I was led hither without my willing it; and my story, although long, comprises many extraordinary things, and whenever our resting-place is fixed, if thy illustrious mind desires it,

HEMISTICH.

> I will of much some little part recount.'

The conversation here ended, and the Crow took hold of the tail of the Mouse and turned in the desired direction. By chance a Tortoise was wandering round the margin of the fountain which was to be their permanent residence. When he beheld from a distance the blackness of the Crow, fear overcame him, and he plunged down in the water. The Crow softly deposited the Mouse from the air upon the ground, and called out to the Tortoise, who, when he heard the familiar voice, came up from the water, and beholding the face of his valued friend, raised to heaven the exclamations of his joy.

STANZA.

> My friend long-lost has come in peace again,
> And wayward fortune has its promise crowned.
> How long sit anguished by the thorn of pain?
> To hail this smiling rose, let joy abound.'

They then warmly accosted one another, and the Tortoise inquired, Where hast thou been this long time? and how camest thou to pass this way now?'[2] The Crow then detailed at length his own history from the time when the pigeons fell into the net to the period of their release, and his desire to obtain the friendship of the Mouse, and his ratifying the bonds of amity with him, down to his arrival at his familiar abode.' The Tortoise having learned the particulars of the case, showed the utmost pleasure at seeing the Mouse, and said,

---

[1] Lit., 'shaking thy sleeve.'

[2] *Hál bar chih minwál guzashtah* might, perhaps, also mean 'in what manner has thy time passed?'

COUPLET.

To this glad-omened place thou hast arrived auspiciously,
Well hast thou come, and on thee peace and benediction be!

My happy fate drew thee to these precincts, and the strength of my fortune raised the star of thy beauty above the horizon of this neighborhood.' The Mouse said, 'How can I sufficiently acknowledge these kindnesses which thou shewest to me? and with what tongue can I repeat thanks for the gracious manner in which thou condescendest to encourage me. It is from the burning heat of the sun of accidents, that I have sought refuge in the shade of thy clemency, estimating the acquisition of the happiness of communion with thee as the goal of my wishes and desires.

COUPLET.

It was favor from above made me ask my way of thee,
And by the eternal guidance I was led thy face to see.'

After they had rested from the toils of the way and had reposed themselves in that abode, which was a place of perfect safety :—secure from the assaults of the army of mischief, and unsullied by the dust of perturbation of rivals; the Crow, turning his face towards Zírak, requested that, if he thought good, he would narrate to the Tortoise the tales and adventures which he had promised the Crow to recount, in order to strengthen the friendship between them, and that they might derive all imaginable gratification from the recital.

COUPLET.

Open thy lips, thy pleasant story tell,
And our heart's mouth with sugar fill as well.'

The Mouse, commencing his story, said to the Tortoise,[1] 'O brother! my birth-place and native country was in a city of the country of Hind, which they call Nádút; and in that city I had taken up my abode in the cell of a solitary recluse, and in the corner of his hermitage had made a cell for myself, and I had several mice as attendants, and every day the numbers of my dependants increased. Now, a devoted disciple brought every morning for the holy man a tray of viands, a small portion of which the recluse used to take for his breakfast, and store up the rest for the evening ; while I used to be on the watch for his going out of the house, in order that I might immediately leap on the table, and after eating such dainty bits as I liked, scatter the rest among the other mice. The holy man employed many stratagems to get rid of me, but in vain; and devised various schemes to kill me, but they were all to no purpose; until one day a friend came as guest to the abode of the recluse. After they had finished the usual salutations and

---

[1] This is the fifth story of the 1st. Book of the Hitopadesha, where the town is called Champaka, and the recluse Chúrá-karna. The relator is there said to be *Múshika-rájá*, 'king of mice or rats,' for the word *múshika* too may mean either a mouse or a rat.

T

the requisite repast, and had spread out the beneficial table of discourse, the recluse inquired of his guest the news at home, and his destination, and the cause of his journey, and motive for his change of place.   Now, the stranger was a man of experience, who had tasted the sweets and bitters of fortune,

COUPLET.

One who for years had ranged o'er land and sea,
And proved the change of varied destiny.

He replied to the recluse in a pleasing manner, and recounted with captivating eloquence what strange cities and marvelous countries he had beheld, and, during his discourse, the recluse kept every moment clapping his hands, in order that the mice might be scared by the sound.   The guest was annoyed at this circumstance, which bore the appearance of an indignity, and enraged at an action which was so removed from due respect, and said, 'O recluse! to clap the hands when one is speaking appears like turning the speaker into ridicule, and I do not think that the character of a jester or the part of a mocker accords with thy position, nor that it is consistent with thy profession to deviate from the highway of good manners towards sarcasm and jokes.

STANZA.

Incline not thou to mockery and jeers,
For ill do these the pious man befit.
Who always as a vain buffoon appears,
Will reap dishonor for his scurril wit.'

The holy man replied, 'Heaven forbid that the thorn of jesting should ever be fastened in the skirt of my condition, and that the dust of raillery should be mingled with the atmosphere of the purity of my heart! This action which thou noticest, is to drive away a host of mice, who have overrun the realm of my board and table, and extending the hand of plunder and spoliation to all that I store up, leave not even a crust on my table safe from their assaults, nor permit me to preserve from their injuries any food in my house.

COUPLET.

Like me a hundred could not drive away,
Their bands descending to bear off the prey.'

The guest asked, 'Are they all bold and blindly audacious, or do some show more temerity than others?'   The recluse answered, 'One of them is so hardy that in my presence he will carry off a thing from the board, and before my very eyes will display his audacity in plundering my viands.' The guest replied, 'There must be some reason for his boldness, and his story has a similar complexion to that of the man who insisted to the wife of the host, that there must surely be some cause why she should barter husked sesamum on equal terms for unhusked.' The recluse said, 'If thou seest fit, tell me, how was that?'

STORY IV.

The guest said, 'In this road that I came, I arrived at night at a certain village and alighted at the house of an acquaintance, and after supper was over and we had done talking, they spread a garment for me to sleep on, and I put on it a pillow, but I did not go to sleep. My host went to his wife, and there being no other screen between me and them than a mat, I overheard their conversation, and what they said on both sides from first to last reached my ears. The man said, 'O wife! I wish to invite a party of the heads of the village to-morrow, and seat them in the presence of this my respected guest, who is a present to us from the invisible world, and prepare an entertainment for them suitable to my position.' The wife rejoined, 'I am astonished, that when thou hast not sufficient in the house for the wants of thy family, and hast not the means of procuring a diram[1] to purchase greens and salt, thou shouldst still, with such powerful resources and ample means, entertain the notion of receiving guests! Well, at least, to-day that thou hast the power to lay up, make a store for the morrow, and leave something behind thee for thy wife and children, that after thy decease, they may not be dependant on any one.' The husband replied,

COUPLET.

Blind is the man, who nought enjoying, yet hoards up his useless pelf,
But blest is he, who much bestowing, still can expend his gold on self.

If the power of doing a kindness and the ability to benefit others be attainable, we must not shrink from it, since, in fact, that will be a store for the next world; and whoever lays up a store for himself in this world will, in the next, be punished with the loss of his soul, for to amass and hoard up wealth is unblest, and its consequences disastrous, as was the case with that Wolf.' The wife asked, 'How was that?'

STORY V.[2]

The man said, 'They have related that a skilful hunter (such that through fear of his net the deer was not stepping forth into the plain, and the mountain-goat, through dread of his artifices and stratagems, would not leave its lair,

COUPLET.

Sharp-sighted, full of quickness and address,
Acute, not mild of heart, but merciless),

---

[1] A silver coin, in value about two pence.
[2] This is the 7th. story of the 1st. Book of the Hitopadesha.

had set a snare, and a deer had been caught in the net.   On his issuing from his place of concealment and coming towards the net, the stag, in fear for its life, made an effort, tore up the net, and started off in the plain.   The hunter was ashamed, and fixing an arrow to his bow, shot at the deer, which fell, and the hunter, coming up, took it on its back and set off home. On the way a wild boar met and charged the hunter, who discharged an arrow at him.   It so happened that the deadly arrow transfixed the hog as he came on, and, infuriated by the pain of the wound, he ripped up the breast of the hunter with his lacerating tusk, and both fell down dead on the spot.   In the midst of this a hungry wolf came there, and saw the man and the hog and the deer slain.   Pleased at the sight, he felt himself supplied with an abundance of delicacies and ample means of support, and said to himself,

COUPLET.

'Time enow must pass ere we,   Such good cheer again can see.

This is the time for reflection and consideration, and the season for amassing and laying up a store, for to be remiss here would be opposed to all prudence and forethought, while if I am profuse, I should be censurable for folly and carelessness.   I consider my advisable course and that most beneficial to be this, that I should consume for to-day's meal, the bow-string, and not string the bow of wasteful expenditure and impropriety, and placing this fresh meat in a retired spot, each day impel the arrow of desire to the target of my wish, and conveying these treasures to a corner, make a magazine for hardness of times and times of hardship.   For the wise have said,

VERSE.

Consume not all, or thou mayest, long, for more
Stand waiting ; want ill suits the hoary head.
Part use, and, of thy goods, part place in store,
Nor at one swoop let all be lavished.'

The Wolf from excessive greediness turned towards the bow-string and began to gnaw it, and at a single motion of his teeth it broke asunder.   The moment the string snapped, the horns of the bow struck him on the heart, and he instantaneously gave up the ghost.

HEMISTICH.

Untasted, all were left, and he, too, died.

And the moral of this story is, that greediness in amassing wealth and the being swayed by distant hopes to lay up stores, has disastrous results and fatal consequences.

COUPLET.

Eat what thou hast to day, nor for the coming future vainly care,
For when the morrow comes, be sure the morrow's bread will, too, be there.

Ah! what a hapless band are they who, from their earliest years painfully accumulate worldly gear and resign it at the close of life with infinite anguish.

STANZA.

How long wilt thou amass? good sir, reflect!
Thou wilt be soon of all by death bereft.
Though Ḳárún's riches e'en thou couldst collect,
Thy greedy pangs would still the same be left:
Light not then flames from which none can themselves protect.'

When the wife of the host heard these words, which bore the stamp of wisdom, and a happy inspiration had whispered in her listening ear the glad tidings that, '*Sustenance is with God,*' she adopted a gentle tone, and said, 'O dear one! I have stored up in the house a little rice sesamum for the children; and now that it has been disclosed to me that storing up is unlucky, I will, to-morrow morning, prepare a meal sufficient for ten persons. Do thou invite whom thou wilt, and make whomsoever thou desirest, thy guests.'

COUPLET.

Next morning, when the glittering orb of day
Washed from its eyes the dust of sleep away.

The wife husked the sesamum and placed it in the sun, and enjoined her husband to keep a good watch till the grain was dry, lest the birds should carry away some of it; and she herself turned to some other business. Sleep overcame the husband; and a dog came up and touched the grain with his mouth. The wife observing this, was too disgusted to think of preparing a dish from it, and therefore taking it up, set off for the bázár. I, too, having some necessary business in the bázár, was going along behind her. I saw her go to the shop of one that sold grain, and she wanted to barter her sesamum for unhusked grain of the same description, measure for measure.[1] The man made a great outcry, saying, 'O woman! surely there is some trick here, that thou shouldest wish to barter on equal terms sesamum which has been cleaned from the husk for that which is still in the husk.'

And I have told this story because that I, too, am of opinion that the said bold mouse has so much strength and hardihood, and courage, from the place of its abode; and the probability is that it has a treasure of coin in its house, sustained by which it exhibits all this prowess; and if the plant of its condition should meet with the autumn of poverty, this freshness and vigor would not be evinced in the coppice of its actions. For they have said, 'He who is moneyless is like a bird that is wingless and featherless.'

---

[1] Lit. '*sá'a* for *sá'a*.' The *sá'a* is a dry measure of the largest description, containing 4 mudds, and each mudd = 1½ ritl.

QUATRAIN.

Sit not supine, devoid of gold—the quest of gold is glorious pleasure :
Gold has a worth, which high and low and all admit, but none can measure.
'Better,' they say, 'to have free choice than to possess a golden treasure;
But hearken not, for gold bestows an unconstraint, which none can measure.[1]

And I feel convinced that the strength of this mouse springs from gold.
Bring a mattock that I may demolish his hole, and see how the matter ends.'
The recluse immediately brought a mattock, and I at that moment was in
another hole and heard what they were doing. Now in my abode there
were a thousand gold dínárs, on which I used to roll, and my mind rose
from one ecstacy to another at the sight of them. In short, the cheerfulness
of my heart and my peace of mind were dependant on that gold. Whenever I
called it to remembrance, I experienced a gush of pleasure in my bosom, and
exultation and delight made themselves felt in my heart. The stranger dug
up the ground until he reached the gold, and what saw he then ?

VERSE.

Coins gaily smiling with their sunny faces fair,
    Than Jamshíd's lustrous cup they seemed more bright :
So handsome they, and florid, with an impress rare ;
    Dear—not to be rejected, nor too light.
He breathed on them and bound his breath of silver there,
    Anon his fingers poised their loveliness :
They the true key to ope time's difficulties were,
    And cheer at once the bosom of distress.

'This,' said he to the recluse, 'is the source of the courage of that Mouse
and that which adorns his vigor; for wealth polishes the intellect and
supports the strength, and hereafter he will not venture on thy table nor
attack thy loaf and viands.' I overheard these words and perceived the
tokens of debility and feebleness, and the marks of amazement and pusilla-
nimity in myself, and felt compelled to desert that hole. The instant, too,
that this unforeseen calamity overtook me, and this frightful accident
descended on my dwelling, I beheld that my dignity waned in the minds of
the mice, and that a prodigious change took place in their wonted respect and
reverence. The flame of my friends' sympathies was quenched, and the pure
fountain of their allegiance and submission was discolored with the dust of
denial and disobedience.

---

[1] The literal translation of these very difficult lines is as follows :—
        'Without gold sit not, for the business of gold has gold :
        Before all the credit of gold has gold.
        They say that choice is better than gold ;
        Hearken not thou, for the choice of gold has gold.'
If any one dislikes my free translation he is welcome to the above.

QUATRAIN.

Fidelity and love desert each heart,
The heliotrope is from my garden reft.
Gold did a hundred means of life impart,
The gold is gone, nor means, nor life, is left.

The mice who subsisted on my leavings, and devoured the scraps from the table of my bounty, and gleaned the harvest of my gifts, still expected my favors, and longed for my entertainments as before. When they failed to realize from me their wishes, they desisted from obeying and following me, and disavowing all feelings of loyalty and submission, loosed their tongues to censure and upbraid me; and deserting my society went over to my enemies and those who rebelled against my authority.

VERSE.

From heaven when blindness darkly on me fell,
I found full many a knave then meet my sight.
'Twas they who used my retinue to swell,
To dog my steps and play the parasite.

And it is a well-known proverb, ' *When the finances decrease, dignity is lowered,*'—when our wealth ends, we lose our friends. And the man who is empty-handed and poor will be sure to fail, seek what he will, and the wish which springs up from his heart's core will not be attained; like rain-water which collects in summer and cannot reach the sea nor unite with the streams, but, destitute of support, is frittered away in the valleys, and arrives nowhere. And the wise have said, ' He who has no brother is poor wherever he happen to be; and he who has no child, his memory is obliterated from the page of time: and whoever is indolent and without supplies will receive no sympathies from his friends—or rather the empty-handed have no friends at all: for whenever a man has himself come to want, the parties who, like the Pleiades, formed the group of his society, will, like the daughters of the Bier[1] become scattered, inasmuch as the friendship of the base and sordid is controlled by sensual motives and worldly advantages.

VERSE.

Long as the cheer which they consume, will last,
Like wasps they hover round with busy hum.
But once thy mansion has to ruin past,
Empty as rebec-case thy purse become,
Aside thy friendship and thy love they cast.
In truth that friendship was an idle dream.
Not friends in them but market curs thou hast,
Who than their friend a bone more precious deem.

---

[1] The stars in the constellation of the Bear are so called. What we have chosen to compare to a bear, the Orientals compare with a coffin. From the scattered appearance of these stars they are contrasted with the Pleiades, which appear to form a compact cluster.

It is related that they asked a great personage, how many friends he had ?
He replied, ' I know not, for I have a fortunate destiny, and an abundance of
wealth and property, and every one professes to be my friend, and makes a
boast of his regard and attachment. If, which God forbid ! the dust of
adversity should blind the eye of fortune, I should presently know who is
my friend, and who my enemy.'   An ally may be known in the time of
disaster, and a friend may be distinguished from a foe in a period of trouble.

COUPLET.

When fickle fortune does a man forsake,
Wife, friends, and children too, their leave will take.'

And it is also recorded in the elegant pages of the wise, that they asked an
eminent personage, what was the meaning of the avidity which people
showed for the friendship of one possessed of wealth.   He replied, ' Riches
are men's idol ; whoever has them, men respect him, and as soon as he loses
them, they cease to congregate about him.'

QUATRAIN.

When the rose her skirt of gold showed in the parterre,
With a thousand songs the nightingale her praises did proclaim.
But, alas ! her leaves were soon scattered to the air,
And then no more did any hear from the nightingale her name.

At this crisis one of the mice who used to glory in my service, and to esteem
one moment of my company as a fund of eternal happiness, and who was
perpetually setting forth his fidelity and sincerity in the path of friendship,
in the following strain,

COUPLET.

So constant is my love, that if a sword my head should smite,
Unmoved, I'd like a taper stand, which burns [1] with steady light,

passed me by as if I were a stranger, and took not the slightest notice of me.
I called him to me and said,

COUPLET.

' Passing, thou payest no regard to me,
Ne'er was the unpropped cypress half so free.[2]

What, I pray, has come to thee, and whither is all that affection and tender
feeling, of which thou didst make such a display, gone ? '   The mouse
frowned, and said with the utmost possible rudeness, ' What a simpleton
thou art ! men don't serve one for nothing, nor do they wait on any one
without a motive.   At the time when thou hadst money and wast generous,
we were all thy servants.   Now thou hast become indigent, and the wise
say that just as an indigent man has no share in the pleasures of this world,

---

[1] That is, ' after it is cut or snuffed.' Such is, I suppose, the point of resemblance in
this very forced and meaningless comparison.

[2] The cypress is always called the free, as being free from curvature, or too straight to
require a prop.

so it is not improbable that he may be excluded from the rewards of the next [according as it is said], '*Poverty falls very little short of becoming*[1] *infidelity.*' The reason is,that a man rendered desperate on account of food for himself and the maintenance of his family, may seek to support himself by unlawful means, and the consequence may be his disgrace and punishment in the next world; and as in this life he succumbs to the distress of penury, so hereafter he may be shut up and incarcerated in the prison of eternal woe.

HEMISTICH.

Like a false darvesh, worldless, faithless he!

'*The loss of this world and of the next, that is a loss indeed.*'[2] Wherefore if we forbear to associate with, and shun the converse of, one who has lost his worldly wealth, and whose reward in the next world is doubtful, we may be held excusable.' I said, 'Cease talking thus, for the faḳír is a king, since they have placed on the head of his excellence, the crown, '*Poverty is my glory,*'[3] and have spread over the shoulders of his nobility, the scarf, '*The faḳír has no wants.*'

DISTICHS.

Above thy ken the darvesh-calling lies,
Look not on darveshes with careless eyes.
Their calling is life's loftiest story; they
From all mankind have borne the palm away.

COUPLET.

All else is accident. Poverty is
Essence. Disease all else: health nought save this.[4]

Wherefore, why dost thou decry poverty? and with what reason dost thou shew aversion to the darvesh?' The mouse replied, 'Alack! what relation has this penury and distress of thine with the poverty extolled by the prophets and lauded by the saints. That poverty implies that the traveler on the road of truth refuses to accept any particle of the wealth of this world or of a future state.[5] He abnegates all to secure all, '*None arrives at the total*

---

[1] Literally, 'that it should become.' The same proverb is quoted in the 'Gulistán,' p. 250 of the translation, ch. vii., st. xix., where I have rendered it somewhat more freely.
[2] Literally, 'a palpable loss.'
[3] This saying of the Prophet is likewise quoted in the passage of the 'Gulistán' cited above: p. 249 of my Translation.
[4] *Jauhar* is the logical term for 'essence,' '*arż*, for 'accident.' Man's original state is that of the naked savage. civilization furnishes him with raiment, etc., but these are mere 'accidents,' of which he is despoiled by death.
[5] I should be glad to strike out the words *sarmáyah-i ákhirat*, did the MSS. allow it. They completely mar the sense. Pious men do not decline the means of happiness in the next world; on the contrary, they refuse to be rich, because riches impede their prospect of happiness in the next world. This is so obvious, that it is a wonder how these words could have been foisted in. Yet some will perhaps think that an exaggerated spirituality is here intended, in which even the rewards of heaven are slighted, and the pilgrim so entirely abnegates self, that he does not even think of his condition in the world to come!

save he who has severed himself from the total.' That poverty is displayed in the darvesh; this of thine in the beggar. A beggar is one thing and a darvesh another. The darvesh is he who voluntarily forsakes the world, and the beggar he whom the world forsakes.

DISTICHS.

A land-fish is the begging darvesh. He,
In shape of fish, yet shudders at the sea.
The true fakír is not on morsels fed,
Give not thy incense-offering to the dead.[1]

The saying, '*Poverty is a treasure of the treasures of God,*' is one of the mysteries of the true Unitarian faith, and the very essence of spirituality and of the glorification of God, and the water of the fountain of the abnegation of self, which washes off the dust of worldly entanglements from the face of the pure soul; and it is a robe of honor from the treasury of solitary devotion with which the hand of omnipotence arrays the purified spirit. The true poverty is the divine alchymy,[2] and its mystery is not to be comprehended in the circle of description either by the lips or the pen.

QUATRAIN.

Forsake his life, this must the darvesh do
As his first step, and then surrender all.
With life forsaken, all things yielded too;
Thus freed, he must again himself enthral.

But darveshes, who are so in mere outward appearance and want, are the roots of all evil, and the means of incurring the enmity of mankind, and of removing all modesty and shame. They subvert the foundation of courtesy and are the sum of evil and calamity, and cut off all strength and honor, and originate meanness and disgrace. And whoever is a prisoner in the circle of want must necessarily tear off the veil of modesty; and when the inscription, '*Modesty is a part of faith,*' is erased from the page of his condition, life becomes disgusting to him, and he is overtaken by trouble and distress, and the guest of comfort removes his effects from the area of his breast, and the army of grief overruns the territory of his nature. The taper of his intellect continues without light, and his understanding and ingenuity and memory and sagacity begin to decline. The advantages of right counsel yield in his case injurious results. In spite of his uprightness he becomes exposed to the calumnious imputation of treason. The good opinion which

---

[1] The *darvesh-i nán* is he who is a darvesh for the sake of the *nán*, 'the loaf,'—as we say. 'for the loaves and fishes.' The meaning of the last two lines is: 'There is a poverty which feeds on scraps and aims at nothing else. The true poverty disregards everything but pious contemplation. Yet the worldly man can as little understand these spiritual things as a corpse can inhale incense.'

[2] Lit., 'The philosopher's stone of ' Be' and it was.' This latter phrase is applied to the Deity, as descriptive of His Omnipotent power.

his friends have of him is reversed, and if another commits a crime the guilt is transferred to him. Whatever he does or says is harmful to him, and every quality for which they laud and panegyrize a rich man is a cause of reproach and rebuke to a poor man. Thus, for example, if a poor man shew boldness, they ascribe it to rashness; and if he choose to be liberal, they call it extravagance; and if he try to be mild, they account it weakness and want of spirit; and if he adopt a grave demeanour, they call him sluggish and torpid; while, if he display eloquence and oratorical powers, they designate him as loquacious; or if he betake himself to the security of silence, they speak of him as a painting in a bagnio; and if he make choice of the corner of retirement, they find that it is owing to madness; but should he meet them with hilarity and sociability, they think it akin to low humor and buffoonery. If he be careful in his food and dress, they call him self-indulgent; and if he content himself with a rag and a scrap, they regard him as a miserable, poverty-stricken wretch. If he reside in one place, he is raw and ignorant of the world; and if he desire to travel, he is then a vagabond and ill-starred. If he pass his life in celibacy, he is one who neglects the injunctions of the law; and if he marry, they term him sensual and a slave to his appetites. In short, an indigent man is repudiated and utterly vile in the opinion of people of the world; and if, together with this condition of penury, they observe him trying for anything, then, merciful Heaven! hatred of him takes fast hold of their minds, and without aiding any of his necessities, they are all annoyed with him. And every distress which befalls men has its origin in desire [according to the saying], ' *Whoever desires becomes vile.*'

HEMISTICH.

From want springs baseness, honor from content.'

When my friend had recited this discourse, I said, 'Thou speakest the truth, and I had heard that if any one be overtaken by sickness to such a degree that all hope of convalescence is cut off; or be involved in calamitous separation of such a nature that it is a vain idea to anticipate re-union, or fall into exile which admits not of return nor affords the means of residence, even these are more easy to bear than penury and indigence; and I now see with my own eyes that this saying proceeded from the fountain of wisdom, and that the speaker of it delivered his sentiments from experience.

QUATRAIN.

The world no greater ill than want can show;
The needy wins no solace for his grief:
The victim of distressful want and woe
Must die; for poverty finds no relief.

And of the evils of want, this is sufficient,—the being compelled to ask men for anything, and to beg for subsistence from such a one as oneself; and death is in every way preferable to poverty and mendicity, since to put one's hand into the mouth of a venomous serpent, and to take deadly poison for one's food, and to snatch away his mouthful from a hungry lion, and to lodge with a furious tiger, is less grievous than to carry one's distresses to the stingy, and to endure the disgrace of begging; for they have said, 'The pleasure of a gift does not compensate for the pain of asking, and the sweets of office do not pay for the distress of removal;' and an eminent personage has said,

VERSE.

Four things at first to great advantage tend,
Yet are not worth four others in the end.
Life is not worth the woe of dying; nor
Will office make thee compensation for
The shame of thy displacement; sin weighs not
Remorse; nor can alms gild the beggar's lot.'

I then turned away from that mouse and hastened again to the mouth of my hole. There I beheld the recluse and his guest dividing the gold, and the former having put his share into a purse, placed it under his pillow. An unlucky covetousness began to tempt me, while I reflected that, 'Could I regain a portion of that gold, my stout-heartedness and cheerfulness would return a second time, and my friends and brethren would seek my service with eagerness, and my court would be restored and my assembly adorned.' Busied with these thoughts I waited only till they lay down for the night. I then stealthily approached the pillow of the recluse. Now his guest was a man of experience, and keeping awake employed his eyes in watching at that crisis, and was in expectation of what I was going to do. He gave me such a blow on my foot with his stick, that I turned back stricken down with the pain of it, and, trailing my leg, crept into my hole. I waited just long enough to let the pain subside a little and I came out a second time with the same covetous intent. This time the guest smote me such a blow on the crown of my head that I was stupified and was compelled to employ all my invention to throw myself into my hole, where I lay senseless, and the pain of that wound gave me a disgust to worldly wealth, and I forgot my poverty and hunger.

COUPLET.

Why should one wail the want of wealth?
Since there is treasure infinite in health.

And I now learned of a certainty that covetousness is the vanguard of all calamities and the vidette of all distresses. Until the bird of greediness carries off the grain, its neck is not encompassed by the collar of the net, and until man binds up the waist of covetousness, the robe of his honor is not exchanged for the sack-cloth of disgrace. Whoever undertakes a journey by sea or submits to any unnecessary risk, is guided by covetousness, and from the darkness of greed, the dust of abasement settles on the page of the countenance of the pious, and the levity of covetous desires reduces the weight of the eminent in the scale of respect.

STANZA.

O brother! be not covetous, for this
The cause of man's disgrace and ruin is.
List to this short advice, if thou would'st fain
From life its vintage of delights obtain.
' O'er thine own feet contentment's border fold,
And thy desire from others' wealth withhold.'

Strangely do they act who seek for happiness in abundance of wealth and know not that a little of it affords comfort; and who look for enjoyment in amassing riches, and do not perceive that by giving it all up they might arrive at a higher pre-eminence.

COUPLET.

Who tear their hearts from worldly things the sole true honor find,
And they have peace who from its gauds and show withdraw their mind.

Wherefore, from this event, my state came to this, that I tore up by the roots the plant of desire from the soil of my heart, and culled the fruits of contentment from the orchard of acquiescence, and cheerfully submitted to the Divine Will, and bowed down my head to the writing of destiny, and said to myself, ' The world, by the contents of these calamities and distresses, supplies a sample of its qualities and defects.   There is no mansion in which the mark of its deceit and perfidy is not found, nor is there a palace on the inscription of which the sign of its assault is not impressed.   Whom did it ever elevate that it did not afterwards cast down? and where did it plant a sapling which it did not afterwards tear up? to whom did it shew favor and not in the end drink his blood? or to whom did it open the door of fortune and not subsequently bring up a thousand troubles?

STANZA.

This world, like to a spouse unchaste and base,
Did ne'er yield joy to those who with her wed;
None on her throne's ascent their footsteps place,
But feel her trenchant sabre on their head.

Such faithlessness deserves not that we toil for it, or grieve for its presence or absence, or for its loss or gain.

COUPLET.

Upon this world the value of our tears we should not set,
Nor for its losses or its gains should suffer vain regret.'

After these reflections I migrated from the house of the recluse to the waste, and there was a pigeon which had a friendship for me, and through its love and attachment arose my companionship with the Crow, and the latter related to me the account of thy courtesy and kindness, and so the zephyr of thy good qualities reached me from the flower-garden of his conversation; and the mention of thy virtues and high endowments led me to seek thee with earnestness and sincerity; and I formed the wish of obtaining, by the happiness of a meeting, the advantage of thy friendship. And I shrink from the horror of loneliness, for solitude is a hard thing, and the terror of friendlessness a difficult matter, and there is no pleasure in the world like the companionship of friends, nor can any grief compare with separation from one's allies and removal from those who sympathise with us. And, thanks be to God Most High! the rose of happiness has begun to bloom from the heart-rending thorn of adversity, and the dark-visaged night of distress has been exchanged for the serene world-adorning morning of repose.

VERSE.

> The day of parting and the night of absence now is past;
> 'T is o'er, my evil star has set, for well the lot I cast;
> The morn of hope which did behind the future's curtain sit;
> Bid it come forth, for gloomy night at length its place must quit.

This is my history which I have fully recounted, and now I have come to be thy neighbour, and hope for thy friendship and alliance.

COUPLET.

> It would befit thee with the file of thy kind gentleness,
> To free the mirror of my mind from the rust-stains of distress.'

When the Tortoise had heard this narrative, he spread the carpet of courtesy, and laying the foundation-stone of affability, said,

COUPLET.

> 'The house that opes its gate to guests like thee,
> The nest of Heaven's phœnix there will be.

What happiness can be weighed against the honor of having thee for a neighbor? and what gladness can compare with the joy of thy[1] society? and even as thou art hoping for my aid and amity, so I too look to and plume myself upon thy love and companionship; and as long as the lamp of life burns on I will, moth-like, sport round the taper of thy beauty.

COUPLET.

> Mote-like, I sun myself in thy love's ray,
> No sword from thee could smite my arms away.

And in this true history which thou hast recounted, a variety of experiences and abundant lessons are contained, and by means of those experiments it is made clear that the man of sense should be satisfied with a very little of the rubbish of this world, and ought to be content with just enough to obviate the necessity of begging; for whoever longs for aught beyond

---

[1] The printed edition here repeats *mujáwarat* from the preceding sentence, by a mistake for *munádsalat.*

requisite lodging and food, steps beyond the limits of justice, and this injustice plunges him bewildered into the labyrinth of calamity and the wilderness of peril ; and he meets with what befell that greedy Cat.' The Mouse inquired, ' How was that ?'

STORY VI.

The Tortoise said, ' They have related that a person had a Cat, and assigned to it as its daily portion just so much flesh as might quench the flame of hunger ; but from the animal propensities which prevailed over the temper of that inconsiderate creature, it failed to be content with its lot.

COUPLET.

Friend ! let thy life in cheerful want be spent.
From greed spring troubles—honors from content.

One day the Cat passed near a dove-cot, and its appetite being excited by the fascinating voices of the pigeons and their harmonious treble and bass notes, it sprang into that citadel.   The keeper of that castle, however, and the warder of the place immediately seized it, and conveyed it from the rose-garden of existence to the furnace of annihilation.   Before it could perfume the head of appetite with the brains of the pigeons, he stripped off its skin, and having filled it with straw, hung it up over the door of the dove-cot.   It happened that the owner of the Cat passed that way, and on seeing the plight of his Cat, said, ' O greedy wanton ! hadst thou been contented with the portion of flesh which fell to thy lot, they would not have stripped off thy skin.'

VERSE.

O soul ! be with a little satisfied,
For sure destruction will from greed betide.
Ḳárún, voluptuons Ḳárún, pondered not,
That safety bideth with the lowly lot.
The lusts unchecked bring evil destinies,
Then do not foster them, if thou be wise.
Wild beast and deer, and bird that wings the air,
Caught in the net, by greed are prisoned there.
Tigers, that all the savage tribe oppress,
Like the poor mouse, are caged through greediness.

And the moral of this story is that thou shouldest hereafter be contented with as much food as will suffice to keep in the breath of life, and with a hole just enough to afford protection from the heat and cold, and not afflict thyself for wealth that is lost.

COUPLET.

My life ! though riches pass away, let not thy heart be sad ;
This carrion is not worth our tears : then for its loss be glad.

And know that every man's nobility is from his virtue, not from his wealth ;

and every one whose mind is adorned with accomplishments, though his stock of wealth be small, is always beloved and honored. So the lion, though he may be bound with chains, yet his awfulness is not diminished. But a wealthy ignorant man is always despised and destitute of weight, like a dog, which, though adorned with a collar and rings, still remains vile and contemptible as before.

VERSE.

He that in folly's prison fettered is,
E'en though a hundred jars of gold be his,
Is but a beggar; while the skill-rich man
Will gold or jewels never deign to scan.

Dismiss, moreover, from thy heart, grief for thy exile, and attach no importance to separation from thy native land and home; for let the wise man go where he will he will be befriended by his own good sense, while the fool will be friendless and a stranger in his own country and the place that gives him birth.

HEMISTICH.

The man of sense nowhere a stranger is.

And be not sad as to what thou sayest, that, 'I possessed a treasure and it has been dissipated,' for worldly wealth and possessions are liable to decay, and their increase or decline are beyond the circle of reliance; and the wise have said, 'Permanence and continuance cannot be expected from six things. The first is the shadow of a cloud, which, even as thou lookest on, passes away. The second is interested friendship, which is extinct in a short time, like the lightning's flash. The third is the love of women, which is quenched by a slight matter. The fourth is the comeliness of the beautiful, which changes in the end. The fifth is the praise of the false, which is devoid of continuous lustre. The sixth is worldly wealth, which in the end arrives at the place of exposure to annihilation, and does not carry out to the end the line of fidelity to its owner.

COUPLET.

By this vile world's adornments, its wealth or triumphs won,
Be not elate, for these will shew fidelity to none.

And it beseems not a man of sense to rejoice at the greatness of his wealth, nor to grieve for his want of riches, since, in the opinion of the magnanimous, the whole world, with its goods and gear, is not worth a straw.[1] Wherefore it is not right to waste the harvest of dear life in acquiring this; nor ought one to suffer a grain of disquietude at its loss or non-attendance, and those who, having become acquainted with that wise saying, '*Lest ye immoderately grieve for the good which escapeth you, or rejoice for that which happeneth unto*

---

[1] *Káh bargí* is not given in the Dictionary, but I presume it to mean the flag or leaf which projects from the stalk of corn and of some grasses.

you,' [1] give reins to the steed of high-mindedness in the plain of content, and who, staking the coin of life in order to acquire the things of solitary devotion and abandonment of earthly connections; are neither led by worldly riches to open to their heart's countenance the portals of rejoicing, nor evince regret and despondency at the loss of them.

STANZA.

Though from thy grasp all worldly things should flee,
Grieve not for them, since they are nothing worth:
And though a world in thy possession be,
Joy not, for worthless are the things of earth.
Since to that better world 't is given to thee
To pass; speed on, for this is nothing worth.

And, in truth, men ought to consider their wealth to be that which they send on before, and to regard that as their property which they store up for themselves in the final state; and righteous acts and words of probity are a possession which cannot be snatched away from any one, nor dissipated by the accidents of fortune, nor the revolutions of night and day. And the advantage of worldly goods is to make ready a provision for the world to come, and to prepare the means of threading the path of that world to which all must return; since, in accordance with the saying, ' *We took vengeance on them suddenly,*' [2] death comes unawares and there is no fixed time nor any appointed period [known to man] for restoring the deposit of life.

COUPLET.

That fair narcissus [3] from its slumber wake, for life is gliding on;
Not e'en the roses fade so quick; ere thou canst close thine eyes, 't is gone.

And although thou art not in need of my counsel, and canst well distinguish between what is for thy advantage and what is detrimental; nevertheless, I wished. to discharge the duty of a friend, and to aid thee to praiseworthy feelings and laudable dispositions; and to-day thou art my friend and brother, and all the assistance that it is possible to render thee, and all courtesy that can be imagined, will in every respect be realised; and even under the impossible supposition that thou shouldst evince unkindness, on my part nothing but the blessed influence of true attachment and the usages of cordial friendship will be displayed.

---

[1] Ḳur'án, ch. lvii. 23; Sale, p. 398, l. 43: 'No accident happeneth in the earth, nor in your persons, but the same was entered in the book of our decrees, before we created it: verily, this is easy with God: and this is written lest ye immoderately grieve for the good which escapeth you, or rejoice for that which happeneth unto you; for God loveth no proud or vain-glorious person, or those who are covetous, and command men covetousness.'

[2] Ḳur'án, Fl. vii. 93; Mar, vii. 96; Sale, p. 118, l. 8: Then we gave them in exchange good in lieu of evil, until they abounded and said, ' Adversity and prosperity formerly happened unto our fathers as unto us.' Therefore we took vengeance on them suddenly, and they perceived it not beforehand.'

[3] A beauty is compared to a slumbering, and sometimes to an intoxicated, narcissus.

COUPLET.

I never will thy side abandon, though thou shouldst abandon me,
And though thou break my heart, I'll never break my plighted truth to thee.'

When the Tortoise had finished these words and the Crow had heard his kindness with regard to the Mouse, his heart was refreshed, and his delight became unbounded, and he said, ' O brother ! thou hast made me glad, and doubled the amount of my joy and pleasure, and hast manifested somewhat of thy virtues. Now, the best of friends is he, in the shade of whose kindnesses and favor, and in the shelter of whose care and protection, a number of those attached to him at all times pass their life, while he keeps open for them the doors of his bounty, and considers it obligatory upon his soul to accept their requests and expedite their requirements; and whoever fails in any part of friendship to his ally, is not fit for a friend. Moreover, it has been related that an eminent personage had a friend. One night this friend came to the door of his house and knocked, and that personage discovered that it was his friend. Thereupon he fell into a lengthened meditation, saying, ' Ah me ! what can be the cause of his coming at this unseasonable time ?' After long reflection, he took up a purse full of dirams, belted on his scymitar, and bade a female slave light a lamp, and go before him. When he had opened the door and had greeted his friend by clasping his hand and embracing him, he said, ' O brother ! I have imagined three causes for thy coming at this unusual hour. First, that some accident has happened and that thou art in want of money. Secondly, that an enemy has risen up to assail thee, and that thou requirest an ally and helper to repel him. Thirdly, that thou art sad at being alone and requirest some one to minister to thee, and I have made ready for all three contingencies, and have come out to thee. If thou hast need of money, lo ! here is a purse of dirams ; and if thou seekest help, behold here am I with a trenchant scymitar ; and if thou lookest for a servant, here is a suitable handmaid.

HEMISTICH.

Whate'er thou willest, thy commands prevail.'

His friend excused himself [for coming so late], and by that fair procedure the bond of reliance on his attachment and love was strengthened.

STANZA.

Art thou sincere in friendship ? then beware
That thy friend find a kind ally in thee !
And of his wishes have a watchful care,
And grant them ere he long expectant be.

And when a benevolent person falls into the whirlpool of disaster, none can befriend him but those of a like disposition ; just as if an elephant should fall into a quagmire, other elephants alone can extricate him; and if in befriending the Mouse thou shouldest meet with hardships, thou must not grieve; and keeping thine eyes on thy reputation and the maintenance of thine honor, must disregard the inconvenience, for the wise man ever labors for distinction and to leave behind him a fair repute; and if, for example, he be compelled, in his pursuit of an honorable name, to risk his life, he will not shrink from it, because he will thus have purchased the imperishable with the perishable, and have sold a little for much.

COUPLET.

Does the world smile on thee?—secure a name,

For all the world can offer is fair fame.

And whoever excludes the necessitous from his good things is not to be reckoned among the really rich; and he whose life is passed in dishonor and disaster such as his foes would wish, his name is not inserted in the roll of the living.

COUPLET.

Sâdi! he whose fame lives can ne'er be dead,

He dies whose good name is dishonorèd.'

The Crow was discoursing thus, when a Deer appeared in the distance running fast. They suspected that somebody was pursuing him, whereupon the Tortoise leapt into the water, the Crow took his seat in a tree, and the Mouse ran down a hole. When the Deer reached the edge of the water, it stood like one stupified, and the Crow cast its eyes around to see if any one was on its traces. Though it looked to the left and right it saw no one. It called therefore to the Tortoise, who emerged from the water; and the Mouse joined them. The Tortoise, observing that the Deer was scared and kept looking in the water without drinking, said, 'If thou art thirsty, drink! and be not alarmed, for there is no cause for fear.' The Deer came forward, and the Tortoise uttered an exclamation of joyful welcome, saying,

COUPLET.

'Beloved comrade! from whence art thou come?

Feel not strange here, for here thou art at home.'

The Deer said, 'I have been used to dwell in this plain alone, and mingle not with those of my race; and the archers, ever stringing the bow of murderous intention, have driven me from this corner to that. To-day I observed an old man lying in wait for me, who watched me wherever I went. I conceived the idea that it was a hunter and that the snare of his craftiness would presently catch my feet; and, running away, I reached this spot.' The Tortoise said, 'Fear not! for hunters never come to the environs of this place, and if thou wishest to associate with us, we will introduce thee into the circle of our friendship; and the pedestal of the association of us three will be supported with a fourth pillar, viz., thyself: for the wise have said, 'The more numerous friends are, the less will they be exposed to the assaults of calamity.'

U 2

COUPLET.

Where'er I come, love and good faith increase,
Joy spreads with calm serenity and peace.

And it is certain that if there be a thousand friends, they must be regarded as
one; and if there be but one enemy he must be looked upon as many.

COUPLET.

In friendship well a thousand may agree,   But all too many is one enemy.'

The Mouse also took up the discourse, and the Crow uttered some
benevolent words. The Deer perceived that they were amiable friends and
pure-minded companions. He mingled with them and sought their society
with his heart and soul.

HEMISTICH.

With a fit friend how sweet is intercourse.

The Deer took up his abode in that meadow; and his friends admonished
him not to set his foot beyond the grazing-ground in their vicinity, nor to
elongate himself from the neighborhood of the fountain which was their
castle of security and peace. The Deer agreed to act in conformity with
their advice. They were passing their time together, and there was a
bambú thicket[1] where they used always to assemble, and sporting, recount
their adventures. One day the Crow, the Mouse, and the Tortoise,
assembled at the trysting-place, and waited some time for the Deer. It did
not come, and this circumstance making them sad, as is the wont of
attached friends, a depression of spirits overcame them. They requested the
Crow that he would take the trouble to fly up into the air and inform them
of their lost friend's condition.

COUPLET.

Pass, Zephyr! o'er my love's abode, this boon refuse me not;
And O! refuse not wretched me news of my loved one's lot.

The Crow in a short time brought them intelligence that he had seen the
Deer prisoned in the net of calamity. The Tortoise then said to the Mouse,
'In this unhappy conjuncture our only hope is in thee, and by thy help
alone can the banner of the Deer's safety be set up.

HEMISTICH.

Haste! for the time of action fleets away.'

The Crow then showed the way, and the Mouse, running off,[2] came to the
Deer and said, 'O kind brother! how hast thou fallen into this difficulty?
and with all thy good sense and sagacity how hast thou yielded thy neck to

---

[1] *Nai basti* does not occur in the Dictionary, but is doubtless equivalent to *nai zdr*. One
MS. however reads *walí basti*, which might mean, 'but there was a thicket,' or, 'but there
was an agreement.'

[2] *Dar tag istddah*, to use a vulgarism, 'setting-to to run.' *Istddan* has frequently this
sense; thus p. 251, l. 10 of the Persian text, *bi-talab-i vai istdd*, 'set-to to pursue him.'

the fetters of deceit?' The Deer replied, 'Opposed to the divine decree, of what avail is shrewdness? and of what use is acuteness and sagacity, if it controvert the mandate of the Supreme Ruler? From the desert of deliberation to the resting-place of destiny, the way is endless; and from the plain of stratagem to the confines of fate, the distance is infinite.

COUPLET.

Proud of a hundred wiles I stood without,
But knew not what, within, they were about.'

The Mouse replied, 'Thou speakest truly,

COUPLET.

Where fate sets up the tent of destiny,
None can the assault by wise-laid plans defy.'

He then occupied himself with severing the bonds of the Deer, and in the meantime the Tortoise having come up, made known his grief and dejection at the imprisonment of his friend. The Deer said, 'O kind friend! thy coming to this spot is yet more perilous than what has befallen me; for if the hunter should come and the Mouse have severed my bonds, I with a single step can save my life, and the Crow will fly away, and the Mouse will conceal itself in the recess of a hole. But thou hast neither the hand to fight nor the means of opposition, nor the front to resist nor the foot to fly. Why hast thou ventured thus gratuitously? and wherefore hast thou been so rash?' The Tortoise replied, 'Dear comrade? how was it possible for me not to come? and with what color could I delay or allow of hesitation? what pleasure has life which is passed in absence from friends? and how can existence be valued which is spent in separation from those we love.

COUPLET.

Lifeless I lived. Let this thee not surprise;
Bereft of friends our life, uncounted, lies.

And I am excusable for coming here, since the desire of beholding thy beauty drew me hither whether I would or not, and the wish of beholding thee deprived me of all patience; and with reference to this trifling distance and necessary journey which has presented itself, the companion of patience has set his foot in the road of annihilation.[1]

COUPLET.

Too sad without thee, God knows! my distress;   The parting day and night of loneliness.

And be thou not pensive, for this instant thou wilt obtain thy release, and these knots being loosed, thou wilt with unconcern hasten home; and on all accounts it is requisite for thee to offer due thanksgiving, and incumbent on thee to render thy grateful acknowledgments that thy body is unwounded and

---

[1] Plainly, 'I could not bear not to take so trifling a journey.'

thy life uninjured; else the remedy would have been beyond the reach of imagination, and the cure would have passed the bounds of possibility.' They were engaged in this conversation when the hunter appeared at a distance, and the Mouse finished dividing the meshes. The Deer leapt forth, the Crow flew away, the Mouse went down into a hole, but the Tortoise remained where it was. When the hunter came up and found the net which held the deer severed, he bit the finger of amazement with the tooth of reflection, and began to look to the left and right, saying, 'Ah! by whom has this deed been done and whose hand has effected this?' His eyes lighted on the Tortoise, and he said to himself, 'Although this contemptible piece of goods cannot soothe my sorrow for the escape of the Deer, and the rupture of the net, yet to return empty-handed is discreditable to the character of a hunter.' He then forthwith seized him and tossed him into his bag, and having tied him on his back, set off towards the city. As soon as the hunter had departed, the friends assembled, and discovered that the Tortoise had been taken by the hunter. Their hearts poured forth lamentations, and they raised their cries and complaints to the summit of the blue sky, and said,

COUPLET.

> 'The day our eyes thy beauty cease to view,
> Look where they will, tears will those eyes bedew.

What pain can equal separation from friends? and what calamity can parallel the absence of our comrades. Whoever is excluded from beholding his companion, and is parted from communion with his rosy-cheeked [favorite], knows that the wanderers in the plain of separation have the foot of bewilderment in the mire, and that the recluses of the cell of affection keep the hands of regret upon their heart.

COUPLET.

> How canst thou, painless, estimate the cruel pang of our regret?
> How tell what those athirst must feel, while by thee flows the rivulet?'

Each of the brotherhood uttered a separate moan, and composed a clamorous and piteous lament suited to his condition, and the tenor of their words had reference to one and the same subject.

COUPLET.

> Without our loved one's sugared lips our hearts exult no more,
> Reft of our friends, the joy of life, and life itself is o'er.

At length the Deer said to the Crow, 'O brother! although our words are extremely eloquent, and the effusions which we utter excessively sweet, yet they do not benefit the Tortoise in the least; and our lamentations and weepings, and bemoanings and disquietude, will not satisfy[1] him. It is more in accordance with good faith that we devise some stratagem, and employ some device which may embrace his release and ensure his escape;

---

[1] *Dar hausilah-i ú nah nishinad*, a remarkable phrase.

and the wise have said, 'The test of four kinds of persons is at four seasons, The courage of the valiant may be known in the day of battle, and the honesty of the upright in the time of lending and borrowing, and the love and fidelity of wife and child may be discerned in the hour of famine, and the truth of friends may be learned in the season of adversity and distress.

COUPLET.

Let me a comrade find in time of woe;   I lack not friends in happy times, I trow.'

The Mouse said, 'O Deer ! I have thought of a trick. The advisable course is that thou shouldest shew thyself to the hunter, and appear like one fatigued and wounded, and let the Crow alight on thy back and make it seem as if he were attacking thee, and assuredly, when the eyes of the hunter fall upon thee, he will plume himself with the idea of catching thee, and will put down the Tortoise with his gear on the ground and make towards thee. As soon as he comes near thee, run limping away from him, but not to such a distance as to cast off his hope of catching thee. Then keep him a good while employed in chasing thee, and do not fail to encourage him and to regulate thy movements. It may happen that I may release the Tortoise and let him run away.' The friends expressed their admiration of his plan, and the Deer and the Crow shewed themselves to the hunter as had been agreed. When the too credulous hunter beheld the Deer limping along, and the Crow hovering round him and pecking at his eyes, he fancied he should be successful in capturing the deer, and putting down his bag from his back set to work to pursue him. The Mouse forthwith severed the ties of the bag and released the Tortoise, and after an interval, when the hunter was well wearied in pursuing the Deer, and, despairing of success, came back to the bag, he could not see the Tortoise, and found the ties of the bag severed. He was overcome with astonishment, and thought to himself, 'No one would credit these extraordinary circumstances which I have witnessed. First, there was the severing of the Deer's fastenings, and his pretending to be wounded, and the Crow's sitting upon him, and the making a hole in the bag, and the escape of the Tortoise ! How are we to explain these acts ?' In the midst of these reflections, being overcome with terror, he said, 'Most likely this is the haunt of fairies and the abode of dívs; I must get back with speed, and break off all desire for the beasts of this plain. The hunter took up the fragments of his bag and his broken net, and taking to flight, vowed that if he could escape from those wilds, for the rest of his life he would not suffer himself to think of that plain; and he would, out of kindness, warn other hunters not to enter that wilderness.

HEMISTICH.

' For there the net secures nought but the wind.'

And when the hunter had gone away, the friends re-assembled and returned to their dwelling-place free from care and safe, and content and peaceful;

and thenceforward neither did the hand of calamity reach the skirt of their affairs, nor the nail of trouble lacerate the cheek of their condition or proceedings; and by the happy influence of their agreement and the beauty of their unanimity, the knot of their friendly intercourse was secured, and the bond of their society strengthened.

STANZA.

The single thread an old dame's strength might break,
    But Zál[1] were weak to rend its twisted ply.
Sugar, alone, the heart to burn will make,
    The roses' unmixed scent the brain will dry.
Rose-sugar, sugared-rose, is best to take
    For vigor, useless if imbibed dividedly.

This is the story of the agreement of friends and the narrative of the reciprocal aid and support of companions, and of sincerity of attachment in prosperity and adversity, and of the maintenance of regard in the time of tranquillity and of trouble, and of the discharging social obligations in the season of enjoyment and of hardship, and how these friends displayed steadiness in perfect devotion during the mishaps of time and the vicissitudes of fortune; and, consequently, by the blessing of unanimity and mutual aid, they obtained release from such mortal perils; and, casting disasters and calamities behind them, were securely seated, happy and unruffled, on the throne of friendly converse and the cushion of mirth. Now, it behoves a man of sense to feel it incumbent on him to give proper consideration to these tales with the light of his reason and the clearness of his judgment; for since the friendship of feeble animals yields such admirable fruits and choice results, if a body of wise men, who are the cream of mankind and the *élite* of the human race, pursue a similar sincere unanimity, and lay the base of friendship on these rules, and conduct to the end this faithfulness of intention and inward purity; how will not the advantages thereof extend to high and low? and the beneficial effects being manifested on the pages of the circumstances of each individual, to what extent will not the blessing of such a proceeding accrue to the fortunes of great and small?

VERSE.

They who the laws of social converse know,
    Guided by them alone their life will lead.
All that we do without a friend is woe,
    'Tis rare if friendless we in aught succeed.
Whose converse is sincere, and free from wile,
    Grasp thou his skirt, for he will faithful be,
And seek the man whose acts are void of guile,
    Who against fortune's arrow would shield thee
With life. Friends who at core devoted are,
    Their love than life itself is dearer far.

[1] *Zál* signifies 'an old woman,' and is also the name of a famous hero, the father of Rustam. The equivoque cannot be retained in English.

CHAPTER IV.

IN EXPLANATION OF ATTENTIVELY REGARDING THE CIRCUMSTANCES OF OUR ENEMIES, AND NOT BEING SECURE AS TO THEIR STRATAGEMS AND MACHINATIONS.

INTRODUCTION.

The King said to the Bráhman, 'I have heard the narrative of mutually-agreeing friends, and companions fitted for each other and sincere, and I have learned the result of their concord and unanimity, and have become acquainted with the fact that,

COUPLET.
He feels no grief who has a faithful friend,
And one unfriended no delights attend.

Now if you would be pleased to recount the story of an enemy, and how one ought not to be deceived by him, nor to rely on his pretended courtesy and submission. For the purport of the fourth precept is this, that it behoves a wise man, from motives of prudence, not to place any confidence in a foe; since friendship will never spring from an enemy.

COUPLET.
In one now hostile to expect a friend,   Is fire and water in one spot to blend.'

Bídpáí said, 'Of course a wise man will give no heed to the speech of a foe, nor will purchase the hypocritical wares of his deceit and imposture; for a sagacious enemy, for his own purposes, displays the utmost gentleness, and gives his outward conduct a specious appearance at variance with his inward feelings; and employs all the refinements of dissimulation and the arts of deceit, and under cover of them, disposes deep plans and surprising devices. Wherefore it behoves a man of sense and prudence, the more he observes a fawning and obliging demeanor on the part of his foe, to maintain the greater suspicion and watchfulness; and the more his enemy advances the foot of suavity, the closer to draw in the skirt of acceptance; for if he choose to be supine and leave a crevice open, his adversary, who is always on the watch for this state of things, will suddenly open his ambuscade and shoot the shaft of machination at the target of his wish. And in this case, the opportunity for applying a remedy being lost, his regret and repentance will be unavailing; and 'if' and 'would that,' will be in vain; and that will befall him which happened to the Owl from the Crow.' Dábishlím inquired, 'How was that?'

STORY I.[1]

The Bráhman said, 'They have related that somewhere in the country of
China there was a mountain so high that the sense of vision, in order to
reach its top, was wont to halt several times; and the watchman of thought
had never scaled the platform of its summit save with the ladder of fancy.

COUPLET.

Nought to its height, save mental vision, went;
Nought save conjecture measured its descent.

And on that mountain, from whose exceeding loftiness and from the breadth
of whose area,

COUPLET.

Heaven's loftiest summit seemed to be its crest
And earth's expanse seemed stretched out in its breast,

the gardener of Divine Wisdom, purely by His omnipotence, had caused a
tree to grow, such that its branches passed beyond the Pleiades, and its root
had fastened themselves in the bowels of the earth.

VERSE.

Each mighty branch of that gigantic tree,
Rivaled the lote [2] of Heaven's boundary.
Reason among its praises did descry
Roots deeply fixed, and branches in the sky.[3]

And on that many-branched tree there were a thousand nests of crows, and
these crows had a king, by name Pírúz [Fortunate], in allegiance to whom
all continued, and showed submission to his commands and prohibitions in
opening and contracting all matters.   One night the king of the owls, whom
they called Shabáhang [Moving-by-night], in consequence of the ancient
enmity which exists between the crow and the owl, made a night-attack on
the crows with an innumerable army and a blood-thirsty host, and destroyed
a number of them.[4]

COUPLET.

With valiant arm he raised his hand on high,
And low as dust he made his foemen lie.

---

[1] This chapter corresponds to the Third Book of the Hitopadesha, the Vigraha, where
the story, however, is very differently told.

[2] On this *sidratu 'l-muntaha*, Lote-tree of Paradise, sits Gabriel perched.   It is called
al-muntaha as being on the verge of Eden.

[3] After much consideration of this difficult couplet I can make no other sense of it but
what I have given.   The roots were too deep and the branches too lofty for anything
but the intellect to discover their whereabouts.   Such an idea strictly accords with
Persian taste.

[4] *Damár az rúzgár bar dvardan* is a common phrase, but it is difficult to explain it.
Literally it is ' to bring out perdition from the life of any one.'

In that dark night he consumed with the flames of war many of the black-actioned crows, and sketched on the collar of the condition of those gloomy-fortuned ones the writing, '*Kill them wherever you find them*,'[1] and returned from that battle victorious and triumphant and strengthened and glad. The next day when the dark-pinioned crow of night turned its face towards its nest in the west; and the host of stars, like a flock of owls, were concealed in the corner of retirement,

COUPLET.

The world-adorning sun its sabre drew,
And, from the day, night's hosts in terror flew,

Píruz assembled his forces, and introduced the story of the onslaught of the army of the owls, and said, 'Ye witnessed the night-attack of the owls, and saw with your own eyes their courage, and to-day some among you have been slain, and others stripped of their feathers, wounded and with their plumage ruffled. And worse than this is their .hardihood and intrepidity, and their eagerness to harass and annoy us crows, and their discovery of our abode and residence, and their becoming acquainted with our resting-places and our nests; and there is no doubt that the success and victory which they have won over this division will embolden them, and next time they will return more quickly, and on the next occasion will obtain a more effectual advantage than at the first, and will cause those who are already sick of the disease of panic to drink of. the same beverage, and it is probable that if they make a night-attack again in this manner, they will not leave one of our army alive. Deliberate on this matter, and having stated the nature of your advice, devise with one consent how to repel them.

VERSE.

As yet 'tis the first onset of our foes,
Again new arts, new counsels, they devise.
Stop then this current ere it onward flows,
Lest many a mischief from its progress rise.
Strongly to-day oppose disaster's tide,
Lest next day's efforts should in vain be tried.'

When Píruz had finished speaking, five crows from among the leaders of the forces approached the king, and offered the customary prayers and becoming praises. Now these were celebrated among the crows for the excellence of their judgment and their abundant good sense; and renowned for the soundness of their counsels and the justice of their plans. In all

[1] Ḳur'án, Fl. ii. 187; Mar. ii. 192; Sale, p. 21, l. 4: 'Therefore enter your houses by their doors; and fear God, that you may be happy. And fight for the religion of God against those who fight against you; but transgress not by attacking them first, for God loveth not the transgressors. And kill them wherever ye find them, and turn them out of that whereof they have dispossessed you; for temptation to idolatry is more grievous than slaughter: yet fight not against them in the holy temple, until they attack you therein; but if they attack you, slay them there. This shall be the reward of the infidels.'

they were wont to pronounce, the secrets of victory and success were included, and in every way, which they pointed out, the tokens of prosperity and good were apparent.

STANZA.

> They with clear judgment and true wisdom's aid,
>> Time's mirrored surface cleansed from trouble's stain.
> Their perfect reason and just counsel made,
>> The thousand knots of fortune loose again.

The crows were used to rely in all affairs on their advice, and under their guidance undertook measures for repelling disasters; and the king looked upon their judgment as auspicious, and in the matter of counsel did not transgress their sentence. When the eyes of Pírúz fell upon them he honored each with his royal condescension, promised them robes of honor and gifts befitting their condition, and said, 'To-day is the day of trying your intellect and eminent qualities; place on the string of explanation every jewel that you have treasured up in the casket of your mind and set it on the salver of representation; and every coin that you have struck in the mint of your lofty minds on the touchstone of credit you must bring forth from the coining-house of examination to the mart of manifestation.' The crows loosed the tongue of eulogy, and said,

VERSE.

> 'King! may the world in thy safe-keeping be,
> And earth and time still friendly prove to thee!
> Hold thou the key that leads to victory,
> And may thy foemen 'neath thy footsteps lie!

Thine own high judgment will be the most right-counseling, and that which passes through thy luminous mind will be best and most proper. What can we, thy slaves, utter that is not a thousand-fold more visible in the mirror of the imperial intellect? and what can we know that is not many times more inscribed on the tablet of the royal wisdom? However, in accordance with the saying, '*He that is commanded is excusable*,' in whatever we may be interrogated, that, to the extent of our capacity, and the full limit of our ability and power, shall be set forth.

HEMISTICH.

> That which we speak is known to thy high mind.'

The king asked one of them, 'What dost thou say on this head, and how dost thou propose to meet this difficulty?' He replied, 'O king! the wise who lived before us have pointed out to us the stratagem requisite for this kind of occurrence; and said that when any one is too weak to oppose a powerful enemy he must assuredly bid farewell to his property and effects, and birth-place and fatherland; and must avert his face from his wonted dwelling-place and well-known abode: since to wage war is very perilous, and to step into the plain of battle is a great calamity; especially when a defeat has been suffered from an enemy, and it has been reckoned a piece of good fortune to escape from him. And whoever—inconsiderately advancing to avenge himself, pretends to attack foes, the impression of whose arms and hostility he has experienced, is like one who slumbers in the bed of a torrent and who has built in the face of a flood; and to rely on one's own strength, and to be intoxicated with one's own prowess and valour, is far removed from prudence, since the sword has two edges, and the gale of victory can blow from both sides.

VERSE.

> From strife with e'en a weaker man refrain,
> For torrents grow from single drops of rain.
> Nor with more valiant warriors meet in strife,
> Thou canst not smite thy finger 'gainst a knife.' [1]

The King turned to another and said, 'What have been thy reflections, and in what manner dost thou foresee a prosperous issue to this matter?' He replied, 'My sentiments do not accord with what the former minister has said with respect to flight and the desertion of our abodes. Nay, that counsel beseems not men of understanding, since, at the first onset and attack to suffer one's self to be so abased, and to bid farewell to one's home and fatherland, is a cause of disgrace and dishonor.

HEMISTICH.

> At every wound brave men must not give way.

It is more advisable that we should make preparations for battle, and enter upon the war with all possible dignity, and on the most imposing scale.

VERSE.

> Unless we draw the sabre from its sheath,
> None will our name as that of brave men breathe.
> Ourselves will be on honor's road the guide,[2]
> And meet the boastings of the proud with pride.
> So, aided by the world-creating Lord,
> On foes we'll wreak our vengeance with the sword.

The fortunate king may then fondle with the hand of enjoyment the chaste bride of empire, when the water [3] of his fire-dropping scymitar has washed out the name of the malignant foe from the tablet of life; and the renowned emperor can at that time raise to the lip of his wishes the cup of blissful repose, when he has crushed with the stone of victory the goblet of the desire of the insolent-eyed foe. The advisable course at present is that we establish videttes and keep watch on every side whence danger can be expected, and

---

[1] Lit., ' a lancet.'

[2] I give this translation because of the equivocal meanings of *nang* and *zabún*, though it is more likely that the real signification is, 'We shall ourselves shew the way to our dishonor, inasmuch as before the weak we shall play the recreant.'

[3] The word *áb* signifies also 'the lustre of steel,' 'the water of a sword.' Hence its use here, when associated with the epithet 'fire-dropping,' it is exactly suited to the Persian taste, which is the farthest possible removed from that of Helicon.

if the foe assail us, meet him prepared and upon our guard, and keep our
ground manfully in the battle until the face of victory shews itself to the
eye of hope through the dust of the conflict, or our blood be mingled with
the mire of the battle-ground in the field of honor and renown.

HEMISTICH.

Let me but fall with honor, and 'tis well.

And it behoves kings on the day of battle, and at a crisis when their honor
is concerned, not to regard consequences; and, in the time of war, to look
upon life and property as valueless.

STANZA.

Step thou into the battle-field prepared to die, and see
    In the hollow of attainment's bat the ball of thy desire.
Wouldst thou that fortune shew her face as thou wouldst wish to thee?
    Then meet thy foeman front to front, nor from his face retire.'

The King turned the face of attention towards another, asking, 'What
does thy judgment point out and what writing does thy counsel inscribe on the
board of representation?' He replied, 'I will have nothing to do with what
the others say. I think it will be best to despatch spies and employ clever
emissaries, and having thoroughly reconnoitred the position of our enemies,
to discover whether they show any inclination to make terms or not. If
they are content to receive tribute and subsidy from us, and will meet our
friendly advances with the favor of acceptance; we, too, will base our affairs
on peace, and to the extent of our power and the limit of possibility, we will
undertake to pay tribute, and thus relieved from the hardships of war and the
affliction of their night-attacks, we will rest in our own country.

VERSE.

Till with success by prudent plans we meet.
    Better be humble than resist our foes.
When force cannot the enemy defeat,
    Better with gifts the door of mischief close.
Wouldst thou by foeman's malice not be stung?
    With talismanic kindness bind his tongue.

And one fitting policy and wholesome counsel for kings, is—that when the
preponderant power of their enemy is apparent, and there is cause to dread
that his injuries and influence will spread throughout the realm, and that the
people will be exposed to destruction and fall into the vortex of perdition—to
try the throw[1] of stratagem and to meet the doubles[1] of his foe with
gentleness; and having released his subjects from the check[1] of adversity, to
make his wealth the shield of the state and realm—since to challenge the
throw, though the cast[1] of the enemy may be on the carpet[2] of overbearing
power and haughtiness, and to play the piece[1] of opposition madly, in spite of

---

[1] It will be seen that all the terms that follow are taken from the game of backgammon.
[2] Chess, dice, etc., are played by the Orientals on a carpet as by us on a board.

the adversary's superior strength, is far removed from the decrees of reason and diverse from the adornments of experience.

HEMISTICH.

When times are adverse, then yield thou to time.'

The King called up another vazír, and said, ' Do thou, too, point out thy views and explain what enters thy mind.' He said, ' O King! in my opinion, to leave our country and undergo the pain of parting and the affliction of exile, is more to be commended than to break the thread of our hereditary honor, and condescend to a foe who can never be aught but our inferior.

COUPLET.

When will the hawk the puny quail obey ?
When savage lions are of deer the prey.

If we place ourselves in a position to assent to give tribute, and supply provisions to the owls, they will not be satisfied with that, and will exert themselves to the utmost of their power to extirpate and cut us off. And they have said, ' It is right so far to show deference to an enemy, as to enable us to obtain our object of him, and not to carry this feeling to such an excess as that our minds should be degraded and our enemy emboldened.' And they will never be content with a trifling tribute from us; wherefore our remedy is patience and cautious procedure ; and if the exigency arise there is nothing to render war inadmissible, inasmuch as the distresses of war are preferable to the obliteration of fame and honor.

COUPLET.

Better to lie entombed beneath the stone,
Than, living, under vile opprobrium groan.'

The king then called forward the fifth vazír, whose name was Kárshinás [Experienced], and said, ' I have much reliance on thy understanding, which is capable of solving difficulties—and infinite confidence in thy world-illuminating wisdom.

STANZA.

None e'er beheld a solver of the knots of church and state
In straits, like to the counsels of thy penetrating mind :
From these alone men gain their wish, are rendered fortunate,
And by thy spirit's influence the Humá's glories find.

What opinion dost thou give in this matter; and of war, and peace and expatriation, which dost thou select ?' Kárshinás replied, ' My counsel is, not to choose war with the owls save on compulsion, and so long as we can see some other issue for our affairs with them, not to base our proceeding on strife, because they are bold in fighting with us, and we feeble against them. They are both stronger and more terrible than we are, and to despise a foe occasions one to be elated with pride, and pride borders on a fall; and before this I was in dread of their attacks, and I have now witnessed with my eyes that which I feared; and they now will not give us trouble, because among them are cautious people, and a cautious man never feels himself safe from his foe, because when he is near, it is possible that he may make a sudden attack; and when the distance between them is great, it may be that he will turn back upon him; and when he takes to flight, an ambuscade may be expected; and when alone one may suppose that he has devised some stratagem and treason. And, according to this way of arguing, war is now in the knot of suspense on their part, and, supposing that they have the intention of making war, it is not advisable for us to engage them, for he is the wisest of creatures who abstains from war; for that which is lost in war is the coin of life, and there is no equivalent for that.

COUPLET.

> Hast thou the strength of elephants, the claws
> Of lions; yet 'tis best from war to pause.'

The king said, 'If thou loathest war, then what dost thou propose?' He replied, 'Deliberation is requisite in this matter, and the heights and depths of it must be measured with the step of debate; for kings obtain by just counsels and right deliberation those objects which are not attainable with much treasure, and a countless band of ministers and attendants.

COUPLET.

> The sword may one, perhaps a hundred, slay: By prudence a whole host dissolves away.[1]

And the main thing in such matters is the luminous judgment of the king; and the counsel of judicious ministers is a cause of increasing the lustre of intellect, whence arises the perfection of light, as the water of the sea is augmented by the volume of the rivers; and, therefore, whoever does not seek assistance from the opinions of upright councillors whose words are worthy of approval, will, in a short time, lose all he may have gained from the assistance of fortune and the support of successful coincidence; while he who fortunately participates in the blessings of reason, and makes attention to the words of those in whom confidence can be placed his outer and inner garment, his happy destiny will be permanent and his fortune secure. And to-day—thanks be to God!—the king is adorned with perfect wisdom and arrayed with the beauty of right counsel.

VERSE.

> O Thou! whose reason guards the realm of worth,
> Whose wisdom[2] to the eastern orb gave birth;
> Whose counsels true with right opinion's aid,
> The rules of justice on firm basis laid.
> What my thoughts' value gauged by thy clear view?
> What price for beads from jewelers is due?

---

[1] Lit., 'thou mayst break an army's back.'

[2] *Rây* signifies 'the kindling of fire by the stick zand,' as well as 'wisdom,' hence an equivoque here, no trace of which can be preserved in the translation.

But since the king has honored me by consulting me in this affair, and has bestowed on me the dignity of a counsellor, I wish to say some things in answer privately, while I will declare a part of my opinion in public. And just as I am averse to war, so I feel repugnant to yield unqualified submission and degrading compliance, and I will not bow my neck to tribute and the endurance of reproach to which our ancestors refused their consent.

COUPLET.

A weak submission brings foul obloquy,
Than life dishonored better 'tis to die.

A man of a lofty spirit desires a long life that his memory may survive, and his name be perpetuated, and if—which God forbid!—infamy should attach to him, he would prefer a brief career to that.

HEMISTICH.

Good fame without reproach be mine! for death is better far than shame.

And I do not think it expedient for the king to make a declaration of his own weakness; for whoever yields to self-abasement, the doors of calamity are opened upon him, and the path of remedy closed against him.

COUPLET.

Keep a firm heart, nor yield to weak despair;
Where man is weakest Heaven grows darkest there.

And for the other segments of my discourse privacy is required in order that they may be represented to the view of the realm-adorning judgment of the king.' One of the courtiers in the assembly said, 'O Kárshinás! the advantage of consultation is this, that every one of those possessed of sagacity may say his say. Thus it may chance that the shaft of the thoughts of one of them may strike the target of the desired object; and the wise have said, 'A counsel is an assembly of wise men, and wherever a body of men of sense enter upon an affair, the beginnings and issues thereof will be in the best possible way brought under their examination, and the issue of that matter will be combined with victory and success. Thus a sage has said,

VERSE.

'Place not thy hopes on treasure, sword or host;
But from the wise for plans and counsel call:
For prudent counsel will befriend thee most,
Where sword and arrow ineffectual fall.'

Wherefore what can be the advantage of thy proposing to defer thy speech to a private audience?' Kárshinás replied, 'Not every one consulted is worthy of confidence, and state-secrets are not like affairs of ordinary occurrence and common transactions on which advice may be asked from any one. And they have said, 'King's secrets are disclosed by those consulted, or by ambassadors and emissaries.' And how knowest thou that

x

there is no emissary present here at this time, who is listening to our words in order that he may with all speed transmit to the enemy intelligence of all he hears? So they after due consideration of the beginnings and endings thereof, will close up their dangerous apertures, and the arrow of our schemes will fail to reach the desired mark. And on the supposition that an enemy is present not being allowed; perhaps, each one of the bystanders may have a friend and companion, and it is possible that these friends may demand of them the particulars of this meeting, and a statement of what has been said, and in a very short time the exact nature of our deliberations will pass current in the mouths and on the tongues of all, and thus reach the ear of both friends and enemies; and hence it is that they have urged so strenuously the concealment of secrets.

COUPLET.

How truthfully that man of prudence said!
' Guard well thy secret, wouldst thou guard thy head.'[1]

And whoever divulges his secret to another who bears not the stamp of confidence, will repent in the end when regret is unavailing. And no person needs to conceal his secret with such strenuous care as a king, for if any one but he, who is truly a confidant of the king, becomes acquainted with his secrets, the greatest troubles may be expected to arise from it.

COUPLET.

If one beside thyself thy counsel know,
Then for thy counsel soon thy tears must flow.

And there have been many, who have lost possession of realm and royalty, yea, of life and existence, through the disclosure of a secret, just as the King of Kashmír, through revealing his purpose to his vazír, fell in a short time from the pinnacle of princely power into the abyss of helplessness, and the sun of his existence set below the horizon of nonentity.' Pírúz inquired, ' How was that ? '

STORY II.

Kárshinás said, ' They have related that in the city of Kashmír there was a King, who had placed the reins of subjugation upon the head of the bay courser of the sky, and had cast the lasso of possession over the neck of refractory fortune. From fear of the gleam of his lightning-like scymitar, the wind had not the boldness to blow contrary to the straight direction, and through dread of his life-ravishing shafts, whose effects resembled those of the thunderbolt, water had not the power to flow tortuously on the earth.

---

[1] *Sirr* signifies ' a secret,' and *sar* ' the head.' Hence arises an equivoque in the original unretainable in English.

VERSE.

He o'er the world a robe of safety threw,
That freed the sword from shameful nudity.
His justice such,—oppressed spirits grew
Forgetful of their groans' sad archery.[1]

And this potent King had in the unviolated sanctuary of his Haram and behind the curtain of enjoyment,[2] a beautiful mistress, whose dark ringlets lent assistance to the longest winter-night, and whose life-bestowing countenance outvied the full moon in perfect loveliness. If the vigil-keeping recluse had beheld in a dream the image of her beauty, he would —like the chaste-skirted morn—from attachment to her features, have rent the collar of his religious garb.

VERSE.

Of stately aspect and of stature tall,
Her eyebrows arched, her locks in nooses fall.
Just so the cypress finds in the parterre,
Jasmines for cheeks, and violets for hair.

The king's heart was bound to that delicate fair one, so that he regarded the survey of her beauty as the sum of existence, and counted gazing on her ringlets and mole as the principal of life. Every moment the attraction of the love of his mistress drew his soul towards herself, and the curl of her heart-delighting ringlets snatched away the coin of patience from the pocket of his heart.

COUPLET.

It is not of my own free choice I follow her pursuing still,
But lasso-like her ringlets draw me on and on against my will.

And that playful and mischief-exciting fair one, when she saw the bird of the King's heart prisoned in the snare of her fascinating locks, drew the bow of her eye-brow to behind her ear, and let fly the shaft of her glances at the target of his breast; and each hour, with her wily coquetry and sweet blandishments, she tried a new trip[3] against the foot of his heart.

COUPLET.

The art of winning[4] lovers, and the wont of causing feud,
Were like a robe that o'er her form by nature had been sewed.

And through the capricious haughtiness inseparable from beauty, she was not content simply with the attentions of the King, but made other conquests in

---

[1] He made the world so safe that there was no need to bare the sword. Sighs are said to be the arrows of the oppressed, and his justice was such that those who suffered, forgot to discharge them *sahar-gāh*, ' at dawn,' that is, ' at morning-prayer,' which two words I have omitted.

[2] A MS. in my possession has the infinitely better reading of *pardah-i 'usmat* ' in the curtain of chastity,' for the *pardah-i 'ishrat* of the editions, which should decidedly be expunged.

[3] The *band* is here ' a throw in wrestling.'

[4] Or it may be *kushī* ' slaying.'

all directions, and cast the lasso of her fascinations over the neck of the
unfortunate wanderers in the deserts of passion; and finally commenced
operations with a youth of graceful form, who was one of the attendants
on the king, and a stripling of kind disposition, one of the court
favorites, whose tender beard had arrived, like Khizr, on the brink of the
water of life, and the down of whose cheek shewed itself like a hyacinth of
Paradise on the margin of the river Kausar.

COUPLET.

The downy hairs by coral lips appear,
Like heliotropes that grow life's water near.

And the youth too was overpowered by love, so that on the scroll of his
feeling there remained not a character from the volume of patience, nor was
there a breath of life's impression left on the page of his fortunes.

COUPLET.

He that becomes with love acquainted nought will chase his pain away.
He feeds his grief, nor leech nor physic e'er can make his love decay.[1]

The lover and the lady continually carried on question and answer with their
eyes and brows, and conversed by gestures and nods. One day the King
was seated on the cushion of enjoyment, and had fixed his heart on union
with his fascinating mistress, and the youth was standing in attendance, and
all the requisites for entertainment were at hand. The King gazed on the
bewitching beauty of his fair one, and perused on the page of her cheek the
writing, '*In the most perfect symmetry.*' The lady, careless of the King's
regards, cast her eyes upon the youth, and displayed on her lips a smile
which filled Time's lap with sugar.

HEMISTICH.

Smile, and the lap of pleasure fill with sweets !

The youth too, from the corner of his enchanting eye, responded with a
glance, which would have excited in the world a thousand troubles.

COUPLET.

Half-oped the gay narcissus of his eye,
And half looked forth, and half was coquetry.

When the King observed that circumstance, the fire of jealousy began to
blaze in his heart, and now that he had discovered their attachment, he at
once withdrew his affections from association with his mistress.

COUPLET.

'Touch not the tree,' such rule the wise have made,
Which o'er another garden casts its shade.

He then thought to himself, 'To be precipitate in this matter seems far from

---

[1] A MS. in my possession reads *dard parwarad ú muhabbat-i ydr bar na tdft*, which I
prefer to that of the editions, of which I find it difficult to make sense.

the path of reason, and to be over hasty in removing these two persons, who, in point of fact, are my enemies, is not agreeable to prudence, and a due regard for consequences.

HEMISTICH.

Patience, for man, transcends all things that are.

He then passed over that thing as if he had not observed it, and finished his interview according to his established custom, and passed the night until day with the light of the taper of the beauty of his beloved, but his heart burned moth-like in the flame of the fire of inquietude.

COUPLET.

King, lover, drunken and a love so fair,
How could he see her mark another there?

In short, the next day, when the Jamshíd of the sun set up on the dome of the turquoise-coloured heaven the banner of victory and triumph, and the monarch of the planets removed from before the portico of the reclining place of the blue sky the curtain of darkness.

VERSE.

When at the tell-tale morning's chilly spell [1]
The golden bason from the terrace fell.
The fair-cheeked bride, the sun, with maiden grace,
From the sky's purple curtain shewed her face.

The king came forth [and seated himself] on the throne of his glory, and having proclaimed a summons to appellants, himself decided their suits.

COUPLET.

Kings, who to justice favoringly incline,
Of God's own mercy are the shade divine.

And after he had finished transacting business and giving sentence on the suits, he held a private council with the vazír who was his prime minister. The executioner, Anger, importuned him to state to the vazír the occurrence of the night, and, with his advice, to make the offenders taste of the beverage of punishment; and the president, Reason, bade him conceal his secret, and put in execution the command which his heart required. In the end anger prevailed, and he imparted some hints of what lay hid in his heart to the vazír, and asked advice of him on that head. The vazír too gave sentence for putting them to death, and agreed with the opinion of the king, whereupon the destruction of those two persons was determined, and it was resolved to make each of them drink deadly poison, and so plunge them from the shore of existence into the whirlpool of annihilation, and in a way

---

[1] *Dam* means both the 'light breeze' which arises at morn, and also the 'breath of detraction.' Sunrise is compared to a golden basin falling from a terrace. I shall be glad if any critic will throw more light on this strange expression.

known only to the king and the vazír, carry the affair to its conclusion; so that the curtain of dishonor[1] should not be rent, nor the thread of reputation severed.

COUPLET.

> Such things as these 'tis better to conceal,
> Thou wilt repent if thou shouldst them reveal.

The vazír came home from the presence of the king and found his daughter very sad and discomfited. On asking her the reason, he learned that his daughter had been that day in the seraglio of the king, and that she had been treated by the royal lady discourteously in a variety of ways, and had received from her much indignity in the midst of her equals and associates. The vazír was vexed at this circumstance, and said, to soothe his daughter,

COUPLET.

> 'The messenger, the morning-breeze, last night did whispering say
> That the day of trouble and of grief was fleeting fast away.

Grieve not, for in these two or three days the lamp of her life will be extinct, and the flower of her existence will be withered.' The girl in order to ascertain this circumstance, made inquiries into the facts of the case. The vazír recounted somewhat[2] of what had passed between him and the king, and enjoined her most strictly to keep it secret. The girl, pleased at this good news, came out from her father's presence, and shortly after, one of the attendants of the seraglio and servants of the Ḥaram came to apologise to her and comfort her. When the preliminary excuses had been made, the vazír's daughter said, 'It matters not. If the king's lady has for no reason given me pain, she will nevertheless soon get her punishment and reward.

HEMISTICH.

> Soon will my foe be taken from my sight.'

The attendant, too, displayed much gratification and delight at this, and asked, 'Whence dost thou say this? and when will it be that we shall be released from her tyranny and cruelty?' The vazír's daughter said, 'If thou art able to keep my secret, I will disclose to thee this matter and will not conceal a particle from thee.' The attendant swore an oath to her, and the vazír's daughter detailed the whole affair exactly as it stood. Hereupon the attendant hurried back and acquainted the royal lady with the circumstance, and the latter sending for the youth to a private consultation, informed him of the secret, and they together induced others to become their accomplices; and before the King could hear of it, they came to his pillow and plunged the bark of his life into the whirlpool of destruction. Thus by disclosing his

---

[1] 1 confess I should have preferred *nik námi* here, as it would have corresponded better than *bad námi* to *námús*; and besides, to rend the curtain of *dishonor* seems to give a false idea.

[2] Lit.: 'a whiff.'

secret to the vazír, he fell from the post of successful fortune; nay, also from the place of existence, to the narrow strait of ruin and the prison of extinction.

And the moral of this story is, that if kings consult with vazírs, and reap the advantage of their experience and sagacity; nevertheless, it behoves them not to acquaint any one with the secret of their heart, since when they themselves—notwithstanding their divine rank and aid from heaven, and their lofty spirit and noble character—are unable to keep their secrets, how can others who are lower in position and inferior in reason and understanding, preserve it?

COUPLET.

When thine own secret thou canst not conceal,
Why art thou vexed if others it reveal?'

When Kárshinás had recounted this story and had perforated a gem of this beauty with the diamond of fascinating style, another of those present in the assembly, loosed the tongue of objection, saying, 'According to what thou hast said, we must throw up the practice of taking advice, and content ourselves with our own plans and judgment; yet to abandon counsel is not approved by reason and wisdom, and the wise saying, '*And consult them in the affair* [*of war*]' [1] proves that an affair ought not to be undertaken without consultation.

COUPLET.

Unless on counsel thou thy actions base,
Nor law nor reason find in them their place.[2]

And the verse of God's word which enjoins his own Chosen one, the Prophet, to take counsel with the attendants of the court of the prophetical office, is a proof that consultation is a divine command, nay, rather an absolute decree.

COUPLET.

Since counsel is the Prophet's high behoof;
Why from that method dost thou keep aloof?'

Kárshinás said, ' God Most High commanded the Prophet (on whom be the divine blessing!) to consult with others—not that his judgment might be aided by theirs, since the luminous mind of the Lord of Prophecy, (may benedictions and peace be upon him!) which was assisted by the inspiration of God and was adorned with the help of the supreme favor, is a world-displaying mirror, such that the true state of things appears evident and distinct in it—but [the command was given] to attest the advantages of counsel, and to corroborate its benefits, in order that mankind might array themselves with this admirable quality, and turn from self-deceit and

---

[1] Ḳur'án, Fl. iii. 153; Mar. iii. 160; Sale, p. 50, l. 16 : 'Therefore forgive them and ask pardon for them: and consult them in the affair of war; and, after thou hast deliberated, trust in God; for God loveth those who trust in Him.'
[2] Lit. : ' Thou dischargest not the duties of the law, nor givest to reason its just claims.'

opinionatedness towards asking advice of others and sober deliberation; and support their own weak judgment with the aid of that of others; like the light of a lamp, which is augmented by the substance of grease; and the rays of fire, which are increased by the help of wood. Now my words did not imply that we ought to give up consultation, but the meaning which they developed was, that we must conceal the conclusion which we come to from consultation, and keep close our resolve. For the concealment of secrets and the withholding our intentions, contain two most important advantages:— the first is, that it has been proved by experience, that every affair which is kept concealed, is most quickly brought to a successful issue, and the direction, ' *Seek ye help in your momentous affairs*,' alludes to this. The second is, that if that plan should not be in accordance with destiny, and the mind should be unable to perform its purpose, at least the rejoicing of enemies and the mischief-making remarks of detractors will not follow.

COUPLET.

That I fail to win thee does not on my soul so darkly weigh,
    As the sarcasms of my rivals, who against me aye inveigh.'

Píruz said, ' O kind counsellor! I have perfect confidence in thy excessive attachment and loyalty, and of all the vazírs and ministers who wait at this court, I know thee to excel in ability and judgment; whatever then, enters thy mind, of the nature of advice and loyal recommendation, allow not thyself to fail in declaring it.' Kárshinás made obeisance, and said,

COUPLET.

' O thou! beneath whose sheltering justice beasts and birds in safety live,
    Whose wisdom's rays to man sweet rest, and to the race primæval[1] give.

It is incumbent on every servant, when he sees his master devising a measure, to declare that which he sees to approximate nearest to the right; and if he find the royal purpose associated with error, to display the way in which mischief will result from it; and to speak with respectful gentleness; and until he observes his plans and counsels to be thoroughly sound, not to desist. And every counsellor who neglects his benefactor and does not observe what is due from an adviser, nor discharge the requirements of uprightness and confidence, must be regarded as an enemy; and the custom of asking advice of him must be abandoned; and whenever a king thus values and conceals his secrets, and secures a competent minister and an upright counsellor in whom reliance can be placed; and considers the remuneration of those who are serviceable as an obligation according to the laws of princely rule; and recognizes the rebuking and chastisement of offenders as an intimate part of king-craft; it is most probable that his kingdom

---

[1] *Ján* is the name of a Pre-adamite race, according to Muslim tradition.

will remain permanent and his fortunes unshaken, and the hand of the vicissitudes of time will not quickly snatch from him the gifts of favorable destiny.

VERSE.

On faith and justice that thy throne may rest,
Be all thy labor in their culture spent:
And let the world be with thy riches blest,
That thou be glad, and God with thee content.'

The King asked, 'How must secrets be kept hid and from whom?' Kárshinás replied, 'The secrets of kings are of different degrees. Some are of such a nature that the king must keep them concealed—even from himself; that is to say, he must carry his concealment of them to such excess that, as one might say, he himself is not to be the confidant of them, how then could he give even a hint of them to others? And a sage has said, on this head,

STANZA.

'That which should not be mentioned, in thy mind
Keep hidden, and that so rigidly,
That should thy heart long seek the thought to find,
The search may vain and unsuccessful be.'

And there are a few other secret matters in which the position of confidant may be imparted to two persons, and in others it may be extended to three, and it is allowable to go as far as four and five persons. But a secret which the mind may have conceived in the matter of the owls, admits not of being confided to more than four ears and two heads.' After the King had heard these words he turned his face towards his cabinet, and having sent for his vazír Kárshinás, introduced the subject, and inquired, first, 'What has been the cause of the hostility and what the reason of the enmity and spirit of rivalry between us and the owls?' He replied, 'In ancient times a crow uttered a speech, and the owls nourished a spite in their hearts on that account, and laid the foundation of hostility, and that quarrel and feud have continued to this day.' The King asked, 'How was that?'

STORY III.

He said, 'They have related that a flock of birds assembled and came to an agreement, saying, 'We must have a chief and leader, to whom we can have recourse in troublous affairs, that if an enemy come to make war upon us, we may exert ourselves to repulse and get rid of him with this chief's assistance.' Hereupon each of them designated one of the birds as chief, and another exerted himself to bring proofs and arguments to make the nomination abortive, until the turn came to the owl. A party were unanimous to make him chief, and to give the reins of authority into the hand of his management. When they entered upon the consideration of this subject, and commenced arguing as to the acceptance or rejection of him, the fire of mischief blazed up between them, and the discussion passed from the limits of moderation to hostility and contention. Some, through partiality to the owl, set up the banner of prejudice, and others threw the stone of discord into the field of agreement. In brief, it was resolved that they should make another arbiter, who was not a member of that assembly, and that both parties should consent to whatever he directed, and. that they should thus terminate their dispute. It befell that they saw at a distance a crow, and they said, 'Lo! there is one who does not belong to this assembly, we will ask counsel of him; and another thing is, he is of our race; and until the nobles and grandees of every particular kind of birds are not agreed, unanimity is unattainable, and without unanimity, this plan that we propose is impracticable.' Wherefore, when the crow had joined them, they told him the state of the case, and asked him for direction in the matter. The crow replied, 'What vain thought and impossible longing is this? What has the ill-omened owl to do with the office of ruler and governor? and what business has that ill-favoured creature with the dignity of absolute power and authority?

COUPLET.

O Fly! the Símurgh's movement-ground is not for thy manœuvres made,
Much thou troublest us while boastful thy puny force thou dost parade.

What has happened to the high-soaring falcon, which boasts equality of place with the eagle of the sky? and what has befallen the beautiful peacock of graceful form, by the ornament of whose feathers and wings the garden of beauty and elegance is adorned? Where is the Humá of fortunate omen, the shadow of whose auspiciousness sets the crown of exaltation on the head of renowned kings? And the glorious eagle,[1] at the clang of whose victorious pinions and triumphant wings the summits of the mountains quake, why is he absent? If all the birds of noble race were to perish, and the weak and feeble too were lost without a trace, it would be better that the birds should exist without a king, and not consent to the dishonor of being subjects to the owl, and the disgrace of being ruled by him. For he, together with[2] his foul aspect, has a base intellect; and, at the same time that he is a slave to his angry passions, does not refrain from feelings of arrogance; and, besides all this, he is shut out from the beauty of the world-illuminating day, which, according to the sacred verse, '*And destined the day to the gaining your*

---

[1] '*Ukáb* is 'an eagle,' '*akabát* 'mountain-summits,' whence arises a play on words by the figure called Tajnís, of which Orientals are passionately fond, and of which so many examples have already been cited.

[2] The common meaning of *bá wujúd* 'notwithstanding,' will hardly apply here, for there is no reason why ugly men should not be foolish as well as hideous. I have therefore taken the first original meaning of the words, 'with the existence of' 'co-existent with,' or 'together with.'

livelihood,'[1] is the stock of the market of subsistence; and he is excluded from the light of the creation-adorning sun, which, as declared[2] by the text, '*And placed therein a burning lamp,*'[3] is the universe-irradiating lamp and taper that gilds the earth. And what is still worse, passion and levity have got the better of him, and vehemence and absurdity are manifest in all his actions. Abandon this unwholesome project, and base your affairs on wisdom and ability, and control your transactions by the rules of wisdom, and consider it incumbent on you to manage every matter in accordance with sound views, so that ye may always live tranquil and free from anxiety. And your first care must be to appoint among yourselves a president, in whose intelligence and sagacity and good sense and ability you may have perfect confidence and complete reliance. So that whatever circumstances may arise, and whatever momentous affair or accident may take place, he may be equal to the management of it with his judicious mind, like that Hare which pretended to be an ambassador from the moon, and, by skilful management, averted a terrible calamity from his race.' The birds inquired, 'How was that?'

STORY IV.

He said, 'They have related that one year, in the country of elephants, in one of the islands of Zírbád,[4] it happened that no rain fell, and the mother-clouds, from the teat of maternal affection, did not distil a drop into the mouth of the thirsty-lipped ones of the cradle of the earth. The fire of drought made the fountains[5] moistureless as the eye of the hard-hearted; and the springs of water became dry, like the mouth of the longing of the poor. The elephants, impatient of their sufferings from thirst, complained to their king, who commanded that they should hasten in all directions to procure water, and should carry on the search with a diligence that could not be exceeded. The elephants, having traversed all the coasts and borders of that country with the step of investigation, arrived at a fountain, which they called the fountain of the moon,[6] and which by the Persians was named the

---

[1] Kur'an, Fl. lxxviii. 10; Mar. lxxviii. 11; Sale, p. 433, l. 7: 'Have we not made the earth for a bed, and the mountains for stakes to fix the same? And have we not created you of two sexes; and appointed your sleep for rest; and made the night a garment to cover you; and destined the day to the gaining your livelihood; and built over you seven solid heavens: and placed therein a burning lamp?'

[2] An excellent MS. in my possession reads *bih parwánah* 'by the decree'; which is infinitely preferable to the unmeaning *pirdyah-i* of the editions, which is not only devoid of sense, but destroys the symmetry of the corresponding sentences.

[3] Kur'án, ch. lxxviii., 12, as quoted in note 2, above.

[4] The modern Burmah.

[5] *Chashmah* 'fountain,' *chashm* 'eye,' the figure Tajnís again.

[6] The words rendered 'fountain of the moon,' are Arabic, and the Persian translation of them, as will be seen, follows.

'Chashmah-i-máh.' It was a deep pool, and contained an inexhaustible supply of water. The elephant-king, with all his retinue and warriors, proceeded towards the fountain to drink water, and around it certain hares had located themselves, and of course some of them were injured by the elephants. Each one on whom an elephant set his foot, received such punishment [1] that he was obliged to retire from the stage of life; and met with such chastisement as it is impossible to expound the result, except by referring to the area of non-existence.

COUPLET.

Not to the plain in such wild fury rush,
Lest heads beneath thy courser's hoof thou crush.

By one visit of the elephants many of the hares were squeezed and trampled to death.

HEMISTICH.

Who'll live, if thou thus comest twice or thrice?

The next day they went together to their king and said, 'A just king is the protection of the oppressed, and the aid of the destitute. Every one who occupies a throne sits there for the administration of justice, not to lead a life of pleasure.

COUPLET.

Therefore thou didst this throne ascend,
That thou the helpless mightst befriend.

Give us justice and exact satisfaction for us from the elephants, and graciously remedy the sufferings we experience from them; for every moment they may return and, this time, trample under their feet some poor wretches who escaped half dead from their tread.

COUPLET.

When first thou didst thy face display; my heart, my reason, senses, fled,
Now take my life, with life alone this tenement is plenishèd.'

The King said, 'This is no trifling matter, that we should enter carelessly upon it. Let every one of you who is possessed of ability, attend, that we may hold a consultation; for the execution of a resolve before counsel has been taken, is not among the happy qualities of the wise.

COUPLET.

The mind with wisdom richly fraught   Will, unadvised, resolve on nought.'

Now among the hares there was one of sharp intellect, whom they called Bihrúz,[2] and men relied on him for the abundance of his good sense, and

---

[1] The figure Tajnís is here again employed; gúshmálí, lit. 'rubbing of the ears,' is followed by gúshah ' corner :' and málish ' chastisement,' by ma-ál ' result.'

[2] 'Fortunate day.' To say that men relied on this hare seems absurd enough.

his perfect understanding and clearness of mind and excellent judgment. When he perceived that the king was distressed by this matter, he advanced saying,

VERSE.

'Thy helpless subjects, aye regard, O king! with pitying love,
For this the rule and custom is of those who justly reign.
Noi ever from the destitute thy favoring glance remove,
That thus thou mayest from crown, throne, wealth, and rank, enjoyment gain.

If the King think it advisable, let him send me on an embassy to the elephants, and having appointed a commissioner, despatch him with me, that ·he may see and hear what I do and say.' The King said, 'I have no doubt of thy rectitude and good-faith, and truth and honesty, nor shall I ever doubt of it; and I have oft witnessed and heard of thy speech and actions.

COUPLET.

For thy deeds' coin it is enough that them I oft have tried,
And on the stone of trial found that they no alloy hide.

Go with good-fortune, and that which thou deemest to be advisable for the present crisis and adapted to the circumstances, do! And thou knowest that the messenger of a king is his tongue; and whoever wishes to know the title-page of the writing of any one's mind and the interpretation[1] of the secret of his heart, may learn it from the words and actions of his envoy. For if virtue and excellence be visible in the latter, and laudable impressions and praiseworthy conduct discernible in him; they may regard this as a proof of the worthy selection and perfect appreciation of character in the king: while as regards the messenger who is guilty of errors and remissness, the tongue of cavilers will be put in motion, and find occasion for reproach and disparagement. Moreover, the wise have given strict injunctions, and insisted beyond measure, that whoever sends an envoy to a place, must take care that he is the wisest of his tribe, the most eloquent of them in speech, and the most perfect in action. And former kings used for the most part, to send sages on embassies; and Iskandar Ẓú'l-ḳarnain[2] went even beyond them in this, for he disguised himself, and used to go in his own person as ambassador, and say,

COUPLET.

'Great heroes, like the lion-king,   With their own feet their message bring.'

And an eminent person has said, with reference to the despatch of envoys,

---

[1] For *tarjumán* 'interpreter,' I would gladly read *tarjumah* 'interpretation,' did the MSS. allow it.

[2] 'Alexander with the two horns,' or the elder Alexander, of whom many fabulous stories are related by Orientals. The real Alexander is called in distinction, 'Rúmí' or 'bin Filikús' (son of Philip). The two horns are said to allude to the conquest of east and west; but, in my opinion, they owe their origin to a corruption of the tale of Alexander's claiming descent from Jupiter Ammon, who appeared to him under the form of a ram. Horns in general are symbolical of strength, as in Daniel and the Psalms. For an account of this Alexander, see Sale, pp. 226, 227, and the note there marked 'f.'

VERSE.

> ' Wise must he be by monarchs sent,
> And bold in speech and eloquent.
> He must reply to all they ask,
> So as to best fulfil his task.
> In speaking it must be his aim
> For those who hear, his speech to frame.
> Oft has a word too roughly said,
> The world embroiled and heaped with dead.
> And oft another, soft and mild,
> Two nations' hate has reconciled.'

Bihrúz said, 'O king! although I have such share of the knowledge of the rules of an ambassador's duty as I have, yet if the king, the asylum of the world would condescend to arrange on the string of favor, some precious jewels from the casket of wisdom, I will make them the ornament of my career; and regarding them as the decoration of my character and the capital upon which I am to draw, will never seek to swerve in all I do or engage in from that canon; and will carry out to the end, my transactions in accordance with that rule of procedure.' The King said, 'O Bihrúz! the best direction to an envoy and the most useful rule for the discharge of his functions, is this, that his tongue should be employed like a keen scymitar—vigorously and sharply, but the jewel of courtesy and gentleness should be manifest and displayed on his pages; and the light of benignity and politeness evident and conspicuous on all sides of him. Every speech from the exordium of which roughness is apparent, must be terminated at its close [1] with softness and mildness, and if, at the commencement of his discourse, he enter upon his subject spiritedly, with words inspiring terror, he should finish his harangue kindly and soothingly, with amiable expressions and a bewitching suavity.

COUPLET.

> The seeds of hate are from the breast removed by words that soothe,
> And gentle tongues can all the folds of frowning eyebrows smooth.

In short the words of an envoy should be based on the rule of courtesy and rigor, of anger and mildness, of love and violence, of equity and opposition; and he ought to observe the path of binding and loosing, of taking and giving, of rending and binding up, of making and burning,[2] so that he may have a due regard to the honor of his king and the glory of his prince, and at the same time may discover the intention of his foes and their hidden mind. And the essence of all directions on the subject of an ambassador-ship is contained in this,

---

[1] The *maṭl'a* is the beginning of a poem, the *makṭ'a* is the cæsura or pause in reading verses.

[2] These words seem meaningless enough in English, and in Persian are only recommended by alliteration and similarity of sound.

Send one that's wise, nor him with rules restrict.'

Then Bihrúz made his obeisance and came forth from the court of the king and tarried until Night, clothed in sable garb, drew down the curtain of darkness before the palace of the blue sky; and after a time the table-decker of omnipotence publicly displayed the silver salver of the moon on the table of heaven.

COUPLET.

When Eve her musky ringlets did untie,
The moon moved proudly o'er the terraced sky.

At the time when the centre of the moon had nearly reached the circle of the mid-sky and the beams of the lesser luminary were spread over the dusty surface of the earth, whose surface was illuminated by the world-adorning beauty of that taper of the cell of the destitute; Bihrúz set off for the isle of elephants, and having reached their abode, reflected, ' In the vicinity of these oppressors, there is risk of losing my life, and danger of destruction; and, even though they should not assail me, yet foresight demands that one should not encounter the terrible and the oppressive; since they, from their excessive haughtiness and pride, care not for the poor and broken, and if a thousand helpless ones perish beneath the tramp of their power, the dust of that trampling would not reach the countenance of their pride.

COUPLET.

For our lorn state what cares the tranquil sky![1]
What cares the morning, though the taper die!

The advisable course is for me to ascend an eminence, and deliver the message I have in charge, from a distance. If it be accepted, then my object is gained, and if my stratagem succeed not with them, at least I shall escape with life.' He then ascended a height and called out to the king of the elephants, saying, ' I am the envoy of the moon, and no fault attaches to a messenger whatever he may say or hear, *'And the delivery of his message is all that is incumbent on one sent,'*[2] and although a speech may appear disrespectful and rough, it should nevertheless receive a hearing; for whatever message the moon has given, I cannot use my own discretion either in enlarging or contracting it. And thou knowest that the world-traversing moon presides over the bázár of the night, and is the deputy of the lord of day, and if any one imagine ought against him, and listen

---

[1] *Turd chih dárad* is bad grammar, and, even in Persian, bad grammar is inadmissible. I was much pleased, therefore to find in a MS. I have recently purchased, *falak chih dárad,* for which the reading of the editions ought to make way.

[2] Kur'án, xxix. 17; Sale, p. 298, l. 24 : ' If ye charge me with imposture, verily sundry nations before you likewise charged their prophets with imposture : but public preaching only is incumbent on an apostle.' This sentence occurs in several other passages of the Kur'án, *e.g.* at ch. xxiv. 53. It will be seen that I have rendered the sentence more literally than Sale, as the context here requires, and as *al-mubin* is omitted in the present quotation.

not to his message with the ear of attention, he will have struck an axe
against his own foot, and striven with his own hand for his own destruction.'
The king of the elephants was startled at this address, and asked, ' What
is the purport of thy embassy ?'   Bihrúz replied, ' The moon says,
' Whoever sees himself superior to the weak in power and majesty, and
becomes inflated by his own might, and spirit, and strength, and prowess, and
desires cruelly and tyrannically to overthrow the feeble, this circumstance
betokens his own fall, and these feelings plunge him into the whirlpool of
destruction.

VERSE.

Sow not the seeds of pride within thy breast,
Nor suffer malice in thy heart to rest.
How long wilt saddle fury's steed ? for know
If thou spurr'st on, he'll not continue so.
Soon o'er thy head these troublous waves will rise,
And heaven's shaft pierce thy buckler from the skies.
In other scenes must end this course of pride,
And thy powers fail thy onward steps to guide.

And from this haughtiness, through which thou regardest thyself as excelling
other animals, and valuest thyself on thy strength and terribleness, both
of which are on the point of waning, things have come to this pass, and affairs
have reached this climax, that thou hast invaded ·my fountain and marched
thy army to that spot, and, from excess of blind hostility, hast troubled that
water ! What ! dost thou not know that if the swift-winged eagle fly over
my fountain, the lightning of my wrath consumes her offending pinions ; and
if the eye of Taurus,[1] from the meadow of the sky, look thereon with the
glance of appropriation, Arcturus, with his terrible javelin, will transfix that
eye.[2]

VERSE.

A demon coming there must bow his head,
  A bird that flies there too must droop his wing.
Nor e'en the sky, save by some guidance led,
  Could from that air, those confines, itself bring.

And I, from excess of compassion, have thought fit to warn thee by this
embassy. If thou followest up thine own interests and repentest of this
temerity, it is well ! Else I will come in my own person and will slay thee
terribly, and if thou doubtest of this message, come this moment and I will
present myself in the fountain that thou mayest see me with thine own eyes,

---

[1] Name of a very brilliant star.

[2] ' Simdka'r-rámiḥ' and ' simáku'l-'dzal' are the names of two stars called also ' the feet of
the lion.' The former (' simdka'r-rámiḥ') is Arcturus, the latter (' simáku-l-'dzal') is Spica
Virginis; simák means 'fish,' rámiḥ means 'armed with a spear,' and 'dzal' signifies 'unarmed.'
Thus the name of Arcturus would be ' The spear-armed fish.' In speaking of the fountain
(chashmah), therefore, there is that kind of equivoque in the name of Arcturus (viz., ' the
spear-armed fish') which is so pleasing to Persian taste.

and henceforward forbear to dwell near this spring.' The king of the elephants was astonished at this address, and having gone to the fountain, beheld the appearance of the moon in the water. Bihrúz said to him, ' O king! take up a little water, and having washed thy face, prostrate thyself. Perchance the moon, feeling commiseration, will incline favourably to thee.' The elephant stretched out its trunk, and when it struck the water and agitated it, it seemed to the elephant that the moon made a movement. Hereupon the elephant called out, ' O envoy of the Moon! it was, perhaps, because of my putting my trunk in the water that the moon moved.' Bihrúz exclaimed, ' Heavens! on thy knees with speed! that he may be tranquilized.' The elephant bent down and did homage, and promised that henceforward he would not come there, nor bring the elephants to the neighborhood of that fountain. Bihrúz conveyed this news to his king, and the hares reposed in peace; and by that stratagem he averted from them so terrible a calamity.

And I have used this story to show that a clever person is required among you to be your leader, in meeting emergencies and in exerting himself for the repulse of foes. And if at this time a clever and intelligent person had been consulted by you, he would never have suffered the title of king to be inscribed on the name of the owl, and would have put you on your guard against bringing on yourselves the disastrous disgrace of his leadership, for together with the numerous bad qualities that he has, fraud and artifice and deceit and craft are also bound up with his disposition. And there is no fault in kings so great as perfidy and bad faith and trickery and insincerity.

VERSE.

He who to love and faith a stranger is,
Not e'en a trace of friendship can be his.
The breast which traitorous falsehood steeps in night,
There, dwells not e'en the feeblest ray of light.
Be not unfaithful, for amid mankind,
No fault like want of faith deforms the mind.

And kings are the shadow of the Creator—may His glory be magnified!— and without the sun of their justice, the world's surface is not illuminated; and save under the shadows of their beneficence and equity, mankind cannot repose in the cradle of security and peace. Nay, the pavilion of heaven is supported only by the pillar of justice; as it is said, ' *By justice stand the heavens.*'

COUPLET.

If justice measurement did not supply,
Ne'er could, uprearèd, stand the azure sky.

Since the cord of the security of mankind is bound up with the existence of a just king, and the tent-cords of heaven, without the aid of justice and

Y

beneficence, the manifestors of which are the sovereigns of the age, would be rent asunder, and since the command of kings has free course with respect to the life and property of men; and their mandate, like descending fate, pervades and penetrates in the currents of the loosing and binding of affairs; it therefore behoves a king to be faithful and not tyrannical, and to make choice of tenderness towards his subjects and not violence; and to keep the mirror of his breast untarnished by malice; and not to admit on the tablet of his heart the writing of perfidy and deceit: for those unfortunates, who are afflicted by the tyranny of a perfidious king and the cruelty of a false ruler, meet with what befell that Partridge and Quail, from the cat that fasted.' The birds asked, ' How was that?'

STORY V.

The Crow said, ' I had my nest on a tree in the skirt of a mountain, and in my neighborhood there was a Partridge.   In consequence of our proximity, the feelings of friendship between us were strengthened to the utmost, and from constantly seeing him I had become familiar with him, and at our leisure-seasons a conversation would spring up between us.   All of a sudden he disappeared, and the time of his absence was protracted, so that I began to suspect he had perished, and after a long interval a Quail came and took up his residence in the Partridge's abode.   Since, however, I was uncertain as to the fate of the Partridge, I did not quarrel with the Quail for what he did; and I said,

HEMISTICH.
' One goes and straight another fills his place.'

Some time elapsed after this circumstance, and the circling heavens made several revolutions, when the Partridge returned, and seeing another in his abode, began to quarrel, saying, ' Give up my place and vacate my lodging.' The Quail replied, ' The house is now in my occupancy and I am the possessor; if thou hast the right to it, thou must exert thyself to prove it.' The Partridge replied, ' Thy possession is by violence and usurpation, and I hold proofs and documents as to this matter.'   In short, a downright quarrel arose between them, and the fire of mischief blazed higher every instant, and the flag of obstinacy and strife was each moment held more aloft; and however much I tried, by artifice, to reconcile them, it was all in vain, and it was decided that reference should be made to the judge, that he might hear what both parties had to say, and having issued his commands as justice should require, might terminate their dispute.   The Partridge said, ' Hard by there is a cat, pious and abstemious, devout and uninjurious.   Always during the day he fasts, and passes the night-hours in devotion; and from the time when they beat the kettle-drum of the golden-throned Jamshíd of the

sun, in the vestibule of the palace, '*The heaven we have built*,[1] till the time
when they spread the carpet of the sable-vested sovereign of the night in the
expanse, '*And we have stretched forth the earth*,'[1] he melts his precious soul
into the crucible of abstemiousness with the fire of hunger. And from the
hour when the calvacade of the stars and the host of the fixed stars come
rushing into the plain of the sky; and the period when the chamberlains of
omnipotence, with the candle of the world-beautifying dawn which gleams
from the ascending-place of the horizon, display to the inhabitants of the regions
of the earth the tokens of the outposts of the sun, (which warns the world that
this ascetical cat stands taper-like on the foot of devotion and melting with the
heat of religious fervor and the blaze of heavenly love, showers down tears,

VERSE.

His tears wash out all creature-sympathies,
And in want's cell he seeks a heavenly prize;
On both worlds turns his heel, does all disown,
Strange to himself and bound to God alone.)

the breaking of his fast is limited to water and herbs, and the injuring any
living thing and spilling its blood is far removed from his habits. No kází
can be more just than he, nor can we secure any better arbiter to give a
rightful decision between us. Let us go to him, that he may settle our case.'
Both parties consented, and proceeded to the house of the judge. I, too,
following their footsteps, set out—being desirous of seeing this fast-keeping
cat, (which, thought I, is surely one of the wonders of the world), and of
observing his justice in deciding between the litigants. No sooner did that
perpetual faster set eyes on them, than he stood upon his right foot and
turned his face towards the sanctuary, and assuming the air of a pilgrim
engaged in the performance of the ceremonies of devotion, entered upon
a prayer of prodigious length, and with the most intense deliberation
persevered in making genuflexions with the most scrupulous exactness.

VERSE.

The key of hell's gate is that prayer, I trow,
Which thou protractest in the gaze of men:
Since none is worse, more vile within, than thou,
Why honor's gilding for thy outside then?

The Quail was astonished at his demeanor, and the Partridge seriously
contemplated his proceedings. They waited till he had finished his prayer,
and having humbly offered their respectful salutation, requested that he
would be judge between them, and settle their lawsuit about the house,

---

[1] Ḳur'án, li., 47; Sale, p. 385, l. 9: 'We have built the heaven with might: and we
have given it a large extent: and we have stretched forth the earth beneath; and how
evenly have we spread the same!'

according to the decrees of justice. The cat, after they had importuned him
and pressed him excessively, bade them state their case. The Partridge and
Quail then represented the circumstances. 'Young people,' quoth the Cat,
' old age has made a great change in me, and my external senses have suffered
a complete decline. The revolution of the mill-stone of the circling heavens has
sprinkled the dust of decrepitude upon my head, and the wintry hand of the
cruel autumn of life has taken away the moisture of freshness and vigor
from the plant of the garden of existence; and the night [1] of youth, which is
the cause of all strength and energy, has been exchanged for the morning of
hoary age, which is an accumulation of all defects.

VERSE.

Alas! youth's season has gone by; and set,
 For aye, life's joyous sun. Thou knowest how
Hopes, lessening, fade; and still augments regret;
 And all my buoyancy has left me now.

Come nearer and speak louder, and tell me your pretensions again, in order
that I may become acquainted with the claim of the plaintiff and the reply of
the defendant, and may be able to pass sentence, and before I proceed to do
so, I may favor you with some friendly advice, and may deliver some
admonition comprising your welfare in the things of faith and of this world.

COUPLET.

If my advice to-day in vain is spent,
God grant to-morrow thou may'st not repent!

If you will listen to my words with the ear of the heart, and bring them into
the place of acceptance, you will reap the fruits thereof, both in this world
and in that which is to come; and if you are refractory and violate its tenor,
at least, I am absolved as regards my own conscience and honor.

COUPLET.

I will perform the adviser's duty: what   Remains is thy concern, to do or not.

The best thing is, that both of you should seek the path of right and not
choose to swerve from the way of uprightness, nor be deluded by the wealth
and effects of the world, which incline towards the place of annihilation and
decay. Nor, owing to the acquisition of some trifle from the rubbish of this
transitory world by wrong appropriation, deprive yourselves of the final
reward and enduring bliss.' The Partridge said, 'O righteous judge! if men
restricted their endeavors to the pursuit of what is right, and if every one
made the quality of conscientiousness and uprightness his habit, there would
be no need of tribunals nor of troubling judges, and the custom of plea and

---

[1] Youth is here compared to night, and old age to dawn, on account of the black locks of
the young and the silver hair of the old. Otherwise, surely youth more resembles morning,
and old age the declining day.

rejoinder, and of swearing and giving evidence, would be erased from the surface of the book of Time. But when the eyes of each of the two—plaintiff and defendant—is afflicted with the ophthalmia of selfish motives, truth is not visible to them, and, consequently they stand in need of some one whose eyes are brightened with the jeweled collyrium of truth, and around the mirror of whose vision the dust of self-interest has not settled; in order that he may display to them the loveliness of what is right, and bring it beautifully forth to the eye of their heart; and this very subject has been elucidated in a metrical story by one of the eminent persons in the faith.' The cat asked, 'How was that?'

STORY VI.

The Partridge said,

DISTICHS.

'Two parties chose a judge, who shed
Tears on election. 'Wherefore,' said
One, 'these tears? 'tis rather fit,
Since thou art judge, to joy at it.'
'Alas!' quoth he, 'can I, untaught,
Decide where both know all, I, nought?
Those two that strive, in all instructed stand,
While the poor judge sees nought of either hand.
Thus, uninformed and blind to either state,
Could he proceed to slay and confiscate?'
'True! thou art blind,' the litigant replies,
'Thou uninstructed, and the parties wise,
Yet faith to thee the needful light supplies,[1]
In that thou hast no bias: this
The strengthening of thy vision is.
While selfish ends, those wiser twain
Blind, and inter their wits again.
Merit is hid where interest assails,
And o'er the vision casts a hundred veils.
Art thou unbribed, thy sight remains;
But greed brings slavery and chains.
The judge whom justice once has dared to sell,
Ne'er can the tyrant from his victim tell.'

And, thanks be to God! the rust of interest has not darkened the mirror of thy pure heart, and the eye of thy conscience has not been dimmed by the rays of the fire of bribery; and for this reason it is thoroughly certain that thou wilt exhibit to our sight what is right, and wilt appoint the minister of punishment to act against him who draws back his neck from the law.

---

[1] The literal translation of this feeble and obscure line is, 'Ignorant art thou, but the light of the religious party.'

Who from thy will draws braws back his neck, behead!'

The cat said, 'Thou hast spoken well, and truth demands that you both should pluck up the plant of interest from the ground of your heart, and know that he who has right on his side is in truth victor, though his claim be not to outward experience gained; while the wrongful appellant is spiritually baffled and defeated, though practically a decree be passed in accordance with his wish; for ' *Verily falsehood is of short continuance.*'[1] And how well it has been said,

If thou to-day thy reins too much dost loose,
How shalt thou break to-morrow from my noose?[2]

And I say to you, Store up good actions as a treasure for the final state, and trust not in life, which is like a summer cloud; and, like, the rose-garden's bloom, swiftly fleets away; and regarding mankind both high and low, far and near, as your own soul, suffer not yourselves to do anything to them that ye would not like for yourselves.

Do not to others what would grieve thyself.'

In this manner he breathed his spells upon them, until they became friendly with him, and advanced securely and unconcerned, without shunning him or putting themselves on their guard. Then with one spring he seized them both and supplied the kitchen of his stomach with the food of their delicious flesh; and such was the upshot of all his show of prayers and fasting and advice and abstinence, that is to say, it all ended in the gratification of his own foul appetites and impure passions.

And I have adduced this story in order that it may be known that one ought not to place confidence in an unprincipled and perfidious person. And the conduct of the deceitful and hypocritical owl bears this complexion, and his faults are infinite, and his vices innumerable, and this portion, which I have repeated, is but a drop from a boundless ocean, and a mere atom in comparison with the nine revolving heavens.

Did I my voice a million decades raise,   Of hundred thousands I but one could praise.[3]

---

[1] Ḳur'án, Fl. xvii. 83, Mar. 82; Sale, p. 216, l. 16: 'And say, O Lord! cause me to enter with a favorable entry; and cause me to come forth with a favourable coming forth; and grant me from Thee an assisting power. And say, truth is come, and falsehood is vanished: for falsehood is of short continuance.' Sale's note on this passage is, 'These words Muhammad repeated when he entered the temple of Mecca, after the taking of that city, and cleansed it of the idols.'

[2] That is: 'If thou weariest thy steed to-day, how shalt thou escape my lasso to-morrow?'

[3] My best MS. reads *sál* for *ḳarn.* As the reading stands in the edition the literal rendering is, 'If I should praise for a hundred thousand centuries, without doubt, of a hundred thousand, only one would be mentioned.'

And God forbid! that you should choose to act thus, and place him on the throne of sovereignty : for as soon as the royal diadem rests on his ill-omened head, without doubt the stubborn heavens will smite it with the stone of calamity, and whenever the throne-step of dominion is pressed by his inauspicious foot, the etherial vault will wrathfully rain down the fire of disaster upon it; and inasmuch as his nature is impure and his essence imperfect, the effect of your encouragement of him will be lost.

COUPLET.

Our favor should to natures pure be shewn,
Pearls, coral, spring not from the clod or stone.'

After hearing these words, the birds at once desisted from the affair, and abandoned their intention of becoming the subjects of the owl; and that unhappy wretch, remaining stupified and sad in the corner of dejection, said to the Crow, 'O black-faced, impudent one! after removing from before thyself the curtain of modesty, thou hast indulged in these insults against me, and by hurting my feelings, hast brought me to harbor resentment and hostility, and raised a dust of terror that the revolution of Time will not be able to remove in a hundred thousand centuries, and hast kindled a fire of mischief whose fire cannot be quenched with the water surrounding the heaven!

HEMISTICH.

My heart may die, but ne'er will fade the impress of thy wrong.

I know not whether the first advances came from my side, that thou hast displayed all this affection and friendship; or whether thou hast thought fit to come forward by way of commencement with so much courtesy and kindness! Learn, however, that if they fell a tree, a branch will spring from its root, and, increasing in vegetation, it will return to its former state; but when the plant of friendship has been severed by the saw of ill-treatment, the springing up of the shoot of sincere regard is altogether out of the question; and if a wound be inflicted with a sword, it may be healed, and admits of cure with a plaster, but the wound which words inflict can never be cured, and the gash they make no ointment can salve.

HEMISTICH.

That which the tongue has wounded, never heals.

STANZA.

The wound the tongue inflicts upon the heart,
No soothing ointment ever can close up.
And thou, and they who from thy sarcasms smart,
Will be such comrades as the stone and cup.

It is possible to extract the point of an arrow which is fixed in the breast, but the shaft which the tongue infixes in the heart can never be drawn out.

HEMISTICH.

The shaft *that* launches at the heart —its point no skill can e'er extract.

And everything from which injury can be anticipated finds an antidote in something else, except malice, which cannot be obviated by anything. For example fire,—which, though it burns, may be quenched with water; but the flame of rancor cannot be extinguished with the water of the seven seas. Poison, too, though deadly, may have its injurious effects removed from the body by theriaca; but no such antidote can expel the poison of malice from the heart. And from this time forth between my race and thine a tree of enmity has been planted, whose root reaches to the bottom of the earth, and whose boughs stretch out beyond the height of the Pleiades.

STANZA.

When in the breast the plant of malice lies,
'Tis clear and certain what the fruit will be.
And rancor's tree such produce still supplies,
Its flavor will with no one's taste agree.'

The Owl having uttered this speech, departed vexed and distressed; and the Crow, repenting what he had said, fell into a long train of thought, and said to himself, ' It is a strange thing that I have entered upon, and stirred up against my tribe fierce enemies and cruel foes. What had I to do with advising the birds? and it did not become me to deliver these sentiments more than other parties, who are greater and stronger than I am. Surely these sagacious birds knew the faults of the owl better than I, and better understood what measures were advisable in this matter; but they wisely dreaded the termination of this matter and the issue of this debate; and acted in accordance with the purport of the saying, ' *He who holds his peace is safe.*' The tongue has been created in the shape of a sword that men may not use it in play; and sword-play is the practice of merry-andrews, while men of the sword exercise that weapon only in the ranks of war. Without absolute necessity, to bare the sword of the tongue from the sheath of the palate, is the same thing as cutting one's throat and risking one's life.

VERSE.

When once the tongue adopts loquacity,
What marvel that the soul from fear should shake !
Since tongues were formed a deadly trade to ply,
'Twas right them in the shape of swords to make.

And worse than that,—these words were spoken in the owl's very presence; and, doubtless, this increased his fury and resentment, and the hearing[1] abusive words piles wrath on wrath. And they have said that a wise man, though he have perfect confidence in his own strength and might, must not allow himself to make belligerent advances, and to commence a quarrel; but, rely on his own preparations and majesty, and not stir up strife. For,

---

[1] That is, ' *in propriâ personâ.*'

whosoever has a tried antidote, and a variety of drugs collected in his possession, ought not, trusting therein, to volunteer to drink deadly poison.

COUPLET.

What though thou hast an antidote! yet this   No reason to drink deadly poison is.

And sages agree that the effect of deeds is preferable to that of words, and that acting is proved to excel speaking; and the effect of a good action is apparent in the issue of things, and associates the termination of matters with good. But he whose words preponderate over his deeds, and who employs himself in rhetorically setting off to advantage what ought to be done, and embellishes it in men's eyes with fine talking and eloquence, the end of his proceedings will, in a short time, be disgrace and reproach. And the end of words without deeds can be nothing but regret and remorse. And I am that great talker and little doer that did not use salutary reflection as to consequences, nor deliberate sufficiently. And had the crown of prudence adorned the head of my affairs, and had I had a portion from the boundless treasures of wisdom, I should first have consulted some one; and after deciding as to what was to be said, I should have uttered a discourse innocent and unblameable, and in which there could have been nothing mischievous.

COUPLET.

The words I spoke, in truth, were too unweighed,
I pierced a pearl I should not have assayed.

Since, however, I entered upon this subject without the direction of prudent advisers and the counsel of the perfectly sagacious, and uttered some words impromptu which caused disturbance and excited enmity, what wonder that I have been reckoned among the number of the depraved; and that fatuity, ignorance, and absurdity have been imputed to me? And it has become proverbial, that '*the babbler is a dotard*,' in other words, that the great talker is also a foolish talker; and although, in externals, the power of speech is that which discriminates between men and brutes, still sages account the utterer of evil words as below brutes in rank, and regard the dumb as better than those who speak foolishly.

VERSE.

Dumb are the brutes, and man has power to speak;[1]
    Yet the tongue-tied, those who speak ill, excel.
Let men to utter words of prudence seek,
    Or, are they brutish? be they dumb as well.
Shun then the fools, who for ten mortals prate;
Thou, to speak wisely, first excogitate.'

---

[1] There is a clever equivoque in the original here which cannot be preserved in English; *gúyd bashar* is 'man has the power of speech,' and the next line, *gúyd basharr*, is 'speaking wickedly.'

In short, the Crow vexed himself for a time,[1] and gave vent to self-accusations, such as these and then flew away. Such was the commencement of the feud between us and the owls, which I have recounted.'

The King said, ' O Kárshinás ! I have heard thy words, and they contain much that is valuable ; and to associate with the wise, and to make their words the guide of our actions and procedure is a presage of good fortune and success, and a token of arriving at perfection.

STANZA.

Like musk is sweet communion with the wise ;
  It, with a perfume rare, the brain affects.
Each act a hint in wisdom's path supplies,
  And every word to useful ends directs.

And now, after that the dwelling of my heart has been illuminated by the lamp of luminous language, which alone can be the taper of the cells of the recluses of the monasteries of friendship; explain in what way thou hast devised a remedy for the state of our soldiers, who, like moths, are consumed by the fire of the violence of the owls; and what counsel thou hast taken for removing the apprehensions of my subjects and tranquilizing the hearts of the soldiery ?

COUPLET.

The thing, where thou dost use thy subtilty,
Is, from a hundred knots, at once set free.'

Kárshinás unloosed the tongue of gratitude, and said,

COUPLET.

' O King ! may earth obey thee, heaven befriend !
And swift-borne[2] victory in thy van attend !

As to what thy vazírs of luminous mind laid before thee in their statements, with respect to war and peace, and abiding and flight, and submitting to tax and tribute ; my mind is satisfied with none of their proposals; and my hope is that, by some kind of stratagem, we shall obtain success and deliverance; for many persons have gained their wish by the practice of artifice and humble bearing ; and have effected, by stratagem and deceit, what they could not have brought about by war and measures of that kind, as the thieves of the country of Gurgán[3] got by artifice, a sheep from the hands of a holy man.' The King asked, ' How was that ? '

---

[1] I prefer the reading *bárah-i*, 'for a time,' which I find in one MS. to that of the editions *párah-i*, of which I cannot make any sense.

[2] Lit. ' having two steeds.'

[3] I know nothing of this country. As *gurgán* signifies ' wolves,' and the story is about stealing a sheep it is, probably, a name given merely on that account.

STORY VII.

He said, 'They have related that an abstemious devotee purchased a fat sheep[1] for sacrifice, and having tied a string round its neck, was leading it towards his hermitage. On the way a party of thieves, observing the sheep, opened the eye of covetousness, and bound the loins[2] of trickery[2] and deceit, and stood in the recluse's way. The Gurgání rogues felt their hungry appetites excited, but were unable to rush like tigers to clutch the prey; consequently, they had recourse to fox-like stratagem, and resolved to put the recluse in a hare's sleep.[3] After much consideration, the opinions of all were unanimously given for a particular kind of trick, and they agreed that they would, by that trick, deceive the simple-minded and innocent devotee, and so get possession of the sheep. One of them then advanced to the recluse, and said, ' O shekh! whence bringest thou this dog?' And another passed by and said, ' Whither art thou taking this canine animal?' A third met him in front and exclaimed, ' O shekh! what, dost thou intend to go hunting, that thou hast got a dog in thy hand?' Another accomplice came up behind and asked, ' O shekh! for how much didst thou purchase this dog?' In the same way one after another, from every quarter and direction,—they came up to the shekh, and all agreed in saying the same words. One said, ' This is a shepherd-dog.' Another, ' This is a herdsman's dog.' Another sneeringly cried, ' And this man is in a religious garb; why does he pollute his hands and clothes with this dog?' And another rebuked him, saying, ' The holy man is leading this dog to educate him and show him honor for the sake of God.' In this manner all the rogues uttered their wily remarks and all harped on the same string.[4]

COUPLET.

His eyes they closed with their cajolings, while each a different tale repeats :
Thus of his heart the simple lover each by a different method cheats.

From the multiplication of these speeches doubt was engendered in the heart of the pious man, and he said, ' Heaven forbid that the seller of this animal was a sorcerer, and by magic made a dog appear to me like a sheep! My best course is to let this dog go, and run after the seller and get back the money which I gave him as the price of the sheep.' The unfortunate recluse then, from excessive simplicity, let go the sheep and started off after the seller, and that gang seized it and carried it off to their house, and

---

[1] Or 'goat.' In the Sanskrit original (the Hitopadesha) it is a *goat* that is purchased. But at the '*Id* it is proper that a ram should be sacrificed, since a ram was the substitute brought by Gabriel for Ishmael.

[2] Here is a play on words : *kamar* is 'loins,' and *makar* ' deceit.'

[3] That is, ' in a state of carelessness.' Hares are said to sleep with their eyes open. So the careless man is asleep, though his eyes be not shut.

[4] Lit., ' In the same arrangement uttered a letter.'

without loss of time, forthwith slaughtered it. Thus, by means of that trick, the poor recluse lost the sheep and did not recover his money.

And I have brought forward this story, to show that we, too, should employ stratagem, since it is only by deceit and artifice that we can get the better of them.

STANZA.

> When thou canst not in prowess match thy foe,
>   Do not aside, then, craft and shrewdness fling:
> For if too strong for thee the mighty bow,
>   Thou mayest at least, by cunning, snap the string.'

King Pírúz said, 'Bring forward what thou hast to suggest.' Kárshínás replied, 'I will devote myself to this enterprise. And they have decided that the destruction of one individual, which secures the existence and survival of a large number, is in accordance with reason and precept.[1] I think it advisable that the king, in the general assembly and meeting in which both high and low are convened, should be wroth with me and command them to pluck out my feathers and to cast me, smeared with blood and wounded, beneath that same tree, on the boughs of which are our nests. And let the king go with his whole army and encamp in such a place, and await my coming, in order that I may spread the net of deceit in their way, and having arranged my stratagem, may come and unfold whatever the crisis may require to be done.' The king then issued from his cabinet, filled with wrath, and all his courtiers were in expectation as to what announcement would proceed from the private consultation of the king and the vazír, and to what initiatory measures their counsel and deliberation would give rise. When they found the king wrathful, they hung down their heads and pondered; and king Pírúz commanded that they should pluck out the feathers and tail of Kárshínás, and stain his head and feet with blood, and cast him underneath the tree. And the king himself with his army and retinue, set off for the place which had been appointed and agreed upon. By the time these things were done, the sun had set and the tire-woman of omnipotence had brought forward and displayed the brides of the stars upon the platform of the gem-ornamented heavens.

COUPLET.

> When the bright sun had vanished from the eye,
>   Dark night her squadrons marshaled in the sky.

Shabáhang, the king of the owls, was all day consulting with his vazírs to the effect that, 'Since we have become acquainted with the crows' abode, and have wounded and overthrown many of them, if this night another night-attack be made upon them, the day of their existence will be exchanged for the evening of death, and we shall pass two or three days in the corner of our cots in peace.

---

[1] *Nakl* is here used for its similarity of sound to *'akl.* It means 'tradition.'

When foes are dead, one can live sweetly then.

But when night, which is the day of the market of the power and might of the owls, had robed itself with the garment of darkness and the apparel of sable hue, and had gained possession of the throne of dominion over the world, and the leader of the hosts of Zanzabár,[1] set up his black banner with the purpose of making an onslaught, by night, on the horsemen and tribe of the Tátárs,

COUPLET.

An amber[2] mist was o'er earth's surface spread,
And all Heaven's cells with smoke were tenanted,

the king of the owls, with all his troops and followers, put to the vote the matter of the night-attack, and, as the assembly were unanimous for it, they marched towards the abode of the crows.

VERSE.

A conflict-seeking, mischief-stirring band,
All cruel, fearless, and athirst for blood;
Girding the loins of malice, fierce they stand,
And turn their hearts to stone in martial mood.

And when the army of the owls reached the abode of the crows, there was no trace to be found, nor intelligence got of them. The owls moved about in all directions in perplexity, and Kárshinás writhed beneath the tree, and uttered faint groans. An owl, hearing his voice, informed the king, and Shabáhang, with some owls who were his favorite courtiers, and the confidants of the secrets of the king, came to where he lay, and asked, 'Who art thou? and what has befallen thee?' Kárshinás declared his name, and that of his father,[3] and announced his office as vazír, and the nature of his abilities. The King said, 'I know and have often heard accounts of thee. Now inform us where the crows are?' He replied, 'My state is a proof that I cannot possibly be in their secrets.' Shabáhang demanded, 'Since thou wast the vazír of the king of the crows, and master of his secrets, and consulted and confided in by him, through what perfidy has this disgrace been inflicted on thee? and by what crime hast thou deserved this punishment?' Kárshinás replied, 'My master became suspicious of me, and the envious found an opportunity of slandering me, until that happened to me which has happened; and my former services and previous devotion passed all at once into the expanse of annihilation.

---

[1] That is, Zanzibar in Africa. Darkness is here compared to the sable sons of Abyssinia, and the day to the fair-faced Tátárs.

[2] Night is compared to ambergris as being of an ash colour. Amber, on the contrary, is yellow and semi-pellucid.

[3] Observe the idiom, *az án-i pidar*.

For all my service, no reward, no thanks, were given to me,
O God! may never one beneath a thankless master be!'

Shabáhang inquired, 'What was the cause of the king's suspicion?' He answered, 'King Píruz, after your night-attack, summoned his ministers and demanded counsel of each one of them as to this event which had happened, and the turn came to me. He said, 'Point out a remedy for these circumstances which have happened, and devise some stratagem for averting this misfortune.' I replied, 'We have not strength to encounter the owls, for their valor in war exceeds that of ourselves, and their might and terribleness is greater than our prowess and the awe which we inspire. Moreover the reins of the steed of fortune are in the hands of the will of the owl-king, and the step of the throne of success is adorned with the star-reaching foot of their monarch, and to grapple in war with the possessor of happy auspices betokens disaster; and to boast of encountering the lord of prosperity which daily augments, forebodes an approaching downfall.

VERSE.

He who would battle to the prosperous give,
    Strikes his own head off, as one fells a tree.
Elks that would in the haunt of lions live,
    Will in their homes soon make a vacancy.

The advisable course is to despatch an envoy. If they light the torch of war, we must consume our houses with the flames of dispersion, and wander scattered in the corners of the world; and if they make peaceful advances, we will agree to any tax or tribute they may claim from us, and be grateful to them.

COUPLET.

Would'st keep thy head from tribute, turn not back,
Else thou wilt both thy head and crown too lack.'

Our king was troubled and said, 'What word is this that thou speakest? and how dost thou display all this boldness? Thou wouldest frighten me from making war upon the owls, and thou representest my army as of no weight compared with his followers!

VERSE.

Does the foe wish to draw the glittering steel?
    Sharp will he find the point too of my dart.
If I the burning thirst for battle feel,
    I'll wring with anguish every foeman's heart.'

I again loosed the tongue of advice and loyally and faithfully urged my remonstrances, saying, 'O king! swerve not from the right path, nor plunge inconsiderately and without reflection into an affair, led on by the passions of thine own heart. Adopt a spirit of conciliation, for a powerful enemy may be soothed by courtesy and submission, and a refractory quarry may be netted by suavity and gentleness.

COUPLET.

Fair words ensure in either world a peaceful blest repose,
Be kind and courteous to your friends and humble to your foes.[1]

And in accordance with this sentiment is the operation of a furious wind, from which the feeble grass escapes safely on account of its humility, while the tree of many branches, on account of its roughness and obstinacy is torn up by the roots.

COUPLET.

Strive not, for heaven with stubbornness is rife,
And to the stubborn stops the road of strife.

The crows were incensed at my admonitions, and accused me of cherishing a partiality for the owls, and of deserting my own race. The king, led by the words of my enemies, turned aside from my counsel and wounded me in the manner ye behold, and I observed that their purpose was war, and in preparing a stratagem to repel you.' When the king of the owls had heard the words of Kárshinás, he asked one of his vazírs, saying, 'What thinkest thou should be done with this crow?' He replied, 'There is no occasion to think about it. We must clear the face of the earth as soon as possible from the foulness of his principles,[2] and consider it a vast pleasure and complete gain, and we must not let slip the opportunity of slaying him, viewing it as a blessing than which we shall obtain no greater; and in these half-extinct embers I see a fire whose flame it would be impossible to quench.

HEMISTICH.

God save us from this flame if it should once more gather strength.

And whoever lets slip an opportunity; after he has once lost the power, never recovers it again, and it is most probable that his regrets will be afterwards unavailing. And he who finds his enemy weak and alone, will do well to free himself of him; for if his foe escape from that peril, he will gather strength and provide means, and lie in wait for vengeance.

QUATRAIN.

If thy foe scape thee, thou art lost, be sure;
His freedom from thy chain will thee enthrall.
Would'st thou from his annoyance be secure,
Then spare him not, if in thy power he fall.

Forbid it Heaven! that the king should heed his words or listen to his soul-consuming spell, for the wise have said, ' To rely on an untried friend is far removed from a rational procedure; what confidence, then, should be placed in a deceitful and malicious enemy?

---

[1] These lines are quoted from the 3rd Ode of Háfiz, p. 34, where for *talattuf* the lithographed edition reads *muruwat*, which is preferable, if only for the alliteration.

[2] '*Akidah* does not seem to give a very good sense here. I should prefer '*akirah* ' wounded, maimed person,' did the MSS. allow it.

COUPLET.

Since e'en on friends we cannot here depend,
To a foe's words what credit can we lend!'

Kárshinás having overheard somewhat of this discourse, wept sadly, and
exclaimed,

COUPLET.

'My heart e'en now is sad and wounded sore,
Then on my wound make not one puncture more.'

These words made an impression on the heart of the owl-king, and he
turned away his face from that vazír and demanded of another, 'What sayest
thou?' He replied, 'I cannot give my sentence for his execution, for a
magnanimous man, when he finds his enemy weak and helpless, ought
mercifully to alleviate his distress, and display to mankind his own virtues
by the manifestation of pardon and beneficence; and quarter ought to be
shown to a panic-stricken suppliant, and the hand reached out to a miserable
and fallen being.

COUPLET.

No barrier to the good man's path oppose,
And, if thou standest, raise thy fallen foes.

And there are certain things which soften a man towards his enemy, as the
fear of the thief made the Merchant's Wife kind to her husband.' The king
inquired, 'How was that?'

STORY VIII.

He said, 'They have related that there was a merchant who was rich,
but very bad-tempered and ill-favored, and withal old and infirm, and
stingy and morose.

VERSE.

A hellish demon he in ugliness;
And, like a jackdaw,[1] senseless in his prate.
His heart was stony, steeled; and, with distress
Like loss of friends, all hearts did macerate.

And this man of repulsive appearance had a wife of pure manners and
pleasing form, such that the moon of the fourteenth night, by the help of
borrowing the glow of her cheek, could make the dark night brighter than
the shining day; and the world-illuminating lamp of the sun, which is the
candle before the portico of the sky, could not have competed with the
radiance of the taper of her heart-delighting countenance. The tongue of the
age, in praise of that life of the world, warbled these words,

---

[1] I am ignorant of what is intended by the *zágh-i gulkhan,* 'the crow of the stove,' unless
it be a tame crow or jackdaw kept near the fireside; or some noisy apparatus so called.

COUPLET.

Fair is the moon, but yet more fair the beauty of thy face ;
Graceful the cypress, but thy form displays a loftier grace.

And the jewel-scattering pen was inscribing on the pages of description a
particle of her fascinations in this manner,

STANZA.

Fancy might try, in vain, to paint upon the page of thought
Thy image ; for thy winning form with lovelier grace is fraught.
Each charm, which from our ken was hid, in unseen worlds concealed,
Here, gathered in thy lovely self, is to our eyes revealed.

Her husband, with a hundred thousand efforts,[1] sought her favor, and she
was flying from his approaches to a hundred thousand removes, and was not
to be won by his coaxings, nor deceived by his cajolings. And, at every
fresh instance of her cruelty, the man felt his attachment renewed, and every
moment he evinced an accession of love in return for her dislike.

HEMISTICH.

Thy spite is needed to renew my love.

The hand of his desire did not reach the lasso of her locks without sore
fatigue, nor did the flower of his wish bloom in the rose-garden of her beauty
without the thorn-prickings of trouble.

COUPLET.

I am that beauty's slave, which they refuse to let me see;
Those ringlets craze my sense whose touch they ne'er vouchsafe to me.

One night a thief came to the house. It happened that the merchant was
asleep, and the wife being awake, observed the entrance of the thief.
Alarmed at this, she clasped her husband tightly to her breast ; and the
merchant, awaking from his slumbers, found his treasure in his arms, and,
from excessive joy, uttered a shout, saying,

COUPLET.

'Surely my fortune smiles, that thus before my waking eye,
That face I see, that e'en in sleep I hoped not to espy.

What compassion is this which has been shewn me from the unseen world ?
and by what service have I deserved this boon ?

HEMISTICH.

Whence has this love, thou knew'st not, sprung ?'

On looking well about him he perceived the thief, and exclaimed, 'O my
brave fellow of auspicious footstep ! take what thou wilt of my goods, and
carry it away ; for, through the blessing of thy arrival, this cruel, faithless
one has become kind and tender to me.'

And the moral of this fable is, that there are some emergencies, the sight
of which renders nought proper save forgiveness and kindness to our enemy ;
and the condition of this crow is of the number.

---

[1] Lit., 'with a hundred thousand hearts.'

z

Have pity when thou see'st my state, for pity is deserved there.'

The King asked the third vazír, saying, 'What does thy judgment pronounce in this case?' He replied, 'It is best that the king should not strip him of the garment of existence, but rather invest him with the robe of security, and not withhold from him the tokens of encouragement and benevolence, that he, too, in return may look upon the king's service as a rich prize, and open the gates of sincere counsel and loyalty. Moreover, the wise have always labored to detach a party from their enemies; and having thrown the stone of discord among them, by every artifice they can think of, separate them into two bodies; since the disputing of enemies is a cause of encouragement to friends, and of assisting their operations. So the falling out of the Thief and the Demon proved the source of tranquillity to the recluse.' The king asked him, 'How was that?'

STORY IX.

He said, 'They have related that a devotee of pure disposition, abstemious and virtuous, had made his cell in one of the environs of Baghdád, and passed his morning and evening hours in the worship of the all-wise King *(May His name be magnified)*, and by these means had shaken his skirt clear from the dust of worldly affairs; and had perused, from the page of life, the description of its treachery and faithlessness, and had learned that the sweet draught of joy is unattainable without the sting of injury, and that the coin of the treasure of wealth cannot be gained without the pain of the burthen of toil.

VERSE.

Ne'er in that garden blooms a thornless rose,
Nor spotless tulips there their charms unfold:
And yet thou seest sunbeams in its blows,
It gilds thy visage and thou callest it gold.[1]

He had bowed his head in the corner of contentment under the collar of freedom from care, and rested satisfied with the portion that was supplied to him from the invisible world.

COUPLET.

'Tis ours to be content and acquiesce   With our Friend's largess, be it more less.

In short, one of his sincere disciples got knowledge of the poverty and fastings of the holy man, and by way of offering, brought to the hermitage of the shekh, a she-buffalo, young and fat, with whose delicious milk the

---

[1] In these four lines are, as usual, several untranslateable equivoques. Thus, in the third line, *tigh* is 'a sword,' and also 'a sunbeam,' answering to *khúr*, 'the sun:' and *zard kunad* is 'to make yellow'; answering to *zar*, 'gold.'

palate of desire was oiled and sweetened. A thief beheld the circumstance, and his hungry appetite was excited; and he set off for the cell of the recluse. A demon, too, joined him in the likeness of a man. The thief asked him, 'Who art thou, and whither goest thou?' He replied, 'I am a demon, who have assumed this shape, and, putting on this guise, am going to the hermitage of the recluse; for many of the people of this country, through the blessing of his instruction, have began to repent and to be converted, and the market of our temptations has become flat. I wish to get an opportunity and kill him. This is my story which thou hast heard: now tell me, who art thou and what is thy story?' The thief replied, 'I am a man whose trade is roguery, and I am occupied night and day with thinking how to steal some one's goods and impose the scar of affliction on his heart. I am now going, as the recluse has got a fat buffalo, to steal it and use it for my own wants.' The demon said,

HEMISTICH.

'Life of the world! my bosom friend art thou.

Praise be to God! that the bond of homogeneousness is strong between us; and this alone is sufficient to ally us, since the object of both is to assail him.' They then proceeded on their way, and at night reached the cell of the recluse. The latter had finished the performance of his daily worship, and had gone to sleep, just as he was, on his prayer-carpet. The thief bethought himself, that if the demon attempted to kill him he would probably awake and make an outcry; and the other people who were his neighbors, would be alarmed, and in that case it would be impossible to steal the buffalo. The demon, too, reflected that if the thief carried off the buffalo [1] from the house, he must of course open the door. Then the noise of the door would very likely awaken the recluse, and he should have to postpone killing him. He then said to the thief, 'Do thou wait and give me time to kill the hermit, and then do thou steal [2] the buffalo.' [1] The thief rejoined, 'Stop thou till I steal the buffalo, [1] and then kill the hermit.' This difference was prolonged between them, and at last the words of both came to wrangling. The thief was so annoyed that he called out to the recluse, 'There is a demon here who wants to kill thee.' The demon, too, shouted, 'Here is a thief who wants to steal thy buffalo.' [1] The hermit was roused by the uproar, and raised a cry, whereupon, the neighbors came, and both the thief and the demon ran away; and the life and

---

[1] The printed edition here should read *gdomish* for *gdo*, as is shown by what precedes, and by the reading of the best MSS.

[2] In the printed edition, for به دزد دزد we must read ببر دزد *bi-bar duzd*, as the MSS. prove. The first *duzd* is evidently a slip.

property of the holy man remained safe and secure through the quarrel of his enemies.

COUPLET.

When the two hostile armies fall to strife,
Then from its sheath what need to draw the knife?'

When the third vazír had finished speaking, the first vazír was astonished, and said, 'I see that this crow has bewitched you with his wiles and deceit. Beware that ye wake out of the sleep of supineness, and take the cotton of conceit out of the ear of vigilance, and see the necessity of pondering thoroughly on the consequences of this thing. For wise men base their actions especially in guarding against the stratagems of enemies on the rule of real advantage, and are not seduced by false speeches and inconclusive reasoning. While on the other hand the incautious, not heeding this truth, adopt a gentle behaviour on a trifling show of attachment; and, forgetting ancient grudges and hereditary feuds, are pleased to become reconciled, and are ignorant that though a foe shew himself in a thousand forms, the rust of hatred will still remain in the tablet of his heart.

COUPLET.

I said unto thy Indian tresses, 'These will plunder hearts no more,'
Years have flown, and still they practise the same arts they did before.

And still more strange is it that through ignorance a Basrah fringe[1] appears in your sight a precious work from Baghdád, and in your eyes a glass bead seems a royal gem. And your circumstances are like those of the Carpenter who was deceived by the words of his profligate wife.' The king asked, 'How was that?'

STORY X.

He said, 'They have related[2] that in the city of Sarándíp there was a Carpenter who had reached the uttermost limits of stolidity. He had a wife excessively beautiful and extremely lovely. She was a gazelle-eyed charmer who used to strike down the savage lion with her glance of coquetry, and imposed by her fox-like stratagems a hare's sleep on the knowing ones of the world.

VERSE.

A mistress heart-alluring, soul-dissolving, she;
An idol, love-rewarding, fair to view.
The hyacinth her ringlets writhed to see,
And her cheeks bathed the rose in jealous dew.

The carpenter was infatuated with her, and could never rest an instant without seeing her. The wife, compelled by necessity granted him her favors, but drank the cup of desire in the feast of pleasure with others who

---

[1] I follow a MS. in reading *tirás* for the *tardr* and *tarrdr* of the editions.
[2] This is the 7th story in the 3rd book of the Hitopadesha.

were his rivals. In the vicinity lived a youth, in stature like the cypress that grows in the garden of the living spirit, and in face like a fresh rose whose cheeks have been washed in the water of life.

COUPLET.

Not sun and moon together blending could produce that matchless cheek;
And to his beard thou mightest vainly e'en in musk a rival seek.

The fair one's eyes fell upon him, and her heart was bound to him in love and affection. Things between them proceeded from correspondence to intimacy, and from letters and messages to unintermitting enjoyment and intercourse, morning and evening. A party of envious people, with whom the very idea of the union of two lovers was wont to turn bright day into gloomy night, and whom the thought of ' Why should the lamp of converse be kindled between two persons? would consume with the fire of envy and jealousy,

COUPLET.

Wealth and rank did never make envious thoughts arise in me;
But I grudge that any lover happy with his love should be;

having got information of those circumstances, acquainted the Carpenter with them. The poor fellow, though he had not much jealousy, wished to learn the certainty of the matter, and take steps to remedy it. He said to his wife, ' Get some food ready for a journey, for I am going to a village, and though the distance is not great, nevertheless my stay there will be for some days, and I do not know how I shall endure being without thee, nor how I can bear to be melted in the crucible of separation.

COUPLET.

Thou, from whom this cruel parting is unwished, abhorred by me;
Who of his free choice would suffer a removal far from thee?

The wife too simulated affection, and, weeping for joy, let fall some tears from her eyes; and forthwith prepared the provisions, and dismissed her husband. The Carpenter as he was going gave her many injunctions, saying, ' Thou must securely fasten the door, and take good care of the household stuffs, that during my absence thieves may not find an opportunity, and we suffer loss in our property and goods. The wife received these instructions with good will, and swore to observe them, and directly her spouse was gone, sent to tell her lover.

HEMISTICH.

' Come into my garden for the rose is blooming, and no thorn is left.'

Her paramour promised, saying, ' As soon as a watch of the night passes, expect the rising of the morn of union.' The fair one, rejoicing at that promise, made preparations to entertain him.

COUPLET.

Gramercy! happy fortune! if that lovely moon, one night,
In my deserted cottage from beauty's heaven alight.

The Carpenter returned at an unseasonable hour to his house by a secret way. It happened to be at the time when the sun and moon were in conjunction, and the lover and his mistress were in mutual raptures at the sight of one another. At one time the beautiful youth, with his ravishing glances, threw the fire of perturbation into the harvest of her patience. At another, the fair one, like a silver moon, with her fascinating coquetry, made havoc of the reason and senses of the youth.

VERSE.

Two graceful, sense-beguiling idols they,
From head to foot in love's adornments dressed.
His cheek shed lamplike o'er their couch its ray,
Her lip to every wine-cup lent new zest.

The hapless Carpenter waited until they betook themselves to the bed-chamber, and then very softly crept under the bed, that he might observe what they were doing in private. Suddenly his wife's eyes fell on his foot, and she perceived that the departure of her spouse had been a mere pretext to discover the truth of this affair. Whispering to her lover, she said, ' Ask of me in a loud voice whether I like thee or my husband best.' The youth raised his voice, and said, ' O pretty one! I want to know whether the love thou hast in thy heart for me is greater than thy attachment to thy husband?' The woman replied, ' How camest thou to ask this question, and what is the use of inquiring?' The youth, in fear of his life, pressed her for an answer, and took her hand.[1] The woman answered, 'If I am to speak the truth, these accidents happen to women either from trifling and careless-ness, or from wantonness and lust; and they take up with friends without caring about their worth or birth, or without laying stress on their vices or bad habits. And when their sensual wants are satisfied, and their passion begins to wane, they soon regard them as mere strangers.

COUPLET.

They cease their fondling, and their lover quit.
Their passion—not a thought remains of it.

But their husband resembles the life of their bosom, and is precious as the light of their eyes,

HEMISTICH.

One might life indeed surrender, but not e'er relinquish thee.

May she never reap the fruit of life and youth, and means and existence, who does not value her husband a thousand times above dear life itself, and who does not wish for the capital of vitality simply to increase his comfort and his happiness here and hereafter!

---

[1] The printed edition reads *ilḥâḥ burd va dast girift*, 'importuned and took her hand.' The lithographed edition has *ilḥâḥ burd va dast-i zan girift*, 'importuned and took the woman's hand;' and the best MS. I have reads *ilḥaḥ bar dast girift*, 'took in hand,' or ' commenced importuning her,' which I much prefer.'

Without thee, may I ne'er my hope attain !
And, save for thee, I'd e'en from life refrain.'

When the Carpenter heard this speech, tenderness and commiseration arose in his heart, and emotion and pity overpowered him, and he said, 'It had very nearly happened that I had wronged this woman, and had become guilty and sinful in the sight of God. After all, what was this evil suspicion that I entertained of her, while the poor thing was all the time pining for me, and terribly in love with me ; and, in the creed of friendship and path of love one ought not to attach much weight to it if, with all this attachment and friendship that she has for me, she make a little slip ; nor ought one to reckon too strictly with her for follies like these which she may commit, for no creature can be pure from errors and failings.

HEMISTICH.
Where lives there one whose skirt has not been stained ?

And I, blockhead that I am ! have given myself all this trouble, and plunged myself in such distress gratuitously. My best course is now not to embitter their enjoyments, and not to disgrace her before a strange man, since she acts so from mere playfulness and folly, and not intentionally and of set purpose. I ought to fix my eyes on her merits, and close my eyes to her failings.

COUPLET.
Hast thou one virtue, faults threescore and ten ;
Nought but that virtue shines in friendship's ken.'

He then remained sitting in silence in the same place under the bed, and did not utter a word until they had finished their toying, and the flag of gloomy night had been reversed.

COUPLET.
When from night's shade sprang up the charming day,—
Morn's breath from heaven made creation gay,

the stranger departed, and the Carpenter's wife pretended to be asleep on the bed. The Carpenter came gently out from under the bed, and sat down upon it courteously and kindly, and was wiping off the dust of dejection from his wife's face with the sleeve of suavity, and stroked her limbs gently with his hand, until the wily woman opened her eyes, and fixing her eyes upon her husband as he sate at her pillow, started up and said,

COUPLET.
' Welcome the morn that brings my loved one home !
Thanks that the partner of my cares is come.'

She then asked, 'When didst thou safely arrive ?' He replied, 'At the time when thou wast pressing the hand of desire in the bosom of union with that stranger. However, as I knew that necessity was the cause of it, I preserved thy credit, and did nothing to annoy him. And as I am aware of thy kind feelings towards me, and know the friendship thou entertainest for me; and am quite sure that thou art anxious for life only for communion with me, and wishest for sight only to gaze on my beauty; if thou art guilty of these immoralities, it must, of course, be from frailty. Wherefore I felt it incumbent on me to be indulgent to thy friend, and to preserve thy honor. Be of good cheer, and do not give way to alarm or fear, and emancipate thyself from thy terrors, and pardon me for thinking ill of thee, and for entertaining a hundred kinds of bad suspicions of thee. Praise be to God! thou hast not turned out to be what I supposed thee.

HEMISTICH.

All my suspicion was indeed mistake!'

The wife made use of deceitful words; and both sides, forgetting their anger, placed the arms of reconciliation round the neck of satisfaction; and the Carpenter, loosing the tongue of apology, was expressing this sentiment.

COUPLET.

'In no grave light may God thy error see! Since I'm content, may He forgiving be!'

And I have introduced this story, that you too, like the carpenter, who was cajoled by the words of a profligate woman, may not be deceived by the talk of this deceitful crow, nor seduced by his hypocrisy and artifices, which smell of blood.

COUPLET.

Let not the foe malignant thee beguile; He rues it in the end who heeds his wile.

And every enemy who, by means of his distant position, cannot make an assault, advances closer by stratagem; and assuming the part of an adviser, brings himself, by hypocrisy and fawning, into the situation of confidential intercourse. As soon as he has learned the secrets [of his dupe] he looks out for an opportunity, and, with perfect insight, commences his undertaking; and not a blow that he strikes, but like the fire-raining thunderbolt, consumes the fire of life; and, like the arrow of fate, unerringly reaches the target of his wish and the mark of his desire.' The crow (Kárshinás) said, 'O cruel friend! what is the use of all this eloquence? and what results from this useless preamble which thou art linking together? After all, what connection has this cruelty, which has been practised upon me, and this tyranny which has befallen me, with deceit and stratagem? No sensible person is willing to suffer pain himself to give comfort to another, nor have I voluntarily taken upon myself this disgrace and suffering. And every one knows that these tortures were nothing but the requital of my opposition to the crows.' The vazír said, 'This thing that thou hast done is the spring of thy deceit, and thou hast willingly, nay, greedily, submitted to these sufferings; and the sweetuess of revenge which thou hast in mind has made the bitter draught of this pain pleasant to the palate of thy hope; and there have been many who have been willing to die in order to destroy their enemy, and who, to do their patrons and benefactors a service, have cast themselves into the vortex of annihilation, to leave inscribed on the page of their life the character of gratitude and loyalty. So that Monkey gave himself up to be killed, in order that he might avenge his friends.' The king of the owls asked, 'How was that?'

STORY XI.

He said, ' They have related that a troop of monkeys had their abode in an island where were fruits fresh and dry in abundance, and the climate agreed with them perfectly. One day a party of the elders of the tribe were sitting under the shade of a tree, and were talking on all sorts of subjects. At one time, with laughing lip like a pistachio, they discoursed of the impervious nut, and at another they would not open their eyes, which resembled fresh almonds, save to gaze on the beauty of the dry fig. On a sudden, a bear passed by them, and was excessively chagrined at their composure. He said to himself, 'Is it to be borne that I should pass my time in the midst of stony mountains, with saddened heart; and with a hundred thousand efforts get possession of a thorn-top or a root of grass, while these monkeys in this pleasant spot and agreeable station, feast on fresh and juicy fruits and make their repasts on herbage softer than green silk.

COUPLET.

My rivals, rose-like, flourishing in the fair spring of converse, see !
Why should, in autumnal absence, I, all leafless, withered be ?'

He then resolved to enter among that crowd and overthrow with the axe of cruelty, the pedestal of their tranquillity. The monkeys, accepting battle, assembled to the number of nearly a thousand, and making a rush, overthrew [1] and wounded the bear with their blows. The unhappy bear of vain schemes, had not as yet tasted the fruit of his wishes from the plant of desire, when he found the tree of his enjoyment withered, and the cell of his nature not being illuminated by the radiance of the taper of repose, the lamp of his strength went out.

COUPLET.

Before I from the bowl of gladness one short draught of joy could sip,
Cruel fate dashed down the goblet ere it yet had reached my lip.

In short, the bear escaped with the greatest trouble from among the

---

[1] The MSS. supply the *va* between *pardganda* and *majrúḥ*, which the editions wrongly omit.

monkeys, and having conveyed himself to the mountains, raised loud cries
and a vast uproar. A great number of his species came round him, and
seeing him in that state, asked him as to the circumstances of the battle and
the manner of the contumely and blows inflicted on him. The bear
recounted the affair as it had happened, and said, 'Bravo, dishonor! that a
powerful-framed bear should endure this disgrace from feeble monkeys!
never in by-gone days did such a thing befall our ancestors and progenitors,
and until the day of resurrection, this infamy will adhere to our race. Our
advisable course is that we should join together, and by one united night-
attack, change the day of existence for them into the night of extinction, and
blind the eye of their hopes with the dust of battle.

VERSE.

Let us but be by fate unharassed,
   We'll wreak our [1] vengeance on the hated foe;
And in the battle we'll so crush his head,
   To the last day our glory down shall go.'

The bears' feeling of pride was roused, and kindling the flame of implaca-
bility, and loosing the tongue of boasting and vain-glory, they raised to
heaven their fierce and martial shouts.

VERSE.

'Ants are our foes,—a giant serpent we,
   How can they scape the clutches of the strife?
Tis ours to shake the flag of battle free,
   Theirs to relinquish sovereignty and life.'

They then agreed that that night they would engage in kindling the flames
of slaughter, and in the heat of battle and the fire of war, would cast an
igneous shower into the harvest of the life of the monkeys; and at the time
when the golden-clawed lion of the sun turned from the waste of heaven
to that place of fountains [as it is written] 'in a spring of black mud,[2] and
the Greater and Lesser Bear began to stalk towards the confines of the
Northern Pole,

COUPLET.

When the bright sun had turned his back,
Earth darkened,[3] and the air grew black,

at once, the bears of that mountainous region set out for the island of the
monkeys. It happened that the monkey-king with a number of his nobles
and grandees, had made a party to hunt, and that night they remained in the

---

[1] The printed edition has here by a typographical error—*kamin* for *kín*.

[2] Ḳu'rán, Fl. xviii., 84; Mar. 87; Sale, p. 227, l. 4: 'And he (Dhu'l-karnein) followed
his way, until he came to the place where the sun setteth; and he found it to set in a spring
of black mud: and he found near the same a certain people.'

[3] *Durusht*, lit., 'rough,' *i.e.*, hard to be walked over, on account of the darkness.

waste, and the other monkeys, unprepared for the attack of their foes, were reposing each in his own place, when all at once,

COUPLET.

Like ants and locusts, countless warriors swarm,
And spread through earth war's world-convulsing storm.

Before the monkeys were aware, many of them were slain, and a few, crushed and wounded, escaped with life from that sanguinary struggle. When the bears saw that flourishing plain and populous island cleared of the enemy, they drew the foot of continuance under the skirt of residence in that very place, and made the bear that had been maltreated and injured, their commander; and stretching forth the hand of tyranny, they brought within the range of their own possession, every good thing which the monkeys in the lapse of time had stored up for themselves.

HEMISTICH.

Who wasted, O my God! and who amassed? [1]

The next day, when the dark-hearted world became brilliant as the cheek of the beautiful, and the Jamshíd of the sun came forth upon the throne of the sky,

COUPLET.

When morning's host upraised its banner, then
The world drew through the word of night its pen, [2]

the king of the monkeys, unaware of what had happened, was returning to the island, and in the middle of his journey a number of fugitives who had brought themselves semi-animate from the whirlpool of calamity to the shore, came up, and began to call for redress. The king, when he had been informed of the nature of those events, began to bite the finger of amazement with the tooth of regret, and said, 'Alas! for my hereditary kingdom, which has been torn from the grasp of my possession, and alack! for those rich treasures which have fallen into the hands of the enemy. At last, fortune has changed, and has rained down the dirt of adversity on my head, and, at length, she, fickle that she is, has averted her countenance.

STANZA.

Ne'er in this world's flower-garden did one verdure constant see,
Nor upon the cheek of fortune can we trace a changeless hue.
Earth is but a house of cheating, credit there can never be,
Because than it a place of mischief more disastrous none e'er knew.

The others, too, who attended in the cavalcade of the king, beginning to be disquieted, raised lamentations each for his own property and possessions, and

---

[1] That is, 'one hoards, another spends.'
[2] That is, 'renounced allegiance to it.'

wife, and family, and among them was one named Maimún,[1] adorned with an excellent understanding, and distinguished from the rest by the abundance of his sagacity; and on this account they used to hold him in supreme honor, and king and people were in the habit of availing themselves of the benefits of his advice.

VERSE.

> So bright of heart, so clear in wisdom he,
> That by one counsel he could climes enslave;
> Zuḥal[2] his pupil was in subtlety,
> And to 'Aṭárid[2] he pen-lessons gave.

When Maimún beheld the king amazed and his subjects distressed, he loosed the tongue of advice and said,

STANZA.

> 'Be not contentious in disaster, thou!
> 'Tis doubly faulty; for, to me attend,
> First, it will gild with joy thy foeman's brow;
> And next cast down and stupify thy friend.

To be stiff-necked in misfortunes excludes a creature from the rewards of eternity, and makes him notorious for impatience and levity, and in occurrences of this nature, there are but two things of any avail. The first is, to endure and to increase in patience and fortitude; for the tree of patience produces the fruit of desire, and in accordance with the saying, '*Patience is the key of joy,*' to make choice of patience is the key of the portals of salvation.

STANZA.

> Patience, the key that opes the treasury
> Of wished-for things, unlocks each closed-up way;
> And clears the breast from pangs of tyranny,
> As from a glass the dust that thereon lay.

The second is to make use of just judgment and right counsel; for when the lightning of the bright mind of the possessor of sagacity flashes in the night of incident, it can completely efface the darkness of cruelty from the page of the condition of the tyrannously oppressed; and in one night of thought accomplish things which have occupied a thousand years.

COUPLET.

> With the salve of happy counsel, and of schemes that aim aright,
> Be the heart in fragments shivered, there is healing for its plight.'

The king of the monkeys was comforted by the words of Maimún, and asked 'How can this be remedied?' Maimún requested a private audience and said, 'O renowned king! my children and kinsmen have perished by the

---

[1] The Dictionary informs us this word, in Persian, means 'monkey,' in Arabic 'fortunate.'
[2] Saturn: and in the next line 'Aṭárid is Mercury.

hands of this remorseless band; and, deprived of the sight of these dear ones life will afford me no delight, and existence no happiness.

COUPLET.

Without thy face I might survive,—yes, I might linger so;
But yet a thousand deaths, methinks, were lighter than that woe.

And since in the end the goods of life must fall into the whirlpool of annihilation, I desire with all possible speed to transport myself from the narrow strait of worldly things to the expanse of the blissful regions of eternity; and, sacrificing my life, to avenge my friends and beloved ones on those blind and savage monsters.' The King said, 'O Maimún! the flavor of revenge appears sweet to the palate of existence, and the relish of triumphing over one's enemy is necessary for the repose of life, but if thou art no more, [I care not] whether the world be populated or desolate. And wherever the heart is set, it matters not whether the place be tranquil or disturbed.

COUPLET.

Once from this garden be thy transit made,
I care not if the roses bloom or fade.'

Maimún replied, 'O king! in my present circumstances the preference may be given to death over life, and one might choose to perish rather than exist. For the light of the eyes is in gazing on the beauty of one's children, and they have drawn over their countenances the veil of the earth; and the joy of the bosom is bound up in beholding one's domestics and kinsfolk, and the harvest of their peace has been dispersed by the tempest of fate; and the chief pillar of one's maintenance is wealth and property, and the hoardings of one's whole life have been dissipated by the plundering of the enemy. I now wish to show my gratitude for the favors of the king, and to aid, with the ointment of cheerfulness, my brethren, whose hearts are sorrowful and whose minds are wounded; and having offered up the coin of life, to leave my name on the page of Time.

COUPLET.

My heart's wish is to perish gloriously:
Earth yields one object,—'t is with fame to die.

And the king must not mourn for my death, and when he sits with his friends at the mirthful banquet let him call to mind my faithful service.

COUPLET.

With the hand of hope, when gathering the enjoyment of thy bliss,
Call to mind our social converse, and bethink thee still of this.'

The king said, 'How wilt thou prosecute this undertaking, and by which of the doors of stratagem will thou enter upon it?' Maimún answered, 'I have thought of a plan by which I may consume them with the flame of the

Samúm[1] in the deserts of Mard-ázmáí;[2] and it is most probably to be expected that my prognostications will not deviate from the line of truth. The advisable course is, that thou command them to tear out my ears with their teeth, and fracture my hands and feet, and cast me at night in a corner of that waste which was our former abode. And let the king, with his attendants and the party of fugitives, wander at will through all parts and directions of this desert until two days have passed, and on the morning of the third day let them come and settle, free from care, in their own home. For there will be no trace of their enemies, nor afterwards will any injury accrue from that race.' The king, in accordance with the wishes of Maimún, commanded them to tear out his ears, and, after breaking his limbs, to cast him in a corner of that region. He then dispersed his forces, and sate awaiting the appointed time. Maimún, through the whole night, uttered plaintive wailings after a fashion that would have dissolved, in sympathy, a heart of stone. The mountains re-echoed the piteous sound of his cries; and the king of the bears going out for a circuit early in the morning, heard those lamentations; and following the sound, beheld Maimún in that plight. Although he was hard-hearted, he had compassion upon him, and in spite of his ferocity, pity arose in his heart. Busying himself with inquiry into his circumstances, and examining into his condition, he demanded of him a detailed explanation of what had happened. Maimún sagaciously discerned that he was the king of that race, and entered upon eulogiums of him; and after acquitting himself of the usual duties of panegyric, which is due to the position of kings, he said,

COUPLET.

'This earthly frame, soul and shape the same, in flaming fire and water[3] lies;
Look with thine eyes and sympathize, for cruel are these agonies.

O king! I am the vazír of the monkey-king, and went out with him to hunt. On the night of the attack I was not present in the field of battle. The next day the fugitives reached us, and I received intelligence of the descent of your majesty in this place. The king of the monkeys, from the confidence which he had in my judgment, required of me an expedient to remedy this. I, from sincere regard to him, pointed out the service of your majesty, and said, 'The recommendable course is, that we gird up the waist of attendance, and pass the rest of our lives in waiting on the king; and, under the shade of his good-fortune, in security from the reverses of fate, content ourselves with a corner and a crust.

----

[1] In the English dictionary 'Simoom;' but the first vowel should be *a*, according to the Arabic.

[2] Lit., 'man-trying;' *i.e.*, 'perilous.'

[3] That is, 'in woe.'

VERSE.

He that is wise, will ever guide his way
To pious shelter, such as thou art, who,
Oft as thy feet amid the garden stray,
Bear'st off the roses and the spikenard too.'

The king was displeased at my words, and vented many unseemly reproaches on the parties who had become occupants of this region; and when a second time I rebuked him, he commanded that they should inflict all this contumely upon me; and he gave orders, saying, 'Since he is one of the fautors of that monarch, and belongs to his army, the best thing is to cast him down near the island, so that I may see how they will protect him.' Thus they brought me hither, and requited my former loyal services with these subsequent distresses.' He said this, and wept so piteously that the tear-drops began to fall from the pitiless eyes of the king of the bears.

COUPLET.

My groans would make a stone dissolve in blood;
And from my weeping eyes pours Jaihún's [1] flood.'

The king said, 'Where are the monkeys now?' He replied, 'There is a forest, which they call Mard-ázmáí, where they have taken refuge, and are collecting forces from all sides, and every hour they may be expected to come with a fierce and numerous army to make a night-attack.' The king of the bears started and said, 'O Maimún! what is thy advice? and Heaven forfend! that a calamity fall upon us from them.' Maimún replied, 'Let the king be tranquil as to this, and had I but feet, I would conduct a force unexpectedly against them, and bring destruction on those perfidious ingrates.' The king replied, 'I know that thou hast complete acquaintance with their position, and if thou canst conduct us to them, thou wilt cast a chain of obligation on the neck of the condition of this people; and inasmuch, too, as they have wronged thee, thou wilt obtain thy own wish of revenge.' Maimún said, 'How can I do it? for it is impossible for me to go, and for me to move with such hands and feet presents insuperable difficulties.' The king replied, 'I know an expedient for this, and can convey thee by a contrivance.' He then called aloud, so that the leaders of his army and the courtiers presented themselves; and having stated to them how matters stood, he said, 'Be ready, for to-night we will march against the enemy.' All agreed in this plan, and made ready the weapons of war, and, having tied Maimún on the back of a bear, they set off. Maimún guided them by signs, until they arrived at the waste Mard-ázmáí, which was a desert full of fierce heat and devoid of water, such that the spring-cloud was burnt up, in its expanse, from excess of heat; and the swift messenger of the

---

[1] The river Jaxartes.

moon, from the dread nature of that waste, lost its way in the heaven; and the world-measuring intellect was unable to emerge from its difficulties, and the creation-circling imagination knew not the way forth from its stages. A Samúm used to blow in that waste, such that every one who was reached by its effects, melted away; and it made the sand and soil burn like the furnace of iron-smiths; and on account of this fiery wind, no living thing abode in that desert, and no herbage sprang up in that salt and man-devouring wilderness.

VERSE.

A desert vast and full of horror, where,
    At every step, a hundred risks arose;
Its air was flame, its fire igneous air,
    Magnets its stones, and stones its earth compose.

Maimún said, 'Make haste; and, before the white dawn lifts away the veil from the face of the transactions of the world, let us tear away the curtain of their tranquillity from the area of enjoyment; and, ere the king of the Turkish vestment[1] can lift up his gold-embroidered flag, let us subvert the banner of the puissance of those wretches forsaken by fortune.' The bears, with the utmost alacrity, pressed on into that waste, and with their own feet entered into the plain of death and space of destruction. The sun rose, and no trace of the monkeys was to be found; and Maimún still urged them on with speed, and with plausible inventions beguiled them, until the time when the sun rose high, and, with the warmth of his rays, lit up the quarters and districts of that region. The flame of his taper was then kindled to that degree, that whoever looked into the air was consumed like a moth, and whoever set foot on earth was melted like wax.

STANZA.

The frame was heated by the warmth intense,
    Till, taper-like, the lip did radiate;
And such the fiery blast, that Providence,
    Thou wouldst suppose, had thought good to create
    A fiercer hell in this, man's earthly state.

The rays of the sun, exerting their influence, smote the bears with destruction, and the fiery Samúm, beginning to blow, appeared like a smokeless flame. Then the king of the bears turned to Maimún [and said], 'Here is a desert such that our hearts are consumed with the dread of it, and our livers are dried up; and what is this which, like a flame of fire, comes, fierce and hot, towards us?' Maimún replied, 'O cruel tyrant! this is the wilderness of death, and that which comes towards thee is the messenger of fate. Be at ease, for didst thou possess a hundred thousand lives, thou wouldst not save one. And now, soon as the Samúm reaches you, it will consume all to

---

[1] A title of the sun.

ashes, and thou wilt be burned in the fire of that injustice which thou didst inflict on the persons of the monkeys.' They were talking thus, when the flame of the Samúm reached them, and consumed on the spot Maimún, together with all the retinue and soldiers of the bear-king, and not one of them emerged from that wilderness. On the third day, as had been agreed upon, the king of the monkeys, together with his army, came to the island, and found the region unoccupied, and beheld his dominions cleared of the· gloomy presence of his foes.

COUPLET.

Disaster's night has rolled away, the morn of triumph comes at last;
The spring—the joyful spring—is here, the autumn of our grief is past.

And I have adduced this story in order that the king may understand that resentful persons, for the sake of vengeance, will relinquish their own lives, and, to gratify their friends, attach no weight to the sacrifice. And I understand the baseness of Kárshinás from his deceitful speeches, and I know the whole train of the story which has been related.[1] And I have had experience of the crows before, and know the extent of their foresight and sagacity, and the greatness of their deceit and artfulness; and as soon as I beheld Kárshinás in this state, I felt convinced that their cleverness and prudence were allied to some useful end, and that their wisdom and penetration is beyond what were supposed.

COUPLET.

Yes! I had heard thy charms, but see, indeed,
Fact does the tale a thousand times exceed.

The advisable course is, that before he can give us supper we should supply him with breakfast; and ere he can spill our blood, we should give the signal for his execution.' When the king of the owls heard this speech he frowned and said, 'What harshness and merciless procedure is this! that when a poor wretch has undergone a variety of sufferings and torments from his attachment to us, we should stand forth as his tormentors and destroyers, and melt again in the crucible of trial one who has already been wofully stricken. But, perhaps, thou hast not heard that they have said,

COUPLET.

'Make glad the mourner's bosom, and recall
The night of mourning, which may thee befall.'

He then commanded, and they took Kárshinás with the utmost reverence respect, and bore him along with the owl-king. The vazír said, 'O king! since thou hast not heeded my counsel, and hast averted the face of acceptance from my directions, which were essentially wise and purely beneficial; at least live with him as with thy foes, and be not off thy guard

---

[1] For *hilah mí shindsam* my best MS. reads *jumlah mí shindsam*. The sentence is obscure, but probably means that he recognises in the story he has just told a parallel case to that of Kárshinás.

2 A

for the twinkling of an eye as to his artifices and treason. For his coming can have no other object save injury to the affairs of the owls and the promotion of the ends useful to the crows.' The king refused to attend to this advice, and despised the words of that incomparable friend; and the Crow continued to live in his service with the utmost honor, and he omitted no particular of the homage due, nor of the respectful manners suited to the service of princes; and by conciliating each of the favorites and ministers of the king in some way or other, he attached them to himself. Hence his rank was each day advanced, and each day he made greater progress in the affections of the king and his subjects, until he became the depositary of the confidence, and the confidant of the secrets of the king. And when his thorough sincerity and complete probity had been noticed, he rose to be the State-referee and pivot of public affairs of that country. And in commencing affairs of importance, they used to consult with him, and they formed all sorts of schemes according to his opinion and counsel. One day, in the public assembly and general meeting, he said to high and low, 'The king of the crows has causelessly injured me, and tortured me, though I am innocent. Until, then, I wreak my vengeance on him, and get the better of him like a man, how can I find rest or repose? and how relish sleep or food? And I have reflected long, and spent much time in meditating and considering how to obtain this object and compass this end. At last I have come to the firm conclusion that so long as I am in the guise of a crow, and retain their appearance, I cannot arrive at this my wish, nor attain my object. And I have heard from the wise, that when an oppressed and unfortunate person has suffered wrong from an unjust oppressor, and met with persecution from a haughty tyrant, and seeks death and consumes himself with fire, every prayer that he utters in that state meets with acceptance. If the king's wisdom thinks it right, let him command them to burn me. Perhaps, at the moment when the heat reaches me, if I pray to God (may His name be magnified!) to make me an owl, I may, by that means get the advantage over the tyrant, and wreak my vengeance on him?' Now, the owl that had been so urgent for the laceration of Kárshinás was present in that assembly, and said,

COUPLET.

> 'Art thou not bold as the narcissus? like the tulip, dark of heart?
> Then ten-tongued and double-faced, too, cease to play the lily's part.'

The king asked, 'What sayest thou to this speech?' The vazír replied, 'This again is another artifice which is put forth, and a pretence colored with hypocrisy.

COUPLET.

> From hand to foot he's nought but juggleries;
> At his deceit astonished stand the wise.

And should they burn again and again his foul person and impure body, and moisten[1] the ashes with the water of the fountain of Salsabíl and the wine of purification, his unclean nature and base qualities would not be altered; and the malignity of his mind and obliquity of his moral principles cannot be cleansed by water or burnt out with fire.

COUPLET.

Hope not that evil natures good will shew;
For rust, through washing, white will never grow.

And if (this impossible supposition being admitted), his impure person should put on the appearance of the peacock; or, for example, his unclean limbs should be arrayed in the garments of the Símurgh, he would remain just as before, attached to the society of the crows, and friendly with them. Like that Mouse, which, although it had obtained a human form, relapsed into the inclinations suited to its former state, and did not attach itself to the world-illuminating sun, and the bounteous cloud, and the exhilarating breeze, and the firm mountain.' The king asked, 'How was that?'

STORY XII.

He said, 'They have related that a devotee, whose prayers were accepted, had located himself on the bank of a stream, and had washed his hands with the water of contentment from the contamination of worldly affairs. A kite on the wing arrived there, and a young Mouse dropped from its beak on the ground before the holy man; who had compassion on it, and taking it up, and rolling it in his patched gabardine, was about to carry it home. He then reflected that he had better not, lest it should annoy his domestics and do mischief. He prayed, therefore, that God Most High would be pleased to [turn the mouse into a damsel, and thus] bestow on him a daughter. The arrow of the recluse's prayer struck the target of acceptance, and the tire-woman of Omnipotence adorned for him a daughter of graceful form and straight stature, of bright countenance and curling hair, such that the sun of her cheek cast the fire of jealousy into the harvest of the moon, and her musky ringlets wrung sighs from the heart of black night.

COUPLET.

Her graceful form derides the cypress: she
Writes 'gainst the moon the mark of contumely.

The recluse looked and beheld a figure composed of pure grace, and found a maiden reared in perfect elegance. He delivered her to one of his disciples to treat with the same affection as his children. The disciple, receiving with respect the charge of his spiritual instructor, used the greatest endeavors in

[1] My best MS. reads *hall sdzand*, 'should loosen or moisten.' The editions read *gil sdzand*, 'should make clay.'

tending the girl. In a short time she reached the period of puberty, and the holy man addressing her said, 'Dear life! thou hast grown up, and there is no alternative but to unite thy pure gem with another jewel on the string of marriage. I leave this to thy own choice, and whomsoever among men or fairies, yea, even of beings from the highest to the lowest rank thou mayest select, to him I will give thee.' The maid replied, 'I wish for a husband strong and powerful, who may possess multiform might and majesty, and, in rank, may be distinguished by his exalted dignity and high position.' The recluse answered, 'The sun will be the possessor of these qualities which thou mentionest.' The girl replied, 'Aye! I am of opinion that he succumbs to none, but has the mastery over all that exist beneath the sky. Marry me to him.'

> **VERSE.**
> The next day, when the East's Khusrau arose,
>   And stepped forth on the archèd purple sky,
> Time did the gates of light again unclose,
>   And earth began anew its revelry.

In the morning, when, by the command of Him who makes the morn break forth, the sun ascended from the eastern horizon, the recluse communicated to him the circumstances, and said, 'This maiden is exceeding beautiful and amiable; I would have her be thy handmaid, for she has asked of me a husband, strong and mighty.' The sun blushed[1] at hearing this tale, and replied, 'I will point out to thee one stronger than myself, which is a cloud. For this conceals my light and excludes all living creatures from the rays of my beauty.

> **COUPLET.**
> High though the glorious sun does ride,
> A cloud-speck can his radiance hide.'

The recluse came to the cloud, and repeated his former speech. The cloud, perspiring at this address, said, 'If thou choosest me for strength and superiority, the wind is my superior, since it carries me whithersoever it will, and takes me along with it in whatever direction it wishes.' The recluse, acquiescing in this remark, went to the wind, and recited the story of what had passed. The wind writhed from shame, and said, 'What strength and might do I possess? absolute power belongs to the mountain, since it has drawn the foot of endurance under the skirt of majesty, and like the pole reposes in its own centre; and my influence upon it is no more than that of a low sound in the ear of one born deaf, or of the footfall of a little ant on the surface of the solid rock.[2]

---

[1] *Bar afrúkhtah*, lit., 'blazed up,' 'kindled.'

[2] The printed edition has here a mistake,—*ṣamdd* for *ṣammd*, 'hard rock that returns no echo,' which is the reading of my best MS. The lithographed edition reads *ṣdd*, which is meaningless.

The cloud may scatter at the tempest's shock,
Whose rage is vain against the mountain-rock.'

The holy man then proceeded to the mountain, and recited the scroll of the affair. The mountain uttered a deep sound, saying, ' O recluse! the force and strength of the mouse exceed mine, for it pierces my side, and makes its nest in my heart. My breast is rent in a thousand places by its life-exhausting goad, and I know of no expedient to get rid of it.' The maiden exclaimed, ' He speaks the truth. The mouse is his conqueror, and deserves to be my husband.' The recluse then offered her to a mouse, and he, owing to his homogeneousness (for in him the cord of affinity of the girl found its limit), felt an inclination for her in his heart, and replied, ' I too for a long time have been wishing for a charmer, who should be my mate for life. It is necessary, however, that my spouse should be of the same race with myself.' The girl said, ' This is an easy matter. Let the holy man pray that I may become a mouse, and embrace thee with the arms of love.' The recluse saw that there was an evident longing on both sides : he held up his hands in prayer, and prayed to the Lord Most High to make her a mouse. The petition of the saint was immediately honored with acceptance, and the remarkable truth, ' *Everything reverts to its primitive nature,*' was here manifested, for the girl became a mouse, and the recluse bestowed her on that other mouse, and went his way.

COUPLET.
Each thing must to its pristine essence back revert at last, my friend !
Earthy are we, and we must mingle with the earth, too, in the end.

And the moral of this story is that, whatever may be the requirement of the original nature, although other accidental circumstances may divert it, will, in the end, relapse to that same character of its origin. And an eloquent sage has arranged in poetical order this same sentiment, and expresses it in this beautiful language, and with this graceful turn :

VERSE.
The tree that is by nature sour,
  Though thou shouldst it to Eden's garden bring,
And moisten, at the watering hour,
  Its root from the eternal, heavenly spring,
  With purest honey, or some sweeter thing,—
Would still not lose the memory of the past,
But aye put forth its acrid fruit at last.'

The king of the owls, as is the wont of the unlucky, listened not to these admonitions, and imputing the words of his vazír to envy, paid no regard to consequences. The crow, on the other hand, each day adduced some charming tale, and every night some incomparably pleasing narrative, and recited marvelous stories and wonderful anecdotes; until he became the chief

confidant; and obtained perfect information of their most recondite secrets
and hidden affairs. He then watched his opportunity and suddenly set off to
join the crows. The king of the crows seeing him approach, began to
address him joyfully, as follows,

COUPLET.

'Friends! we may now our wish, the object of our heart, enfold;
For here, the solace of our life, our soul, our spirits' joy behold!'

Then king Pírúz asked him, saying, O Kárshinás! what hast thou effected?'
He replied, 'By the king's good fortune, I have effected all that was required,
and have accomplished the object I had in view. Be ready to act! for it is
the time for exacting vengeance and for seeing our enemies as our friends
would have them.' The king said, 'Tell me, concisely, the nature of what
thou wouldest advise, in order that we may follow up the measures of
importance with a right understanding, and that the things that are required
may be made ready.' Kárshinás said, 'In a certain mountain there is a
cave, and during the day-time the owls go and collect in that cave; and in
the vicinity, much dry wood is found. Let the king command the crows to
transport a small quantity there and heap it at the door of the cave, and I
will bring a little fire from the station of the shepherds, who have their
houses in the neighborhood, and cast it upon the wood. Then let the king
command the crows to fan it with their wings so that the fire may be
kindled. Every owl that attempts to come forth from the cave, will be
burnt, and every one that does not come out will be killed by the smoke.'
The king was pleased with this counsel, and he undertook the enterprise in
the way the vazír had seen good. Thus they burned all the owls: and the
crows having won a great victory, were all glad and triumphant, and loosing
the tongue of congratulation, they raised to the star 'Ayyúḳ[1] their joyous
shouts at this splendid triumph.

VERSE.

'Fortune, at last, the monarch's wish allows;
At last fulfils the promise of success.
The joys sedition held back from our vows,
Now, by one happy stroke, our nation bless.'

The king and the army, deeply obliged by the laudable efforts and acceptable
and illustrious acts of Kárshinás, were lavish in the honors they awarded
him, and they viewed it as requisite and incumbent on them to go to excess
and profuseness in praising him. He, in his turn, invoked benedictions on
the king and lauded the others suitably to their respective conditions. In
the midst of this, the king gave utterance to these words, 'The auspiciousness of thy counsel and thy fine judgment in overturning our foes and

---

[1] A bright red star, which follows the Pleiades.

smiting them on the head, and in gladdening and cheering our friends, have been evinced in a peculiar manner.' 'Kárshinás said, 'All that has succeeded in this respect, has been from the greatness of the good-fortune of the king and his auspicious destiny. I beheld, too, the token of this victory on that very day when those ill-fated ones displayed such designs and permitted themselves to practice such cruelty upon the weak and helpless, and formed the desire of appropriating our fatherland and ancient country.

COUPLET.

In lusting for thy country then, red grew that black-souled traitor's eyes;
But yellow soon his face became, and earth grew dark; in death he lies.'

Again the king asked, 'How couldst thou for so long a time endure the society of the owls? and how put up with them who in disposition are so opposite to thee? For I know that the good cannot endure the society of the wicked, and that it is the nature of the generous to flee the very sight of the sordid. And they have said that it is better to live with an evil serpent than against one's will to gaze upon a bad companion.

COUPLET.

Though of grief's poison thou shouldst die, when parted from a comrade sweet;
'Twere better far than with a stranger purest honey e'en to eat.'

Kárshinás said, 'The case is as the king has pronounced; and there is nought more galling to the spirit than so unsuitable a companion.

HEMISTICH.

'Tis hell to view a mate that suits us not.

But a wise man, to please his master and relieve his care, turns not away from difficulties, and goes forth with joy to meet every labor that occurs to him, and willingly accepts it. And the man of high spirit does not at every disappointment and difficulty plunge himself into the place of grief and whirlpool of distress. For in every affair, the issues of which are combined with victory and triumph, though it may be necessary to undergo trouble in the commencement and endure degradation, the effects thereof will not be so great; since no treasure can be won without pain, and no rose gathered without the annoyance of a thorn.

COUPLET.

Give not vent to angry wailings, for in seeking aught, be sure
They alone attain to gladness, who can sadness first endure.'

The king said, 'Narrate somewhat of the sagacity and wisdom of the owls.' He replied, 'I did not see a single man of quick parts among them, save that one person who advised my execution. But they thought his judgment weak and did not give ear to his counsels with the hearing of acceptance; and did not reflect thus far, that I had fallen a perfect stranger among them, and that I had held a high station among my own tribe and was noted for my intelligence and prudence, and that I might be devising some stratagem, and might have an opportunity of playing the traitor. They neither from their own good sense understood thus much, nor did they make any account of the words of their counsellors, nor did they conceal their secrets from me; in consequence they suffered what they did suffer and arrived where they did arrive. And they have said, ' Kings should use the utmost caution in preserving their secrets, specially from despairing friends and alarmed foes.

STANZA.

The friend, who has lost hope in thee,
 Ne'er to thy confidence invite.
Nor to the fear-struck enemy,
 Is it to tell thy secrets right.'

The king said, ' It appears to me, that oppression was the cause of the destruction of the owls.' Kárshinás replied, ' Even so; every king who enters upon a course of tyrannical conduct, it quickly happens that the foundations of his fortunes are subverted. Moreover, kingly rule may continue to exist with infidelity, but not with tyranny and injustice, ' *Dominion endures notwithstanding infidelity, but it will not remain with tyranny.'*

VERSE.

Give up thy course of tyranny and wrong
At once—for ne'er was life of tyrant long.
Know, when a king perverts his judgment, he
Does that which for himself, too, scath will be.

And they have said, that every one who does four things must expect four things. Whoever acts tyrannously must look with certainty for his own destruction; and whoever is greedy of the society of women, must be prepared for his own disgrace; and he that is gluttonous in eating must expect to be ill; and whoever relies on imbecile and unwise ministers, must bid adieu to his kingdom. Moreover it has been recorded amongst the sayings of the wise, that six persons must retrench their longings for six things, and cut off the hope of obtaining them. First, an oppressive and tyrannical king must cease to expect the permanence of empire, and continuance of good fortune. Secondly, a haughty and arrogant person must in like manner abandon the hope of men's praise, and of being commemorated with honor. Thirdly, ill-humored persons must not hope for many friends. Fourthly, an impudent and disrespectful man is not to look for high rank. Fifthly, a niggard must not expect benefits. Sixthly, a covetous man must not hope for innocence, for covetousness plunges a man in crime; and wherever it and avarice set up the tent of permanence, honor and truthful dealing remove thence. And as the king of the owls was very covetous and greedy to slay the crows and

CHAPTER IV. STORY XIII.

devastate their country, he consequently chose to swerve from the path of justice and uprightness, and became lost in the waste of disappointment, and in the end fell himself into the abyss of contempt and the pit which he had dug for others.

STANZA.

Devise not evil against men,
Lest thou bring evil down on thine own head.
Dost thou not see what toil he then
Endures, who digs a pit that I may tread
Therein? But when 'tis ended—after all,
Not I—the digger down himself will fall.'

The king said, 'How can any one fully acquit himself of the gratitude due for this obligation? For thou hast endured infinite labor, and waited graciously on thy enemies against thy will, and hast undertaken the service of one from whose society the heart shrank with abhorrence; and had thy foes listened to the words of their monitor, vast danger was to be anticipated to thy life.' Kárshinás answered, 'He may truly be called a brave man, who when his resolve is firmly taken to accomplish a thing, first washes his hands of life, and detaching his heart from the hope of surviving, sets foot in the arena of warriors.

COUPLET.

Brave hearts, who erst won fortune's ball and conquered in the strife,
Stepped boldly to the battle-field and washed their hands of life.

And if he sees it advisable at present to submit to wait on another inferior to himself, he adopts this course in order to attain his object. Thus the Snake seeing his own interest therein, was willing to serve the frog.' The king inquired, 'How was that?'

STORY XIII.

Kárshinás said, 'They have related that the infirmity of age had taken effect on a Snake, and that complete debility had supervened upon him. Through loss of strength, he was unable to pursue his prey, and was bewildered in his proceedings how to obtain food. Life was impossible without food, and to hunt for that which was wont to be his food, had, through want of strength, become impracticable. Accordingly he thus reflected, 'Alas! for the strength of my youth, and woe is me for the season of my prosperity; and now to expect the return of the days of my juvenescence, and to hope for the recurrence of my animal vigor is a thing of the same complexion as to light a fire from water, and to desire to remove thirst with fire; and, notwithstanding all this, would that there were permanence even to the season of old age, and that this brief period, too, could be relied upon!

The time of youth has passed away, and coming age has shewn its sign :
  Alas ! for days when we were young, for boyhood's friends—a happy train !
E'en age itself a blessing deem, for of the life thou callest thine,
  Each moment that now flies thou wilt—except in dreams—ne'er see again.'

The Snake felt that what was passed could not be recalled, and he therefore
busied himself with taking thought for the future, which is the most
important business, and said, ' In lieu of the strength of youth I have a
little experience which I have acquired, and a trifle of prudence, the clue of
which I have during a long life laid hold of.   I must now base my proceedings
on abstaining from injuring others, and every degradation that is presented
to me I must gratefully accept it.   I must begin, too, to consider how I may
obtain, for the remainder of my life, what may be the means of support.'
He then went to the brink of a spring of water in which there were a number
of frogs, who had a potent king, and one who was obeyed and renowned.
The Snake cast himself down there in the dust of the road, like to mourners
with their bosoms rent, and to sufferers on whom calamity has fallen.   A
frog speedily made up to him, and asked him, ' I see thou art very sorrowful,
what is the cause of it ? '   The Snake replied, ' Who deserves more to grieve
than I, whose maintenance was from hunting frogs ?   To-day an event has
happened to me which has rendered the pursuit of them unlawful to me,
and if I seriously designed to seize one, I could not.'   The frog went away
and told the king.   The king of the frogs was amazed at this strange
circumstance, and coming to the Snake, asked him, ' What is the cause of
this accident that has befallen thee?[1] and what act has brought down this
upon thee ? '   The Snake replied,

' I heave this sigh thus soul-afflicting from a heart of broken troth,
Self-cause, indeed, is all my woe, why should I be with others wroth.

O king ! audacious greed plunged me into the mesh of calamity, and mischievous covetousness opened upon me this gate of trouble, and this befell as
follows.   One day I attempted to seize a frog, which fled from me and took
refuge in the house of a holy man.   My appetite led me to follow him into
the house, which happened to be dark.   The son of the holy man lay there
asleep, and his great toe coming against me I fancied it was the frog.   From
the ardour of my greediness I closed my teeth upon it, and the child died on
the spot.   The holy man discovered the fact, and, from regret for his son,
attacked me, and I, turning towards the open country, fled with speed, and
the recluse pursued me and imprecated a curse on me, and said, ' I desire of
my Creator that He will make thee base and powerless, and cause thee to be
the vehicle of the frog-king.   And, verily, thou shalt not have power to eat

---

[1] The printed edition, by a typographical error, omits *bar* before *tú*.

frogs save what their king shall bestow on thee as alms.' And now, of necessity, I have come hither that the king may ride upon me, and I have acquiesced in the Eternal command and the will of God.

HEMISTICH.

To fortune's insults I have stooped the neck.'

The matter pleased the king of the frogs, and he thought that it would redound to his honor and advantage; and he always seated himself upon the Snake, and indulged in vain-glorious airs in consequence, and sought to magnify himself above those of his own species. Some time passed in this way. At last the Snake said, 'May the life of the king be prolonged! I cannot do without food and sustenance, that I may support life thereon, and fulfil this service.' The king said, 'The case is as thou sayest; I cannot[1] do without my steed, and my steed cannot have strength without food.' He then fixed two frogs as his daily allowance, that he might use as his regular supply for breakfast and dinner. The Snake maintained himself on that allowance; and inasmuch as the attention he paid to the frog-king involved a benefit to himself, he did not find fault with it.

QUATRAIN.

The hand that elsewhere thou with shame wouldst see,
When stern occasion presses, thou shouldst kiss:
And what chagrin and foul reproach would be,
In time of want thou wilt not take amiss.

And I have adduced this story to make it apparent that if I, too, was patient, and endured abasement with a view to the destruction of my foes, and the welfare of my friends, which were involved in that abasement, I did not experience such a sensation of disgust. Moreover, courtesy and humility are readier means to uproot an enemy than war and contest. As when fire furiously assails a tree, all that it is possible for it to consume is as much as is on the face of the earth; while water gently and softly undermines the roots of every tree (even of those that are[2] larger and stronger), to such a degree that there is no farther hope of its abiding in the same place.

COUPLET.

Be mild, for things though hard and troublous too,
Thou mayest by kindness and by mildness do.

Hence they have said that indulgence and counsel are better than valor, since, however brave and mighty a warrior may be, he can but match ten persons, or, at the utmost, twenty; and if any one would choose to exaggerate, he might say a hundred, and a thousand would be the climax. But a

---

[1] The MSS. show that *nist* should be supplied after *guzir*, though wanting in the editions.
[2] The editions read *ḳawiytar nah báshad*, but my best MS. omits the negative.

wise man, by a single right-aiming scheme, may thrust a whole country into perplexity, and may, by one plan, overthrow a powerful army, and embroil a populous kingdom.

VERSE.

By one wise counsel thou mayest bring about,
That which a mighty army could not gain.
Thy sword may let a foeman's life-blood out,
But plans well-laid a conquered clime obtain.'

The king said, 'Thou hast obtained a wonderful triumph over our enemies, and thy hand has won a marvelous victory!' Kárshinás answered, ' All this success is not attributable to the goodness of my plans and the excellence of my deliberations, but the splendour of the good fortune and the felicitous auspices of the king lent their aid in this matter. And they have said, ' If a party form the design of doing a thing, and a body of people take steps in any enterprise, that one will attain his object who is distinguished by a high sense of honor ; for it is the peculiar property of honor that the affair of its possessor progresses ; and if all are equal in this point, he will be successful who has the greatest firmness and sincerity of purpose ; and if they be on the same footing in this respect too, that one will win the end in view, whose friends and allies are most numerous ; and if here also there be no difference, his will be the triumph, who is aided by fortune and befriended by destiny.

VERSE.

When o'er hope's horizon rises fortune's brightly-shining star,
How swiftly every wish is won !
But if fortune does not aid thee, it will all thy efforts mar,
Turn to the sea, 't will from thee run.'

The king said, ' They thought not so much of us, and did not imagine that we could be designing to revenge ourselves, for they saw that we were few, and they accounted us weak.' Kárshinás replied, ' There are four things, a little of which must be thought a great deal. The first is fire, a little of which is as mischievous in burning as a great deal. The second is debt, since the shame of being dunned for one dirham is the same as for a thousand dínárs. The third is sickness, for, though the health may be but little disturbed, yet its concomitants are debility and want of spirits. The fourth is an enemy, who, though he may be weak and contemptible, will in the end effect his purpose. And I have heard that a Sparrow in spite of its feeble condition, obtained vengeance on a powerful snake.' The king asked, ' How was that ?'

STORY XIV.

Kárshinás said, 'They have related that two sparrows had made their nest in the roof of a house; and, contenting themselves with a single grain, so lived. Once on a time they had young ones, and both the mother and father used to go out in search of food for their support; and what they procured, they made up into grains and dropped into their crops. One day, the male Sparrow had gone out somewhere. When he came back, he beheld the female sparrow fluttering in the greatest distress around the nest, while she uttered piteous cries. He exclaimed, 'Sweet friend! what movements are these, which I behold in thee?' She replied,

COUPLET.

'A thorn, my bosom piercing, makes me rain tears from my eyes;
There's a grief, my heart consuming, that forces from it sighs.

How shall I not lament, since, when I returned after a moment's absence, I saw a huge snake come and prepare to devour my offspring, though I poured forth piteous cries and said,

COUPLET.

Thou mayest have overwhelming might, yet dread thy feeble enemy;
For ever on the target lights the arrow of the morning-sigh.

It was all in vain, for the snake said, 'Thy sigh will have no effect upon my dark-mirrored scales.' I replied, 'Dread this, that I and the father of these children will gird up the waist of vengeance, and will exert ourselves to the utmost for thy destruction.' The snake laughed and said,

COUPLET.

'He that does o'er the lions's self prevail,
When will such foe to such as thou art quail?'

And I, since I have been in nowise able to oppose him, raise these cries, and no one heeds them.

HEMISTICH.

I raise much clamor, but redress there's none.

And that cruel oppressor has devoured my young, and has also taken his rest in the nest.' When the male Sparrow heard this story, his frame was wrung with anguish; and the fire of regret for the loss of his offspring fell on his soul. At this moment, the master of the house was engaged in lighting his lamp; and, holding in his hand a match, dipped in grease and lighted, was about to put it into the lamp-holder. The Sparrow flew and snatched the match from his hand and threw it into the nest. The master of the house, through fear that the fire would catch to the roof, and that the consequences would be most pernicious, immediately ran up on the terrace, and began clearing away the nest from beneath, in order to put out the fire. The snake beheld in front the danger of the fire, and heard above the sound of the pickaxe. It put out its head from a hole which it had near the roof, and no sooner did it do so, than it received a blow on its head from the pickaxe.

And the moral of this fable is, that the snake despised its enemy, and made no account of him, until in the end that enemy pounded his head with the stone of vengeance,

COUPLET.

Weak though thy foe may be, for prudence sake,
Esteem him strong, and due provision make.'

The king said, 'The successful management of this affair, and the downfall of our foes, was through the blessing of thy counsel, and the happy influence of thy loyalty. And in every affair in which I have relied on thy word the result has developed itself well and favorably. Whoever commits the reins of the management of important affairs to a wise vazír, the hand of reverse never reaches the skirt of his good-fortune and the foot of calamity never circles round the region of his happiness; and thus it has happened to me from the excellence of thy judgment and wisdom.

COUPLET.

Where'er I turn, where'er direct my will,
I have strong help, for thou art with me still.

And of all thy good qualities this is the most perfect, that though thou hast remained for a long time in the enemy's dwelling; neither did thy tongue utter anything at which they could take offence, nor did any action spring from thee which could occasion aversion in them, or distrust.' He replied, ' O King!

HEMISTICH.

That too from thy good auspices arose.

For I had no pattern in all that I did, save the king's good qualities and virtuous habits, and what I borrowed, to the extent of my abilities, from the imperial virtues, that I made the exemplar of my own actions, and, Praise be to God! in the king are combined excellence of judgment and correctness of deliberation, with dignity, and majesty, and valor. Nor do the minutest parts of an affair remain hid from him, nor is the place for haste and delay, nor the suitable time for mildness and wrath, concealed from him. In the commencement of every undertaking, the measures that are expedient for to-day and to-morrow, and the steps requisite for the present and future conjunctures, are perceived by him; and he is cognizant of the modes of remedying the consequences thereof; and at no time, neglecting to be cautious, does he let slip the dignity of the state and the reputation of the Government.

And whoever of his own choice enters upon hostility with such a king draws with a thousand cords death upon himself, and repels life from himself by a thousand removes.

STANZA.

Fate drags the foe with hurrying steps along,
From life's fair threshold to the realms of death.
Each one who thee with hostile thoughts would wrong,
'Twere strange if fate should spare him half a breath.'

The king said, 'During this long interval of thy absence, I have neither tasted sweetness in my food and drink, nor have I enjoyed my sleep or repose; and now, praise be to God!

COUPLET.

To the zenith of perfection has arisen fortune's sun,
And the downfall of our foeman's baffled fortunes has begun.'

Kárshinás said, 'Of a truth whoever suffers from the calamity of a powerful enemy and a victorious foe, distinguishes not between night and day, and light and darkness; nor discerns his foot from his head, nor his slipper from his turban, until he is liberated from him. And the wise have said, 'Until the sick man is completely cured, he derives no pleasure from his food, nor does the porter rest until he has set down the heavy burthen from his back, nor does the lover find ease till he attains to the happiness of union with his mistress, nor is the fatigue of the traveler abated till he alights at the station, nor does the frightened man breathe in comfort until he is freed from his powerful enemy.

COUPLET.

When from his foe one is at length set free,
He turns his rein towards tranquillity.'

The king said, 'What view didst thou take of the qualities and character of their king in the battle and at the social board?' Kárshinás replied, 'His actions were based on presumption and self-conceit, and pride and indulgence. He neither possessed any share of right reflection nor did he distinguish right judgment from erroneous projects, and all his followers were like him, save one person who strongly urged my death.' The king asked, 'What was the proof of his understanding and wisdom?' Kárshinás replied, 'In that his settled opinion was that I should be slain; and in truth that opinion was combined with right reasoning. Secondly, that he withheld not his advice from his master, though he knew that he would not hear him, and in offering his advice, he preserved the bounds of respect.' The king asked, 'What is the etiquette to be observed in advising kings?' Kárshinás answered, 'Those who address monarchs should speak with courtesy and humility, and should incline from bluntness and roughness towards benignity and gentleness, and having shown the most perfect consideration for the honor of their lord,

should not exhibit boldness and audacity; and if in his actions or words—
any fault is observable—should employ words of true but kind admonition, and
use sweet illustrations and fascinating stories, and recount in the midst of the
tale the faults of others—and the vazír of the king of the owls possessed all
these qualities, and omitted not one particle in this respect; and I heard
with my own ears, that he said to the king, 'Dominion is a lofty station and
elevated rank. One cannot by one's own endeavor set the foot of desire on that
step, nor can one reach that degree save by the aid of fortune and the
assistance of destiny; and since it is attainable only by these fortunate
coincidences we ought to hold it dear, and show strenuous exertion for
retaining its laws and preserving its customs by justice and equity.

QUATRAIN.

O thou! to whom an empire's sway is given,
Wouldst thou be blest, eschew then tyranny.
Not by a hundred swords are realms so riven,
As by, if just, one injured victim's sigh.

And now it is more in accordance with a right course to avoid carelessness in
action, and not to look superciliously on measures of importance, since the permanence of a state and the continuance of good-fortune are attainable only by
four things. By perfect caution, which beholds the face of to-morrow in the
mirror of to-day; and by a universal fortitude, against whose resolve weakness
and infirmity make no way; and a right-aiming judgment, which swerves not
from the path of moderation towards error; and by a keen sword, which, like
the world-consuming lightning, casts fire into the stacked corn of the life of
its opponent.

COUPLET.

Ne'er in the garden of the state will justice flourish green,
Save it be watered from the fount of the sabre flashing keen.'

He said all this and no one heeded his words, and his advice was not
honored with acceptance.

HEMISTICH.

Till things from right and left all topsy-turvy turned.

Neither did they derive any benefit from his wisdom and sagacity, nor did he
himself escape from that calamity by his own intelligence and ability. And
here the truth of the subtle saying, '*There is no counsel to him who is not
obeyed,*' was thoroughly demonstrated.

VERSE.

How can his counsel advantageous seem,
From whose persuasions all men turn away?
A sage has said, 'The most judicious scheme
Is faulty, if its author none obey.'

This is the story of being cautious of the deceitful snares and treacherous
frauds of an enemy. For although he may be extremely humble, and

abase himself much; nevertheless, it is far removed from the path of wisdom to be deluded thereby. For a single lone crow, in spite of his weakness and feebleness, in that manner chastised powerful and numerous enemies; and this happened in consequence of their weakness of mind and poverty of understanding. Otherwise, had those owls possessed a particle of prudence, that crow would never have attained his object, nor have seen, even in sleep, the face of that triumph. And it behoves a wise man to survey this history with the eye of self-admonition; and to hear this ensample with the ear of understanding; and to know of a truth that it is not right to place confidence in an enemy, nor to despise a foe, however contemptible he may seem; and however much he may hear his enemy boast of attachment, or perceive him adduce causes for the confirmation of friendship, not to be elated thereby.

STANZA.

Whate'er his boasted friendship, still the foe
Will ne'er by wise men be believed a friend.
The venom of the snake is changeless, though
By casting off his skin he seem to mend.

And there is a second moral in this story which bids us to secure sincere friends and loyal and attached companions, since that may be regarded as the most profitable of treasures and the most advantageous of transactions. For the friendship of Kárshinás and his aid and assistance issued in such results to the crows, that they arrived from the dangerous place of terror and dismay at the station of security and peace. And if any one show himself to be equitable and amiable, know that he may at the same time have zealous friends, and may also pluck away the skirt of avoidance from perfidious foes. And thus he will arrive at all he could desire and at the summit of his wishes, '*And God is the Lord of successful assistance.*'

COUPLET.

With cordial friends in glad delights repose;
And pluck the skirt of converse from thy foes.'

CHAPTER V.

OF THE DETRIMENT OF GIVING WAY TO NEGLIGENCE, AND OF PER-
MITTING THE OBJECTS OF DESIRE TO ESCAPE FROM ONE'S
HANDS.

INTRODUCTION.

The king said to the Bráhman, 'Thou hast narrated the story of being
cautious of the deceit of enemies, and not being beguiled by their words, and
of guarding oneself from the injury of the hypocrisy and fraud of foes, and
from the calamity of the perfidious and insidious schemes of enemies although
they should appear in the guise of friends. My request now is, that thou
wouldest explain the story of one who exerted himself to gain a thing, and
after having obtained the object of his desire, indulging in carelessness, threw
away what he had gained.' The Bráhman opened the mouth of praise, and
recited from the page of eulogy these panegyrical verses.

STANZA.

'O Thou, auspicious-footed king of kings!
  Heaven's stars glad power from thy aspect gain.
Blest as the spot waved o'er by Phœnix' wings,
  Become the countries which thy shade obtain:
How of thy might shall I the glorious things
  Recount? Laud be to thee! and, yet again,
  High laud! albeit thou art above our praises vain.

It is not concealed from the penetrating mind of the king, which is the
happy site of infinite benevolence, that it is easier to acquire than to
preserve a thing. For many precious things may be obtained through a
happy contingency and the assistance of fortune, and the aid of destiny;
without the woe of exertion and the pain of labor. The retention of them,
however, save by clear counsels and proper measures, is impracticable; and
whoever is destitute of the ornament of caution and foresight, and who does
not[1] walk vigorously in the plain of good sense and a regard for consequences;
what he has acquired soon falls into the plain of spoliation and ruin, and
nothing is left in the grasp of his option but regret and contrition. Just in this
manner the friendship of one so attached as the Monkey, was gained without
the trouble of labor and exertion, by the Tortoise, and through folly and
ignorance was lost by him; and the wound of his fatuity and stupidity found
no healing-plaster.' The king inquired, 'How was that?'

---

[1] I can make no sense of *rájil bdshad*. It appears to me that a negative is absolutely
required, prefixed to the verb, and I translate accordingly, though no MS.supports the reading.

STORY I.

The Bráhman said, 'They have related that in one of the islands of the Indian Ocean [1] there were many monkeys, and they had a king whose name was Kárdán.[2] The foundation of his empire was raised on much awe, and a perfect administration of justice; and the basis of his grandeur was strengthened by a will which brooked no delay, and a justice dealt out to all. His subjects, through the glad influence of his beneficence, placed the side of happy repose on the couch of security and peace, and the inhabitants of that country loosed the tongue of benediction and propitiation in praise of his unlimited liberality.

COUPLET.

Wrong he repressed, and aid to justice lent;
God was well-pleased and man with him content.

He lived a very long time in happiness and prosperity, and passed from the spring of youth to the autumn of old age and weakness. Then the symptoms of decrepitude beginning to show themselves in his members, cheerfulness began to pack up its marching equipage to leave his heart, and light to quit his eye; and the plant of vigor, which had produced the fruits of desire, began, under the Samúm of debility and helplessness, to wither, and the lamp of mirth was extinguished by the violent blast of calamity and trouble, and the carpet of pleasure was folded up by the invasion of diseases and sufferings.

VERSE.

Seek not the signs of youth in aged men;
For to their source, streams ne'er return again.
Age must all passion from its thoughts remove,
Since with old age, expires the reign of love.
When age lets fall its snow-dust on the head,
Know that all hope of unmixed joy is fled.

And the custom of perfidious fortune is no other than this, that it changes the freshness of the rose-garden of youth into the dismal thorn-thicket of old age and makes turbid the sweet water[3] of wealth with the rubbish of the abasement of poverty. The happiness of its day is not separable from the suffering of its gloomy night; and its atmosphere, which shows at first so clear, is not without the dust of damage and injury.

STANZA.

Life's joys with sorrows infinite the fates together weld;
Then not for pleasant-tasted wine in fortune's goblet seek.
For who the water-lily in the garden ere beheld
But saw the tulip spotted with the tear-drops from its cheek?

---

[1] Lit., 'the green sea.'

[2] 'Knowing affairs,' 'experienced.'

[3] I have no doubt a play on words is intended here, as '*aẓb* means 'sweet water,' and '*aẓab*, ' water covered with weeds.'

This old husband-slaying beldam, which they call the world, presents herself to mortals in the apparel of a young bride, and with her fleeting jewels and untrustworthy ornaments, brings the heart of foolish simpletons into the snare of her love.

COUPLET.

This world's gear is but a pastime, to beguile poor infants fit;
Foolish are those simple mortals who are led astray by it.

And notwithstanding that she makes all this outward adornment a means of deceiving the victims of the plain of supineness, and employs this false stock of allurements for the demented ones of the bázár of appetite and lust; yet none of those who have bound her with the nuptial knot have succeeded in placing the hand of desire in the bosom of their wish, and not one of all who have brought[1] themselves into the net of union with her have for a single night reaped enjoyment according to the wish of their heart.

COUPLET.

A fair bride is the world; but yet, be wise!
For none may wed this coy and curtained prize.

The puerile ones of the end of the street, ' *This present life is no other than a play, and a vain amusement,*'[2] lie in her calamitous net, and are attached to her bewitching person, and are ignorant of the foulness of her interior, and the falseness of her promises, and the baseness of her nature, and the impurity of her disposition.

DISTICHS.

This world's enjoyments, like a serpent's skin,
Are chequered, soft, and venom-full within.
Rich men and poor, by her delusions bound,
Rejoice like one who dreams of treasure found.

And a wise man, the eyes of whose heart have been enlightened by the jeweled collyrium, ' *The world is a bridge, pass over it,*[3] *but do not repair it,*' gives no heed to its fleeting and delusive tales, nor sets his heart on the pursuit of its vain dignities and useless riches, and since he knows the instability of the world, and the uncertainty of its possessions, he turns his face to search for enduring happiness.

COUPLET.

Plant thou a root whose produce blest, eternal joy shall be;
For in life's garden spring fleets by, and autumn now we see.

---

[1] My best MS. inserts *khwudrá* before *dár dvarad*, which I think a great improvement on the reading of the editions.

[2] Ḳur'án, Fl. vi., 32; Mar. 31; Sale, p. 94, l. 17. 'This present life is no other than a play, and a vain amusement; but surely the future mansion shall be better for those who fear God: will they not, therefore, understand?'A similar expression occurs also at Ch. xlvii. 38, lvii. 19, of the Ḳur'án.

[3] For the reading of the edition *fá'atabarúhá*, I would suggest *fá'abarúhá*, which is the reading of my best MS., and is evidently the correct one.

In short, the rumor of the old age and decrepitude of Kárdán being spread abroad, his royal dignity and kingly awe suffered vast diminution; and a complete infraction and absolute weakening found way to the pillars of his princely majesty, and royal power and renown.

COUPLET.

Thou mayst high fortunes—such as Jamshíd's—share,
Yet hoary locks will bring with them despair.

It happened that one of the kinsmen of the king, a blooming youth, arrived there, on whose countenance were found the tokens of happy fortune, and in whose movements and attitudes the signs of auspicious destiny were conspicuous. When the nobles beheld in him suitableness for the rank of king, and merit deserving the high office of ruler; and observed his vigor in promoting a rigid administration of justice, and in repressing tyranny, and in perfectly arranging the course of indulgence and protection of the people,

HEMISTICH.

Thou, whose cheek bears the stamp of kingly sway!

they suffered his friendship to take a firm hold of their minds, and having brought their hearts into the bond of obedience and devotion to him, they said to one another,

VERSE.

' When garden-wards morn's breath begins to blow,
'Tis fitting that the young trees bow to it.
When the musk-willow blooms, 'tis spring, although
Their withered leaves the old trees' boughs then quit.

This blooming youth, the plant of whose existence has obtained its growth on the margin of the rivulet of courtesy, possesses all the qualifications[1] to make the garden of the kingdom, through his means, full of foliage and fruit.

HEMISTICH.

Behold this cypress, proudly stepping, make a garden of the world !'

And he, too, getting round the soldiery with caresses, and the people with conciliatory demeanor, presented each with a dress of honor suitable to his rank, and gratified them with the glad announcement of his munificent intentions, and with promises of land, and the good tidings of office and promotion; so that by a simultaneous movement of high and low they removed the broken-down old king from his office, and without a struggle or difficulty committed the reins of authority over the kingdom to the grasp of the sway of the young man.

COUPLET.

On earth the throne with joy at this wide spread,
And o'er the sky the crown upraised its head.

---

[1] One MS. reads here *sázad* for the *sázand* of the edition, and I should much prefer the former reading, if the awkward and unnecessary *bi-daulat-i ú* could be got rid of.

The hapless Kárdán, when he was stripped of the robe of royalty, not being able to endure that indignity, made choice, through hard necessity, of expatriation; and withdrawing himself to the sea-shore took up his abode in an islet which possessed abundance of trees and much fruit, and contenting himself with the fresh and dry fruits which were to be found in that wilderness, consoled himself, saying,

HEMISTICH.

'With water and dry food content, I'm monarch of the sea and land.'

In this manner in that wild spot, adopting the character of resignation, he traversed with the step of abstemiousness the paths of worship and devotion ; and night and day employed himself in making up for the time he had spent in the intoxication of sovereign power; and prepared, by penitence and contrition, provision for the road to a future state, and made ready with daily offerings of words and homage to God, a stock for his final journey; and rubbed off with the aid of the dawning light of old age the dimness which is imparted to the mirror of the breast by the darkness of the night of youth.

COUPLET.

Age dawns at last; for one short breath, arise, and off thy slumbers shake!
At morning-time it is not well to slumber on—Awake! awake!

One day having ascended a fig tree, in which he passed most of his time, he was gathering figs. Suddenly one of them slipped from his paw and fell into the water, and the noise it made reaching the ear of the Monkey-king his frame thrilled with pleasure, and delight pervaded him. Every minute, to gratify himself in that way, he kept on throwing another into the water, and amused himself with the sound. It happened that a Tortoise had come on his travels from the other side of the water to that island, and stopping under that tree, was wishing to repose there for a day or two, and afterwards return to his wife and family. In short, at that very time when the Monkey was eating the figs, the Tortoise was in the water under the tree. Every time that a fig dropped into the water he devoured it with the greatest avidity, and fancied that the Monkey was throwing it in for him, and that he thought fit to shew this winning behaviour and kindness for his sake. Where- upon he reflected thus, 'Here is a person who, without previous acquaintance, shews this beneficence towards me. Now, if the link of friendship and the bond of amity should be established between us, it is evident what a vast amount of favor and kindness would be manifested by him. And putting aside[1] worldly advantages, the companionship of such a person, in whose nature such virtues and admirable qualities are bound up, and on the pages of whose condition the pen of grace has written the verse of generosity and liberality,

---

[1] Observe the expression, kata'-i nazar, which is here used adverbially.

is one of the invaluable prizes of fortune. And assuredly, with the furbisher of his society, the dust of ennui may be effaced from the mirror of the heart; and by the light of his presence, the shades of disaster may be removed from the atmosphere of the bosom.

COUPLET.

When the heart's royal mirror [1] dim I find,
I ask from God a friend of serene mind.

He then resolved on seeking the society of the Monkey; and, raising his voice, offered the customary salutations, as is prescribed. Next he represented the wishes he had formed for his friendship and companionship. The Monkey returned a favorable answer, and evinced the utmost rapture and the strongest inclination for his society, saying, 'To shew an eagerness for amicable intercourse with comrades, and to seek strenuously to increase the number of our friends, is a praiseworthy quality and an amiable attribute; and whoever has a real friend and a pious brother derives exaltation and success in both worlds.

VERSE.

They who the friendship of the pious share,
Have what in both worlds will them lustre lend.
Not few are this world's blessings—true! but where
Can one be found, so precious as a friend!'

The Tortoise said, 'I aim at thy friendship and companionship, but I know not if I possess the requisite fitness for it.' The Monkey said, 'The wise have furnished scales for trying friendship, and have pronounced that although it is bad to be friendless altogether, yet it is not every one who is suited to be a friend; and friendship ought to be formed with one of three kinds of persons. The first kind consists of men of learning and devotion, since, by the blessing of their society, happiness may be obtained in this world and the next. Secondly, people of amiable qualities, who will conceal the errors of a friend, and will not withhold their advice from a comrade. Thirdly, such people as are devoid of selfishness and greediness, and who base their friendship on sincerity and true attachment. And it is a divine precept to shun the friendship of three classes. The first is the profligate and debauched, whose energies are expended in gratifying their carnal appetites, and whose companionship is neither a cause of happiness in this world, nor a means of obtaining mercy in the next. The second class is the false and traitorous, whose society is an excruciating torment, and whose converse is a huge misfortune. They will be ever speaking untruths of thee to others, and will bring from others to thee alarming and mischievous messages contrary to the truth. The third class is the fatuous and imbecile, in whom no confidence

---

[1] Lit. 'The heart, that is a royal mirror, has dust; I ask of God the society of the clear-minded.'

can be placed for securing advantage and in repelling injuries; and it often happens that what they have thought to be essentially good and advantageous, is absolutely bad and injurious.

COUPLET.

> How from his friendship canst thou aid obtain,
> Who knows not good from ill, nor loss from gain?

And the apophthegm which they have uttered on this subject, viz., that 'A wise enemy is better than an ignorant friend,' may signify that when a foe is adorned with the ornament of good sense; he, being invested with foresight, does not inflict a wound till he sees a fitting opportunity; and hence, by observing in his movements and posture, the symptoms of revenge, it is possible to guard oneself against him. But a friend who is destitute of any share of the riches of wisdom, although he may attempt to make himself useful in deliberating on the measures advisable to be adopted, will render no service. And it is probable that the person he attempts to befriend will be caught in some dangerous strait through his defective judgment and mistaken opinions. Just as, from the Monkey that stood sentinel, it almost happened that the vessel of the life of the king of Kashmír fell into the whirlpool of destruction; and if the Thief, who was a wise enemy, had not cried out, it would have been impossible for that affair to have been remedied.' The Tortoise inquired, 'How was that?'

STORY II.

Kárdán said, 'I have heard that in the country of Kashmír there was a great king, who possessed such a treasure that it was too heavy even for mighty mountains to support, and such an army that the thought of reckoning its numbers never entered the idea of the intellect which observes the slightest minutiæ. He had set up the banners of empire and success on the dome of the azure sky, and had inscribed the verses of his justice and benevolence to his subjects on the page of the revolutions of night and day.

VERSE.

> The world obeyed his all-pervading law,
> And kings his threshold, stooping, kissed with awe.
> To justice he, and faith, their basis gave,
> And teeming realms through him new nations have.

And this king had a Monkey upon whom he used to place reliance in perilous circumstances, and there was no point of royal bounty which he failed to observe in rearing him. From the excessive attachment with which the Monkey was indued, he was distinguished by the king's special favor. Every night he held in his hand a dagger, brilliant as a drop of water, and kept guard at the pillow of the king, nor did he let slip from his hand the clew of that service, until the tumult of the rise of the true morn roused from the bed of sloth the careless slumberers on the couch of pride.[1] It so happened that a clever thief from a distant city came into that country, and one night determined that he would shew his skill and get some booty. Putting on the dress that sharpers wear, he traversed the streets accordingly. With the same intentions, another thief, who knew but little and was inexperienced, had come forth. Owing to their homogeneousness they joined each other, and he that was the foreigner asked, by way of taking advice, 'To which quarter should I go? and whose house should I undermine?'[2] The unwise thief replied, 'In the stable of the Ra'is[3] of the city there is a fat and fleet ass, and he values him exceedingly, so that to keep him safe he has put a strong chain on his fore and hind legs, and has set two slaves over him. Our advisable course is to go first and steal that ass, and at the corner of the market-place of the city there is the shop of a glass-blower, into which we will break, and bringing out new and valuable glasses will lade them on that ass, and come back with our wishes accomplished.' The clever thief stood amazed at his words, and was about to cross question him well about the matter, when all of a sudden, the night-patrol made his appearance. The clever thief dexterously concealed himself behind a wall, and the fool was taken. The watch asked him. 'Where wast thou going?' He replied, I am a thief, and my intention was to steal the ass of the Ra'is, and break into the shop of a glass-blower, take his glasses, and carry them off home.' The patrol laughed and said, 'Bravo! this is the sort of thief we want, who for an ass that is so watched puts his life in the balista of calamity, and who thrusts himself into danger for glasses, ten of which they sell for a dáng.[4]

HEMISTICH.

Thou didst not buy thy life for money, hence thou dost not know its worth.

If thou wert to undertake such perils for the treasures of the king, then indeed reason would hold thee excused.

HEMISTICH.

Let him, who bears the burden, carry off the guerdon[5] too.'

With these words he tied his hands and dragged him away to prison. The clever thief thus received a warning from the intellect of the foolish one, and deriving some experience too from what the patrol said, soliloquized as follows, 'This thief was an ignorant friend to me, and the patrol was a wise enemy, and that friend by his folly was plunging me into the vortex of

---

[1] Or it may be, *gharúr*, 'the world.'

[2] Oriental thieves enter houses by mining under the walls which are generally built with little or no foundation.

[3] The Ra'is is the chief citizen, a sort of alderman.

[4] A small silver coin.

[5] In every case where, as in this line, there is a jingle of words like 'burden' and 'guerdon,' let the reader remember it represents a similar effect in Persian; and has been often arrived at with considerable trouble.

destruction, and but for this wise enemy, the affair would have passed beyond my control, and ended in my being put to death. Now, just as the patrol said, it behoves me to make for the treasury of the king. Perhaps my main object and my fullest wishes may then be gained.' He then went very softly under the palace of the king, and began to make a mine, and the livelong night, in his covetous desire for gold went on cutting through the stone with his steel instrument.

COUPLET.

> So on the stones his massive crowbar rang,
> That fire and water [1] both at once outsprang.

As yet the sharper that travels by night, the sun, had not completed boring a passage beneath the wall of the horizon, when the thief's mine was finished and he emerged at the spot where was the bedchamber of the king. There he beheld the monarch sleeping on a golden throne, and a variety of costly furniture around the royal pillow, and divers sorts of gems scattered over the borders of the imperial carpets. Wax candles, white as camphor [2] were lighted up like the countenances of wealthy men of rank, and were consuming the poor moth, as the hearts of fasting darveshes is consumed by the flame of despair.

COUPLET.

> Betwixt me and the moth this difference see, the flame burns both, 'tis true ;
> But, while its wings alone are scorched, I lose my heart and spirit too.

The thief looked about him and beheld the monkey with a poniard in his hand, standing at the king's pillow and casting vigilant glances to the left and right. The thief was astounded at this sight and said, ' How has a contemptible creature such as this, to whom it would be too much honor to climb up a lamp-post, set his foot on the carpet of the prince ? and whence has a sharp sword, with which is bound up the stability of the realm and nation, fallen into the hands of one so unstable ? ' The thief, immersed in the ocean of these meditations, and overwhelmed in the vortex of these cogitations, was looking on, when, on a sudden, some ants fell from the ceiling of the apartment upon the breast of the king, which was the mirror that adorned the world, and began to crawl about, and the irritation of this, affected the heart of the king. The monarch, his slumber unbroken, yet sensible of the tickling of the ants, smote his hand upon his bosom, and the Monkey ran to that side and perceived the ants that were crawling on the king's chest. The fire of wrath was kindled in his breast, and he exclaimed, ' Whence comes it that in spite of a guardian such as I am, the star of whose eye, like the rolling planets, has never, any night, beheld the face of sleep,

---

[1] The word *áb* signifies not only ' water,' but also 'the polish of steel.' Perhaps therefore this strange expression means that the steel was polished by collision with the stone and sparks of fire struck out. Or, the *áb* may refer to the perspiration of the man, and the *átish* to the sparks struck out from the stone.

[2] Or, 'perfumed with camphor,' according to some.

these dusky ants have the audacity to set foot on the breast of my lord?'
Then stimulated by his ignorant zeal, and enraged at the ants,[1] he drew his
dagger, that he might make a blow at the king's breast and slay the insects.
The thief gave a shout, calling out, 'Rash churl! hold thy hand or thou
wilt overturn a world from its foundation.' With these words he leaped
forward and tightly grasped the monkey's hand which held the dagger.
The king was roused from his slumbers by the shout of the thief, and
beholding this posture of affairs, asked the thief who he was? The latter
replied, 'I am thy wise enemy, who had come hither in quest of thy wealth
and the attainment of my own ends. And had I paused for a moment in
defending thee, this kind ally and attached friend would have saturated thy
chamber with gore.' When the king had learnt the state of the case, he
prostrated himself in gratitude for his escape, and said, 'Aye, truly! when
infinite grace befriends us, the thief becomes the guardian and the foe a
friend!' He then rewarded the thief and admitted him among his favorites,
and having chained the monkey, sent him to the stable. Thus a thief, who
in hope of a treasure, girt up his waist for a night enterprise, and made a
breach in the wall of the treasury, inasmuch as he was robed in the vest of
wisdom, had the crown of fortune placed upon his head; while a monkey
who thought himself the friend and confidant of the secrets of the king, in
that the thorn of ignorance adhered to his skirt, was stripped of the apparel
of honor.

VERSE.

Wise foes though deadly evils they may be,
Excel friends who are ignorant.
What the fool does is all calamity,
And all his usefulness is scant.

And the moral of this story is, that it behoves a wise man to pave the
way to friendship with the wise and to flee for leagues from the society of
ignorant friends.

VERSE.

Flee not a prison with friends to thy mind,
But those unsuited e'en in gardens shun;
Thou wilt a prudent foeman better find,
Than with a fatuous comrade to be one.'

When the Tortoise had heard this story, which comprised much useful
instruction, he said, 'O ocean of wisdom! thou hast adorned with the
princely gem of knowledge the ear of my heart. Now be pleased to recount
how many kinds of friends there are.' Kárdán said, 'The wise have
pronounced that of people who pretend to be friends, there are three sorts.
The one kind are like food, since their presence is indispensable, and without

---

[1] Readings differ here very considerably, but I think that of the editions as good as any.

the survey of the brilliance of their beauty the taper of social intercourse gives no light.

COUPLET.

A friend's face is the lamp that gilds the mansion of the heart,
'Tis this alone that does to it its usefulness impart.

And another class resemble medicine, being such as are occasionally required; while a third sort are like pain, as being of no use at any time. And these last are the hypocrites and impostors, who have a face and a tongue for thee, and who yet do not quit the path of agreement with thy enemies.

VERSE.

Before thee, they are kindlier than light,
And yet behind, than shadows falser far:
Warm—but in inward feeling frigid quite;
Quick—but at heart they dead and lifeless are.[1]

Wherefore it behoves a wise man to shun this kind of enemies with friendly faces, and to flee for refuge to sincere friends and cordial companions.

HEMISTICH.

Break from thy foe and lay hands on a friend.'

The Tortoise said, 'What procedure is one to adopt in order to fulfil all the requirements of friendship?' The Monkey answered, 'Those who are adorned with six qualities, there are no short-comings in their friendship. The first is he, who, when he discovers a fault, does not try to divulge it. The second is, he who, if he becomes acquainted with a virtue, magnifies it tenfold. The third is he who, if he does thee a favor, does not always bear it in mind. The fourth is he who, if he receives a benefit from thee, does not forget it. The fifth is he who, if he sees thee commit a fault, does not twit thee with it. The sixth is he who, if thou excusest thyself, accepts the excuse. And whosoever is not indued with these qualities, is totally unfit for friendship; and if thou choosest to become his friend, repentance will come at last. And most people are devoid of these qualities, and consequently a true friend is like the philosopher's stone; and attachment without a flaw, resembles the 'Anḳa, whose flight is towards the nest of non-existence.

QUATRAIN.

He that can not the lines of friendship trace,
With him in unison thou canst not tread:
The glass alone displays a friendly face,[2]
Of what avail, since with a breath 'tis fled?'

---

[1] I have freely rendered these very difficult lines, about the real meaning of which I am in some doubt. The last two lines are, perhaps, literally; 'Warm, but more melancholy than the liver: Alive, but more dead than the heart itself.' But the *az dil* may signify 'at heart,' as I have translated it.

[2] This line means, either that a mirror is the only unsullied surface; all human breasts are stained with some selfish or evil quality: or, that a mirror shews a true friend, even oneself; yet this image vanishes if one breathe on it.

When the conversation had proceeded thus far, the Tortoise said, 'I opine that I shall plant my foot firmly in friendship, and not omit a single particle of the rites of companionship. If, then, thou wilt honor me with the exaltation of thy friendship, and place on the neck of my heart the chain of obligation, which will abide till the resurrection, it will not be alien to thy beneficent character.' The Monkey, with courteous demeanour, descended from the tree, and the Tortoise likewise stepped out of the water under the tree, and they embraced one another, and pledged themselves to brotherhood. Thus both the horror of his solitary life was removed from the heart of the Monkey, and the Tortoise, too, was succored by his amity. Every day the plant of unity sprouted more abundantly between them, and the garden of companionship and attachment gained an increase of adornment and freshness. So that the Monkey forgot his kingdom and sovereignty, and the Tortoise, too, failed to remember his family and home.

COUPLET.

Our friend is with us, wherefore, then, should we yet seek more joy than this?
The treasure of his converse is to our fond hearts sufficient bliss.

A long time passed thus, and the period of the absence of the Tortoise was protracted. His partner became anxious, and intense anxiety and boundless solicitude found way to her, and life-consuming separation burnt up her heart with the fire of regret.

COUPLET.

Absence is such a wound, that with it were a mountain's bosom scarred,
It would smite stones upon its breast, and raise an outcry heavenward.

At length she introduced the subject of her regret for the absence of her spouse, and the tale of her love, to one of her own race.

STANZA.

'My friend is gone, but yet my heart the longing for his face retains:
Like the sad cypress hence my foot down-sunken in the clay is left.
I with his beauty wished to soothe the growing torture of my pains,
He hid his face, and as before the story of my grief is left.

I know not in what quarter my poor spouse has been stayed in the mire, or in what slough the foot of his heart has sunk down. Would that by the rising of the moon of his return the gloom of the evening of separation were dispersed! and that by the manifestation of the display of his beauty, the love-thoughts, which tend to madness, were banished!

COUPLET.

How blest were I, did that fair rose return once more to the parterre!
This soul, which has the body left, if it again were harbored there!'

When her companion beheld all this distress of mind, she said, 'O sister! if thou wilt not take it ill, or suspect me of evil motives, I will acquaint thee with his condition.' The wife of the Tortoise replied, 'Kind friend, and

confidante of my hidden secrets ! how can I possibly suspect thy words, or
think they proceed from interested motives? and how could I meet thy
advice with evil surmisings and opposition? and it is long since I have
tested the coin of thy friendship on the touchstone of trial, and found it
unalloyed.

HEMISTICH.

I know thy words are true, without a doubt.'

The friend rejoined, 'I have heard that thy husband has happened to form
a friendship and good understanding with a monkey, and dedicating his
heart and soul to his amity, regards his society as surpassing all other
blessings, and intercourse with him as superior to all other delights; and
allays with the water of his proximity the fire of regret for separation from
thee, and solaces his time with the beauty of this friend in exchange for thy
image.' When the female tortoise heard these words, the fire of jealousy
spread through her brain, and she exclaimed,

COUPLET.

'Blood is the ocean of my heart, for he by others is caressed ;
And while my lap is filled with tears, he in another's lap is blessed.

O cruel fortune ! thou hast given to the wind of dispersion the harvest of my
peace of mind, and hast destroyed, with the scorching blast of sorrow, the
field of my hopes.   Thou hast made the friend, who was the companion of
my sad heart, the associate of others, and hast thrown into their embrace the
beloved one, with joy at whose sight I used to depict on the carpet of pleasure
the painting of my wish.   And thou wouldest imagine that the faithless one
had never read from the page of association the writing of love, and wouldest
say that that apparent stranger had never in his whole life inhaled from the
garden of friendship the scent of attachment.

COUPLET.

That froward one, who nothing prized the value of a wretch like me,
Is now estranged, nor sees in what his better, happier course would be.'

Her friend rejoined, 'Now what was to be, has been ; it is useless to indulge
in vain regrets.   A plan must be devised which shall comprise the restoration
of thy tranquillity.'   They then busied themselves with perusing the book
of artifices, an account of the measures of which is rendered by the verse
'surely your cunning is great,'[1] and find no plan better than the destruction
of the Monkey.   They therefore schemed how to contrive this; and the
spouse of the tortoise, at the suggestion of her intimate friend, feigned
herself sick, and sent one to the Tortoise with this message,

---

[1] Ḳur'án, Fl. xii. 28; Mar. 29; Sale, p. 176, l. 22 : 'And when her husband saw that
his garment was torn behind, he said, This is a cunning contrivance of your sex: for surely
your cunning is great. O Joseph, take no further notice of this affair: and thou, O
woman ! ask pardon for thy crime ; for thou art a guilty person.'

COUPLET.

' For me, sick, yet to ask has he the will?
Bid him come quickly, for I'm breathing still.'

The Tortoise, having received the intelligence of the indisposition and sickness of his spouse, asked permission of the Monkey to go home, and renew the duty of visiting his wife and children. The Monkey said, ' O friend, partner of my cares! thou must with all possible speed favor me again with thy society, and not leave poor me in this retired solitude alone and friendless; and, indeed, the grief of being parted from thee will not leave me alone, nor will the pain of separation suffer me to be without a companion.

COUPLET.

No friend for many a lonely night have I, but only grief for thee:
Alas! for him to whom no friend but sorrow yields kind sympathy.'

The Tortoise replied, ' Kind friend and solace of my soul! a necessary journey has befallen me, and an event has occurred which leaves me without option; otherwise, I should never of my free and willing choice remove myself from thy society, nor would I be absent for a single moment from attending on thee by my own desire.

COUPLET.

Yes! were it not that I from thee must go, I'd leave thee never,
No thing that lives could wish its frame should from its spirit sever.'

Then, willing or not, he bade farewell to the Monkey, and turned his face homeward; and, when the familiar fatherland was honored and adorned with the step of the Tortoise, friends and kinsfolk came round and raised their shouts of welcome to the star 'Ayyúk[1]; and the Tortoise, with a party of his intimate friends, entered his abode. He beheld his wife stretched on the bed of death; and on the garden of her cheek, instead of a nosegay of the red Arghawán-flowers, the yellow rose expanding.

HEMISTICH.

From grief, a reed; from weeping, like a hair.[2]

Although he laid before her the offering of salutation, he was not honored with the boon of reciprocation; and however much he paved the way with courtesy and tenderness, he discovered no sign of his being heeded; nor did his blandishment and soft address reach the place of acceptance; nor his kindness and caresses yield any result.

COUPLET.

Take from her street thy stock of grief, thy wailings, O my heart!
These unsought goods will ne'er find there a sale-time or a mart.

---

[1] A certain bright red star, which follows the Pleiades.

[2] There is a very good play on words here, which I find it impossible to retain in English. The Persian has,—From (*ndlah*) ' wailing,' she became (*ndlí*) ' a reed;' from (*múyah*) ' weeping,' she became (*múí*) ' a hair.'

He then inquired of her adopted sister who had appointed herself to the attendance on her sick bed, 'Why does the sufferer not open her lips to speak, nor disclose to me, distracted as I am, what she has on her mind?' The bosom-friend heaved a cold sigh and said,

COUPLET.

'Doctor! pain thyself no longer, for thy time is vainly spent,
Love is not like other ailings, nor admits medicament.

How can an illness which is irremediable, and sufferings for which a cure is hopeless, obtain leave from the heart to breathe a word? And by what energies could it be furnished with the means of conversation?' The Tortoise began to weep, and was excessively distressed, saying, 'What medicine is this which cannot be found in this country, and which we cannot succeed in obtaining by contrivance and artifice? Speak with all despatch! that I may traverse sea and land in search of it, and seek for it from far and near, and from friend and stranger. If, like a fish, I must descend to the bottom of the deep, I will proceed taking steps with my head; and if, like the moon, I must hasten to the summit of the sky, I will mount by the noose of contrivance to the battlements of heaven. I will freely give my life and heart in quest of this remedy, and devote this essence of water and clay, (which is a metaphor for the continuance of existence), in order to gain this cure.

COUPLET.

What thing is life, that it should not be offered for thy sake?
My heart for thee I could devote—a free-will offering make.'

The waitress at the sick bed replied, 'This is a kind of pain which is peculiar to women, and which takes place in the womb, and admits of no cure save the heart of a monkey.' The Tortoise answered, 'Whence can this be procured, and how can it be obtained?' The bosom-friend who originated this guileful device, and was the real agent in proposing the remedy for the disease, replied, 'We, too, knew that the procuring of this sanative would be difficult, and the toil of securing this remedy which resembles the elixir-vitæ, would be great, nay, immense. We therefore sent for thee, in order, in fact, that thou mightest take the last sight of thy faithful friend and say thy last farewell, since to this unfortunate there is no other hope of her pain being alleviated, nor is the blessing of health in any other manner recoverable.

COUPLET.

Save blood I see no sharbat that befits my fell disease,
Through life's vista only sorrow seems assigned to give me ease.'

The Tortoise was grieved and agonised beyond measure; and however much he revolved the means of securing a remedy, he saw no escape save in killing the monkey, and felt himself compelled to regard his friend with greed. Clear-counselling reason loosed the tongue of admonition, and said,

'O ungenerous one! with perfidious hand to destroy the former basis of friendship and unanimity which had been firmly laid down between thee and the Monkey, is far removed from generosity and honor.

COUPLET.

Shame, if by woman's blandishment
Thy vest should be with falsehood rent.' [1]

And dark passions began to reproach and tempt him, saying, 'To abandon the cause of a wife, on whom is dependent the prosperity of the house and the prop of maintenance, and the means of living and the safeguard of treasure and property; and thereby to observe the regard due to a friend who has no homogeneousness with thee, nor affinity to thee, appears to be removed from a due regard to the transactions of life.

COUPLET.

I swear it by the rights of friendship!—dust e'en of an ancient friend
All the blood of new companions does a thousand times transcend.'

At last, his affection for his wife prevailing, he resolved to shatter with the stone of treachery the candle of good faith, and to make the scale of loyal attachment kick the balance through fraud and deceit. He, unhappy being that he was, knew not that the mark of insincerity is the brand of misery, the impression of which is not found save on the face of the condition of the ill-starred, and the quality of promise-breaking is a character of infamy which is not inscribed except on the tablet of the forehead of the vile. And whoever has, by perfidy and hypocrisy, reached the degree of notoriety, no man of piety desires his converse; and he that is noted for faithlessness and inconstancy is admitted by no one to the rank of acceptance; nay, people consider it necessary to shun meeting him, or holding conversation with him, and regard it as expedient to disown his actions and all knowledge of his affairs. [2]

COUPLET.

The old man, rest his soul! who drained with me the wine-cup bright,
Oft bade me shun their converse, who of promises make light.

After the Tortoise had formed this design against the Monkey, he saw that until he could get him to his own house, it would be impossible to secure his object. For this purpose he returned to the Monkey, whose longing to see him was quite overpowering, and whose desire to behold him exceeded the bounds of restraint. As soon as his eyes fell on the beauty of his friend, from the excess of his delight, he commenced, in joy-exciting strains, this song,

---

[1] 'To rend the vest,' is here an expression for acting 'unchastely,' 'dishonorably;' in the latter sense as applied to the tortoise.

[2] We have here the first of three pages of excessively obscure and difficult Persian.

2 c

COUPLET.

'A thousand thanks be paid to God, that one so loved as thou,
At length, and after dark suspense, to me hast showed thy brow.'

Then after warm inquiries concerning the welfare of the Tortoise, he requested that the condition of his children and relations might be made known to him. The Tortoise replied, 'Pain at separation from thee had entirely overpowered my heart, so that I could not derive pleasure from the warmth[1] of my meeting with them, and gladness and mirth displayed not themselves at the companionship of my wife and family. Every moment that I bethought myself of thy solitude, and the separation which has befallen thee from thy followers and retainers, and that I reflected on thy friendlessness, and the isolation from thy kingdom and prosperous fortune, in which thou hast been involved; my pleasure became embittered, and the clearness of the draught of happiness was discolored, and I said to myself, 'O ungenerous one! is it allowable for thee to sit here in the expanse of the garden of ease on the cushion of enjoyment, while thy faithful friend, in the thorny brake of exile, makes his dark couch upon the earth?

COUPLET.

Befits it that thyself shouldst here, rose-like, be gaily blooming?
While fortune thy thorn-wounded friend to lameness there is dooming.

Therefore I have come with the strong hope that thou wilt think it right to honor me, and that thou wilt adorn and gratify my house and children with the sight of thee, in order that my kinsfolk may recognize the rank I hold in thy friendship, and that my friends and connections may be proud and elated thereby. Thus both my heart may be soothed by union with thee, and, at the same time, my position may derive lustre from thy beauty, so that, by the good fortune of thy footsteps, my dignity may be elevated, while thou wilt experience no abatement of estimation in accepting my invitation.

COUPLET.

What lustre wilt thou lose, O moon! if thou shouldst pass before me,
Or through my lattice thou shouldst cast a beam of radiance o'er me?

Moreover I desire to seat in thy presence a party at the banqueting-table, and thus, perhaps, I may in some degree discharge what is due to thy virtues.' The Monkey said, 'Forbear these ceremonies, for when the chain of friendship is firmly riveted, and the knot of affection and companionship is rightly adjusted, there is no necessity for undergoing the trouble of entertainment and the ceremonial usages of general hospitality, as persons of formality and etiquette observe them. For they have said, '*He is the worst of brothers for*

---

[1] The word *dtish* seems to me meaningless here. One MS. reads for *faraḥi*, *ḥarak*, which may mean, 'the fructifying property of the male palm!'

whom ceremony is required.' Yes! truly he is the worst of friends and of brethren for whom ceremony is necessary, and for whom the load of troublous etiquette must be endured.

HEMISTICH.

One might live happy did forms not exist.

And with regard to the reciprocal friendship and amity which exist on my part towards thee, if thou observest an excess with reference to thee, for that too, be not sorrowful, since the pride I feel in thy virtues is greater, and my need of thy support and sympathy more urgent, inasmuch as I am cast far from my country and home, and kindred and dominions, and servants and retinue; and am calamitously involved in the disgrace of exile and the abasement of a solitary life and loneliness. Had not God Most High, by the blessing of thy society, conferred a fresh favor on me and bestowed on me the boon of thy friendship in a distressful and forlorn state such as mine then was, who would have extricated me from the injurious claws of fortune? or who would have plucked me from the hand of the affliction of separation from my friends?

COUPLET.

In this solitary mansion, in this trouble-peopled state,
'Tis thy sight that makes us glad, and our spirit thus elate.

Wherefore by the force of these circumstances, thy claim upon me is greater and thy kindness towards me more abundant, and this being the case there is no occasion for this trouble and irksome ceremony; and in friendship the purity of faith is the thing to be relied on, not the preparation of the materials for entertainment; and the offering of mental gratification is what is looked for, not the arrangement of substantial fare.

COUPLET.

A friend devoid of outward shew is wanted: have we such,
What if in forms he wanting be! that does not matter much.'

The Tortoise said, 'O companion of real sympathy! and O friend and partaker of my secrets! my object in inviting thee is not that same regard for the requisites of entertainment and the preparation of eatables and drinkables, but rather that separation should decamp from between us, and that the ennobling privilege of unbroken intercourse should be secured.

HEMISTICH.

Distance and nearness have no place in love.

Should the distance of east and west[1] intervene between two lovers, even then, inasmuch as their solace is in the remembrance of each other and the

---

[1] *B'udu 'l-mashriḳayn,* lit. 'The distance between the two Easts.' It seems somewhat forced to suppose that the West is to be reckoned one of these. Hence, the two farthest points at which the sun rises, viz., the tropics, have been suggested in lieu of the above explanation.

mutual happiness of their hearts in picturing each other's beauty, their
actual distance will not prove a veil in the road of their spiritual meeting,
and they will incessantly gaze on the incomparable beauty of each other,
with the vision of their mind and the mind of their vision.

COUPLET.

Am I united with my friend in heart,   What matters if our place be wide apart!

And a grave authority has said with regard to this,

QUATRAIN.

'What though our hands hold not the coin of union!
Yet in our souls abides each other's thought;
We may not taste in outward sense communion,
Our spirits, blending, set that care at nought.'

The Tortoise again applied the arrow of entreaty to the bow of supplication,
and began to launch it at the target of his desire, and, at length, aided by the
strength of his good fortune, reached the goal of his wishes. The Monkey
[at last] said, 'It is a canon in the code of honor to seek to gratify a friend,
and I will not remain at this distance from mine, but regard as a blessing
this pilgrimage to thy brethren and connections. However, it is a matter of
difficulty for me to pass over water, and to cross this sea which intervenes
between the wilderness, where I am, and thy island is for me an impossibility.'
The Tortoise replied, 'Set thy mind at ease, for I will take thee on my back
and convey thee to that island, in which are found both security and
happiness, and plenty and peace.' In short, inasmuch as the Tortoise
employed these gentle words, the Monkey desisted from his opposition,
and, tamed by the lash of flattering and courteous expressions, surrendered
to him the reins of control. So the Tortoise taking the Monkey on his
back, set out homewards. When he arrived in the midst of the sea, the
vessel of his mind sank down in the vortex of meditation, and he
reflected, 'What thing is this that I have taken in hand? and what result
can it have but dishonor?

COUPLET.

Who turns obliquely from the bowers of faith,   The thorn of anguish will his bosom scath.

For the sake of weak-minded women to adopt perfidious measures towards
friends completely wise, is not the wont of those of a liberal spirit; and to
let the clue of God's favor slip from the hands to please the devil, is a source
of damage and loss.

HEMISTICH.

Forbear! forbear! for good men act not thus.'

In this manner he halted in the midst of the water, and disputed with
himself, and the signs of irresolution were apparent in his movements. This
gave rise to suspicion in the mind of the Monkey, and he asked, 'What is
the cause of thy pondering? Perchance thou beginnest to find the carrying of
me difficult, and hence, being overloaded, thou proceedest so deliberately?'

The Tortoise answered, 'Whence sayest thou this, and from what dost thou draw this inference?' The Monkey replied, 'The marks of thy contest with thyself, and thy embarrassed purpose are evident. Perhaps if thou wouldest acquaint me and bestow on me the honor of an explanation, thou mayest by the aid of my advice, which is worthy of confidence, emerge from the whirlpool of perplexity to the shore of safety.' The Tortoise answered, 'Thou sayest truly—I was plunged in meditation, and all my doubt is, that as this is the first time that thou bestowest on my abode the good fortune of thy visit, and my wife is sick, as a natural consequence our domestic arrangements will not be free from confusion, and the due rites of hospitality and obligations of civility, will not be discharged, and this will be a cause of shame and discredit.

HEMISTICH.

And though my fault be pardoned, I should blush.'

The Monkey said, 'Since the sincerity of thy purpose is certain, and thy eagerness in seeking to gratify me, well ascertained, if thou shouldest postpone this ceremony and omit the compliments and observances which among strangers it is the duty of hosts to pay, it would certainly seem more agreeable to the course of friendship and amity.

COUPLET.

Through forms a stranger men to friendship lead;
Where amity exists, of forms what need?'

The Tortoise proceeded a little further, and stopped and began afresh to ponder the same thing, and said, 'Women urge me to break my promise and my faith, and I know that sincerity is not to be found in them, and that to expect truth and humanity from them is far removed from the procedure of wise men.

COUPLET.

Forbid it, one in woman's nature should for gentle feelings look!
Ne'er amid the brackish desert, roses home ungenial took.

Wherefore, to be deceived by their guile, and to hurry towards unfaithfulness and ungenerous conduct, how can this be done by the followers of rectitude and uprightness? or how can this be practised by men of piety and honesty?' The Tortoise, busied with these reflections, stopped where he was. This increased the suspicions of the Monkey, and becoming uneasy, he said to himself, 'When doubt of his friend arises in the heart of any one, he must have recourse to the asylum of counsel; and, gathering up his skirt, must secure himself by courtesy and gentle demeanour. And should that suspicion turn out to be true, he will have preserved himself from the other's malice and perfidy; while, should it prove false, he will not expose himself to censure, inasmuch as he will have been strict in observing caution and forbearance.

COUPLET.

Is he thy friend? thou restest then in peace;
If he plays false—thou wilt thyself release.'

He then called out to the Tortoise, and said, 'What is the reason that every moment thou givest reins to the courser of thy imagination in the plain of reflection, and makest the diver of thy thought plunge into the ocean of bewilderment?' The Tortoise replied, 'O brother! pardon me that the indisposition and illness of my wife, and the distressful condition of my children, owing to their mother's sickness, keep me absorbed in thought.' The Monkey rejoined, 'I knew that thy affliction was on account of the illness of thy wife. In truth, they have said that, 'To be ill is less grievous than to see illness.'

HEMISTICH.

Count not him well who suffers for his friend.

Now tell me what her disease is, and what is the method of cure? For every ailment there is an appointed remedy, and for every kind of suffering there is a means of cure manifest and distinct. It is necessary that reference be made to physicians of auspicious minds, of fortunate breath and happy footstep, and in whatever way they may direct, exertion must be made for the prescribed remedy.' The Tortoise replied, 'For the cure the physicians have pointed out a medicine which is not to be obtained.' The Monkey inquired, 'What medicine is that which is not to be found in the shops of druggists, or in the repertories of medicine-vendors? If thou wilt tell me, perhaps I may have knowledge of it, and may furnish a clue to it.' The Tortoise candidly answered, 'That rare medicine which has plunged me in the vortex of bewilderment is the heart of a monkey.' The instant that this word reached the ears of the Monkey, his breast, though in the midst of water, was on flames; and the smoke of despondency ascending to his head, his eyes began to grow dark. By a strong effort of his mind, however, he supported himself, and said, 'O soul! seest thou not that through a shameful greediness and avidity, thou hast fallen into this dread vortex? and, owing to carelessness and incaution, thou art overtaken in this mighty danger? And I am not the first that has been deceived by the hypocrisy of foes, and has given heed to the speeches of the perfidious, and has been pierced to the heart by an arrow aimed deceitfully by those who pursue their own selfish ends.[1]

HEMISTICH.

This furious flame full many a one has burnt.

Now I know of no help save stratagem and artifice, nor can I find any aid except in prudence and wise counsel. If, which may God avert! I am cast

---

[1] Lit. 'From the thumbstall of the deceit of the lords of selfishness.'

on the island of the tortoises, there will be a knot in the concatenation of my affairs, which the hand of thought will be weak too to undo. For if I do not resign to them my heart, I shall remain a prisoner, and perish of hunger; and if I wish to fly, I must throw myself into the water; and that plan, too, is rife with destruction. But I deserve a thousand-fold this punishment and requital, in that I left my own happy and secure wilderness without thought of the consequences, and yielding the reins of control to the hands of the tortoise, set my heart on seeing his island.

COUPLET.

Mad that I was thy ringlets to resign! What guilt deserves so stern a chain as mine !'

He then said to the Tortoise, 'I comprehend the means of curing that virtuous matron, and the remedy for her is in my hands an easy one. Give thyself no anxiety, for our women suffer much from these disorders; and we give them our hearts and suffer nothing from it, but find it quite easy to extract our hearts from within our breasts, and to replace them again. Moreover, we are able to live without them; and I am not in a position to grudge this trifle to thee; for the wise have said, 'It is not good to be niggardly of four things to four persons. First, one ought not to withhold from kings that which they require for the public weal. Secondly, one ought not to deprive meritorious darveshes of that which they ask in God's name, for the performance of alms and the providing good deeds. Thirdly, needy scholars, who would desire to obtain the wherewithal for acquiring science, and who advance with the step of sincerity in pursuit thereof, them we ought to assist on their way. Fourthly, we ought not to grudge, or require to be importuned for, that which may be the means of tranquillizing the minds of cordial friends, provided it lies within our reach.'

COUPLET.

Is then the heart so dear a thing that we should pause to offer it,
Or shrink to pour life's golden shower where those we hold far dearer sit ?

And hadst thou informed me in my own abode, I would have brought my heart with me, and it would have been a goodly thing indeed if, on my arrival, thy spouse had obtained complete restoration to health. And I have become so weary of my own heart, that it never recurs to my thoughts except with the wish to part from it; and, inasmuch as grief and melancholy have usurped every quarter and part of it, and a throng of troubles have over-run its limits, there is nothing more hard for me to bear than the society of my heart; and I long to sever the cord of connection with it, that I may escape from the thought of my separation from my wife and family, and the grief of the abandonment of my country and wealth; and that my soul may be set free from these excruciating afflictions and consuming horrors.

COUPLET.

This drop of blood they call the heart [this region of regrets and care],
O God! how long shall moon-faced ones injurious play the tyrant there ?'

The Tortoise said, 'Where is thy heart that thou didst not bring it with thee ?' The Monkey responded, 'I left it in my house, since it is the custom of my kind, that when they go to visit a friend, and wish the day to pass pleasantly, and the skirt of their enjoyment and mirth to be unreached by the hand of grief, not to take their hearts with them; for that is a gathering-place of pain and affliction, and a source of grief and annoyance. Every moment it stirs up thoughts which trouble the pure fount of enjoyment, and sour the season of mirth and happiness. Thus, too, from its vicissitudes, they have named the heart by a name which signifies change.[1] Every instant its inclinations are directed to somewhat new, either of good or ill, gainful or injurious.

COUPLET.

Each moment, some new fancy it alluring,   It speeds away, in one place ne'er enduring.

And, inasmuch as I was coming to thy house, so much did I wish that I should be thoroughly and perfectly free from solicitude in seeing thee and beholding thy friends and connections that I therefore left my heart there. And very unlucky is it, that I should hear of this means of curing thy chaste spouse, and not have brought my heart with thee. And as thou knowest how I stand in respect of friendship to thee, it is possible that thou mightest excuse me, but the whole body of thy kinsmen and friends will suspect that notwithstanding such previous amicable ties and friendly antecedents which have existed between me and thee, I have grudgingly withheld this trifle, and slight thee in a manner in which no injury would recoil on myself, while benefit would accrue to those connected with me. If thou wouldest return, that we may come again ready and prepared, it would be better.' The Tortoise forthwith turned back, and in the fullest confidence of obtaining his object, and succeeding swimmingly in his hopes, conveyed the Monkey to the shore. The latter at full speed ascended a tree, and having offered the thanks and acknowledgments [due for his escape], seated himself at the end of a bough. The Tortoise waited some time, and then called out, 'O friend beloved! the opportunity for going is fleeting away,

COUPLET.

Take pity ! for our need has reached its bound ;
Come forth ! our patience has its limit found.'

The Monkey laughed, and said,

---

[1] *Kalb* means 'turning,' as well as 'heart.' From the word in its former sense comes *inkiláb*, 'vicissitude.' Our word 'heart,' is no doubt from the Sanskrit *hrid*, which is derived from *hri*, 'to take.' The equivoque, therefore, is unretainable in English.

COUPLET.

'Bethink thee ever, all thou didst pretend
Of faithful love, proved falsehood in the end.

I have passed my life in kingly sway, and I have experienced many heats
and chills of fortune. Fortune snatched back from me her own bestowings,
and heaven required of me that which it had conferred; and I became
numbered with the wretched, and fell into the circle of the ill-starred. Yet I
am not of such a nature as to have remained altogether destitute of the fruits
of experience; so as not to know what happens, and not to discern a quarter
in which reliance can be placed, from one where only hypocrisy is to be
found. Cease these words, and forbear henceforth to take thy seat among
the generous. Leave off thy boastings of fidelity, nor speak of sincerity and
honor.

COUPLET.

O speak not thou of faithfulness where feast the frank and free;
For not an atom of good faith its fragrance sheds on thee.

And if any one makes an initiatory display of virtues, whatever they may be,[1]
and talks of his manliness and honor, one may discover his real metal in the
time of trial, and test his coin on the touchstone of experience.

COUPLET.

How good, if trial such a touchstone were,   That liars would a blackened visage bear!'

The Tortoise exclaimed loudly in great grief and said, 'What suspicion
is this that thou entertainest of me? and what quality is this that thou
imputest to me? Heaven forbid that anything contrary to thy good
pleasure should ever have passed through my mind! or that any ill-
design or perfidious scheme with reference to thee should have crossed my
thoughts. And though thou shouldest cast a hundred thousand stones
of despite in my face, I will not remove my face from the dirt of thy
threshold; and though thou shouldest pierce my breast again and again
with the sword of contumely, I will not remove my heart from thy society.'

The Monkey retorted, 'Fool! think not I am like that Ass of which the
fox said, that it had neither heart nor ears.' The Tortoise said, 'How was
that?'

STORY III.

He said, 'They have related that a lion had become afflicted with the
mange. Together with constant fever, he was worn out with itchy torments,
and at last by reason of the irritation, the numberless thorns of disquietude
pierced his heart and his vigor flagged, and abandoning all motion, he
relinquished the pleasures of the chase. Now in this lion's service was a

---

[1] I am doubtful of this rendering, but I can make no other meaning of this obscure
sentence.

fox, who used to gather up the scraps from his table, and the remnants of
his repast, and who gained strength and food from the blessing of his
leavings. When the lion was unable to pursue the chase, the affairs of the
fox came to distress. One day from the meagreness of the supplies and the
overpowering violence of hunger, he began to reproach the lion, and said,
'O king of beasts! anxiety for thy indisposition, has made the beasts of this
jungle sad, and the lassitude of thy state and the impression of thy
despondency, pervade all thy attendants, nay, the whole body of thy
subjects.

COUPLET.

> A hundred thousand beings tremble for thy life,
> Shocked at thy failing strength, a world with care is rife.

Wherefore dost thou not apply some remedy to this disease, and direct
attention to the cure of this heart-tormenting pain?' The lion, groaning
with pain, said,

COUPLET.

> ' A thorn lies buried in my heart, no needle can remove it thence;
> And lo! my heart is changed to blood, and nought can dull its aching sense.[1]

O fox! I have now a long time suffered agonies[2] from this cruel disease,
and from this itching I waste away daily. My body from attenuation
has become like a hair, and not a hair is left upon it; and I know not how
to cure this illness, or how to allay these sufferings. A physician, in whose
words I have complete confidence, has, indeed, lately pronounced that I
must eat the ears and heart of an Ass, and that all other remedies will be
unavailing. Since then I have been rendered anxious by the thought how
this wish can be accomplished, and by what stratagem of my friends I can
obtain this desired object.' The fox replied, 'If the royal command is
condescendingly uttered, I that am the nearest of the attendants of the court
will gird up the waist of inquiry and step forward on the road of search, and
my hope is that by the blessing of the imperial auspices and the happy
influence of the perpetual fortune of the king, what is desired will be gained.'
The lion asked, 'What kind of artifice hast thou imagined? and what
device hast thou read from the volume of imposture?' The fox answered,
'O king! it occurs to me that it is impossible for you to issue forth from this
jungle; since, after your body has been denuded of hair, and the gloriousness
of your beauty, and the majesty of your appearance, have suffered some
deterioration; to move out and exhibit yourself to friends and strangers
would be injurious to the royal dignity and kingly awe. Wherefore, the
advisable course appears to me to be this, that I should bring the object of
your desire into this jungle, in order that the king of the beasts may tear

---

[1] Lit. 'And this thorn comes not forth from my heart.'
[2] Lit. 'I drink blood from this anger.'

him to pieces, and at pleasure eat that which he may desire.' The lion replied, 'Whence wilt thou bring him?' The fox answered, 'In the vicinity of this wilderness there is a spring of water, which from its abundance resembles the sea of 'Umán,[1] and by its sweetness and purity represents the fountain of life.

COUPLET.

Its ripples pure as beauty's cheek,   Its waves of life's own sweetness speak.

And a washerman comes there every day to wash clothes, and an Ass, which carries burthens for him, grazes daily around that spring. Perhaps I may, by a stratagem, lead him to this jungle. Let the king, however, vow that, after eating his heart and ears, he will bestow the rest as alms on the other beasts.' The lion vowed and promised accordingly, and confirmed his words with an oath; and the fox, in hopes of a plentiful feast, directed his steps towards the spring of water, and as soon as he saw the Ass at a distance he performed the customary salutations, and began to address him in a soft voice, and politely opened the path of conversation.

COUPLET.

With honied tongue, and language soft and fair,
Thou mayst conduct a mammoth[2] with a hair.

He then asked, 'What is the cause that I see thee suffering and lean?' The Ass replied, 'This washerman is constantly imposing work on me, and neglects to take care of me; I perish of distress for forage, and he cares not a grain for it; and the harvest of my life is almost carried away by the wind of extinction, and he takes not so much account of it as of a blade of grass.

VERSE.

I've got no kind friend to supply my famine;
Of hay and barley I ne'er heard the name e'en.
Under this load each day my blood devouring,
I with my tongue, all night, the walls am scouring.
Reproach me not, then, if I'm lean and wasted,
For blood and dirt are all the food I've tasted.'

The fox replied, 'O simpleton! thou hast feet and the power of moving; why, then, d_st thou choose this drudgery, and why tarry thus miserably beset?' The Ass rejoined, 'I am a notorious bundle-carrier, and go where I will there is no getting free of this toil. Besides, I am not the only ass especially devoted to this labor: all my brethren are overtaken in the same troubles, and groan under the like burthens.

COUPLET.

Each has of pain his fated portion: none   Can by free passport this allotment shun.

---

[1] The sea betwixt Ethiopia and India.
[2] 'Elephant' in the original, a word never intended for verse.

And after much consideration I have come to the firm conclusion that since the cup of trouble is to be quaffed everywhere, and the garment of vexation and endurance of suffering to be put on in all places, I must rest quiet in the house of some one, and not endure the reproach of fickleness for a life which, as it passes, disappoints our expectations.

HEMISTICH.

'Tis naught to wander on from door to door.'

The fox said, ' Thou art wrong,

HEMISTICH.

Thou canst not die of famine, for I'm here.

In accordance with the text, ' *Verily God's earth is spacious*,'[1] to the earth's plain ample space has been given; and the royal mandate, ' *Go through the earth*,'[2] was sent down for those who suffer oppression and endure tyranny.

STANZA.

Go! travel, should thy station please thee not,
    Thither to move from hence is no disgrace.
And if too narrow be on earth thy lot,
    The earth God made is no contracted space.'

The Ass said, ' Let one go where he will, he will obtain no more than what is destined. Wherefore, to choose to be covetous, and on the top of other loads to undertake voluntarily the hardships of travel, is far removed from what is reasonable.

DISTICHS.

The allotted portion reaches every seeker.   So
    Our own impatience is our trouble's spring.
God's blessings freely to all creatures flow;
    His hands to all the destined bounty bring.'

The fox said, ' These words have reference to an exalted state of reliance on God, and every one is not able to attain this rank. The command of the Lord God (may His name be glorified!) was on that account issued, that in this world of causes, subsistence should be conveyed to each by the intervention of some means, and the Causer of Causes, in respect to each one of those who subsist by Him, displays in a different manner the means of supply.

HEMISTICH.

Strive thou to earn—all earners are God's friends.

And if thou art content I will take thee to a meadow, the ground of which,

---

[1] Kur'án, ch. xxix. 56; Sale, p. 301, l. 1: 'O my servants, who have believed, verily my earth is spacious; wherefore serve me.'

[2] Kur'án, ch. vi. 11; Sale, p. 92, l. 27: 'Say, Go through the earth, and behold what hath been the end of those who accused our prophets of imposture.'   Vide also Sale, p. 298, l. 27, where the same expression occurs; as also p. 44 of this book where, by an error, p. 82 of Sale is quoted for p. 92.

like the houses of the vendors of jewels, is adorned and lustrous with the radiance of a variety of gems, while its air, like the tray of the perfumer, is aromatized and scented by its fragrant breeze with the odor of the purest musk. [1]

VERSE.

Its air delightsome, and its plains wide-spread,
Its trees fruit-burthened, and their branches green :
The rose breathes fragrant, and the dove o'erhead,
Murmurs its wooings soft ;—as when, between
Two lovers, vows are pledged, where parting long has been.

And before to-day I have given advice to another ass, and led him to that Eden-like spot, and at this moment he walks proudly, at perfect ease, in the expanse of freedom from care, and feeds in happiness and health in the garden of security and peace.' In short, the fox, employing his subtle language, used such wheedlings, and uttered such cajolings, that the bread of his deceit was baked in the oven of imposture, and the cauldron of the Ass's desire began to boil with vain longing, and he said, 'It is not right to turn aside from thy directions, which spring from pure friendship and compassion, nor allowable to disregard thy injunctions, which are the essence of kindness and commiseration.

HEMISTICH.

Whate'er thou biddest, with my life I'll do.'

The fox went first, and brought him near the lion, who, from excessive eagerness, sprang at him at once, and inflicted a wound on him, but owing to excessive weakness, failed of his object. The Ass turned to flight, and the fox, astonished at the feebleness of the lion, began to reproach him, saying, ' Well now ! what was the advantage of uselessly tormenting an animal? and what end has been served from being hasty in a matter, the opportunity for commencing which was not fleeting away? Prudence required thee to restrain thyself, and firmness of purpose pointed out to thee not to relinquish the hold on the reins of option, so as not to repent in the end.

HEMISTICH.

Of what avail repentance now, when things have passed beyond thy power ?'

These words annoyed the lion, and he thought to himself, ' If I admit that I have not kept a guard on my actions, I shall lay myself open to the charge of unsteadiness and want of fixed purpose ; and if I shall have recourse [2] to the temptations of appetite as my apology, I shall be branded with greediness and levity and rashness ; and if I acknowledge my want of strength, the imputation of weakness and impotence follows, and sundry bad consequences,

---

[1] For the reading of the editions I would gladly substitute *bih nasím-i 'ambar shamím-i ú muṭayyab va muʻaṭṭar*, did the MSS. allow it.
[2] Observe this somewhat uncommon use of *tamassuk jústan*.

which are not for the public good, will result therefrom. My advisable
course is not to reply to the fox, save roughly and with asperity, and to
prohibit him from speaking thus in future.' He then said, 'It is excessively disrespectful for subjects to inquire into, or pry after, the recondite
intention of what kings do, whatever that may be.

COUPLET.

Submissive bow thy head; why meddle thou with this or that?
What has the poor fakír to do with mandates of the autocrat?

And the real circumstances of the actions of kings cannot be known to every
one of their servants. The capacity of subjects is unable to comprehend
that which the judgment of monarchs requires, [as it is said] '*None but
their beasts carry their burthens.*'

HEMISTICH.

Not to poor quails the falcon's craw belongs.

Cease this questioning, and employ some stratagem that the Ass may
come back, and thus the sincerity of thy faith and the excess of thy
friendship will be manifest to me, and thou wilt be distinguished by my
favorable notice and favor above thy peers and fellows.' Thereupon the
fox went again to the Ass, and with the utmost courtesy went through the
customary benedictions and salutations. The Ass turned away his face
and said,

COUPLET.

' 'Twere shame to suffer for a friend like thee,
Who, faithless, dost but aim at treachery.

O worthless deceiver! thou didst begin by promising me my freedom; and
in the end thou broughtest me into the claws of the lion.

HEMISTICH.

This action could arise from none but thee.'

The fox replied, 'O simple one! what fancy hast thou formed, and what
thought hast thou suffered to pass through thy mind? The instant thou
sawest the talisman, thou wast scared from the pursuit of the treasure;
and, before thou didst behold the asperity of the thorn, thou didst relinquish
the spectacle of the garden. Know that what thou sawest is a talisman,
which sages have made and excogitated by way of caution, on account of
the beasts and reptiles which repose in this spot; because this meadow is
adorned with a variety of delicious viands, and a diversity of exquisite
fruits. And did this magic spell not exist, wherever there is a beast in the
world, it would come to this place, and the affairs of the inhabitants of
this wilderness would become embarrassed; and now, on account of this
talisman, a great variety of animals do not resort to this secluded haunt;
but each one that comes hither, and beholds this shape and appearance
which thou sawest, hovers no more about this meadow. Thus the

inhabitants of this wilderness pass their time in freedom from care, and in happiness. And we impart to every one, for whom we have a friendship, the mystery of this talisman; and we make known the true state of this enchantment, which is nothing but mere show, to him, in order that, without fear of distraction, he may attain to these incalculable blessings.

DISTICHS.

> ' What,' quoth the Fox, ' a lion seems to be,
> Is but a talisman and witchery;
> For I, of weaker frame than thou art, still
> There night and day feed safely at my will.
> And, but for that vain phantom's groundless fear,
> Each suffering wretch would fly for refuge here.

And I intended to warn thee beforehand, that if thou shouldest see anything of the kind thou shouldest not be afraid. But I was so transported at meeting thee that it escaped my memory. Now that thou hast full knowledge of that empty form, come back, since my directions will issue only in thy honor.' In this manner he tempted and cajoled the unfortunate Ass till he trod again the path of folly; and, beguiled by his seductive persuasions, proceeded towards that jungle. The fox went before him, and having conveyed to the lion the good tidings of the Ass's approach, besought him not to move from his place, and not to step beyond the circle of dignified repose. Nay, he desired him not to heed the Ass at all, however near he might pass by him until he should get full power and a good opportunity to accomplish his purpose. The lion heartily assented to the fox's advice, which was so loyally given, and stood on his feet in a corner of the jungle like a magical figure without life. Then the fox said to the Ass, ' Come here! that thou mayest see the real truth of this enchantment, and mayest know that it is altogether incapable of motion, and devoid of all idea of doing mischief. The Ass advanced boldly, and however near he grazed to the lion he did not see him move in the least. By gentle degrees he became accustomed to him, and gradually grew familiar with him; and being altogether at his ease, with reference to him, fell to work with the grass. Then the luckless Ass, who had suffered a long time from insatiable hunger, on now beholding the table of invitation spread before him, and on finding the tray of dainties ready, began to eat, and did not pull the rein until he reached the boundary of repletion. When he was quite full he lay down before the enchanted lion in the middle of the meadow. Thereupon the lion, finding him off his guard, made a spring and tore open his belly. This done, he said to the fox, ' Keep watch! till I go to the spring of water and perform my ablutions, after which I will eat the heart and ears of the Ass, since the physicians have prescribed them as the remedy of this disease.' The lion accordingly turned in the direction of the fountain, and the fox ate up the heart and ears of the Ass, which were the daintiest parts of him. When the lion had finished the requisite ablutions, and had returned, however much he searched for the heart and ears, he could not find a trace of them. He then said to the fox, 'Where are these two parts, which are to cure me, gone? and who has taken them away?' The fox replied, 'May the king live for ever! this Ass had neither ears nor heart, for had he had a heart, which is the place of the reason, he would not have been deceived by my artifices; and had he had ears, which are the organs of hearing, he would, after having had ocular demonstration of the terrors of your majesty, have distinguished my false words from the truth, and would not have come with his own feet to the edge of the grave.'

And I have adduced this story in order that thou mayest know that I am not without heart and ears; and thou hast not omitted any refinement of artifice, but by my own penetration and sagacity I have found thee out, and I have exerted myself much, so that when affairs had become perilous, they were smoothed again; and life which had reached the lip, again shed the radiance of animation over my frame.

COUPLET.

Wounded, 'twas not my fate by thee to die ;
Else thy stern heart failed nought in cruelty.

And hereafter hope not for companionship with me, and relinquish the idea of my return, which belongs to the impossibilities, and rest assured that,

QUATRAIN.

Wert thou the moon, I'd gaze less on the sky ;
The cypress wert thou, I'd the garden quit :
Hung it on thee, I'd life itself not buy ;
Thy name I'll ne'er recall, nor think of it.'

The Tortoise answered, 'Thou sayest the truth, and it is all one whether I protest or deny. I own I have inflicted on thy heart a wound, which, as long as existence lasts, cannot be salved. And the brand of perfidy and cruelty has so set its stamp on my countenance, that its erasion enters not into the area of possibility. I feel that I must make up my mind to quaff the bitter beverage of separation, and must oppose my body like a shield, to the poisoned sword of parting.

VERSE.

'Twere fit that I in bloody tears should lie,
That I so true a friend have cast away ;
Whoe'er himself so wrecked his hopes as I ?
Who thus his ruin did himself assay ?
Though all my life I would forgiveness win,
I could not purchase pardon for this sin.'

Thus he spake and downcast and shame-stricken turned back, and during the rest of his life he bewailed his separation from such a friend, and said,

COUPLET.

Fate wrote this cruel treatment in my loved companion's lot,
Else, heaven forbid!—the thought of wrong in my breast harbored not.

This is the history of one who, having acquired wealth or secured a friend, loses him through folly or neglect, and so falls into perpetual remorse; and however much he beats his head on a stone, or a stone on his head, it is all in vain. It behoves men of understanding to make the instructions of this story the guide of their conduct, and to set a high value on a desired object when it is gained, whether it be worldly substance or a soul-bound friend. Whatever of this nature is let slip is not to be re-acquired by wishing, and regret and chagrin will prove unavailing.

STANZA.

Prize high a wished-for object, when 'tis won;
Nor let it slip, lest thou shouldst feel regret.
Full many a spendthrift, when his gold is done,
Must under want's stern trials, cashless, fret.
For by-gone treasures back shall ne'er return,
Though clothes be rent and hearts with anguish burn.

CHAPTER VI.

ON THE CALAMITOUS RESULTS OF PRECIPITATION, AND THE INJURIOUSNESS OF HASTE.

INTRODUCTION.

The world-conquering king, distinguishing the clear-minded Bráhman by the honor of his address, said,

COUPLET.

'Praised be thy soul! in God's[1] own secrets wise.
Praised be thy words! unveiling mysteries.

Thou hast narrated the story of one, who after securing the object of his desire, chose to be careless in preserving it, and hence the treasure passed from his hands and he was plunged in regret, and though panged with distress for his bereavement,[2] obtained nought but remorse and grief. Now recount the tale of one acting precipitately in the pursuit of his desired object, and continuing devoid of the advantages of counsel and deliberation, and point out in what such conduct and procedure finally issued, and what fruit men reap when they sow in the field of action the seed of haste?' The Bráhman loosed his tongue in praise of the great king, and said,

COUPLET.

'King! still on thee may earth's enactments rest,
And all earth's garden with thy rule be blest!

Whoever bases not his actions on patience and steadiness, and does not strengthen the foundation of his proceedings by firmness and constancy, the final tendency of his doings is towards reproach, and the conclusion of his affairs will issue in repentance. And the most praiseworthy quality with which the Most High God has adorned men, and by the blessing of which he has bestowed on mankind the grade of a dignified position, is, that graceful one, long-suffering; and that eminent virtue, constancy.

COUPLET.

Patience is reason's treasury. We speak
Of brutes and devils when we name the unmeek.

And they have cleverly said, as to this, 'That if thou wilt convert *Hilm* it becomes *Milh*,'[3] that is, meekness is the salt of the table of qualities. Thus

---

[1] *Kun fakán*, 'Be, and it was;' a title of the Deity.

[2] Or, more literally, 'amercement,' 'mulct.'

[3] The word ‎حلم‎ *hilm*, 'meekness,' read backward is ‎ملح‎ *milh*, 'salt.' Hence the witticism here.

when any one outstrips his peers in the acquisition of various excellencies, and carries off the ball of superiority from those of his time in the display of numerous virtues; if he combine therewith, roughness and haste and levity, his other good qualities, like insipid food, are relished by none; nay, his frivolity and want of steadiness cause him to be regarded with aversion. Thus it has been said, '*But if thou hadst been severe and hard-hearted, they had surely separated themselves from about thee.*' [1] And notwithstanding all those perfections which centred in his Holiness the Lord of created things, (On whom be the choicest blessings and most perfect benedictions!) he was graciously addressed as follows, by the Lord of Lords, saying, 'O Muhammad! if thou hadst been rough-tempered and hard-hearted, and prone to anger and resentful, assuredly the legions of stars—as it is said, '*My companions are like the stars,*'—which are now assembled round thee like the Pleiades, would be dispersed like the daughters of the Bier.[2] Moreover, the possessor of God's friendship, and the Full Moon of Faith, Abraham the friend of God, (On our Prophet and on him be the blessings of The Merciful!) is praised for this quality, there, where he says, '*Verily Abraham was pitiful and compassionate.*'[3] For the mild person is beloved of all hearts, and the minds of high and low are all inclined towards him.

COUPLET.

In patience reason's prop we see,   And man disgraced by levity.

Precipitation is altogether alien from men of sense, and the thoroughly wise man regards it as a temptation of the devil; as it is said, '*Patience is from God, haste from the devil,*' the meaning of which they have thus explained,

DISTICHS.

Hurry and rashness from the devil spring,
But patience, meekness, are from Heaven's King.
See from God's hand creation slow arise,
And six days' labor claimed by earth and skies.
Else with two letters [4] He possessed the might,
Sudden to make new worlds' upstart to light.
Lo! in this course instruction to us sent;
'Use patience, for with it success is blent.'

---

[1] Kur'án, Fl. iii. 153; Sale, p. 50, l. 14. The same quotation occurs at p. 2 note of this translation, *q.v.* Through a typographical error the page of Sale is there given 30 instead of 50.

[2] The constellation of the Bear.' See note 1, page 279.

[3] Kur'án, Fl. ix. 115; Mar. 117; Sale, p. 152, l. 20: 'Neither did Abraham ask forgiveness for his father, otherwise than in pursuance of a promise, which he had promised unto him: but when it became known unto him that he was an enemy unto God, he declared himself clear of him. Verily Abraham was pitiful and compassionate.'

[4] That is, with the *k* and *n* in *kun*, 'be,' as in the common title of the Deity, 'Be, and it was.' See the preceding page, note 1.

2 D 2

And whoever in his proceedings surrenders the reins of choice to the grasp of precipitation, assuredly in the end his affairs will draw towards contrition, and the issue of his doings will be disappointment and regret.

COUPLET.

Who dares to act without due thought and care,
Will sink at last in sorrow and despair.

And there are many anecdotes and innumerable stories à-propos of this subject which are written and commemorated in the pages of nocturnal conversations and elegant annals, and among these is the story of the Holy Man, who rashly stepped into the plain of precipitate action, and, staining his hands with innocent blood, destroyed [1] the unfortunate Ichneumon; which displays the ill effects of this precipitation.[2] The king asked, 'How was that?'

STORY I.

He said, 'They have related that a Devotee after long celibacy[3] desired to put in practice the injunction, ' *Matrimony is my commandment, therefore he who turns away from my commandment is none of mine,*' and act in accordance with the mandate deserving of obedience, ' *Marry and beget children.*' He therefore conferred with one of the pious men of the time, and asked his blessing and his permission. The devotee [whom he addressed] responded, ' Thou hast formed a very praiseworthy project, since matrimony is beneficial as relates to subsistence here, and is perfectly advantageous and protective in matters of religion, and by it is obtained a safeguard to household chattels, and, moreover an abundance of children, from which results a continuance of one's name.

STANZA.

Ne'er on a man does radiant fortune smile,
  Till a spouse light home's cheering lamp for him.
Pass not thy life a celibate, the while
  Thou mightest, bird-like, those glad gardens skim,
  Where pleasures reign, and joys the goblet brim.

Nevertheless use thy endeavors to secure a tender partner, and avoid an unsuitable companion.' The Devotee asked, 'What sort of wife ought one to make choice of?' The other replied, 'A wife that is affectionate, and prolific, and sedate, that is to say, one that holds her husband dear, and brings him many children, and avoids crime. And a virtuous wife bestows new light on every house into which she enters.

---

[1] Lit. ' Gave his head to the wind.'

[2] The Dictionary gives for *siyákat* only ' driving,' ' urging onward.'

[3] This meaning of *tajarrud* has been omitted in the Dictionary.

STANZA.

Sweet is the converse of a virtuous wife;
Happy his fate who such a spouse possesses;
Who aids him here and in his future life.
Companionship man's lot here truly blesses,
When fortune grants a friend, our trouble less is.'

The Devotee asked, 'The society of what wife ought we to shun?' The other replied, 'Three kinds of wives ought to be avoided, a widow anxious to marry again; a woman who places her husband under an obligation; and a complaining woman. Now the first is one who has had a husband before thee, and has been separated from him by death or divorce, and ever remains longing to regain his society. The second is one who possesses property, and effects, and who, by her wealth, imposes on thee an obligation. The third is a wife who, when she sees thee, speaks with a feeble voice, and feigns herself to be ill when she is not, and the sight of such a wife is a renewal of death every hour.

VERSE.

In a good man's house an evil wife
Is his hell above in this present life.
From a vixen wife protect us well;
Save us, O God! from the pains of hell.' [1]

Again the Devotee who wished to marry, asked, 'Of what age shall I choose a wife?' The other replied, 'It must be a young maiden of tender years, since old women steal away the roses from the cheek, and converse with them brings on debility and weakness.

STANZA.

The wife, whose back is crooked as a bow,
Her mind is like an arrow, straight,[2] thou'lt learn.
Girls, who, while young, do nought but joy bestow,
In their old age to deadly poison turn.

And wives, from ten years old to twenty years, are places of security and promise; and from twenty to thirty years, they are the solace of the hearts of and lovers, and the delight of the souls of those who eagerly pursue them; their from thirty to forty years, controllers of the property and the children, and displayers also of high feelings; and from forty to fifty years they aim at name and reputation, and employ on those present, artifices and finesse. But after they have passed fifty years, they become dark calamities, and the destruction of property and rank, and withered gardens, and rain-penetrated mansions, and fallow fields, and serpents without treasure, and mines of trouble and annnoyance.

[1] These lines are quoted from the 'Gulistán,' ch. ii., story 32, (p. 134 of my translation).
[2] 'Straight,' is here an adverb to 'thou'lt learn,' not an adjective agreeing with 'arrow.' The original is intentionally ambiguous here, thus affording a play on words, as if, while her back was crooked the woman's mind was straight.

VERSE.

Wives, that on that side fifty tread,
　　'Twere best to shun, by stepping on this side :
For, though one may from fifty's claws have fled,
　　'Tis but, at last, to sixty be tied.'[1]

The questioning Devotee again asked, 'What sayest thou as to beauty and good looks?' The other replied, 'The best thing in the matter of women is chastity and amiability. If to these be added the blessing of beauty it is like adding light to light.

COUPLET.

All holy spirits will that form surround,
Where beauty, chastity, and worth are found.

But a beautiful and comely woman, if she be unamiable, is a mortal calamity and a perpetual source of annoyance; while an amiable woman, although she be plain-featured, is a kind companion and an ornament of the family.

VERSE.

A kindly partner, and a gentle friend,
　　E'en though not fair,—does yet the eyes illume :
But not thy heart to a cross mistress lend,
　　Though flowers beneath her footsteps seem to bloom.

And two or three couplets from the 'Results of Meditation,' composed by that illustrious author, which relate to this subject ought to be borne in mind.

VERSE.

A modest, chaste, and an obedient wife,
　　Lifts her poor husband to a kingly throne :
What though the livelong day with toils be rife !
　　The solace of his cares at night's his own.
If she be modest, and her words be kind,
　　Mark not her beauty, or her want of grace ;
The fairest woman, if deformed in mind,
　　Will in thy heart's affections find no place :
Dazzling as Eden's beauties to the eye,
　　In outward form ; foul is her face within.
Better in dungeon, bound with chains, to lie,
　　Than mark at home a wife of frowning mien.
Better bare feet than pinching shoes. The woes
　　Of travel are less hard than broils at home.
Contentment's door upon that mansion close,
　　Whence wrangling women's high-pitched voices come.
Be woman's eye to strangers blind ; to those
　　Abroad, let it be dark as in the tomb.'

---

[1] That is, If a man survive the society of a wife who has reached fifty, his fate is only the more deplorable, for she will grow older and uglier every day.

In short, after extensive inquiry and infinite pains, the Devotee, through the aid of his lofty fortune, and the help of his noble spirit, obtained a wife of a great family and an illustrious stock. The reflection of her countenance gave radiance to the morn, and the hue of her curling ringlets aided the perfumer of evening in intensifying his gloom. The azure sky had never beheld her equal, save in the mirror of the sun; and the swift-sighted limner of the imagination had ne'er looked on the like of her lovely semblance, save in the world of dreams.

VERSE.

The glories of thy sunny cheek the world of beauty warmly kiss;
Like the full moon, thou hast arisen amid the sky of loveliness;
Thy countenance the brightest rose, thy form the fairest cypress is;
That ever grew in beauty's bower, or 'mid the flowers of comeliness.

And, together with this beauty of form, she was adorned with excellence of disposition, and the graces of her body were set off by those of her mind. The Devotee, in his daily prayers, returned thanks for such a blessing; and having thus commenced his intercourse with that partner whose face resembled the beauties of Eden, he desired to beget a son. And no wise person bases his desire for children on mere sensual appetite, nor yields his body to the task save in quest of a virtuous son, who, in procuring the blessings asked for by prayer, is equivalent to the perpetual offering of alms.

COUPLET.

From woman's pain, and what man's toil has done,
Is formed the fair amusement of a son.

And when an interval had passed, and the desired event did not happen, the Devotee, losing hope, began to place the face of supplication on the ground of entreaty, and to let fly the arrow of prayer from the bow of sincerity; and since he was altogether absorbed in the path of prayer, according to the saying, ' *Who heareth the afflicted when he calleth upon him,*' [1] the shaft of his supplication reached the target of acceptance.

DISTICHS.

The man, whose heart is moderate and pure,
His prayer will reach the All-Glorious One, be sure.
Rapt from himself, the prayer is not his own;
The prayer he utters is from God alone:
Vain is the creature, but the prayer is true;
Divine the prayer, and the acceptance too.

Then after his despair the gates of the heavenly favor were opened with the keys of mercy, and the wife of the Devotee became pregnant. Greatly

---

[1] Kur'ân, xxvii. 63; Sale, p. 288, l. 2: ' Is there any other God equal with the true God? yet the greater part of them know it not. Is not he more worthy who heareth the afflicted, when he calleth upon him, and taketh off the evil, which distressed him; and who hath made you the successors of your forefathers in the earth?'

did the holy man rejoice, and his wish was all day long to renew the mention
of his son, and, after the performance of his daily devotions, his tongue did
nought but utter his name. One day he said to his wife, 'O partner of my
life, and sympathizing friend! may it quickly happen that the princely pearl
may reach the shore of manifestation, from the shell of thy womb: and that
a fair son may step gracefully from the cabinet of the unseen to the plain of
evidence, and that I may give him a good name and a becoming title. Then,
may I next engage to the utmost of my power in his education and instruction, that he may learn the precepts of the law, and that I may exert myself
fairly in correcting and improving his manners. So will he become adorned
with the demeanour which is fitting for a spiritual walk in life; and thus, in
a short time, rise to fill an eminent station in the faith, and be a venerated
leader possessed of miraculous gifts. I will then wed him at the proper
season to a religious lady, and from them will spring children and grandchildren, and through this blessed channel our seed will be perpetuated, and
our name will, by means of our descendants, endure on the page of existence.

STANZA.

His name, with rolling time, will circle on,
Who leaves his own memorial in a son.
Hence men recall the memory of a shell
Through the rich pearl, once tenant of its cell.'

The wife replied, 'Sweet friend and venerable leader of the faith! these
words befit not a posture of adoration on the carpet of prayer, nor do they
demand the ejaculation of thanksgivings. In the first place, thou hast set
thy mind on a son, and it is possible that I may not bear a child, and if I
should, it is likewise possible that it may not be a male, and though this
should be the case, it is again possible that it may not survive nor be blessed
with life. In short, the conclusion of this affair is not to be discerned, and
thou, like a besotted visionary, hast taken thy seat on the steed of desire,
and galloped the courser of thy hope—like foolish persons infatuated with
their own longings—in the plain of expectation.

STANZA.

Thou canst not speed by hope and mere desire,
Nor by loud talk and boasting aught effect.
Thousands, consumed with longings vain, expire.
And fortune grants them nought their hearts expect.

And thy words resemble the conduct of that Religious Man, who besmeared
his own face and hair with honey and oil.' The Devotee inquired, 'How
was that?'

STORY II.

She said, 'They have related that a pious man had a house in the vicinity of a merchant, and lived happily through favor of his neighborly kindness. The merchant continually sold honey and oil, and made his profits by that traffic in unctuous and sweet commodities. Inasmuch as the pious man lived a blameless life, and ever sowed in the field of his guileless heart the seed of the love of God, the merchant reposed implicit confidence in him, and took the supply of his wants upon himself. And in this very thing is the use of riches,—to win over the hearts of the poor, and to raise up a perpetual provision from perishable wealth.

COUPLET.

Win, O rich man! the heart's love of the poor,
For golden treasures are a fleeting store.

The merchant, too, considering the opportunity of doing good a blessing, sent every day somewhat from the stock, in the buying and selling of which he was occupied, for the support of the Devotee. The latter used somewhat of this and stored up the rest in a corner. In a short time a jar was filled by these means. One day the pious man looked into that jar, and thought thus to himself, 'Well, now! what quantity of honey and oil is collected in this vessel?' At last he conjectured ten mans to be there, and said, 'If I can sell these for ten dirams, I can buy for that sum five ewes, and these five will each have young every six months, and each will have two lambs. Thus in a year there will be twenty-five, and in ten years from their progeny there will be herds upon herds. So by these means I shall have an abundant supply, and will sell some, and lay in a handsome stock of furniture, and wed a wife of a noble family. After nine months, I shall have a son born to me, who will study science and polite manners. However, when the weakness of infancy is exchanged for the strength of youth, and that graceful cypress grows up in the garden of manhood, it is probable that he may transgress my orders, and begin to be refractory, and in that case it will be necessary for me to correct him, and I will do so with this very staff which I hold in my hand. He then lifted up his staff, and was so immersed in thought, that, fancying the head and neck of his rebellious son before him, he brought down the staff, and struck it on the jar of honey and oil. It happened that the jar was placed on a shelf, beneath which he sate with it facing him. As soon as his staff reached the jar, it broke it, and let out the honey and oil all over the head and face and vest and hair of the pious man.

HEMISTICH.

And all these schemes at once dissolved away.

And I have adduced this tale in order that thou mayest know that without positive certainty it does not do to plunge into such projects as these, nor is it right to be led on by 'Would that!' and 'Perhaps,' and 'Haply,' and 'It may be.' They have said, too, that when any one takes 'If,' and 'Perchance,' for his partner, the offspring will be sure to be 'Would that I had not!'

COUPLET.

'If,' was to 'It may be,' in wedlock given,
The child that sprung from them, was, 'Would to heaven!'

It behoves a wise man not to base his proceedings on mere imagination, nor to admit into his heart vain thoughts, which resemble the ill-omened temptations of the devil.

STANZA.

Long years we schemed that in time's onward course,
  Or thus, or thus, should be the issue—Then,
Our rule in such a region should have force,
  Or gold or silver treasures meet our ken;
At length we learned that this was idle thought,
God's will alone is to existence brought.'

The Devotee received this advice with the ear of his soul, and was roused from the sleep of self-deceit, and abandoning those words, no longer indulged in unwarrantable expectations. But when the time of gestation was concluded, and the period of the imprisonment of the fœtus in the womb was finished; a son of fair visage and lovely form was born, such that the tokens of beauty and accomplishments bespoke his perfection, and the signs of admirable gifts shone and gleamed on the forehead of his condition. The Devotee beheld the morn of hope begin to smile from the dawning-place of desire, and the nightingale of his pleasure commenced singing on the rose-shrub of joy.

COUPLET.

A fair gem from the boundless sea of Grace, was brought to light,
Upon the sky of Law divine a new star glittered bright.

The Devotee indulged in raptures at the beauty of his son, and fulfilled a variety of vows which he had made; and girding up his loins in attendance on his son's cradle night and day, drew through other matters the pen of oblivion, and expended all his energies in [promoting] his growth and strength, and grace and freshness and vigor.

COUPLET.

How long shall I on thee bestow my breath like morn's young breeze?
That thou mayest blossom like a rose, to gladden and to please.

One day the mother of the child desiring to take a warm bath committed him, with many injunctions, to the care of his father, who, besides, had nothing else then to do. Some time passed, and a confidential person, sent by the king of the country, came to request his attendance, and there was no possibility of delay. He was, of necessity, compelled to go out of the house. Now they had an Ichneumon, in whose charge they left the house, and through him their minds were altogether set at ease; and he used to display the utmost exertion in ridding them of noxious reptiles, and beasts that bite or sting. The Devotee came out and left the Ichneumon with his son. To be short, no sooner had he left the house than a large snake shewed itself near the cradle. When the Ichneumon saw that dart-like, armour-wearing snake, and that malignant creature swift to wrath, which, when quiescent, assumes the shape of circle—that arrowy-paced reptile, which at times, like a curved bow, joins its extremities,[1]—

STANZA.

Straight as a dart, anon, like buckler, round ;
Anon in noose-like circles flows its form [1] ;
No cloud within, two lightnings forked are found,[2]
No sea, but waves roll there—a mimic storm,

making for the cradle, and intending to kill the child, it leapt up, and seizing his throat, imprisoned him in the ring of the noose of death ; and, by the blessed influence of its defence, the boy escaped from that whirlpool of destruction. Shortly after, the Devotee returned, and the Ichneumon, smeared with blood, ran to meet him, in exultation at having done a good deed. The Devotee imagined that it had killed his son, and that these stains were from his blood. The fire of wrath was kindled in the stove of his heart, and the smoke of precipitation entered the aperture of his brain ; and his reason, through the murkiness of the fumes of rashness ;—which like the cloud of tyranny, is the cause of darkening the world,—covered its face with the veil of concealment. Before inquiring into the matter, or examining into the real state of the case, he smote down his staff on the Ichneumon, and broke the vertebræ of its back, and knocked its head into the casket of its chest. But when he entered the house he beheld the child sleeping in safety in the cradle, and a huge serpent lying there torn in pieces. Then the smoke of remorse ascended from his heart, and he began to smite his breast with the stone of regret, and complaining and lamenting said,

COUPLET.

Hereafter, I and grief are one, and every man this well must see,
For me to have a cheerful heart, impossible and strange would be.

----

[1] The letter | alif resembles the serpent when straight, but the latter when coiled up is like the sign ‿ jazm, which denotes that the letter is quiescent. Such is the meaning of this frigid metaphor.

[2] That is, 'the tongue.'

Alas! that the fire of this distressing accident cannot be extinguished by the water of excuses, and that the dart of the shame of this troublous transaction will not be repelled by the shield of extenuation. What unjust action is this that I have committed! and what unsuitable act is this that my hands have done!

COUPLET.

'Tis right that I my blood should drink, in shame for this distress,
'Tis fit that I my life resign for this unhappiness.

Would to God that this son had never come into existence from nonentity, and that I had not set my love and affections upon him! so that this innocent blood would not have been shed on this account, and I should not have happened to embark in this unholy business. And what answer shall I give to my Creator for this, that I have causelessly destroyed one that dwelt in the same house with me; and have slain the guardian of my home, and the protector of my beloved son, without reason? And what excuse can I offer to my fellow-creatures for this? And, hereafter, the chain of censure will not be removed from my neck, and the writing of infamy will never be obliterated from the page of my affairs.

COUPLET.

My name an ensign is for all reproach and calumny,
Would that that name was lost, nor sign nor trace remained of me.'

The Devotee writhed under these thoughts, and wept piteously at this distress and affliction; and when his wife returned and beheld this state of things, she loosed the tongue of reproach and said,

HEMISTICH.

'These cruelties I never knew thee use.

Pray, is this thy thankfulness for the divine blessing in bestowing on thee thus, by an unusual mercy, a son in thine old age? and oughtest thou thus to show thy gratitude for God's grace in delivering thy darling from the deadly wound of the snake?' The Devotee, with a loud exclamation of sorrow, replied, 'Dear friend! speak not to me thus,

HEMISTICH.

For questions pang me, and replies abash.

I, too, am aware that I have been neglectful in the performance of the thanks due to God, and in the recognition of the value of His inestimable benefits; and that I have swerved from the straight path of patience, which is the road of those who travel in the way of '*Let God alone be thy stay!*' And now, by reason of my impatience and unthankfulness, I am neither named in the register of the enduring, nor inscribed in the page of the grateful, and thy reproach at the present moment is like a sting inflicted on a part already wounded; or using salt as the ointment for a sore.

COUPLET.

When lovers' hearts are rent in pieces, tauntings, added to their woe,
Are like wounds with sabre given, which with the needle's point they sew.'

The wife said, 'Thou speakest truth, there is no advantage, now, in
reproaches, and from this action that thou hast done, there is this experience
to be gleaned, that the conclusion of rashness is repentance and shame; that
levity and instability, in all matters, is reprehensible; and that he who acts
precipitately, is sure to be excluded from his object.

COUPLET.

From Ahraman [1] ill deeds and rashness came;
These pang the spirit and afflict the frame.

And thou art not the only one that has fallen into this snare and opened this
door of mischief upon himself; for ere this, many such occurrences have
happened, and innumerable similar incidents have taken place. Thus I have
heard that a King put his unoffending Hawk to death, and for years his
heart was consumed with the fire of regret, and his breast inflamed with
the burning of repentance.' The devotee asked, 'How was that?'

STORY III.

She said, 'They have related that in ancient times [2] there was a King
fond of hunting. He was ever giving reins to the courser of his desire in
the pursuit of game, and was always casting the lasso of gladness over the
neck of sport. Now this King had a Hawk, who at a single flight could
bring down the Símurgh from the peak of Káf,[3] and in terror of whose claws
the constellation Aquila kept himself close in the green nest of the sky.

VERSE.

When that bold falcon stretched his pinions wide,
Heaven's bosom was pierced through with dread;
When to the sky with upward flight he hied,
The eagle of the spheres his feathers shed.

And the King had a prodigious fondness for this Hawk, and always cared
for it with his own hands. It happened that one day the Monarch, holding
the Hawk on his hand, had gone to the chase. A stag leapt up before him
and he galloped after it with the utmost eagerness. But he did not succeed in
coming up with it, and became separated from his retinue and servants; and
though some of them followed him, the king rode so hotly that the morning
breeze—which in the twinkling of the eye encircles the world—could not
have reached the dust he raised, nor could the north wind in spite of its
velocity, attain to the dust of his horse's hoofs.

---

[1] The spirit of evil, according to the creed of the fire-worshippers.
[2] The heading of this story has been omitted in the index of the printed edition.
[3] Mount Caucasus.

COUPLET.

Unmeasured has thy swiftness been :   So swift, no trace of thee is seen !

Meantime the fire of his thirst was kindled, and the intense desire to drink overcame the King.   He galloped his steed in every direction, and traversed the desert and the waste in search of water, until he reached the skirt of a mountain, and beheld that from its summit limpid water was trickling.   The King drew forth a cup which he had in his quiver, and riding under the mountain filled the cup with that water, which fell drop by drop, and was about to take a draught, when the Hawk made a blow with his wing, and spilled all the water in the goblet.   The King was vexed at that action, but held the cup a second time under the rock until it was brimful.   He then raised it to his lips again, and again the Hawk made a movement and overthrew the cup.

HEMISTICH.
Brought to the lip they then forbid the draught.

The King, rendered impatient by thirst, dashed the Hawk on the ground, and killed it.   Shortly after a stirrup-holder [1] of the King came up and saw the Hawk dead, and the King athirst.   He then undid a water-vessel [2] from his saddle-cord, and washed the cup clean, and was about to give the King to drink.   The latter bade him ascend the mountain, as he had the strongest inclination for the pure water which trickled from the rock; and could not wait to collect it in the cup, drop by drop, and therefore he desired the attendant to fill a cup with it, and come down.   The stirrup-holder ascended the mountain and beheld a spring like the eye of hard-hearted misers, giving out a drop at a time with a hundred stintings; and a huge serpent lay dead on the margin of the fountain; and as the heat of the sun had taken effect upon it, the poisonous saliva mixed with the water of that mountain, and it trickled drop by drop down the rock.   The stirrup-holder was overcome with horror, and came down from the mountain bewildered, and represented the state of the case, and gave the king a cup of cold water from his ewer.   The latter raised the cup to his lips, and his eyes overflowed with tears.

COUPLET.
A little water then he drank; the burnings of his heart were stopped ;
The fluid that his lips imbibed, back from his flooding eyelids dropped.

The attendant asked the reason of his weeping.   The king drew a cold sigh from his anguished heart, and said,

COUPLET.
' So deep my grief, that I to none can tell the secret of my woes ;
And yet my tale is such, that I must still my lips perforce unclose.'

---

[1] The *rikábdár* is a running footman, who sometimes assists himself when the pace is great, or the journey long, by holding the stirrup of the grandee whom he attends.

[2] The *mitharah* is a vessel with a spout from which they pour water in making their ablutions.

He then related in full the story of the Hawk and the spilling of the water in the cup, and said, 'I grieve for the death of the Hawk, and bemoan my own deed in that without inquiry I have deprived a creature, so dear to me, of life.' The attendant replied, 'This Hawk protected thee from a great peril, and has established a claim to the gratitude of all the people of this country. It would have been better if the King had not been precipitate in slaying it, and had quenched the fire of wrath with the water of mildness, and had turned back the reins of the courser of his passions with the vigor of endurance, and had not transgressed the monition of the wise, who have said,

COUPLET.

Do not the courser of thyself so strain,
That thou canst not, at will, draw in the rein.'

The King replied, 'I repent of this unseemly action, but my repentance is now unavailing, and the wound of this sorrow cannot be healed by any salve; and as long as I live I shall retain on my bosom the scar of this regret, and lacerate the visage of my feelings with the nail of remorse.

HEMISTICH.

What can I do? the deed was mine: for self-made ills there is no cure.'

And I have adduced this story in order that it may be known that many such incidents have occurred, where, through the disastrous results of precipitation, men have fallen into the whirlpool of repentance; and, owing to their abandonment of deliberate and cautious procedure, have sunk in the vortex of calamity.

VERSE.

Men without gravity soon pass away.
Man's nature should be stable as a rock.
Soon does the lightning's sudden flash decay;
And base minds only cannot bear a shock.
And he who acts in haste unthinkingly,
Crushed by disaster's stone his glory's base shall be.'

The Devotee replied, 'O partner of my life, and ornament of my existence! thou hast consoled me with this story, and salved my wounded heart. And I know that I have many to share with me this guilt; and just as their stories have been recorded on the page of time, so shall my tale also be narrated. So that, whoever is incautious in his actions, and participates not in the advantages of gravity and placidity, may be warned by this narrative, and derive a salutary[1] lesson from this history.

This is the story of one who, without deliberation, carries the intention of doing anything into execution, and engages in a matter without thought. And it behoves a man of understanding to make experience his guide, and to

---

[1] Observe this somewhat unusual sense of '*itibár*.

furbish the mirror of his judgment with the directions of sages and the admonitions of the wise; and on all occasions to incline towards reflection and counsel, and to turn away from the path of rashness and levity, in order that good fortune and prosperity may, in abundant and successive waves, reach the shore of his happiness, and the help of welfare and good gifts may be added to his virtues and courage.

STANZA.

Wouldst thou bear off the ball of joy with effort's crooked bat,
    Then to the hand of patience thou thy heart's reins yield.
Urge not the courser of neglect on hurry's plain, for that
    Will hurl thee down at last, disgraced upon the field.
Haste thee will into peril plunge—that, though a century
    Thou strugglest on, thou never wilt thyself thence free.
Then be not rash, nor from the glass of calmness turn thine eye,
    For wisdom can in calm and patience only be.'

CHAPTER VII.

OF VIGILANCE AND DELIBERATION, AND OF ESCAPING FROM THE INJURIES OF FOES.[1]

INTRODUCTION.

The king said, 'I have heard the story of a person who thoughtlessly and unreflectingly threw himself into the sea of regret and repentance, and through impatience and want of endurance, was caught in the snare of penitence and remorse. Now, if convenient, detail to me the purport of the Seventh Precept; and narrate the story of a person captured by his enemies; and explain the history of one surrounded by powerful foes, both on the left and on the right, and before and behind, and against whom many opponents have risen up, who, rushing upon him, cut him off on all sides. Thus he beholds himself in the claws of destruction and the grasp of ruin, and deems it requisite to form a connection and friendship with one of them; nay, to enter into a treaty and agreement with him, in order to escape safely: Say how shall he advance in this matter? and when, by the aid and assistance of one of his enemies, he obtains liberation from that calamity, how is he to fulfil his promise? And after having made the first courteous overtures, by what contrivance is he to keep open the path of concord?' The Bráhman replied, 'In general, friendship and enmity are not durable, because they are for the most part accidental, and that which is accidental quickly perishes. Consequently many friendships decrease with the lapse of time; nay, become entirely annihilated. In the same manner enmities, too, change and become erased from the tablet of the breast. The affection and animosity of the people of this world are like the clouds of spring, which sometimes pour down, and at other times withhold their showers; they have, therefore, no permanence nor stability.

QUATRAIN.

Whene'er my heart to friendship turned, on near
Inspection the sought friend an enemy
Was found. So worldly hate is changeful here
Nor on our worldly friends can we rely.

There is as little dependence to be placed on the love and hatred of mankind, as on the partiality of a prince, the beauty of the fair, the voices of

---

[1] This chapter corresponds with the Third of the Sanskrit 'Pancha-Tantra;' the Eleventh of the Arabic 'Kalílah Damnah;' the Ninth of the Persian ''Iyár Dánish;' and also the Ninth of the Hindústání 'Khirad Afróz.'

young singers, the fidelity of women, the favor of the deranged, [1] the generosity of the drunken, the attachment of the populace, or the flattery of foes; for in none of these can you place any reliance, nor can you set your heart upon their duration.

COUPLET.

'Tis pleasant, promises of love with friends to alternate,
But what avails it? for to them is no abiding state.

For there have been many friendships which, after reaching the very extreme of union and attachment, and, after being founded in sincere and pure attachment, and mounting in the course of time to the very pinnacle of heaven, have been, by some fatal misfortune, [2] changed from the most unalloyed affection to the extreme of hate, while their moisture was dried up by the scorching wind of separation. Again, long animosities and hereditary quarrels may be annihilated by a little kindness, and a foundation of friendship laid and strengthened in an excellent manner. Hence it is that men of understanding do not give up treating an enemy with courtesy, nor at once cut off all hopes of reconciliation. Neither do they place implicit reliance upon every friendship, nor feel perfect security and confidence therein. And of the perfect sayings, which have flowed from the source of the Great Prophecy, this significatory sentence is one that has been honored by manifestation, ' *Love thy friend moderately, not to the very extreme.*'

STANZA.

Friendship should ne'er be so exactly true,
That not a hair could find its way betwixt.
So hatred, too intense, we should eschew,
Keeping it with a dash of kindness mixed.
He that is equable in mind will move
Justly between extremes of hate and love.

Wherefore, as it is well known that small confidence is to be placed in the friendship or animosity of mankind, it behoves a wise and prudent man not to reject the overtures of an enemy to reconciliation and friendship, which may be the means of averting evils and of attracting benefits; but on the contrary, he should make use of every means in his power, as the exigencies of the moment may require, for the accomplishment of his purpose—in order that by happy influence of foresight and reflection, the door of good-fortune may be opened and the moon of prosperity dawn from the horizon of success. And of the various examples which have been quoted on this subject, that of the Rat and Cat is one.' The king asked, 'How was that?'

---

[1] Stewart translates, 'the favor of ministers.' He must, therefore have read *diwdnán* for the *diwdnagán* of the editions and of the MSS. in my possession.
[2] Lit., 'wounded eye.'

STORY I.

He said, 'They have related that in the wilderness of Bard'a, there was a tree, which in height surpassed all trees, and was pre-eminent in the forest by its size and firmness.

COUPLET.

Trees that bear fruit best decorate   The garden, and enrich its state.

And under the tree was the hole of a Rat of greedy nature and subtle disposition, sagacious and sharp-witted, who by a single deliberation could loose a thousand knots of difficulty, and in a half-instant could devise a hundred various artifices.

COUPLET.

Rich in expedients and in juggling lore,
That rat saw schemes a hundred years before.

And in the neighbourhood of that tree, a Cat, too, had its abode, and sportsmen used very frequently to resort thither and spread their nets in the vicinity. One day a hunter spread his net close to that tree, and fastened a little flesh in the front of it. The greedy Cat, unaware of that circumstance, came on the scent towards the flesh, and, before its teeth could reach it, its neck was caught in the meshes of the net.

QUATRAIN.

'Tis greed that does enmesh all living; greed
That makes us follow most unrighteous gain;
Greed robs all creatures of the rest they need,
And steeps their being in perpetual pain.

In short, the Rat, too, in quest of food, came from its hole, and cast its eyes cautiously all around, and looked to the right and left, and down and up. Suddenly its eyes lighted on the Cat; but although its sight waxed dim on beholding it and its hope of old age and continued existence was attenuated, it was nevertheless not dismayed,[1] and looked well in that direction. It then observed that the Cat was entangled in the bonds of calamity, and returned heartfelt thanks to the sportsman, and expressed its gratitude for the captivity of the Cat. All at once it perceived an ichneumon crouching in ambush, and with the arrow of attack fitted to the bow of preparation. It then turned towards a tree and beheld a raven, which from the top of the tree meditated pouncing upon it. So the Rat was overpowered with terror and fear, and dismay and dread got the mastery over it.

COUPLET.

Ah! for my hapless fortune! onward, still,   It leads me where I find a greater[2] ill.

The Rat bethought himself, 'If I advance, the Cat will seize me, and if I go

---

[1] Observe the phrase *dil az já burdan*, 'to be dismayed.'
[2] I read with the MSS. and Stewart *bishtar* for the *pishtar* of the editions.

back the ichneumon will fasten on me, and if I stop where I am, the raven will pounce on me. What shall I do, then, in this calamitous position? and by what stratagem avert this danger? To whom shall I tell my distressful story? and from whom seek a medicine for my irremediable woe?

COUPLET.

I have no confidant from whom to ask advice in my affairs,
No sympathiser whom to tell my weary bosom's cares.

Now the doors of calamity are open, and the road to the halting-place of safety very far and distant. Various perils have unveiled their face, and the path of retreat is closed. Yet, notwithstanding all this, I must keep up my heart and fix my eyes on the road of liberation, for the cup-bearer, fortune, if he sometimes gives us to taste a draught of the beverage of our desire, at other times mixes the poison of his wrath with the sharbat of happiness.

COUPLET.

Fate's cup-bearer changes often, thou thy sorrows then assuage,
Now he gives the wine of favor, now the bitter dregs of rage.

A man of firm courage is he who does not suffer his lip to laugh with joy when arraying himself in the robe of good-fortune, nor permits the eye of grief to shed the tear of regret at drinking the draught of trouble.

COUPLET.

Grieve not, nor let thy heart be glad at this world's joy or sorrow,
For know! the scene that now seems fixed, aye changes on the morrow.

Now, there is no better refuge for me in this whirlpool of calamity, than the shade of good sense, nor any kinder friend than the teacher of wisdom. And whoever possesses a strong mind, does not allow terror to find access to it, nor suffers dread and alarm to encompass his heart. And from the saying of the sages, it is to be learned that the minds of men of understanding should be like the sea, the measure of the depth of which cannot be known, and whose bottom can only be reached by divers of experience. And whatever secret or confidential things fall into it, they never reappear, and, however vast the torrent of calamity and disaster which flows into it, its capacity is sufficient to contain it, and the signs of discoloration are not perceptible in it. For if trouble reach such a point as to obscure the understanding, and despondency affect the mind to such a degree that the intellect is overpowered, men become incapable of deliberation, and the advantageous influences of experience and sagacity fail them.

STANZA.

That man is firm whose will no shocks can break,
    Though round the earth he wander like the sky.
Him, like the Simurgh, tempests cannot shake,
    His stubborn thoughts the hurricane defy.
Nor like the sparrow at the feeble breath
Of puny blow-pipe will he sink to death.

But whoever permits a variety of doubts to find way to him, and suffers the suggestions of 'Perhaps' and 'Perchance' to agitate his bosom, the basis of his counsel is ruined, and the market of his deliberations and reflections is marred. Let him look as much as he will into the mirror of his heart, inasmuch as it is disturbed and darkened by the rust of doubt, he cannot see in it the face of his desired object, and however much he peruses the tablet of reflection, as the eye of his vision is dimmed by the ophthalmia of vain fancies, he cannot read from it the writing of his wish. And on this head an eminent authority has said,

STANZA.

'Strive to be resolute; half measures shun:
For from weak doubts, a hundred dangers rise.
A firm mind mirrors clear what's to be done,
But troubled waters cheat the gazers' eyes.'

No measure will suit me better than to make peace with the Cat, for in the extremity of danger he stands in need of my assistance; and just as I see a prospect of being delivered from these perils by his aid, so he, too, will be rescued from that imprisonment by my help and friendly offices. Now if the Cat will listen to my words with the ear of understanding, and will make use of a wise discrimination, and place confidence in the sincerity of what I say, and not impute it to cunning hypocrisy and deceit, and believe it pure of the evil mixture of wiliness and imposture, and the disgrace of dissimulation and interested motives, we may both effect our escape through the blessing of uprightness and unanimity, and my other enemies, being disappointed of their expectations, will go, each of them, about his business.[1]

HEMISTICH.

When friends are with us, bid our foemen wait.'

Then, after these reflections, the Rat approached the Cat, and asked him what was the matter? The Cat answered in a doleful voice,

COUPLET.

'We grieve,—bear witness to our inward pangs,
Parched lip, and drop that from our eyelid hangs.

I have a body imprisoned in the fetters of distress, and a heart consumed with the flame of suffering and affliction.' The Rat replied,

COUPLET.

'I have a secret, but to tell thee it,[2]   Time presses, and I find no season fit.'

---

[1] Observe the phrase *pai-i kári giriftan*, 'to go about one's business;' and a little lower in the hemistich, *pai-i kári nishastan*, which, according to Stewart, signifies 'to wait one's leisure.'

[2] Stewart translates, 'I am acquainted with a secret, unknown to thy mouth.' He takes *bá dihán* with *nihání*, and is thus compelled to give an unusual meaning to *bá*. In any case, the *bá dihán* comes in very awkwardly, unless we suppose that a lover is speaking, and the secret message is a kiss.

The Cat said, with the utmost humility, 'Utter without ceremony whatever occurs to thy mind, and it behoves thee not to admit of any delay by suppressing it.' The Rat answered, 'Never did any hearer hear aught from me but the truth, and falsehoods meet with no acceptance in men's hearts.[1] Know, therefore, that I have always rejoiced at thy distress, and have ever regarded thy disappointment as the source of my own happiness; and my prayers have always been expended for thy loss and ruin. To-day, however, I am thy partner in misfortune, and I have projected a means of escape for myself, which involves thy release also; and for this cause I am now thy friend, and knock at the door of reconciliation.

COUPLET.

This friendship mingles selfish ends, tis true ;
Yet ends that good to thee, not harm, will do.

And it cannot remain hidden from thy understanding and sagacity that I am now speaking the truth, and that in speaking thus I can have no feeling of treachery, nor any bad intention. Moreover I will produce two witnesses to the sincerity of my purpose; one is the ichneumon, which is crouching in ambush behind me, and the other the raven, which is on the look-out for me at the top of the tree, and both of them have the same object, that is my destruction.[2] As soon, however, as I draw nigh to thee their hopes will be averted from me, and the desire of each of them will be altogether cut off. If thou wilt set my mind at ease, and give me a solemn promise sufficient to tranquilize my heart, I will escape under the shadow of thy good-fortune. Thus both my object will be attained and thy bonds too will be severed.

HEMISTICH.

This fact will benefit both me and thee.'

The Cat, after hearing these words, fell into thought, and was immersed in a sea of reflection, wishing to measure all the sides and parts of this discourse with the step of consideration, and to test the purity of this proposition with the touchstone of deliberation. The Rat saw that time pressed excessively, and that the Cat was busying himself with prudential considerations. He therefore called out, 'Listen to my words, and rely on the goodness of my disposition, and the purity of my intentions, and, accepting my kindness, no longer delay. For a wise man does not suffer himself to hesitate in action, and regards procrastination in important matters as inadmissible.

HEMISTICH.

Be not remiss, but prize the time to act.

---

[1] Stewart renders, 'Falsehood possesses no estimation in my breast;' but as *dilhá* is plural, I have rendered it as above. Literally the sentence is, 'To a false word in hearts there is no illumination.'

[2] *Damár az nihád-i man bar ávardan*, lit. : 'To bring ruin out of my nature.'

Just as I rejoice in thy fidelity, do thou also be pleased [at the opportunity of] prolonging my existence; for the deliverance of each of us is dependant on the surviving of the other; and my case and thine is exactly like that of the boat and the boatman, for the boat reaches the shore by the exertions of the boatman, and the boatman performs his business with the aid of the boat. Now, my sincerity will be shewn by trying it, and my haste is simply lest the opportunity be lost.

HEMISTICH.

I fear that fate will give no respite more.

And I think that it is clear to thy heart that my words are not wanting in corresponding deeds, and that my actions preponderate over my promises. Now I have given a promise of friendship, and I will faithfully perform it, and do thou also nod thy head in assent, and declare thy compliance.

COUPLET.

Sign, for our eyes attend expectant now,   Upon the corners of that archèd brow.'

The Cat hearkened to the words of the Rat, and beholding the beauty of truth on the pages of his condition, rejoiced, and said to the Rat, 'Thy words seem true, and from the tenor of thy discourse comes the odor of sincerity. I therefore accept this compact, and listen with the ear of my soul to the word of God, (may His Name be glorified!) who said, '*Peace is good*,' and I will not overstep the purport of this saying,

QUATRAIN.

'While peace is possible, so long, knock not
Upon war's door, and while thou mayest seek
For honor, shun an ignominious lot.
Break not love's ewer, but to all be meek.'

And I hope that by the auspicious influence of sincere friendship both parties will be liberated, and I take upon myself the duty of requiting and recompensing this favour, and accept the obligation of being thankful to all time for this kindness. And I, too, after the same fashion that thou hast promised, plight my troth, and my hope is,

HEMISTICH.

To quite fulfil this promise I have made.

Now, say what I must do, and how I must conduct myself towards thee?' The Rat replied, 'When I approach thee thou must observe towards me the utmost reverence and becoming respect, that my foes, by observing that, may be acquainted with the confirmation of the ties of social converse and sincere friendship between us, and may so retire baffled and discomfited. Then I, with my mind free from care, will remove the bonds from thy feet.' The Cat assented to this arrangement, and the Rat advanced with the utmost confidence. Then the Cat displayed all the forms of friendly and respectful salutation, and addressed him most cordially, and observed towards him a variety of courtesies and ingratiating and flattering ceremonies. When the ichneumon and raven beheld this state of things, they abandoned all thoughts of making prey of the Rat and departed. As soon as the Rat, owing to the protection of the Cat, was delivered from those two perilous enemies, he began to sever the bonds, and fell into reflection how to escape from the mesh of a third calamity, and he commenced his work slowly. The Cat sagaciously discerned that the Rat had fallen into long and protracted thought. He feared lest he should make off without severing the meshes, and leave him tied by the leg. He therefore began to expostulate with him in a friendly manner, and said, 'Thou hast soon become weary, and my confidence in the fervor of thy professions and the goodness of thy disposition was very opposite to this. Now that thou hast gained thy object, and hast been successful in the wish of thy heart, thou seemest to be lax in fulfilling thy engagements, and art meditating some means of evading the discharge of thy obligations. For my part, I have long known that fidelity is a medicine not to be found in the shop of the druggists of this age; and that sincerity is a gain not to be met with in the treasures of the present time; and that good faith is a second Símurgh, of which but the name exists; and that gratitude resembles the philosopher's stone, the truth of which no one has ever ascertained.

COUPLET.

Seek not fidelity.   From none thou wilt now hear its name :
To search for the elixir or the Simurgh were the same.'

The Rat answered, 'God forbid that I should mark the face of my condition with the brand of infidelity, and enter the good name, which I have through so long an interval acquired, in the volume of the breakers of promises. I well know that fidelity is the ladder of ambition, and the provision for the road of happiness. It is an elixir which transmutes black earth into gold, and a collyrium which imparts sight to the eye of the blind. The nostril of every soul which has not snuffed up the scent of faithfulness has no share in the perfumes of the odoriferous plants of good qualities, and the eye of every heart which has not beheld sincerity, is devoid of participating in the sight of the rays of amiable natures.

HEMISTICH.

Dirt fill the head, void of the brain of faith!'

The Cat said, 'As thou art thus sensible that good faith is the tire-woman of the bride of affection, and the mole of the cheek of beauty and comeliness, it behoves thee, too, to adorn the cheek of thy condition with this cosmetic. For no bird of the heart will warble among the branches of the affection of that garden, in which the plant of fidelity does not grow, and no cheek which is destitute of the mole of good faith will receive a single glance from any intelligent person. And hence they have said,

COUPLET.
' She who combines not love with constancy,
Delights me not, though Eden's nymph she be.'

And whoever is not clothed with the garment of fidelity, and does not fulfil
the promise which he plights, will meet with what that Farmer's Wife met
with !' The Rat asked, ' How was that ? '

STORY II.[1]

The Cat said, ' They have related that in one of the villages of Fárs there
was a Farmer of the utmost experience and the most abundant good sense.
He had often tasted the bitters and sweets from the cup of fortune, and had
experienced many hardships and pleasures in the struggles of life.

COUPLET.
A world-wide traveler, a man of sense,   Gifted with shrewdness, wit, and eloquence.

Now this farmer had a wife whose countenance was the taper of his bed-
chamber, and whose sweet and ruby lips were as olives[2] to the drinkers of
wine. She blended a hundred colors like the early spring, and, like fortune,
indulged in a thousand coquettish artifices.

COUPLET.
Some blessed spirit, it may be, her body did compose ;
Such grace and beauty could not spring from water and the rose.

Notwithstanding all the skill that the old Farmer possessed, he passed his time
in want and poverty, and sowed the seed of reliance on God in the field of
' Consign the affair to the Almighty ' ; and, indeed, it is always the habit of
perfidious fortune to exclude the deserving and meritorious from her favors,
and to exalt to the summit of success and honor the worthless and undeserving.

VERSE.
The devious meet with ample measures,
Straight-goers get but blades of grass.
Flies feast on sweets and candied treasures,
And glorious Humás filthy bones amass.

Thus the old Farmer, though famous for his perfect skill in agriculture, not
having the implements for following the business, passed his life in want of
employment and penury. One day his Wife, from excessive distress, loosed
the tongue of reproach, saying, ' How long is this abiding in the corner of
our hovel to continue, and how long is precious life to be wasted in want
and scarcity of means. Surely from motion comes promotion;[1] and although,
from the tribunal of bounty, they have written the free passport, ' Sustenance

---

[1] This story is not in the Arabic, but has been introduced by Husain Vá'iz.
[2] This is Stewart's rendering of nuḳl. The Dictionary only says that it signifies ' fruits or
sweetmeats sent round at entertainments.'
[1] I have chosen these words to preserve the jingle in the original between harakat and
barakat.

is from God,[1] yet the signature which they have impressed on the corner thereof is also ' *The industrious is the friend of God.*' Wherefore industry must be regarded as the means of support, but we must recognise the Lord God as the true provider.

COUPLET.

'Tis true the cause whence comes thy food is industry, but yet
We must not Him, the Source of Food, Causer of Cause, forget.

It therefore appears to me advisable that thou shouldest step forward in the path of industry and acquire supplies by every means in thy power.' The Farmer replied, 'My dear life! what thou hast said approximates to the truth, nay, is beyond all manner of doubt or imputation of selfishness. But I have for a long time acted as master in this village, and most of the farmers of this place have been at some time my laborers. Now that my estate is ruined, and that I have parted with the implements of agriculture, there is no resource left me but to work as a common laborer, but I cannot bring myself[2] to endure the disgrace of working for those who were once my own laborers.

COUPLET.

I cannot eat the crumbs of those who once upon my leavings fed,
Nor bear their burthens who for me once toiling gained their hireling bread.

But if I must needs make choice of some profession, it is best to pack up and depart from this place.

HEMISTICH.

O'er us in foreign lands no foes exult.

Come! let us emigrate to some other place and there support ourselves as best we can.' The Wife was driven to extremity by poverty and destitution, and consented to the hardships of exile. Joining, therefore, in the purpose of her spouse, they set their faces thence towards the neighborhood of Baghdád. One day, in the midst of their journey, tired and weary, they took refuge under the shade of a tree, and, to dispel their fatigue, conversed on a variety of subjects. The Farmer said, 'Dear friend! we have chosen the pains of exile, and are proceeding towards a country where no one is acquainted with us, and where we are acquainted with no one. And it is possible that the men of that country may be oppressive, and tyrannical, treacherous and deceitful, and God Most Holy and Most High has adorned the tablet of thy incomparable beauty with the inscription, ' *In the most perfect symmetry.*' Heaven avert that by craft and subtlety, or by force and violence, they should assail thee; and thou, too, through the pride of youth and the hope of conquest, should incline to them and turn away from this poor old man, and consume my aged head in the flame of absence; and if,

---

[1] Stewart affirms this to be a quotation from the Ḳur'án. I am unable to find it there.
[2] Observe the phrase, *bá khud rást nami tawdnam dvard.*

which God forbid! things should turn out in this manner, it would be no longer possible for me to survive.

COUPLET.

I fear not death, but when I'm dead, I fear,
That thou shouldst be the life of others here.'

The Wife replied, 'What words are these which pass thy lips? and what is this thought which has entered thy heart?

COUPLET.

Long as I live I'll be thy willing slave,
And prove thy handmaid e'en beyond the grave.

Had I entertained such thoughts as these I would not have undertaken the fatigues of the journey, nor would I have impressed on my suffering heart the brand of separation from my country. And my desire is to preserve [inviolate] till the day of resurrection, the vow of the first night when I placed my foot in the chamber of thy society.

COUPLET.

Till the last day I will my troth fulfil,
Lest thou shouldst say I kept that promise ill.

And if thou wishest it I will pledge my faith anew, and promise that so long as the peacock of life adorns the garden of my body, the parrot of my tongue shall not sweeten its palate save with the sugar of gratitude to thee; and while the Humá of vitality continues to canopy my head with the shade of prosperity, I will never suffer the bird of my heart to be caught in the net of any one. Should I precede thee in traveling the last journey, I shall then have fulfilled my engagements, and if my fate should be to linger some days after thee, my promise is unaltered and my faith unchanged.

COUPLET.

If fate a few days' respite should allow,
Stedfast my word, unchanged will be my vow.'

The Farmer was tranquilized by these words, and his Wife having plighted her faith in the manner that has been related, confirmed her promise with oaths; and the old man laid his head contentedly on the knee of his beloved spouse, and fell asleep. Shortly after this, a cavalier arrived there, mounted on a horse of Arabian breed, and clad in princely apparel. The Farmer's Wife looked up and beheld a youth, such that if the pupil of the eye had beheld his countenance in the darkest night, it would have supposed that the true morn had arisen from the curtain of the eastern horizon; and if the human sight had cast a glance, through the veil of darkness, on his beautiful cheek, it would have imagined that the world-illuminating sun had displayed itself glittering from behind the veil [of the clouds]. His cheeks were like the damask[1] rose, and his beard like the twisted hyacinth. One would say that the limner of divine wisdom had drawn, on the page of his cheek, a circle of liquid amber with the compasses of invention, or that through the culture of the husbandman of nature, a delightful verdure had grown up round the fountain of his life.

VERSE.

O'er the bright moon of thy visage thou hast drawn a club of musk,[2]
 And in the hollow of the club hast caught that fair moon, like a ball.
Round the margin of thy spring of life grows up a herbage dusk,
 That is the young down of thy cheek, which we may well, then, Khizr call.
With thy black ringlets thou hast made a canopy of loveliness,
 And o'er thy face's glittering sun hast drawn this ebon-colored dress.'

When the Farmer's Wife beheld the perfect beauty of that cavalier, the sovereign of love occupied with his conquering forces the kingdom of her heart, and reason, which is the lord of the mansion of the body, packed up its goods to depart; and the tongue of her condition began to warble this couplet,

COUPLET.

' Thou hast a mounted hunter come, and of my soul and frame made prey,
The reins of patience thou hast snapped, and led the steeds of sense astray.'

On the other side the youth looked and beheld a beautiful woman, such that the tire-woman of the Divine skill had adorned her enchanting face with the cosmetic of grace, and the polisher of the decree of the Holy One had lent illumination to her cheeks through the light of beauty. Her countenance was such that the radiant sun was consumed[3] with envy at it, and so dark were her locks that the musk of Cathay was tortured with jealousy at them.

VERSE.

Silver her breast, fir-like her stature tall,
 Her every limb seemed lovelier than the rest.
Both eyes with arrows pierced the hearts of all,
 And sugar from her lips acquired new zest.
With extracts of the cane those lips were rife,
 Say rather, sweetened from the spring of life.

---

[1] I find no authority for this version of *siráb*, except Stewart's translation : *siráb* properly means 'moist,' 'bathed in raindrops or dew.'

[2] I beseech the candid reader who would judge of the difficulties of a translator from the Persian, to examine these lines. Well may Stewart say that is is impossible to translate them literally, or to understand them, without reference to a dictionary. The round face of the youth is compared to the moon ; and his black ringlets to a bat used at the game of *chaugán*. These bats have a hollow in them to catch the ball more readily : so the ringlets are said to have caught in the space between them the moon of his face. The down of his beard is compared to herbage growing near the water of life ; and as Khizr or Elias is said to have drunk of the water of life, occasion is taken for an equivoque upon his name, and *khazar* 'verdure.'

[3] *Táftah.* Stewart translates this ' eclipsed,' a meaning it could hardly bear, but he may have had a different reading.

The neck of his soul became instantly bound with the chain of love, and the foot of his heart entangled with the noose of desire.

COUPLET.

When love led on its forces my heart life's banner furled,
And patience, back retreating, took refuge in the world.

Now that youth was the son of the king of that country, who had come out with the intention of hunting, and had got to a distance from his retinue. When his eyes fell upon the two captivating gazelles [1] of that disturber of cities, a piercing shaft from the bow of her eyebrows reached the target of his breast. Thus, though himself pursuing the chase, he was caught in the snare of love. Hereupon he exclaimed, ' O envy of fairies ! and O point of adoration to the idols of 'Azur! [2] who art thou ? and by what chance camest thou hither ?

COUPLET.

O thou fruit thus fairly ripened ! from whose garden mayest thou be ?
O thou verse [3] anew descended ! on whom bestowest thou dignity ?'

The Farmer's Wife heaved a cold sigh from her afflicted heart, and said, ' O wakeful Fortune ! dost thou inquire after the state of one whose happiness slumbers, or dost thou ask the story of these sleepless eyes?

COUPLET.

A secret, cureless grief have I,   A heart's pang without remedy.

The partner of my fortunes is this infirm old man, and my distracted heart is linked with sorrow and melancholy. The origin of my distress [4] is this that thou beholdest, and the conclusion of my career must be such as thou seest. I pass my time in hardships, and have no enjoyment in life.' The youth replied, ' O desire of the hearts of the afflicted ! and solace of the minds of distracted lovers !

HEMISTICH.

Fie ! that such hawk as thou should thus be caged.

Is it to be tolerated that thou with this enchanting countenance shouldst choose to be the companion of a used-up old dotard ; and possessed as thou art of such a stock of loveliness and beauty, shouldst pass thy time in poverty and want ? Come with me ! that I may seat thee on the throne of honor, and make thee the queen of this country, and set up the banner of thy glory and greatness throughout the confines of this realm.

---

[1] That is, ' eyes.'

[2] Abraham's Father, who is said to have made idols of exquisite beauty.

[3] The *áyat* is a verse of the Ḳur'án. The lady is compared to a new verse of that book freshly revealed.

[4] *Libás* signifies generally ' apparel,' but also ' spouse.' Thus an equivoque may be intended. Stewart translates it here ' wretched state,' and I have followed him, but I know of no authority for such a rendering.

VERSE.

To days gone by, now bid adieu!
Fortune and life begin anew.
Enter the door of bliss with me,
Fate smiles: let us, too, mirthful be.
Be gay! my life, my soul, is thine,
Fill thou the cup, I'll drink the wine.'

As soon as the Farmer's Wife heard the happy tidings of union with her lover, she forgot the promise she had that moment made; and shattered the cup of compact with the stone of inconstancy and untruthfulness. When the youth saw that she was inclined to him, he said, 'Life of the world! look on this opportunity as a blessing, and rise and come to me, that I may mount thee [on my steed]; and before the farmer awakes we shall have traversed a considerable distance.' The Farmer's Wife lifted her husband's head from her knee, and rested it on the ground; and, mounting nimbly behind the youth, clasped the girdle of his affection with the hand of reliance. At this moment, the Farmer awoke, and beheld the youth mounted and standing there, and his wife clasping with the hand of union the waist of his desire. A sigh issued from his breast, and he said,

COUPLET.

'My love has torn her heart away, the heart that to her friend was given:
The ties, the ties of former days are all, alas! asunder riven.

Prithee, faithless one! what plot is this that thou hast devised, and what stratagem is this that thou hast ungratefully concocted?' His Wife answered, 'Cease thy persuasions and waste not thy breath in trying to lure me from my purpose. For to expect fidelity from the fair, is like attempting to unite the star Canopus with the Pleiades; and to look for constancy from those who make a practice of dealing cruelly, is like planting a rose-bush in the fire of a lime-kiln. But, perhaps, thou hast never heard what they have said,

COUPLET.

'Learn constancy,' I cried, 'from lovers.' 'Nay!'
Said she, ''tis not the moon-faced fair one's way.'

The old man rejoined, 'Thou hast stepped beyond the limits of right dealing, and hast opened the door of cruelty with the key of injurious conduct. Fear lest thou shouldest be overtaken with the retribution of thy broken vows, and the disastrous consequences of thy breach of promise should descend upon thee.

HEMISTICH.

Forbear! lest thou repent at last, when penitence is vain.'

His wife, paying no attention to his words, said to the youth, 'Make haste! that having escaped from the tortures of the desert of separation, we may convey ourselves to the halting-place of union.' The prince then began to gallop through the waste his fleet, desert-crossing, river-passing steed, which was such, that the fierce northern blast was unable to keep up with it, nor could swift-winged fancy arrive at its traces.

VERSE.

> Rose-hued [1] like lovers' tears, it, swift of pace,
> More fleet than Khusrau's Shabdiz,[2] sped along.
> Like lightning-flash, its one bound could efface
> The limits that to east and west belong.

In the twinkling of an eye they were lost to the Farmer's sight, yet the hapless old man, in spite of the anguish of exile and the pangs of separation, set off after them.

HEMISTICH.

The afflicted ask the road, and follow on.

And he thought to himself, 'The promises of women are devoid of faith, and their faith of continuance.

HEMISTICH.

Forget their memory, for they faithless are.

And I, relying on her words, have abandoned my well-known country and my familiar fatherland, and now I have not the face to return, nor the power to pursue them. What, then, is to be the conclusion of my career, and what the end of my unhappy state?

COUPLET.

> Without or head or foot I seek my heart the wide world round,[3]
> What shall I do? for my affairs nor head nor foot is found.'

However, after the lovers had gone to the distance of three farsakhs,[4] they came to a fountain and a shady tree. The lady was tired, and the youth, too, felt fatigued. They said, 'Let us rest here a moment, and, after we are refreshed, let us begin our journey again.' They then dismounted from the horse, and took refuge under the shade of the tree, and sate some time at the brink of the water, and talked of various matters. The youth gazed with expanding eyes on the lovely countenance and musky ringlets of that enchanting fair one, and beholding the curls of perfumed hair falling on the roseate cheeks of his mistress, like the braid of the hyacinth on the leaf of the jasmine, he exclaimed,

---

[1] Stewart translates *gulgún* 'beautiful and of various hues.' Orientals, however, represent lovers as weeping tears of blood. The courser, therefore, may have been of a rose or roan color.

[2] *Shabdiz* signifies 'Night-color.'

[3] Stewart justly says of this impracticable couplet, 'This verse cannot be literally translated.' Nevertheless, to get the words into metre at all, I have been obliged to be literal. To be *bí sar o pá*, signifies 'to be wretched,' in Persian. Whereas, in the second line, the phrase is to be taken literally, 'without head or foot,' as in Stewart's version, which is, 'I travel round the world, although destitute of the means, in pursuit of my love; but how can I succeed, who have neither head to direct me, nor feet to carry me.'

[4] The *farsakh*, of which the Greeks made 'parasang,' is about three miles.

COUPLET.

'Those musky tresses on thy cheek, a resting-place of roses find,
I know not how thus wondrously they night with day have thus combined.'

On the other hand, that enchanting beauty, casting her eyes on the fascinating stature of that stripling—who was a plant in the garden of loveliness, more luxuriant than the branch of the Túba-tree, and surveying the loftiness of that graceful cypress and the attractions of that branch of joy, uttered this verse,

COUPLET.

'How have they thus symmetrical the date-tree of thy stature made!
How to one spot thus dextrously a hundred thousand charms conveyed!'

In the midst of these speeches the importunities of nature seizing the collar of the Farmer's Wife—she wished to renew her ablutions, and, through delicacy, she went some distance from under the tree, and proceeded to the side of a jungle which was near the fountain; but before she could get there, a ferocious lion—from dread of which the celestial lion dared not to move a step in the heavenly mead, and Taurus in the pasture-ground of the sky, was afraid to breathe, through terror of his claws,

VERSE.

Onward advanced with savage roar and rush.
Through fear of him the heavenly lion fled.
Beneath his talons poisoned torrents gush;
His sword-like teeth a gory deluge shed.

No sooner did the lion get sight of her, than he carried her off and bore her into the jungle. When the youth heard the terrible roaring of the lion, and beheld his mistress carried off into the jungle, he threw himself, with all haste, upon his swift steed, and galloped into the desert,

HEMISTICH.

He saw the danger, and forsook his love.

In terror of his life, the prince sped on, nor looked behind him; and the fair one, a prisoner in the claws of the lion, reaped the seed which she had sown in the field of infidelity.

HEMISTICH.

All reap at last the actions they have sown.

Meanwhile, the old Farmer, who was following them, came up limping and halting; and having reached the edge of the fountain, and finding no trace of them, uttered a cry of distress and said,

COUPLET.

'Alas! my love has gone away, nor calmed my bosom's storm,
A hundred promises she gave, nor yet did one perform.'

He then bethought himself of the time when they were united, and called to mind the feelings of their early wedded life; and, weeping bitterly, steeped his cheeks in the tears of regret.

COUPLET.

How fair the day when first we met in union's flowery ground;
And Rose and Bulbul-like the power of laughing converse found.

Alas! that the rays of the brightness of union have been exchanged for the gloomy impressions of separation; and that the spring of mirth and happiness has faded under the scorching blast of the autumn of inconstancy and affliction.

VERSE.

But yesterday a union with such blissful transports rife,
A parting that the world consumes to-day.
Alas! that fate did enter in the volume of my life,
These joys one day should bloom, the next, decay.

After much weeping and infinite lamentation, he observed the footsteps of his beloved leading towards the desert. Instantly he fearlessly followed the track, and arrived at the moment [1] when, the lion having torn open her belly and devoured part of her entrails, had departed. The old man at this sight was distracted with grief, and perceived that the disastrous results of her infidelity had reached her and that she had been overtaken with retribution for her perfidy and with punishment for her breach of faith. For a while he looked at her and wept over their attachment and his own forlorn state.

COUPLET.

From his lips his sighs arose to the starry Pleiades,
From the lashes of his eyes tears flowed streaming to the seas.

And the moral of this story is, that whoever lets slip from his hand the thread of good faith, places on his own feet the fetters of punishment, and puts the chain of calamity round his neck.

COUPLET.

When to a spot ingratitude has passed,
It makes a dreary desert there at last!'

The Rat said, 'I am aware that hypocrisy and deceit are altogether at variance with the sincere disposition of the benevolent and the practice of the good. Moreover, the advantages of thy friendship and the benefits of thy amity, have this very moment accrued to me, and the desires of my enemies, by the salutary influence of thy friendship, have just now been averted from me. Therefore it is most in accordance with honorable feeling, that I should look upon it as a duty, to requite this and loose thy bonds. But a difficulty has occurred to me and a doubt has risen up before me; and, until the dust of this anxiety is removed from the eye of my deliberation, it is impossible for me to loose all thy bonds.' The Cat rejoined, 'It appears, then, that thou hast still some apprehension of me; and yet the fact is, that

---

[1] Stewart translates *mahalli* here 'spot,' which meaning also it may bear.

I have pledged myself to good fellowship with thee, and have recited to thee a volume of reproaches against breach of faith; be assured, then, that it is impossible for me to act contrary to my promises and engagements. And relinquish the distrust that formerly existed between us; for the obligation of this new alliance has removed the principle of our former enmity, and my expectation of thy sincerity and anticipations of thy gratitude, are confirmed. Do not approach, therefore, to the ruinous practice of deceit and fraud, nor impair and deform the beauty of thy virtues and the mirror of thy good qualities with the rust of fraud and perfidy.

COUPLET.

> Keep pure the mirror of thy heart, for nought can rival purity,
> Break not thy plighted word, for nought with truthful principles can vie.

A man of upright nature and good disposition, on receiving so much as a single gracious look from any one, steps forward in the plain of sincere attachment, and raises the foundation of friendship and special regard to the pinnacle of the sky, and moistens and refreshes the plant of courtesy with the drops of sincere kindness. If by chance any suspicion or alarm should spring up in his mind, and the rankling of doubt develope itself in his heart, he immediately effaces it and does not suffer the thought of it again to approach the area of his imagination. Especially, too, when a compact has been ratified between him and his friend, and confirmed by solemn oaths. And it should be understood that the end of the faithless is infamous, and punishment soon descends on the perfidious; and a false oath lays waste the foundation of life, and to act contrary to promises speedily overthrows the sub-structure of existence.

DISTICHS.

> Man's promise is the root, himself the tree,
> The root with carefulness must cherished be.
> A broken promise is a rotten root,
> Struck from the list of gracious trees its shoot.[1]
> Unfaithful dealing is an idiot's act,
> The pious keep their oaths[2] and guard their pact.

And I am in hopes that thou, with a right feeling of gratitude, wilt forget former injuries, and wilt not exert thyself to break the promise which thou hast made.' The Rat replied,

COUPLET.

> 'Whoever breaks his oath of faith to thee,
> His heart and soul by mishaps wounded be!

---

[1] Stewart translates this obscure line, 'And the tree is cut down from the number of the sound,' which on first reading is rather difficult to understand. I have no doubt an equivoque is intended on *shumár* 'number,' and *shimár*, 'a hard wood of which the handles of axes are made.'

[2] I notice, for the benefit of the student, two misprints in this page in the printed edition. Here we have *matsdk* for *mísdk*, and at line 3 of the same page (370), *mankazat* for *mankaṣat*, 'loss.'

But the mental scruples, which I have before mentioned to thee, cause me to ponder and hesitate; otherwise, God forbid! that I should not fulfil my promise, or fail to release thee from these bonds.' The Cat rejoined, 'Explain to me the purport of thy thoughts, that I, too, may look into the matter with the eye of deliberation, and be able to judge of the solidity of thy reasoning, and the extent of thy wisdom.' The Rat answered, 'My doubts arise from this, that friends are of two kinds. First, there are those who contract friendship with perfect sincerity, and the utmost ardor and eagerness, without any admixture of self-interest or cupidity, or the debasement of hypocritical or feigned intentions. Secondly, there are those who make advances in some emergency with a view to some object they covet or are interested in. Now, the first class, who with pure faith and sincere intentions open the doors of friendly intercourse, are in every respect worthy of confidence, and at all times one may feel secure of them, and to whatever gratification they may point, there will be no swerving from the path of wisdom.

DISTICHS.

Like soothing, grateful ointment, is a friend;
But to the worthless no attention lend,
A friend thy venom will as sugar prize,
And in thy failings merit recognize.

But as for those who in some exigency make friendship a shield to repel injury, or the means of attracting and drawing to themselves advantage, their feelings will not preserve an even tenor. At one time in the season of enjoyment they will spread the carpet of pleasure, and anon at a critical moment, when their wishes are thwarted, they will look askance at their friend.

COUPLET.

Like milk and sugar now they friendship shew,
Anon more cruel than the axe or bow.

A sagacious man, therefore, should delay the accomplishment of some of the wishes of such persons, and not all at once surrender to the grasp of their power the reins of his own option. But in the execution of their affairs he ought to hang back under some plausible pretexts, and bring them to a close by slow degrees. He is bound also to look to his own safety, for self-preservation is a duty. And provided he acts in this manner, he will both be celebrated for the lustre of his kind deeds, and will also be conspicuous for the excellence of his judgment and prudence. Now, I shall act towards thee in the manner that has been pointed out. I will in no wise hold back from releasing thee, to which I have pledged myself; but I shall employ the utmost caution in taking care of my own person, and in guarding myself; for the enmity between me and thee exceeds even that of the parties from whose assaults I have been preserved by thy favor. My object in making

2 F 2

peace with thee was to get rid of them, and I regarded it as a duty; and the
gentleness which thou, too, didst display, arose from the exigency of the
moment, and to avert evil. It is now, therefore, indispensable for me to look
to the issue of the matter, and not all at once to neglect caution and foresight:
for they have said,

COUPLET.

'Be careful, aye, to make thyself secure,
And ne'er aside the rules of prudence fling.
Who rears his actions on a basis sure,
Will reason's structure to perfection bring.'

The Cat said, 'O Rat! thou art[1] exceedingly sagacious and wise, and up
to this time I was ignorant of the extent of thy intelligence, nor did I know
that the amount of thy knowledge and skill was of such a degree. I have
derived advantage from these words of thine, and thou hast given into my
hand the keys of the doors of experience and wisdom. I wish, now, that
thou wouldest disclose to me in what manner both my bonds may be loosed
and thou, too, mayest remain safe. Tell me how it is possible that this can
be effected?' The Rat laughed and said,

HEMÍSTICH.

'For every pain they have a cure too fixed.

My idea is to sever thy bonds, but to retain as a security for my own life the
principal knot, and to look out for an opportunity when thou hast something
in hand of more importance than an attack upon me, and when thou art not able
to attend to me, and hast no leisure to do me an injury. I will then sever
that knot also, in order that thou mayest be delivered from confinement, and
I may escape from harm.' The Cat perceived that the Rat was perfect
master of his own affairs, and would not be moved from his course by flattery
or deceit. He therefore unwillingly consented to that arrangement. So the
Rat severed the knots, but one that was the principal one he left as it was.
Thus they brought that night to an end with conversation. As soon as the
'anká of the morning came flying forth in the eastern horizon,[2] and spread its
light-bestowing pinions over the regions of the world,

COUPLET.

The sky its sword, the sun, from scabbard drew,
Night gathered in her skirt of sable hue,

and the hunter appeared in the distance. Then the Rat said, 'The time
is come to release myself from my promise, and to fulfil completely what I
had engaged to do.' The Cat, too, when his eyes lighted on the hunter, made

---

[1] *Búdah-i*, 'thou hast been;' *i.e.*, during the time of our acquaintance without my
knowing of it.
[2] This appears more accurate than Stewart's version, 'As soon as the Phœnix of the
morning had bent his flight to the eastern horizon.'

sure of his own destruction, and expected to be put to death, when at that moment the Rat divided the remaining knot. The Cat, in terror for his life, forgot the Rat; and running off,[1] mounted to the top of a tree; and the Rat, having escaped from such a danger, crept into a hole. The hunter beheld the meshes of the net broken and the knots severed, and was overpowered with astonishment. He took up the remains, and went away disappointed. After some time had passed the Rat put his head out of the hole, and seeing the Cat at a distance, was afraid to go near him. The Cat called out to him,

HEMISTICH.

'Since thou hast seen me, feign not the reverse.[2]

Wherefore dost thou fly me? and why dost thou think fit to shun me? Art thou not sensible that thou hast acquired a dear friend, and hast gained a valuable store for thy children and descendants, and companions and friends? Come forward, that I may requite thy goodness by my kind behaviour, and that thou mayest experience in the most approved fashion the recompense of thy courage and humanity. For my part, I know not with what tongue to express my acknowledgments of thy favors, or in what words to discharge my thanks for thy compassionate kindness.

COUPLET.

I smile, anon I blush; am glad, yet in a pensive mood;
For for thy gifts I cannot pay my debt of gratitude.'

The Rat, however, just as before, kept to the border of the carpet of separation, and, avoiding the court of companionship, turned his countenance towards solitude and timidity, and inscribed the legend of this proverb on the register of his mind, ' *This is an age of refractoriness, not a season of gratitude*;' and repeated in a mournful voice, ' How beautifully have they said,

STANZA.

' Such is the age, that from excess of wrong,
 The life or goods of none secure can be.
To whom can we attribute kindness mid a throng
 Who think they do a favor not to injure thee?'

It appears to me that this is a season for retirement and a time for divesting oneself of business, and after this I will have no intercourse with any one, but relinquish all converse with my contemporaries.

HEMISTICH.

Would my friend me as comrade have? No! let him be his own.'

The Cat replied, ' Act not so, nor withhold from me thy presence.

---

[1] I am doubtful of the exact sense of *pái kashán* here. Stewart omits it.
[2] I follow Stewart in translating thus. I am persuaded, however, that an equivoque is intended, as the Persian may equally well mean, ' Pretend not not to have seen me as thou art my sight;' *i.e.*, dear to me as sight.

Neither destroy the claims of friendship and the respect of old acquaintance. For whoever, by much exertion, has acquired a friend, and, without cause, supinely permits him to pass beyond the circle of friendship, will remain excluded from the happy results of companionship, and his other friends, having lost all hope in him, will abandon his alliance.

COUPLET.

Think poorly of the man who friends has none,
But worse of him who loses those he won.

Now thou hast conferred on me a vital obligation, and I owe to thy kindness the blessing of life. The vow, therefore, of friendship which I have pledged to thee is safe from the incidents of change, and the amicable compact which I have formed is secure from the damage of being broken.

COUPLET.

Thou mayst scent the gale of faithfulness and of truth without decay
Till the final judgment, from each flower that blossoms from my clay.

And as long as my life lasts I shall not forget thy claims, and I will use all possible efforts to shew thee kindness and honor in requital of what thou hast done for me.

COUPLET.

Thanks for thy favors, clust'ring roselike, which upon thee rest so well:
And am I not a lily, too, them with a hundred tongues to tell?'

Although the Cat made use of speeches of this description, and confirmed what he said by the most solemn oaths, wishing to raise the curtain of separation from between them, and to open the path of intercourse, it was all, in fact, of no avail, and the Rat replied, 'Whenever enmity arises from accident, it may be removed simply by intercourse and urbanity manifested by both parties. In such cases there is no fault to find with persons mixing cheerfully together. But when there is an inherent hostility, though they may, to outward appearance, lay the foundation of friendship, there is no reliance to be placed thereon, and caution and circumspection must not be a jot abated, for the harm thereof is great and the result disastrous. Wherefore it is best that as the connection of homogeneousness does not exist between us, thou shouldest wean thy heart from my society, for I naturally flee from thy society with all my soul. And whoever associates with those of a different species will meet with what befell the Frog.' The Cat asked, 'How was that?'

STORY III.[1]

The Rat said, ' They have related that a mouse had taken up its abode on the brink of a fountain, and had fixed its residence at the foot of a tree. A Frog, too, passed his time in the water there, and sometimes came to the margin of the pool to take the air. One day coming to the edge of the water he continued uttering his voice in a heart-rending cadence, and assuming himself to be a nightingale of a thousand melodies, he set free with his distressing tones the birds of the hearts [of his audience] from the cages of their bodies.

COUPLET.

'Tis true his execrable voice was harsh and bad enough,
But tone and execution joined made him completely rough.

At that time the mouse was engaged in chanting in a corner of his cell. Directly he heard the uproarious yelling of the Frog he was astounded, and came out with the intention of taking a look at the reciter; and while occupied with listening to him, kept smiting his hands together and shaking his head. These gestures, which seemed to display approbation, pleased the Frog, and he made advances towards acquaintance with him. The tongue of understanding was warning him not to associate with one of a different species, but the vanity of his disposition was inclining him towards the mouse. In short, being mutually pleased with each other, they became inseparable companions, and used to narrate to each other entertaining stories and tales.

DISTICHS.

With hearts, as at a game of draughts, they played,
Nor suffered doubt their bosoms to invade.
Oft to the mouse the joyful Frog would hie,
And tell the tale of five years' life gone by.
An eager tongue denotes a friendly mind,
Ill-will is tokened by a tongue confined.

One day the mouse said to the Frog, ' I am oftentimes desirous of disclosing to thee a secret, and recounting to thee a grief which I have at heart, and at that moment thou art abiding under the water.

COUPLET.

'Tis hard for me where thou art to repair.
And where I am my heart is filled with care.

However much I shout thou hearest me not, owing to the noise of the water, and in spite of my crying to thee, the sound cannot reach thee, because of the clamor of the other frogs. We must devise some artifice by which thou

---

[1] Stewart omits the translation of this story.

mayest know when I come to the brink of the water, and thus mayest be
informed of my arrival without my shouting to thee.' The frog said, ' Thou
speakest the truth. I, too, have often pondered uneasily, thinking, should
my friend come to the brink of the water, how shall I, at the bottom of this
fountain, learn his arrival? and how absolve myself of the anxiety which he
will be enduring to gain sight of me? And it sometimes happens that I, too,
come to the mouth of thy hole, and thou hast gone out from another side,
and I have to wait long. I had intended to have touched somewhat on this
subject to thee, but thou thyself, with the kindness thou possessest, has set
forth the circumstance, and with candor of heart hast made known the
hidden feelings of my own mind. Now the arrangement of this matter rests,
too, with thee.

HEMISTICH.

Thy judgment fair lays every project well.'

The mouse replied, 'I have got hold of the thread of a plan, and it appears
to me the best thing to get a long string, and to fasten one end to thy foot, and
tie the other tight round my own, in order that when I come to the water's
edge and shake the string, thou mayest know what I want ; and if thou too
art so kind as to come to the door of my cell, I may also get information of
this by your jerking the string.' Both parties agreed to this, and the knot of
friendship was in this manner firmly secured, and they were also kept
informed of one another's condition. One day, the mouse came to the water's
edge to seek the Frog, in order to renew their friendly converse. All of a
sudden a crow, like an unforeseen calamity, flew down from the air, and
snatching up the mouse, soared up with him. The string which was tied to
the leg of the mouse drew forth the frog from the bottom of the water, and,
as the other leg was fastened to the Frog's leg, he was suspended head downwards in the air. The crow flew on, holding the mouse in its beak, and lower
down the Frog hanging head downwards. People witnessing that extraordinary sight, were uttering in the road various jokes and sarcasms, ' A
strange thing this, that contrary to his wont a crow has made prey of a frog,'
and ' Never before was a frog the prey of a crow.' The Frog was howling out
in reply, ' Now, too, a frog is not the prey of a crow, but from the bad luck of
associating with a mouse, I have been caught in this calamity, and he who
associates with those of a different species deserves a thousand times as much.

COUPLET.

Woe worth the friend of different race ! 'twere best
To seek a well-matched comrade—O my guest !'

And the citation of this story carries with it this beneficial advice, that no
one ought to associate with one of a different race, in order that like the
frog, he may not be suspended on the string of calamity. And for my own

part I have no desire to mingle with those of my own race, then what must
I feel towards those of another?

VERSE.

Leave the gay crowd, thou! who wouldst be alone,
And thy own self thy own companion be.
The Simurgh won by this the bird-king's throne,
And is called thirty [1] though but one is he.'

The Cat rejoined, 'Since thou hadst no wish for society, why didst thou
show, in the commencement, all that courtesy? By thy friendly and polite
manner, thou capturedst me, and when I have become foot-bound in the
snare of friendship, thou severest the cord of union and beginnest to separate.

QUATRAIN.

With truth, O cup-bearer! at first, thou to me the fair goblet didst offer,
But soon I grew drunken, and thou from thy hand didst that goblet resign.
Since at last thou intendedst the lees of sorrowful parting to proffer,
Say, why at commencing present to my lips the sweet draught of pure wine?'

The Rat replied, 'At that time I stood in need of thee; and a wise man,
if he fall into a difficulty from which he may hope to extricate himself by
the aid of an enemy, will undoubtedly have recourse to conciliatory measures
and exert himself to display the proofs of his regard. Afterwards if he
should foresee any injury to himself, he will shun his society, not through
enmity or perversity, nor from aversion or arrogance, but just as the young
of animals follow their mothers for the sake of the milk, and when they are
independent of that nature, abandon their society without any previous
distrust. Nor does any intelligent person impute that conduct to enmity;
but when advantage is withheld, it appears more reasonable that the
connection should cease.

VERSE.

He by whose aid we can secure our ends,
His presence joy to heart and soul will bring.
But he, whose converse nothing good attends,
From meeting him some mischiefs swift will spring.

Moreover my nature and thine have in their origin been predisposed to
hostility, and the fame of our enmity has reached the hearing of all, and it
is imbedded in our dispositions; and no great dependance can be placed on a
friendship which has arisen of necessity, in order to expedite something
imperatively required, nor can much weight be attached to it. For when
the necessity is removed things will assuredly return to their original state.
Thus water, so long as it is set over the fire, will keep warm, but when it is
taken off will become cold as before. And every one knows that the rat has

---

[1] There is an absurd pun here on the word *simurgh*, which, if written separately, *si murgh*
signifies, 'thirty birds.'

no more dangerous enemy than the cat, and I am convinced that thou hast no inclination towards me, save that thou wishest to prepare a draught for thy breakfast of my blood, and to use my flesh to supply thy morning meal. And no sophistry will avail to allure me to thee, or to make me rely or confide in thy friendship.

HEMISTICH.

When did cats feel maternal love for rats?'

The Cat said, 'Dost thou speak these words in earnest, or, in point of fact, dost thou merely jest and banter?' The Rat replied,

HEMISTICH.

'With life at stake what room is there for play?

I speak this in solemn seriousness, and I am convinced that it is safer for a weak creature like me to shun the society of a powerful one like thee, and for a weak man to abstain from a contest with a strong one. For if he happen to act at variance with this rule, he will receive a wound which will not be curable with any plaster.

COUPLET.

The weak man who a strong defies,   Will fall so as no more to rise.

I am now of opinion that it is advisable for me at present to be fully on my guard towards thee, and that thou shouldest be wary of the hunter, and then between me and thee there will be a purity of faith which can be relied on. For the best foundation for a sincere friendship is coincidence of sentiment and mental acquaintance.[1]

COUPLET.

If I and thou in soul approximate,   It matters not if place us separate.'

We must confine ourselves to this, for closer union is impossible, and the point of conjunction is quite beyond the circle of discussion.' The Cat began to be much agitated, and uttered lamentations mingled with tears, and outcries fraught with anguish of heart, and said,

STANZA.

'Tis fortune's wont, with disappointment's steel,
    To separate companions. I can, then, do nought.
When soul from body parts, see! what all feel;
    And yet to part with friends with fiercer pain is fraught.'

With these declarations they took leave of each other, and turned to their respective homes. Now, a wise man of clear intellect will draw the following lesson from this story. In time of emergency he will not let slip an opportunity of making truce with an enemy, and when his object is attained, he will not neglect to observe the requisite caution. Praise be to God! the Rat, notwithstanding his weakness and helplessness when encom-

---

[1] That is, according to Stewart, 'distant intercourse.'

passed by a variety of perils, and surrounded by powerful foes and mighty enemies, by having recourse to ingenious stratagems drew one of them into the net of amity, and by means of his friendship escaped from the torrent of calamity, and having found an opportunity, discharged his promises, and fulfilled the duties of caution and foresight. If persons of wisdom and understanding, and people of sagacity and penetration, will make these experiences a pattern for their own undertakings, and take these directions as their guide in performing the important business of life, both the commencements and the conclusions of their affairs will be linked and attended with abundant success; and happiness in this world and blessing in the next will accompany them in their fortunate career.

STANZA.

They who the guidance of the wise obey;
  Danger will ne'er their happy state come nigh.
The waters of experience allay,
  For them the dust of troubles; so that it
Will never rest upon their fortunes high.
  And who their greatness prudently commit
To cautious keeping—in their dignity
  No evil influence will work decay.

CHAPTER VIII.

ON AVOIDING THE MALEVOLENT, AND NOT RELYING ON THEIR PROFESSIONS OF ATTACHMENT.

INTRODUCTION.

The world-adorning King said to the Sage of fortunate judgment,

COUPLET.

' O Thou! who like the latter morn, from head to foot, art pure and true;
And, like to Wisdom's primal ray, art wholly wise and learned too.

Thou hast with discourse free from the reproach of fault, and arrangement clear of the brand of doubt and suspicion, related the story of one who, when overpowering enemies and triumphant foes assailed him, and there was no way for flight on any side, and a safe egress was not to be imagined; yet sought assistance from one of those foes and arranged a peace, and by the aid of his alliance escaped from the injuries of the others, and remained secure from danger, and peril, and mischief, and calamity, and having faithfully performed his promise made at that crisis to his foe, yet preserved his own person from him, and, by the blessing of caution and the happy influence of sagacity, arrived from the whirlpool of calamity on the shore of safety and salvation.   Now, I respectfully request thee to recite the story of the rancorous and malignant, whether it is better to shun and avoid them, or to mix with them and join in their mirth.   If one of them should make con-ciliatory advances, and manifest a desire to be courteous, ought one to listen to him, or altogether deny to his offers a place in one's consideration?'   The Bráhman said,

COUPLET.

O thou! far-seeing like the mind, from wisdom's early rise;
Like reason, from commencement of creation skilled and wise.

Whoever is assisted by the grace of the holy spirit, or is supported by the aid of perfect reason, will undoubtedly see that it is incumbent to practise in all his affairs the utmost caution, and will well discern the divisions of good and ill, and the positions of gain and detriment; nor will it be concealed from him that it is more safe to withdraw from friends who are displeased, and from companions who have been injured.   And to avoid the ambushed wiles of the malicious and the perils of the treachery of those who pretend to sell wheat, while they are vendors of barley, is a cause of security from danger.   And this especially is the case, when one sees with the eye of understanding a change in his friend's internal sentiments and an alteration in his confidence, and surveys with clearness the doubtings of [his former friends'] mind and the suspicions of his heart.

VERSE.

> Is thy foe vexed and injured? then, beware!
> Who has been hurt will strive to wound again:
> His first advances may be kind and fair,
> At last he'll make thee suffer rueful pain.

And whoever discerns in the resentful the signs of hostility, must take care not to give them a good opportunity[1]; nor to be deceived by their oily language and shew of courtesy. Nor must he neglect caution and vigilance, and foresight; for if he act contrary to this principle, he will make a target of his life for the arrow of calamity, and kindle the fire of anguish in the area of his breast.

COUPLET.

> To feel secure from enemies, is fraught with many an ill;
> Who sows neglect, his garner must with heart's affliction fill.

And of the number of stories, which have been inscribed on the volume of the minds of the venerable, that of Ibn-i Madín and the Lark possesses great beauty and perfect excellence.' The king asked, 'How was that?'

STORY I.

The Bráhman said, 'They have related that there was a king, whose name was Ibn-i Madín, possessed of a lofty spirit, and clear intellect. He had raised the lofty edifice of his kingdom by the exertions of power to the dome of Arcturus; and, with the aid of the geometrician, grandeur, had carried the extensive pedestal of his glory beyond the pinnacle of the heaven of heavens.

COUPLET.

> A king with angel-retinue; as Jamshíd fortunate;
> Throned on the moon and sun; and like the sky in lofty state.

And he had an attachment of the strongest kind for a Lark. Now this Lark was a bird of perfect beauty, and enchanting voice, and pleasing form, and graceful shape. The king was always talking to it, and was delighted with its sweet answers and pleasant tales.

VERSE.

> Sweet are winning words and fair,
> And honeyed tales the heart rejoice.
> And he, who does these rich gifts share,
> Will be the nobles', princes' choice.

---

[1] The editions read *muḥmil-i nikú*; but I would substitute the reading of the MSS., *mahall-i nikú*, which appears to me to be undoubtedly the true reading.

It happened that the Lark laid an egg, and brought forth a young one in the palace of the king. The latter, from excess of fondness [for the bird] ordered it to be brought into the seraglio and the attendants of that part of the palace were commanded to take the greatest care in cherishing it and its young. Now that very day a son was born to the king, on whose forehead shone the rays of nobleness, and on the pages of whose condition gleamed the lustre of happy fortune.

STANZA.

He was a moon, that in perfection's sky
 Arose ; and ne'er through countless years was such
Beheld ;—clear-hearted, of bright destiny,
 And radiant footsteps, gilding all they touch ;
Of form angelical, well-starred, august ;
 That noble seedling did fresh life impart
To the rose-garden of the empire : just
 As the fresh north wind stirs the foliage of the heart.

As the young one of the Lark grew up, the prince too advanced, and a vast attachment arose between them ; and the royal child was ever playing with that young bird, and every day the Lark used to fly to the mountains and plains, and to bring two fruits of a kind unknown to men ; or, if known, unprocurable by them. One fruit it gave to the prince, and with the other it fed its own young one, and both relishing what was thus given them, ate it with enjoyment and eagerness, and the beneficial effects thereof were most rapidly visible in invigorating their bodies and strengthening their frames. Accordingly, in a short time they grew much.

COUPLET.

They sprang up tall in stature ; flourishing Like the fresh grass in time of early spring.

And through those services the Lark was daily more honored and esteemed ; and its place in the king's favor and regard advanced every hour. Some time passed in this way, and time wrote many leaves—white and black—the leaves of day and night. One day the Lark had gone away and its young one leapt on the young prince's bosom, and, with the claw of violence, inflicted a wound in his hand. The fire of wrath blazed up in the prince, and plunged him into the whirlpool of inconsiderate action and violence, so that he cast dirt into the eyes of honorable feeling, and magnanimity, and, giving to the winds the ties of friendship and long acquaintance, seized the bird by the leg and, whirling it round his head, dashed it with such force against the ground, that it was instantly crushed [1] and perished on the rack of destruction.

---

[1] Lit., 'became equal with the ground.'

COUPLET.

Alas! the rose's tender branch, which did but now its blossoms spread,
Too soon, before the chilly breath of autumn, has those blossoms shed.

When the Lark returned, it beheld its young one killed. There was cause to fear that the bird of its life would take wing from the cage of its body. From horror at that circumstance, a mourning arose in its heart—the type of the lamentation at the last judgment. And from the occurrence of that catastrophe, grief took up its place within the Lark's bosom as ineffaceable as characters on stone. It raised its lamentations and outcries to the height of the moon and the planet Mercury.

COUPLET.

'Ah me! the light that did anoint my eyes' far seeing gaze is lost,
The leaf of joy in my sad heart, is gone, and all my hopes are crossed.'

After much lamentation and infinite regrets, the Lark thought to itself, 'Thou hast kindled this flame of calamity, and it is thou that hast sold the goods of tranquillity for the uproar of distress. Humble [1] as thy state is, thou shouldest have made thy nest on the top of a wall. What hadst thou to do with the seraglio of the sultán? and when thou oughtest to have been engaged in rearing thy young, why didst thou employ thyself in the tutelage of the king's son? Hadst thou been satisfied with thy corner and thy morsel, thou wouldest not this day have been involved in this calamity, and wouldest not have suffered grief from these circumstances. And sages have said, ' Hapless is any one who is thrown upon the society of the tyrannical, for the rein of their good faith is very relaxed, and the basis of their fidelity is very weak. They have always the cheek of honor lacerated by the injuries of oppression, and they fill up the fountain of generosity with the dirt of insincerity and injustice. Neither has former companionship any weight with them, nor do they regard previous services and the ties of attendance.

COUPLET.

In the service of a person quite devoid of grateful sense,
Must thou not thy time let perish, without thanks or recompense.

In the school of the revengeful they regard the forgiveness of offences, which is the attribute of liberal men, as inadmissible and prohibited. And ingratitude, which brands the impious, they think allowable and admissible in the law of pride. Pray, then, what advantage can one derive from associating with parties who forget the previous services of their sincere friends? or what benefits can result from attendance on a class who allow the friendly connection of interested associates to pass from their memory?

---

[1] The printed edition has here _khdri_ for _khudrí_; and in the next line _mashghúl shud_ for _mashghúl báyad shud._'

COUPLET.

One who is blind to friendship's rights, 'twere shame
To mention, in the rank of men, his name.

And I have associated myself with a tribe who make no account of the
perpetration of things of great magnitude, where themselves are the offenders,
while they regard a trifling fault on the part of others as excessive.

COUPLET.

Have they a failing of their own? they call 't
Virtue; and name thy virtue a huge fault.

And I, in fine, will not let slip the opportunity of revenge and the hour of
requital, and I will not rest nor allow myself to repose until I have exacted
vengeance for my young one from this merciless tyrant and cruel oppressor,
who, without just grounds, has slain one born at the same time, his play-
mate, and companion and friend, and without a cause has destroyed the
sharer of his house and bed.

COUPLET.

I'll set all love, all pity, too, aside,   And fuel for my burning hate provide.

He then sprang remorselessly in the face of the prince, and tore out the
world-surveying eyes of that refresher of the visual organs of the empire,
and, flying away, settled on a pinnacle of the castle. Intelligence of this
was conveyed to the king. He wept for the eyesight of his son, and wished
to entice the bird into the net of deceit, and having imprisoned it in the cage
of calamity, to command that the punishment due to its offence should be
carried into execution. He then came under the castle-wall, and standing
opposite the Lark, said, 'Friend of my existence! come down from this
height for thy life is safe.

HEMISTICH.

What though thy musky tresses erred? 'Tis past.

Now destroy not our intercourse, nor cause the plant of my enjoyment to
wither.' The Lark replied, 'O king! it is the bounden duty of all to obey
thy command. After wandering for a long time in the desert of reflection I
had arrived at the confines of this thought, that for the remainder of my life
I should regard the royal palace as the sanctuary of my wishes, and the shrine
of my prosperity, and not gallop the steed of my energies, save in the court of
this lord. My idea was that I might be happy and tranquil under the shade of
thy favor, like the doves in the temple of Makkah; and, exerting myself in the
path [1] of honourable and kindly feeling, I might arrive at the elevation of a
pure unruffled content. Now, however, that they have thought fit to slay my
young one in the seraglio like a sacrifice offered by pilgrims, how can I have

---

[1] For the *marwaṭ-i maruwat* of the editions, I feel inclined to read, with some MSS.,
ṭarīḳah-i maruwat, and I have translated accordingly. However, some may prefer *marwaṭ*,
as referring to the temple of Makkah mentioned just before.

any desire left to circumambulate[1] this house. And yet, notwithstanding all this, if I were aware of anything equivalent to sweet life, I would acquiesce and take service with the ladies of the sacred precincts of the seraglio, but,

COUPLET.

The bird once scared that has escaped the net,
Will for no grain its terror then forget.

And moreover the traditionary saying, '*The believer will not be stung from one hole twice,*' is proved correct : and it behoves an acute person not to try the same thing twice, nor to suffer a second time from the wound of the same animal.

COUPLET.

Hast thou e'er heard the saying of the wise ?
' *He will repent who the once tested tries.*'

And, again, it is clear to the luminous mind of the king that an offender cannot live secure. For if his punishment in this temporary state be delayed, yet that of the eternal world is still to be expected by him. And if, by the aid of lofty good-fortune he escape the former, he must taste the bitterness of chastisement through the sufferings of his children and grandchildren ; and he must in this way experience the abasement of the tortures and disastrous results which his crime entails. For the temper of the world is a security for the quality of requital, and the disposition of fortune guarantees the character of proportionate rewards. Accordingly the king's son devised treachery against my young one ; and from me, without my option, but in the way of requital, affliction fell upon him. And it is impossible that any one should drink a draught from the cup of oppression, and not suffer from the intoxication of calamity ; or plant the seedling of injustice in the garden of action, and not reap the fruit of torture and anguish.

COUPLET.

Fools that sow seeds of colocynth, must not
Expect to reap sweet cane will be their lot.

But, perhaps, the king has not heard the story of Dánádil[2] and the thieves, and the retribution which befell the latter has not reached the royal ear ? ' The king asked, ' How was that ? '

STORY II.

The Lark said, ' They have related that in the city of Rakkah there was a darvesh, adorned with estimable qualities and commendable manners, and the plant of his actions was beautified with the flowers of virtuous feelings and excellent habits. Inasmuch as he possessed a heart rendered

---

[1] The word *tawáf* signifies the circumambulation of the K'abah by pilgrims, which they are enjoined to do seven times.

[2] That is, ' Wise-heart.'

2 G

wise by a knowledge of spiritual truth, they used to call him Dánádil and the people of that city entertained a strong regard for him.

COUPLET.

He to whom wisdom does all truths impart,
Is the soul's friend, the ointment of the heart.

At one time in his life he set out on a pilgrimage to the Sacred House,[1] and entered on his journey without a friend or companion. A party of thieves came up with him; and, suspecting that he had considerable wealth, formed the desire of slaying him. Dánádil said, 'The worldly wealth that I have with me is no great matter, beyond what will suffice as provision for the way on my pilgrimage. If your wishes are satisfied by that amount, it is of no consequence, take the things and leave me alone to bring this journey to an end in reliance on God and destitute of other support; and to make of the dust of the temple's threshold a collyrium for the eye of my expectation.

COUPLET.

I'll to his dwelling go, my head upon his threshold lay,
And make collyrium for my eyes of dust from his doorway.'

The merciless robbers, giving no heed to these words, drew their swords to put him to death. The hapless darvesh looked in every direction like one aghast; and, as is the wont of those in distress, sought for aid and deliverance. In that terrible desert and fearful and alarming wilderness, not a living creature met his sight; save that at that time a flock of cranes was flying above their heads. Dánádil called out, 'O cranes! I have fallen captive in this desert into the hands of cruel men, and, save the Lord of the unseen world, no one is acquainted with my condition. Do ye exact vengeance for me from this gang, and require my blood at their hands?' The robbers laughed and said, 'What is thy name?' He replied, 'Dánádil.' 'Marry,' quoth they, 'thy heart has not a particle of wisdom. We are sure that thou art a fool. And whoever is devoid of reason there will ensue nothing very bad from killing him.' Dánádil replied, ' *Surely thou wilt see when the dust is cleared away,* ' I will here recite in your ear somewhat as to retribution, and I will bring under your observation a trifle with respect to the requital of actions; but yet a class of whose nature the characteristic is, ' *They are deaf, dumb, and blind, therefore will they not repent,* ' [2] what knowledge have they of this matter?

---

[1] The temple at Makkah.

[2] Kur'án, Fl. ii. 17; Mar. 18; Sale, p. 3, l. 7: 'These are the men, who have purchased error at the price of true direction: but their traffic hath not been gainful, neither have they been rightly directed. They are like unto one who kindleth a fire, and when it hath enlightened all around him; God taketh away their light and leaveth them in darkness, they shall not see; they are deaf, dumb, and blind, therefore will they not repent.'

COUPLET.

If one with prudence, too, possessed an ear,
He would these sayings with deep pleasure hear.'

However much Dánádil addressed them, the ear of their understanding was insensible to his truthful discourse, and the visual faculty of their sight did not behold the manifestation of the beauty of reality. They killed him and took his effects. When the news of his murder reached the people of the city, they were sad and felt much regret for his loss, and were ever on the look-out to catch his murderers. At last, after a considerable interval most of the inhabitants of that city had assembled on the day of 'Íd in worship, and the murderers of Dánádil also had taken their places in one corner in that meeting. In the midst of the prayers, a number of cranes passing through the air flew over the heads of the robbers, and uttered such plaintive cries, that from their wailing the people stopped reading the daily lessons, and the repetition of the names of God. One of the robbers laughed, and said sneeringly to a comrade, ' They are certainly requiring the blood of Dánádil.' It happened that one of the inhabitants of the city overheard this speech, and told it to another. In a short time they informed the governor of it. They were then seized, and after a short inquiry they confessed, and the retribution for the innocent blood [they had shed] having reached them, they met with the suitable retaliation.

STANZA.

Throughout this world, who did e'er string the bow
Of wrong, that on him was not swiftly hurled
Eternal curses, shaft-like, and he so
Became a butt for vengeance? In this world
Who thinks to play the tyrant, will ere long
A warning prove to those he fain would wrong.

And I have adduced this story in order that the king may know that my boldness in wounding the prince was inspired by retributive justice and the requirements of retaliation. Else whence could a feeble bird have strength for such a deed? And since this action has been perpetrated by me, the command of reason, the controller, is, that I should not obey thy mandate ; nor, relying upon thee, be led by the cord of treachery and deceit into a pit.

HEMISTICH.

'Tis best I shun the service of the king.'

The king replied, ' What thou hast said is allied to truthfulness and prudence, and fraught with the advantages of wisdom and the beneficial results of good sense, and I know that, in accordance with the saying, ' *The beginner is the most in the wrong,*' the fault was my son's, since without any previous offence on its part he killed thy young one. Thus, then, by way of retribution, as it is said, ' *The retaliation of evil ought to be an evil propor-*

tionate thereto,' [1] thou hast exacted a rightful quittance. Nay more, I am thankful that thou didst not proceed to slay him, and wast satisfied with destroying his sight. Now, neither hast thou any rancor left, nor have I any wish to injure thee. Believe my word, and do not foolishly persevere in withdrawing and separating thyself, and know that I regard revenge as a failing in man, and look upon forgiveness as one of the virtues of noble minds. I will never smite the hand of rejection upon the forehead of virtue, nor turn the face of acceptance towards vice. Nay, my desire is to do good in return for evil, and if an injury befall me from any one, to recompence him with a benefit.

QUATRAIN.

'Tis not our practice to be pretexts seeking,
Good-will and truthful speaking are our mood.
And those who wrath upon us have been wreaking,
Have we the power, to them we aye do good.'

The Lark replied, 'My return is altogether impossible; for the wise renounce the companionship of a friend who has been alienated; and it is recorded among the maxims of sages, that although men may shew an increase of courtesy and conciliation to persons whose feelings have been wounded, and regard it as incumbent on them to treat such persons with respect and kindliness, still their suspicions and aversion will augment, and this being the case, it becomes necessary to avoid them.

STANZA.

My friend! when thou hast any one offended,
Be not on soothing him intent:
The more he sees thy services extended,
The more his doubts of thee augment.'

The king rejoined, 'O Lark! cease these words, for thou art as a son to me, nay, even dearer still, and I have not the same affection for any of my kinsmen or connections, that I have for thee. No one ever plans mischief against his own kin, or entertains vengeful or hostile feelings towards his intimates.' The Lark answered, 'The wise have delivered their sentence as to relations, and have spoken in detail as to the circumstances of each; and have thus pronounced, 'Mother and father are real friends; [2] and brothers are as comrades and attached companions; and a wife is in the position of one who shares in social intercourse; and daughters are equivalent to antagonists, and all other kinsfolk are no better than strangers. But men

---

[1] Kur'án, Fl. xlii. 38; Mar. 39; Sale, p. 360, l. 27, 'But the reward, which is with God is better, and more durable for those who believe, and put their trust in their Lord; . . . . . . and who, when an injury is done them, avenge themselves, (and the retaliation of evil ought to be an evil proportionate thereto;) but he who forgiveth, and is reconciled unto his enemy, shall receive his reward from God; for He loveth not the unjust doers.'

[2] From these lines we may learn the distinction between *dúst* and *rafíḳ*, and *ydr* and *dahná*; these words being in fact a descending series.

wish for a son to perpetuate their name, and regard him as the same as soul and body, nor do they allot to any one a share in the value and regard they set upon him. Thus I can never be to thee in the place of a son; and even supposing that thou shouldest hold me as a son, yet when calamity comes upon thee, and misfortune and disaster assail thee, thou wilt cease to regard me, for however dear one may hold another, and however much he may say, 'I prefer thee to myself and would not withhold my life for thee;

HEMISTICH.

What then is life, that it for thee I should forbear to sacrifice?'

when trouble arises and things come to such a point that life must be renounced, a person will undoubtedly convey himself from the strait of that peril to the open expanse of safety, and will in no wise sacrifice the ready coin of existence for another.

COUPLET.[1]

A man should from no risk or peril fly,   Nor for the sake of others fear to die.

But perhaps the king has not heard the story of the Old Woman and Muhastí, and has not been informed of what happened to them?' The king said, 'Explain to me how that was.'

STORY III.

The Lark said, 'They have related that an indigent Old Woman had a daughter, by name Muhastí, such that the full moon envied the brightness of her lustrous cheek; and the world-illuminating sun, from the reflection of her enchanting countenance, sate down perspiring with shame.

VERSE.

Maid of soft words, that stole the sense away,
  And robbed the sweetmeat-maker of his worth :
Did she but one coquettish grace display,
  It raised a thousand troubles on the earth,
  And her one look to thousand broils gave birth.

All of a sudden the blighting glance of unpropitious fortune having fallen on that rose-cheeked cypress, she laid her head on the pillow of sickness; and in the flower-garden of her beauty, in place of the damask-rose, sprang up the branch of the saffron. Her fresh jessamine, from the violence of the burning illness, lost its moisture; and her hyacinth full of curls, lost all its endurance from the fever that consumed her.

COUPLET.

Her graceful form, with lengthened sufferings spent,
  Was like her perfumed musky tresses—bent.

The Old Woman hovered round her daughter, and with eyes moist as vernal

---

[1] This couplet is evidently out of its place. It should follow the hemistich, otherwise it directly contradicts the speaker's sentiments.

clouds, was saying tenderly and sorrowfully, 'Life of thy mother! may my life be a sacrifice for thee, and may the head of this infirm one, wearied out in the corner of distress, be the dust of thy feet! I will make myself an offering for thee, and redeem, with the half life I possess, thy existence.

HEMISTICH.

Does thy head ache? then for it me devote.[1]

Every morning she used to say, with many sighs and lamentations, 'O God! spare this young inexperienced maid, and take in her stead this broken-down old woman tired of her life.

VERSE.

What of my life remains to me,
Take and increase her life withal.
Though dwindled to a hair I be,
From her head let not one hair fall.'

In short the Old Woman, in accordance with the love of mothers and maternal tenderness, day and night exerted herself in prayer and supplication, and freely offered to bestow the life which was left to her for her beloved child. One day it happened that a cow belonging to the old woman returned from the desert, and entered the kitchen; and induced by the smell of soup, put its head in to a cauldron, and ate the contents. But when it tried to extricate its head, it was unable to do so. Thereupon, becoming furious, it went out of the kitchen with the pot just as it was, on its head; and ran from one corner to another. At the time the cow came back the Old Woman was not in the house, and was ignorant of those circumstances. When she came home and saw an object of that form and appearance going round the house, she imagined that it was Izráíl, who had come to seize the soul of Muhastí. Forthwith she uttered a shriek, and said most piteously,

VERSE.

'Angel of death! Muhastí am not I;
I am but a poor old woman, full of woe.
Then if thou would'st remove her spirit, why,
She is within that chamber, thou must know.
Yes! if Muhastí is required by thee,
Lo! she is there; take her, but let me go.'
Thus whom she valued in security,
She soon surrendered; seeing danger near.
Know! if the question is to live or die,
To every man himself will prove most dear.

And I, this day, have divested myself of all connections and separated myself from all mankind, and I have been so plentifully supplied with things in thy service that the caravan of my strength is loaded therewith, and is unable to support any farther burthen.

---

[1] Lit., 'Turn me round thy head.' This means 'devote,' as in the ceremony of taking another's calamities upon one. *Vide* Kánún-i Islám, p. 92, note.

I fear my body is too feeble, and this burthen cannot bear.

And what living being can endure that they should give the corner of his heart to the fire of injustice, and its fruit to the winds of destruction? and having cast the light of his eyes into the gloom of extinction, should deprive him of the joy of his life? And when I think of my precious offspring, that was the light of my tearful eyes, and the delight of my afflicted breast, the sea of regret rolls its billows, and plunges the vessel of patience into the whirlpool of perturbation, and the flame of the fire of bewilderment, rising higher, consumes at once the goods of endurance and toleration.

STANZA.

> I wander in a world of grief, and to the sea that circles round me
> None can find a limit; surely shore or limit none is there.
> I said I would, by patience, flee the watery prison-house that bound me.
> Lo! the ship of patience founders, nought is left me but despair.

f And in addition to all this, my life is not safe; and to be cajoled by this politeness and feigned courtesy, appears to me to be far from the practice of wise men. Consequently I repeat the verse, ' *Would to God that between me and thee there was the distance of the east from the west!* ' [1]

COUPLET.

> Sure separations would be better far,   Than meetings which the cause of sorrow are.'

The king rejoined, ' If what thou hast done had been without previous provocation, caution and avoidance would have appeared more proper than intercourse. But thou hast acted on the principle of retaliation, and thy deed has been done by way of requital. And the tongue of righteous adjudication enjoins nought else, and the judge of equity, in return for such an act as emanated from my son, directs a recompense of such a nature. Wherefore, what can be the reason of thy keeping aloof? and what the cause of thy aversion? Reflect, I pray, that before my son was born thou wast the companion of my hours and the partner of my life. And when my son made his appearance from the concealment of non-existence in the expanse of entity, paternal love required that I should feel delight in his society. In this I associated him with thee, and passed my life in intercourse with thee and in fond conversation with him. And now that the malignant eye of fortune has inflicted an injury on the jewel of his sight, the enjoyment that I felt in seeing him is broken off; but the gratification of thy discourse, and the joy

---

[1] Kur'án, Fl., xliii. 37; Mar. 36; Sale, p. 362, last line: 'Whoever shall withdraw from the admonition of the Merciful, we will chain a devil unto him; and he shall be his inseparable companion: (and the devils shall turn them aside from the way of truth; yet they shall imagine themselves to be rightly directed:) until, when he shall appear before us at the last day, he shall say unto the devil, Would to God that between me and thee there was the distance of the east from the west!'

of addressing and being addressed by thee remains.   Act not in such a manner that this too shall be altogether destroyed; and that I, for the remainder of my life, should become a permanent worshiper in the temple of grief, and pass the time with sorrow, and chagrin, and vexation, and despondency.   And the case betwixt me and thee is like that of the Musician and the King.'   The Lark inquired, 'How was that?'

STORY IV.

The king said, 'They have related that a King had a Musician of a pleasant voice, and a sweet performer, who, by his enchanting melodies bore the foot of reason out of the stirrup, and wrested the reins of self-possession from the hand of patience and endurance.

COUPLET.

Of tones more soft, of voice more sweet than he,
This crooked-backed organ-maker none could see.[1]

The King held him in high esteem, and was ever pleased with listening to his delightful songs and gladsome lays.

COUPLET.

List to the minstrel, for his jocund measures, joy around him spreading,
Now with bass, and now with treble, are Venus bright with Saturn wedding.

And this Musician was instructing a clever slave, and kindly imparting to him lessons in playing and singing, till, in a short time he surpassed his master, and carried the harmony of his performance and the melody of his song to such a pitch, that the fame of his recitations and odes went beyond the conception of the thought or imagination; and the ears of high and low were altogether filled with the rumor and celebrity of his skill and execution.

VERSE.

With his delightsome trills he did succeed
In kindling in the mart of joy, fresh fire:
And Venus' self[2] with both her ears gave heed,
As soon as he began to touch the lyre.

The King, having heard of the slave's accomplishments, deigned to patronize and encourage him; and this was continued until he became a confidential attendant and an intimate favorite, and received especial marks of distinction. The King was ever charmed with his exhilarating strains, which supplied a specimen of the miracles of the Messiah, and was inspired with a desire for the banquet of enjoyment, by the sound of his world-melting lute, which inflamed the hearts of lovers.   At this, the spirit of envy being stirred in the

---

[1] I presume the sky is meant here, but must plainly avow my ignorance of the true signification of this line, and would thankfully receive an explanation.

[2] *Náhid*, 'the planet Venus.'

heart of the master-musician, he killed the slave; and news of this deed reached the King. The monarch commanded the offender to be summoned into his presence: and when they had conducted him to the place of punishment, the King, with a terrible countenance, began to rebuke him,[1] saying, 'Didst thou not know that I was fond of gaiety? and my enjoyment was of two kinds:—first, in public, at thy playing; and secondly, in private, at the singing of thy slave. What induced thee to kill the slave, and thus deprive me of half my enjoyment? I will this moment command them to cause thee to drink of that same potion which thou gavest to him, that hereafter none may venture on a similar act.' The words of the King recalled to the mind of the Musician his wit,[2] and he replied, 'O King! I have done ill that I have destroyed half the King's enjoyment; but how will it be if the King should kill me and so put an end to his own gratification?' The King was pleased at this answer, and bestowing on him a reward, absolved him from the punishment of death.

And my intention in adducing this story is that, through my son, one portion of happiness and delight is spoiled, and thou, also, soundest the note of separation. It is almost come to pass that the back of my hope, like the figure of the harp, has become bent; and that my afflicted breast, like the heart of the lute, has been lacerated with the nail of regret. And in the end a forcible separation must take place between friends; I pray thee, do not exert thyself to bring about a voluntary parting, and give not from thy hand the skirt of contentment.

COUPLET.

I pray thee, make thyself not strange, since, as thou knowest, from each other,
The envious sky itself disparts true friends, and brother from his brother.'

The Lark replied, 'Anger is hidden in the closet of the heart, and resentment is concealed in the cell of the bosom, and as it is impossible for any one to be aware of it, credence cannot be given to what is spoken by the tongue, for in this matter the tongue does not speak in truthful style of the purport of what lies hidden in the mind, and language does not discharge the duty of uprightness in signifying what is hoarded up in the soul. Hearts, however, in accordance with the saying, '*Hearts bear witness to each other,*' are reciprocally true witnesses, and testimony that can be relied on.

COUPLET.

Enough! heart-secrets known are to the heart;
To tongue and lips that knowledge why impart?

And to what thy tongue is saying, thy heart does not assent; nor is thy tongue truthful in making known what thy heart contains.

---

[1] *Az rúi-i haibat,* 'in a terrible manner.'
[2] Lit., 'poesy.'

HEMISTICH.

A hundred lives be given for him whose tongue and heart agree together.

O King! I well know the terribleness of thy fury, and am well aware of the awfulness of thy punishments.

COUPLET.

Than mountains graver far the wounds, at times, thy stirrups bring;
More light than gentle breeze thy reins, when charging on, O King!

I can never be secure from thee, nor repose for a moment from dread of the injury of thy assault. And I am not of that class to one of whom the physician said, 'Medicine for the eyes is more fitting for thee, than physic for a stomach-ache.' The King asked, 'How was that?'

STORY V.

The Lark said, 'A man came to a physician, and being tortured with pain in his stomach, rolled about on the ground, and wept bitterly at the violence of the pain.

HEMISTICH.

'Doctor! I pray thee cure me, for 'tis past my power to bear.'

The physician, after the fashion in which men of skill give the precedence over all other things to the rules for ascertaining causes and symptoms, in order that after diagnosis of the disease they may proceed to the use of a remedy which would be the cause of a speedy recovery, inquired of him, 'What hast thou eaten to-day?' The simple fellow replied, 'I have eaten a piece of burnt bread, and with that piece of food, which was only of the size of one's finger, I have inflamed the oven of my stomach.' The physician bade his servants bring medicine for clearing the eyesight and strengthening the vision, that he might apply it to the man's eyes. Hereupon the patient screamed out,

COUPLET.

'Prithee what time for gibes and jokes is this?
This sudden death and mortal torture is.

O physician! have done with bantering and leave these jests. I am groaning with pain in my stomach, and thou art applying to my eyes collyrium made of precious stone! What has medicine for the eyes got to do with pain in the stomach?' The physician replied, 'I want to clear thy eyesight that thou mayest discern between black and white, and so not eat burnt bread again. Wherefore a cure for the eyes is more requisite for thee than physic for the stomach.'

And my aim in improvising this story is, that the king may not fancy that I am one of those who cannot distinguish between consumed and consummated,[1] or discriminate raw from ripe.

---

[1] I have used these words to express the equivoque on *sukhtah* and *sákhtah*, 'burnt,' and 'made.'

COUPLET.

Praise be to God! my wisdom thus far reaches,
'Twixt good and ill the difference it teaches.'

The King said, 'Between friends, many thing happen of the nature of that which has taken place betwixt thee and me, and it is not possible that the road of variance should altogether be lost between man, and the path of contention and altercation be closed up. But every one who is adorned with the light for reason, and decorated with the ornament of understanding, exerts himself to the utmost of his power to quench the flames of wrath; and to the extent of his ability pours the water of meekness on the fire of rage; and is aware that in drinking the beverage of forgiveness, though it may seem excessively bitter, the sweetness of pleasure is included; and that to endure the hard taste of long suffering, though it resembles poison, yet comprehends the antidote joy.

VERSE.

Be not thou wroth, for wrath doth grief contain:
  Swallow thy rage, and 'twill be sweet to thee.
The lightning flashes but to give men pain;
  But ayo to swallow is thy wont, O sea!
And hence thy breast is ne'er with dust [1] o'erspread,
Though showers descend all stone-like on thy head.'

The Lark replied, 'It is a well-known fact, that ' *Whoever treats sin as a trifle, falls into mischief*,' or he who takes a grave thing lightly will suffer for it. This grave matter, therefore, cannot be treated with levity, and in this serious affair one must not choose to be remiss. I have spent my life in viewing the trickery[2] of the juggling heaven, and played away my precious hours in surveying the marvels of deceitful fortune. Assuredly I have gained much assistance from the stores of experience, and derived the utmost profit from the earnings of prudence, and the principal of good sense and sagacity. I have discovered for a certainty, then, that the sparks of free option and the flame of uncontrolled power consume the substructure of promises; and the needle of the pride of prosperity sews up the eye of shame and good faith with the thread of despotism. And when the lion of kingly terror smites the ground with the tail of revenge, cringing and vulpine artifices are unavailing. It is best for me not to allow myself a hare's sleep,[3] and, shuddering at the fury of the tiger, let me, like the deer, take the way to the woods, for it is in no way possible for a weak antagonist to contend

---

[1] To have dust on one's head or breast is a sign of woe or disgrace, which the sea is said to escape because it swallows everything, as the meek man is said *farú khwurdan*, to swallow his anger.

[2] *Muhrah bázi*, 'passing off shells for pearls,' or something equivalent to what is vulgarly called 'thimble-rig.'

[3] Hares are said to sleep with their eyes open. Hare's sleep then is a proverbial expression for the waking slumber of the careless.

with a powerful enemy. Just as that King improvised a story on this subject for his enemy.' The King asked, 'How was that?'

STORY VI.

The Lark said, ' They have related that in the country of Turkistán there was a King, the Humá of whose unrivaled spirit spread over the nations of mankind the shade of welfare and winged victory and success, and the 'Anká of whose exalted banner raised the head of elevation beyond the nest of the peacocks of the gardens of the sky. His perfect justice bestowed on the affairs of state-administration the most exact order, and his bounty, in which all participated, conducted to a careful completion the important transactions of the crown.

VERSE.

A Khusrau crown-bestowing, throne-conferring he,
Did treasures scatter o'er the crown and throne,
And, earth-subduing, kept it in security.
Him men as Jam and as Sikandar own.

It befell that a doubt arose in the mind of one of the Pillars of the State, and he averted his face from the heaven-resembling vestibule of the King, and, having deceived the King, brought one of his enemies to engage in battle and open hostility with him. When the King learned that his enemy had averted the face of obedience from the shrine of submission, and that the temptations of the rebellious and the seductions of the refractory had penetrated to the foundation of his faith; and that with furious intentions and insensate hopes he was fostering the thought of dominion and chieftainship; and that with a heart full of ancient grudges he was cherishing the expectation of success and elevation; he despatched to him a letter teeming with kindly counsels, and an epistle replete with kingly advice. However, the haughty foe, from the excess of his arrogance and pride, paid no attention to it, and wherever he imagined a rebellious band to exist, drew them to himself by the noose of invitation.

COUPLET.

Some desperate few he gathered round him then,
Who sought the field when war grew hot again.

In short, when the King saw that the draught of the medicine of gentleness could not cure their gross temperament, which had altogether turned aside from the path of true moderation, he sent to him a message of the following nature, 'I and thou resemble the glass and the stone. Strike either the stone on the glass or the glass on the stone, in both cases the glass will break and no harm will happen to the stone.'

Now the advantage of adducing this story is that it may be clear to the luminous mind of the King that I, too, am like the glass, and am unable to encounter the wrath of the King, which is firm and crushing to his enemies as a rock.

COUPLET.

Encounter not, my heart! with them, the steely-hearted fair,
For thou, of glass composed, couldst not the shock of anvils bear.

Though the King adopts an attitude of conciliation, and desires to soothe with the oxymel of excuses the bile of timidity; still in the school of wisdom it is unlawful to accept the excuses of the rancorous and envious, while it is a command, which it is incumbent on all to obey, to reply with rejection and denial to the peaceful requisitions of the hostile.

STANZA.

Friends eloquent this maxim told to me,
Rely not on a foe that speaks thee fair;
But if he look for evil things from thee,[1]
Be not deceived, nor do his faith impair.'

The King said, 'It is not allowable, on bare suspicion, to sever intercourse and overthrow a friendship, nor is it right, on a surmise which springs from the imagination, to calamitously involve a comrade in the pangs of separation. On a slight doubt to lay aside ancient acquaintance and a well-constituted friendship, and on a trifling uncertainty to let go from the hand the string of the promise of companionship and amicable engagements, is not the custom of men of truth.

VERSE.

This was thy faith! thy promise this! and I was all unknowing;
Thy promised love was nought but hate from rancor's fountain flowing.
Thy every word is cruel, as the heart whence 'tis proceeding!
Could then thy heart be hard as this, and I so all unheeding!

Nay, now, the quality of fidelity is found even in a dog, which is the lowest in rank of all animals and the most vile in degree. Why, then, dost thou not draw back thy foot from the plain of faithlessness, and fulfil the compact which thou didst make during our intercourse and friendship?

HEMISTICH.

Couldst thou it learn, 'twere well, indeed, to shew fidelity.'

The Lark replied, 'How can I lay the foundation of fidelity? On that side the pillars of attachment are overthrown, and the traces of fulfilment of promise altogether effaced. And it is impossible that the king should relinquish those things which cause my terror, and turn away from watching for an opportunity of revenge. Now, as he cannot lay hands upon me by violence and force, he wishes to draw me into the grasp of his revenge by artifice and deceit; and one ought to fear the rancor which has fixed itself

---

[1] If he dread thee, and therefore, though hating thee, try to conciliate, reject his offers, and give him just ground for his fears by inflicting all the evil possible upon him.

in the hearts of kings. For, through the haughtiness of kingly power, they are pertinacious in the matter of vengeance; and when they get an opportunity, they grant no respite for time to plead extenuating circumstances or to offer excuses. And resentments in the breast are like cold charcoal, for though at present no effect is perceptible from them, as soon as the flame of wrath reaches them, they warm up, and the blaze of fury, rising, consumes the world. And the smoke of revenge which ascends from the fire of resentment has dried many brains and moistened many eyes. And it is impossible that as long as a particle of the charcoal of resentment is left in the mine of the breast, one can be secure from the injuries of the flame of wrath.

HEMISTICH.

Wrath blazing forth consumes both land and sea.'

The King answered, 'It is strange that in this matter thou takest a one-sided view, and altogether lettest slip the other side. Why may it not be that the preambles of dread may be exchanged for the happy influences of attachment? and after the obscuration of contention the serenity of kindly feeling make its appearance?' The Lark said, 'If any one were able to display perfect courtesy and kindness in the due observation of all that regards the other party, and would exert himself to secure the goodwill and happiness of his friends; and regard it as a duty to aid and assist in the obtaining advantages for them, and the repelling detrimental and disagreeable things from them; it is possible that timidity might be removed from between them, and that both the resentful one should be pacified and the heart of the fearer be perfumed with the gentle breeze of security. But I am unequal to the task of entertaining thoughts of this nature, such as would obliterate the springs of resentment and promote the advancement of amity and concord. Should I return to the service of the King, I shall always be in terror and alarm, and every moment I shall behold death afresh. Wherefore it is better to choose avoidance rather than such a return, and to exchange return for separation.

COUPLET.

When the rose of union blooms not on the branch of fortune's tree,
'Tis joy in the waste of absence, pierced with thorns our feet to see.'

The King said, 'No one has any power to benefit or injure any one without the will of the great God (may His name be magnified!) so that which befalls any one, whether it be little or much, small or great, happens only by the eternal decree, and through the previous command of Him who suffers no decline. Inasmuch, therefore, as the hand of a creature is unable to create or revivify, it is impossible that it should be the cause of annihilating or producing anything. Thus the deed of my son and thy retaliation occurred through the decree of God and the will of the Almighty, and they were but the means of carrying into execution that order. Do not, therefore, call us to account for the decrees of heaven, nor reprove us for that which has been fated by God, but acquiesce in the dispensations of providence.

VERSE.

Our sole course is submission to our lot;
Patience alone befits us in distress.
Whate'er fate's pen may write, oppose it not,
Or from His way who wills it, find egress.'

The Lark replied, ' The weakness of created beings to avert the decree of the Creator is manifest and ascertained; and it is apparent and clearly delineated on the pages of the thoughts of people of verity, that the varieties of good and ill, and different degrees of advantage and detriment take place according to the intention and requirement of the ordinance of the Almighty, (may His name be magnified!) and that the averting or prevention of them, or their acceleration or postponement, is not to be effected, ' *There is no repeller of His decree, and no retarder of His mandate.*'

COUPLET.

None here may question why 'tis thus, or wherefore things that happen are:
For He that does events pourtray, beyond such questions lieth far.

And notwithstanding that all sages have been unanimous as to this matter, no one has affirmed that one ought to neglect caution and vigilance, or that self-preservation from disagreeable and calamitous things, ought to be deferred. Nay, they have said that we must provide the means for all things, and commit the completion of affairs to the Causer of Causes.

DISTICHS.

To study ways and means is God's decree
To all beneath the sky's blue canopy.
By causes chained seek not from cause to fly,
Yet doubt not the First Cause is Deity.
Art thou through causes to their Cause supine?
Canst thou from Him to those veiled ones incline?[1]

And the recondite saying, '*Be wise and trust*,' supports this assertion.

HEMISTICH.

In trustful hope, bind thou the camel's knee.'

The King rejoined, ' The sum of this discourse is, that I am desirous of a meeting with thee, and find in my own mind an abundant longing for thy society, and in spite of all this earnest desire that exists on my part, I perceive nothing on thy part but the tokens of chagrin.

---

[1] By *rú púshhd* here, I imagine 'causes' are compared to 'brides;' the point of resemblance being in the veil that sometimes covers the former, and the latter always.

COUPLET.

We love thee, and thou tak'st our love amiss,
Since hearts to hearts incline, what state is this ?'

The Lark said, 'Thy strong desire lies in this—to appease thy heart by killing me; and the state of the case is, that my soul does not at present desire to drink the beverage of death, or incline to put on the apparel of extinction; and as long as the reins of option are in my hand, I repudiate the acceptance of these things, and look upon the avoidance of them as the essence of salutary counsel.

HEMISTICH.

Unlike the cane, heads shoot from trunks no more.

And I this day can infer the feelings of the King from my own heart, for could I obtain the power and ability, I should not be satisfied, save by the destruction of the king's darling[1] son; and I feel sure that owing to the distress of his son, the sole wish of the king, too, is for my destruction. Moreover, he that obtains information as to what is concealed in the mind of the unfortunate is he that has been consumed by the fire of the same grief, and who from that source has drunk the sharbat of bitterness. Parties at their ease are ignorant and careless of this state of things, and those nursed in luxury, and who have experienced nought but happiness, are free from the knowledge[2] of pain.

COUPLET.

Thou in whose foot not e'en a thorn has broken—how canst thou
Tell what the warriors feel, whose heads before the sabre bow?

And I see with the eye of understanding that whenever the king recalls his son's [loss of] vision, and I think of my own 'light of my eyes,' a difference will be visible in our internal feelings, and a change will manifest itself in our tempers, and one may judge what will spring therefrom, and what circumstances will then arise. On these grounds separation is more prudent than meeting, and distance more expedient than personal vicinity.

HEMISTICH.

Since such the union, parting then is best.'

The King said, 'What good can there be in that person who cannot overlook the offences of his friends, nor relinquish feelings of spite and annoyance. And a wise man, of perfect understanding, possesses the power of non-retaliation to such an extent that during his whole life he does not refer to it, nor at any time does any trace of it, little or much, appear on the page of his heart. He accepts, too, with the utmost readiness, the prayers of forgiveness of the guilty, and the excuses of offenders. [Thus

---

[1] Lit., 'lustre of the eyes.'
[2] Lit., 'devoid of the ornament of pain.' This sounds absurd in English, but the Persians are ever straining after a metaphor, however ridiculous.

it is said], ' *The worst of the wicked is he who will not accept an excuse*'; in other words, he is worst among the bad who accepts not excuses, and harbors in his heart resentment against one who apologizes.

HEMISTICH.

A frank avowal hides with me all sin.

And I, for my part, find my mind pure in all I have said ; and I do not discover in my heart a trace of the form of wrath, or the fury of anger, or the idea of revenge ; and I have always preferred forgiveness to punishment, and have always thought that, however great the offence may be, the quality of forgiveness will be greater.

COUPLET.

Greatly in error may inferiors fall ; But great men's pardon will outstrip it all.'

The Lark replied, 'This is all true, but I am an offender, and the criminal is always an alarmist ; and my case is like that of a person in the sole of whose foot there is a wound. If from the strength of his natural firmness he acts fearlessly, and consents during a dark night to walk through a stony place, there is no escape from opening afresh that wound, so that his foot will be incapable of work, and it will be impossible for him to move even on soft ground. Now my acceding to the service of the king is of the same nature ; and, according to law and the canons of my creed, it is a positive duty that I should abstain from it. So it is said, ' *And throw not yourselves with your own hands into perdition*;' [1] and sages have remarked, ' Three persons are far from the path of wisdom, and separated from the road of knowledge. The first is he who relies on the strength of his own nature, for such a one undoubtedly casts himself into peril, and his own rashness causes his destruction. The second is he who discerns not the proper amount of food and drink, and eats so much that his stomach is unable to digest it ; and this person is, in fact, the enemy of his own life. The third is he who is deceived by the speech of an enemy, and beguiled by the promise of one from whom he cannot be safe, and the conclusion of his affair will certainly turn out to be abasement and repentance.

COUPLET.

Be not too careless of a foe's deceit,
But ponder, turn the rein, and thence retreat.'

The King said, 'O Lark ! though I enter by the door of courtesy, and point out to thee the road of welfare and friendly admonitions, thou remainest

---

[1] Ḳur'án, Fl. ii. 191 ; Mar. 197 ; Sale, p. 21, l. 19 : 'A sacred month for a sacred month, and the holy limits of Mecca, if they attack you therein, do ye also attack them therein in retaliation ; and whoever transgresseth against you by so doing, do ye transgress against him in like manner as he hath transgressed against you ; and fear God, and know that God is with those who fear him. Contribute out of your substance toward the defence of the religion of God, and throw not yourselves with your own hands into perdition ; and do good. for God loveth those who do good.'

as before in thy bitterness, and shakest the skirt of thy acceptance free from hearing my advice. Now, advice, with reference to a person who will not accept it, is useless; as was the advice of that Devotee to the Wolf.' The Lark asked, 'How was that?'

STORY VII.

The King said, 'They have related that a holy man of virtuous manners—whose august time, after the performance of his daily portions and prescribed prayers, used never to be spent save in exhorting the servants of God—as he passed through a desert place, beheld a Wolf which had opened the mouth of greediness and appetite, and had fixed the eye of covetousness on the road of search. It had devoted its whole spirit to injuring the innocent, and to depriving some animal of life, in order that it might take a part of it to gratify its own rebellious lusts.

COUPLET.

See that unjust contentious caitiff, who
For one self-gain a hundred wrongs would do.

The holy man, who observed him in that state, and who perused from the page of his forehead the writing of violence and oppression, in accordance with his natural tenderness and innate clemency, began to admonish him and said, 'Take care not to approach the sheep-flocks of men, nor to assail the oppressed and the helpless. For the end of injustice is divine punishment, and the conclusion of oppression results in disgrace and torture in the world to come.

VERSE.

'They who have chosen an unjust career,
  Do gyves on their own hands and feet impose.
What though they should some days their heads uprear,
  Yet fortune in the end all such o'erthrows.'

In this manner he discoursed and used unbounded urgency in persuading him to abandon cruelty to the flocks of men. The Wolf said, 'Be so good as to cut short thy advice, as there is a flock grazing behind this waste spot; I fear lest the opportunity for carrying off a sheep should be lost, and then regret will be unavailing.'

Now the object of adducing this story is to shew, that however much I exhort thee, thou persistest obstinately in thy purpose, and givest no heed to my words.

COUPLET.

Say no more! The kindly-hearted are not dull or hard to teach,
Oft a word will win them, and their love a thousand years will reach.'

The Lark replied, 'I have listened to your exhortations, but I have taken counsel of the preacher, wisdom. I regard him as intelligent who always keeps open the door of caution, and places before himself the mirror of experience. I have come to the place, where I am, through excessive fear and terror, and I wisely stand on the brink of the road to escape, and propose to myself a journey in order that I may not fall into the hands of any one; and it is forbidden me to delay longer than this, and to continue in this perplexity and hesitation would justly expose me to censure. For I know that the King looks upon the shedding my blood as lawful, and considers as permissible all that is conceivable in the code of honor. Wherefore my stay is irksome, and it is incumbent on me to depart quickly.

HEMISTICH.

I'm gone, for longer stay delights me not.'

The King rejoined, 'Here the means of support are ready for thee, and the doors of happiness and tranquillity open to the face of thy heart. It is altogether inexpedient[1] to choose voluntarily the hardships of travel and uncertainty as to arrangement for supplies.' The Lark replied, 'Whoever makes five qualities the provision for his way and the stock of his existence, go where he will, attains his objects, and acquires friends and comrades in whatever direction he may turn. The first is, to put away evil actions The second, to clothe himself in good conduct. The third is, to shun such things as will expose him to slander. The fourth is, to supply himself with a train of virtues. The fifth is, at all times to observe the duties and graces of social intercourse. One who combines all these qualities will nowhere be left in destitution, but people will cause the dreariness of his exile to be exchanged for the pleasures of friendship.

HEMISTICH.

No town, no country, sees the wise man strange,

And when a man of understanding cannot be safe in the city of his birth, and in his fatherland, and among his own kinsmen and relations; he must of necessity choose to separate from his friends and connections, since for all these substitutes can be found, but there is no substitute for his own person.

VERSE.

If things proceed not to thy wish at home,
Be not a captive in woe's house through blindness.
Go forth, nor wilt thou be unfriended; roam
Where'er thou wilt, thou there wilt meet with kindness.'

The King said, ' For how long wilt thou go, and what length of time wilt thou stop away?' The Lark replied, ' O King! expect not that I will come back when I am gone, nor imagine a return after this departure; and this dialogue of ours strongly resembles that of the Arab and the Baker.' The King inquired, ' How was that?'

---

[1] Observe the phrase *hich wajahi na dárad*, which is not unlike our vulgar expression,— 'to be all nohow.'

STORY VIII.

The Lark said, 'They have related that an Arab of the desert came into the city of Baghdád and saw the shop of a Baker. Round loaves, like the moon's orb, arose from the horizon of the counter, and biscuits of a starry brightness had ascended to the pinnacle of the shop. Their solar beauty laid the hand of amazement on the face of the sun, and envy[1] of the biscuit rent the collar of the afflicted bread.

STANZA.

> Of fair, round form, hot, new-made loaves upon the Baker's counter lie ;
> Thou wouldst suppose each was the sun, world-lighting, rising in the sky.
> The oven sparkles like the fire they lit, God's prophet-friend[2] to try ;
> For from it, roselike, issuing forth, fresh loaves each moment meet the eye.

In short, when the poor Arab, who obtained a gasp of life from the smell of the bread, saw the face of the loaves, he rent the upper coat of patience, and advancing to the Baker, said, 'O sir! how much wilt thou take to give me my fill of bread?' The Baker thought to himself, 'This fellow will have his fill with one man of bread, and two mans will be the outside he can eat, and beyond three mans he cannot get, do what he will.' He then said, 'Give me half a dínár and eat as much bread as thou canst.' The Arab gave the half-dínár and sate down on the brink of the water of the Tigris. The Baker kept bringing the bread, and the Arab went on moistening it with water, and eating, until the price passed half a dínár and reached four dángs,[3] and having gone beyond that too, came to a whole dínár. The Baker then lost all patience, and said, 'O brother Arab! I adjure thee by that God who has bestowed on thee this miraculous power of eating, tell me how long thou wilt continue eating?' The Arab replied, 'O sir! be not impatient, for as long as this water continues to flow I also will continue to eat.'

Now the object of adducing this story is, that the King may know that as long as the water of life flows in the ducts of my body, I have no resource but to eat the morsel of fear and alarm, and to consider it impossible to take up advantage from the table of union. And fortune throws separation between us in such a manner that the thought of union is nothing but a vain fancy; and, hereafter, whenever desire prevails, I will inquire of

---

[1] The editions have a misprint here, *súr* for *súz*, which might delay the student. The passage is somewhat obscure. Perhaps *shamsí* and *sang pukht*, though not found in the Dictionary, are kinds of biscuit, in which case it will be difficult to name them properly in English, as 'sun-cake,' and 'stone-bake,' would sound somewhat ridiculous.

[2] Ḳur'án, Sale, p, 70, l. 16. Abraham is called 'the friend of God.' Hence this Patriarch is known among Muḥammadans by the term *Khalílu'lláh*, 'friend of God.' For an account of Abraham's dispute with Nímrúd, and that tyrant's casting him into a fire, which changed into a pleasant meadow; see Sale, p. 247, and the notes there.

[3] A *dínár* in Hindústán is worth 2⅖ rupees, or 30*d*. See Ḳánún-i Islám, p. 59. A *dáng* is the one-sixth of a *dínár*.

the morning-breeze happy tidings of the King, and will behold in the mirror of imagination, the perfect beauty of his majesty.

If I cannot meet my loved one, I'm content to think of him;
Sure the moonbeam is the best light for the votary's closet dim.'

The King let fall the drops of regret from the fountains of his eyes, and perceived that that sagacious bird would not come into the snare, and that the desired vengeance would not move gracefully forth from the cabinet of non-existence into the expanse of being. Again he began to strew the grain of deceit, and employed a variety of promises and asseverations. The Lark said, ' O King! of noble fortune and of brilliant crown and throne, although thou arrangest the substructure of favor and offerest a variety of kindnesses as to the matter of safety and security, and ratifiest the same by attestations worthy of approval and becoming assurances; yet it is impossible that I should draw the ring of servitude through my ear or spread over my shoulder the cloth of obedience.

Waste words no more—they take no hold of me.'

The King perceived that he could not extract from the foot of the Lark's heart, the thorn of timidity with the needle of deceit, nor bring back with the strong arm of perfidy, the arrow which had left the string. He [1] said therefore, ' O Lark! I see that from the flower-garden of union, nought but the perfume will reach the nostril of desire, and that the face of inter-view will not appear save in the mirror of hope.

He's gone who was the water in the rivulet of mirth,
Or glossy curl that beautifies the ringlet of desire.
Alas! the time of joy, to which our union glad gave birth,
Is past, as words in visions fade, and, shadow-like, expire.

I desire, however, that by way of a souvenir, thou wouldest utter two or three sentences by the repetition of which the signs of happiness will be observable on the pages of life, and that thou wouldest rub out, by the polisher of friendly admonition, the rust of neglect from the mirror of my mind, which has been clouded by the dust of grief.

Leave for my sake some words that may memento of thy dear self be,
Than good advice thou canst not leave a better souvenir of thee.'

The Lark said, ' O King! the affairs of mortals are carried on in accordance with destiny. And therein they have allotted to none a discretionary power as to augmentation or the reverse, or anticipation or postponement. Nor

---

[1] I would recommend, that, in accordance with the best MSS., instead of *malik guft*, which is the reading of the editions, we should read simply *guft*.

can any one know if they have affixed to his name the diploma of happiness, or have entered him in the roll of the wretched. But it is incumbent on all to direct their affairs according to the requirements of right reason, and to use their utmost endeavors in the observance of caution and vigilance. If their counsel accords with destiny, they are of themselves established on the throne of prosperity and the cushion of dignity and state. But if circumstances turn out adverse, it both happens that friends accept the excuse, and railers, too, fail in finding an opportunity for disparagement.

STANZA.

'True,' said the wise man, 'fate precedes, but still
    Neglect in no case thine own plans—for should
Thy counsels coincide with the high will
    Of destiny, then thine own actions would
Secure thee fruit to thy heart's wish. But say
That fate is adverse, still all whom the ray
    Of sense gilds, view thy fall in lenient mood.'

And, moreover, it should be known that the most visionary of possessions is that of which there is no fruition; and the most negligent of kings is he who does not apply himself to protect his country and coerce his subjects; and the most execrable of friends is he who deserts his friend in the time of distress and adversity; and the most unserviceable of wives is she who agrees not with her husband; and the worst of sons is he who refuses to obey his parents; and the most desolate of cities is that in which there is neither security nor cheapness; and the most unpleasant intercourse is that in which the hearts of the associates are not right to each other. And as suspicion has arisen in my intercourse with the King, it is most proper to relinquish it; and it is most in accordance with the advisable course to exchange the language of friendship for the terms of truce.

QUATRAIN.

We're gone and let us then a heartfelt farewell find,
    And with the water of both eyes turn earth to clay.
Hast thou been wronged? yet let thy every word be kind,
    And if thy head has ached, put now the thought away.'

With these words the Lark brought the discussion to an end, and flying from the battlements of the castle took her way to the desert. The King bit the finger of regret with the tooth of amazement; and after lamenting some time, turned his face towards his palace with grief exceeding computation or conception, and with chagrin that overpassed the bounds of comprehension, and said,

VERSE.

'Where shall I tell? that in this torturing pain
    My leech himself life's trembling cord would break.
And how amid my friends can I complain,
    That thus my loved one acted and thus spake?'

This is the story of being cautious of the perfidious ambushes of the resentful, and of avoiding to test the sincerity of their entreaties and be-wailings, and of placing confidence in the hypocritical friendship of foes; and of not being deceived by the fraud and artifice which they employ to secure their revenge. And let it not be hid from the man of understanding that the intention of narrating these things is no other than this, that the prudent man ought to regard every one as a guide in the accidents of fortune and in the disasters of life, and to base his proceedings on the requirements of reason and good counsel, and in no wise to rely on an enemy that has been vexed, and not to sit down secure from the calamitous effects of deceit and the danger of guile.

QUATRAIN.

Wouldst thou be never leagued with grief or woe?
Hear, then, a word than finest pearl more pure:
Ne'er shew supineness with a wounded foe,
Nor of the proud and spiteful feel secure.

CHAPTER IX.

OF THE EXCELLENCE OF CLEMENCY; THAT IT IS THE BEST ATTRIBUTE OF KINGS, AND THE MOST PLEASING QUALITY OF THE MIGHTY.

INTRODUCTION.

Dábishlím said respectfully to the perfect sage, the Bráhman of profound mind, 'I have heard the story of one whose heart was not tranquilized by the caresses of an enemy whose feelings had been wounded; and who, when he saw the signs of hostility and marks of rancor remaining, was not to be shaken from the path of caution, though his foe did his utmost to conciliate him. Now the fires of eager desire have been kindled within me, and so long as a shower from the fountain of the Ninth Precept does not reach my consumed heart, the burning impatience of my mind will not be allayed. I entertain a confident hope that you will narrate a story which shall comprehend the subject of the clemency of kings and their indulgence, and that you will recount whether, when a king, after the infliction of severe punishment on his attendants, beholds in them the evident tokens of crime and transgression, he ought again to shew them favor or not? Also, whether or not it would be in accordance with prudence to place confidence in such persons, by restoring to them their offices?' Bídpáí, with a pleasing voice and in an exhilarating style, replied, 'If kings close up the door of forgiveness and clemency, and in whatever quarter they discover a slight offence, command the offender to be chastised, their attendants will lose all unmixed confidence in them, and not rely on them farther. And from this state of things two calamities will arise—first, all affairs will be paralysed and conducted with remissness; and secondly, offenders will be deprived of the sweet taste of clemency and the favor of indulgence. Moreover one of the greatest princes has said, 'If people knew what gratification the palate of my soul finds in forgiveness they would bring no other offering to my heart than errors and offences.

VERSE.

> Did the offender know what bliss to me
>   Arises from the pardon of a sin,
> He 'd ever err intentionally,
>   And with excuses some new crime begin.'

There is no ornament more becoming to the state of princes than clemency, and no more brilliant evidence to the perfection of the worth of the noble among the sons of Adam than pardon and indulgence. And the import of the miraculously-gifted saying of His Highness the Prince of Mankind (On him be the choicest benedictions and blessings!) viz., '*Ha! I will teach you, who is the strongest of you,—he who governs himself when in anger*,'—graciously points out that one may discover the power of a man by his quenching the flame of wrath, and that the proofs of manliness and magnanimity may be learned by the capacity to swallow down the distasteful beverage of anger.

COUPLET.

Think not that manly virtue is in courage and in strength alone:
Do thou thy anger overcome, and I will thee as perfect own.

And the most admirable quality of kings is to make high-minded reason their guide in all that befalls them, and at no time to suffer their character to be deficient in graciousness and due severity. But their indulgence ought to be of such a nature as not to verge towards weakness; and their severity should be such as to be clear from the reproach of cruelty, so that their rule may be adorned with the two characteristics of beauty and grandeur, and the axis of the state may revolve on the display of terror and the good tidings of hope. Thus neither will the attached despair of a kindness which will be void of limit, nor will the rebellious set foot in the world of audacity through fear of punishment.

COUPLET.

Imperial Jamshíd swayed his people's mind,
While mingled hopes and fears their thoughts confined.

And the sages of the true religion *(May God reward them with good!)* have said that God Most High hath given His people virtuous qualities by the admonitions of the Ḳur'án and the instructions of that holy book, and hath given them a longing for approved customs and laudable habits. Thus all, whoever they may be, to whom infinite happiness lends aid and assistance, and eternal wisdom supplies support and countenance, will make the mandates of the Ḳur'án the point of adoration of their hearts and the sanctuary of their souls; and they will ever, with heart and soul, turn towards the honored shrine of this temple of security and peace. And of the number of the said admonitions is a verse which comprehends all the truths of this assertion above made, and its word is most high, '*Who bridle their anger, and forgive men; for God loveth the beneficent*.'[1] And one of the leaders of religion has, with the tongue of verity, explained this verse in the following manner: To restrain anger is, not to go to excess in punishment; and forgiveness is, to obliterate the trace of aversion from the page of the heart; and beneficence is, to return a second time to a friend that has offended and

---

[1] Ḳur'án, Fl. iii. 128; Mar. 134; Sale, p. 47, l. 16 : 'And run with emulation to obtain remission from your Lord, and paradise, whose breadth equalleth the heavens and the earth, which is prepared for the godly ; who give alms in prosperity and adversity; who bridle their anger and forgive men : for God loveth the beneficent.'

made his excuse ; and the sum and substance of the verse is to base one's proceedings on kindness and gentleness, and to observe carefully in all matters politeness and benignity. For it has been handed down among true traditions, that if benevolence could be represented in a bodily shape the splendor of its beauty would so glitter and shine that no eye would be able to endure the sight of it, and no one would ever have beheld a more graceful form, or a more comely appearance. And an eminent personage, in a single couplet of the following stanza, expresses all this.

STANZA.

' When God has given thee o'er a culprit sway,
    Forgive and bind him so to be thy slave.
Their own bad actions do the guilty slay,
    The scent of pardon lifts them from the grave.
Could we in outward shape sweet mercy see,
Than sun or Jupiter more bright she 'd be.'

And should this matter be duly pondered, it will undoubtedly be discerned that the dignity of man is increased by the excellence of a forgiving and beneficent disposition. Wherefore our best efforts should be directed to the cultivation of these two qualities. Moreover, it is not hidden [from our knowledge] that man cannot be devoid of faults and negligence, and offences and failings. If, then, every offence brings out a manifestation of severity, and every crime developes a corresponding punishment, a general injury will be occasioned, which will spread through the departments of finance and government.

VERSE.

To grasp the sword with wild impetuous haste
    Causes remorseful gnawing of the hand,
Forbid it that a kingly crown be placed
    On heads that cannot their own wrath command.

Again, it behoves a king to estimate the extent of the friendship, and the sincerity of the counsels, and the merits and ability of the person who has exposed himself to aspersions; in order that, if he be of the number of those who can aid in the counsels of the state, or from whose advice assistance may be anticipated in the events which time brings about; the king may then exert himself to restore his own confidence in him, and take speedy measures to encourage and promote him. Let him regard this course, therefore, as free from danger and doubt; and restore his heart, by conciliation and entreaty, to its wonted tranquillity. For there is no limit to state emergencies, and it is also certain that kings stand in need of efficacious advisers and trustworthy officers, who deserve to be entrusted with secrets, and possess aptitude for discretionary powers in the affairs of government. Wherefore it befits the regal position to promote those parties who are adorned with perfect understanding, and hortatory powers and merit, and abstinence from what is forbidden, and are graced with rectitude and uprightness, and piety and honesty; and who are distinguished from their fellows by gratitude and good advice, and loyalty and attachment. And as a means thereto, they ought to learn what office suits each, and to what department each should fittingly be attached; and to appoint each individual to some business, according to his capacity and the extent of his judgment and valor, and in proportion to his understanding and ability. And if in any one, together with merit, be found a fault, of that, too, kings should not be neglectful; for no creature can be found faultless. And they have said,

HEMISTICH.

Seek not a faultless friend lest thou shouldst all unfriended live.

And in this particular, caution is requisite to such an extent, that if any one should embarrass matters which he is called upon to superintend, he should he removed from the government; and if another, by his very abilities, should disturb his department, he, too, should be avoided. For though this is a state of things which is impossible, that abilities should prejudice anything, nevertheless, the above injunction has been given in order that it may be known that to obtain one's object, even men of ability and merit may be discarded; whence it will be the more expedient to elongate oneself from people fatuous and prone to error. Consequently, from the right understanding of this subject, and the recognition of these points, it becomes the duty of kings that they should execute the diligent exploration of the matters, and inquire into the employments, which they commit to the care of their officers and superintendents, so that they may be minutely[1] conversant with the affairs of finance and government. And in this, two important advantages are discernible. One is that it will be thence known who of the superintendents are cherishers of the subjects, and who are their oppressors. Thus the king must take care to caress those who are tender towards the people, and support them in that course; and obliterate from the book of employment his name who cares not for those under him, and enter it in the register of disgrace.

VERSE.

Thy folk to pious men entrusted be,
For he builds up the state, who rules himself.
The nation's tyrant—thy worst foe is he,
Who grinds thy subjects to increase thy pelf.
'Tis wrong that he a nation should enthrall,
Against whose hand men lift their hands in prayer;
Evil will ne'er the virtuous man befall,
But evil-doers their own lives ensnare.

[1] Observe the phrase, *nakír ú kitmír*, lit., 'the groove in a date-stone, from which the stalk grows, and the thin pellicle that covers the stone;' hence, any minutiæ.

And further, when this idea has been impressed on the minds of all, that the king keeps the rewards of the actions of well-doers at hand in the best possible way, and thinks it incumbent on him to punish traitors in proportion to their guilt: then the good, being inspired with hope, will not be remiss and supine towards acting rightly; and mischievous persons, becoming alarmed and terrified, will not act with audacity and fearlessness as regards sedition and wrong-dealing to others.   Now the tale of the Lion and the Jackal is a story suited to these premises.'   The King asked, 'How was that?'

STORY I.

The Bráhman said, 'They have related that in the country of Hindústán there was a Jackal, by name Farísah,[1] who had averted his face from the world, and had turned his back on its vain affairs.   He lived among his fellows and those of his own race, but he abstained from eating flesh and spilling blood and hurting animals.

COUPLET.

His lips he crimsoned with the blood of none,
And did with carefulness bad actions shun.

His comrades commenced a wrangle with him, and began a dispute, the tendency of which was towards strife and contest, and said, 'We do not feel satisfied with this disposition of thine, and we blame thy judgment in this procedure.   Inasmuch as thou dost not turn away from our intercourse, thou oughtest to agree with our habits and character, and since thou dost not snatch away the skirt of consentaneousness from our society, thou shouldest not withdraw thy head from the collar of coincidence.   Moreover, to pass precious life in prohibition, and to keep thyself incarcerated in the prison of austerity, is of little utility.   Besides, it is right to demand what is due as thy portion of the enjoyments of the world, that thou mayest have thy share of the drink, ' *And forget not thy portion in this world*.'[2]   Nor is it right to relinquish eating and drinking which form an essential support of life, in order that thou mayest comply with the command, '*Eat and drink*;'[3] and thou shouldest know well the fact that yesterday cannot be recalled, and it befits us not to make sure of gaining the morrow.   What is the use, then, of losing to-day? and of foregoing the enjoyment of [present] pleasures?

---

[1] This signifies 'catching and breaking the bones of the prey.'

[2] Kur'án, xxviii. 77; Sale, p. 296, l. 5: 'And forget not thy portion in this world; but be thou bounteous unto others, as God hath been bounteous unto thee: and seek not to act corruptly in the earth; for God loveth not the corrupt doers.'

[3] Kur'án, Fl. ii. 57; Sale, p. 8, l. 1: 'Eat and drink of the bounty of God, and commit not evil in the earth, acting unjustly.'

COUPLET.

Come! from life a blissful moment now in secret borrow,
For not one can tell us here the changes of to-morrow.'

The Jackal replied, 'Since ye know that yesterday is past, and will return no more, and that a sensible man does not rely on the morrow, lay up something to-day in store, that may serve as provision for the [final] journey.

COUPLET.

Ransack to-day each corner for the things
To feed thee in to-morrow's journeyings.

And the world, full as it is of faults, has at least this one merit, that it is, as they have called it, the seed-ground of the final state, and the seed that thou sowest therein, the same thou wilt reap in the resurrection; [as it is said], ' To-day is the sowing and to-morrow is the harvest.'

DISTICHS.

Strive thou to-day to sow with might and main,
To-morrow leaves thee not a single grain.
Art thou neglectful now to sow this earth?
Thou wilt not then be half a millet worth.

It behoves a man of sense therefore to expend all his energies in securing a recompense in the final state, and this he may do by the performance of alms and pious works; and he should set his heart on enduring happiness and eternal delights, and this is to be brought about by forsaking the affairs of this deceitful world and fleeting abode.

COUPLET.

Do not thou thy heart, I pray thee, on this fleeting threshold place!
Elsewhere they the firm foundations of joy's mansions for thee trace.

To-day that ye have the power and canst do so, gallop the steed of abstinence in the plain of holy warfare, and store up for sickness the fruits of health, and acquire interest from the capital of youth for the flagging market of old age, and from the advantages of life prepare provisions for the journey through the desert of annihilation and extinction. A sage has said, 'To day ye have the power and lack the knowledge, and to-morrow ye will have the knowledge and lack the power,' [according to the text] ' Alas! that I have been negligent in my duty to God.' [1]

COUPLET.

What use the power since I wist not too?
And when I wist I lacked the power to do.

---

[1] Ḳur'án, Fl. xxxix. 57; Mar. 56; Sale, p. 348, l. 9: 'And follow the most excellent instructions which have been sent down unto you from your Lord, before the punishment come suddenly upon you, and ye perceive not the approach thereof; and a soul say, Alas! for that I have been negligent in my duty to God; verily, I have been one of the scorners; or say, If God had directed me, verily I had been one of the pious; or say, when it seeth the prepared punishment, If I could return once more into the world, I would become one of the righteous.'

Worldly enjoyment, like the lightning's flash, is unenduring, and its sufferings, too, like the dark shadow of a cloud, have no continuance. One ought not, then, to become attached to the gain of its good things, nor to grieve at the hardship of its trials.

COUPLET.

What though it yield! its smiles no joy bestow :
And its withdrawal is not worth our woe.

The sum of the matter is, that to devote the heart to attachment to this cell of misery appears to be far removed from nobility of mind; and to erect an edifice in the channel of the torrent of annihilation seems inconsistent with perfect foresight. [Thus it is said] '*Pass over it and do not build it :*' this hired mansion and place, soon to be abandoned,

HEMISTICH.

Try not to build, but leave it to decay.'

The other animals replied, 'O Farísah! bid us not abandon the enjoyments of the world, for it is a world excellent for the purpose for which it was created, which was that we might reap advantage from it, and enjoy the fruition of its delights. And the recondite saying, '*And we provided good things for their sustenance,*'[1] is a proof of this assertion.' Farísah replied, 'The real excellence of the world consists in its being the implement[2] by which a wise man obtains a good name and enduring mention; and by the means of which he acquires provision for the journey to that place to which all must return; so that, in accordance with the saying, '*Honest wealth is a good thing,*' riches become the cause of his happy end, not the means of his punishment and disgrace. And ye, if ye desire happiness in this world, give ear to these words; and, for the sake of pleasant food, the gratification of which does not extend beyond the gullet, do not think it permissible to destroy an animal, and be content with what ye can get without molesting or paining others, and do not exceed such a quantity as will suffice for the sustenance of the frame and the support of the body. Nor require of me to conform to you in that which is contrary to law and reason. For my mere association with you does not lead to harm, but my participation in blameable actions would be the cause of my being punished; and if ye mean to annoy me by these vexatious importunities, give me leave rather to abandon your society, and betake myself to the corner of retirement.

HEMISTICH.

I'll hie me to some quiet corner, and on mankind shut my door.'

---

[1] Kur'án, Fl. x. 93; Mar. 91; Sale, p. 161, l. 4: And we prepared for the children of Israel an established dwelling in the land of Canaan, and we provided good things for their sustenance: and they differed not in point of religion, until knowledge had come unto them; verily thy Lord will judge between them on the day of resurrection, concerning that wherein they disagreed.'

[2] Observe this sense of *dast afráz :* it is not given in the Dictionaries.

When Farísah's companions saw that his foot was firmly planted on the carpet of abstinence and piety, they were convinced, and became ashamed of having spoken these words, and loosed the tongue of apology to excuse themselves. As for Farísah, he in a short time attained such eminence in piety and virtue that the recluses of that country were in the habit of imploring spiritual succor from his soul; and those who were hastening over the tract of religious improvement continually besought the aid of the favor of his directing glance. After a short interval the fame of his austerities and uprightness was diffused through the environs of that region, and the celebrity of his devotion and religious life penetrated the adjoining parts of that territory. Now, hard by the place where Farísah lived, there was a jungle, abounding in streams and springs of water, and trees of various kinds. In the midst of it was a meadow, such that the garden of Iram from envy of its freshness withdrew its face beneath the veil of concealment, and the invigorating influence of its cool northern breezes bestowed immortal life on the fainting heart.

VERSE.

Its rapture-giving plain did life renew,
    Its breeze, invigorating, banished care.
Fringing its streamlet's lip, all moist with dew,
    Verdure upsprang such as one might compare
    To the soft down of tender stripling fair.

And in that spot many wild animals and beasts of prey had collected, and by reason of the amplitude of the expanse and the delightfulness of the air various beasts and reptiles reposed there, and their king was a lion, terrible and dreadful, a monster, frightful and awe-inspiring.

COUPLET.

His roar was louder than the thunder crash,
His eyes like lightning fire seemed forth to flash.

The whole body of the inhabitants of that jungle were constrained to obey him and passed their time under the protection of his majesty, and in the asylum of his awe. They called him Kámjúí,[1] and under this title his fame had spread through all parts of that country. One day, Kámjúí was conversing on divers subjects with his grandees, and had opened the road of various discourse. In the midst of the conversation the story of Farísah was introduced, and such were the encomiums of his perfect virtue and blameless life that from all quarters reached the ears of the monarch, that he wished with heart and soul for his society.

COUPLET.

They did to him a place, though yet his cheek beheld was not,
As to the pupil of their eyes, upon their eyes allot.

---

[1] That is, 'seeking enjoyment.'

In short, as the desire of Kámjúí to converse with Farísah passed all bounds, he sent some one to require his attendance; and Farísah, on his part, in obedience to the imperial command, presented himself in the world-sheltering court. The king having received him with the prescribed forms of respect, bestowed on him the honor of a seat in the high assembly, and tested his real condition in various points of devotion and spiritual knowledge. To be brief, he found that Farísah was a boundless sea in developing virtuous excellencies and high accomplishments, and saw that he was a gem-scattering treasure in the knowledge of the particulars of perfect truth. Again, he made trial of him in the matter of subtlety and in the transaction of important business, and in eloquence of speech and justness of deliberation; and found the coin of his condition of full value on the touchstone of acceptance.

HEMÍSTICH.
Gold that is pure, why should it dread the test?

Kámjúí was pleased with his society, and cultivated an intimacy with him. After some days he called him to a private audience, and said, 'O Farísah! my realm is of wide extent, and the transactions of it are vast, and they brought to my royal hearing the tidings of thy piety and abstinence, and I

HEMISTICH.
Held the unseen more dear than if I saw.

And now that I have seen thee, what I see exceeds what I heard; and hearing proves inferior to the sight.

COUPLET.
I heard earth's regions did not hold a second such as thou,
I see thou dost a thousand-fold surpass that rumor now.

I will now place confidence in thee, and entrust to thee the affairs of government and finance, so that thy rank being elevated by my patronage, thou wilt be admitted into the class of my special and intimate favorites, and wilt be distinguished through the blessings of my condescension and the happiness of my favor, from thy fellows and brethren, yea, even from all thy contemporaries, by the honor of my selection and the excellence of thy dignity.

COUPLET.
Who on my glorious threshold lays his head
Will gain a throne ere yet a week be fled.'

Farísah replied, ' It behoves kings that for state-affairs they should select proper helpers and becoming assistants; and, moreover, it is requisite for them not to force an employment upon any one against his consent. For when they by compulsion thrust [1] office upon a person, who is unable to execute

---

[1] Lit., 'hang it round its neck.'

it rightly, and is incompetent to the proper discharge of its duties, the disastrous result thereof recoils upon the king, and the sin of the disobedience of the functionary comes back upon the ruler.

Now the drift of this discourse is, that I am averse to affairs of state, and possess no knowledge nor experience in them. And thou art a king of great majesty and a monarch of high dignity; and in thy service are many wild animals and beasts of prey, endued with strength and ability, and noted for their qualities of uprightness and honesty, and who are anxiously looking out for such employment. If thou wilt be pleased to bestow on them thy favor and regard, they will keep the royal mind at ease from all anxiety as to the management of affairs of importance, and will be pleased and benefited by the presents and offerings which they will obtain for undertaking office.' Kámjúí answered, 'What advantage hast thou from thus rejecting my offer? and what profit dost thou see in repelling my proposals? And for my part, I will assuredly not excuse thee, and with thy will or against it will hang the chain of undertaking this affair on the neck of thy care.

HEMISTICH.

Willing or not, thou dost belong to me.'

Farísah said, 'The business of the king should devolve on two kinds of men. Of these, one is the acute, uncompromising person, who with extreme energy and boldness, pursues his object; and having succeeded by craft and subtlety, does not become a butt for the arrow of opposition. The second, is a careless and weak-minded individual, who has become habituated to degradation, and who cares not for dishonor, and disregards the loss of reputation and character.[1] Now such a person is not exposed to envy, nor does any one oppose or strive with him. And I am not of these two classes. I am not swayed by cupidity, so as to play the traitor; nor have I a low disposition so as to endure patiently the load of infamy.

STANZA.

By God! whose hand in all things we discern,
Who made the wise self-guidance to retain.
My soul the empire of both worlds would spurn,
If bought by one dishonorable stain.

The king must abandon this idea, and excuse me from undertaking the burthen of this task; for it is now a long time since I have sewed up the eye of pert cupidity with the needle of contentment; and have consumed with the flashing fires of abstinence, the vain ware of avarice, which is subject to so many wants. And should the king contaminate me again with worldly matters, the same thing will befall me which befell the Flies who had settled in the vessel of honey.' The Lion asked, 'How was that?'

---

[1] In one MS. 'aib is well supplied before na dárad.

STORY II.

Farísah said, 'They have related that one day a pure-minded fakír, whose step was firm in the path of spirituality, was passing along the bázár. A poor man,[1] a confectioner, who had a fellow-feeling for the indigent,[2] requested the holy man that he would rest for a moment at his door. The spiritually gifted fakír, to gratify him, took his seat there; and the master sweetmeat-maker, by way of imploring a blessing, filled a cup with honey and set it before the darvesh. The Flies (according to their custom of rushing upon sweet things, and of not suffering themselves to be driven away, however much one may try to get rid of them,

HEMISTICH.
The shop of the confectioner, that is the place for flies,)

all at once settled in swarms on the cup of honey. Some alighted on the side of the cup, and a few threw themselves into it. The confectioner seeing that the attacks of the Flies went beyond all bounds, flourished a fan for driving away insects; those that were at the side of the cup, easily took wing and went off; while the feet of those who had seated themselves within, having stuck in the honey, when they tried to fly, their wings became smeared with the honey, and they fell into the snare of destruction. The pious darvesh was greatly amused, and began to utter wild cries of delight. After the sea of the shekh's mind grew calm, and the waves of the ocean of ecstacy and rapture had abated, the confectioner said, 'O holy man! I have not withheld from thee material sweetmeats, and do thou not withhold from me that spiritual matter which was disclosed[3] in thy recent transports.

HEMISTICH.
Thy sweet lips open and pour sugar forth.'

The shekh replied, 'They represented to me in this cup of honey the vile world, and the greedy and covetous competitors for it, and a secret and inspired voice said to me, 'Know that this cup is the world, and this honey its dainties; and these flies those that pursue them. And those that sit on the side are the contented fakírs, who are satisfied with a small morsel from the table of the world; and the others, which are inside the cup, are

---

[1] I would rather, with some MSS., omit the *darvesh* that precedes *halwdgar* in the editions.

[2] Lit., 'who had a share in the taste of poverty.'

[3] There is an equivoque here on *halwá*, 'sweetmeat,' and *halwd shudah*, 'descending and being revealed,' which cannot be retained in English. For *hall shudan* is 'to descend,' and *wd shudan* is 'to be disclosed,' and the two compounds are here put together for the sake of the equivoque.

the greedy and covetous, whose conceit is, that as they are inside they will get the greater share; but they are ignorant of the import of the saying, '*Food is allotted.*' However, when 'Izráil waves the fan of departure, those that are on the side fly away easily and return to their nest '*in the assembly of truth, in the presence of a most potent king;*'[1] while those that are seated inside, the more they struggle, get their feet the deeper entangled, and remain in the strait, '*Afterwards we rendered him the vilest of the vile,*'[2] and the issue of their affairs terminates in eternal misery and ruin.

VERSE.

Why, as the price of one poor morsel paid
Should we all this indignity endure?
Contentment choose—be this thy stock-in-trade,
Treasure without it there is none—be sure.'

And this story has been adduced in order that the king may not besmear the wings and feathers of my happy state with the honey of the world. It may be that when the time for demanding restitution of my spirit arrives, I may be able to travel easily the road to the final state.

COUPLET.

So spend thy life, that should they say 'Depart!'
Thou mayst the call obey with all thy heart.'

Kámjúí replied, 'If any one keeps his eyes fixed on what is right, and standing firm on the path of equity omits no particle of justice, and protects the oppressed from the sparks of the injuries of the tyrannical, and listens with a pleased heart and smiling countenance to the words of the afflicted, assuredly in this world his fortunes will be honored with permanency, and in the next he will attain to the exaltation of high dignity and blessedness.' Farísah said, 'If in officiating under kings all obligations are fulfilled, the perfume of final salvation may then reach the nostrils; but in this world the state of a courtier cannot possibly be permanent or unchanging, nor can his office continue for a long time fixed and secure; for as soon as one has been exalted by being granted nearer access to the king, even friends begin to view him with estranged looks, and foes, too, make his life a target for the arrow of calamity. And when a party coalesce, in hostility to him, of course he cannot be safe, nor can he live tranquilly. Nay, though he should set his foot on the top of the planet Saturn, he will not secure his head.' The Lion answered, 'Since thou hast obtained my favor, do not plunge

[1] Ḳur'án, liv. 55; Sale, p, 391, l. 29: 'Moreover, the pious shall dwell among gardens and rivers, in the assembly of truth, in the present of a most potent King.'
[2] Ḳur'án, xcv. 5; Sale, p. 447, l. 18: 'By the fig, and the olive; and by Mount Sinai and this territory of security; verily we created man of a most excellent fabric; afterwards we rendered him the vilest of the vile: except those who believe, and work righteousness; for they shall receive an endless reward.'

2 I 2

thyself into imaginary dangers, for the sincerity of my good opinion is a bar to the mischievous plots of slanderous enemies. With a single chastisement I will close up the path of their machinations, and convey thee to the utmost limit of good cheer and safety.

HEMISTICH.

Are friends with us ? what matter if foes plot !'

Farísah rejoined, ' If the king's intention in thus raising me and bringing me into notice, is to do me a benefit, it would be more suitable to his imperial kindness and condescension and his infinite justice and impartiality to leave me to go about safe and at my ease in this desert; and of all the good things of this world to content myself with water and herbs, and so keep aloof from the injury of the envy and malice of friend and foe. And this is certain that a short life in peace, and happiness, and freedom from care, and health, is better than a long one in fear and dread, and mental fatigue and labor.

COUPLET.

One breath, with ease of mind, is better far
Than thousand years, which disappointments mar.'

Kámjúí responded, ' Thou must put far from thy thoughts the irritating doubts of fear, and allocating thyself with me, must take on thy responsibility the administration of affairs.' Farísah replied, ' If the case is so, and all my deprecation and rejection are unavailing, I must have a letter of immunity, that when high and low rise up against me,—the former in the hope of getting my post, and the latter through fear of their sinking lower,—the king may not be alienated from me by their whisperings, and may think it right to ponder and weigh their insinuations, and may fulfil all that is proper in examining [1] into my case, and the mischievous accusations of those who seek to do me hurt.

COUPLET.

Be not displeased at every slanderous word,
Friends are soon left, if foes be lightly heard.'

The Lion made a covenant with him, and gave him a promise, and then delivered to his charge his effects and treasures; and distinguished him above all his retainers and attendants by unbounded favor. He deliberated too on affairs of importance with him alone, and revealed the state-secrets to none but him. Every day the Lion's confidence in him increased, and his intimacy with the lion, and the esteem in which the latter held him augmented, until their friendship reached the utmost limit possible, and their union was thoroughly cemented. Farísah was not absent one moment from attending on the lion, nor could Kámjúí rest an instant without his society.

HEMISTICH.

'Tis thus, when friendships reach the utmost bound.

---

[1] I would, in accordance with the best MS. supply *iḥtiyáṭ* after *shardiṭ*.

This state of things became irksome to the favorites of the Lion, and a body of the Pillars of the State came to an agreement hostile to Farísah, and bound themselves by a promise of acting consentaneously in opposition to him. They passed whole days in devising his ruin, and whole nights in compassing his removal. At last all unanimously resolved to accuse him of treason, in order that the mind of Kámjúí, which never swerved from the path of justice and uprightness, might be estranged from him, and that the Lion's belief in his honesty, which quality he conceived to be perfectly manifested in him, might be shaken. 'Thereupon' (thought they) 'great openings may be obtained, and endeavours may be used for humbling and overthrowing him.

COUPLET.

By slow degrees we may advances make,   Till the foundation of his power we shake.'

They then suborned an individual to steal a portion of flesh which they had set apart for the Lion's breakfast, and hide it in Farísah's cell.

COUPLET.

And when the Lion, golden-clawed, next day,
From heaven's den began to take his way,

the nobles and ministers formed rank in attendance, and the notables and officials presented themselves at the court of the king. Farísah had gone on some business of the utmost importance in some other direction. The Lion was waiting for his return, and uttered not a word except in praise of his ability and understanding and knowledge.

COUPLET.

'Theme of my tongue, life's solace is his name,
No moment flies but I repeat the same.'

The time for the Lion's meal arrived, and his savage appetite being excited, he was overpowered with the violence of his hunger. The more they sought for the flesh which was apportioned to the king, the less they found it. The Lion was exceedingly enraged, and at this crisis Farísah was absent and his enemies present. When they perceived that the fire of the Lion's hunger was joined to the heat of his wrath, they began their mischievous tricks; and finding the oven of his fury hot, they shut in their unleavened bread. One of them said, 'There is no alternative but we must acquaint the king, and represent all we know as to his majesty's advantage or detriment, though it may not suit certain persons.' Kámjúí, his attention being thus drawn, said, 'It behoves loyal attendants and attached retainers at no time to neglect the duty of giving advice, and in recognition of the obligations they are under for favors received, to report at fitting times what they know and can tell.

COUPLET.

They only loyal, grateful are, in sooth,
Who never from their king conceal the truth.

Report what thou hast heard, and say what thou hast seen.' One of those traitrous slanderers and ill-judging sycophants replied, 'They have informed me that Farísah conveyed that flesh towards his own house.' Another, in a doubtful way, interposed with a remark intended to answer a different purpose than the apparent one,[1] and said, 'I cannot believe this, for he is an inoffensive and trustworthy animal.' Another, commencing craftily, exclaimed, 'We must be cautious in this matter, for everyone has his friends and enemies, and through interested motives they assert things which are not the fact, and we cannot quickly know men's characters, nor can we be easily informed of men's secrets.' Another, interposing with greater boldness, said, 'Such is the case, and intelligence of secrets and acquaintance with men's minds are not readily acquired. But if the flesh be found in his house, whatever is rumored of his treason among high and low, and small and great, will be true.' At this crisis, Kámjúí lost the reins of self-control, and exclaimed, 'What do men say with regard to him? and how do they establish his treason?' One of those present, who was in league with the adverse faction, said, 'O king! the report of his perfidy and deceit has been widely diffused among the inhabitants of this jungle, and if he be a traitor he will never carry his life out safe from this whirlpool, and the disastrous results of his treason will quickly reach him.' Another of the interested ones loosed the tongue of mischief, and said, 'A number of persons did certainly always spread this report of him, but I hesitated to credit it. Now that I hear this history, it has almost come to pass that the gloom of my doubt is exchanged for the light of certainty.' Another added, 'His frauds and deceit before, too, were not hidden from me, and I have such a one and such a one as witness that the affairs of this pretended saint would end in disgrace, and that some grave offence and enormous crime would be perpetrated by him. On this head they have said,

HEMISTICH.
'The false of heart will be disgraced at last.'

Another said, 'It is strange that, notwithstanding pretensions to religious poverty and pure-mindedness, and the ascetic's garb and good intentions, a person should not be ashamed to adopt perfidy; and strange, too, if this couplet is not inscribed by the tongue of his condition on the page of discourse,

COUPLET.
My pious garb does no such virtue show;
It o'er a hundred hidden faults I'll throw.'

Another, joining in the conversation, in a plausible manner, said, 'This pure and abstemious person, during these many days, used to weep, and

---

[1] I am obliged to use these eleven words to translate *maghlatah*.

externally pretended to regard the administration of public affairs as a calamity, and misery, and misfortune, and trouble; and if, in spite of all this, his perfidy is proved, there will be room for astonishment.' Another said, ' When in such a trifle as this, viz., the portion set apart for the king's breakfast, he could shew his greediness, one may guess what bribes he will have taken in affairs of vital importance, and what enormous sums he must have squandered from the king's treasury.

COUPLET.

The fowler that not sparrows e'en will spare,
Think what he does when game and quails are there!' [1]

When the nobles found the plain of effrontery clear, they began to gallop the steed of abuse, and raised in the expanse of the heart of Kámjúí, the dust of suspicion and doubt. The ministers, too, turning the reins of discourse towards calumny and wicked slander, impressed in the mind of the king some envious and hypocritical remarks.[2] One of them said, ' If this thing turns out true, it will not be simple deceit, but plain proof of ingratitude and treason to his benefactor; and, undoubtedly, by this audacious act he will have thrown contempt on the king, and set aside the imperial honor and dignity.' Another adopted the language of advice and admonition, and said, ' O friends! blacken not the writing of your own proceedings by these fatuous words, and in accordance with the saying, ' *Would any of you desire to eat the flesh of his dead brother?*'[3] do not bite the flesh of your brother with the tooth of reproach. For it may be that the story of his treason is false, and ye will all become criminal and guilty. If the king will at once issue his command that they search his house, the dust of doubt will be removed from the path of truth. For if the flesh be in his dwelling, it will be a clear proof of the truth of these words, and the suspicions of high and low will terminate in conviction. But if it be a palpable calumny, and the lost flesh is not found in his cell, all must loose their tongues in asking forgiveness for their fault, and entreat Farísah to pardon them.' Another said, ' We must make haste if these prudent measures are to be adopted, for his spies surround us on all sides. Every moment he will get intelligence of what is going on, and will neglect no measures that may be required to remedy the matter.' At the conclusion of the debate one of the privy councillors of the king boldly came forward and said, ' What is the advantage of investigating

---

[1] In my copy of the lithographed edition, there is great confusion here. The story of the Fakír and the cup of honey, is inserted here out of its place.

[2] I read with the best MS., *rakami chand az gúnah-i hasad bá zark*, instead of the *rakami chand az har gúnah-i hashw va párah-i zard.*

[3] Kur'án, xlix. 12; Sale, p. 380. l. 24: 'Inquire not too curiously into other men's failings; neither let the one of you speak ill of another in his absence. Would any of you desire to eat the flesh of his dead brother? Surely ye would abhor it.'

this affair, and what is the use of inquiry into this matter? For even, if the crime of that corrupt traitor should be clearly proved, he will by hypocritical and false pretences turn away the mind of the king from inflicting retribution, and will employ some astonishing device, by which he will throw doubt upon all in spite of their certainty in this matter.

COUPLET.

He in evasion has such mighty skill,
He can make doubt look truth-like at his will.'

In short, at this crisis, when the Lion was hungry and furious, they said so much after this fashion, that his heart was penetrated with a feeling of aversion to Farísah, and in accordance with the saying, ' *Whoever listens, doubts,*' various thoughts passed through his mind, and he gave orders to summon Farísah to his presence. That hapless one, unaware of the impression made by the wiles of his enemies, began his return, and as the skirt of his honesty was pure from the stain of this false accusation, he came boldly into the presence of Kámjúí. The Lion asked, ' What hast thou done with the flesh I committed to thy charge yesterday?' Farísah replied, 'I conveyed it to the kitchen, that they might bring it to the king at breakfast-time.' The cook, too, was one of the conspirators. He came forward to deny [what Farísah had said;] and asserted most pertinaciously, 'I know nothing about the circumstance, and thou gavest no flesh to me.' The Lion then sent a party of commissioners, who searched Farísah's abode for the flesh; and, as they had hid it themselves, they soon brought it to light and took it to the Lion. Farísah perceived that his enemies had effected their purpose, and that they had found their opportunity and accomplished an affair, the threads of the counsel of which they had been long weaving. He said to himself,

COUPLET.

' The wall hides now the sunshine of my bliss,[1]
For long long years I feared a day like this.'

And of the number of the vazírs was a wolf, who to that moment had not uttered a word of reproach, and who reckoned himself among the just, and made as though he would not take a step without certain and convincing proof, nor meddle with the matter till he had full cognizance of all the circumstances, and vaunted his friendship for Farísah, and made a strenuous show of protecting him. When these things had taken place he advanced, and, in declaration of his opinion, said, ' O King! the fault of this villain has been found out, and the guilt of this dishonorable wretch has come to light. The king's advisable course is that the command for his punishment should be

---

[1] Lit., ' The sun of my mirth has arrived on the top of the wall.'

carried into execution with all possible despatch ; for, if this be overlooked, other criminals will doubtless be freed from dread of chastisement, and will wax more audacious every moment.

HEMISTICH.

Business would cease if punishment were not.'

The Lion commanded them to remove the Jackal, and plunged into a long and deep meditation. Meanwhile a lynx, who was one of the special favorites of the king, began to say, ' I am astonished at the luminous mind of the king—from the radiance of which the sun acquires its power of diffusing light, and under the defence of which the taper of heaven's dormitory illuminates its face,—as to how the acts of this traitor, and the perfidy of this paltry cheat, have been hid from it, and how unobservant the king has been of the impurity of his foul mind, and the deceitfulness of his wily nature, and why the king delays his execution, notwithstanding such an enormous crime, and such a shameful action, and disturbs with the straw and rubbish of reflection the stream of punishment, by the drops of which the tree of justice is refreshed and invigorated.' Kámjúí, roused by these words, said, ' What hast thou to say ?' The lynx replied, ' O king ! sages have said, ' *He, whose administration is good, his rule will endure ;*' the regulations of a needful severity are the cause of a government's continuance. Whoever draws not out the sword of punishment from the sheath of vengeance cannot repel the arrow of mischief with the shield of defence ; and he who does not hack to pieces the foundation of injustice with the axe of wrath will not be able to plant the seedling of his wishes in the flower-garden of life.

VERSE.

Where laws of wholesome rigor cease to reign,
    The base of safety, too, is overset :
For 'tis from it these gardens fruit obtain
    From the clear fount of righteous strictness wet.

And whoever seeks the king's welfare must inflict punishment on the guilty, nor shew him favor though he be the friend of his heart and the beloved of his soul. As the Sultán of Baghdád, for the public weal, inflicted punishment on his own beloved mistress.' Kámjúí said, ' How was that ?'

STORY III.

The lynx represented, ' They have related that in the capital of China there was a king, who, in observing the canons of justice, had, like Jamshíd, made the world-displaying goblet of reason the mirror of his life ; and, like Alexander, sought for the living waters of equity in his attention to the rules of government.

COUPLET.

From his impartial sway, injustice fled   A hundred leagues, to regions of the dead.

He had a son of fair countenance and sweet disposition, who captured the hearts of mankind with the lasso of suavity, and, with the grain of beneficence and courtesy, brought into the snare of his attachment the birds of the souls of high and low.

COUPLET.

Never did Mother World one of such stainless temper bear,
Nor ever did Time's eye with him one so unmatched compare.

This son formed a desire of seeing the Holy Sanctuary, which is another term for that in the well-known passage, ' *Verily the first house appointed unto men to worship in* [*was that which is in Becca*]*;*'[1] and from the corner of his heart was manifested a strong inclination to circumambulate that most excellent place, round which religious processions move, by which is meant the abode of peace, according to the saying, ' *Whoever entereth therein shall be safe.*[2] Having accepted with the words 'Here I am!' the invitation of the summoner,[3] [who says] '*And proclaim unto the people,*'[4] he formed a fixed determination of entering on a pilgrimage to the sanctuary of the K'abah.

STANZA.

The hope to circumambulate the temple of thy street,
   Consigns a train of pilgrims to the wilderness of care.
Exclaiming, 'Here am I !' we climb, and mount with willing feet
   Upon thy sacred quarters, 'Arafát;[5] and clustering there
A hundred caravans of souls await
The summons, ' Enter ye the holy gate !'

After he had obtained leave to depart from his father, he set off by way of the sea, and embarked with a number of retainers in ships such that the expanse of heaven appeared insignificant in comparison with each vessel, and the page of the sky shewed like a diminutive scrap in juxta-position with a single sail of each barque. They put in motion the footless, water-traversing coursers, and taking up their abode in that wooden house in which the roof was below and the pillar above,[6] they committed the reins of disposal to the rapid wind.

---

[1] Ḳur'án, Fl. iii. 90; Mar. 96; Sale, p. 43, l. 36: 'Say, God is true ; follow ye therefore the religion of Abraham the orthodox ; for he was no idolater. Verily the first house appointed unto men to worship in, was that which is in Becca; blessed and a direction to all creatures.' Becca is another name for Mecca, the Arabs using the *m* and *b* promiscuously in several words.

[2] See the passage of the Ḳur'án quoted above. The next line is, ' Therein are manifest signs : the place where Abraham stood ; and whoever entereth therein shall be safe.'

[3] I would read *dá'i-rá* did the MSS. allow it, governed in the dative by *ijábat zadah.*

[4] Ḳur'án, xxii. 28, Sale, p. 253, l. 28: 'And proclaim unto the people a solemn pilgrimage : let them come unto thee on foot, and on every lean camel, arriving from every distant road; that they may be witnesses of the advantages which accrue to them from the visiting this holy place; and may commemorate the name of God on the appointed days, in gratitude for the brute cattle which he hath bestowed on them.'

[5] 'Arafát is a mountain twelve miles from Makkah, whence pilgrims make a procession to the Holy Monument on another mountain at a little distance. On 'Arafát Adam met Eve after a separation of 200 years.

[6] That is, the deck was below the mast or pillar.

COUPLET.

Moon-like, they in the waters [1] hold their dwelling,
Towards the shore their swift-sailed barques impelling.

Having traversed a distance, in a short time they arrived at the revered Makkah, and having performed the proper ceremonies and rites of the pilgrimage, they bent their steps to kiss the threshold of the sacred Mausoleum of His Highness the Sultán of the throne of prophecy, and the Khákán of the court of honor and majesty.

COUPLET.

That hot-reined, soaring cavalier, he for whose use were given
As leather for his stirrups twain, the expanses nine of heaven.

(May God pour His blessings on Muhammad the chosen, and on his family the pure ones, and on his companions the excellent!) ; and were made felicitous by kissing the sublime court of the Prophet.

COUPLET.

To kiss thy portals' sacred dust, the wish of every saint is this;—
And harder than all hardest things, to lose [2] this long-hoped, much-sought bliss.

And thence they came with a caravan of Khurásán towards Baghdád. The king of that place, hearing an account of the prince, came out to meet him, and observed towards him the respectful and honorific ceremonies which were fitting and requisite, and having prepared for him proper entertainment and allowances, and a suitable place to alight in, he besought him to tarry there certain days. When they had recovered themselves from the fatigue of the journey, and had resolved on returning to their own country, the prince made many apologies to the Sultán for the trouble he had given ; and having replied to his attentions with the gifts of thankfulness and gratitude, sent to his seraglio, by way of present and good-will offering, a Chinese damsel ; and he himself having packed up his traveling effects set out for Khurásán. The Sultán, after the ceremony of accompanying his guest some way on the march, and the discharge of the customs of valediction ; returned to his seraglio, and sent for the damsel. He beheld a form of such beauty that the Limner of Creative Power had never drawn the like on the tablet of existence, nor had the eye of the painter of imagination ever beheld in the volume of fancy so graceful a shape. Her enchanting locks enchained a world with the lasso of mischief, and the world-illuminating moon, from its high station, had painted a diadem on the ground before her face. With one arch movement of her eyebrow, she placed the claims of other pretenders

---

[1] There is an equivoque here, which cannot be retained in English. The *burj-ábí* may mean 'the sign Aquarius,' or 'a mansion in the water.'

[2] Here again is an equivoque not retainable in English. *Khák búsí,* is 'kissing the ground;' and *burdan ba-khák,* lit., 'to bear to the ground,' means—like the German 'zu Grunde gehen,'—'to be ruined or lost.'

to beauty on the shelf of oblivion, and with a single coquettish glance of her half-intoxicated eye, she gave to the wind of inebriation the piety of anchorets.

DISTICHS.

A lamp to lovers, where to couch her cheek;
Her lip, the zest and wine that topers seek.
Her form, the lofty fortune of the just:
Her curls, the shrine that vigil-keepers trust.
Sweeter than sugar, baleful [1] envy owns
Her words. Her lips shame rubies into stones.' [1]

At the graceful movements of that free cypress, the foot of the heart of the king of Baghdád sank in the clay; and by tasting her wine-colored lip, he became intoxicated and bereft of sense without the intervention of wine.

COUPLET.

'Chained to her slender-waisted [2] form,' her captive said, 'I languish,
Ah! to my sorrow-wasted [2] heart what suffering this, and anguish!'

However much the Sultán, who had lost his heart, exerted himself [to escape this thraldom] it was all in vain; and though commanding reason poured the water of admonition on the fire of love, its flame did but blaze forth the more.

COUPLET.

Words will not stanch these flowing tears, nor stay the torrent of these eyes,
And chiding but augments the more the torture of love's agonies.

Giving himself up to the society of the damsel, the Sultán, all at once abandoned the thought of his people's sufferings, and attention to the affairs of the State. And whenever a king engages in dissipation, and ceases to inquire into the condition of the oppressed; and, fixing his ears on the soft sounds of the lute and lyre, listens not to the wailing of each afflicted heart, troubles in a short time arise, and sedition and disorder, growing rampant, the issue of affairs is disastrous to mankind.

VERSE.

When monarchs time in revelry employ,
Then sets the star of their ambitionings.
Libra [3] the constellation is of joy,[3]
And there the planets wane and sink for kings.

Some days passed in this manner, and the Pillars of the State and ministers of the king, distressed at their monarch's indifference, beheld the condition of the city and of the country involved in disorder. A number of them,

---

[1] I have kept the equivoque here more successfully than the extravagance of Persian allusions generally permits: *dar tang mándan*, said of sugar, means, 'to be in a bale,' and signifies generally 'to be distressed;' *dar sang raftan* has the two meanings that 'to be petrified' has in English.

[2] Here again is an equivoque on *tang*, which signifies 'slender' and 'sad.'

[3] *Mízán*, 'Libra,' may also mean 'convivial tables.' I know not if an equivoque is intended.

unfolding the hand of prayer, turned their faces to [ask help of] hermits and saintly men; and soliciting benedictory intercessions from pure-minded darveshes, made offerings for the restoration of the Sultán's state. The prayers of these disinterested personages reached the target of acceptance. At night the Sultán saw, in a dream, one advancing towards him, say,

COUPLET.

'King! if they ask, what will thy answer be,
There, where thou fearest, and where none fear thee?

What thing is this that thou hast taken in hand? and hast withdrawn thy hand from attending to the oppressed. It has almost come to pass that affairs are irremediable and thy empire overthrown. Rise! and betake thyself to thy concerns,

HEMISTICH.

Else coming mischiefs will spring from thyself.'

The king, in terror at this circumstance, awoke. He then performed his ablutions, and loosed his tongue in excusing himself, and praying to be forgiven, and employing himself in remedying the past, issued a command that that damsel should not again intrude on his privacy. And although he could not rest without her, and his heart was never tranquil except in meditating on her beauty, still, through fear of God and dread of the decline of his kingdom, he gave this order. The damsel waited two or three days, and then one night, feeling a longing desire for the king's society, she entered his chamber with a face like a fresh rose-bud [1] which the morning-breeze has caused to blow; and with ringlets like the twisting hyacinths buried in an envelope of purest musk.

VERSE.

With hyacinth and jessamine her perfumed hair was bound,
A posy sweet of violets her clustering ringlets seemed;
Her eyes, with love intoxicate, in witching sleep half drowned,
Her locks to Indian spikenard like, with love's enchantments [2] beamed.

Again at sight of her beauty the king was despoiled of his senses, and tumultuous love robbed him of his reason and understanding.

COUPLET.

Now love returned, and madness came again,
And her arch looks again inflict sweet pain.

For several days more he remained captivated by her beauty, and infatuated with her locks and mole,[3] passed his time in delights; and again

---

[1] *Gul-barg*, 'rose-leaf;' but *shiguftah* will hardly apply to a leaf. However, Persian writers care little for such inconsistencies.

[2] Lit. 'From desire her Indian spikenard in a twist.' I commend this to the lovers of purely literal translation.

[3] The mole takes a conspicuous place in the enumerations of the beauties of a Persian mistress. Ḥáfiz tells us he would give Bukhárá and Samarḳand (as we should say Vienna and Paris) for the mole of his fair one.

the messengers of the invisible world summoned him with infallible warnings
to the path of rectitude.   The king came to himself and said, 'There is no
remedy for my sufferings but to get rid of this mischief, and no hope of a
cure for my affairs save in the annihilation of this calamity.'   Hereupon he
commanded a chamberlain saying, 'Take this disobedient damsel, who without
permission entered my chamber, and cast her into the Tigris.'   The chamberlain led the damsel away, and reflected thus with himself: 'This is the
beloved mistress of the king, and perhaps to-morrow he may repent and
require her of me again.   Then if I have put her to death, the hand of
thought will not reach the skirt of remedy.'   He therefore concealed her in
his house.   The king, who was sad at what he had done, when he returned
from his seat in the public hall into his private apartments, was overcome
with the desire of seeing his mistress, and tortured with regret.   Again
reproaching himself, he allayed the ferment of his mind with the arguments of
reason. One night, to dispel his grief, he quaffed a goblet of pure wine, and
forgetting the admonitions of reason and the warnings of prudence, became
impatient at the recollection of his enchanting fair one.   Summoning his high
chamberlain, he inquired into the fate of his beloved, and said with the most
terrible threats, 'If thou bringest her not here this night I will bring thee
to punishment.'   However much the chamberlain began to excuse himself, it
was all in vain, and beholding the dreadful wrath of the king he saw himself
on the verge of destruction.   Through necessity therefore he conveyed the
moon-like beauty to the king's chamber.   Again the foundation of delight
was laid, and the materials of mirth set ready.

VERSE.

We're here, 'tis night—our mistress is before us,
    The cup is near, the wine of rosy hue.
The flowers bloom and autumn has passed o'er us,
    Hail, joyous spring ! and winter sad, Adieu !

In short, three times the king commanded her to be slain, and the
chamberlain acting cautiously, delayed the execution.   At last the affairs
of the state came to a complete stand.   The Sultán perceived that there was
no remedy for this calamity but from his own hand, and that he could not
hope to get rid of this misfortune by the aid of another.

HEMISTICH.

'No other's hand can manage this affair.'

For he saw that whomsoever he might command to slay the damsel would
assuredly, out of caution, delay the execution.   Therefore the king prepared
himself to put her out of the way, yet he was unwilling to destroy any one
openly, without some palpable treason on their part.   At last, one day,
standing on the terrace of his palace, he was gazing on the Tigris, and the

damsel, in attendance on him, was contemplating from a distance the beauty of the king. The Sultán, dreading the future, reflected on the fatal consequences of his supineness. He saw that the time was come, and said to himself, 'Though I bring on my head innocent blood, yet a hundred thousand hearts will be solaced which now by my neglect of them, are immersed in blood. And though this girl is dear to me as my life, yet it is of still greater importance to have regard to the condition of my distressed people.' He then bade her approach nearer to look at a vessel. When the damsel had come close, the king gave her a push, and threw her into the Tigris; and evincing much grief, gave out as though she had of herself fallen into the water. He then commanded them to draw her out of the river, and burying her, and beginning to mourn for her, he fulfilled the most rigorous conditions of that rite. Thus, for the public weal, he with his own hand, took away the life of her whom he adored.

HEMISTICH.

For one good end kings will a hundred slay.'

And I have adduced this story in order that the king may know that it is better to take care of the welfare of the state than to shew indulgence to one traitor, and more advisable to remove one person whose existence is a general injury, than to exclude a thousand others.' By these wily insinuations the fire of the lion's wrath was kindled, and he sent a message to Farísah, 'If thou hast any excuse to offer for this offence, make it known.' As Farísah was innocent, and [as it is true what] they have said, 'When a man's hand is short, his tongue is long;

HEMISTICH.

The innocent are ever fearless found,'

he sent back a rough message, and his reproachful words did but help the mischievous flatteries of his opponents. The fire of Kámjúí's wrath rose higher, and putting aside all covenants and promises, he gave a positive order to put Farísah to death. They conveyed tidings of this to the mother of the Lion, who saw that he was acting precipitately, and had disregarded clemency and forbearance, and exchanged patience and calmness for levity and precipitation. She thought to herself, 'I must go with all speed and release my son from the temptations of the accursed devil. For whenever anger gets the mastery over kings, Satan bears sway over them, and leads them to do whatever he wishes; and the same meaning may be understood from the import of the true tradition, ' *When the sultán is furious, the devil exercises dominion over him.*'

COUPLET.

Wrath is a flame from Satan that proceeds,
And in the end it to repentance leads.'

First of all she despatched some one to the executioner, saying, 'Pause ere thou slayest the Jackal, until I speak to the Lion.'   She then came to Kámjúí, and said 'O son, I have heard that thou hast given orders to put Farísah to death.   What was his crime? and what fault has he committed?'   The Lion recounted the circumstances.   His mother said, 'O son! cause not thyself to wander in the wilderness of perplexity, nor exclude thyself from the quality of justice and beneficence.   And the wise have said, 'Eight things depend on eight things.   The honor of a wife on her husband; and the reputation of a son on his father; and the knowledge of a pupil on his teacher; and the strength of an army on its general; and the spiritual gifts of religious men on their faith; and the security of subjects on their king; and the government of a king on justice; and the excellence of justice on reason and vigilance.   Now the principal things in this matter are two.   One is to know one's followers and attendants, and to place each in the position proper for him, and to promote him in proportion to his ability and skill.   The second point is, to suspect them in what concerns one another, for there is a constant strife between those who are most in favour at the courts of kings, which cannot be extinguished except by their utter annihilation.   Wherefore if the King listens to the accusations of one against the other, and attends to the calumnies of that one with reference to this, there will be no more confidence between the Sultán and the Pillars of the State.   Hence whenever they wish they will be able to bring a loyal servant under suspicion, and trick out a traitor in the garb of loyalty.   Consequently the innocent are overtaken in the whirlpool of calamity, and the guilty pass their time on the shore of escape in safety and security.

COUPLET.

> Broken-hearted in their prison languish all the innocent;
> While the guilty stand afar off ever smiling and content.

And without doubt, the result of this procedure will be that those present will decline office, and the absent will hang back;[1] and the execution of the supreme commands will be delayed, and a thousand embarrassments will accrue to the Pillars of the State; and the ill consequences which proceed from this are beyond the limits of computation, and exceed the power of reckoning.

STANZA.

> Let not the ear to selfish men be lent,
>   For they will injure both the faith and State.
> As sycophants through thee grow eminent,
>   So will thy greatness and thy power abate.
> If to the envious thou dost yield consent,
>   Of thy free-will thou ceasest to be great.'

---

[1] This appears to be the meaning of *taḳa'ud namúdan* here, and indeed I find it given on the margin of one of the MSS.

The Lion said, 'I have not been induced by any one's words to issue this command with reference to Farísah. Nay, my disposition towards him was unchanged, until his treason was palpable.' The lioness replied, 'It is not right for kings to alter their minds, especially with reference to the confidential advisers of the court, without perfect certainty. And as to what thou saidst that his treason was fully proved, this matter is still veiled in doubt; and the truth will then be evident when the curtain falls from the face of this affair. And it was but fitting that thou shouldest have found room in the amplitude of thy clemency for so slight a fault which they impute to Farísah on suspicion; and that thou shouldest have kept in full view of thy mind his previous services; and the virtuous efforts and illustrious acts which he performed at the door of this palace ought not to have been effaced from the tablet of thy memory; nor ought the words of those devoid of merit, unattested, to have met with a favorable hearing as to the meritorious of approved capacity.

VERSE.

The mean man grudges others their success,
And so the miser would the fly expel
From the same cup. Endless the tricks, finesse,
That knaves who neither act nor prosper well
Will try, lest fortune should true merit bless.

O son! we ought to recognise, in all circumstances that occur, and in all events that take place, far-sighted reason and world-adorning judgment as a just oracle and perfect discriminator: for the excellence of man's nature is ennobled by the clearness of his intellect.

COUPLET.

Of human greatness reason is the base,
'Tis this exalts the rank of Adam's race.

And Farísah had reached in thy court a high station and exalted rank, and had attained great eminence and lofty position. In public assemblies thou wast accustomed to speak in his praise, and in private thou honoredst him by taking counsel with him. Now, it behoves thee to break thy resolve of violating thy covenant, and not to exert thyself for the destruction of the base of that edifice which thou hast erected with the hand of thy own encouragement; and to guard thyself from the exultation of enemies and the rejoicing of the envious, so that, as is required by thy grave and dignified position, having judged it necessary to make due investigation, and, having practised caution and employed inquiry to the fullest extent, thou mayest be excused in the eye of reason, and be clear in the opinion of the wise from the stain of false accusation. And this crime which they impute to him is too paltry for a wise man like him to soil with its dust the mirror of uprightness, and to defile the skirt of honesty with the impurities of trifles such as these. And

2 κ

I know that greed and appetite could not overcome his abstinence and contentment; and that covetousness and lust could not gallop the steed of hope in the plain of his vision and knowledge. Moreover, during this long period that Farísah has been an attendant of this court he has never eaten flesh; and, previous to that, too, he was famed and celebrated for this quality. His abstaining from eating animal food was in every mouth, and had reached all ears.

HEMISTICH.

Not so prolonged would vain words be.

And the probability is that enemies put the flesh in Farísah's abode. And it is not to be supposed that this is too much for the deceit of the fraudulent, or the envy of the invidious to effect. For among the envious there has been one who, in expectation that it might be injurious to another, was a consenting party to his own death, as that wretched merchant ordered the slave to kill him.' The Lion requested to know, 'How was that?'

STORY IV.

The lioness said, 'They have related that there was in Baghdád an envious man, who had a neighbor a poor man and a pious, who passed his days in traversing the waste of fasting with the step of abstinence, and his nights in traveling the roads of worship by the path of nocturnal prayer and spiritual conflict.

COUPLET.

His heart, a lamp of love, he did illume;
And every other thing, save God, consume.

The inhabitants of Baghdád turned the face of confidence towards that holy man, and his goodness was talked of in their assemblies and public meetings and the great men of the city used to notice him kindly and by way of present, and, to secure his blessing, used to send offerings of money and goods to him. On these several accounts the envious man envied his good neighbor, and made various attempts to injure him, but every arrow of deceit which he discharged from the bow of calumny was rendered nugatory by the shield of innocence and the armor of piety. At last he was reduced to despair about this, and was utterly wearied. He then bought a slave, and made a point of according to him all possible kindnesses and rewards, and fulfilled all the requirements of compassionate feeling and care towards him. He used constantly to say, 'I am cherishing thee for a particular object, and bringing thee up for a thing of the greatest importance, and I hope that thou wilt extricate my heart from that load, and free my sad soul from that care.

COUPLET.

With the tears I fondly cherish, with the pangs that wring my frame,
I am hopeful, yes! I feel that I shall quench this cruel flame.

After a considerable time had passed, and the slave became firmly obedient, and submissively disposed, he several times begged with the tongue of entreaty to undertake the promised affair, and to enter upon the business in which the wish of his master was contained, and said, 'I am not able to express by the force of language the various favors and kindnesses which thou hast lavished on this helpless person, nor by the aid of description can I distinctly set forth the condescending attentions and benefits with which thou hast distinguished this humble slave.

COUPLET.

Thy favor makes thy slave a lily seem,
Each limb a tongue of praise, and thou the theme.

I desire, in return for these demonstrations of kindness, that I may shew my devotion, and perform service in requital of these benefits.

COUPLET.

The coin of life I'll sacrifice for thee,   And for thy ends my soul shall offered be.'

When the master saw that his slave aimed at shewing his gratitude and was ambitions of proving his attachment, he raised the curtain from before the affair and said, 'Know and understand that I am tired of my life by reason of this neighbor of mine, and I wish by some means or other to bring a misfortune upon him. In spite of all the artifices I have set on foot, and the expedients I have contrived, the arrow of my counsel has not reached the target of desire; and the fire of envy blazes forth every moment in my heart and makes life odious to me. And from chagrin on his account I loathe the enjoyments of life, and am disgusted with my own existence. I have cherished thee during this long interval, that thou mayest this night kill me on my neighbor's terrace, and leave me there and depart; in order that, when they see me there in the morning a corpse, they may, as of course they will, apprehend him on suspicion of the murder; and so he will be despoiled of his property and life, and his character for goodness and virtue will be destroyed, and men's faith in him will end in being marred, and he will no longer be able to boast of his piety and austerity. And to men's sorrow the meaning of this couplet will come true with regard to him, in that they have said,

COUPLET.

The pious man affects too much: O God! his curtain draw away,
And to the world his hidden vice and naughtiness display.'

The slave replied, ' O master! relinquish this thought, and set about managing this affair differently; and if thy wish is to get rid of the holy man, I will slay him, and will set thy heart at ease with regard to him.' The master rejoined, ' That is a complicated and long affair. Perhaps

2 K 2

thou mayest not get him into thy power, nor be able to kill him so quickly, and I have no more patience or endurance left. Arise! and perform this service, and make me satisfied with myself; and lo! I hand over to thee a writing of manumission, and I give thee a purse of gold, with which thou wilt be able to support thyself all thy life, that thou mayest depart from this city, and take up thy abode in another country.' The slave replied, 'O master! no wise man entertains this thought which thou hast formed; and no one who has drawn in the perfume of good sense, sets forth such a scheme as thou hast set forth. For the misfortune of an enemy may, indeed, be desirable in one's lifetime; but when thou hast passed beyond the circle of existence, what gratification will there be to thee from his execution? and what advantage from his being racked and imprisoned?

COUPLET.

Bid the tulip cease to grow when I have left the gay parterre;
Cypress! wave not in the garden, when I am no longer there.'

However much he spake after this fashion, it was of no avail; and, when the slave saw that his master's inclinations lay that way, he cut off his head on the terrace of his neighbor's house, and left his body, which was a disgrace to the expanse of creation, in that spot, and taking his deed of manumission and the bag of dínárs, he set off for Iṣfahán, and took up his residence in that abode of peace. The next day they found the malevolent merchant lying slain on the terrace of the good man. Thereupon, they seized the latter and detained him in prison. However, as the murder of the accursed envious man was not proved according to law against him, and the majority of the notables and other inhabitants of Baghdád gave their testimony to his virtuous and blameless conduct, no one opposed his acquittal. Still they did not remove his fetters, and he remained for some time imprisoned in the same manner. After an interval, a merchant of distinction saw the slave in Iṣfahán, who asked about the family of his master, and also about the neighbor's. In the midst of the conversation, they came to speak of that good man and his imprisonment. The slave said, 'A strange and cruel injustice has been inflicted on that innocent person. The fact is, the thing was done by me at the command and order of my master, and that holy man is quite ignorant of the whole transaction.' He then detailed all the circumstances, and the rich merchant took a number of persons to witness what he had said; and, on their return to Baghdád, they recounted the story of what had taken place, and the particulars of what had occurred. Thus that true believer obtained his release, and the envious man became a mark for the arrow of execration; while his pious neighbor uttered, with the tongue of his circumstances, this exulting stanza, which is the produce of the mind of an eminent personage,

STANZA.

'Some rude ones, moved with envy, on my name
  Did slanderous breathe, and their foul falsehoods, like
A forge, made hot.   In error's night, the same
  Did, with fraud's bow and envy's arrow, strike
The hair of selfish aims.   Yet to me came
  From all their labors good in place of ill,
  While their bad deeds were worse rewarded still.'

And I have adduced this story in order that the king may condescend to
perceive what actions are done by envious men, and when their feelings
towards one another are such, how can birds high in the air, and fishes down
in the sea, and beasts in the expanse of the wild plain, be safe from the
assaults of the malevolent?   And those of thy attendants are not far to seek,
who are now inferior to Farísah in dignity, and before held a more honorable
position than he does, who have probably contrived a scheme against him,
and stir up this treason to degrade him.   Pause in thy haste and in these
precipitate measures, and adopt a merciful and dignified procedure, and
deliberate well in this affair, planning its remedy in a manner becoming thy
greatness.   Since to-day thou hast pulled in the reins of punishment, and
to-morrow the real state of the case will be known and its details understood,
one of two things must follow.   If he was not worthy of death thou hast
exercised a merciful intervention in his behalf, and not impressed on the
volume of thy acts innocent blood.   While if, in fact, he deserves to be
slain, the option is left and there is no excuse for delaying his punishment.

Thou mayst the live man put to death; but, slain,
Thou canst not him resuscitate again.'

The Lion listened to the words of his mother, and having weighed them
in the scales of reason, perceived that they contained advice free from selfish
ends, and admonition adorned with the ornament of benevolence.   He
delayed the punishment and commanded them to bring Farísah into the
presence, and having summoned him to a private audience, said, 'I have
tried thee before and seen and approved thy qualities and dispositions, and
thy words find more acceptance with me than the speeches of thy enemies
and of those who envy thee.   Return again to the discharge of thy duties,
and as to what thou hast said or heard in what has taken place, grieve not
over it nor think of it.'   Farísah said, 'Although the king has spread the
shade of his favor on the head of my condition ,and manifested towards me all
the bounty that kings can evince, nevertheless, I cannot emerge from the
chagrin of this calumny, save when the king thinks of a remedy and devises
an expedient, that the real truth of the affair and the exact state of the case
may be known.   Notwithstanding that I am assured of my own perfect
honesty, and have the most perfect security in the verdict of acquittal, which

my own heart supplies, yet the more cautious the scrutiny your majesty may
be pleased to use, the more apparent will be my sincerity and uprightness.
And I know that my advantage and welfare is bound up in this matter.

COUPLET.

Grieve not, my heart! for gibes of envious men ;
There may be good here if thou look'st again.'

Kámjúí said, 'In what manner can inquiry be made? and by what
expedient can the investigation be carried on?' Farísah replied, 'The
parties who made the false accusation must be brought hither, and your
majesty must, in the way of searching inquiry, demand of them what they
meant by accusing me in particular of this treason, when I have not eaten
flesh for years, and passing over those who eat flesh and cannot do without
it. And assuredly when the king is urgent in inquiring into this point, they
will give the true account of it. And if they are contentious, by terrifying
them with threats of punishment, intelligence may be obtained of the particulars; or if that, too, fails, by holding out hopes of mercy and promising
favors, the veil of doubt may be removed from the face of certainty; so that
my innocence and unstained honor will be clear to all the court.

COUPLET.

Each secret that lies veiled beneath the night,
When day appears, will all be brought to light.'

Kámjúí said, 'I will inquire the state of the case of them by threatening
them with punishment, not by promising them pardon and indulgence, for
clemency must not be expended in the case of one who acknowledges malice
and envy towards my confidant and trusted minister.' Farísah said, 'In
all cases where pardon is bestowed by those invested with absolute authority
and power, it is rightly bestowed, as it is said, 'Forgiveness is to be found with
power.' The right method of action is, to pass over the offence of an
adversary even when we have complete power over him. For the obtaining
power over an adversary is an estimable blessing, and our gratitude for such
a blessing can only be shewn by pardon and forgiveness of his fault.

COUPLET.

Has victory o'er a foe thy struggles blessed?
Then by forgiveness be thy thanks expressed.'

When Kámjúí had heard the words of Farísah, and beheld the marks of
truth and right counsel impressed on the pages of those words; he sent
separately for each of those parties who had stirred up this dust of mischief,
and used the most strenuous exertions, even to the limit of excess, to discover what was concealed, and to develope the intricate points. Moreover
he urged them much, with the promise that, if they would state the truth,
the pages of their offences should be washed with the water of forgiveness ;
and, in addition, they should also be rewarded with honors and gifts

from the king. At last some of them acknowledged the facts, and the rest, too, being compelled to confess, disclosed truthfully the real state of the case. Thus the sun of the integrity of Farísah came forth from under the cloud of doubt, and the dust of uncertainty was removed from before the eye of conviction.

HEMISTICH.

We 've tried it, and the state of each is known.

The mother of the Lion said, ' O my son ! thou hast granted immunity to this faction, and to recall it is impossible ; but let this be an example to thee, whence thou oughtest to take warning, and hereafter not open the ear of attention to the slanders of any calumniator. Nor till clear proof and demonstration of positive certainty is obtained, which may release thee from doubt, must thou listen to the idle tales of interested persons, nor assent to what they may say of the faults of another, however pithy[1] and laconic their words may appear. For a thing of little magnitude, by degrees, reaches such a point that the remedy of it does not come within the sphere of possibility. And the source of great rivers, like the Nile, and the Euphrates, and the Jaihún, and the Tigris, is but a very small spring, which by the accession of other waters reaches that magnitude that it is impassable save in ships. Wherefore it is necessary to keep back words, whether trifling or the reverse, that are uttered in defamation of any one, and to close the path to the remarks of others that the conclusion of the affair may not terminate in mischief.

COUPLET.

A spade may, at its head, the new-born stream restrain,
Which, full, an elephant would try to ford in vain.'[2]

Kámjúí replied, ' I accept this advice, and I perceive that without clear proof it is not good to suspect any one.' His mother answered, ' O king! the person who, without evident cause, is angry with his friends, is one of those eight classes of people of whose society sages have commanded us to beware.' Kámjúí replied, ' Recount to me the detail of this classification.' The lioness continued, ' The wise have traced on the leaves of the pages of admonition that it is proper to shun the society of eight classes, and equally incumbent on us to converse and associate with eight other classes. However, the eight persons from whose intercourse we ought to pluck the skirt of agreement are as follows :—The first, is he who does not recognize the debt he owes to benefactors for benefits received, and stigmatizes himself by ingratitude and unthankfulness. The second, is he who is angry without cause, and whose anger overpowers his gentler feelings. The third, is he who

---

[1] *Mújiz va mukhtaṣar*. I doubt the meaning of these words here. ' Trifling and unimportant' would suit the context better.

[2] These lines are quoted from the ' Gulistán ' of S'adí. See my Translation, p. 39, l. 11, where they are rendered somewhat differently.

through long life becomes proud, and thinks himself freed from the necessity of discharging his duty to his Creator and his fellow-creatures. The fourth, is he who bases his proceedings on perfidy and deceit, and in whose sight these qualities appear venial. The fifth, is he who opens up to himself the path of falsehood and perfidy, and who withdraws from truth and uprightness. The sixth, is he who gives a swing to his appetite in matters of licentiousness, and accounts sensual gratification as the principal object [1] of his wishes, and the K'abah of his hopes. The seventh, is he who is characterised by a deficiency of modesty, and conducts himself with impudence and disrespect. The eighth, is he who is causelessly suspicious of persons, and who, without clear proof and demonstration, distrusts the wise. But the eight persons with whom we ought to unite, and whose society we ought to regard as a blessing, are the following :—First, he who regards it as a duty to be thankful for kindness, and who is careful to discharge the duties which he finds devolve upon him. The second, is he the knot of whose friendship and the promise of whose attachment is not broken by the accidents of fortune and the vicissitudes of uncertain time. The third, is he who feels it incumbent on him to shew respect to men of education and honor, and is disposed to reward and requite them by word and deed. The fourth, is he who keeps himself from perfidy, and lying, and pride, and haughtiness. The fifth, is he who is able to control himself in the moment of anger. The sixth, is he who raises the standard of generosity, and who exerts himself to the utmost in obtaining the wishes of the hopeful. The seventh, is he who clings to the train of modesty and honor, and never oversteps the line of good manners. The eighth, is he who is by nature the friend of good and virtuous men, and shuns the debauched and irreligious. And whoever associates and unites with this class that has been mentioned, and who shuns and avoids the parties that have been named before, by the blessing of the said associates the defect of objectionable qualities diminishes in him, and his temperament approximates to the true equilibrium : for when vinegar, with all the sharpness and sourness that is natural to it, is mixed with honey, it escapes from its original acidity, and becomes the means of dispelling so many ailments.[2]

STANZA.

Go! and, like vinegar, thy acid blend
  With honey, and, disease expelling, so
Make glad the soul. Seek a life-valued friend,
  And be not dead of heart, for thou shalt grow
Reanimate through him that is thy life. Attend,
  Like their own shadow, on the good ; which done,
Fame, round the earth shall bear thee like the sun.'

---

[1] Lit., 'point to which the face is turned in prayer.'
[2] The drink *sikanjabín* 'oxymel,' is here alluded to, which according to Oriental writers is good to cure biliousness, etc.

When the Lion saw the results of the care[1] and the excellence of the intervention of his mother in obviating this embarrassment, and remedying what had happened, after performing what gratitude and thankfulness prescribed, he said, 'O queen of the age! by the blessed influences of thy admonitions and the favors of thy advice,

COUPLET.

Light in the way that had grown dark, has shone,
And things once difficult, have easy grown,

and an able minister and faithful officer has emerged from the whirlpool of calumny, and I have acquired information as to the character of each of my attendants, and I shall know hereafter what kind of treatment to adopt towards each of them, and how to commence in rejecting or accepting their words.' His confidence in Farísah then increased, and having offered many apologies, and shewn him much courtesy, he called him before him and said, 'Thou must regard this aspersion as the cause of an increase of my confidence, and the source of an augmentation of my reliance in thee, and thou canst continue the superintendence of the affairs, which was committed to thee, according to the former fashion.' Farísah replied, 'This does not come right so, nor is the knot of my affairs loosened by these caresses. The king slighted his former promises, and gave to the accusations of my enemies a firm place in his mind.[2]

QUATRAIN.

Thou! who hast from thy heart expunged all truth,
And sided wholly with my enemies,
If this the love thou show'st to all—in sooth
There breathes not one worth loving in thy eyes.'

Kámjúí replied, 'Thou must not take to heart any of these things, for neither didst thou fall short in thy service, nor I fail in my regard. Be of good cheer! and betake thyself to thy duties with the fullest reliance on my protection.' Farísah replied,

HEMISTICH.

'Fresh head and turban are not mine each day.

This time I have escaped, but the world is not void of envious and slanderous persons, and as long as the favor of the king towards me continues, the envy of the malignant will be unchanged. Moreover, from the king having listened to my calumniators to the extent that he has, my enemies have learned, that he is easily won over. They will therefore every moment get ready some new embroilment, and will incessantly thrust in their insinuations; and every king that has lent his ear to the words of the

---

[1] One MS. reads *mauk' i-i iḥtimám*.

[2] As I can make nothing of the reading of the editions here, I read with the best MS. I have, *va maḥál-i dushmandn-rá dar zamír tamakkun dád*, which is simple and intelligible.

mischievous traducer, and given heed to the falsehoods and wiles of the backbiter and defamer, his service is a risking of life; and to sport with one's life is not the habit of the wise.

HEMISTICH.

My life will not be re-bestowed each day.

And if the king's judgment sees fit, I will, by a single word, make my excuse for declining service clear.' The king said, 'Say on.' Farísah continued, ' In that the king showed compassion upon me in this occurrence, and placed fresh confidence in me, and even augmented his former trust in me, he has acted with graciousness and indulgence, and that may be regarded as a surpassing blessing, and a favor exceeding description. But in that he issued his command for my punishment,[1] with such rash haste and without inquiry being made, he displayed such precipitancy, that I have lost my confidence in his royal generosity, and have ceased to hope in his imperial kindness and infinite compassion. For he causelessly cancelled his former favors, and unreasonably obliterated my previous services, and on a false accusation—and that too of such a paltry nature that had it been proved would not have deserved such importance to be attached to it—authorised a cruel punishment. Now a king ought to be such that even a gross act of treason would not sully the quality of his mercy, like the King of Yaman,[2] who, notwithstanding an offence of the gravest nature, did not disgrace his Chamberlain, and covered his bad action with the veil of clemency.'   Kámjúí inquired, ' How was that?'

STORY V.

Farísah said, ' They have related that in the capital of Yaman there was a king, from whose clear countenance beamed the light of the morning of justice, and on the face of whose acts and the forehead of whose desires the rays of the light of equity were manifest.

VERSE.

A king, that heaven in his court's way showered,
From bright Orion and the Pleiades,
Largesse. Like Kisra, or like Kai, empowered
He banqueted. Obeyed were his decrees,
Like those of Farídún. Most blest his tread
[Success and fortune followed where he led].

One day he was displeased with his Chamberlain and forbade him his palace.[3] The hapless Chamberlain had not fortitude to meet the eye of the king, and yet thought it not advisable to depart from that city. Compelled

---

[1] The printed edition omits va after siydsat-i man, and thus the sense of the passage is lost.
[2] Yaman = Arabia Felix.
[3] Observe the phrase, khdnah bar vai zindan sákht.

by necessity he remained seated in the corner of his house, and was at one time weeping over the embarrassment of his affairs, at another laughing at the marvelous vicissitudes of fortune.

COUPLET.

In weeping for my piteous state the livelong night I thus beguile,
I now like wasting taper weep, anon, I tearful sadly smile.

At last from the deficiency of means, and his numerous family, and the embarrassment caused by their utter destitution, he came to the conclusion that he ought to convey himself into the king's presence, either that his neck might meet the sword of punishment, or his head be adorned with the diadem of acceptance. One day, when the king had a great entertainment and there was a general levée, the Chamberlain sent to all his friends, and having borrowed a horse and a robe, sate thereon, and entered the king's palace. The warders and chamberlains supposed that the king had renewed his favor towards him, and that they had given the steed and the robe to him by command of the Sultan; wherefore no one opposed his entrance. So the Chamberlain boldly entered the court and stood in his proper place. Now the king had taken his seat at a banquet of wine, and was indulging in mirth with his guests. When he saw the Chamberlain, the fire of wrath began to blaze forth; and the executioner, Anger, demanded the chastisement of the offender. Again, on reflection, he was unwilling to disturb the convivial meeting, and to exchange the enjoyment of the sweet wine for the ennui of vexation and annoyance. His natural clemency sought to get the preference by pardoning the crime, and his innate generosity viewed the offence as not committed.

HEMISTICH.

Drink wine, be kind, and trust the rest to me.

When the Chamberlain looked on the face of the king, and found the freshness of his mirth and his hilarity unchanged, he applied himself busily to his duties; and having tightly bound the skirt of service on the waist of attendance, he lent a hand in everything that was being done, and engaged in every duty; until, having obtained a good opportunity, he concealed under his tunic a golden dish, which weighed a thousand miṣkáls. The king perceived that action of his, and understood that narrowness of means and his distressed condition were the cause of this boldness. He therefore deputed clemency to conceal that offence. At the end of the party, those who had charge of the dishes were making search and accusing the people, and their aim was to extract a confession from them by intimidation and threats. The king asked one of the grandees, 'What has happened to these people that they are in such excessive perturbation?' The nobleman represented the matter as it was. The king said, 'Let these people go, for they have not got the dish. He who has it, will not give it back; and he who saw it

will not tell.' The Chamberlain went out and supported himself for a year
on the price of that dish. The next year, at the very same time, there was
a special banquet and a general levée. Again the Chamberlain introduced
himself in the crowd. The king called him up and whispered to him, 'Is
the dish all spent?' The Chamberlain turned the face of supplication
towards the ground, and said,

COUPLET.

'O happy prince! be evil eyes from thy moon's fortune far away!
And thy life's mansion to all time replenished and abundant stay.

What I did was for a set purpose, and I thought that the king would
see me, or some other would detect it, and convey me to punishment; for,
from the sufferings of hunger, I was sick of my life. While, if what I did,
remained under the veil of concealment, at least I should secure food for
some days. These were my feelings, and I am certain that the truth of my
statement will not remain hidden in the mirror of the most luminous mind.

COUPLET.

That heart-irradiating lamp full well my pain and anguish knows;
And in this plaint its pure idea a witness to my sufferings shews.[1]

The king replied, 'Thou speakest truth, and there is room for commiseration in thy case.' He then bestowed on him marks of his favor, and
committed to him the same post which he formerly held.

Now the object of citing this story is to shew that the heart of the king
ought to be like the billowy sea, so as not to be discolored by the dirt and
rubbish of calumny; and the centre of his clemency should be like the stately
mountain, firm in a position of stability, so that the furious wind of anger
cannot move it.

VERSE.

Not with good minds does wrath assimulate;
Nor in hot places will the citrul grow.
Crumbling to dust, vile things their former state
Abandon; while the mountains undergo
No change; but as they were, continue so.'

The Lion responded, 'Thy words are true, but bitter and rough. Now
an antidote ought to be sweet, that the patient may find it easy to swallow;
and it is possible that the mind of a sick person may loathe a nauseous
medicine, even though he knows that his recovery depends upon it, and hence
he remains excluded from the blessing of health.

COUPLET.

Who, by sweet speech, could win our hearts to mirth,
Why should his mouth to tart response give birth?'

---

[1] This English may appear devoid of meaning, but it is a literal translation. The
original idea is so strained as to be almost unintelligible.

Farísah replied, 'The king's heart is rougher in confirming falsehood, than my words in uttering truth. And since he hears with facility deceit and slander, it would be better if the listening to what is true and wholesome, were not so displeasing to him. Nor, I pray, let him impute this speech to boldness and disrespect, for it comprehends two things of the utmost utility. The first is, that those who have been unjustly treated, find a relief in appealing and in venting their grief, and their minds are cleansed from the dust of grief in lamenting and exclaiming against oppresssion. Moreover, it is better that I should disclose all that is in my heart, that present or absent I may be the same to the king, and that nothing may remain that in future may rankle into hostility. The second thing is, that I wished that the sagacious judgment and world-adorning justice of the king should pronounce on this case. But the decision could be pronounced only after hearing the statement of the injured person; consequently, it appeared imperative, that the latter should state the case of his wrongs to the physician of the court of justice.

HEMISTICH.

How can one hide his ailment from the leech ?'

Kámjúí replied, 'The case is so; but in liberating thee from this whirlpool, we conferred on thee an infinite benefit; and liberation from the vortex of destruction, after the order for punishment had been issued, is a more manifest favor and a more thorough instance of bounty.' Farísah rejoined, 'As long as life lasts I shall be unable to return thanks for the kindness of the king, nor in ages could I acquit myself of my debt to the royal beneficence; and this pardon and condonation after the order for retribution and chastisement, surpasses all other favors; for other benefits have relation only to the sustenance of the body, while this is the cause of tranquillity as regards life itself.

COUPLET.

With favor on my life and heart thou didst thy look of kindness cast;
My life is pledged to gratitude, and my heart, blushing, owns the past.

And before this, too, I was always the king's sincere, obedient, loyal, and attached servant, and I considered my life and soul due as a sacrifice to obtain his approval and to execute his commands; and what I now say, is not to attach blame to the king's judgment in this affair, or to reproach his prudence and wisdom; but it is an enduring custom, and an inveterate habit, for the ignorant to envy those who possess merit and ability, and it appears impossible to close the path of envy from reaching the eminent and wise.

HEMISTICH.

The rose of worth and merit blooms not free from envy's rankling thorn.

And an eminent personage has said on this subject,

STANZA.

'Some worthless fellow may speak ill of me,
  'Tis that my merit does his soul distress;
Little care I that men should envious be,
  Who is not envied can no worth possess.'

And from the sage's blessing, '*Return envied*,' the same subtle sense is intelligible.' Kámjúí said, 'What need one care for the envy of foes and the machinations of the envious? for false words carry no weight[1] with them, and the schemes of the worthless, with respect to the excellencies of people of merit, are like an obscure star in the Lesser Bear in the sun's splendor, which causes it to remain hid. Falsehood is always defeated and truth triumphant, according to the saying, '*And the word of God is triumphant :*' the glory of the wise man is not broken by the breach of the envious person, nor is the innocent man stained by the calumnies of the defamer.

STANZA.

What if a worthless foe should thee defame ?
  Copper can never take the place of gold.
In spite of taunts obscure, the sun will flame
  With equal brightness. When will pebbles hold
The market-price that gems can justly claim ?

And be thou henceforward secure, that the mischievous attempts of the envious cannot injure thee, for I have learned the truth of their interested remarks, and will not meet them with assent.' Farísah replied, 'In spite of all this, I fear lest, God forbid! my enemies should find an opportunity of interfering between us, not by envy, but by way of advice.' The Lion asked, 'In what manner can they interfere ?' Farísah answered, 'They will say, 'In the heart of such a one alarm has sprung up, inasmuch as thou didst give an order for his punishment; and his brain has become intoxicated with pride, because thou hast augmented thy favor towards him, and at this very time he feels himself wronged by your majesty; and one whose suspicions are excited is not fit to be trusted, nor ought he to be promoted in thy service.

HEMISTICH.

Be not supine with him whom thou hast galled.'

And when they essay to move the king's mind with this artifice, it is not improbable that suspicion will be excited on the king's part too; and in point of fact, there is ground for kings not feeling secure of a servant, who has been wronged or disgraced from his post, or removed from his office; or whose enemy, who was formerly inferior to him in rank, has

---

[1] Lit.: 'are not lighted up,' 'have no lustre.'

been preferred before him.' Kámjúí replied, 'How can this affair be remedied? and by what plan can the gates of this approach be closed?' Farísah made answer, 'Their words on this score would be very unfounded, and would have nothing but a mere erroneous semblance. For after such occurrences the confidence of both parties becomes more clear; and hence, even if in the mind of the master dissatisfaction has arisen, owing to his discovering some neglect in the service of his minister, yet, after giving vent to his anger, and inflicting the punishment deserved, that resentment will, without doubt, diminish, and no apprehension, little or much, will be left. Moreover, the king will for the future understand the little dependance to be placed in the false reports of messengers, and will give no more heed to the idle whispers of the interested, while the excessive attachment and sagacity, and perfect skill and honesty of the other party become better established. Moreover, even if in the heart of the servant, too, alarm and dread have existed, yet, after having received his chastisement, he feels secure, and ceases to anticipate evil.

COUPLET.

I was in grief, and from that grief got free;
In trouble, yet I found security.'

The Lion asked, 'In how many ways does distrust originate among servants?' Farísah replied, 'In three ways: in the first place, if the subject possess a high dignity, which through the supineness of his master is impaired. Secondly, if enemies sally out against him, and by reason of the king's withdrawal of favor, make an overpowering attack against him. Thirdly, if property and wealth, that he may have acquired, pass from his hands through the king's want of kindness.' Kámjúí asked, 'How can these things be remedied?' Farisah replied, 'By one thing, which is, that the favor of his master be regained, and fresh confidence be reposed in him by the king; so that both the rank which he had lost be restored to him, and his rival, too, who had got the better of him, be rebuked; and the property of his, which had been dissipated, be re-collected. For an equivalent can be found for everything save life, specially in the service of kings and great men. And since the king has been pleased to remedy the condition of this his slave, and since I have entirely regained the royal favor and approval, what grievance can yet remain? or how can my enemies find an opportunity to speak? Yet notwithstanding all this, I hope that the King will hold me excused and not draw me again into the net of calamity, and permit me to wander in this wilderness secure and content, and with sincerity of heart offer up daily portions of benediction and praise.

COUPLET.

By day thy praise I'll study to proclaim.
All night repeat due portions of the same.'

Kámjúí answered, 'Keep a stout heart! for thou art not of those servants that calumniators should make their voices heard respecting thee, and convey to the place of acceptance words tending to asperse thy character. Moreover I have thoroughly proved thee,[1] and learned that in adversity thou art indued with patience, and in prosperity art conspicuous for thy gratitude; and that thou rejectest all that is contrary to honor and uprightness, and regardest it as a plain obligation to observe generosity, and at the same time honesty in all thy orders. Wherefore rely on my protection and favor, for my confidence in respect to thy ability and truth and sagacity and probity has been doubled; and in no possible way can the words of thy opponents hereafter find a hearing; and whatever wiles they may contrive will be construed into a palpable attack.

COUPLET.

> Henceforward we no listening ear will lend,
> To envy's words malignant 'gainst a friend.'

Farísah replied, 'With the existence of all this condescending kindness, what fear should I have of the malice of enemies? and possessing the happiness of the imperial favor, what need I fear from the dissatisfaction of my rivals?

COUPLET.

> What care I for the arrows now of envy's bow that aims awry;
> For now that my arch-eyebrowed one I've gained, I may its shafts defy.'

Then with the utmost assiduity he entered upon his duties, and each day the degree of his authority was augmented, and the rank of his elevation and promotion doubled, until through the abundance of his right-mindedness and rectitude the royal confidence was entirely reposed in him, and he became the depositary of the state-secrets, both financial and political.

COUPLET.

> His tree to such an elevation grew,
> That higher than high heaven, its shade it threw.

This is the story of kings, with regard to what happens between them and their followers; and how, after the manifestation of their dislike and displeasure, they return to gracious and indulgent feelings. And let it not be hidden from the wise, what an amount of profitable instruction they have wrapped up in the composition of these stories and narratives. Whoever is favored by the assistance of heaven, and aided by the divine auspices, will expend all his energies in trying to understand the directions

---

[1] The reader will have exclaimed again and again 'Ohe jam satis!' was there ever anything so wearisome and inane, so full of repetition, as these speeches of the stolid Kámjúí and the luckless Farísah?

of the sage, and lavish all his zeal in unveiling the dark sayings of the wise; and will have recourse to the physicians of the hospital of spirituality, the exhilarating care-dispellers of truth; in order that by the blessing of the curatives of these spiritual doctors he may escape from the error-blending ailments of ignorance and fatuity.

VERSE.

> Of thy soul's guide the cure of teaching ask,
>   For man's worst ailment is his ignorance.
> If darkness should the sullied mirror mask,
>   Vainly in it the fairest face may glance.
> Recluse, monk, Ṣúfí, children are astray;
> The man is he who walks in God's own way.

CHAPTER X.

ON THE SUBJECT OF REQUITING ACTIONS BY WAY OF RETRIBUTION.

INTRODUCTION.

Dábishlim reverentially blessed the sage Bídpáí, and said, 'I have heard the story of Farísah and Kámjúí, and it is a tale for the intelligent as to what happens between kings and their servants in the matter of disagreement and treason, and forgiveness and punishment, and a return to the renewal of favor and an augmentation of confidence in trustworthy and able men, with a view to the ordering of the state and the furtherance of salutary measures. It also refers to the not transgressing in the direction of falsehood and the being open to conviction through true and wholesome words; and the advantages of these directions are such as to be beyond the limits of computation. Now be pleased to relate the story of one, who for the preservation of his own condition and the defence of his own person, does not desist from injuring others and inflicting harm on animals; and does not give heed to the admonitions of the sagacious, until, in consequence, he is overtaken with a retribution similar to his own acts.' The sage responded, 'None but a fatuous person proceeds in acting injuriously to dumb animals, except one who is ignorant, and cannot discern between the light of good and the darkness of evil, and the advantage of gain and disadvantage of loss: and who, swayed by his fatuity, wanders in the wilderness of error, careless of the consequences of his actions; and the visual faculty of whose eyes falls short of the termination of his deeds, wherefore he is not indued with sight to behold the nature of retribution. He, however, the eye of whose thought [1] is illuminated by the jeweled collyrium of the eternal guidance, and the flower-garden of whose heart is perfumed with the odors of the herbs of the everlasting favor, will never suffer himself to act towards a fellow-creature, in a way he should not himself approve if done to him.

HEMISTICH.

Allow not that to others, which thyself wouldst disallow.

And thou must know that every action has its appointed recompense, which will assuredly reach the doers; and they must not be elated by any delay that may intervene, for in accordance with the saying, ' *Assuredly God grants*

---

[1] *Sar*, lit., 'head,' which, indeed, may be the meaning here.

delay, but does not overlook,' there may be a respite but not an entire
overlooking : there is time allotted for two or three days' delay, but the idea
of escaping punishment and retribution is a vain one. Every seed which
they sow in the field of action, will, before much time elapses, yield fruit.
Wherefore every one that desires good must sow nothing but the seed
of good.

QUATRAIN.

Dost wish no evil should to thee occur ?
Then, all thou canst, try evil not to do.
Since, whether thou dost rightly act or err,
Thy acts recoil ;—look that thou dost not rue,
Through acting ill, loss to thine ownself too.

And if anyone wishes by deceit and misrepresentation to veil his own
misconduct, and to trick out his hypocrisy and artifice in the apparel of
righteous actions, to such an extent that men may praise him, and that the
mention of his virtues, pervading all districts and regions, should extend far
and near, by these means the result of his blameable actions will never be
averted from him, but the fruits of his internal baseness and the impurity of
his mind will reach him. Just so, if a husbandman should sow—for
example—the seed of colocynth in the ground, and having covered it
with earth, should give out that he had sown sugar-cane there, and all
persons should believe that sugar-cane would grow up in that land, still
indubitably his crop would not be changed by that artifice, and that same
seed of colocynth which he sowed, would produce to view its fruit.

DISTICHS.

Hast thou done ill ? hope not unscathed to go :
Acts are the seed God's power makes to grow.
At times a veil to thy bad deeds is lent,
God grants thee thus a season to repent.
That he requites, we from His word may learn ;
' If ye go back, we also will return.' [1]

And it may be, that when anyone finds the reality of the retributive system ;
and when the mystery of the verse, *' And whoever shall have wrought good of the
weight of an ant, shall behold the same. And whoever shall have wrought evil
of the weight of an ant, shall behold the same,* [2] has penetrated his heart, that he

---

[1] Lit., ' If ye return to it, we also will return to it.' These words more ' in extenso ' occur
at Kur'án, xvii. 8 ; Sale, p. 210, l. 14 : ' Peradventure your Lord will have mercy on you
hereafter : but if ye return to transgress a third time, we also will return to chastise you ;
and we have appointed Hell to be the prison of the unbelievers.' Sale's note is, ' And this
came accordingly to pass ; for the Jews being again so wicked as to reject Mohammad,
and conspire against his life, God delivered them into his hands ; and he exterminated the
tribe of Koreidha, and slew the chiefs of that of Al Nadìr, and obliged the rest of the
Jewish tribes to pay tribute.'

[2] Kur'án, xcix. 7 and 8 ; Sale, p. 450, l. 19 : ' On that day men shall go forward in distinct
classes, that they may behold their works. And whoever shall have wrought good of the
weight of an ant, shall behold the same. And whoever shall have wrought evil of the
weight of an ant, shall behold the same.'

will turn from his evil acts, and expressing his repentance of his cruel and
injurious conduct, will adopt as his path, the way of clemency and kindness.

HEMISTICH.

This, too, may happen by the help of God.

And among such discourses and similar narratives, is the story of the rank-
breaking Lion and the Archer.'   The king asked, ' How was that ? '

STORY I.

The Bráhman replied, ' They have related that in the country of Aleppo,
there was a jungle full of various trees and containing gardens and streams.

COUPLET.

Rose, willow, poplar, box and cypress made,
Bough within bough a thick o'er-hanging shade.

And in that jungle there was a Lion,[1] a monster, ready for war and conflict,
of elephantine bulk, such that Bahrám in the sky was like a wild ass before
it, and the celestial lion, from the awe of its terribleness, fled beneath the
earth like the energy infixed there by omnipotence.[2]

VERSE.

When it its tusks in furious anger showed,
An anvil's self dissolved with fear and dread.
Like coals of fire [3] its two eye-balls glowed,
Its mouth a cave with daggers keen was spread.

It was always busied in shedding blood and incessantly besmeared its jaws
with the gore of animals. A lynx, who was its attendant, on beholding
things going on after this fashion, felt alarmed at the consequences of this
cruelty and the fruits of this blood-thirstiness, and bethinking itself of the
commination, ' *Whoever abets an oppressor, God will give that oppressor power
over him,*' desired to abandon that service.

COUPLET.

Of tyrants' converse ever stand in fear !
Burns must be dreaded when the flame is near.'

Thus reflecting he turned his face toward the desert, on the edge of which he
saw a mouse, which was most busily employed in gnawing the root of a tree

---

[2] I know not the meaning of the *mddah* inserted here in the editions after *búd*. It
cannot be ' female,' for at p. 438, l. 18 of the Persian text this lion is addressed as *ai malik*,
' O king !'

[2] It is utterly impossible to render this passage intelligibly. *Gáo-i zamín* would signify
literally, ' the cow of the earth,' but it also bears the meaning which I have given to it in
the translation. [See Burhán-i Ḳáṭ'i.] The equivoque must be entirely lost in English.

[2] The *kánin* is ' a chafing-dish,' or ' a fire-place ;' ' the place where live coals are kept
for warming a room.'

and in severing with its serrulated teeth the material of its fibres. Meantime the tree with the tongue of its condition, was addressing it thus, ' O cruel tormentor ! why art thou overthrowing with the axe of injury, the foundation of my life ? and why dost thou sever with the sword of injustice, the strings of my existence, or in other words, my roots, with which I imbibe water ? and thus exclude men from the happiness of my shade and the advantage of my fruit.

COUPLET.

Abstain from ill, for ill will ill requite,
Badness is madness [1] in good people's sight.'

The mouse paying no attention to his complaints, employed himself in the same cruel proceeding, when suddenly a snake with open mouth came out from a lurking-place, and making a spring at the mouse, all at once swallowed him.' The lynx carried away fresh experience from these circumstances, and learned that the injurious person meets with nought but injury, and he who plants a bramble gathers not the rose of his wish.

COUPLET.

Thou look'st for good, and yet dost evil do !
The guerdon of ill acts is evil, too.

And at the same time that the snake, after finishing the deglutition of the mouse, coiled itself under the tree, a hedgehog came up, and seized the tail of the snake with its mouth, and pulled it. The snake, from excessive inquietude dashed against it, until all its body was transfixed with the points of its quills, and it yielded up its life to the ruler of hell. The lynx clearly beheld on the page of certainty another writing. But when the snake was disabled, the hedgehog put out its head, and devoured such parts of the snake as were fit for its food, and again drawing back its head under the curtain of concealment, lay in the shape of a ball on the plain of the desert. The lynx was watching the state of the hedge-hog, when all of a sudden a hungry fox came there, and beheld the hedgehog, which was a tit-bit for it, in that posture. The fox knew that owing to the sharpness of the thorns it could not inhale the perfume of the rose of its desire, nor open the door of its wish with the key of artifice and contrivance. He, therefore, threw the hedgehog on its back and dropped some drops of urine on its belly. And the hedgehog, under the idea that it was raining, drew its head from out of the curtain of concealment. Then the fox leapt up and seized his neck, and having bitten off its head, greedily devoured the rest of its body, so that the skin alone was left. The repast was not quite done when a bounding dog came from a corner like a ravenous wolf, and tore the fox to pieces, and having appeased its canine appetite with a part of it, went to sleep in a retired spot. The lynx was observing these marvels,

---

[1] Lit., ' ferine brutishness.' I have, however, translated as I have, in order to preserve in English the jingle on the words *badí*, ' badness,' and *dadí*, ' brutishness.'

each of which was a clear proof of the certainty of retribution, and was in expectancy as to what was next to come from the secret chamber of fate into the expanse of the plain of destiny, when suddenly it beheld a leopard, which rushed out from the corner of the desert, and before the dog was aware, tore its heart from its breast with his life-lacerating teeth. It happened that the leopard had sprung out without observing the ambush of a hunter, who was sitting close by with an arrow fitted to his bow. When he saw the leopard busy with the dog he discharged a heart-piercing shaft at it, which entered its right side and came out at the left.

COUPLET.

Heaven praised the adroitness of that hand and aim,
And earth approval murmured of the same.

The leopard was as yet scarce fallen to the ground when the hunter nimbly stripped off its skin from its head. Just then a horseman came up there, and took a fancy to that leopard's skin, which was very beautifully spotted and colored. The hunter, however, being loath to part with it, their proceedings ended in a quarrel and deadly strife, and in the midst of their contest the horseman drew a finely-tempered sword, and rode at the hunter, and before the latter could shake himself free, the horseman made his head roll on the plain, and snatching up the leopard's skin, set off on his road. He had as yet not gone a hundred paces, when his horse fell on its head, and the rider, being hurled to the ground, broke his neck.

HEMISTICH.

Fate did not him two instants' pause allow.

These experiences augmented the conviction of the lynx, and coming to the Lion, he demanded permission to quit that jungle. The Lion replied, 'Thou reposest under the shade of my good fortune, and hast a share from the tray of my beneficence, and the table of my generosity. What may be the cause of thy departure from this station, and of thy abandonment of my service?' The lynx answered, 'O King! an idea has exhibited itself to me, and a thought has raised its head from the environs of my heart, which if I conceal, I fear I shall melt; and if I tell, I am in terror lest I should lose my life.

COUPLET.

What my heart feels 'tis hard from thee to veil,
From fear of God more hard to tell my tale.

But if your royal highness will pledge me your faith in a manner which it will be quite inadmissible to break, I will truthfully state how the case stands.' The Lion assured him of his safety, and pledged himself accordingly, and confirmed his promise by oaths. Then the lynx said, 'I observe that the inclinations of the king are restricted to the injury of God's creatures, and the reins of his power are turned to the annoyance of the innocent.

Hearts are wounded by the claw of his tyranny, and breasts lacerated by the scar of the sufferings he inflicts.

COUPLET.

Go! dread remorse and leave thy cruel way,
And fear the terrors of the judgment-day.

And I am much alarmed at this state of things, and am aghast at these circumstances.' As the Lion had that very moment given his promise, he put up with this hard language, and said, 'Since no wrong is done to thee, and my tyranny does not reach thee, of what use is it to withdraw?' The lynx replied, 'The first of two reasons is, that no generous-minded person can endure to see oppression, nor can bear to hear the groans of the victims.

VERSE.

Thy being does all living things distress,
And their afflictions truly please me not.
I am half sallow at my helplessness,
And this my grief is caused by their sad lot.

The second reason is, my fear lest the baneful results of these actions should reach thee, and I too, owing to my association with thee, should be consumed in the fire of punishment.

HEMISTICH.

The fire once kindled burns both moist and dry.'

The Lion said, 'How hast thou learned the disastrous result of evil actions? and by whom hast thou been taught the happy consequences of acting well?' The lynx replied, 'All whose nostrils have inhaled the fragrance of the flower-garden of understanding know that whoever sows the seed of injury will reap nought save the harvest of detriment, and he who plants the young tree of benefit will gather only the fruit of tranquillity. They have compared the world, which is the place of retribution, to a mountain, because whatever thou sayest, good or bad, thou hearest, by way of echo, the response of the same.

DISTICHS.

This world a hill is, and our acts a shout,
And back the hill to us the echo spurns.
Though long the shadow that a wall throws out,[1]
That shadow dwindling to the wall returns.

And I have this day beheld with the eye of certainty the realities of retribution, and have seen with my own sight the nature of recompense.' He then began and recounted, in the manner he had observed it, the story of the mouse and the snake, and the hedgehog and fox, and the dog and leopard, and the hunter and the horseman. He then added, by way of admonition, 'O king! the mouse that gnawed the root of the tree became the food of the

---

[1] As the shadow, though long, comes back to its original source, the wall; so our cruelties, though it may be after a long interval, recoil on ourselves.

snake; and the snake that injured him was overtaken with the calamity of the hedgehog; and the hedgehog that killed the snake fell into the snare of the artifice of the fox; and the fox, which spilled the blood of an animal, was destroyed by the hungry dog; and the dog, on account of this injustice, was crushed under the paw of the leopard; and the leopard, through the disastrous influence of its own cruelty and injuriousness, was made a target for the shaft of fate; and the hunter, owing to his unprovoked attack and mercilessness, lost his life; and the horseman, through his pitiless shedding of innocent blood, was left with his heart crushed and neck broken. Thus the actions of each, since they were based on injury to others, proved, by way of retaliation, injurious to himself. Wherefore it is incumbent on persons of understanding to abandon evil, and to keep aloof from the evilly disposed; and it is a sacred and necessary duty for the wise to reduce their own conduct to rectitude, and let their disposition be towards good actions.

COUPLET.

'Tis the first sign of Wisdom's course begun,
Through every circling year ill acts to shun.'

The Lion was so infatuated with the pride of his own strength, and so intoxicated with the arrogance engendered by his own might and prowess, that he looked upon the words of the lynx as mere idle tales, and regarded his admonitions as a jest; and the more he talked in this fashion the higher rose the flame of the Lion's cupidity and greediness.

COUPLET.

Thou, who dost preach to me 'gainst love, waste not
Thy words—they do but make my flame more hot.

The lynx saw that his advice had the same effect on the heart of the Lion that the foot of a little ant has on a rock, or on steel; and that his warnings exercised no more influence on the breast [of that savage] than the point of the lance of a thorn on the cuirass of a hard stone.

HEMISTICH.

Aye! when will thorn-points pierce through solid stone? [1]

He therefore quitted the Lion and went out into a retired place. The Lion, incensed by what had occurred with the lynx, followed close upon him, but the lynx concealed himself in a thicket of thorns. The Lion passed by him and beheld two fawns feeding in the plain of that desert, while their fond mother was, guardian-like, watching their movements. The Lion attempted to seize them, and the deer called out, ' O king! what wilt thou gain by making prey of these two little ones? or what will it advantage thee

---

[1] The equivoque is lost in English. In the original, khár, 'a thorn,' cannot, it is said, pierce khárá, 'a hard stone.'

to devour them? Cause not my eyes to weep at separation from those who are the solace of my sight, and broil not my heart with the fire of parting from those who are pieces of my liver. Thou too, in fine, hast children. Think of them! lest the same befall them that befalls mine.

HEMISTICH.

Do that to me thou wouldst wish for thyself.'

It happened that the Lion had two young ones, the sight of which made the world bright to him, and he wished for the power of vision simply to gaze on their forms. At the very time that he was about to pounce on the fawns, a hunter, too, was employed in that jungle in capturing the lion-whelps. Here the Lion, giving no heed to the lamentations of the doe, killed her fawns, and then the hunter slew both the lion-whelps and flayed them.

COUPLET.

Of thine own children, sure thou art the foe,   On others' children who inflictest woe.

The doe, flying from the presence of the Lion, and suffering the pangs of separation from her own beloved ones, was running in various directions distractedly. All at once the lynx came up to her, and asked what had befallen her? and, when he had learned what had happened to her, his heart was consumed at her distress, and he began to lament with her.

COUPLET.

' Whene'er my heart for my love's suffering weeps,
Walls groan, and every door the cry repeats.'

After outcries, and wailing, and sighs, and weeping, and lamentation without end, the lynx consoled her, and said, ' Grieve not! in a short time he will meet with his punishment and the requital due.

COUPLET.

The taper did the moth consume, 'tis true ;
Burned in its wax it soon will perish too.'

However, in the other direction, the Lion returned to his jungle and saw his young ones stretched in that manner upon the ground. Hereupon he raised his outcries and roarings to the sky, and said,

COUPLET.

' Anguish has reached my bosom, for the solace of my life is sped;
Alas! my state has come to this that hope and patience' self are fled.'

The Lion raised so huge an uproar, and commencing a piteous outcry, lamented in such wise that the wild animals of that wilderness wept at his bemoanings, and he expressed his distress in such a fashion that the birds of the air, from sympathy with his sufferings, lamented also.

COUPLET.

Blood, like a torrent, flows from my moist eyes,
Why speak of friends, e'en foes must sympathize.

In the neighborhood of the Lion lived a jackal who had shaken his skirt free from worldly associations, and who perused, from the page of resignation and reliance on God, the subtle saying, ' *Whoever is contented, is full.*'

COUPLET.

In Resignation's plain he mounted went,   And in the waste of Trust he pitched his tent.

He came to the Lion to condole with him, and said, 'What is the cause of all this lamentation and groaning?' The Lion stated the facts. The jackal said, ' Practice patience, and take to thyself fortitude, for never did any nostril inhale from the flower-garden of the world the perfume of constancy. Nor did any palate ever taste from the hand of the cup-bearer Time the wine of happiness without the smack of suffering.[1]

QUATRAIN.

To look for fortune's constancy is vain ;
Nor hope Time's circling course repose will bring.
There is no better medicine for the pain
Of wounded hearts than to endure the sting.

Compose thy heart for a time and open the ear of attention while I read to thee two or three maxims from the volume of wisdom, and point out to thee the true state of the transactions of this perfidious world.' The sea of the Lion's mind was calmed from its tumultuous state, and he listened heedfully to the admonitions and counsels of the jackal with the ear of acquiescence. When the latter saw that the Lion was disposed to hearken to his words, he began a captivating harangue, and said, 'O king! there is an ending appointed to every beginning, and there is a predestined conclusion to the commencement of every affair. Whenever the period of life is finished and the time of fated extinction has arrived, a moment's respite is impossible, [as it is said], *Therefore when their term is expired, they shall not have respite for an hour, neither shall they be anticipated.*'[2] And we may expect joy to follow on the traces of every grief, and after all mirth we must anticipate lamentation.

COUPLET.

Like the breeze for years I wandered life's enchanting gardens round,
Wheresoe'er I found a flower, there I always thorns too found.

In all situations one ought to acquiesce in the divine decree, and lay aside complaints which are altogether unavailing.

COUPLET.

Resign thy life ! fate's aim is such, that it
Not by one hair's point fails the mark to hit.'

---

[1] Lit, ' wounding.'

[2] Kur'án, Fl. vii. 32; Mar. 35; Sale, p. 110, l. 22: 'Unto every nation there is a prefixed term : therefore, when their term is expired, they shall not have respite for an hour, neither shall they be anticipated. The same expression occurs also at chap. x. 50; xvi. 63.

The Lion said, 'Whence has this calamity reached my young ones?' The jackal replied, 'This, too, has reached thee from thyself, for thou hast inflicted on others twice as much as the Archer of destiny has inflicted on thee. And this is the requital of thy own deeds which has reached thee, [for it is said], '*As thou judgest, thou shalt be judged.*' And thy case is very like that of the Seller of Wood, who said, 'Whence did this fire fall among my wood?' The Lion asked, 'How was that?'

STORY II.[1]

The jackal said, 'They have related that in former times there was an oppressor who used to buy the wood of poor people, by violence and injustice, and having made a great difference in the price, used to give for it less than it was worth, and forcing it in winter on rich men, would take from them double its value. Thus both the poor were driven to despair at his cruelty, and the rich, too, were bewailing his tyranny.

COUPLET.

The bosom of the poor by him was burned,
The hovel of the wretched overturned.

One day he took by force the fire-wood of a poor man, and gave half the price to that destitute wretch. The darvesh raised to heaven the hand of supplication, and turned the face of prayer towards the point of adoration of the humble and submissive.

COUPLET.

Think not safe thyself, O tyrant! from the curses of the poor;
For the prayer of midnight weepers is a fount whose drops are gore.

At this time a devout person came by, and having heard how matters stood, loosed the tongue of reproach against that tyrant, and said,

COUPLET.

'Fear the poor man's arrowy shower in the ambuscade of night,
For his shaft's point wounds the sharper the more wretched is his plight.

Act not thus towards the helpless, who have no protection save the court of the divine king; and indulge not in cruelty towards the afflicted, who rain down tears all night, like a taper from burning of the heart. Do not lay waste with the wrongs of injustice, the mansion of the breast of the poor, and pour not into the goblet of vengeance, in the place of ruby wine, the heart's-blood of the bereaved.

---

[1] This story is related, in somewhat different language, in the 'Gulistán,' chap. i., story 26. See page 81 of my translation.

HEMISTICH.

Quaff not this cup, lest pain come with the morn.'

That proud oppressor was offended at the words of the pious man, and frowning insolently and with fatuous displeasure, said,

COUPLET.

'Go thy way, old man; henceforward cease this irksome vain tirade,
Ten score stacks e'en[1] of this nonsense with one grain were dearly paid.'

The darvesh turned his face away from him and hastened to the retirement of his own privacy. It happened that that very night the tyrant's stack of wood caught fire, and extending thence to his house and residence, burnt clean up[2] all the property he possessed, and deposited that tyrannical person from his soft bed in warm ashes. It came to pass, in the morning, the same pious man who had rebuked him the day before, came to that quarter; there he beheld the tyrant, who was saying to his friends, 'I know not whence this fire caught my house?' The devout personage replied, 'From the smoke of the hearts of the poor, and the burning of the bosoms of the afflicted.

COUPLET.

'Beware of the sigh of the wounded heart,
For the secret sore you'll too late discern.'[3]

The tyrant hung down his head, and said to himself, 'One ought not to transgress justice. The seed of oppression that I have sown will yield no better fruit than this.

COUPLET.

Our seed has ever been the seed of wrong;
Behold the fruits that to such seed belong!'

And I have cited this story, in order that thou mayest know what has befallen thy sons, is in requital of what thou hast done to the children of others; and they have all used the same complaint and lamentation that thou hast used; and, again, all have been compelled to be patient. Wherefore, as others have patiently endured the pain thou hast inflicted, do thou also be patient under the wrongs that others have wreaked on thee.' The Lion replied, 'Impress these words on my mind, by corroborating them with arguments and proofs.' The jackal answered, 'How old art thou?' The Lion replied, 'Forty years.' The jackal rejoined, 'During this long interval, of what has thy food been?' The Lion replied, 'Of the flesh of animals and men of which I made prey.' 'Then,' said the jackal, 'had the animals on whose flesh thou hast fed thus long

---

[1] The _khirman_ signifies 'harvest,' and also 'corn piled up in a large circular stack.'

[2] An exact translation of the original _pák bi-súkht_.

[3] These lines occur in the 'Gulistán' in the place quoted above, but the two lines that rhyme to them are here omitted.

neither father nor mother? and did not their kinsfolk express in wailings and lamentations their regret for separation from these thy victims, and their distress at losing them? If on that day thou hadst seen the conclusion of this affair, and hadst shunned to spill blood, this event would not now have occurred, and such an adventure would never have taken place.

DISTICHS.

Thou! who didst ne'er to others pardon grant,
When wilt thou solace for thine own self find?
And, say! while all in terror of thee pant,
Who will spread ointment on thy wounded mind?

And shouldest thou persevere in this line of conduct, and adhere to the same sanguinary and cruel course, be prepared! for thou wilt experience many such things; and so long as people are afraid of thee thou wilt not inhale the perfume of security and peace. Deck thy character with kindness and clemency, and make no approaches to the harming other animals, and the molestation of this one or that. For he that molests others, never sees the face of happiness, and the injurious person never arrives at his object and wish.

HEMISTICH.

None, from this bow, e'er struck the butt with their desire's shaft.'

When the Lion heard these words, and the real state of the case was revealed to him, he perceived, that the result of an action based on harm to others, can be nought but disappointment and disaster. He then reflected, 'Life's spring, for such is the season of youth, has been exchanged for the autumn of old age and debility; and every moment I must expect to tread the path of annihilation, and undertake a long and far journey. There is nothing better for me to do than to prepare the provisions for the road to that place, whither all must return; and than that, forsaking injuriousness and oppression, I content myself with scant food, and feeling no solicitude as to more or less, abandon all care of the having or not having.[1]

STANZA.

Be glad! nor grieve thy bosom here with thoughts of 'is,' 'or,' 'is not,'
For 'is not,' is the source of all that is to us accruing.
Since from this two-doored inn to move man finds it must be his lot,
What need we care, if life's support[2] should stand or fall in ruin?'

He then desisted from eating blood and flesh, and satisfying himself with fruits, took the path of contentment. When the jackal saw that the Lion had commenced eating fruits, and that if he persevered therein, an

---

[1] Lit., of 'is,' and 'is not.'
[2] Lit., 'portico and dome of subsistence.' So, at least, I would translate the words *riwdk va ṭdk-i m'aishat*. I may add that the lines are very pretty in the original.

amount of food, which would suffice a jackal for a year, would be consumed in ten days, he was vexed, and came to the Lion again and said
How is the king employed?' The Lion replied, 'I have abandoned
the world, and have girt up my loins to spiritual conflicts and abstinence.

COUPLET.

Since from this world's azure ocean pleasant water none can drink,
Sated with its false[1] emotions from its margin back I shrink.'

The jackal replied, ' The case is not as the king is pleased to say ; nay,
the injury which he inflicts on others, is even greater now than before.'
The Lion responded, 'From what cause is any one now injured by me?
I neither stain my mouth with blood, nor do I spread out my claws to
harm any one.

COUPLET.

Did they me piece-meal with wrong's dagger tear,
None should from me the marks of vengeance bear.'

The jackal replied, ' Thou hast withdrawn thy hand from thy own
natural food, and eatest of the allotted portion of other animals, to which
thou hast no right; and the fruits of this jungle will not suffice for thy
maintenance for ten days. Thus, those whose subsistence is dependent on
these fruits will quickly perish, and the curse of this will hang round thy
neck, and it is possible that the punishment of it will reach thee even in
this world, and I fear lest thy condition should be like that of the Hog that
violently seized the monkey's fruits.' The Lion said, 'Explain, how was
that ?'

STORY III.

The jackal said, ' They have related that once upon a time the aid of
divine grace was extended to a monkey, and, withdrawing from those of his
own race, he took up his abode in a retired spot in a certain wilderness.
Now, therein were some fig-trees; and the monkey bethought himself, ' An
animal cannot dispense with food, and in this jungle the only eatable thing
is figs. If I devour all the figs while they are fresh, I must pass the winter
without supplies. I cannot do better than each day shake down the figs of
one tree, and after eating as much thereof as will support life, dry the
remainder, that both the summer may pass comfortably, and that during
the winter, too, I may be well off.

COUPLET.

One must in summer toil for household stuff,
If in the winter he would have enough.'

---

[1] Here again is an untranslateable equivoque : *db khwurd* has two meanings, ' draught of
water,' and 'halting-place.'

Accordingly he finished several trees, and having eaten a little of their fruit, he stored up the remainder. One day, having climbed up one of the fig-trees, he, as usual, was eating some of the fruit and gathering some to dry, when all of a sudden a Hog springing away from a hunter rushed into that jungle. Whenever it came to a tree it found no fruit on it, till it came to the foot of that up which the monkey was, gathering the figs. When the monkey's eyes lighted on the Hog his heart was pained, and he said,

COUPLET.

'This unexpected woe from whence befell?
From this unlooked for curse—God! keep me well.'

When the Hog saw the monkey he called out 'Bravo!' and having uttered the usual benedictory expressions, said, 'Dost thou wish for a guest?' The monkey, too, deceitfully returned a hypocritical answer, and said,

COUPLET.

'A graceful cypress to the garden of my hope has hither come,
And providence has sent a guest to glad my poor and humble home.

May the arrival of thy auspicious footstep be blessed and fortunate! If thou hadst previously favored me with a message informing me of thy high advent, assuredly the conditions of hospitality should have been fulfilled in a manner suitable to my circumstances. At present the shame that I feel is owing to the want of the means of entertainment.

HEMISTICH.

A poor man's troubled by an unexpected guest.'

The Hog replied, 'We are just off our journey, and could most eagerly partake of whatever thou hast at hand.

HEMISTICH.

Cease these excuses—what thou hast produce.'

The Monkey shook the fig-tree, and the Hog kept on eating with the utmost avidity, till not a thing was left on the tree and on the ground. He then turned to the Monkey, and said, 'O gracious host! the fire of my hunger is still burning fiercely, and my greedy mind is still in distress to obtain food. Shake another tree, and bind me to thee as thy debtor.' The Monkey willing or not shook another tree, and in a very short time not a trace of the fruit of that tree too was left. The Hog pointed to another tree. The Monkey said, 'Dear guest! exceed not the bounds of generous sentiment! that which I have devoted to thee was a month's provision for me, and I cannot offer thee more.

HEMISTICH.

I can no farther kindness shew than this.'

Hereupon the Hog grew angry and said, 'This wilderness has been for a long time in thy possession, and now it shall belong to me!' The Monkey replied,

'To take away the territory of another is unlucky, and the conclusion of an oppressive and tyrannical course is not to be commended, but deprecated. Give up the thought of acting intemperately, and hold back thy hand from wrong and injustice; for oppression of the weak yields no happy result, and the molestation of the friendless bears no good fruit.

COUPLET.

Thou mayst, by biting him, draw blood, 'tis true;
But should thy teeth ache,[1] what then wilt thou do?'

At these words the fire of the Hog's wrath waxed hotter, and he said, 'I will forthwith bring thee down from this tree, and pour into thy bosom what thou deservest.' He then ascended the tree to throw the Monkey down. He had, however, hardly fixed himself on the first branch, when it broke, and falling head downwards he proceeded to the pit of hell.

And I have adduced this story, since thou too usurpest the fruit of others, and makest their allotted sustenance thy food. When these parties die of hunger, enmity to thee will settle in the hearts of their children, and being ever employed in speaking ill of thee behind thy back, they will not cease for one moment to curse thee. And if the impression of thy tyranny pervaded the world before, so now the rumor of thy pious abstinence is rife on all tongues. Yet in both cases animals cannot escape thy persecution, whether it be in a state of violence and mischief, or in the array of virtue and rectitude. And pray what devotion is this? that thou shouldest be as busied as ever in pampering thy body, and forbear to turn from sensual and corporeal gratifications to the securing intellectual and spiritual delights.

COUPLET.

Thou art the slave of carnal joys, else were it truly otherwise,
Is there a pleasure that beyond the confines of possession[2] lies?'

When the Lion heard this discourse, he relinquished his fruit-diet also, and, contenting himself with water and grass, increased his daily portions of worship and adoration; and, in season and out of season, repeated to himself the purport of these truth-distinguished couplets,

VERSE.

O heart! this heart-afflicting world now quit!
And through the circling heaven's close gorge proceed.
For wise men's notice this world is unfit;
Then with calm fortitude abandon it.

---

[1] The meaning of these obscure lines I take to be as follows: 'Thou mayest bite the poor man, and thus draw blood from his heart; but if, by the retribution which is sure to follow, thou undergoest the toothache of remorse, what wilt thou do then?'
[2] Lit., 'thy life.'

And since the bowers of heaven may be thy meed,
Bestir thyself, and from this thorn-road pass;
Nor let insatiate longing to amass,
    Thee, like some bold and fearless diver, lead
To plunge into a sea of griefs; through them
Were dearly purchased, e'en a royal gem.'

This is the story of a violent evil-doer, holding the inhabitants of the world in thraldom under his oppression, and regardless of the disastrous results; till in the end he becomes involved in the same calamity which he inflicted on his fellow-creatures; after which he recognises the right way and the path of rectitude. Similarly, the Lion, until he beheld both his beloved sons roasted on the fire of regret, removed not his heart from blood-thirstiness and evil actions. But when he gained this experience, he turned his back on the deceitful world, and thought it no longer admissible to give heed to its unsubstantial gauds, and was in no wise led to purchase the smiles of this faithless one.

COUPLET.

This writing on the portico of Eden's garden [1] lies.
'Woe! woe to him who purchases this false world's coquetries.'

And it behoves men of sense to comprehend well these directions, and store up these experiences for their present condition and future state; and to lay the foundation of their affairs in this world and that to come on the same one maxim, viz., that whatever they would not approve of for themselves and their children and their connections, they should not suffer to be done to others; in order that the commencements of their undertakings and the conclusion of their affairs, may be adorned with a good name and honorable celebrity, and that they may remain secure in this world and in that to come from the consequences of ill-actions and the baneful results of oppression.

VERSE.

The world 's not worth the raising one emotion
    Of sorrow in a single heart. Beware
    Ill acts! which wise men shun with care.
The world is like a deep and and troubled ocean,
    Peopled with monsters ravening for their prey.
    Who keep the shore, the wise, the blest are they.

---

[1] I am doubtful whether I have rightly translated *jannatu 'l Mávai*.

2 M

CHAPTER XI.

ON THE DETRIMENT OF SEEKING MORE, AND FAILING IN ONE'S OBJECT.

INTRODUCTION.

The world-subduing king after hearing this agreeable story, said, ' O eloquent and right-counselling sage! thou hast set forth with clear proof[1] and perspicuous reasoning, the apologue of an evil-doer who without thought of consequences, went to excess in injuring and molesting [others], and on being himself involved in similar calamities, had recourse to repentance and contrition.   I now request that thou wouldest recount a narrative comprising the import of the eleventh precept; and that thou wouldest set forth the true particulars of a person aiming at something not suitable to his condition, nor in accordance with his circumstances.'   The perfect sage, in a style which in purity and clearness resembled the water of life, and in sweetness and richness was the foster-sister of the beverage of the sugar-cane ;

VERSE.

Words that in clearness did outvie the gem,
So sweet, that sweetness could not rival them.
Should to the ear those wondrous accents come,
E'en Plato's self they'd strike with wonder dumb.

said, ' O king! asylum of the world!

COUPLET.

Thy step tread ever on the skirt of hope !
Thy realm, thy life be boundless in their scope!

Ancient sages have pronounced, ' *For every action there are men, for every place its* [*proper*] *saying.*'   In the wardrobe of the invisible world they have sewed on the lofty[2] stature of every person the garment of his own actions, and have carefully prepared for each in the treasury of the Divine bestowal, the robe of his special transactions suitable to his figure.   Each individual has his task, and every man his actions that suit him.

---

[1] I prefer to insert, with some MSS., *bih* before *burhání*, and to read *bi-burhání rúshan*, rather than to take *burhání* as in apposition with *maṣal*.

[2] The adjective *wálá*, 'lofty,' is most inaptly introduced here, merely for the sake of the jingle with *bálá*, 'stature.'   So, if we were to attach any sense to it in this sentence, we might infer that only tall men are indebted to these invisible tailorings, or that all men are tall.

VERSE.

They did not make the fly, to deck
It in the peacock's star-bright pinion.
Nor magnified each insect speck,
With fabled 'Anká's wide dominion.
And vinegar in vain may pine
To catch the luscious taste of wine.
The sullen thorn stands dry and bare,
When will the rose breathe fragrant there?

The cupbearer of the divine favors presents from the wine-cellar of '*Every party rejoiceth in that which they follow,*' [1] a cup suited to the condition of each, nor does He exclude one single person from the beverage of His bounty or the fountain of His grace.

COUPLET.

There is not one, who does not there his fit allotted portion find,
To one a sip, to one a cup, to all their rightful share 's assigned.

Wherefore every one ought to employ himself in that profession which the eternal Artificer has entrusted to him, and take steps to conduct that business by gradual progress, to the stage of perfection.

COUPLET.

A pack-saddle maker,[2] the best of his trade,
Surpasses a hatter, whose hats are ill made.

And whosoever quits his own employment and betakes himself to a business unsuited to him, and turns away from what he has received by hereditary descent or long previous acquisition, will undoubtedly be overtaken with embarrassment and perplexity. Consequently, by the way which he is then pursuing, he will not arrive at the wished-for station, and the return to his former road becomes impossible. Thus he remains stupefied and aghast between the two.

HEMISTICH.

No passage onward—no returning back.

Wherefore it behoves a man to plant his foot firmly in the path of his own profession, and not to be led by desire to stretch forth his hand to every branch of vain longing, and to lay aside the quest of greater things, since for the most part the final issue thereof is disappointment; and let him not soon or lightly surrender a thing whence he has experienced profit, and whose

---

[1] Kur'án, xxiii. 55; Sale, p. 260, l. 17 : This your religion is one religion; and I am your Lord, wherefore fear me.   But men have rent the affair of their religion into various sects : every party rejoiceth in that which they follow.'   The same expression occurs again in the Kur'án at Ch. xxx. 31.

[2] The point of these lines is somewhat lost in English; as with us there is little reason why a hatter should claim precedence over a saddler.   The Oriental idea no doubt is, that he who makes gear for asses and other beasts, is below him who ornaments the noblest part of man, his head.   Of course, the word rendered 'hatter,' is more properly 'turban-maker,' or 'cap-maker.'

fruit he has found to be advantageous,[1] so that he may act in accordance with the import of the high tradition, '*Whoever has had a thing bestowed on him, let him cling to it,*' and may escape from bewilderment and distress; and the words of the holy Maulaví,[2] who is a mine of the jewels of spirituality, alludes to this same circumstance, in the passage where he says,

COUPLET.

'For the fig-vendor, say, my friend!
What better than his figs to vend?'

And of the stories that befit these premises, the story of that Devotee who spoke the Hebrew tongue is one, and of the versatile Guest who wished to learn that language.' The king asked, 'How was that?'

STORY I.

The Bráhman said, 'They have related that in the land of Kinnauj (Kanoj) there lived a man pious and abstemious, and continent and religious. He was assiduous in satisfying the conditions of the daily duties of devotion, and he performed with sincerity the customary ceremonies of worship. The clearness of his purity had obliterated the opacities of earthly connections, and the transparency of his nature removed from before the eyes of the spiritual the curtain of the obscurities of terrestrial concerns. The border of his prayer-carpet was the alighting-place of the manifestations of grace, and the threshold of his closet was the theatre of the exhibitions of the infallible world.

VERSE.

His crown was of the 'C'[3] of God's 'Code' made,
 The heart his throne, his prayers the ladder were.
His will was in th' angelic world obeyed,
 The kingdom of God's Oneness owned his care.
Devils he slew, angelic in his mind,
And when he moved he left dull earth behind.[4]

He expended all his energies in restoring life to the ceremonies of the law, and employed all his zeal in fulfilling the duties of a righteous life. The bird of love of the world did not find a nest in the region of his breast, and the beams of his regard from the sun of his mind did not fall nor shine on this dark earth.

---

[1] The expression *natíjah-i chízí* is somewhat unusual. I almost suspect the reading to be corrupt here.

[2] A famous Súfí doctor and poet, who wrote in A.H. 600 = 1203 A.D. His name was Jalálu 'd-dín Muḥammad ibn Muḥammad u'l-Balkhí u'l Konaví.

[3] Of the ش *shín* of شرع *shar'a*.

[4] Lit., 'He placed his step on the air.'

COUPLET.

Happy they, who pure as the sun have past !
Nor on this world a shadow e'en have cast.

And notwithstanding[1] all this piety and abstinence, whatever was his portion from the treasury of *' Unto God belong the stores of heaven and earth,'* [2] he devoted to [the reception of] guests, and used to bestow the provisions of his own dinner and supper, through the strength of his liberality, on deserving darveshes.

COUPLET.

O'er the ethereal sky he raised the stars of generousness,
In bounty's sign, for great the power that liberal gifts possess.[3]

One day a traveler came to his cell as guest, and the pious man, as is the custom of bountiful hosts—viz., that their table appears without the vinegar of frowns—advanced to meet him with a fresh countenance and open brow, and displayed the utmost joy and cheerfulness at his visit. After offering his salutations, and the arrangement of the repast, they spread the carpet of conversation. The Holy Man inquired, ' Whence art thou come ? and to what country is it thy intention to go ?' The Guest replied, ' My story is a long one, and it is a narrative compounded of many points of true experience and subtleties of comparison. But if your illustrious mind feels disposed to hear it, some particulars may be set forth by way of summary.' The Devotee replied, ' Whoever has the ear of intelligence open will be able to derive some advantage from every story, and may pass by the bridge of comparison to the road of true wisdom.

COUPLET.

From every play we may a hint obtain,
From every story some advantage gain.

Do thou without hesitation recount thy history, and state unreservedly what advantages and detriment have accrued to thee from this journey.' The Guest replied, ' O holy man of the age, and incomparable saint ! know that I am originally from Europe, and I was employed there as a baker. I was always heating the oven of my bosom with the fire of covetousness, and yet, with a thousand difficulties, I obtained but a single loaf from the table of fortune.

COUPLET.

My kidneys turned to blood, ere I could win
My destined loaf, that lay fate's oven in.

---

[1] Or, it may be, ' together with.'

[2] Kur'án, lxiii. 7 ; Sale, p. 410. l. 12 : ' These are the men, who say to the inhabitants of Medina, Do not bestow anything on the refugees who are with the apostle of God, that they may be obliged to separate from him. Whereas unto God belong the stores of heaven and earth : but the hypocrites do not understand.'

[3] These untranslateable lines are a string of puns on the words *işdr*, 'giving,' *aşír,* ' ethereal,' *aşar*, ' effect,' or ' power.' It is impossible to convey the slightest idea of these equivoques in English.

Now I had a friendship with a farmer, and the road of companionship was incessantly trodden by us, and the customs of amicable intercourse observed. The farmer, out of friendly feeling and to assist me, used to send to my shop the grain that I required, and took the money for it as time came round, and when[1] there happened to be a delay[1] sometimes in the payment, he was easy with me. One day he took me to an entertainment at one of his gardens, and discharged all the duties of a host, as is customary with liberal people. After we had finished eating our meat, we engaged in conversation. He inquired, 'What amount of profit dost thou make by thy trade? and what is the extent of thy stock and interest?' I gave him some slight inkling of my condition, and said, 'The stock in my shop is twenty kharwárs[2] of wheat, and the profit I obtain thereon is just enough to support my wife and family, and that may be[3] about ten or twelve kharwárs.

COUPLET.
Since I no trade more gainful have than this,
This then my craft and occupation is.'

The farmer exclaimed, 'Holy God! the profit of thy profession is not of that degree that one could build thereon. I fancied that in thy trade the profit was great and the income immense.

HEMISTICH.
It was a downright error, what I thought.'

I rejoined, 'Sir! what kind of business is thine? and what are the profits and capital in it?' He replied, 'In my business the capital required is small and the interest vast. Save the seed that we sow the whole crop is clear gain. And in this business we are not content with a return of ten for one.' I was amazed, and said, 'How can this be?' The farmer answered, 'Don't be surprised, for there is still greater profit than this. When a single poppy-seed, which is the smallest of all seeds, takes root well in the ground and germinates, it sends up near twenty shoots,[4] and possibly even more. And at the end of every shoot is a poppy-clump, so that one cannot reckon the number of them; and hence thou mayest imagine that the profit of my business is beyond the range of calculation, and the gain of farming greater than can be computed. And the agriculturists of the field of wisdom have said that زرع zar'a (sowing) is a word of three letters, and that its two first letters are زر z-r (or zar) 'gold,' and its last letter is ع 'ain, and that, too, is a name for gold, wherefore this business is gold upon gold.

---

[1] The printed edition, by a typographical error, omits chún before muḥlati. For the va furṣati of the editions, I would prefer to read, with some MSS., bi-furṣati.

[2] Lit., 'ass-loads,' a measure equal to 100 Tabríz maunds.

[3] The lithographed edition omits búd after tawánad.

[4] The Persian word for our 'shoot,' here, is tír,—lit. 'arrow.'

COUPLET.

Since Zara's two first letters 'gold' express; and that behind
Means also 'gold,' in this word then 'gold upon gold,' we find.

And, according to the belief of the alchymists, the department of husbandry is viewed in such a light that the philosopher's stone[1] is supposed to allude to agriculture : as it is said,

COUPLET.

To seek the red-hued sulphur[2] is to squander life in vain,
Turn to black mould and there the one sole alchymy obtain.'

When I heard these words from the farmer, a longing for the gains of agriculture entered my head, and shutting up the door of my shop I busied myself with preparing farming implements. Now, in the quarter of the town in which I resided, there was a darvesh famed for his perfections, and noted for his excellent qualities.

COUPLET.

All outward show relinquishing, a lonely life he spent;
All luxuries he put aside, with requisites content.

When he learnt that I was leaving my own business, and going to employ myself in a different profession, he sent for me, and loosing the tongue of rebuke, said, 'Master baker! be content with that which has been given thee and don't seek for more, for the quality of greediness is an unlucky one, and the end of the greedy is to be deprecated. But whoever holds in his hand the coin of contentment is the king of his own time, while he that is a prisoner to the baseness of avarice is on a level with devils and brutes.

COUPLET.

Be patient, and thy loaf of barley break,
Lest thou the wheat[3] that ruined Adam take.'

I replied, 'O shekh ! I get but little advantage from this business in which I am engaged, and I have found out that the profits of farming are great.   I have formed an idea that I may, perhaps, be benefited by the latter occupation, and that I may subsist more easily.'   The old devotee answered, 'For a very long time the means of thy subsistence have been procured by this business, and the beverage of thy life has, by this employment, been purified from the rubbish of anxiety ; while the undertaking in which thou art at present designing to embark is an affair full of toil. Peradventure thou mayest not be able to labour assiduously in the duties required, nor to discharge fitly what it demands.   Nor is everything which shews its head from the secret chamber of desire possible to be acquired according to our wish.

---

[1] *Kibrit-i aḥmdr*, lit. 'red gold.'
[2] *Gúgird-i aḥmar*, another name for 'the philosopher's stone.'
[3] Some Muḥammadans suppose that 'wheat' was the forbidden fruit.   See Sale, page 5, note 'c.'

COUPLET.

Know, my friend! the way is long, longer far than words express,
From the street of our desires to the market of success.

Meddle not with that which concerns thee not, and withdraw not thine
hand from thine own employment, for whoever leaves his own trade and
undertakes a thing unsuited to him will meet with what that Crane met
with.' I asked, 'How was that?'

STORY II.

The darvesh replied, ' They have related that a washerman was wont to
be busy in his avocation on the bank of a certain river. Every day he saw
there a Crane, which sat on the river's bank, and used to catch the creatures
that are found in the mud, and contenting himself therewith, went back to
his nest. One day there came a swift-winged hawk, which made prey of
a fat quail, and after eating part of it, left the rest and flew away. The Crane
thought to himself, ' This animal with such a puny body makes prey of large
birds, and I of such a huge stature content myself with a trifle ; and this state
of things is evidently owing to my mean spirit. Why should not I too have
a share of magnanimity? My advisable course is hereafter not to stoop to
small matters, and not to cast the noose of my efforts save on the battlements
of the highest heavens.

VERSE.

The cloud when thirsty seeks the purple ocean,
Nor bows its head to sip the humble dew.[1]
Hearts that are stirred by proud and high emotion,
Stoop not to mean things, nor for trifles sue.'

He then forsook the chace of worms, and was on the watch to pursue
pigeons and quails. Now the washerman had from a distance observed the
proceedings of the hawk and the quail. When he saw the amazement of the
Crane, and how it gave up its own employment, he was astonished, and
opened the eye of amusement. By the will of fate a pigeon appeared in that
direction, and the Crane flying up made a stoop at it. The pigeon turning
along the edge of the water, outstripped the Crane, which pouncing down
behind, fell on the bank of the river, and his leg stuck in the mud.
The more he tried to fly away, the more his foot sank in the thick mire, and
his feathers and wings became more and more besmeared with the mud. The

---

[1] I feel very doubtful of the meaning of the first two lines of this verse. Readings differ
very considerably, yet none seem good, I have translated very freely. The literal version
would, I apprehend, be, 'The cloud runs, because it is thirsty, to the blue sea; it bows not
its head to moisture. They are live-hearted who fly upward: from the effect of spirit they
fly upward.'

washerman came up and seized him, and set off home. In the way a friend met him and asked, 'What's this?' The washerman replied, ' *This is a crane that wanted to hunt,*' and that wished to play the part of a hawk, and so destroyed itself.'

And I have adduced this story that thou mayest know that every one ought to attend to his own business and quit that which does not belong to him.'

When the old darvesh had cited this tale, the temptings of my covetousness increased, and refusing that speech access to the ear of attention, I persevered in the same idea. So I abandoned the business of a baker, and with the trifling capital I possessed purchased implements for farming, and having sown a quantity of grain, fastened the eye of expectation on the road of looking for the crop. In the meantime my means of subsisting myself and my family became straitened, because what I expended daily had been as regularly procured in the baker's shop, and now it was necessary for me to wait a year expectant, until the profit should arrive. I said to myself, ' Thou hast committed an error in not listening to the words of thy venerable seniors, and now thou art in distress for thy current expenses, and there is no channel by which income is obtainable. Thy best course is to get a sum by way of loan, and having re-opened thy baker's shop, return to thy own business.

COUPLET.

From his own business, he who turns aside,
'Twere best that he should there again subside. [1]

I then betook myself to one of the rich merchants of the city, and having taken up a sum on credit, I opened my shop a second time, and leaving one of my servants to superintend that business, I myself was busy with my farming. Now I started for the country to manage the cultivation, and anon I returned to the market to set off my shop. When two or three months had passed in this way, my servant swindled me, and not a particle either of stock or profit was left. At the same time a variety of misfortunes befell my crops. The tenth of what I had expended was not realised. I then went to the same neighbor, and detailed to him my case, and told him the circumstance of my taking two things in hand, and my losing by both. The aged darvesh laughed and said, ' How like thy case is to that of the man of two kinds of hair, who gave up his beard to his wives!' I asked, 'How was that?'

---

[1] The reader must pardon the bad rhyme of these verses, as the rhyming words are intended to express the jingle of *sar gashtah* and *sar rishtah*.

STORY III.

The darvesh said, 'They have related that a person had two wives, one old and the other young; and he himself had hair of two colors. Now he was fond of both his wives, and passed a day and a night in the apartment of each; and his habit was, when he entered the apartment of one of his wives, to put his head in her lap and go to sleep. One day he went to the room of the elderly wife, and, according to custom, put his head in her lap and went to sleep. The old lady gazed on his face and hair, and said to herself, 'In the beard and whiskers of this person there are some black hairs; I can't do better than pluck them out, that all his beard may appear white, and that young wife of his may not fancy him; so when he perceives that that wife is not fond of him but loathes him and has an aversion for him, the flame of his affection, too, will be quenched and he will remove his heart from her and will give himself up altogether to me.' She then pulled out all the black hairs she could from his beard.

HEMISTICH.

The beard that lies in women's hands were better far plucked out.

The next day that person was in the apartment of his young wife, and in his accustomed manner put his head in her lap and went to sleep. The young wife observed some white hairs in his beard, and thought to herself, 'I must pluck out these white hairs that his whole beard may appear black, and when he sees himself with black hairs he will of course be disgusted with the society of his old wife, and will be attached to me. Thereupon she, too, pulled out as many white hairs as were required at the time. After some time had passed in this manner, one day that person stroked his beard with his hand; he found that the hairs were gone and that the harvest of his beard was scattered to the wind. At this he raised a cry of distress, but all his lamentation was vain. Now thy case is just similar. Part of thy capital and interest thou didst expend on thy baker's shop, and part thou wastedst on thy farming business, and now when thou lookest about thee, thou hast neither baked bread in the oven of subsistence nor a stack obtained in the tillage-ground of life.

COUPLET.

One day in this, the next in that, goes by;
Thou look'st, and now nor this, nor that, canst spy.'

When I heard this story I perceived that what the old darvesh said was true, and that from this procedure I had got nothing but regret and remorse, and that all I possessed would not suffice to pay my debts. I looked upon it, therefore, as the best thing I could do in accordance with the direction, '*Flight from what is insupportable is agreeable to the laws of Apostles,*' to fly from that city, which I accordingly did by night. I went on stage by stage, in terror and alarm, until I had traversed a long distance. After the lapse of a considerable interval, I heard that my children were dead and that my creditors had taken possession of my effects—under a valuation—in payment of my debts. Thus hopeless of returning to my country, I journey on from stage to stage and from one place to another: and I seek a solace for the pain of my heart, from every gentleman I meet with, and place the ointment of gratification on the wound of the fatigues of travel by interviews with men of God: till this moment, when the mirror of my heart has been purified from the rust of cares by the furbishing instrument of proximity to your honor, and the sharbat of my enjoyment has been prepared with the sweetness of the sugar-raining conversation of my lord.

COUPLET.

Thanks be to God! though grief has wrung my soul,
In seeing thee I've reached my wishes' goal.

This is a sample of my history, which I have narrated.' The Devotee responded, ' I have inhaled from thy words the perfume of sincerity, and my heart has borne testimony to the truth of thy discourse; and if during some days thou hast undergone the affliction of exile and the toils of travel, still thou hast gained good experience, and hast acquired perfect information of the manners and customs of divers nations, and mayest live hereafter in peace and tranquillity.

HEMISTICH.

Grief's eve is ended, and joy's morn begins.

The Guest was pleased with his host, and the host, too, viewing the society of his guest as a piece of unexpected good fortune, shewed his satisfaction by his friendly unceremoniousness. Now the Devotee was one of the children of Israel, and knew the Hebrew language well; and though he was versed in most languages, and could converse in a majority of tongues, nevertheless, as the Hebrew was his mother-tongue, his fluency therein was conspicuous, and he always spoke in that tongue to his domestics. Although the European stranger was, in point of fact, ignorant of Hebrew, still he liked to hear the Devotee speak in it, and constantly besought him to do so. The latter, too, to gratify his Guest, and on account of his liking for the language, loosed the tongue of eloquence, and satisfied all that rhetoric could demand in speaking the Hebrew tongue well. Thus the Guest became a lover of the language, and from the excessive sweetness of the Devotee's discourse, and the tastefulness of his conversation, he formed the desire of learning Hebrew from him.

VERSE.

His sugar-raining lips, aye, smiling sweet,
Of honeyed sayings shed a ceaseless treat.
When the Guest saw of sweet words such supply,
Like parrot he the sugared feast would buy.

Some days passed, and the veil of ceremony being removed from between them, their character of strangers was exchanged for that of united friends, and from the premises of acquaintance the conclusion of intimacy was obtained.

COUPLET.

To their hearts' wish they may together sit,
When banished forms no more prohibit it.

Then the Guest boldly commenced the praises of the Devotee, and said,

COUPLET.

'Thou! whose speech opes perfection's cabinet,
While on thy words the seal of grace is set,

what ornament of discourse and embellishment of style is this ? It is such that the eye of the reason of those of penetrating sight never saw more perfect eloquence, and the ear of the intelligence of those who can appreciate rhetoric never listened to more beautiful language.

COUPLET.

Of thy discourse I know not what I fitly can affirm ;
I cannot call it prophecy, nor yet it magic term.

I trust that thou wilt teach me this language, and I respectfully entreat that thou will not withhold from me instruction in this dialect; for, without previous introduction, thou hast fulfilled towards me all the dues of courtesy in treating me with honor and respect; and without the premission of the antecedents of friendship, thou hast been careful to display manifold attentions in thy hospitable reception of me. To-day, that the bond of our amity has been confirmed by means of our long intercourse, I am in hopes that thou wilt be pleased to shew kindness and link my request with acceptance, and draw on the page of my condition with eagerness and pleasure the writing of discipleship, in order that it may become a cause of the increase of the matters of mutual esteem, and that thus the daily portions of the commemoration of kindness and the fashion of gratitude may be observed.

COUPLET.

I can do nought but still thy praise declare ;
Thy servant I, the nursling of thy care.'

The Devotee replied, ' Why should I grudge or demur to do this ? being as it is to raise a person from the abyss of ignorance to the pinnacle of knowledge, and to conduct a learner from the lowest place of the low of defective understanding to the rank of highest of the high of perfection. However, it occurs to me that between the Hebrew language and that of Europe there is an immense disagreement and huge difference. Forbid it! that in this study thy mind and intellect should be altogether wearied out on account of its being altogether incompetent to comprehend and recollect it. And in that case both my labor will be wasted and thy time lost.' The Guest replied, 'Whoever steps forward to acquire anything must undoubtedly prepare himself to undergo hardships, and he who turns his face in the direction of the K'abah[1] of his wish, must not think of the suffering in the desert of toil.

COUPLET.

When, in the hope to reach the K'abah, in the desert thou dost tread,
Arabia's thorn[2] may hold thee back, but be not thou discomfited.

And I am so much in earnest in this resolve, that if every hair on my head became a thorn I would not turn my face from this enterprise; and though every eyelash on my eyelids were changed into a lance I would not glance at any other business.

HEMISTICH.

He who would win a treasure must, as well, endure the toil.

And all suffering that is endured in the pursuit of learning turns into enjoyment in the end, and the labor of the student is never thrown away. In this way that Hunter, by means of a slight inconvenience which he submitted to for the sake of learning, and by an insignificant service which he performed towards the wise, obtained complete affluence, and arrived from the narrow strait of want in the expanding plain of independence and abundance.' The Devotee asked, 'How was that?'

STORY IV.

The Guest said, 'They have related that a poor man was practising a hunter's profession, and contenting himself with capturing birds and fishes, so passed his existence; and when employed in capturing fish, his whole frame became eyes, like a net; and when in pursuit of birds, he made a gin of every hair of his body.

HEMISTICH.

Nor bird, nor fish, could from his net escape.

One day he had set his net, and, with a thousand difficulties, had brought three birds into its vicinity, and he himself was sitting in a place of ambush, waiting until he could secure the neck of those hapless birds in the mesh of his snare. In the midst of this state he heard a noise of wrangling, and in

---

[1] The black temple at Makkah. Study is here compared to the wearisome and dangerous pilgrimage of the Hajj.

[2] What the *khár-i maghailán* may exactly be, I do not know. The Dictionary merely says, 'a thorn different from the acacia.' It is probably the same thorn, exceedingly sharp and strong, called in Africa the 'Wait a bit' thorn.

fear lest the birds should, by reason of the sound, fly away, he issued from his ambuscade. He then beheld two students, who were disputing on a point of law, and their discourse had ended in quarreling. The Hunter besought them much, saying, ' Do not make a noise, that these birds may not be scared away, and thus my labour lost.

HEMISTICH.

Breathe not a word, lest the net's prey be scared.'

They retorted, ' If thou wilt give us a share in the game, to each of us a bird, we will consent to thy request, and will not indulge in strife and angry vociferation.' The hunter replied, ' Friends, I am a poor man with a family, and the food of several persons depends on these birds, and after you have carried off two birds, how shall I go home? and how shall I solace ten persons with one bird.' They answered, ' Thou art employed every day in this business, and it is a long time since we have met with this sport. It is altogether impossible that we should dispense with these birds. Either we will call out so that the birds will fly away, or thou shalt agree to give each of us a bird, so that we may take them for our lecturer to see, and give the other students of the college an entertainment.' In vain the Hunter complained, saying, ' Your professor did not knit my net, nor did the hands of the students twist my cord. I have not set my net in ground bequeathed for religious purposes; nor have I scattered grain as bait from the granaries of the college; nor am I bound by law to bestow upon you my game by way of thirds or two-thirds.' All his words, however, had no effect; and at last he promised them the birds; which, having pulled the string, he caught in the net. Then he commenced his entreaties and lamentations again, saying, ' Have pity upon me! and shorten the hand of covetousness from carrying off these birds.' They replied, ' Cease these words and fulfil the promise thou hast made.' The hunter saw there was no alternative, and gave each of them a bird. He then said, ' Since, forsooth, I have submitted to your annoyance, and have presented you with gifts and somewhat to conciliate your good-will, teach me the word about which you were disputing; perhaps some day it may be of use to me.' They replied, ' We were disputing about the word ' hermaphrodite,' and were contending as to the rights of inheritance of such a person.' The hunter inquired, What is the meaning of the term ' hermaphrodite?' They answered, ' In point of fact it means one who is neither male nor female.' The Hunter stored up the word in his memory, and went home very much out of spirits, and related to his family the circumstances, and they contented themselves with a scant repast, and so passed the night. The next day, when the golden-pinioned bird of the sun came flying abroad from the nest of the horizon, and the silver-encrusted fishes of the stars, from dread of the cords of the solar rays, turned to flight on the expanse of heaven,

COUPLET.

Heaven like a hunter, with a golden net,   Did the sun, fish-like, in its meshes get,

the old fisherman, having taken up his net, set off for the river's side, and, with complete reliance on God, let down the net into the water. Fate decreed that a fish of beautiful form and exquisite shape should be taken; such that the armorer, water, had never reared one clad in scales like it, and the eyes of mermen[1] never beheld in the expanse of waters an equal beauty[2];

VERSE.

Its belly clear a silver whiteness shewed,
Bright as the fountain of the sun its eye.
Chameleon-like, its back with colors glowed,
Whose varying tints would thought itself defy.

The fisherman was amazed at its shape and appearance, and thought to himself, ' In all my life I never saw a fish like this, nor gazed upon so splendid a prize. My best course is to carry it alive to the Sultán as a free-will offering, and by such a service get myself a great name among my fellows.' Hereupon, he cast the fish into a vessel of water, and set off for the king's palace. It so befell that, by the Sultán's command, they had made in the royal garden in front of the palace, where the king was wont to sit, a basin of marble and alabaster for a fountain, and had put in it various kinds of fishes.

COUPLET.

Fish of silver therein play;   Golden rings their ears down weigh.

And they had set afloat a skiff, shaped like a crescent, on the surface of that heaven-resembling reservoir.

COUPLET.

Of aloe-wood a barque there too,   Like crescent seemed in sky of blue.

Every day the monarch came to the brink of the basin to enjoy the sight, and was pleased with the sportive swimming of the fish and the movements of the vessel. At that same time, too,

COUPLET.

He gazed upon the water fair,   Watched moon and stars reflected there.

when all at once the fisherman[3] came in, and offered to the king's inspection that beautiful and exquisite fish. The king was excessively pleased at the sight of the fish, and commanded them to give the Fisherman a thousand

---

[1] Such I suppose to be the meaning of *mardum-i dbt*, though the word does not occur in the Dictionary.

[2] *L'ubatí*, lit., ' doll,' ' plaything.'

[3] The word *ṣaiyád* is rather a difficult one to translate, as the class so designated are at once fishermen, hunters, and fowlers. So the old man in the present story. It seems odd to call him a fowler when fishing, and a fisherman when catching birds.

dínárs. One of the vazírs who held a rank, which allowed of his taking a liberty, and an office which permitted him to speak boldly, loosed the tongue of admonition and whispered to the king,

COUPLET.

'May thy clear heart a fountain be of light,   And thy high fortunes no reproach invite![1]

Fishermen are numerous and the sea is full of fish: if the king bestow a thousand dínárs for every fish, neither will the gold in the treasury suffice for it, nor will the revenues of the country be adequate. It is a settled thing, too, what the price of a fish ought to be, and how much one ought to give to a fisherman for a reward. A present ought to be proportionate to merit, and a reward suitable to the service done.

COUPLET.

A tank that holds a hundred tons—no more,
Admits not that two hundred should flow o'er.'

The king responded, 'I have promised him a thousand dínárs; and how can it be admissible to break that promise?' The vazír replied, 'I have a scheme for this, so that your promise shall not be broken, and too much money not be lost either. My advice is, that you ask him whether this fish is male or female? If he says it is a male, we will tell him to bring a female, and he will receive a thousand dínárs. And if he says it is a female, we will say, 'Bring a male and take thy gold.' Of course he will be at a loss how to do this, and then having satisfied him with some trifle, we will acquire his goodwill.' The king then turned to the Fisherman, and said, 'Is this fish a male or a female?' The old Fisher was a man of experience, and a cunning fellow. He guessed what the secret intention of the king and the vazír was by that question, and sent down the diver of thought into the sea of deliberation, to see how he could secure the pearl of an answer, which he could place on the tray of representation. At last that same word which the day before he had learned of the students flashed across his mind. He answered, 'O king! asylum of the world! this fish is a hermaphrodite, that is to say, it is neither male nor female.' The sultán was much pleased [at this rejoinder], rebuked the vazír for his scheme, and adding another thousand bestowed two thousand dínárs on the Fisherman, and made him one of his special favorites and counsellors.

And the lesson to be drawn from this story is, that the Fisherman by one word which he committed to memory, and through the two birds with which he obliged the students, obtained two thousand dínárs, and was honored with the sultan's favor; wherefore no loss accrues from toil after learning, and from waiting on learned men. Moreover the wise have said,

---

[1] Here is an equivoque on *sar sabz*, 'fortunate head,' and *sar zanish*, 'reproof.'

VERSE.

Get learning, that thou mayest honored be ;
Man is worth nought,[1] of learning when bereft.
Knowledge will raise thy fortune and degree
From the remotest line where shoes are left,[2]
To the mid-circle of the company.'

The Devotee said, 'Now that thou importunest me, and art resolved to traverse the road of inquiry in the desert of study with the step of labor, I, too, as far as is attainable, will impart instruction and communicate knowledge; and will not omit a particle in causing thee to understand questions and in making clear the rules.' The Guest betook himself to that study, and passed a considerable time in learning the Hebrew language. His mind, however, was in no wise disposed to be a recipient of that tongue, and was altogether devoid of capacity for comprehending its subtleties. The more instruction he received, his skill in the practice of it became less ; and, however much he planted the sapling of instruction in the garden of thought, the more the fruit of disappointment increased on the branch of hope.

COUPLET.

Unaided from the store of heavenly grace,
No toil avails, no wished-for thing takes place.

One day the Devotee said to him, 'Thou hast undertaken a difficult matter, and hast laid on thy mind a huge weight. Thy tongue will not speak fluently in this dialect, and thy intellect is not suited to this tongue. Relinquish this design, and set not thy foot in a plain which is not proper for thy equitation.

STANZA.

For that, which thou by no means e'er canst win,
To waste thy life in vain attempts, were shame.
List to the sages' counsel, nor begin
A course, if thou canst ne'er conclude the same.

To give up the tongue of one's progenitors, and to toil at a language and business opposite to that of one's ancestors is far removed from the path of rectitude. The Guest replied, 'Imitation of the dead in their errors and ignorance is the very extreme of servility and fatuity; and in this matter I will not imitate any one, nor will I quit the road of right investigation, for imitation is the noose of the torments of devils, and right investigation the guide of the paths of sincerity and truth. And the

---

[1] *Pishíz,* ' a fish scale ;' also ' a small coin.'
[2] This I take to be the meaning of *ṣaff-i nid'lat.* It is well known that Orientals on entering a room leave their shoes or slippers. Some of the lowest domestics are left to take care of these, and form the outside of the company, which goes on by regular ranks till the upper centre is reached, where the chief personage is.

recondite saying, '*Verily we found our fathers practising a religion,*[1] is a
rebuke to the children of the play-ground of imitation that they should come
from the perilous place of doubt into the stronghold of conviction, and gaze
with the eye of certainty on the brilliancy of the light, '*He directeth whom
He pleaseth into the right way.*'[2]

DISTICHS.

Whose sight base imitation does not mar,[3]
Sees in the light of truth all things that are :
There is between the mimicked and the true,
The difference of the[4] voice and echo too.
'T is imitation that has ruined men,
Two hundred curses rest upon it then ! '

The Devotee said, 'I have done my duty in advising thee, and I fear that
the end of this struggle will issue in regret, and now thou art able to speak
in the European language, and can discourse in the dialect of thy wife and
kindred. It is probable that if thou art continually repeating Hebrew phrases,
the practice of this language will be hidden from thee, and thou wilt lose the
other language too. Thus thy case will resemble that of the Crow that tried
to learn the gait of the mountain-partridge and so forgot his own.'   The
Guest asked, 'How was that?'

STORY V.

The Devotee said, 'They have related that one day a Crow was flying
and saw a partridge, which was walking gracefully on the ground, and with
that sweet step and graceful gait enchanted the heart of the looker-on.

COUPLET.

Thy graceful gait bore off at once my heart, in rapturous ecstasy,
With witching step approach once more, that I may shed my life for thee.

The Crow was pleased with the gait of the partridge, and amazed at its
symmetrical movements, and agility and elasticity. The desire of walking in
the same manner fixed itself in his mind, and from the core of his heart, the
insane longing to step proudly, after the same fascinating fashion, made its
appearance. He forthwith girt his loins in attendance on the partridge, and

---

[1] Kur'án, Fl. xliii. 21 ; Mar. 22 ; Sale, p. 362, l. 14 : 'And they say, If the Merciful
had pleased, we had not worshipped them. They have no knowledge herein : they only utter
a vain lie. Have we given them a book of revelations before this ; and do they keep the
same in their custody ? But they say, Verily we found our fathers practising a religion ;
and we are guided in their footsteps.'

[2] Kur'án, Fl. ii. 136 ; Mar. 143 ; Sale, p. 16, l. 15 : 'The foolish men will say, what hath
turned them from their Keblah, towards which they formerly prayed ? Say, Unto God
belongeth the east and the west : he directeth whom he pleaseth into the right way.'

[3] Lit., 'He, who beyond the curtain of imitation has sprung.'

[4] I confess myself quite unable to translate these lines. I have no idea what داود
means, and the dictionaries supply no information.

abandoning sleep and food, gave himself up to that arduous occupation, and kept continually running in the traces of the partridge, and gazing on its progress.

COUPLET.

'O partridge! on thou proudly steppest with a sweet enchanting grace;
Halting and lame I follow after, ever limping on thy trace.'

One day the partridge said, 'O crazy, black-faced one! I observe that thou art ever hovering about me, and art always watching my motions. What is it that thou dost want?' The Crow replied, 'O thou of graceful manners and sweet smiling face!

COUPLET.

Thy step has robbed me of my heart, and now I thee pursuing,
Search on and on lamenting, and my lost heart vainly ruing.

Know that having conceived a desire to learn thy gait, I have followed thy steps for a long time past, and wish to acquire thy manner of walking, in order that I may place the foot of pre-eminence on the crown of the head of my fellows.' The partridge uttered a merry laugh, and said, 'Alack! alack!

HEMISTICH.

Ah me! how great the gulf 'twixt thee and me![1]

My walking gracefully is a thing implanted in me by nature, and thy style of going is equally a natural characteristic. Nothing can obliterate natural dispositions, and no pains can alter the inherent bent. My going is in one way, and thy mode of procedure is quite another.

HEMISTICH.

Behold from where to where our roads diverge![2]

Leave off this fancy and relinquish this idea.

HEMISTICH.

Cease! for this bow suits not thy arm to draw.'

The Crow replied, ' *The commencement forces.*' Since I have plunged into the affair, no idle stories shall make me give it up; and until I grasp my wished-for object, I will not turn back from this road.

COUPLET.

We have the ship of patience launched on the strong sea of pain;
And we will perish there or win the jewel we would gain.'

So the unfortunate Crow for a long time ran after the partridge, and having failed to learn his method of going, forgot his own too, and could in nowise recover it.

And I have adduced this story in order that thou mayest know that thou hast undertaken a fruitless task, and art using unavailing efforts. And they

---

[1] Lit., 'Where art thou and where are we?'
[2] This is the 1st line of the 5th Ode of Ḥáfiẓ, p. 36, lithographed edition.

have said that the most fatuous of creatures is he that plunges into a thing
unfitted to his nature and unsuited to his degree; and this affair has, in point
of fact, exactly the same character as thy leaving the baker's business and
embarking in agriculture, and in the end the clue of both things having
escaped from thy hand, thou hast been left in the grief of exile and the
calamity of friendlessnes.

COUPLET.

I said, I would my life surrender, that I might that meeting gain,
I gave my life, but in the end I could that meeting not obtain.'

The Guest would not meet the advice of the Devotee with acceptance, and
in a short time forgot the language of his fathers, and failed to learn Hebrew.

HEMISTICH.

That from him slipped, and this he failed to grasp.'

This is the story of one who quits his own profession and undertakes a
thing which does not suit him, and this chapter is closely connected with the
caution and prudence requisite in kings. Thus every ruler who wishes to
sway with a vigorous hand his kingdom, and to whom the tranquillity of his
subjects, and the promotion of his friends, and the extermination of his
enemies, are desirable objects, will think it right to give the minutest attention and consideration to these matters. Such a king will not suffer a
worthless and naturally incompetent person to contest precedence with those
of a noble and pure nature. For many low people fancy themselves rival
competitors of the experienced cavaliers of the field of honor, and in the
exercising ground of competition[1] consider their own lagging carrion as
equal in the race with the lightning-paced Burák of the others' spirit, while
in point of fact, if they traveled by relays, they would not so much as come
up with the dust that their more noble competitors raise.

COUPLET.

How the bright goblet of Jamshíd shall earthen cups to rival try?
Though decked in pearls[2] and rubies it their worthless boasts may still defy.

Wherefore the observation of this precedence in the rules of administration
is of the highest importance, and if, which God forbid! the difference of
ranks disappear from among the rulers of men, and the lowest sit in the
same scale with the mediocre, and these latter put themselves on an equality
with the noblest; the awe of royalty is impaired, and interruption and
disturbance appear in the royal administration of affairs. On this account
former kings used to take care that men of low nature and origin should
acquire learning and the art of writing, and know questions in accounts and

---

[1] I am doubtful of this meaning of *kafáf*.

[2] One MS., for *bidurr ú l'al*, reads *bidaur-i l'al*, 'in the circulation of the wine.'

numeration, because that should this custom come to prevail, that men of business should enter the circle of the great, while great men would be unable to transact the operations of men of business, the ill effects thereof would of course be all-pervading and widely spread.   Thus the means of support of high and low would be absolutely interrupted, and in consequence of these circumstancies retardation would take place in affairs, and in the course of time the effect thereof would be apparent.   Wherefore it behoves a sensible man to think it incumbent to preserve the sections of the admonitions of the wise, and the advice of the sage, in order that having reaped the advantage of their beneficial influence, the fruits of experience may be made available for his career in life, and his transactions may remain preserved and safe from the imputation of faultiness, and the brand of neglect.

VERSE.

Him in the world thou mayest call truly wise,
Whose ear heeds counsel and heart subtleties.
Words are like pearls, the speakers they who dive;
Ere they win princely gems they long must strive;
In those dark shells so hardly brought to light,
Lies many a pearl with secret wisdom bright.

CHAPTER XII.

OF THE EXCELLENCE OF MILDNESS, AND CALMNESS, AND TRAN- QUILLITY, AND COMPOSURE, ESPECIALLY IN KINGS.

INTRODUCTION.

Again the august king of kings turned to the illustrious sage, and in a style sweetly eloquent,

COUPLET.

Said, eulogizing him, ' O matchless sage!   Ne'er was thy equal witnessed by this age.

Thou hast narrated the story of one who having turned from the profession and language of his forefathers, betook himself to a thing unsuited to his condition and unconformable to his habits; and for whom, after that the object of his desire had been hid from the eye of his intention, return to his original business became impossible.

HEMISTICH.

He yields up this, and that eludes his hands.

Now relate what are the most admirable qualities in kings, and which are most closely connected with the welfare of the State, and the continuance of fortune, and stability of affairs, and the conciliation of hearts? And I have seen in the Twelfth Precept that it behoves monarchs to make mildness the ornament of their career, and patience the principal of their dealings. Yet I am in doubt whether mildness be a preferable quality for kings, or generosity or valor? Do thou, with thy sagacity which solves difficulties, undo the knot of the string of this problem, and with thy judgment, which points out the right, elucidate in the best possible way the mystery of this question?'

VERSE.

When the sage teacher heard this question, he
The door of wisdom's treasury set wide,
And said, ' O Khusrau! sway and fortune be
Ever, as now, with thy command allied!

Know that the most praiseworthy characteristic and approved quality, whence both the person of kings will inspire awe and be most respected, and whence, too, as well soldiers as other subjects, will be made to feel content, is mildness and good-nature. And from the verse, ' *If thou hadst been severe and hard-hearted, they had surely separated themselves from about thee,*[1] and from the words, tending to virtue, of the Sulṭán of the throne of prophecy and the felicitous lord of the empire of glory *(On him be the choicest benedictions of those who pray !)* it is to be understood that happiness in this world and what we hope for in the next are the consequents of mildness and good-nature. *Thus it is said,*[2] *' Of the happiness of man is excellence of disposition, and the meek man is all but becoming a prophet.'* And as to these three qualities, of which the king is enamoured, it is better that he should know to which to·give the preference. All three are requisite, but valor is not always required, and in a whole life there may be but once a necessity for its display. But generosity and mildness are always wanted; wherefore these too are better than valor. Again, the advantages of generosity are restricted to a certain class; and it is only a particular body of individuals who can share in the benefits of the royal bounty. On the other hand, small and great stand in need of mildness, and the blessings of good temper extend to high and low, the civilian and the soldier. Wherefore it follows, as a matter of course, that mildness is superior to the other virtue.

VERSE.

> He is, in truth, the best of human race,
>   Who aye maintains a mild and kindly mood.
> Man's goodness is not in the charms of face;
>   The temper's sweetness is his fount of good.

And a sage has said, ' Were there between me and all mankind but a single hair, and all of them unanimously tried to break it, it would be impossible that it should break ; because if they left it slack I would tighten it, and if they pulled it tight I would slacken it. In other words, the perfection of my mildness and scope of my forgiving nature are of such extent that I can live at peace with all mankind, and can put up with the vulgar and the learned, the innocent and the criminal.

COUPLET.

> While he pursues his selfish ends, his cords around me rest;
> If he will not obey my will, I'll follow his behest.'

And be it known, that gravity and composure are a more graceful ornament of kings, and meekness and endurance a better decoration for the rulers of the world [than generosity or courage], because the commands of princes are absolute as to the life and goods and landed property of mankind, and their directions to do or not to do a thing prevail without restriction over the

---

[1] Kur'án, Fl. iii. 153, Mar. 160; Sale, p. 50, l. 14: 'And as to the mercy granted unto the disobedient from God, thou, O Muḥammad ! hast been mild towards them? but if thou hadst been severe and hard-hearted, they had surely separated themselves from about thee.' See also p. 2 of this translation, note 7, where this verse is quoted, and where by a misprint the page of Sale is given as 30 for 50.

[2] Lit., ' as he said.'

lowest and the highest, and the mean and the great. Wherefore, if their
dispositions are not adorned with mildness and conscientiousness, it is
possible that by a single harsh act they may estrange the minds of a whole
nation, and by a rash and precipitate deed chafe and displease the whole
world, and thus many lives and possessions will fall into the place of
destruction and alienation.

QUATRAIN.

Each order given by a reigning king,
    Should after long reflection be expressed;
For it may be that endless woes will spring,
    From a command he paused not to digest.

And if a king wash from the face of the age the dust of want with the
water of generosity, or consume with the fire of valor the harvest of the life
of the hostile; yet, if he have no share of the stock of mildness, he will, by a
single act of tyranny, make turbid the fountain of bountifulness, and by one
violent deed raise up a thousand mortal enemies. While, on the other hand,
if he fall short in the matter of generosity, and be slack in the field of
courage, he may still conciliate his people and his armies by courtesy and
blandness, and by his mildness and amiability, and by these qualities bind
men to loyalty and chain them to his service;

VERSE.

'T is best thy face be smiling as the rose,
    That through all parts thy name spread fragrantly.
Mankind will look with favor upon those
    Who gild the world with their humanity.

And together with mildness, a king must have a share, also, of dignified
composure, for mildness without firmness is not devoid of fault. Thus if one
endure many annoyances; and manifest, in the most extreme degree, the
quality of patience, if it conclude in precipitancy and terminate in rash
and inconsiderate action, all those instances of long-suffering will be wasted,
and he will be unsuccessful.

COUPLET.

Be thou in the path of patience ever stable as a rock,
He who shows the most composure will be freest, too, from shock.

It behoves a king, too, at the time of showing mildness, not to suffer
himself to be swayed by his inclinations; and at the time of anger not to
allow himself to listen to the tempter; for rage is a torch of the devil's fire,
and a branch, the fruit of which is chagrin and repentance. Mildness is one
of the qualities of the prophets; and rage a canine passion and one of the
temptations of the evil one. It is agreed, too, among men of profound
wisdom and those possessed of true piety, that until a person has got the
mastery over anger, he cannot reach the rank of the just. It is also
written in the remarkable sayings of the wise, that they made representation

to an eminent personage, saying, ' Express in one word the various branches of a good moral nature, that it may be the easier to grasp it.' He responded, ' To forsake anger comprehends all virtuous qualities and excellent disposi- tions, and to allow wrath its free course, includes all reprehensible acts and disgraceful deeds.

DISTICHS.

Anger and spite to brutes and beasts belong,
Class then the wrathful with the bestial throng.
Thy anger springs from hell—is a part so
Of that dread whole, and of mankind's arch-foe.
Art thou a portion then of hell ?—Beware !
For parts to wholes, by nature's laws, repair.

And moreover it must be known that the requirement that a king has of a vazír who is able to give him perfect advice, and of a prudent and eminent counsellor, is in order that, if the pride of power and the haughtiness of regal sway should lead him aside from the path of mildness and clemency, his right-counselling vazír, having brought him back by advice to the path of rectitude, may cause him to tread firmly in the road of calmness and com- posure ; and having by the antidote of admonition destroyed the tendency to swerve from justice, may bestow on him the quality of stability in the way of safety; that by the bestowal of the grace of the Creator, and the happy influence of mildness and composure, and the loyalty of the counsels and purity of the intentions of his fortune-bringing vazír, he may be successful and triumphant in all his affairs : and that in whatever direction he may turn, victory and conquest may be his companions and attendants, and fortune and success his aiders and assistants.   And if on some occasion he should issue his commands in any affair in accordance with his passions, and in obedience to his deceitful lusts, and deliver a decree without reflection and sure thought, and not according to foresight and prudence, then by the clear judgment of such a faithful minister the evil of his injustice may be alleviated; and the remedy of the confusion, and reparation of the error may not remain in the area of impossibility, as was the case in the contest of the King of Hindústán with his tribe.'   The world-adorning king asked, ' How was that ? '

STORY I.

The Bráhman said, ' They have related that in one of the countries of Hindústán there was a king by name Hílár, possessed of immense treasures and hidden stores and wealth and money without end.

COUPLET.

His spear that fostered wealth was of his realm and tribe the guard,
His victory-spreading sabre took, the faith, the world itself, in ward.

And he was distinguished from the princes of his time by a variety of illustrious actions, and was conspicuous among successful rulers by many glorious deeds.   He had two sons, such that the bright sun borrowed splendor from their radiant countenances, and the shining moon moved distractedly in the field of the sky at the beauty of their cheeks, and the delicate grace of their faces.   One with stature like an arrow drew towards himself, like the horns of a bow, the quadrigesimal fasters of the corners of pilgrimage,[1] and the other, with ringlets like the chains of the demented, brought to the sick-bed of suffering the limbs of those who tore their hair.   At sight of the symmetrical stature, delightful to the heart, of the one, the straight cypress had its foot plunged in clay through amazement; and from jealousy of the fascinating movements of the other, the mountain-partridge forgot its own gait.

COUPLET.

This like the tulip, with its shining face :

And, rose-like, that diffused attractive grace.

And together with comeliness of form, they were also adorned with excellence of manners, and they decked the young plant of their beauty with the flowers of goodness and perfection.   Their outward form was exceeding graceful, and their inner nature excessively enchanting.

COUPLET.

Ne'er did heaven's eye such forms, such souls too, find ;

Praised be their form, and yet more praised their mind !

They called one Suhail-i Yamaní, and the other Máh-i Khutaní,[2] and their mother, 'Irán-dukht, was a ravishing beauty, in envy of whose delicate cheek the bride of the sun was hidden behind the veil of inquietude, and from shame at whose falling ringlets the curling hyacinth was writhing and in folds.

VERSE.

A beauty, graced with parted, curling hair ;

A hundred amorous signs her love express.

Her cheek—the rose and violet mingle there,—

The violet keeps the rose in safe duresse.

From ring of purest musk her locks flow loose,

And on the sun's neck cast their glittering noose.

The king's heart was excessively attached to this incomparable gem, and bound in affection to those two peerless sons : and without the sight of their beauty, the repose of his mind and the joy of his bosom were lost.   Moreover he had a vazír whom they called Balár, and the meaning of this word in their language is 'Auspicious face.'   And he was a sage illustrious for the

---

[1] That is, 'of those who came to see him.'

[2] That is, 'Canopus of Arabia,' and 'Moon of Tátary.'

solidity of his understanding, and famed and celebrated for the accuracy of his judgment. The proofs of his sagacity and experience, and the testimonies of his acuteness and attachment, were clearly displayed upon the face of his actions and the forehead of all he did; and the tokens of his sincerity and loyalty, and the happy influences of his special goodness and zeal to give satisfaction, were evident and conspicuous in his virtuous efforts and intense and glorious labors. The tongue of the age used to chant the praises of his perfection after this manner, and sought to attain the delineation of a trifling portion of the laudation due to his worth and greatness with these couplets,

VERSE.

O Âṣaf! thou, in whose assembly high,
Heaven's chancellor of small account would be.
And where the busy pen thy writers ply,
E'en Mercury's unreached by fate's decree.[1]

And the king's private secretary, whose name was Kamál, was a penman such that the planet Mercury[2] would be unable to draw the bow of his description, and the celestial amanuensis could not, with the step of consideration, mount the ladders of his edifices. Thou wouldest say that his reed, clothed in elegance, was the magazine of the secrets of eloquence; and the noise of his pen, marked with ingenuity, was the dawning-place of the lights of rhetoric. Every pearl of reasoning which he perforated with the diamond of reflection was strung by the arranger of his penetrating intellect on the string of lucid words and elegant expressions; and every coin of truth that he weighed with the balance of deliberation, the broker of his right-judging thought submitted with perfect recommendation and complete description to the inspection of the purchasers of the bázár of subtlety.

STANZA.

His speech with soul-expanding sense was fraught;
The structures of his pen bade hearts rejoice;
His reed to utter such sweet sounds he taught,
As put to shame the parrot of the voice.

And for his own especial riding the king had a white elephant, which was wont to hasten into the battle-field like the world-traversing wind, and to pierce with his rock-crushing tusks the bosom of stony-hearted mountains. Iron is ever hidden in mountains, but it, reversing the usual order of things, was a mountain hidden in iron; and hills are ever quiescent in one place, and destitute of pillars; but he, contrary to custom, was a moving mountain on four pillars.

---

[1] This idea is evidently borrowed from the Hindú notion that Vṛihaspatih, 'the planet Jupiter,' is the preceptor of the Gods. So Mercury is here called fate's registrar.

[2] Here is an unretainable equivoque. Tir means 'arrow,' as well as 'the planet Mercury.'

VERSE.

His head, vermilion-painted, rubbed the sky,
  Twilight assumed from it a pinky hue ;
His trunk, like to a lasso, circling flew,
  It seemed a dragon fall'n from mountain high ;
His feet were huge,[1] and terrible to view,
  'Neath them the trampled earth to finest powder grew.

He had also two other elephants of very majestic size, like the mountain
Alvand[2] in the hugeness of their limbs. With their trunks, like bats in the
game of chaugán, they drove the heads of rebels like balls along the field,
and with their column-resembling fore-feet they crushed the necks of the
refractory. Their crystal-like tusks brought forth spouts of coral from the
breasts of the king's foes, and with their ivory pickaxes they displayed from
the mines of the bodies of enemies heaps of rubies of Badakhshán.

VERSE.

Clouds they, whose drops the points of daggers are ;
Towers, but their ramparts are the ranks of war :
The tusk of this, in Mars' heart fixèd fast,
That's trunk, like lasso, o'er the Pleiads cast.

Moreover he had two dromedaries which could traverse mountains and
sandy plains, and which in one night could cross a whole clime, nay, in a
single instant could measure with their feet a world. They shewed with their
necks and ears the exact resemblance of a bow and arrow, and exhibited
with their fore-feet and breasts the similitude of a mace and shield. At the
time of running they made the surface of the earth appear like a shield, and
when traveling they bore off with their feet, which resembled the bat in the
game of chaugán, the ball of precedence from the swift-paced courser of the
moon.

COUPLET.

Sand-crossing, hill-resembling, they, content at heart, still onward sped;
Till morn each night they carried loads; all day upon the thorn they fed.

Besides these he had a fleet-paced, fiery steed, with silver hoofs and bridle
of gold ; which, when his reins were slackened, outstripped the world-
traversing moon ; nor could the earth-crossing north-wind come near the
dust which it raised. Thus, so long as the bay courser of the sky has circled
round the globe of earth, none had ever beheld the equal of that steed, and
while piebald time has traversed the space of ages, no one had ever heard
of such a horse.

---

[1] Lit., 'Large as a shield.'
[2] A high mountain near Hamadán.

VERSE.

Sky-circling, and earth-traversing, that horse
Drank water at the fountain of the sun ;
Each time that, bathed in sweat, it ran its course,
Rain-showers fell and lightning 'twixt them shone ;
And when it hastened to the battle-field,
A hundred breezes to its pace must yield.

And he had a sword adorned with jewels and embellished with precious pearls. One would have said that they had studded a blade of grass with drops of dew, or adorned a sheet of blue sky with royal pearls. The black marks of its original high temper, looked on its diamond blade, like the feet of ants, and on its blue-enameled surface the wings of flies were exhibited. It was not a sword, it was rather a cloud that showered blood or fiery-flashing lightning.

VERSE.

'T is like a verdant leaf in greenness, yet
A branch of Arghwán in war's orchard is.
Hid in the stream the lotus' leaves are set,
A lotus that has water in't is this.'

The king's heart was wholly bound up with these things that have been mentioned, and he always boasted of superiority in all these possessions over the monarchs of all the countries of Hind. Now there were in his kingdom a number of Bráhmans, who regarded themselves as the followers of Brahmá, and acknowledged his prophet and chose to turn aside from the true faith and the right way, and caused people to stray in the waste of error and the gulf of ignorance. However much King Hílár[1] bade them desist from misleading and deceiving his subjects, they, unheeding his rebuke, did not forsake that reprehensible habit. At last the affair came to this, that the king, through religious zeal and in defence of the faith, slew nearly twelve thousand of them. Their houses he gave up to be plundered, and their wives and children he led into captivity. But four hundred persons of the number who were adorned with the accomplishments of science, and were gifted with a variety of knowledge, he made to wait on the imperial throne. These, against their will, having girt the waist of service, traveled the road of obedience, and watched for an opportunity of revenge and a chance for wreaking their vengeance. One night the king was reposing[2] on the couch of enjoyment, when he heard seven terrible voices. Through dread of these he awoke, and fell into thought and reflection. In the midst of this, sleep again overpowered him, and in a dream he beheld two red fishes, from

---

[1] The editions have here, by a typographical error, *Hílár* for *Hílár*, which, as will be seen by the beginning of the story, was the king's name.

[2] For the *mashghúl búd*, one MS. reads *khuftah búd*, which I should prefer, as more applicable to sleep.

the brightness of which the eyes were dazzled, stand on their tails and call
to him, Bravo! Again he awoke and entered into a long train of thought,
and then went to sleep once more. A second time he saw two ducks of
various colors, and a large goose, which flew after him and at last alighted
before him and began to utter benedictions. Again he awoke, and remaining
bewildered at what had occurred, once more slumbered, and saw a green
snake with yellow and white spots, winding about his leg; and that ugly
serpent was twisting itself on that branch of sandal-wood. The king awoke
in terror, and was sad at those strange spectacles which he had beheld in the
curtain of fancy. Again the genius of sleep drawing him by degrees, bore
him off to the world of dreams. This time he beheld that he was bathed
from head to foot in blood, like a branch of coral, and, as it were, adorned from
top to toe in rubies of Badakhshán and precious stones of a red color. The
king awoke and began to be sorrowful, and wished to call to one of the
officers of the seraglio,—suddenly, sleep overcame him, and he beheld that
he was mounted on a swift white mule, which, like leaping lightning,
crossed over mountains and yet was easy-paced as dear life itself. It seemed
as if he turned the reins of his steed towards the east, and sped on alone.
However much he looked about him, he saw none of his attendants, save two
chamberlains,[1] and these on foot. From dread of this occurrence, he started
up from sleep once more; and then the sixth time relapsed into slumber.
He then saw a fire which was kindled on the top of his head, and the flames
of which encompassed all quarters. From beholding this circumstance he
awoke again, terrified. The seventh time falling insensible from the wine of
sleep, he saw a bird, which perched on his head and pecked the crown of
it with its beak. This time the king uttered a shout, such that the
attendants round about the royal chamber raised cries, and some of them
rushed aghast to the foot of his bed. The king re-assured them and sent
them away; and from dismay at those deadly dreams, he, like a serpent
whose tail has been cut off, or a snake-bitten man, continued writhing in
anguish, and kept saying to himself, 'What strange variety of horrid sights
was this which the pen of omnipotence caused to rise up! and what
troops of calamity were these which poured forth one upon another!

COUPLET.

Before one tumult ceases, others rise;   Upstart new horrors, ere the first one dies.

Ah me! to whom can I reveal the nature of these occurrences? and what
sage can I invoke to solve this difficulty? Whom can I make the confidant
of these secrets? and with what person can I hazard the throw[2] of relating
this story?

---

[1] *Farrásh*, lit., 'carpet-spreaders.'
[2] *Nard*, lit. 'dice,' 'draughts.'

To whom can I this pang confide, of whom demand the cure?'

In short, with a thousand sufferings he passed that night till the dawn of day, and was complaining of gloomy night for its tardy progress and its length, and exclaimed,

VERSE.

'If thou, O night! art not the judgment-day,
Wherefore brood o'er me grievous as in death?
O morn! why vex my heart with long delay?
Ah! breathe, if still thou hast the power of breath!'

Thus he continued till the time when the cheek of bright morning began to shine from the curling ringlets of dark night, and the perfumed taper of the sun began to be visible in the expanse of the azure sky in place of the ambergris-hued tapestry of darkness.

COUPLET.

The brain of earth, scorched by the solar flame,
From slumber to the whirl of frenzy came.

As soon as the hand of Providence removed the veil of darkness from before the beauty of the world-illuminating day, and the monarch of the planets took his seat on the enameled throne of the sky, and conveyed to the ears of mortals the proclamation of justice-dispensing light,[1] the king arose and summoned the Bráhmans, who were solvers of difficulties and perfect in the science of the interpretation of dreams. Then, without pondering on the consequences, he related to them, in the manner he had beheld them, all his dreams. The Bráhmans having heard these terrible circumstances, and seeing the marks of fear and dismay on the countenance of the king, replied, 'These visions are portentous, and during the lapse of time no one has ever beheld dreams of such horror, nor has the ear of any interpreter of dreams listened to such an account as this. If the king will grant us permission we will consult together and refer to books which have been written on the art of interpreting visions, and will consider thereof with the most careful scrutiny. Then having represented the interpretation with accuracy, we will devise a plan for averting the injury and evil.

COUPLET.

The wise man all he says will ponder well;
But fools are indiscreet in what they tell.'

The king gave them permission, and they, issuing from his presence, held a private meeting; and from the foulness of their minds and the impurity of their thoughts, began to agitate the chain of revenge, and said to one

---

[1] When the king mounts his throne in public, the crier announces that the royal court is opened for the administration of Justice. In the same way, light is dispensed when the sun takes his seat on the throne of the sky. Such is the comparison.

another, 'This cruel tyrant has but lately slain several thousands of our tribe, and given to the wind of spoliation our goods and wealth. To-day we have got hold of a clue, by means of which we may wreak[1] our spite on him, and remedy and alleviate the distress of our affairs. And since he has made us his confidants in this matter, and has placed confidence in our interpretation and representation, we must not let slip the opportunity, nor make a long delay in exacting retaliation.

COUPLET.

Our foe is with the pangs of grief opprest,
Upon him then![2] and think the moment blest.

Our best course is to speak boldly in this matter and terrify him with the strongest threats, and say, 'These visions are a proof that seven great perils, such that there is mortal danger in each, are to come. The means of averting these evils is as follows: that they should kill with the sword of high temper a number of the Pillars of the State and of the ministers of the king, and of those animals on which he is wont to ride, and pour their blood into a laver, and let the king sit for a time in that blood, and we will breathe spells over him, and will rub some of the blood upon his body. Afterwards having washed his person with pure water, we will anoint him with unguents, and will bring him back to his court safe and free from care.'[3] Then after that, by this stratagem, we have destroyed his nearest attendants, in the lapse of time, when he is alone, we will settle his business. Thus, though during these days, the foot of our heart has been wounded by the thorn of his injuries, still there is hope that we shall pluck the rose of our desire with the hand of our wish, and we shall see our powerful enemy fallen as we could desire into a position of weakness.

COUPLET.

Our heart has felt oppression's thorn, but we may still aspire,
To pluck the rosebud of our wish in the garden of desire.'

Wherefore, thus perfidiously and traitorously having conspired together against their master, they went again to the king, and said,

COUPLET.

'King! may thy throne and rank perpetual be,
And month and year auspicious be to thee!

It has been in a general way signified to the luminous mind of the king that the interpretation of these dreams exhibits nought but the assault of calamity, and pain, and woe, and trouble, and we have thought of a good

---

[1] The phrase in Persian is *kínah báz tawánim khwást*, lit., 'we may ask back our spite.'

[2] Lit., 'bring smoke (or a sigh) out of him.'

[3] The reading of the editions, *báz ravím*, is clearly incorrect, and I would substitute that of a MS., *barím*, 'we will bring.' For these words are part of the Bráhmans' speech to the king, who was not interested in their safe return, but in his own.'

way of averting the injurious effects of these occurrences. If the king will receive with the hearing of acceptance our words, which will be spoken with the truest desire for his welfare, and the purest intention to gratify him, the evil which is about to follow these dreams will assuredly be averted. But if he refuse to hearken to our directions he must be prepared for a great calamity; nay, even for the decline of his empire and the extinction of life itself.' The king feared, and falling into the circle of dismay, his heart failed him, and he said, ' Ye must declare the particulars of this advice, in order that in every way, which enters the range of possibility, exertion be made to remedy this. They, beholding the oven of deceit hot, shut into it the leaven of guile, and thus continued, ' Those two fishes which stood on their tails are the sons of the king; and that serpent which wound round his leg is Irán-du<u>kh</u>t, and those two colored ducks are the two elephants, and the large goose is the white elephant, and the swift mule is the easy-paced courser of the king, and the two chamberlains on foot are the dromedaries, and the fire that shone on the king's head is the vazír Balár, and the bird which struck its beak into the king's head is the secretary Kamál, and that blood with which the king's body was besmeared is caused by the high-tempered sword which they smite on the king's head and stain his body with. Now we have devised a remedy for the injurious effects of these dreams in the following manner : that they should slay with that sword both the king's sons, and their mother, and the secretary, and vazír, and the elephants, and the horse, and the dromedaries, and having taken some of the blood of each, collect it in one place, and having broken the sword, bury it with the corpses of the slain under ground. Then we having mixed the blood with river-water will pour it into a laver, and causing the king to sit there, will repeat spells and benedictions, and afterwards write talismans with that blood on the forehead of the king, and smearing his shoulders and breast with that mixture of blood and water, will allow three hours to pass. Then we will wash with spring-water the king's head, and having dried him, will make an unguent with olive oil, so that the pernicious effects will be altogether removed : and except this contrivance no help will avail.

COUPLET.

T'avert these ills, (may they thy lot ne'er be !)
Sole plan is this that we have told to thee.'

When the king heard these words, the fire of regret consumed the goods of patience and composure, and the blast of dismay gave to the winds the stock of his endurance and mildness; and he said, ' O foes with friendly faces ! and O foolish men ! death is better than this plan of yours, and to drink the beverage of fate preferable to this proposal full of mischief. When I shall have slain this group, some of which are precious to me as my own soul'

2 o

and all of whom are the pivot of the state and of its wealth, and the source of
the ornament of my grandeur and renown, what enjoyment shall I have in
life, and what advantage shall I reap from continuing to exist?

COUPLET.

> I would have life, that I may reap sweet converse with my well-loved friend;
> And if that source of joy should fail; true, life may last, but to what end?

But perhaps ye have not heard the story of Sulaimán (on whom be peace!)
and the Heron, and the purport of their conversation has not reached you?'
The Bráhmans humbly asked, 'How was that?'

STORY II.

The king said, 'I have heard that Sulaimán (*the blessing and peace of God
be upon our Prophet and upon him!*) was a king whose revered command was
adorned with the honor of rapid execution. Jins,[1] men, animals, and birds,
bound the girdle of submission and obedience to him on the waist of their
souls. The writer of destiny had ornamented the diploma of his kingly
office with the signature, '*Give me a kingdom which may not be obtained by any
after me*,'[2] and the groom of omnipotence had placed the saddle of his
authority on the east wind as his steed; so the verse, '*It blew in the morning
for a month, and in the evening for a month*,'[3] affords a description of his
riding.

VERSE.

> Heaven was his servant, and the sun his slave,
> Fortune obeyed him, earth his bidding did.
> Genii and men devoted service gave,
> And ranks of beasts and birds his portals hid.

One day one of the cherubs of the oratories of the angelic world came to
see him, and presented to him a cup full of the water of life, and said,
'*The Creator of all! May His greatness be glorified and His power magnified!*'
has given thee free choice, and has said, 'Quaff, if thou wilt, this cup; and,
till the end of time, be free from tasting the beverage, '*Every soul shall
taste of death.*'[4] And if thou wishest, quickly lift up thy foot, and from the
corner of the prison of humanity, betake thyself to the pure garden and
expansive air of divinity.' Sulaimán (On him be peace!) reflected within

---

[1] Genii.

[2] Kur'án, Fl. xxxviii, 34; Mar. 37; Sale, p. 341, l. 31: 'We also tried Solomon;
and placed on his throne a counterfeit body. Afterwards he turned unto God, and said, O
Lord forgive me, and give me a kingdom, which may not be obtained by any after me; for
thou art the giver of kingdoms.'

[3] Kur'an, xxxiv. 11; Sale, p. 322, l. 30: 'And we made the wind subject unto
Solomon: it blew in the morning for a month, and in the evening for a month.'

[4] Kur'án xxi. 36; Sale p. 245, l. 17: 'We have not granted unto any man before thee
eternal permanency in this world: if thou die therefore, will they be immortal? Every soul
shall taste of death: and we will prove you with evil, and with good, for a trial of you; and
unto us shall ye return.'

himself, that the coin of life is a stock with which it is possible to secure in the bázár of the resurrection abundant profit; and that the space of existence is a field, in which can be sown the seed of happiness in both worlds and the plant of eternal felicity.

COUPLET.

Too short the hand of this life is,   To reach to such enduring bliss.

Wherefore, in every point of view, one ought to choose the continuance [1] of existence rather than the allurements of extinction and annihilation; and, for the two or three days that the reins of delay are in the hand of option, exertion ought to be used to secure the favor of the Almighty.

HEMISTICH.

'T is life that's past in serving those we love.

Again he reflected, saying, 'The chiefs of the Genii and of men are present, and the leaders of the beasts and birds. I must consult with them, and whatever their unanimous opinion may be, that I must propose to myself as my rule in this matter.' He then took counsel with all the fairies, and men, and birds, and all the animals, as to drinking the beverage of life. All bade him drink it, and were comforted and glad at his life being perpetuated, in which, too, the welfare of the inhabitants of the world would be included.

COUPLET.

'Enjoy the fruit of life eternal and of never-ending days,
For 'tis the prayer which night and morning, old and young, too, for thee raise.'

Sulaimán said, 'Is there any one of all my subjects that is absent from this assembly?' They replied, 'Yes! the Heron has not come to this meeting, and is not informed of this consultation.' Sulaimán (On him be peace!) sent the horse to summon him, but the Heron declined to come. Again he commanded the dog, saying, 'Go! and bring the Heron.' The dog came to the Heron, who acquiescing in his words, presented himself before Sulaimán. Sulaimán said, 'I wish to consult thee, but before I tell thee the subject, solve a difficulty I have.' The Heron expressed his inability, and said,

HEMISTICH.

'Who then am I, that of me that illustrious mind should think?

Thy slave has not power to solve any difficulty, nor does he deserve that such a king, as thou, should honor him by consulting him. It is not, however, strange that the great of lofty station should inquire into the circumstances of their humble subjects.

COUPLET.

Thou art the sun and I a mote most insignificant,
It is not strange the sun to motes its fostering rays should grant.

If my lord, pre-eminent for the dignity of the prophetic office, will favor me with a declaration of that difficulty, that which passes through my feeble

---

[1] *Nashd* 'growing,' also 'an agreeable smell.'

mind shall be represented.' Sulaimán (On him be peace!) rejoined, 'After man, the most noble animal is the horse, and the basest of animals is the dog. What is the meaning of this, that thou wouldest not come at the summons of the most noble animal, and didst accept the invitation of the meanest?' The Heron replied, 'Although the beauty of nobility is outwardly apparent in the horse, and the most perfect gifts are luminously and evidently displayed in him, yet he has not fed in the mead of faithfulness, nor drunk one drop from the fountain of gratitude.

COUPLET.

Not from thy steed expect to find a sense of favors ever,

A horse—a wife—a scymitar—these three were faithful never.

And notwithstanding that the dog is notorious for his baseness, and well-known for his impurity, still he has eaten the morsel of constancy, and habituated himself to the custom of gratitude.

COUPLET.

The dog wears in his ear the ring of love,

Nor for one morsel will unthankful prove.

And I, in accepting the invitation of my lord, who is the fountain of fidelity and the confluence of all truth and sincerity, did not listen to the words of an unfaithful animal, but gave heed to the address of a faithful one.' Sulaimán (On him be peace!) approved of this reply, and disclosed to him the question as to drinking the water of life. The Heron said, 'Wilt thou drink that water alone, or wilt thou give a part thereof to thy friends and kinsmen also?' Sulaimán (On him be peace!) said, 'They have sent it specially for me, nor have they granted a portion of it to others.' The Heron replied, 'O Prophet of God! how may this be, that thou shouldest continue alive and every one of thy friends and companions and children, and of those who are attached to thee, perish before thee? I cannot imagine that there could be enjoyment in such a life, nor can I suppose that there could be happiness in an existence which would be an incessant scene of separation.

STANZA.

Prize high the converse of thy friends, for know! the coin of life-time here

Was given but to scatter at the feet of those that we hold dear.

Oh! life is precious but to view the flowers that in the world appear,

This spectacle is joyous but when friends and those we love are near.'

Sulaimán (On him be peace!) applauded what he said, and declining the envenomed draught of separation, sent back the water of life untasted to the place whence they had brought it.

And I have cited this story to show that without this group of beings I do not wish for life, and see no difference betwixt my own death and their extinction. Moreover, as a matter of course, every kingdom verges to decay, and every monarch is on the brink[1] of departure and migration; and, in the end, this perilous journey must be traveled by all; and in this fearful catacomb,[2] for the sake of two or three days' transitory existence, why should I take steps towards so perilous and grave a measure? and why, with my own hand, lay waste the foundation of my greatness, and the basis of my enjoyment? Can ye not devise some other scheme? and contrive in a more simple manner a remedy for this misfortune?

HEMISTICH.

For I, what this demands, can ne'er fulfil.'

The Bráhmans answered, 'May the king live long! the words of truth are bitter, and faithful counsel appears harsh. We are amazed at the State-enlightening judgment of the king, in that he esteems the lives of others as equally precious with his own life and person, and for their preservation surrenders his precious existence and his hereditary kingdom! He ought to listen to the advice of his well-wishers, and to repose confidence in the words of the disinterested, and to consider his own person and his broad dominions as an equivalent for all losses. It behoves him therefore without hesitation or change of purpose to enter upon this affair, which will be a cause of universal joy, and of tranquillity to high and low. It is certain too that a wise man is attached to others for his own sake; and it is not hidden from the king that it is with a hundred toils that man arrives at sovereign power, and the keys of the treasures of dominion are acquired only by infinite exertion. To decide then on relinquishing the high estate of life, and to abandon the throne of glory and good-fortune appears far removed from the path of good sense. And so long as the king himself lives, he will not want for wives and offspring, and as long as his kingdom is stable, there will be no deficiency nor scarcity of articles of convenience and luxury, or of clever and faithful servants.

HEMISTICH.

If nought is left—while thou art—all remains.'

When the king heard these statements, and saw the determination with which they delivered these words, he was very sad, and went from the hall of audience into his private apartments, and from the dais of his palace set his face towards the retirement of the house of sorrows.

COUPLET.

Since I, alas! to none can tell the story of my woes and grief,
I'll to myself lament, and in the cell of sorrow seek relief.

Then, having placed the face of supplication on the ground, he let loose the water of regret from his eyes, and his heart being roasted with the fire of

---

[1] Observe this somewhat rare sense of *sharaf*.
[2] That is, 'the world.' The words are *laḥd-i ḵẖuftani*, 'grave in which we must sleep.'

despair, he gave the harvest of patience and composure to the wind of spoliation, and said, 'This cloud of mischief, which rains down the shower of calamity, whence has it made its appearance? and this troop of griefs, which has made spoil of the goods of life alone, by what channel has it found its way to invade me?

COUPLET.

> While I sate uninterrupted with my friend, and sang elate,
> Who showed grief the way to enter? who told sorrow of our state?

How forsooth can one call the death of beloved ones a matter of small importance?[1] and what enjoyment can one derive from life without [seeing] the beauty of sons and spouses? and of what use will my kingdom be to me without my sons, who are the light of my eyes, and the fruit of my heart, and who are my solace in the present life, and my hope after treading the path of death?

COUPLET.

> Of nought do fathers stand in so much need,
> Nought's dearer, than sons worthy to succeed.

And Irán-dukht (from the well of whose chin the fountain of the radiant sun is but a drop, and the dawning light of the bright moon but a glimmer from the reflection of her brilliant face; whose cheek is like the time of happy fortune, fresh and joyous, and whose locks, like the nights of adversity, are dark and raveled;

VERSE.

> Her cheek is peerless like the sun through all sublunar space,
>   The young moon stole its crescent from those archèd eyebrows twain;
> The fountain of day's glory is my fair one's radiant face,
>   And rubies from her red red lips, do added lustre gain;)

possesses the power of fascinating by her society, and of exhilarating the soul by her companionship; and without her what fruition can I have in life? And if my vazír Balár (whose luminous judgment is a light-increasing sun in every night of emergency, and the ray of the taper of whose intellect is a gloom-dispelling light in the darkness of every critical event;

COUPLET.

> Without the aid his restless pen aye brings,
> No rest were certain for the throne of kings;)

were not before the throne of my glory, how would the building up of the State, and the lustre of administration, and the plenishing of the treasuries, and the acquisition of desired objects, be possible? And when the page of the counsels of the secretary Kamál (of whose fingers the sublime limner of the sky is a pupil, and of the tray of whose eloquence Mercury of elegant style is but a crumb-eater; whose words delight the heart like a string of pearls, and whose handwriting, like scattered gems, increases joy;

---

[1] Or it may be, 'How can one easily give the word for the death of those we hold dear?'

COUPLET.

Water and fire together are commingled in his diction's grace,
And in his writing's beauty, we darkness at once and light can trace,)

is withdrawn from our sight, how can the affairs of the provinces and the
events of the neighboring country be known? or by what device will
information be obtained as to the circumstances of our enemies and the
intentions of our foes? And whenever the line of extinction is drawn
through the volume of the life of these two faithful counsellors and efficient
officers, which are to the frame of the kingdom like helping hands[1] and
watchful eyes, of course the benefits of their advice and the results of their
ability will be cut off from the State. Then, supposing this to be the case,
the lustre of affairs and arrangement of matters will belong to the class of
impossibilities. Again, without the white elephant (whose body shines like
the lunar orb, and who is beautiful and swift as the revolving sky;

COUPLET.

Girt like a fortress in an iron net;
His tusked blows could castles overset;)

how could I advance to meet the foe? Moreover, without those two other[2]
elephants (which, in the ranks of war, like tumultuous floods, bear down
the enemy; and, like a whirlwind, carry off men from amid the battle;

COUPLET.

With their huge trunks the lasso's circles making,
And in these fetters valiant warriors taking;)

how, in the day of conflict, shall I break through the hostile ranks? and
how, in the moment of strife, shall I overturn the army of my opponents?
And if, too, I had no longer any rapid dromedaries (at the time of whose
speeding forth, the courier of the east wind is unable to distinguish, even
from a distance, the dust of their footsteps; and the messenger of the northern
breeze cannot frame the notion of being able to accompany the pulverized
atoms which their passage stirs up;

COUPLET.

Thorn-eating, head-upraising like fire, these,
And through the desert traveling like the breeze.)

how shall I obtain information as to what passes around? and by what
conveyance transmit the imperial commands through the kingdom? So,
without that fleet steed, of rapid pace and steely sinews, and lightning
movements, and dazzling speed (which would kindle in the heart of the
Rakhsh of Rustam the brightness of the lightning of the fire of calamity;
and the nimbleness of whose motions would make the rose-colored tears [of
envy] roll from the eyes of the Shabdíz of Khusrau,

---

[1] I read with the MSS., *dast-gír*, for the *dast-gírd* of the editions.
[2] I do not know the exact meaning of *pishízah* applied to an elephant. The word
properly signifies 'the scale of a fish.'

COUPLET.

A steed that in a single rush would strain,
Though long as hope, quite through the extended plain.)

how could I hope to spread the carpet of enjoyment? and in what manner could I carry off the ball of hilarity from the plain of mirth with the bat of pleasure? Lastly, without the sharp sword (which is of the form of water, so that the fire of sedition is quenched by the water of its terror, and is fiery in its dealings, so that the honor[1] of the State is sustained by the awe it inspires;

COUPLET.

Thy blue sword shows its water on its blade,
Like violet fresh with drops of rain o'erlaid.)

what impression shall I make in war? And when I am left destitute of these instruments and with my own hand render useless a number of my supporters, what enjoyment can I reap from my kingdom? and what relish can I derive from life? And in truth,

HEMISTICH.

If 't is so passed—we cannot count it life.'

To be brief, the king dived for a while day and night, in the ocean of reflection, yet found not the gem of counsel by which he could grasp the clue of hope. The mention of the king's reveries was spread among the Pillars of the State, and the abstraction of the monarch became known to all the favorites of the imperial court. The vazír Balár bethought himself, 'If I am the first to endeavor to lay bare this matter, and before a hint is given me from the king, if I open the subject, it will be far removed from due respect and reverence. While, on the other hand, if I choose to be supine and adopt a course of hesitation and delay, it will not be comformable to sincere and marked attachment.' He therefore went to Irán-dukht and after offering the usual salutations, began to utter benedictions, and said,

COUPLET.

'Thou who on high[2] hast set the curtain of thy chastity,
While Gabriel[3] attentive waits the haram of thy honor by!

It is not unknown to thy sublime mind, that from the day when I obtained the honor of insertion on the string of the attendants of this court—whose pomp resembles that of heaven,—to this moment, the king has concealed nothing from me, and has not thought it right to enter upon affairs, either small or great, without consulting me. Yesterday he once or twice summoned the Bráhmans and conferred with them; and to-day he continues in private and sits thoughtful and dejected. Now thou art the queen of the

---

[1] An equivoque is intended, as dbrú is lit., 'water of the face.'
[2] Bar 'alliyín, 'in excelsis.'   [3] Rúh-i amín, 'the faithful Spirit.'

time and the partner of the affections of the prince ; and the people, and soldiers, next to the king's favor, look hopefully to thy bounty; while thy commands, after the mandate of the king, are regarded by them as second in the management of affairs.[1] It is advisable that thou shouldest go to the king, and, having learned the state of the case, favor me with information regarding it, that we may engage with all despatch, in such measures as may appear salutary. For the Bráhmans are perfidious and malevolent, and I fear lest by their deceptions they may induce him to steps which will result in regret and repentance ; while after an event has taken place, remorse and contrition are unavailing.

HEMISTICH.

Before th' event precautions should be used.'

Irán-du<u>kh</u>t replied, 'Reproofs have passed between me and the king, and some angry hints have been thrown out. I am ashamed while this is the case, to intrude on the king's privacy and to loose my tongue to ask an explanation.' The vazír rejoined, 'O queen of the world! *Reproof is the offering of dear friends,*—chiding is a cause of the stability of friendship's basis, and a reason of the permanence of the foundation of attachment and cordiality.

COUPLET.

Thou mayst be froward, and I, too, may chide !
Friends are by faults and chidings best allied.

On this occasion thou must put aside this lovers' quarrel, for since the king is overwhelmed with anxiety, and long and painful excogitation has made him sad, his servants and attendants ought not to show such boldness [as to intrude], and save thyself, none can open this door with the key of advice. Moreover, I have repeatedly heard the king say, 'Whenever Irán-du<u>kh</u>t comes to me—though I be sad—I appear joyful, and am freed, by her auspicious presence, from the fetters of grief and despondency.' Go, then, and discover this affair, and thus[2] confer a vast favor on all the royal retinue in court.' Irán-du<u>kh</u>t then approached the king, performed the usual obeisance, and said,

COUPLET.

'Far be from thee both care and pain, and fortune's ills as well !
Thou art our heart's ease and life's joy, and dost our griefs dispel.

What is the reason of thy gloom, and the cause of thy anxiety? and if any thing has reached thy ears from the Bráhmans, it is right thou shouldest acquaint thy slaves, in order that, aiding therein, they may perform the services due from them.' The king replied, 'It is not proper to ask a question as to a thing which is of such a nature, that if an answer be given

---

[1] Lit., 'loosing and binding.'
[2] *Mutawajjih* may perhaps be translated, ' by attending to our request.'

it will prove painful to the mind, [for it is said,] '*Do not ask about things, which, if told to you, would annoy you.*'' Irán-du<u>kh</u>t answered, 'If this suffering is to fall on the body of the king's dependants, it matters not, for the safety of the royal person is a remedy for all calamities.

HEMISTICH.
A thousand lives be offered up for thee!

And if (which heaven forfend!) the thing has reference to the precious person of your Majesty, even then, too, let us not give way to perplexity, nor on any account sit down desponding; but let us show manly deter- mination (for '*firm purpose is of the purposes of kings,*') in company with the qualities of patience and composure. For complaining does but augment suffering, and impatience makes our enemies happy and joyous, and our friends vexed and chagrined. And in whatever befalls man, when he has recourse to the strongest handle[1] patience, in the end the face of his desired object appears; and we may justly regard that as the best of objects in which the favor of God is not lost.

COUPLET.
O heart! bear patiently disastrous things,
For patience in the end good fortune brings.

And it befits the king, when an affair of importance arises, and a critical event occurs, not to suffer the means of remedy and mode of averting it to remain uncertain or concealed from his perfect penetration and abundant sagacity; especially as there is no deficiency of power and ability; and the means of dispelling despondency and of removing care and solicitude are ready and prepared.

VERSE.
Thou hast treasure and retainers; kingly pomp, wide realms hast thou,
From thy lonely chamber stepping, plant thy banner on earth's plain.
Set thy face toward thy object, let thy grief be banished now,
Make thy friends rejoice, and from thy heart remove the load of pain.'

The king said, 'If of what the Bráhmans pointed out to me, they were to whisper a single letter in the ear of a mountain, its sides, like that of the glorious[2] mountain Sinai, would be rent asunder, and the description, '*And the mountains shall be dashed in pieces,*[3] would be shown to apply to it; and if they were to give a hint of it to the bright day,

---

[1] '*Urwatu'l wuṣḳa*, a proverbial expression, signifying, the dictionaries tell us, 'genuine religion,' but here, 'the best course.' I have thought it best to translate the phrase literally.

[2] I know not if the epithet *tajallí* is applied especially to Sinai, in that the glory of the Lord appeared there, as it is said, Exodus, xix. 18: 'And Mount Sinai was altogether on a smoke, because the Lord descended upon it in fire;' or, simply.

[3] Ḳur'án, lvi. 5; Sale, p. 394, l. 18: 'When the inevitable day of judgment shall suddenly come. . . . When the earth shall be shaken with a violent shock; and the mountains shall be dashed in pieces, and shall become as dust scattered abroad.'

sadness would turn it to the color of gloomy night, and the sign, *Darkness one over the other*,[1] would be manifest in it.

COUPLET.

Cursed were the moon did it not clothe itself in mourning at this woe;
Shameless the cloud whence at these horrors tears sanguineous did not flow.

Do thou, too, importune me not as to this, nor be over instant in investigating it; for neither have I the power to tell it, nor thou fortitude to listen to it.' Again Irán-dukht urged him exceedingly to tell; and the king, to gratify her, having made known somewhat of what was hidden in his breast said, 'In one of these nights I saw a thing, and alarmed by the horror of it, I disclosed it to the Bráhmans to explain and interpret it; and those accursed ones viewed it as expedient that men should slay thee, together with thy two blessed and noble sons, and the pure-minded vazír, and the eloquent secretary, and the white man-destroying elephant, and the other gigantic army-crushing elephants, and the waste-traversing, thorn-eating dromedaries, and the steed of fair paces, with the high-tempered sword, in order that the calamitous effects of that dream might be averted.' When Irán-dukht heard these words, the sigh[2] of grief rose from the fire-temple of her heart to the aperture of her brain, and she was near shedding drops of regret from the fountain of her eyes. However, inasmuch as she was wise and discreet, she swallowed that life-dissolving grief, and with heart unmoved, said,

COUPLET.

' If for thy love I'm called to perish, may thy life so ransomed be!
May thousand lives, and like me, hundreds, fall a sacrifice for thee!

The king ought not to be sorrowful on this account, for of what use are the lives of his slaves, if they are not devoted to his advantage? As long as his august person is safe, and the position of his authority fixed, he will not want for wives and children, nor will his servants and royal equipment decrease. But when the ill effects of the dream are averted, and the royal mind is freed from this sorrow, the king must not place confidence in this perfidious sect; and if they exhort the king to slay a number of individuals, he must not take this step without reflection; for the shedding of blood is a grave matter, and to subvert the foundations of the existence of a living being is a troublous thing; and if, (we take refuge from it with God!) the blood should turn out to be wrongfully spilt, the end thereof will be disastrous, and its punishment enduring torment;

---

[1] Ḳur'án, Fl. xxiv. 40; Mar. 41; Sale, p. 269, l. 1 : 'But as to the unbelievers, their works are like the vapour in a plain, which the thirsty traveller thinketh to be water, until, when he cometh thereto, he findeth it to be nothing; but he findeth God with him, and he will fully pay him his account; and God is swift in taking an account : or as the darkness in a deep sea, covered by waves riding on waves, above which are clouds, being additions of darkness one over the other ; when one stretcheth forth his hand, he is far from seeing it.'
[2] Or, 'smoke.'

and repentance and regret, and remorse and anguish, will be then unavailing; for to recall the past and to restore the dead to life is beyond the circle of human ability.

HEMISTICH.

Not by my hand nor thine can this be done.

The king must understand that the Bráhmans are not friendly to him, and though they have dived into science and learned some problems as far as they have, still the sages of the faith are unanimous on this point, that one of an evil and accursed nature cannot derive beauty from any ornament, and that neither learning nor wealth can bestow on him the adornment of good faith and benevolence. For the impurity of a dog is unchanged, though they throw a chain of gold round his neck; and the filthiness of a hog will not be altered into cleanliness, though they were to encase his teeth with the same precious metal; and the subtle saying, '*Like an ass that carries books*,' confirms the truth of this

COUPLET.

If knowledge touch the heart, it is a friend :
A snake, if it does but to shew extend. [1]

And knowledge is like a sword with which all may be slain. Those who are pure of mind and of unsullied natures, put to death with that sword the lusts and appetites, than which man has no worse enemy. Some on the other hand, who are devoid of spirit and of impure dispositions, afflict with that same sword the understanding and the spirit through which alone man is ennobled. Thus, they turn what ought to be an instrument for repelling their foes, into an implement for injuring their friends. And that perfect sage [2] alludes to this, where he says,

DISTICHS.

A base man's mind with science to expand,
Is to put weapons in a robber's hand.
Better to arm a drunken negro, than
To lavish learning on a wicked man. [3]
Such natures base will practise but deceit,
And with more skill their wily arts repeat. [4]

---

[1] Lit., ' When learning knocks on the body it is a snake.' The only merit I can discover in these lines is the play on the words *ydrí*, 'a friend,' and *márí*, 'a snake.' This merit, such as it is, seems to me altogether to vanish in the reading of the editions, which exhibit *bárí bavad* in the first line, which would be therefore, ' When learning strikes the heart it is a load.' I read, therefore, with the MSS., *ydrí*.

[2] Maulaví Rúmí.

[3] The reading of the editions here is evidently incorrect. Literally translated it signifies, ' Better than that a base man should not come to learning in the hand,' *i.e.*, ' be acquired by learning,' which is obviously reversing matters, for the learning is to come to the man, not the man to the learning; nor is there any difference in the Persian idiom and our own in expressing such an idea. A MSS. reads *bih kih drad 'ilm nd kas rd bidast*, whence I conjecture the true reading to be, *bih kih drad 'ilm-rd nd kas bidast*.

[4] These impracticable lines literally translated are, ' Learning artifices, burnt livers, Learnt shameful deeds and tricks.'

And their object in this interpretation is, to secure an opportunity for revenge, and that the wounds which have been inflicted on their hearts by the royal chastisement should, by this guileful artifice on which they have imposed the name of salutary regulation, be salved over.   They will first remove out of their way your sons, which are like the king himself, and are the counterparts of the gracious Sháh, in order that the king may be left without an heir.   Next they would take away the united nobles, who are the Pillars of the State, and on whose ability depends the populousness of these realms, and the plenishment of the treasuries, that the people may become turbulent[1] and the army dispirited.   They would destroy, too, the other means of empire, such as the elephants and camels, horse and weapons, that the king might be left alone and helpless.   For my own part I, this poor slave, am of no account; and many like me are to be found in the service of the king; but [let me say] that when they find the king isolated, this vengeful purpose will in the lapse of time be manifest, and that which they have for years concealed in their minds, they will bring from volition to execution.   And hitherto they could but contemplate this with impotence and perplexity, but when, having obtained full power, they get the reins of option into their hands, their purpose is to excite tumults in the kingdom, and set open the gates of mischief.   For in case the king destroys his followers, both the soldiers will become dejected and the people suspicious ; and when the civilians and the military are of two hearts and ten tongues, this becomes a cause of triumph and exaltation to foes, and, supposing this to be the case, territory and wealth depart from the grasp, and soul and life fall into imminent peril.   And kings ought not to be careless of the deceits and artifices of their enemies ;

VERSE.

Be not secure of foes that would thee harm,
For traitrous are they and defiled with sin.
To outward sight they breathe of friendship warm,
But malice, rankling, lurks their breasts within.[2]

Yet, notwithstanding all this, if in what the Bráhmans have deemed advisable, there is any relief[3] or relaxation of anxiety to the king, of course it is not fit that there should be any delay; but if there be room for postponement, one measure of caution may yet be adopted, which at the king's command, I will utter.'   The king gave the required permission, and said, 'What thou sayest is in my belief clear of all suspicion of doubt, and will assuredly be acceptable and listened to with attention.'   Irán-dukht continued, 'The sage Káridún, who is the founder of the pedestals of eminent

---

[1] *Dilír*, 'bold,' 'audacious.'   Might not *dil-gír*, 'dejected,' be a better reading?
[2] Lit., 'Within he knocks on the door of ill faith.'   I have put the nominative to ' breathe' in the plural for the sake of the verse.
[3] I read with the MSS. *fardkhí.* I can make no sense of the *farji* of the editions.

qualities, and the traveler of the roads of virtue and excellence, and who is gifted with a disposition, which is a storehouse of the precious things of spirituality and wisdom, and endued with an intellect, which is a mine of the mysteries of special manifestations and merit.[1]

COUPLET.

His mind, illumined, lifts the veil that hides fate's mysteries,
His pure heart is acceptable to heaven's all gracious eyes.

has at this time made choice of a retirement in a cave in the mountain Khazrá,[2] and continually observes the recitation of faith in the unity of God and abnegation of self. Though, by origin, he is related to the Bráhmans, yet in sincerity, and uprightness, and good faith, and rectitude, he has the pre-eminence over them. His sight is more perfect as to the issue of affairs, and his right-aiming counsel is more comprehensive of the propulsion of calamity and accident. If the king's judgment acquiesce, this sage must be honored by being made a confidant, and the circumstances of the dream and the interpretation of the Bráhmans must be communicated to him. There is no doubt that he will truly instruct the king as to every particular thereof, and will not withhold any circumstance of the explanation of what is at present hidden. If his interpretation correspond with that of the Bráhmans, all doubt will be extinguished, and it will be right to execute the same resolve; and if his directions are contrary, the luminous mind of the king will decide between right and wrong, and will discriminate sound advice from perfidy.' This speech pleased the king, and he immediately mounted his horse and went to the sage Kárídún, and having obtained the felicity of an interview with the divine sage, who was a gathering-place of endless virtues, he performed the required respectful salutations. The sage, too, fulfilled the courtesies due, and said,

COUPLET.

'Since Eden's prince has entered here, my hut is changed to Paradise.
To Canaan wafted Joseph's scent, has lent new lustre to these eyes.

What is the cause of the procession of the fortune-attended train hither? Hadst thou conveyed thy mandate, I myself would have attended at the court, for it is in accordance with what is right that servants should attend to minister.

COUPLET.

Attendance and the claim to serve, to me
Commit, O Lord! and thou my sultán be.

And, moreover, one may see on the royal face the marks of disturbance, and the traces of grief are physiognomically discernible on the august countenance. The king must state the case, and recount the cause of his sadness.

---

[1] A rare sense of *kadam*.
[2] That is, 'green.' The word also signifies 'heaven.'

The king narrated in full detail the circumstances of the vision, and the interpretation of the Bráhmans. Kárídún shook the head of astonishment, and having bitten the finger of amazement, said, 'The king has committed an error in this, for this secret was not to be disclosed to that sect, and this story ought not to have been related to that body of men.

HEMISTICH.

Secrets are suited not for every ear.

And let it not remain hidden from the royal mind, that these perfidious advisers are not suitable interpreters of these things, because they have neither reason to guide them, nor their faith rightly planted. Now the king's happiness ought to be augmented by these dreams, and he ought, as a thank-offering, to bestow on deserving objects an infinite abundance of alms; for the proofs of happiness and the testimonies of honor and exaltation are manifest and clear on the pages of the explanations of these events. Every moment, events which are to occur will be in accordance with his wish; and every hour the affairs of his glory and greatness will be in order of arrangement.

COUPLET.

Heaven will obsequious, Time thy slave, the sky thy captive, be.
Fortune will serve thee, realms obey, and life and hopes agree.

And I will at this very time, fully deliver the interpretation of every thing that has occurred, and repel with the shield of wisdom, the arrow of the artifices of those counsellors.

HEMISTICH.

If thou an arrow hast, I've, too, a shield.

First, those two red fishes which stood on their tails, are ambassadors, who will come from Sarándíp and who will present to the king two strong elephants with four hundred ratls[1] of red rubies, in envy of whose color the heart of the pomegranate will be filled with blood; and the body of fire, in jealousy of their rays, will hide itself in the secret chamber of the stone. And those two ducks and the goose, which flew after the king and alighted in front of him, are two horses and a mule which the King of Delhi will send to his Majesty as a present; and those two steeds will have voices of thunder, the fiery spirit of lightning, keen sagacity, and unflagging energy.

STANZA.

On the earth's face their hoofs the crescent stamp,
Their forkèd ears darts on the air imprint.
Their strength of joint no stirrup's weight can damp,
Nor dragging reins their generous ardor stint.

And that mule is a carrier, fleet as the wind—spirited as fire, such that it

---

[1] *Ratl* is, says the Dictionary, a pound of twelve ounces.

passes swift as lightning over roads and narrow gorges; and like the thunderbolt, with the wound of its hoof brings fire out of stone.

COUPLET.

> Silver-hoofed, with reins of gold; fleet of pace, it speedeth on;
> Heaven's orchard is its pasture-ground, its drinking-place the sun.

And that snake which twisted round the king's foot, is a sword of fiery efficacy and of high temper, which in the day of battle showers from the fountain of its blue water a torrent of liquid rubies, and scatters o'er its diamond-colored surface, particles of carnelion and coral sand.

COUPLET.

> Conquest and triumph ever on thy lustrous sword attend!
> Nay, victory in it does with an outward figure blend.

And that blood with which the king found himself stained, is a scarlet robe ornamented with gems which they will bring as an offering to the royal wardrobe from the imperial city Ghaznah. And that white mule on which the king was mounted, is a white elephant which the Sultán of Bíjánagar is sending for the royal service, and the king will enjoy the pleasure of exercise on that elephant. It will be huge as a cloud, and, in the ranks of war, will make its emerald-colored trunk like a lustrous ruby with the blood of the brave; and with its dragon-taming tusk,[1] which is united to a mountain of iron, it destroys a whole world in an instant of time.

COUPLET.

> A form whose mountain-hugeness fills the waste
> Unpillared, on four pillars—moved with haste.[2]

And that which blazed like fire on the august forehead of the king, is a crown which the King of Sailán[3] is sending as a gift; which is such a diadem that the ornament of its circlet may vie with the highest region of the blue-colored heaven; and by the radiance it showers, it will make every hair of the sovereign that wears it a string of jewels.

COUPLET.

> Upon the sky where shines the moon, reflected fall its radiant beams,
> And, like Muḳanna's[4] magic work, a second Queen of Night it seems.

And the bird, which struck its beak on the King's head, betokens that some slight disaster is to be looked for, but the consequences are not so important or injurious. The utmost of it is, that the king will for

---

[1] The printed edition here correctly reads *bi-dandán* instead of the meaningless *bidán* of the lithographed edition, and of some MSS.

[2] Extravagance of metaphor can no further go. The first line seems to me corrupt, but I find no variety of readings.

[3] Ceylon. But we have had the King of Sarándíp, *i.e.* Ceylon, sending two elephants and four hundred raṭls of rubies before. This, however, is a trifle to interpreters of dreams.

[4] Muḳann'a, the Veiled Prophet of Khurásán, of whom Moore has sung so well. He was a thaumaturgist who raised an appearance like the moon from a well at Nakhshah. He flourished A.H. 163.

some days avert his face from a dear friend and an affectionate companion; and the conclusion of it will be beneficial and fortunate. This is an account of the interpretation of the visions of the king, and in that he saw them at seven successive times, this shows that envoys will arrive on seven distinct occasions with the presents of princes to his august court; and the king will be gratified and delighted by the receipt of those valuables, and the acquisition of those precious things. Moreover, he will be rendered felicitous by the stability of his good-fortune and the continuance of life; and it behoves the emperor of the world hereafter not to make worthless persons the confidants of his secrets; nor until he has tested the wisdom of a man, to consult with him in an affair of importance.

COUPLET.

Thou shouldst a man a hundred times test well;
And not till then to him thy secrets tell.

And it is the very essence of wisdom to regard it as a sacred duty to shun altogether the society of audacious, impure, base, and unprincipled men; and not to arrange the precious jewel of one's own self on the string of men fatuous, of mean spirit, and accursed nature.

COUPLET.

See how the water murmurs at its lot,[1]
When it meets comrades that do suit it not.'

When the king had heard this discourse, he immediately made repeated prostrations in thankfulness, and expressed his acknowledgments to that auspicious-minded old man, who, like the Messiah, had given to his lifeless heart unbounded happiness; and said, 'The divine favor has bestowed on me the aid of success, and guided me to your highness wise and joy-bestowing, so that by the happy influences of the blessed spirit of your holiness, the difficulties of distress have been exchanged for the advantages of tranquillity.

COUPLET.

God sent one voiced like Jesus, who away,
Removed the griefs which did my soul down weigh.

Praise be to God! a praise, lasting and eternal!' Then the king, with glad heart, bestowed the honor of his alighting on the settled abode of his greatness; and for seven days, in succession, envoys arrived with gifts and offerings, and in the same manner as the perfect sage had announced conveyed to the place of representation, the purport of the messages with which they were charged. On the seventh day, the king summoned to a private audience his sons, and the vazír Balár, and Irán-dukht, and

---

[1] That is, The river murmurs and frets when it encounters stones, sticks, or other obstacles.

his secretary, and said, 'I committed a strange fault in disclosing my dream to my enemies; and had not the mercy of God been a bar to their artifices, and the counsel of Irán-dukht not opened the hand of remedy, the directions of those accursed ones would, in the end, have achieved my destruction, and that of all my kin and retainers. And whoever is befriended by the Divine Felicity, and supported by the Eternal Power, he will assuredly hold dear friendly advice, and enter upon affairs with deliberation and reflection; and cautiously avoiding a disastrous result, will take care not to quit the place of prudence and spot of vigilance. And they have said,

HEMISTICH.

'He finds no rest who unreflecting acts.'

He then issued his commands, that as the minds of those his beloved, owing to such circumstances, could not be clear from grief, it was fitting that these presents should be divided among them, and that a special share should be given to Irán-dukht, who, by the delivery of her sentiments, had remedied this affair. The vazír Balár said, 'Thy slaves are for this, viz., to make themselves the shields of calamity in emergencies, and thus not to withhold their lives and spirits;

HEMISTICH.

He that would serve thee must not care for life.

And if by the assistance of fortune and the succor of felicitous destiny, service of this nature and the fulfilment of this duty be attainable, and it become possible to lay down one's wealth and life in the path of the service of one's benefactor, a reward and gifts are not to be looked for, nor are presents and requital to be expected. However, the Queen of the Age has exerted herself much in this matter, wherefore of these gifts the crown adorned with jewels, or the scarlet robe ornamented with gems befits her; and the king ought to present her with whichever she chooses to accept.' The king commanded them to carry both of these things into a private chamber, and he, himself, with the vazír Balár, entered. Now there was in the haram, another damsel whom they used to call Bazm Afrúz.[1] She possessed a form such that the sun of the east from shame on her account, veiled his face with the curtain, '*Until the sun is hidden by the veil of night,*'[2] and the fresh rose-leaf, through the diffidence it occasioned, retired into concealment behind its verdant screen.

---

[1] 'Lighting up the banquet.'

[2] Kur'án, Fl. xxxviii. 31; Mar. 34; Sale, p. 341, l. 27: 'When the horses, standing on three feet, and touching the ground with the edge of the fourth foot, and swift in the course, were set in parade before him in the evening, he said, 'Verily I have loved the love of earthly good above the remembrance of my Lord; and have spent the time in viewing these horses, until the sun is hidden by the veil of night: bring the horses back unto me.' Solomon is the person here spoken of; he is said to have forgotten the time of evening prayer in looking at these steeds.

VERSE.

Small mouth, and oval-face, and archèd brow,
Check like the red rose on a verdant bough :
    With smile of honey like the sugar-cane,
    Neat, pleasant, charming, sweet, and succulent.
    Each time she smiled she added a new pain
    To wounded hearts, and them with salt besprent.

The king was warmly attached to her, and although Irán-dukht was, by her beauty and piquancy, a mischief to the whole world; and by her grace and elegance, a cause of agitation to the age; still the king used to give Bazm Afrúz a turn with her, and was one night out of every two in the chamber of the former. This day the king commanded them to call Bazm Afrúz, and they brought the crown and the robe, and the royal mandate was issued that whichever Irán-dukht chose, the other should fall to Bazm Afrúz. Irán-dukht was more inclined towards the crown, and that golden constellation with gems for stars pleased her most. Feeling disposed towards this, she looked towards the vazír Balár to see that he approved of her choice. Balár signaled with his eyes towards the robe, and in the midst of his glance the king looked towards him. Irán-dukht saw that that interchange of looks was observed, and she snatched up the crown in order that the king might not discover their consultation ; and Balár kept his eyes just as they were, that the king might not observe the signal. And for forty years after that he waited at court, whenever he approached the king he preserved the same strabism, lest the king's suspicion should become certainty. Thus, but for the cleverness of the vazír and the queen's own shrewdness both would have lost their lives.

COUPLET.

Who makes good sense the pivot of life's course
Will through the bonds of woe a passage force.

And when Irán-dukht had had her wishes crowned by accepting the diadem, Bazm Afrúz also was rendered happy [1] by choosing the scarlet robe. Now, according to the custom aforesaid, the king passed one night with her and one night with Irán-dukht. And it happened that one night, when it was the turn of Irán-dukht, the king, in accordance with the stipulation, went to Irán-dukht's chamber, who with a face lit up with joy and enchanting locks,

COUPLET.

(She with fresh musk had washed each several hair,
And in life's water bathed her visage fair ;)

---

[1] Here are two untranslateable puns : *sar afrázi yáftan,* ' to be exalted,' ' to be successful,' might mean, if literally translated, ' to obtain an ornament for the head ;' and *surkh rúi shudan,* ' to be honored,' means literally, ' to be red-faced,' which of course the lady would be from the reflection of the scarlet robe. In such puerilities and insipidities do Persian writers delight.

had set her golden crown on her head, and holding in her hands a golden
dish filled with rice, presented herself before the king. He ate a morsel
from the dish, and allocating himself in propinquity to her, illumined the
eye of his heart with surveying her beauty. At this moment Bazm Afrúz
passed by them clothed in the scarlet robe, with cheeks like a blossoming
rose and a face like the moon when two weeks old.

VERSE.

A scarlet robe her symmetry displayed,
  Like cypress with red tulips for a margin.
Her Turkish eyes for hearts kept ambuscade;
  Her eyebrows twain 'gainst breasts were shafts discharging;
Her cheeks shone brightly from her heavy tresses,
Like moonlight gleaming from night's dark recesses.

When the king beheld her he drew back his hand from the food and an
overpowering inclination of his mind towards her, and a sincere longing for
her society, removed the rein of self-possession from the grasp of his power,
and detached the guiding-strings of repression from the hand of choice.
Approaching Bazm Afrúz, therefore, he loosed his tongue in eulogy and
applause,

COUPLET.

'O cypress! treading gracefully, O young rose newly blown!
Eyes, stature, cheek, to match with thine not e'en in sleep I've known.

By thus coming thou hast opened the doors of joy in my breast, and by this
graceful approach thou hast given to the winds the harvest of my patience
and composure.

HEMISTICH.

Hail! fortune, made [thrice] blest by thy approach.'

He then said to Irán-dukht, 'This crown which thou hast taken is worthy
the head of Bazm Afrúz, and in choosing it thou hast turned from the path
of right-dealing to the region of error.' The jealousy of love seized the skirt
of Irán-dukht, and the flame of the fire of jealousy fell in the chafing-dish
of her breast. At these words she blushed, and like one distraught, dashed
the plate of rice upside down on the head of the king, and besmeared therewith the royal face and hair. Thus the interpretation of the dream which the
Sage had given, by the occurrence of that contretemps, turned out true. The
fire of the king's wrath was kindled. He called the vazír Balár, and told him
the hasty act of which she had been guilty and said, 'Take this foolish
woman from my presence and cut off her head,[1] in order that she may know
that such as she are not of such importance that they should dare to do such
audacious things, and we pardon them.' Balár led the queen out and thought
to himself, 'In this matter it is not right to be precipitate, for this woman is
peerless in eloquence and wit, and has no equal in sagacity and intelligence;

---

[1] Lit., 'strike the neck.'

and the king will not rest without seeing her, and by the blessing of her pure spirit and the auspicious influence of her clear judgment, a number of persons have been saved from the whirlpool of destruction. It is possible that the king will deny that he authorised such haste, and irrespective [1] of the king's displeasure, precipitation in such matters does not appear advisable. I have no better course therefore than to base this transaction on deliberation, in order that I may not be ashamed when questions are put, and answers given thereupon.

COUPLET.

When Ḳáẓís write with caution their decree,
They will not by the rulers [2] censured be.

I must pause, then, two or three days. If the king evinces repentance, at least the opportunity of remedying the affair will not have gone by. But if he is obstinately bent on putting her to death, and urgent for it, there will be no difficulty in slaying her. Moreover, by this delay I secure three positive advantages; first, the merit of preserving an individual; secondly, the acquisition of the king's favor if he repent of her execution; thirdly, the gratitude of all the people of the realm for preserving to them such a queen as she is, whose beneficence is communicated to all, and the marks of whose good works are widely and completely diffused.' He then conveyed her to his own house with a number of confidential attendants, who used to perform the service of the king's seraglio; and he commanded them saying, 'Take charge of her with the utmost caution, and consider the utmost care obligatory as to the respect and deference to be shewn to her.' He then himself, with his sabre stained with blood and with downcast head like the mournful, entered the king's chamber and said, 'I have performed the king's command, and have punished and chastised that disrespectful one, who had set her foot on the carpet of audacity.' The king's anger was upon the whole somewhat appeased, and the tumultuous billows of the ocean of wrath were calmed. When he heard these words, and recalled the thought of her beauty and perfections, and her good sense and judgment, he was excessively sorrowful. Yet he was ashamed to shew signs of irresolution, and to give an urgent command and one for the infraction of it close together, for it is self-evident that conflicting orders are attended with numerous disadvantages. He then began to reproach himself, and said, 'This is thy [3] fault in that thou hast set clemency and long-suffering on one side, and, for a slight offence, which, in point of fact, might have been forgiven, hast exposed to destruction thine own mistress. Thou oughtest not for a fault so trivial to have issued such an order, but to have assuaged the fire of wrath with the water of forgiveness.

---

[1] I think I may assign this sense to ḳiṭ'a-i naẓar.

[2] Dastár bandán 'wearers of turbans,' that is, 'great men or learned doctors.'

[3] In the Persian the pronoun here changes from the second to the first person, a change which would be awkward, if not ungrammatical, in English.

VERSE.

A piece of fire that furious man will be
    Whose breath the flame of rage up-kindles high;
His fiery wrath exceeds all just degree
    Who ne'er gives vent to a remorseful sigh.' [1]

However, when the vazír perceived the signs of penitence on the countenance of the king, he said, 'The king ought not to be pensive, for the
arrow which has leapt from the string cannot be brought back, nor can
the slain person be resuscitated either by strength or gold, and to give way
to unavailing regret renders the body emaciated and the heart sad, and
nought can be gained thereby but the distress of friends and the gratification
of foes. Every one, too, who hears that the king issued an order, and
repented immediately it was carried into execution, will become distrustful
of the firmness and steady determination of his majesty. But it behoved the
king to have been more gentle in this matter, and to have avoided harshness
and severity; and like the Letter-possessing King, to have mastered his
resentment, so that there would have been no room for repentance. But,
if his command is given, I will recount to him a story. The king replied,
' Of course narrate how that was.'

STORY III.

The right-counseling vazír said, 'They have related that in the capital
of Yaman there was a king of a bright spirit, of an old judgment, and young
fortune. The eye of the swift-revolving heaven, in the long intervals of its
journeys, had never seen on the sky of empire a sun like him; and the ear
of time, which tests mankind, had, in the space of ages, never heard of a
governor who possessed his qualities.

VERSE.

Bright as the sun, at feasts his cheek was lit with beauty's flame;
    He, dragon-like, consumed the world in war.
And, by wide-spreading bounty, knew the way men's hearts to tame;
    Fortune obeyed, nor would his wishes mar.

Now this king was fond of hunting. One day, in a hunting-ground, he
galloped his steed joyously to left and right, and threw around him on every
side the gaze of vigilance. In those environs he saw no quarry, either
animal or bird, nor did he behold a single creature which was fit to be the
prey of a king. The monarch looked about him astonished at these circumstances. Fate decreed that a poor wood-cutter, from excessive want
and poverty had put on a garment made of deer-skin, and had cut down a
quantity of brambles in that jungle; and, being excessively fatigued by that

---

[1] Here *dúd* is again ambiguous, signifying both 'smoke,' and 'sigh.'

labor, had reclined against the side of a rock. The king's sight fell on him from a distance, and imagining it was a deer, he directed a heart-piercing arrow against it.

VERSE.

> A fiery dart, which diving, blood 'gan spill,[1]
> Like heaven's bolt, upon that wretch did light.
> Mischief distinguished not 'twixt good and ill,
> And thus he erred although he aimed aright.

In short, when the king came up to the quarry and beheld the man with his breast transfixed, and his heart full of blood, he was sorely grieved and distressed, and began to tear the face of repentance with the nail of self-reproach; and being afflicted at that rashness and precipitation which had caused him this regret and contrition, he made many excuses to the wood-cutter, and, for salve-money, bestowed on him a thousand dínárs of red gold. Downcast he then turned his reins towards his capital, and condescended to alight at the door of the hermitage of a pious recluse, who was celebrated in that city for his sanctity and holiness, nay, was renowned and famous all over the world for his guidance and spiritual directions. He then begged of the holy man a piece of advice, which might augment his dignity in this world, and in that to come be a cloak to offences. The pious man, by way of exposition and gracious explanation, said, 'O king! a quality which ensures happiness in this world, and felicity in the world to come, is the controlling angry feelings, and at the time when wrath is about to overpower us, to make choice of mildness.

VERSE.

> Who kindles up the flame of wrath on high,
> Hope not from him the ways of courtesy.
> When hot the champings of thy spirit wax,
> Pull back the reins until thy fury slacks.'

The king said, 'I know that the taste of the bitter beverage of long-suffering is much relished by the palate of reason, but in the time of anger I cannot make mildness ruler over my passions; and at the moment when they are inflamed, I cannot bring myself under control.' The pious man replied, 'I will write three letters, and do thou deliver them into the hand of a select officer, and a confidential and faithful person; in order that, when he beholds the marks of an alteration of temper on thy countenance, and perceives the fire of thy anger and inconsiderateness to be kindled, he may read one of them to thee. It is probable that when the lesson it inculcates is made evident thy mind will be soothed. And if he finds that the flame of thy rage has not been quenched by the water of that admonition, let him call in the aid of the second; and if the rebellious spirit is untamed

---

[1] The first line seems to intend a play on words, on *sh'ulah*, 'flame,' and *ghark*, 'immersion in water;' *dar dvardan* is 'to bring forth,' 'to produce.' The arrow then produced 'immersion' in the body. The conceit is most forced.

by that also, let him show the third letter to thee. I am in hopes that the misfortune of that harshness will thus be exchanged for tenderness and kindness; and when the darkness of resentment is dispelled, assuredly the rays of clemency and gentleness will replace it.

HEMISTICH.

When fiends retire, good angels come instead.'

The king was pleased with these words, and the recluse having written three letters, gave them to one of the king's attendants. The meaning of the first letter was, 'While thou still retainest the power do not place the reins of choice in the grasp of the possession of thy passions, for they will plunge thee into the whirlpool of everlasting destruction.' The contents of the second letter were, 'In the time of wrath be merciful to those in thy power, in order that in the hour of retribution thy superiors may be merciful to thee.' And the substance of the third writing was, 'In issuing thy commands, do not overstep the bounds of the law, and under no circumstances abandon what is just.

VERSE.

What though, as king, thy mandate speed unchecked!
Play not the tyrant—cruel deeds are baneful.
Thy lips may, like the rose, with smiles be decked;
But victims' eyes, like clouds in March, are rain-full.
Nor boast the palace-garden of thy sway,
Soon thou must all forsake and pass away.'

The king took leave of the devotee, and returned to his capital; and continually, in the assembly where he issued his commands, especially in the moment of his wrath, they recited to him these three letters; and, for the reliance which he placed in them, they called him the 'Letter-possessing King.' Now this monarch had a concubine, of fair face and pleasing manners, in stature like the cypress, moon-cheeked, ruby-lipped, silver-chinned, partridge-gaited, parrot-speeched,

COUPLET.

Moon-faced, of musky fragrance, hearts' delight,
Soul-expanding, heart-deceiving, and moon-bright.

The intoxicated narcissus was enamoured of her love-sick eye, and the agate of Yaman had its heart crimsoned with blood at her sweet vermilion lips. The beauties of the region of Cathay were captives in the fetters of her curling tresses; and the coquettes of Kashmír had their hearts chained by affection for the links of her ringlets full of windings and curls,

COUPLET.

Fair one! is there, can there be, a beauty wanting to thy cheek?
Of love's brightest fascinations have we aught there still to seek?

The beauty of her condition derived lustre from the mole of modesty; and the bride-chamber of her beauty was adorned with the ornament of chastity and continence. The king's heart was so attached to her good qualities, that he withdrew himself from the society of his royal lady, and from dalliance with his other female slaves. The king's bride, from jealousy of him, was always shedding the tears of poignant regret; and in order to get rid of the damsel, through resentment and envy, stirred up all kinds of stratagems. In short, she disclosed her vexation to the tire-woman of the seraglio, and asked her aid in killing the king, and removing the girl. The tire-woman answered, 'Inform me what thing the king so admires in the damsel, and what part of her it is that he gazes on most?' The queen replied, 'It has been observed, when they have been sleeping together, that it is her apple-like chin, which, from its excessive clearness, thou wouldest say is a fruit suspended near the water of life; or a soft quince, which the hand of Omnipotence has placed upon the citron of her throat, upon which he bestows many kisses, and expresses by his gestures

COUPLET.

'Invite me not, O holy man! to enter Eden's garden fair,
The apple of her chin outvies the fruits, the flowers that blossom there.'

The tire-woman rejoined, 'I have found out an easy way to remove the king with all despatch. Our advisable course is for thee to give me some deadly poison, that I may mix it with indigo, and go to the apartment of the damsel, and make a mole with it somewhere about her chin and throat. So when the king, in a state of inebriety, applies his lips to it, he will die on the spot, and thou wilt be quit of this distress.' The queen was delighted at these words, and got ready for her what she wanted, and the tire-woman, in the manner described, compounded an artful mixture, and having placed it in a casket of guile, went to the girl's chamber, and with black artifice placed a mole on the chin of that moon, and thus lodged dark-visaged Hárút[1] on the brink of the water of Bábal.

---

[1] See Sale's Ḳur'án, p. 12, l. 22, 'But the devils believed not; they taught men sorcery, and that which was sent down to the two angels at Babel, Harût and Marût.' On this passage Sale has the following note (t) :—'Some say only that these were two magicians, or angels sent by God to teach men magic and to tempt them. But others tell a longer fable; that the angels expressing their surprise at the wickedness of the sons of Adam, after prophets had been sent to them with divine commissions, God bid them choose two out of their own number to be sent down to be judges on earth. Whereupon they pitched upon Harût and Marût, who executed their office with integrity for some time, till Zohara, or the planet Venus, descended, and appeared before them in the shape of a beautiful woman bringing a complaint against her husband (though others say she was a real woman). As soon as they saw her, they fell in love with her, and endeavoured to prevail on her to satisfy their desires; but she flew up again to heaven, whither the two angels also returned, but were not admitted. However, on the intercession of a certain pious man, they were allowed to choose whether they would be punished in this life or in the other; whereupon they chose the former, and now suffer punishment accordingly in Babel, where they are to remain till the day of judgment. They add, that if a man has a fancy to learn magic, he may go to them

COUPLET.

That mole is placed upon her chin, a tempting bait, a dangerous snare;
O God! from fortune's evils shield, and aye protect the good, the fair.

Now the king had a slave who possessed the entrée into the seraglio. It so happened that he overheard behind a curtain the conversation of the queen and the tire-woman, and saw with his own eyes the latter go to the chamber of the slave-girl, and put the mole on her cheek. The call of loyalty and gratitude impelled him to acquaint the girl with that deceit. He could however find no opportunity, and the king, too, was in a state of intoxication, and it was noways possible to make known to him that secret. At length the king, according to his familar and wonted custom, entered the apartment of the girl, and from excessive intoxication fell asleep. As, however, grateful affection laid hold of the skirt of the slave, he softly approached the pillow of the damsel, and with the corner of his sleeve wiped away the mark of the indigo from her chin. Meanwhile the king awoke, and beheld the slave with his hand extended to the girl's chin. The heat of jealousy placed him on the fire of wrath, and with his diamond-like sword he made at the slave. The latter ran out from the private chamber, and the king issued in pursuit of him with his scymitar drawn. A confidential officer was standing there, and held the letters in his hand. When he beheld the king incensed, he advanced and displayed one letter. The ocean of the king's fury, however, was not calmed thereby. He then uttered the contents of the second, yet the fire of mischief was not quenched. But when the third letter reached the place of representation, the king allowed himself to be somewhat composed and calmed, and swallowed the bitter draught of anger. He then called the slave kindly to him and said, 'Why didst thou do this bold deed?' The slave truthfully detailed the circumstances; whereupon the king called his bride, and exerted himself to an extraordinary degree in inquiry into that treason, and examining into that deceit. The queen denied the facts, and said, 'The slave lies, and I have often noticed this abandoned and worthless wretch doing similar things to the girl. But I was ashamed on the king's account to make known his impudence. Besides it might possibly have been supposed that I was calumniating them through jealousy. Now, Praise be to God! the king has seen it with his own eyes. To admit of any pause therefore in destroying the traitor is injurious to the royal character for justice, and when anger takes place in its proper season, it is doubtless many degrees better than clemency.

COUPLET.

The thorn is but for burning, it   For placing in the collar were unfit.'

---

and hear their voice, but cannot see them.—This story Mohammed took directly from the Persian Magi, who mention two rebellious angels of the same names, now hung up by their feet with their heads downwards in the territory of Babel. And the Jews have something like this of the angel Shambozai, who, having debauched himself with women, repented, and by way of penance hung himself up between heaven and earth.'

The king looked towards the slave, who said, 'O king! prosperous, and the means of the tranquillity of the age! it is possible that the remains of this powder may still be in the tire-woman's box. If the royal order be issued for her attendance, perhaps this doubt will altogether be removed.' The king commanded, and they brought the tire-woman and her box into the presence, and gave her a little of that indigo powder to eat. The instant she swallowed it she died; and when the true state of the case was thus made known to the king he imprisoned the queen, and gave the slave a writing of liberation, and committed to his charge the government of some districts of that kingdom. So that world-protecting monarch, inasmuch as he adorned the face of his own proceedings, with the ornament of clemency, was saved from being harmed by the tire-woman; and by the blessing of his gracious endurance, escaped the injury of that black deed; and a secret of such peril was made known to him, and he was enabled to discern between friend and foe.

And I have adduced this story that in the mirror of the clear judgment of the king, this beautiful idea may shew itself, that kings ought in no affair to act precipitately, nor without reflection and due thought, to order anything to be put in execution.

STANZA.

Like a fierce fire, or a raging ocean,
  Commands of monarchs may destroy a world.
It fits not then in times of wild emotion,
  The thunders of their will be round them hurled.'

The king said, 'I have erred in giving this order, and the words passed my lips in a moment of anger. At least, then, thou oughtest, as befits the character of prudent counsellors, to have observed, therein, due deliberation. And it is strange that thou shouldest have chosen to be so precipitate and put to death such a peerless lady.' The vazír replied, 'For one woman the king ought not to suffer his august mind to be so troubled that he may not be kept back from the enjoyment of intercourse with the other servants of his seraglio.

COUPLET.

What, has the cypress perished? Yes! but Nárvan[1] flowers the eye still bless:
The tulip's gaudy bloom is o'er, then mark the jasmine's loveliness.'

When, from the tenor of the vazír's words, the king understood that Irán-dukht had been slain, a sigh issued from his bosom, and falling into the whirlpool of grief, he was saying to himself,

COUPLET.

'Freely, O breast! indulge in grief; for lo!
My heart stands girt to emulate thy woe.'

---

[1] *Nárvan* or *Nárwun* is, perhaps, the pomegranate, or a species of cherry.

Alas! for the beauty of the flower-garden of youth, which, like the rose's promise, has been short-lived : and alack ! for that plant of the garden of prosperity, which by the calamity of the autumn of separation has shed its leaves.

VERSE.

> Now prostrate in the dust, alas! the cypress of thy stature lies,
> And earth, alas! and yet, alas! that priceless gem o'ercanopies.
> The place for it, thy place indeed, thy fitting place was on our eyes.
> Alas! and yet again, alas! that peerless gem in dust now lies.'

He then turned to his vazír and said, 'I am filled with grief at the death of Irán-dukht.' The vazir replied, 'Three persons are always the prisoners of grief, and fettered by woe. The first, is he who expends his energies in doing ill. The second, is he who does not do good when he has the power. The third, is he who acts without reflection, and whose conduct, being of this nature, issues in remorse.' The king said, 'O Balár ! thou didst not pause in putting Irán-dukht to death, and by the trouble thou tookest to no good purpose, she perished.' The vazír replied, 'The labor of three persons is vain : first, that of a person who clothes himself in white, and practices the trade of a glass-blower; next that of a washerman, who with costly garments stands in the water and washes clothes; thirdly, that of a merchant, who secures a good wife, and having left her at home chooses to take a long journey. And I did not exert myself to secure her death; I did but obey the king's command, and in this matter it is your majesty on whom censure rightly falls; since, though his prudence does not fall short in noticing the issues of affairs, and his visual faculty comprehensively surveys the terminations of things, still in this mandate his penetrating sagacity failed to discern, and his right aiming foresight missed the deliberation due.

COUPLET.

> Prudence ought to have swayed the royal word:
> Had it done so, these things had not occurred.'

The king responded, 'Cease these words and bethink thyself of this, that a longing to behold her keeps me sad, and I know not how to prepare a cure for this sorrow.' The vazír replied, 'The hand of remedy reaches not to the skirt of this business, and in this transaction regret is unavailing; and whoever plunges into a thing without reflection, and undertakes a matter in which repentance is of no use, will meet with what that Pigeon met with.' The king demanded, 'How was that?'

STORY IV.

The vazír said, 'They have related that a pair of Pigeons had collected some grains of corn in the beginning of summer, and stored them up in a retired place as a hoard for winter. Now that corn was moist, and when

summer drew to a close, the heat of the atmosphere had had such an effect
upon the corn, that it dried up and appeared less than it did at first.   During
these days the male Pigeon was absent from home.   When he came back
and observed that the corn appeared to be less in quantity, he began to
reproach his partner, and said, 'We had laid up this grain for our food in
winter, that when the cold became excessive, and from the quantity of snow
no corn was to be found on the fields, we might support ourselves with this.
At this time, when pickings are to be met with in mountain and plain, why
hast thou eaten our supplies? and why hast thou swerved from the path of
prudence?   Hast thou not heard, pray, that the sages have said,

COUPLET.

'Now that thou hast food in plenty do thy best it up to store,
That thou may'st still have abundance when the harvest-time is o'er.'

The female Pigeon said, 'I have eaten none of this grain nor have I
used any of it in any way whatever.'   As the male Pigeon saw that the
grain had decreased, he did not believe her denial, and pecked her till she
died.   Afterwards in the winter when the rain fell incessantly, and the
marks of dampness were evident on door and wall, the grain imbibed
moisture and returned to its former state.   The male Pigeon then discovered
what had been the cause of the apparent loss, and began to lament and
to bewail his separation from his affectionate partner.   Thus he wept
bitterly and said, 'Grievous is this absence of my friend, and more grievous
still that repentance is unavailing.

COUPLET.

With prudence act, for haste will cause thee pain
And loss, and to regret the lost is vain.'

And the moral of this story is, that it behoves a wise man not to be
precipitate in inflicting punishment, lest, like the Pigeon, he suffer from the
anguish of separation.'   The king said, 'If I was hasty in word, thou, too,
didst show precipitation in deed, and hast plunged me into this distress.'
The vazír replied, 'Three persons plunge themselves into distress.   One, is
he who is careless of himself in battle, so that he receives a severe wound.
The second, is he who has no heir, and amasses wealth by unlawful means,
which will be dissipated by accidents, and bring him punishment in the end.
And the third, is the old man who ties the marriage-knot with a profligate
and youthful wife, and sets his heart upon her; while that wife every day
prays to God for his death, and disagrees with him.'   The king rejoined,
'From this deed one may derive proof of thy rashness.'   The vazír replied,
'Rashness is shewn in the conduct of two persons.   One, is he who deposits
his money with strangers.   The other, is he who makes a fool arbiter between
himself and his adversary.   And I have not chosen to act precipitately in
this affair.   The utmost that I have done is to seek to obey the king in

executing his commands.' The king replied, 'I am much grieved for Irán-dukht.' The vazír answered, 'It is fitting to grieve for five kinds of women. The first, is she who has a beneficent nature and a noble mind, and graceful form and perfect chastity. The second, is she who is wise and long-suffering, and sincere and attached. The third, is she who chooses the advisable course in everything, and who is kind whether absent or present. The fourth, is she who makes agreement and submission her under and upper garment in good and bad, in welfare and adversity. The fifth, is she who is of fortunate presage and happy augury, and the blessing of whose footstep is manifest to her husband; and Irán-dukht was adorned with all these virtues. If the king evinces grief for her loss it will be but what is right; for without a faithful partner, there is neither enjoyment in life nor happiness in existence.

COUPLET.

It is not so pleasurable, friendless, lone to live;
Life, alone and friendless, cannot so much pleasure give.'

The king said, 'O Balár! thou art bold in thy language, and dost overstep the bounds of respect; and I am of opinion that it is necessary to remove to a distance from thee.' The vazír replied, 'Distance is desirable from two persons. One, is he who regards good and bad as equal, and imagines that future rewards and punishments do not exist. The other, is he who outwardly preserves himself pure from things prohibited by law, and inwardly from interdicted pastimes.' The king answered, 'Do we appear vile in thy sight, that thou thinkest fit to dare to utter these words?' The vazír replied, 'The great appear contemptible in the eyes of three classes of persons. The first, is the impudent servant, who, in season and out of season, in sitting down and getting up, and at supper and breakfast, takes his place with his master; and whose master, too, jokes with him, and relishes his ribaldry. The second, is the villain domestic, who has the control of his master's goods, and opens the hand of embezzlement thereupon, so that in a short time his wealth surpasses that of his master, and he thinks himself the better of the two. The third, is the servant who, without deserving it, has confidence reposed in him, and, becoming acquainted with the secrets of his master, is puffed up with that honor.' The king said, 'I have tried thee, and thou wert better untried.' The vazír replied, 'Eight persons cannot be tried save in eight positions: the brave man in battle, and the farmer in cultivation, and great men in the hour of anger, and the merchant in the time of reckoning, and a friend in the season of need, and men of a generous nature in the time of adversity, and the pious man in storing up the rewards of the final state, and the learned man in the moment of discourse and discussion.' In short, how much soever the king continued making displeased rejoinders to the vazír, so much the more did the latter give back answers sharper than the points of darts dipped in venom; and placing on his tongue[1] words in keenness like a sword of diamond, kept uttering them; and the king, patiently submitting to them, perseveringly swallowed those bitter draughts.

VERSE.

He that is rational, is patient, too;
But senseless he whom anger masters. True,
Patience, at first, seems sour as poisonous things,
It turns to honey, when it inward springs.

At length, the vazír loosed the tongue of eulogy, and said, 'May the shade of the glory of the king, the shadow of God, be perpetuated over the faces of mankind, and may the sun of his grandeur continue to shine from the pinnacle of exaltation and the summit of greatness! I, thy slave, who with the steps of boldness have traversed the plain of audacity, and have ventured to chagrin your exalted majesty with the abundance of my galling remarks, have done so to test your nature, endowed with amiable qualities; and thanks be to God Most High! that if any one seeks for the king's like, and would trace out one resembling him,

HEMISTICH.

Save in the glass and stream's reflection, one can nowhere find his peer.

What a noble nature is this, adorned with the beauty of mildness and virtue! and how precious is this character which is beautified with the ornament of patience, and composure, and amiability! And assuredly greatness is restricted to such a person, and the name of nobility belongs solely to the like of one so glorious.

VERSE.

Greatness is not in fame and rumor solely,
Nor magnanimity in vain conceit.
The name of 'noble' is to none more wholly
Due than to him whose praise mankind repeat
As virtue-gifted, and in temper sweet.'

The king said, 'O Balár! thou knowest well that I have based the affairs of my empire on clemency and compassion, and laid the substructure of my rule on tenderness and forbearance. And if sometimes directions have been isued for the correction of a party who, from arrogance, evinces a refractory spirit, and of those who enter avowedly and openly into a position of contest and strife, this is done to preserve the respect due to the government, and to keep in order the regulations of the empire. Otherwise the expanse of the ocean of my lofty spirit is not so limited as that it should roll the waves of anger on the excitation of such words as these.

---

[1] Lit., 'breath.'

STANZA.

No willow I whose leaves each breath makes tremble,
Nor straw that shrivels as fire onward climbs.
The shout-returning hill I nought resemble,
Nor cloud which winds make weep a hundred times.'

The vazír said, 'A commandment of that nature is rare, and [it is said],
' *The rare is like the non-existent,*' and [the king's] mildness has remedied it
this day, for in no history have they recorded that a fortunate monarch and
a powerful ruler with a sharp sword and potent will, has been seated on the
throne of his greatness; while an offending servant, standing in his
lowly position, has uttered disrespectful words; and, stepping beyond his place,
has given his tongue free license. What, in such a case, could prevent the
due chastisement being enforced, save vast clemency and perfect pity?

HEMISTICH.

The more I err, the more thy grace abounds.'

The king responded, 'When a slave acknowledges his crime and sees
with his own eyes the trace of guilt on the pages of his own conduct, of
course he will be in a position to be excused; and the beneficent man has no
alternative but to accept an apology.

HEMISTICH.

The generous will excuses aye admit.'

The vazír answered, 'O king! I confess my guilt, and my offence is that I
have thought it permissible to postpone the execution of the king's mandate,
and have delayed to put Irán-dukht to death, and pausing through fear of
this terror-exciting word, and through dread of this rebukeful address, have
avoided precipitation in slaying her. Now it is for the king to order and
command.

COUPLET.

Whether thou art gracious, or thou wavest the unpitying sword,
I have bowed my neck before thee, as a captive to his lord.'

As soon as the king heard these words, the signs of delight and
exultation, and the evidence of joy and gladness were evident on his
august countenance. He erected to the summit of the highest heavens the
banner of the performance of the praises of God; and, having performed
the prostrations of infinite thanksgivings, he raised his joyful shouts beyond
the top of the ethereal sky and said,

VERSE.

Glad tidings these, O Fortune! that my wish the door has entered in;
The hapless lover finds once more his soul the body centred in.
She, like the rose, at whose perfume, smiles did the spirit's lip illume, [1]
With radiant cheek, more bright than flowers once more my door has entered in.'

[1] The lithographed edition omits this second couplet.

He then continued, 'I was left in amazement in that thou continuedst to speak in such wise as to lead me to the belief that Irán-du<u>kh</u>t was slain; yet I well knew thy sincere attachment and judiciousness, and could not but think that thou wouldest delay the execution of that order.' The vazír replied, 'My rejoinders were made in order that I might thoroughly understand the king's purpose, and see whether he repented of that order or not. If I had found your majesty still bent on her death, I should have secretly hastened the despatch of that affair. Since, however, the king's mind is more inclined to suffer her to live, I have made known my fault and offered my excuses for the delay.' The king responded, 'Thy caution and prudence are the more conspicious to me in this affair, and my confidence in thy sagacity and discernment has been augmented; and I have accepted the service which thou hast done, and the fruits thereof will reach thee with the utmost speed. Thou must now, this instant, proceed to Irán-du<u>kh</u>t, make known all the circumstances and convey to her many excuses, and respectfully request, in the best way possible, that she will come hither, which alone will be a key to the gates of the acquisition of our desires and the capital of joyful union and delight.

COUPLET.

Come! for to meet thee is my prayer, the prayer I'm still repeating!
My ear is straining for thy voice—my eyes to give thee greeting.' [1]

Balár came out from the king's presence and conveyed to Irán-du<u>kh</u>t the good news of her safety and the happy tidings of her being about to meet her royal lover.

COUPLET.

O heart! complain not, like the bud, thy bloom thou canst not hasten,
The morning gale a breeze shall bring and thy closed state unfasten.

Irán-du<u>kh</u>t, obeying the royal mandate, hastened to wait on the king; and having performed the requisite obeisance, loosed the tongue of gratitude and thankfulness. The king said, 'Thou must ascribe this obligation to Balár, seeing that he fulfilled all that prudence could require, and paused in executing this purpose.' Balár said, 'I had the most complete confidence in the perfect clemency and compassion of your imperial majesty, and the excess of your benevolence and infinite mercy; and my consideration sprang thence into existence; otherwise, how could a slave venture to delay in executing the command of the sultán?' The king replied, 'O Balár! be of stout heart, for thy hand has free scope in my dominions, and thy command has obtained equal weight with my own, and there shall be no opposition to whatever thou mayest say or do in loosing and binding, and commanding and prohibiting.' Balár answered, 'Your majesty's former

---

[1] Lit., 'upon thy road.'

favors and bounteous acts outstrip all our services, and could I obtain a life
of a thousand years' duration, I could not return thanks for one in a thousand
of those bounties.

COUPLET.

> The lily may its hundred tongues all use,
> 'T will fail to render to the spring its dues.

But the prayer of your slaves is this, that hereafter your majesty will not
evince precipitation in your acts, that the purity of the conclusion may be
free from the obscuration of repentance.' The king responded, 'We have
deigned to listen to this counsel with the ear of acceptance; and for the
future we will not issue a mandate without consultation and asking
approval.'[1] He then bestowed on the vazír and Irán-dukht, robes of honor
of great value, and having moved joyfully forth from the dark cell of
separation into the bride-chamber of union, he set in bright array the
assembly of mirth.

COUPLET.

> A noble banquet they in order set,
> And in joy's flower-garden, smiling, met.

A beautiful cupbearer poured from a silver goblet pure wine to be quaffed[2]
by the gay companions, and the delicious liquid irrigated the plant of
enjoyment on the rivulet of their bosoms.

COUPLET.

> Bravo! the wine, to pleasure giving birth,
> Made brisk the mart of jollity and mirth.

Sweet-voiced minstrels with harmonious concert of every kind of stringed
instrument were bringing the bird of the heart into a state of fluttering
excitement, and the melodies of song were inviting to the banquet of mirth
and joy. The delicate trills of the harp imitated the warblings of the bird of
a thousand songs, and the ravishing and tender tones of the lute effaced the
rust from the mirror of the breasts of the intoxicated.

VERSE.

> Singers like Venus with their sweet-toned voices,
> And goblets flashing bright like Mercury:
> The sound of mirth each swelling breast rejoices,
> Just as each fickle mind would wish the tone to be.

The remainder of the day and all the night they spent in festivity.

COUPLET.

> Next day, when morn with world-illuming ray,
> Conducted night auspiciously to day,

the king gave a public levée and sate on the throne of justice, and the vazír
Balár, having performed the required obeisance, demanded on his own behalf

---

[1] *Istijázat* seems an unusually strong word for a despot to use. It signifies 'asking
leave.'

[2] Lit., 'into the palate.'

and as representative of the wife and children of the king, justice on the Bráhmans, and recounted the interpretation of the dreams as they had delivered[1] it in the manner aforesaid. Wherefore the king's command was condescendingly uttered, that they should summon the sage Kárídún into the presence, and the king committed to his decision the punishment of the Bráhmans. At the suggestion of Kárídún, they impaled some of them, and casting the majority under the feet of elephants, crushed them to an equality with the dust of the road; and the sage said, ' This is the punishment of traitors and the chastisement of the perfidious.

VERSE.

> Who from its sheath the cruel dagger take,
> Heaven with the same will them decapitate.
> And none their face like anvil rigid make,
> But must the avenging hammer's blows await.'

After getting rid of his enemies, the king committed to his vazír the government of his kingdom, and yielding himself up to the delights of love with Irán-dukht, he fully satisfied the requirements of pleasure.

> Hold dear the night of love and mirth, and take thy fill of pleasure;
> The fortunes of the coming day no foresight e'er can measure.

This is the story of the excellence of mildness and composure, and their superiority to the other qualities and habits of kings and princes; and let it not remain hid from the intelligent, that the advantage to be derived from the recital of this narrative, is the admonition of the readers and warning to the hearers, to make the experience of those who have preceded them, and the directions of the wise, a pattern for their own proceedings; and to base their religious and worldly affairs, and the substructures of their transactions of to-day and to-morrow on the rules of wisdom, and the pedestal of prudence; and to turn from impetuosity and rashness towards gravity and calmness. And whoever is distinguished by the eternal favor, assuredly the head of his spirit will be adorned with the diadem of courtesy, and the shoulder of his pre-eminence will be decked with the scarf of clemency; for courtesy and clemency make an enemy a friend, and exalt a friend to the position of a kinsman.

VERSE.

> Dost thou consort with Meekness—Courtesy?
> Thy rival will prove faithful as ' a comrade of the cave.'[2]
> Thou among men make none thy enemy,
> That with thee time may circle on as thy true friends would have.

---

[1] For *bar namṭ-i mazkúr takrír kardah búdand*, one MS. reads *ghalaṭ takrír kardah búdand*, ' as they had wrongly interpreted.'

[2] *Yár-i ghár*, a name of Abú-bakr, who was with Muḥammad when he lay hid in the cave during his flight. Hence, any intimate companion.

CHAPTER XIII.

ON THE SHUNNING THE SPEECHES OF THE PERFIDIOUS AND TRAITOROUS BY KINGS.

INTRODUCTION.

COUPLET.

The ancient sage, who the world's conflicts knew,
[In language sweet] thus wisdom's veil undrew.

And when King Dábishlím had heard this story from the sage Bídpáí, he offered praise, from the signification of which the perfumes of friendship would reach the nostrils of the saintly, and whose import gave intelligence of the royal diplomas of the happy tidings of tho morn of felicity, and said,

COUPLET.

'O thou! from whom, in problems dark, the reason light has won;
And by whose sense thought's knotty points are all with ease undone,

I have heard the description of the advantage of mildness and endurance, and the detriment of impetuosity and rashness; and have comprehended the superiority of composure and mildness over the other virtues of princes and qualities of potentates. Now recount a story illustrative of kings retaining faithful and loyal servants, and point out what class of persons best appreciate the value of patronage, and return thanks most fully for the benefits conferred on them.' The Bráhman, in reply to the praises of the king, having arranged the offering of benediction, said, 'May the most perfect share and most universal portion of every rare gift of fortune which unveils its face from the fabric, '*Assistance from God and a speedy victory,*' [1] and every felicitous boon which is displayed on the ornamented bride's seat, '*For victory is from God alone,*' [2] be particularly bestowed on his highness the ruler of the kingdom!

---

[1] Kur'án, lxi. 13; Sale, p. 408, l. 14: 'Believe in God and his apostle . . . . . . And ye shall obtain other things which ye desire, namely, assistance from God, and a speedy victory.'

[2] Kur'án, Fl. iii. 122; Mar. 126; Sale, p. 47, l. 5: 'And this God designed only as good tidings for you, that your hearts might rest secure: for victory is from God alone, the mighty, the wise.' I take this opportunity of correcting a little slip in that wonderfully accurate work, G. Flügel's 'Concordance of the Kur'án,' the only one I have yet found. Under *md* should be inserted 'chap. iii. 122,' as is proved by this passage and by referring to النصر.

VERSE.

O may the garden's nurse erase, with th' eastern breeze's aid,[1]
The dust from off the tulip's face and the Arghwán's blushing cheek!
May the glory's parterre, whither gales from Paradise have strayed,
Safe continue from the ravage of the winds of autumn bleak!

The most powerful assistance in the matter, whereof the king has spoken, is to discern the proper field for employing [each individual]; and it behoves a king to test the coin of his servants with a variety of experiments on the touchstone of trial; and to make himself acquainted with the assay-value of the judgment, and knowledge, and sincerity, and prudence of each; and so to rely on their temperance, and integrity, and good faith, and honesty. For the capital stock for the service of kings is truthfulness, and truthfulness cannot exist without the fear of God and uprightness. And the beginning of all knowledge is fear[2] and awe [as it is said], '*Such only of his servants fear God as are endued with understanding.*'[3] Every servant of the king that fears God, the king, too, will have strong grounds for reliance on him; and the people will see in him a prop of hopefulness.

VERSE.

One who fears God be o'er thy people set,
For 'tis the pious man builds up the State.
One who dreads Heaven for thy vazír get,
Not one who fears the king and his own fate.

And assuredly it is not fit that a liar and an untruthful man should be raised to a position of confidence, and should obtain the power of access to the king's secrets; for thence troubles will arise, and the injurious effects thereof will be evident for a long, long period.' The king said, 'This subject requires detailed explanation, for men without birth, or dignity, or real worth, may be adorned with some attractive qualities, yet in the end their affairs, commencing a retrograde movement, will become the cause of shame to their patrons.

COUPLET.

He that is by nature base, though faithful he at first may be,
Will alter in the end, and prove bent on acting cruelly.'

The Bráhman said, 'The distinct exposition of this matter is, that three qualities are required for the servant of a king. The first is uprightness in action, for a trustworthy man is approved both by the Creator and by

---

[1] Lit., 'hand.'
[2] See Proverbs, c. i. v. 7: 'The fear of the Lord is the beginning of knowledge.'
[3] Kur'án, Fl. xxxv. 25; Mar. 28; Sale, p. 328, l. 29: 'Dost thou not see that God sendeth down rain from heaven; and that we thereby produce fruits of various colors? In the mountains also there are some tracks white and red, of various colors; and others are of a deep black: and of men, and beasts, and cattle, there are whose colors are in like manner various. Such only of his servants fear God as are endued with understanding: verily God is mighty, and ready to forgive.'

creatures, and is fit and worthy to be entrusted with the secrets of kings and the management of state-affairs. The second is truthfulness in speech, for the blemish of falsehood is a huge crime, and it is an indispensable duty for a king to shun those who speak falsely. And if all good qualities were collected in a person, and he were celebrated for his gratitude and thankfulness, yet if he be false in speech he is not worthy of confidence. The third quality is a generous nature and high spirit; for a mean man, and one destitute of magnanimity does not rightly appreciate the value of what is bestowed on him, and of the bounty shewn to him. And from whatever direction the wind comes, thither his inclinations are evinced.

HEMISTICH.

When the wind changed, he, as it veered, veered too.

And they have said, with relation to the unfaithful,

COUPLET.

Plant firm thy foot in friendship's path, unshaken as the ground;
And be not, like the breeze, each hour in a new quarter found.

And it behoves a king to fix his eyes on the virtuous qualities of his servants, not on their comeliness or strength,[1] for the beauty of the servants of princes is reason and ability, and their strength is knowledge and sagacity. And when any one is adorned with the ornaments of excellent qualities, and is free from the practice of corrupt habits, and unites in himself hereditary virtue and acquired merit,[2] and who issues from the crucible of trial pure and unsullied in the manner that has been mentioned, it is right that the king should observe every beneficial measure in encouraging him, and deliberately and by regular degrees elevate him to the different ranks of favor and stages of authority. Thus his honor will be established in all eyes, and his awe in all hearts. And the sages have said, 'It behoves a king, in encouraging his servants, [to proceed] like a skilful physician. For, as the latter, until, in the first place, he has fully ascertained and distinctly inquired into the state of the sick man, and the duration of his indisposition, and the nature and extent of his sickness, and its causes and symptoms; and until he has acquired perfect acquaintance and complete knowledge both on general and particular points, and the evidences of the pulse and urine, does not commence the remedies, nor ventures on prescriptions; so a king, too, ought to acquaint himself with the circumstances of each of his attendants minutely and generally, and inform himself of his method of action, and manner of speech, and mode of procedure. Then let him begin to promote him and raise him to power, and not place confidence in any with too great

---

[1] I am doubtful of these meanings of *tajammul* and *istizhár*, but they seem to suit the passage.

[2] The *kih* after *muktasab* in the editions had better be expunged.

facility, lest it prove a source of regret and repentance. And the principal point is, that the attendants of princes should be trustworthy, and to be depended upon; as well that the secrets, financial and administrative, may continue safe, as also that the soldiers and people may be preserved from injury and harm.   For if, which heaven forefend! one of the favorite courtiers be led into the evil quality of treason, and his words be honored with acceptance by the monarch, it is possible that he may plunge some innocent person into destruction, and thus cause disgrace to his prince, and bring upon him evil consequences in the end.   And among the narratives which relate to this subject is the story of the Goldsmith and the Traveler.' The king asked, 'How was that?'

STORY I.

The Bráhman said, 'They have related that in the royal city of Ḥalab,[1] there was a famous king and prosperous potentate, and many princes of that age had drawn the ring of fealty to him through the ear of their minds, and most of the rulers of the time had taken upon the shoulder of their heart the cloth of obedience to his will.

STANZA.

A leader through whose goodly justice earth with wholesome laws was blest,
  A Cæsar from whose radiant spirit that bright epoch guidance gained.
Wherever his imperial will the stirrup of advancing pressed,
  Thither triumph and good-fortune with him, too, their coursers reined.

And this king had a daughter sun-faced and moon-visaged, the light of whose cheek had imparted splendor to the countenance of the sun, and the scent of whose musky ringlets perfumed the nostrils of the age.

VERSE.

Her ruby lip the seal of Jamshíd's ring;
  Her mouth was smaller than a signet's circle.
Her cheek did to the air fresh pinkness bring;
  A hundred horse-shoes, envious glowed at her curl.
The Magians in their prayers turned to her cheek,
  Her mouth was what love's mendicants would seek.

The king kept this gem unique from the eyes of all others, and continued to cherish her like a royal pearl, in the shell of concealment and virtuous privacy.   One day they were preparing an ornament for this maid, and they had occasion for the services of a clever goldsmith, such a one as might be perfect in his craft.   Now in that city was a Goldsmith, who deserved to have the glowing ball of the sun for his melting operations, and for whose silver-smelting the bright crucible of the moon seemed a fitting laboratory.

---

[1] That is 'Aleppo.'

In valuing precious stones his quickness was such, that the instant he saw a shell, he knew the worth of the pearl inside it; and in assaying metals, his skill was so great, that, without experimentalising with a touch-stone, he used to announce the quantity of alloy and pure metal.

VERSE.

His craft he plied assiduous day and night,
Such was his craft all that he did to gold
Was turned: each thing with gold and silver dight,
He fashioned so as no one else could mould.

The king had heard his fame, and had seen some of his beautiful works and excellent articles, wherefore he, on this occasion, sent for him to the seraglio, and held a consultation with him as to the preparation of the ornament. The Goldsmith was a young man of prepossessing countenance and sweet tongue. During the conversation, the king's heart took pleasure in his words, and the royal mind felt an inclination to meet him constantly. And he, day by day, by the astonishing skill of his performances and his admirable discourse, was fascinating the king; and every hour the latter, too, shewed him more favor and honor, until he became the confidential visitor of the seraglio, and the princess, upon whom sun and moon had never cast their shadow, admitted him to interviews [seated] behind a curtain.

HEMISTICH.

He to whom the heart is opened finds in his friend's Ḥaram place.

And this king had a vazír celebrated for the solidity of his judgment, and notorious and well-known for the rectitude of his counsels. The writing of his world-subduing pen was the victorious chronicle of triumph, and the effect of his universe-adorning thought was the fringe of the robe of majesty. The pious and the great used to place confidence in his clear judgment, and the landowners and leaders of the faith had the stock of life augmented by his pen, which was gifted with the miraculous powers of K͟hizr.

COUPLET.

Thy pen, great Heaven! did singly, for religion and the state,
Life's water in a hundred springs from one ink-drop create.

When the vazír saw that the king went beyond the bounds of moderation in his patronage of the Goldsmith, and carried his undue attentions to him, and consideration for him, to the limit of excess, he, out of pure attachment and loyalty, at a proper opportunity and a convenient time, on a pretext which was not beyond the circle of congruity, turned the reins of the courser of his discourse toward the affair of the Goldsmith, and said, 'O king! former

---

[1] The editions wrongly omit the negative before *garddnidah.* A few lines above the printed edition has '*izár* for '*izáz.*

sovereigns introduced not artizans into the circle of men of authority, nor raised them above their peers and fellows. But now the king has made this person the confidential visitor of his ḥaram, without previously ascertaining, as he ought and should have done, his qualifications. It strikes me, however, that this person has not a generous nature, nor is of a guileless temperament; for his discourse is always restricted to the injuring and annoying others, and his energies in the discharge of orders or prohibitions are not expended in the place or time they ought to be. From such a a person, therefore, faithful procedure and grateful habits are not to be expected.

COUPLET.

He that expects the base will faithful be,   Hopes to find fruit upon the willow-tree.

And I have observed that whenever your majesty is disposed to reward or show favor to any one that mean base fellow is ready to wish himself dead from chagrin.   And the wise have said, 'It is a characteristic of low-minded people that they cannot bear to see another person liberal to another.'

VERSE.

The base are loath that others should succeed :
The miser from the cup the fly will scare.
When thou to meat a low-bred wretch dost lead,
'Tis not his portion only he eats there ;
But sour chagrin as well that others too may share.

And those persons are more worthy to be admitted to the king's society who unite honorable descent with the nobility of merit.   And it is right to shun the company of an ignorant low-bred man, for from associating with persons of this class various mischiefs arise, and those who are base by nature and inwardly impure have no regard for honesty nor care for uprightness ; and when these qualities are absent, we may expect from such a sordid wretch every fault which enters the limits of possibility.

DISTICHS.

He that of honest feelings has no share,
What wonder if he guilty acts should dare !
Of all bad things, dishonesty the worst,
Includes all crimes by which mankind is cursed.'

The king replied, ' This young man has a comely form and beauty of form is a sure indication of mental grace, for, ' *the external is the index of the internal,*' and the wise have said, ' the beauty of the preface announces the excellence of the body of the work.

COUPLET.

From a fair preface wise men understand,   That finer beauties may within be scanned.

And in that His Holiness of Prophetical dignity (*on him be the best and choicest blessings !*) pronounced, ' Read the letter of your requirement to one

the page of whose cheek is adorned with the verse of beauty and comeliness;
and expect goodness from one of a bright countenance, for the cheek of his
condition will be adorned with the mole of excellence, ' *Seek for good from
fair-faced women*,'—he intimated that beauty of outward appearance denotes
mental grace.

COUPLET.

Suspect not evil of a man,   If outward grace in him you scan.'

The vazír answered, ' In the school of wisdom they do not read the
chapter of beauty of form, and they do not think the verse of perfection to be
in reality aught else but amiable qualities of the mind.   For there are many
persons who ravish men's hearts by their grace of form, but when they strike
the coin of their spiritual nature on the touchstone of trial, they find
them good for nothing.   And it has been entered among the stories of sages
that a philosopher saw a handsome youth, and his heart yearned towards him.
He went forward and made trial of the coin of his real qualities, but he found
no precious metal worth speaking of.   So he turned away and said, ' It is a
goodly house if there were but some one in it ! '

COUPLET.

Walk in the spirit; for two canes may be alike, yet that
Gives forth sweet sugar, whilst of this one can but make a mat.'

The king replied, ' From grace of form we may infer symmetry of mind,
and one of a well-proportioned mind is worthy of notice.   Moreover since
during this long period he had no patron, it is possible that some of his
qualities may have deviated from the right path; but now we bestow on him
the eye of patronage, that he may acquire praiseworthy feelings to a degree
of perfection.   For the effect of such fostering influence is to turn a flint into
a beautiful ruby, and a lustrous heart-expanding gem.   So too by the
auspiciousness of aid black blood becomes fragrant civet-raining musk, and a
drop of rain is changed into a peerless royal gem.

QUATRAIN.

Through fostering influence water a gem
  Becomes; and navel blood-drops change to musk
Of rarest scent, when blessing hallows them.
  So the transmuting stone, on iron dusk
  And valueless; does such influence hold,
  As changes it to pure, unsullied gold.'

The vazír replied, ' O king! to give encouragement to one that has no
original purity of birth is unfitting, for it is not every stone that becomes a
jewel, nor does all blood change to fragrant musk; and if a base person were
educated for a thousand years, it is impossible to look for goodness from him.

COUPLET.

Though one should tend the willow with the selfsame care
As aloes, aloe-scent would still be wanting there.

And were they to endeavour to change and alter the sordid man a hundred times, his original nature would remain unaltered, and a man of eminence has pronounced on this head,

STANZA.

> Men who with low mean origin are cursed,
>   By changing fortune changed none e'er will see.
> So if the word Sag-magas [1] be reversed,
>   Its anagram will aye Sag-magas be.

And since this truth is well-established, it behoves a person not to associate with such sordid wretches that he may not be overtaken in the whirlpool of disgrace, like that Prince, who from companying with a Shoemaker was plunged into the abasement of slavery, and through his friendship with a Jeweler arrived on the borders of the plain of destruction.' The king asked, ' How was that ? '

STORY II.

The vazír said, ' They have related that in the territory of Fárs, there was a king of good dispositions and an amiable nature, who had placed the foundation of his sway on the benevolent inclination to cherish his subjects, and who on the throne of royalty fully satisfied the requirements of a widely-diffused clemency.

COUPLET.

> His greatness oped the hand of justice to the whole of human kind,
> And by his awe, oppression's feet, too, were in fetters firm confined.

A son was born to him on whose countenance the signs of rectitude and nobleness were found, and on whose face the marks of world-subjugating triumph were conspicuous.

COUPLET.

> When Mercury beheld his day of birth appear,
> He straight pronounced, ' Lo ! perfect bliss [2] is here!'

And on the shoulder of this boy there was a black mole of the size of the palm of one's hand.   The king was disturbed at the sight of this, and inquired of the wise men of the time what that mark denoted.   They replied, 'We have seen in ancient books that whoever has such a mark, many dangers will befall him, but in the end he will be a great conqueror and subduer of the world.'   The king was pleased at these happy tidings, and kept the eyes of fostering care fixed on his condition.   And in the neighbor-hood of the king lived a Shoemaker, devoid of any nice sense of honor and

---

[1] *Sag-magas* ' dog-fly.'   The word does not occur in the dictionary, and I know not which of the detestable insect-brood is intended.

[2] *S'ad-i akbar* signifies, also, ' the planet Jupiter,' which is said to be the most auspicious star.   So Venus is called *s'ad-i asghar*, ' the lesser felicity.'

from birth a lewd fellow. The king observed towards him the rights of neighborly feelings, and had assigned to him a regular pension and a fixed stipend. And he always passed his time tranquilly and in easy circumstances under the shadow of the king's favor. When the Prince reached the age of four[1] years, being naturally of a frolicksome temper, he used constantly to come to the Shoemaker's little room and spend the time in play. The vazír being informed of this state of things, exerted himself to prohibit and prevent this, and said, ' The sapling of the temper of children is very susceptible, and turns in whatever direction people incline it, and remains fixed so.

VERSE.

The branch, when tender, which is bent awry,
    If thou dost straighten it will then come right :
But if two years or three should once pass by,
    To straighten it will then exceed thy might.

My advice is that the king should restrain the Prince from associating with the Shoemaker, that his reprehensible qualities may not suddenly infect the royal youth, nor plunge the peerless spirit[2] of that luminary of the heaven of empire into the abyss of abasement; and that various perils which are to be thence expected may not occur.

HEMISTICH.

From a foul spirit spring all hateful things.'

The king responded, ' He is a mere child, and has taken a fancy for the Shoemaker, and he is very dear to me. It is probable that if I keep him back from associating with the man, he will be vexed, and his chagrin would tend to distress my heart. I will wait a little till he grows older, and can discriminate between good and bad. We will then, by admonition, bring his conduct into the right way.' The vazír was silent, and the king sent for the Shoemaker, and bestowed many favors upon him, and having given him hopes of his imperial bounty for the future, said, ' Thou art my neighbor, and this darling of mine has become attached to thee, and his wish is that thou shouldest be his familiar friend and companion, and protect him from fire and water.' The Shoemaker kissed the ground of service, and said,

COUPLET.

' May the rose of the king's garden kindle up the world with light !
May the lamp of his night-hours like day's radiant torch be bright !

I, your slave, do not find in myself capacity for this post, nor perceive in my

---

[1] There is an absurd mistake in the editions here, viz., *chahdrdah* for *chahdr*, which latter is the correct reading, as is proved by the MSS. and by what follows at p. 511, l. 14, of the Persian text, printed edition, when after ten years the Prince is said to reach his fourteenth year. Besides had he been fourteen, how could the cobler have carried him backwards and forwards to and from the palace ?

[2] *Fardwash*, though not occurring in the Dictionary, is evidently a compound of the same kind as *máhwash*, etc.

own person merit enough for such a dignity, which is the ultimate object of ambition.[1] But the imperial regard possesses the miraculous powers of the philosopher's stone, and can make black earth pure gold, and change rude stones into perfect gems.

COUPLET.

The earth thou treadèst proves instinct with life;
Stones at thy look with golden ore grow rife.

My hope is that under the imperial auspices, the duties of attendance will be in such manner fulfilled that they may attain the honor of approval.' In short, he accepted the service of the Prince, and boldly taking him up brought him to his own hut, and then carried him back again to the king's palace. And at times it happened that the Prince stopped all night in his little room, and the king showed his satisfaction at his familiarity with the Shoemaker; while the latter undertook the service of the Prince in such a way, that every day his favor with the king increased, until he became altogether the favorite, and, by reason of his devoted attendance, he carried off the ball of elevation from his compeers.

HEMISTICH.

With the bat of service thou mayst win [right quickly, honor's] ball.

Day after day he used to take the Prince to wander over flower-gardens, and kept him till night employed in sight-seeing and amusement; and sometimes he spent the night too in gardens and places of entertainment. Once on a time, it became necessary for the king to take a journey; and, when he had formed a fixed intention of going, with a body of his particular attendants, he sent for the Shoemaker, and delivered the Prince anew to his charge, and uttered a number of injunctions that he would attend to his safety. The Shoemaker promised zealously to obey the king's commands, and girt himself afresh to his duties. Now in the environs of the city, the king had a garden, which was a type of the garden of Paradise above, and a model of the delightful region on high in the highest heaven. The breeze shook from the tresses full of curls of its violets, a profusion of pure musk; and the perfumer of the northern gale bore away from the entangled ringlets of its wild roses[2] fresh ambergris. The odoriferous shrubs of Eden from the perfumes of its flowers moist with dew, sought to augment their freshness; and the blossoms of the trees Sidrah and Túba borrowed the quality of gracefulness from the variety of its lofty branches.

---

[1] It appears to me that *ndm,* which is found in the editions before *ast,* were better omitted, as is done in some MSS.
[2] As a substantive is absolutely required in this sentence after *pur shikan,* I read with the lithographed edition and MSS. *nasrinash,* for the *mushkinash* of the printed edition, of which I can hardly make sense. Besides, *nasrin* is also an island where ambergris is found, so that by it we obtain an equivoque, of which the Persians are so fond.

VERSE.

That garden seemed like Paradise in beauty,
 Like Houris' eyes its Eden-flowers were shining.
The jasmine, with narcissus' bowl, did duty
 Cupbearer-like; and ebrious, reclining
The violet and red rose, hung : with ringlets
 O'er shoulder cast, the hyacinth stood pausing;
The Nasrín to the breeze unveiled, [1] and springlets
 Murmured softly. Fresh pain to lovers causing,
  The nightingale and bell-voiced Durráj [2] sung;
  And ravished nature on their accents hung.

The Prince very frequently used to betake himself to pleasant rambles in this garden, and at the very time when the king had chosen to travel, the royal youth had formed the wish of repairing thither according to his wonted custom, and had set off for the garden with a few of his slaves and attendants who always waited upon him. The Shoemaker observed that that day the prince wore on his head a golden crown, and a garment [3] ornamented with jewels, on his person. The low nature and sordid spirit of that wretch tempted him to deceit and treason, and he thought to himself, ' This dress and crown are as valuable as the capital of a hundred merchants, nay, equal to the whole contents of a thousand seas and mines. Just now his father is a long way off from the capital, and his mother and all the people of the seraglio are secure of my fidelity. My best plan is to carry off the boy, and having conveyed him to some remote city, sell his ornaments and apparel for an astonishing sum, and pass the rest of my life in happiness and ease.

COUPLET.

Propitious is the time—arise! to use thy blessings understand;
Since fortune turns her face to thee, then let her not elude thy hand.'

In the end, that wretch of evil end,[4] from the greedy desires of his perfidious spirit, kindled the fire of mischief; and, pouring the face-water [5] of integrity on the ground of injustice, formed a design against the son of his lord and master. He then imparted his intentions to a shrewd slave, who was his confidant, and found means to ply each of the other attendants with the wine of insensibility; and, having reduced the Prince, too, to the same state, he laid him in a large box. Then when night came, he fastened the box on the back of a quick-traveling she-camel, such that the swift-revolving moon applauded the rapidity of her progress, and the creation-traversing sky eulogised her fleet movements.

---

[1] Lit., ' exposed the cavity behind the ear.' [2] The Durráj is perhaps the pheasant.

[3] The *jámah* is a long gown, having from eleven to thirty breadths of cloth in the skirt, which at the upper part is folded into innumerable plaits ; and the body part, being double-breasted, is tied in two places on each side. See Kánún-i Islám, Appendix, Dress, iii.

[4] The double use of the word is in accordance with the original.

[5] *Ábrú,* lit., ' face-water,' but used to express 'honor.'

VERSE.

In fleetness she outrivaled e'en the sky;
Was linked in running with the moonbeams fair.
Like rushing floods she downward now would fly,
Anon like vapor spring aloft in air.

And he himself mounted a cream-colored steed, which sped like the life of the prosperous, and came on like sudden death. In going it tripped up[1] arrows, and its bounds consumed the heart of lightning [with jealousy]. Were they to have given it the rein, it would have carried off the ball of speed from thought itself; and had they struck it with the lash, it would have leapt from the globe of earth to the dome of heaven.

VERSE.

Deep the blows of his tramplings, the hoofs of his speed,[2]
Stamped the Earth-Fish's[3] immense back, the moon's countenance.
Not the sky e'en in swiftness from him took the lead,
Nor the wind to compete with him dared to advance.

And he set the slave also on another wind - rivaling, iron - champing, lightning-paced, thunder-snorting, world-crossing courser.

COUPLET.

Earth-traversing like wishes, wild[4] as lust without control,
Like youth's season fleetly passing, and precious as the soul.

And he took two other, sumpter-horses, and so carrying them with a supply of food for the way, they set their faces to the journey, and by the time that day dawned, they had traveled a vast distance; and having rested in the early morning a short space, they mounted again, and beginning with fiery haste, like lightning, to traverse the road, they passed far beyond the frontiers of the king's dominions, and arrived in another country. In the other direction the attendants and slaves of the Prince, stretched out insensible, did not recover their consciousness till mid-day. At length the gardener being apprised of their condition poured oil of almonds and stale vinegar on the brains of each, so that they came back to their senses, and seeing no trace of the Prince and the Shoemaker, they set off for the city and acquainted the boy's mother with the circumstances. The queen mounted and came to the garden, but from that delicate rose no perfume reached her nostrils.

VERSE.

I hastened to the garden, but my graceful cypress was not there,
And I missed my new-blown flower that was so smiling and so fair.
On every side, like spring-clouds, I was weeping in despair,
But to glad my tearful eyes came no more my cypress there.

---

[1] Observe the phrase *pai zadah*.   [2] Lit., 'at the time of running.'
[3] *Samak* is 'the fish on which the earth is supposed to rest.' An allusion this to Hindú mythology.
[4] Lit. 'wide-stepped.'

However, when the mother found no tidings of the light of her eyes, she uttered shrieks, and raising shrill outcries to the height of Arcturus, commanded that they should traverse with the step of search every part and quarter of the garden, and seek diligently throughout the environs and neighborhood of the city and adjoining country. And when after extensive inquiry and infinite trouble the messengers could in nowise reach the station of their desired object, but came back in despair, and represented how matters stood, the queen's tender nature[1] began to melt in the fire of separation, and, like a taper, she was consuming in the flame of absence, and was made to understand, by the tenor of her condition, the purport of this couplet.

COUPLET.

This night my brain is so on fire that I me down will never sit,
Till taper-like I am consumed, and of this body's garment quit.

Thus she passed the night, the livelong night, in anguish of heart till morning came; and her sorrow then culminating, she heaved a cold sigh from her distracted breast and said,

COUPLET.

Morn-like one breath is left me now, where shall my lover meet my eyes?
Ah! saw I him, I, taper-like, my life for him would sacrifice.

At last the message, '*Return unto thy Lord*,'[2] having arrived, the taper of her life was extinguished by the violent wind of '*Every creature which liveth on the earth is subject to decay*.'[3]

HEMISTICH.

She left this garden and the thorn of sorrow in our feet[4] remained.

The servants of the seraglio represented what had happened, to the king, and the latter, returning to his capital, reposed his greatness there, and gave full vent to all possible lamentation and grief for the loss of his wife and son. At length, having bowed his head on the line of endurance, he adopted the course of patience.

COUPLET.

When to the sage—my guide—I had recourse in like distress and pain,
He said, 'Escape is none, *but we must back to him return again*.'[5]

---

[1] There is a mistake here in the printed edition, which might delay the student, '*azizi* for *gharizi*.

[2] Ku'rán, Fl. lxxxix. 28; Mar. 29; Sale, p. 444, l. 13, 'On that day none shall punish with his punishment; nor shall any bind with his bonds. O thou soul which art at rest, return unto thy Lord, well pleased with thy reward, and well pleasing unto God; enter among my servants: and enter my paradise.'

[3] Kur'án, lv. 26; Sale, p, 392, l. 22: 'Every creature which liveth on the earth is subject to decay: but the glorious and honorable countenance of the Lord shall remain for ever.'

[4] Perhaps this expression refers to the queen herself. She died without having had the thorn of grief, for the loss of her son, extracted from her foot.

[5] Kur'án, Fl. ii. 151; Mar., 158; Sale, p. 17, l. 27: 'We will surely prove you by afflicting you in some measure with fear, and hunger, and decrease of wealth, and loss of lives and scarcity of fruits: but bear good tidings unto the patient; who, when a misfortune befalleth them say, We are God's, and unto him shall we surely return.' A similar expression occurs in Kur'án, Ch. ii., 43, etc.

Meantime, however, the Shoemaker having conveyed the Prince to the country of Damascus, after he had expended the jewels, sold him to a merchant, with whom the Prince lived ten years, and grew up into such beauty that he made the market of Egyptian Joseph flat.

COUPLET.

Say! what was Joseph? though for him musk's price were not too high,[1]
But such thy worth that we might thee at life itself well buy.

Whenever that delicately-educated cypress came forth from his house, a thousand despairing lovers were ready to devote their lives on the road of affection, and from every corner and direction were holding up their hands in prayer for the long life of that straight-statured youth.

COUPLET.

Wheree'er he passed in beauty by, to avert ill glances there,
Forth from their sleeves a thousand hands were stretched aloft in prayer.

The merchant was a discriminating and sagacious person, and possessed thorough shrewdness and penetration. He said to himself, 'It is not for my gain or advantage that I should be attended any more by this slave, for if I keep him concealed in the house he might just as well not exist; and if he issues from the house the fire of mischief is kindled, and no one can look upon his face with composure.

COUPLET.

Beware, spectator! for my love is near,
Then close thine eyes if life to thee be dear.

My best course is to take this slave as a present to the King of Fárs, for he is a munificent monarch. It is certain that he will bestow on me a reward equal to twice the value of the slave.' So the merchant took him to Fárs and presented him to the king by way of offering, and after ten years that he had been torn from his father's bosom, having now, like the full moon, reached the station of the fourteenth,

COUPLET.

A sweet and merry sweetheart of just fourteen years have I,
To whom the moon of fourteen days bows down in fealty.[2]

he arrived once more in the capital of Fárs. The king, ignorant of his son's condition, honored the merchant's offering with acceptance, and sent the new comer to the circle of his favorite slaves, and every day bestowed more and more attention on him, until in a short time he obtained pre-eminence over all his fellows. And, meantime, he had formed a friendship with a Jeweler,

---

[1] According to the Kur'án p. 175, l. 14, Sale's translation: Joseph was sold cheap, for it is said, 'And they sold him for a mean price—for a few pence—and valued him lightly.' Sale's note is, 'Namely twenty or twenty-two dirhams, and those not of full weight neither; for having weighed one ounce of silver only, the remainder was paid by tale, which is the most unfair way of payment.'

[2] Lit., 'Is heart and soul with a ring in its ear.'

2 R

who always waited in the treasury, and to whom was assigned the charge[1] of the precious stones and ornaments. To him the Prince was always doing acts of kindness; and every present that the king gave him, he sent a gem of it to the Jeweler as his share. When, however, the latter perceived the unlimited confidence which was reposed in the slave, his sordid nature formed a vain desire, and he said to himself, 'I will beguile the slave to bring me the king's own signet-ring, and by help of that seal I will plunder the treasury and will carry off an abundant store and immense treasure therefrom.' Wherefore he said to the slave, 'Sweetheart! every day thou dost lavish a variety of kindnesses on this mean individual, and I wish to requite some of those acts by an acceptable service. There is an inscription on the royal signet of the king of such a nature, that whosoever becomes possessed of this inscription on the seal, obtains absolute power and the whole territory of the world is secured to him.

COUPLET.

Just like the seal of Sulaimán, such that inscription's sway,
Who it possesses, him the realm of Jamshíd will obey.

If thou wilt undertake this task, and, at the time when the king is contentedly indulging in a sweet sleep,[2] wilt remove that ring from his finger and bring it to me in order that I may take off the impression for thee, the throne of royalty will soon be adorned with the glory of thy beauty, on condition that thou conferrest on me the post of vazír.

HEMISTICH.

Thou from the table of thy fortune apportion me a share.'

By this artifice the Jeweler beguiled the Prince, so that at night-time he entered the king's bedchamber, and having extended the hand of audacity to the king's signet, by degrees gently drew it off. The king awoke and said to the slave, 'Why didst thou venture on this bold act? and what didst thou want with the ring?' The Prince was unable to utter a word, and the flame of the king's wrath being kindled, he called an executioner and commanded him to put the slave to death. The executioner first of all pulled off the Prince's garment from his neck, and at once that black mole on his shoulder was exposed to view. At sight of the mole the king swooned, and the executioner withheld his hand from inflicting the blow. When the king recovered his senses, he kissed the head and eyes of his son, and said, 'Light of my eyes! the society of the perfidious Shoemaker plunged us into the flames of separation.' The youth too made excuses and said, 'The friendship of the Jeweler incited me to this disrespectful action.' Then the king commanded the Jeweler to be severely punished, and admonished the Prince that in future he

---

[1] Observe this rare sense of *ḳimat*.
[2] Lit., 'A sugar-sleep.' One MS. reads, instead, *dar bistar-i khwáb*, 'on the bed of sleep.'

should draw in his skirt from the society of base persons, that he might not be overtaken in calamities such as those.

And the advantage to be derived from this story is, that it may become evident to the noble mind of the king that the company of people of bad origin makes the king a slave, and the slave downcast. And the Goldsmith is of the number of those whose society ought to be shunned, but now the king has carried his patronage of him to the limits of excess. The advisable course is, that in favoring and exalting him, moderation should be observed; lest a downright mischief, the remedy of which will be beyond the bounds of possibility, should be the consequence.' The king gave no heed to the words of the vazír, and said, ' Sovereign princes do not commence an affair without the guidance of fortune, nor enter upon important matters without the aid of inspiration. What have lofty connections and old family to do with nobility of nature and perfection of qualities? It is the tokens of excellence and good manners, not the vanity of birth and connections, that cause respect and secure honor and advancement.

VERSE.

> Let thy own worth expand thy chest with pride,
> Nor boast thy long antiquity of race.
> The age of pearls with lustre 's not allied,
> But does their hue with yellowness deface.

That person may be regarded as noble and great, whom the reigning monarch distinguishes by his favor: and a mighty potentate said, ' *We are fortune; whomsoever we have raised has been raised, and whomsoever we have put down has been put down.*' So in truth whomsoever we exalt, the head of his loftiness rises above the top of the twin-stars, near the pole of the Lesser Bear; and whomsoever we degrade, the luminary of his fortune falls into the abyss of obscurity. Should the gale of our favor blow over a salt-marsh, it becomes the envy of the rose-garden of Iram; and when the lightning of our wrath scatters its fire, it consumes a thousand stacks of reputation.

VERSE.

> Whom from their presence monarchs chase away,
> They from heaven's peak to earth precipitate.
> And whom, like morn, with favor they survey,
> From them they strip the sackcloth of their state.

And we have raised this young man, and elevated the head of his honor to the summit of exaltation. Our hope is that the opinion we have formed of him will not prove erroneous.' The vazír saw that the king was firmly resolved to encourage him, and he therefore held his peace, and made no further opposition in the matter. However, when some days had passed, the Goldsmith, seeing the hand of choice open, placed his foot beyond the centre of moderation; and began, through hope and fear and promises and threats, to

encroach on men's property.   One day there was occasion for certain precious
stones for an ornament for the princess, and they could not find such as they
wanted in the king's treasury, nor were they procurable in the jewelers'
bázár.   The Goldsmith, being engaged in inquiries for the gems, learnt that
the daughter of a merchant possessed the valuable stones that were required.
Hereupon he sent some persons to her to ask for the jewels, but the girl met
them with a refusal, and however much they urged her, it was all in vain.
In short they sent for her, and the Goldsmith said [1] to the princess, 'I have
heard that this merchant's daughter possesses some royal pearls, such that
from the time when the jeweler of the sky gave to view the radiant jewels
of the stars in the emerald-colored vault of heaven, none have beheld pearls
of such purity and brilliance as those lustrous ones; and so long as the nurse
of ocean has tended the pearl unique [2] in the cradle of its shell, the diver of
the sight never saw the equals of those incomparable gems.

COUPLET.

Starlike [3] in beauty and in brilliance, they
Bear from the moon the palm of light away.

And she has also certain rubies of an excellent water, which, like a mother, the
radiant sun has with a hundred difficulties nourished in the mine's womb; and
the stony mountain, notwithstanding all its hard-heartedness, has kept, with a
thousand acts of tenderness, in its inmost bosom.

COUPLET.

Like drops of wine which in the time of snow,
In vestments red to stony hardness grow.

She is also the owner of some pieces of green emerald, such that the eye of
the spectator is blinded by looking on them, while by viewing that delicious
green color the pupil of the eye has its light augumented.

COUPLET.

It aids the vision, and to me it seems
That from its hue the eye derives new beams.

And in her jewel-casket are also some carbuncles, which, like the flowers of
Persian pomegranates seem to sparkle with fire in the sight of those who
survey them: as well as some turquoises of pleasing color, so clear that
heaven appears to have acquired its beautiful enamel from their hue.

COUPLET.

Rubies Canopus-like [4] in their red hue,   Turquoises patterns of ethereal blue.

The princess should command the girl to bring hither her jewels and sell

---

[1] The printed edition has here *sargar farmúd*; but *farmúd* is only applied to kings or
people of high rank.   I therefore prefer the *guft* of the lithographed edition.
[2] This word also signifies 'orphan.'
[3] Lit. 'Like the planet Venus.'
[4] In the Persian it is 'patterns of carnelion-colored Canopus.'

them to us at the current price; and if she does not agree readily and of her own good-will, they ought to be taken from her by severe and rigorous measures.' Thereupon the princess sent to compel the merchant's daughter to bring the jewels. The girl protested that she had no such gems and produced the small pieces she possessed. The Goldsmith did not approve of them, and incited the princess to put her to the torture. The king's daughter was intoxicated and out of herself with the cup of fatuous termination, ' *They (women) are deficient in intellect,*' and the insinuations of the tempter of mankind combining therewith, and the pride of royalty, and of prosperity, and the temptations of violent passions lending their aid, she commanded the merchant's daughter to be racked, and in a short time that weak helpless one, by the wound of the talons of the eagle of punishment, fell into the claw of destruction. Whereupon the relations of the merchant's daughter raised their complaints and outcries to the summit of the ethereal sky, and the pure-minded vazír inscribed this state of things on the tablet of the king's mind. From the smoke of such dishonor, which arose from the window of the seraglio, the cell of the king's breast was darkened, and in a gracious manner he showered honors on the heirs of the merchant's daughter, and giving them an abundance of money, made them satisfied, and removing his daughter from the eye of his favor, left off patronising the Goldsmith. And by the disastrous influence of the society of that accursed and cruel villain, the noble princess fell from her elevated position of respect; and the Goldsmith, fearing the vengeance of the king, absconded. The mother of the princess looked upon it as advisable that the latter should leave the city for a few days, and stay for a time in the royal garden residence;[1] and when the lightnings of the hurricanes of the imperial anger were appeased, and the flame of the world-consuming wrath of the king had been quenched, the princess should return to the seraglio. The latter accordingly proceeded to the garden, and the Goldsmith being apprised of this circumstance, came to wait upon her. When she beheld him, she was seized with emotion, and exclaimed, ' O unlucky wretch of ill-omened appearance !

COUPLET.

If they should paint thy image on a wall,

Fye! that on it one look, one glance should fall.

Art thou come back to stir up some new mischief? and employ some fresh artifice to gratify thy covetousness and selfish interests? away with thee! for to see thee again is painful to me, and that I should address thee any more is impossible.' The Goldsmith came out in despair from the presence of the princess, and directing his steps towards the jungle, went on distracted

---

[1] *Chár bágh* is the name of a celebrated royal garden in the environs of Isfahán. In both editions چاہ is given for چاخ by a typographical error.

and perplexed. Night came on, and dark clouds fixed their gloomy pavilion in the expanse of air, and set down the lamp of the stars. The hapless Goldsmith, at such a time, when they had sifted over earth's surface the powder of darkness,[1] and had poured the lamp-black of ink on liquid pitch,

COUPLET.

That was a night, like negro's visage, black;
Its gloom spread up and darkened the moon's back;

advanced like one distraught. It happened that, to capture wild beasts, they had dug a pit in that desert, and a tiger, and a monkey, and a serpent had fallen into it. The Goldsmith, who had cruelly dug pits in the path of mankind, having come round that way, fell into the pit on the top of the animals.

DISTICHS.

Thou who in cruelty dost dig a pit,
Know for thyself, too, thou preparest it.
Silk-worm-like round thyself no meshes lead,
And for thine own sake, what thou dost take heed!

This group that were at the bottom of the pit were restrained by their own sufferings from molesting one another, and for several days remained at the bottom of the pit in the same fixed position. Till one day a pilgrim,[2] one of the inhabitants of the city, having set out on a journey, passed by them, and having observed their situation, was amazed, and thought to himself, ' Well! to be sure, this man is one of the children of Adam, and being overtaken in this vortex of calamity, is nearer the wilderness of death than the encamping-ground of life. Humanity requires that by every attainable means I should release him, and store up the merit of this action for the ' *Day in which neither riches nor children avail.*[3] He then let down a cord, and the monkey, clinging to it, reached the mouth of the pit. The second time the snake was the first to get up. The third time the tiger struck his claws into the rope; and when all these three had reached the level ground, they blessed the pilgrim and said,

COUPLET.

' 'T is fortune's act, no work of ours, if, on some blest occasion rare,
One sought like thou, at utmost need, arrives to grant the sufferer's prayer.

Know that thou hast conferred a vast favor and thorough kindness upon each one of us, as we firmly feel and acknowledge, but at this time we

---

[1] Lit., 'Indigo.'

[2] *Saiyid* may mean 'a pilgrim' or 'a traveler,' but it is clear from p. 516, l. 20, of the Persian text, that this was a religious traveler, one who being a Saiyid or having other claims to holiness, went about and received contributions.

[3] Ḳur'án, xxvi. 88; Sale, p. 279, l. 12 : 'And cover me not with shame on the day of resurrection ; on the day in which neither riches nor children shall avail, unless unt o him who shall come unto God with a sincere heart: when Paradise shall be brought near to the view of the pious, and hell shall appear plainly to those who shall have erred; and it shall be said unto them, ' Where are your deities which ye served besides God ? '

have not the power of returning and requiting it.' The monkey said, 'I pass my time in the skirt of the mountain which lies near the city; if thou wilt be so courteous as to honor my dwelling with thy fortunate footstep, the debt I owe will be remembered.' The tiger said, 'I, too, have made my home in the vicinity of the city in such and such a jungle, and if thou wilt please to pass that way I shall, perhaps, as far as my power goes, discharge the dues of service.' The serpent added, 'I have chosen my abode in the wall round the city; if thou comest thither and good-fortune should befriend me, I will to the extent of my ability shew my thankfulness for this benevolent act. We would now, however, offer a piece of advice, to which it is thy bounden duty to listen. Do not get this man out of the pit, for he seems to be a false person, and deems it right to requite good with evil. Be not deceived with the outward beauty of his appearance, and be not off thy guard as to his inward foulness and the impurity of his disposition.

COUPLET.

Leave outward form, seek mental purity,
A man in shape may worse than brutes e'en be.

And most of the people of the age are engaged in adorning their outward appearance and neglecting their inward man : consequently,

HEMISTICH.

Josephs to sight, they yet are wolves at heart :

especially this man who for several days has been our companion, and whose habits and qualities we thoroughly understand : in his face we have assuredly not seen the tokens of a generous spirit, nor inhaled the odor of fidelity from the flower-garden of his qualities.

COUPLET.

From the fair seek not for faith, for none yet did glad inhale,
From time's flower-garden here, of perfect faith the scented gale.

And if thou wilt not act on our suggestions, there may be a day that thou wilt repent of what thou hast done.' The pilgrim gave no heed to their words, and let down the rope, and did not listen to their disinterested advice with the hearing of acceptance, but raised the Goldsmith to the mouth of the pit. The latter thanked the pilgrim and told him some portion of the king's harsh treatment and his own perplexity, and, moreover, he made request that he would pass one day with him, in which case he would perhaps be able to recompense him. The pilgrim replied, 'At present I have placed the foot of reliance on God in the path of the prosecution of my journey, and I shall make a tour of two or three days in various parts of the world. But I pledge myself that, if fate spares me and destiny so decrees, I will secure the honor of thy society again.

HEMISTICH.

If life remains I'll wait on thee again.'

With this promise they took leave of one another, and both returned to their own roads. The pilgrim set his face towards his journey, and the Goldsmith went back to the city, and concealed himself in a retired spot. Meanwhile the king, being ashamed of having patronised the Goldsmith, and blushing at not having listened to the advice of his vazír, shewed no regard towards his daughter. Nay, however much the nobles, employing the kind offices of mediation, besought him [to forgive her], their request did not reach the place of acceptance. In this state of things a year passed away, and the pilgrim—having visited some few districts and countries, and gathered three hundred pieces of sterling gold—at length, feeling the sensation of love of country, bethought himself, 'Although in absence from home things are prosperous with me, and my worldly wealth and future happiness are hourly on the increase, still the air of my own country suits me best, and the water of the fountain of my native land is more gratifying to the palate of my heart.

COUPLET.

Though they may make narcissus pots of silver or of gold,
Yet for that flower is better far its own true native mould.'

He then turned his face homeward from exile, and arriving at night-time at the skirt of the mountain, which was the monkey's abode, he halted there. When a little of the night had passed, two thieves, sanguinary and trouble-exciting, such that Mars the dagger-user was on his guard against their bosom-piercing shafts ; and Arcturus, the javelin-holder, held before his face the shield of fear from dread of their life-chasing swords,

COUPLET.

Like the eyes of cruel fair ones, full of blood, of stern demeanour,
In the gore of men to stain them they their trenchant blades made keener,

came to his pillow, and having possessed themselves of his money and goods, tied his legs together tightly with the noose of a lasso, and cast him so bound into a dreadful ravine, which was a long way from the public road. The hapless one said to himself, 'While thou hast a gasp of life still left, and readest a line from the page of existence,

HEMISTICH.

To wail befits not, but to offer thanks.'

All night long the pilgrim lay there bound, and bowed his neck to the decree of fate and the mandate of destiny ; at length, when it dawned, from the pain of his hands and feet losing control of himself, he exclaimed,

COUPLET.

'Did my heart's wailings reach they would prevail,[1]
But I see none to listen to my wail.'

---

[1] The first line of this couplet admits of more than one rendering. Thus it might also signify, 'If my complaint were to reach a heart, it would rend it :' taking the second verb as from *kandan*, 'to tear out,' to rend.'

He was raining down the tears of anguish from his eyes, and was groaning with the agony of his afflicted breast, and exclaiming, 'Alas! I perish in this woeful strait, and no one has any knowledge of my condition, and with all this life-consuming pain I have fallen into the whirlpool of extinction, and the scent of remedy does not reach the nostrils of hope.

COUPLET.

Whose heart is touched for this my sorrow, for poor broken-hearted me?
Save my own heart, I've no one near me, who will show me sympathy.

At this time the monkey, having come forth in quest of food, passed by the ravine, and heard a lamentable cry, and discovered in the sound something familiar. Making for the ravine he arrived in the very nick of time[1] for the pilgrim. When he beheld his friend bound in the bonds of calamity, he gave loose to torrents of tears from the fountain of his eyes, and said, 'O dear friend! how didst thou fall into this place? and what is thy story?' The pilgrim replied, 'Kind friend! in the toil-house of the world there is no blessing of enjoyment without the distress of suffering, and in the ruinous heap of perfidious fortune, there is no treasure of prosperity to be got without the dragon of trouble and woe.

COUPLET.

No buyer from this shop has ever stingless honey borne,
None gather in this flower-garden dates without a thorn.

And when a person has learned this secret, and the reality of this circumstance has been revealed to him, he ought not, like an autumnal cloud, to let fall the drops of regret at the pangful thorn of the world, nor, at the display of its fresh-cheeked flowers, ought he to indulge in mirth like the season of spring; for its grief has no continuance, nor its joy any stability.

VERSE.

In this existence, so soon to expire,
   The being or not being should not make us gay;
It gives us water, puts us on the fire,
   Freely bestows a thing then forthwith snatches it away.
It gives, it snatches back, and has no shame;
Taking and giving, its task is this, the same.'

He then told the whole story of the thieves, and of their carrying off his gold, and throwing him, bound down, there. The monkey said, 'Be of good cheer! for,

COUPLET.

There is much cause for hoping in despair,   And night's far limit is the morning fair.

And I will exert myself, as far as I am able, to remedy the mischief, but the most important affair at present is thy liberation.' He then broke

---

[1] Note the phrase, *bi-sar-i waḳt*.

the pilgrim's bonds, and conveyed him to a house that he had made of twigs
and bushes. Then he presented fruits moist and dry, and made representation,
saying, 'To-day, come not forth from this lodging, and with a heart free from
care place thy head on the pillow of repose, until I come back.' With these
words he left the pilgrim and took up the trace of the thieves,[1] and proceeded
in pursuit of them. They, however, carrying away the goods and gold had
traveled all night, and in the morning, spent and exhausted, arrived at a spring
of water. Overpowered with drowsiness they undid the pilgrim's things
from their backs, laid themselves down[2] and went to sleep[2] with hearts free
from solicitude and minds at ease. At breakfast-time, the monkey came up
with them just in the nick of time, and finding them off their guard, took
advantage of the fortunate opportunity, and having torn open the bundle of
clothes, first of all took out the bag of gold, and carrying it to a retired place,
hid it in the ground. He then came back, and as they were still slumbering
he took another piece of the pilgrim's dress, and concealed it in a spot. In
short, having carried away all the pilgrim's things,[3] together with some of the
thieves' traps,[4] of which he managed to get hold, he put them in different
places, and took up his position on a tree at some distance, waiting to see
what they would do. After some time had passed, the thieves awoke, and not
finding a trace of the gold or the things, they began to run about in all
directions in a state of consternation and dismay. One who surpassed the
other in shrewdness said, 'Brother! this fountain is not a place which men
frequent; and besides, there is no vestige of men's steps near the spring. It
must therefore be the abode of demons and fairies, and we have come here
securely, and stretching out our limbs, have gone to sleep. This mischief has
been done by their people, and we may yet be thankful that they sought not
to slay us. Our best course is to run away as fast as possible, and make
our heels save the moiety of life that is left us.

VERSE.

Spirits this desert throng unblest: [5]
  Here are strait quarters, room enow for trouble.
They who are here content to rest,
  Feel chills hepatic ; or, like bile, next bubble.
And he who chooses to alight here,
  Is sure to lose his head or night-gear.'

---

[1] Note the phrase, *pai bar dáshtah.*

[2] Observe the difference between *khuftan* and *dar khwáb raftan.*

[3] Observe in *rukhút*, the Arabic plural of a Persian substantive.

[4] As the somewhat vulgar word 'traps' exactly corresponds to *waslhá*, I am obliged to
use it.

[5] As these verses are put into the thieves' mouth, and seem intended to be jocose, I have
tried to preserve the vein. In the fourth line the second sentence is, literally, 'melts like
bile,' but the idea is merely that the victim is hot and cold by turns , or to use a somewhat
vulgar expression, 'shivers and sweats.' The word rendered 'night-gear' is *kuláh*, 'a
turban,' 'a hat' or 'cap,' or even 'a night-cap.'

The thieves, then, with terrified hearts took to flight, and the monkey, being free from anxiety as to their return, went back to his house and told the pilgrim what had happened, and for that night took charge of him. In the morning, when the thief of night began to fly with his robes of gloom from the sun's fountain of light; the solar world-wandering pilgrim, being freed from the bounds of darkness, set his face towards his destined journey.

COUPLET.

When in the skies' expanse appeared to sight,
The sun's pure gold from 'neath the heap of night;

the monkey took the pilgrim to the spring of water and brought to him his gold and clothes, and what he had taken from the thieves. The pilgrim was satisfied with what belonged to him, and did not possess himself of their things, but bidding the monkey farewell, set out for the city. His way happened to lie through that jungle which was the haunt of the tiger, and that savage animal showed itself in the distance like a raging lion. The pilgrim, terrified at the sight of it, was about to take to flight, when the tiger called out, 'Be not alarmed !

HEMISTICH.

I bear thy favours, grateful, yet in mind.'

He then advanced, and, thanking him much, besought him that he would wait there a short time. The pilgrim, to oblige him, halted, and the tiger went roaming in every direction in search of a present worthy of his guest, till at last he came to the door of the king's garden-palace. Entering there he saw a maiden, who was sitting on the margin of a marble basin, and wearing a precious ornament on her neck. The tiger killed her with a single stroke of his paw, and, bringing the ornament to the pilgrim, expressed his regret [for the insignificance of the offering]. The pilgrim, on his part, met his apologies courteously, and departed towards the city. Meanwhile, as he remembered the circumstance of his acquaintance with the Goldsmith, the thought passed through his mind, 'I have witnessed the good-faith of brutes and wild animals, and their acquaintance bears such excellent fruit as this. If the Goldsmith should hear of my arrival, of course he will show the most exuberant joy at my coming, and will think it incumbent on him to take infinite pains to give me a kind reception. Moreover, by his aid and assistance, those pieces of pure gold may be sold at their full price, and this ornament, which is a treasure of gems, may be passed off at a good sum ; for his skill in this matter, and his knowledge of the current price of these several articles, is greater than that of other men. It was morning when the pilgrim reached the city, and at that time the report of the murder of the king's daughter had spread through the city, and the people poured aghast and amazed to the king's palace. The Goldsmith, too, had come forth from his retirement to make inquiry into the circumstance, and was wanting to find one of his friends, and ascertain what had occurred. All of a sudden he saw the pilgrim, and, displaying the utmost joy, conducted him with respect and reverence to his own abode. After the usual inquiries, he again minutely detailed his adventures, and his exclusion from attendance on the king, and the degradation of rank which had befallen him, and the sums of money and property that he had lost. The pilgrim consoled him, and said, 'O brother! if thy means of support have been impaired, and the pillars of thy opulence have been crushed by the hurricane of accidents, grieve not, for I have some pieces of sterling gold, and also an ornament containing many jewels; and thou art sagacious in discerning the worth of gold and gems. Sell them carefully and kindly, and take what thou wilt, for there will be no difficulty as to that.' The Goldsmith sent for the ornament, and when he saw it, he beheld the ornament of the princess. Then putting on a cheerful countenance, he said to the pilgrim, 'The value of these jewels exceeds the power of the calculator of the imagination to compute. Be of good cheer! for I will this very moment set thy mind at ease; and so, rest thou here in peace until I return.' The Goldsmith then reflected, 'I have got a fine opportunity, and secured a rare advantage. If I am remiss and let this slip, I shall prove myself quite devoid of all the advantages of caution and cleverness. Previous to this, the king's mind has been changed towards me, and at this moment, when they have conveyed to him the news of his daughter's murder, of course he is grieved and anxious, and on the look-out for the assassin of his daughter.[1] I can have no better recommendation to him than to consign the pilgrim to the king's hands, that he may bring him to justice. Perhaps, the king, being pleased with me, I shall again rise to my former station.' He then resolved on treachery, and went to the palace and announced that he had caught the murderer of the princess, and secured the ornament. The king sent for him, and seeing the ornament, sent some persons to bring the pilgrim into his presence. When the hapless pilgrim saw who was the instrument of this deed, he said,

COUPLET.

'Thou hast in friendship slain me, and yet none
Was e'en, by foes, so cruelly undone.

This is my punishment, and I deserve a thousand times as much.' The king supposed that he was a criminal, and that he was uttering these words in acknowledgment of his misdeeds; and the ornament, too, was corroborative of that suspicion. He commanded, therefore, that they should parade him round the city, and having imprisoned him, should the next day, when they had finished putting him to the usual torture, inflict on him retaliation for

---

[1] The lithographed edition reads here, rightly as I suppose, *mi ṭalabad* for the *mi ṭalabid* of the printed edition and of some MSS.

his crime. While they were conducting him round the city, the snake on the top of the wall had opened the eye of survey. When it beheld its friend in that state, it set off after him; and after they had shut him up in prison, approached him, and having learnt how matters stood, cried out and said, 'Did I not tell thee that a man of base nature has no gratitude, and in return for kindness and assistance will perform acts of perfidy and cruelty? Thou didst not listen to me, and I, that very day, when thou didst turn away thy face from the suggestions of thy friends, and refuse attention to advice devoid of any suspicion of self-interest, well knew that the issue of thy affairs would have no other result but repentance.

COUPLET.

I ceased that day hopes of Farhád to have,
When to Shírín his blind heart's reins he gave.'

The pilgrim replied, 'Kind friend! from the salt of these reproaches which thou scatterest on my wound, nothing, now, but heart-burning and distress of mind can be derived. And my sufferings from neglecting that advice are already sufficient.

HEMISTICH.

The townsfolk shun me and all men revile.

Now excogitate some remedy, which may be a repellent of this misfortune, and a cure for this disaster.' The snake rejoined, 'Yesterday I wounded the king's mother, and all the city-people are at a loss how to heal her. Keep this grass and early in the morning when they come to thee and ask of thee the means to cure her, go and wait on the king, and after thou shalt have recounted what has befallen thyself, give him this grass that his mother may eat it and recover. Perhaps in this way thy liberation and escape may be attainable.' The pilgrim thanked the snake, and the latter returned to his own hole; and in the morning having ascended the terrace of the king's palace [1] called out from a chink, 'The remedy for the person bitten by the snake is with the innocent pilgrim whom the king yesterday imprisoned.' At that time the king was seated at his mother's pillow, and suffering through grief for the loss of his daughter, together with sorrow for his mother's wound, was in consultation with the doctors as to the remedy for the poison of the serpent. And however many antidotes for poisons and repellents they used, it was all in vain. When the voice reached the king's ear he said, 'Go ye and see what person is on the terrace, and whence he utters those words?' Notwithstanding the search made by the guards, they saw no man on the terrace, and they were led to the conjecture that an invisible monitor had pronounced the words. They went, therefore, and brought the

---

[1] *Kushk*, the word from which our 'kiosk' comes:

pilgrim out of prison, and taking him to the king, busied themselves with
inquiring after the matter of the remedy.   The pilgrim said, ' O king !

COUPLET.

May the high court of thy justice and thy gracious majesty,
The K'abah of the wishes of the wants of mankind be !

The cure for this poison is in my possession, and the queen of the world
shall this very moment obtain perfect recovery.   But I hope that first of all
I may be allowed to convey to the august hearing a brief summary of my
own affliction.   And it befits the king's justice that for an instant he should
open the ear of attention to listen to the state of the oppressed.

VERSE.

So sleep that thou mayest hear the wail of pain,
   If one who seeks for justice cry to thee;
He is not suited o'er the world to reign,
   Whom in such court we careless slumbering see.'

The king's heart felt the truth of the pilgrim's appeal, and he said in a
gracious manner, ' Relate thy case from beginning to end, and fearlessly
recount thy whole story.'   The pilgrim, with that boldness which belongs to
the truthful, courageously recited his own history; and the writing of his
innocence from that crime was clear to the luminous mind of the monarch.
Then they mixed that grass with some milk and administered it to the
queen, and the effect was her immediate recovery.   Thereupon, the king
clothed him in a robe of honor worthy the munificence of royalty.   Meantime the Goldsmith was waiting for the pilgrim at the foot of the scaffold, in
hopes that he would be put to death as quickly as possible, and so the pieces
of gold would remain with him, while he himself would acquire his former
credit and rank near the king.   All of a sudden the royal mandate arrived
that, instead of the pilgrim, they should impale the Goldsmith, and that this
should be made the final result of his calumnious accusation, [and that thus it
might be shown] that if a traducer should plunge anyone into calamity, on
the falsehood of the charge being apparent, and the selfish motive which had
been concealed in that accusation coming to light, the very same punishment
which he desired should be inflicted on that innocently-suspected person,
should be carried out with regard to that lying sycophant.   In this very
same manner they impaled that ungrateful faithless wretch who had never
seen the face of generous feeling nor inhaled the perfume of honor, and thus
they cleansed the expanse of creation from the blot of his unclean person,
which was the confluence of perfidy and mischief, and the fountain-head of
oppression and injurious acts, and he arrived at the reward of his actions and
the just recompense of his deeds.

VERSE.

Here in this hall of retribution, he
 Who evil does, injures himself alone.
Do good if thou wouldst live on happily;
 And in thy acts and thoughts let truth be shewn.

This is the story of kings, with regard to their choice of favorites, and the investigation of the affairs of those who are nearly connected with them. And if the king of Ḥalab had not favoured that man of low origin and bad manners, his daughter would not have assailed the life of the innocent, nor have been killed by the tiger's paw in retribution. So if the king had not opened his ears to hear the words of the persecuted and oppressed, right would not have been discriminated from wrong, nor truth from falsehood. Moreover it behoves kings not to patronise any one incautiously, nor to issue, offhand, a mandate for the punishment of any; and to be quite certain that good actions will never be thrown away, nor the requital of bad deeds be in anywise delayed. Consequently, at this time when the chamberlain of fate has set up the court of their glory, and the controller of destiny has committed to them the opportunity of prosperous fortune and kingly sway, they ought to exert themselves that they may do things which will be the source of their good fame in this world, and of their advancement and salvation in that to come.

STANZA.

From time to time high heaven surveys with favoring glance some later man,
 And fortune grants, in every age, to some new sway, earth's wide domains.
And since success in lasting flow in no one's destiny we scan,
 Most blest is he whose glorious name new glory each new cycle gains.

CHAPTER XIV.

ON ABSTAINING FROM REGARD TO THE VICISSITUDES OF TIME, AND THE BASING ONE'S ACTIONS ON THE DECREES AND WILL OF GOD.

INTRODUCTION.

When the clime-adorning king had heard this story full of advantage, which may be regarded as a treasure fraught with the gems of wisdom, and a store-house filled with the coins of admonition, being bound heart and soul in obligation to the perfect and accomplish sage, he said,

STANZA.

'Thou from the ocean of whose radiant mind,
The weary wanderers in inquiry's plain,
To slake their thirst, pure streams of wisdom find!
Whose counsel's hand, from wisdom's face again
Withdraws the veil of doubts and errors vain!

I have already wearied your highness, possessed of wisdom, beyond all bounds, and have carried the excess of my importunities to the limits of disrespect, and the point has been almost reached for the chain [1] of your sublime discourse to be severed. Since then, you have acquainted me with the signification of the thirteenth precept, and I have heard the tale of kings in reference to their patronage of counsellors and near dependants, and have been informed of the mischiefs which spring from associating with the mean and base: now be so condescendingly gracious as to set forth a detailed explanation of the last precept and discourse on this subject, viz.: Why the beneficent and intellectual sage is fettered by the bonds of calamity, and broken by the wounds of adverse fortune, while the vile ignorant person, fatuously careless, passes his life in ease and enjoyment? why neither the former is assisted by his good sense and sagacity, nor the latter overthrown by his ignorance and fatuity. . Say, moreover, what kind of stratagem is to be employed to secure advantage and repel injury? and by what counsel one may enjoy the happy influences of felicity, and by what service our roads may lead to the halting-place wished-for?' The Bráhman replied, 'O king! there are first steps and sources of

---

[1] Lit, 'Tent-rope.'

felicity, which when a person has secured, he will become more deserving of rank and authority, and more fit for an honorable and exalted position; but the results and fruits thereof are dependent on the Divine decree and God's will; and the king's command may be viewed as the first source of all, and means and appliances will, if destiny so requires it, prove abortive and ineffectual. For many wise persons who have been in the enjoyment of deserved good-fortune, have suddenly been excluded even from food sufficient for a single day; while many ignorant persons, without the aid of puissance and virtue, have been seated on the throne of sovereignty.

STANZA.

They royal treasures on the base bestow,
Yet cannot for the worthy crumbs afford;
Spontaneous give high places to the low,
But ne'er, e'en by mistake, [1] a place afford,
To men of learning in the outer ward.

And assuredly this state of things cannot but be in connection with the Divine decree and the command of God Most Holy. And although one may possess perfect understanding, so that in that way he might procure a maintenance; or a very lucrative profession, whence he might provide the means of support; or fascinating beauty by which he might capture hearts, and so secure advantages: yet when the Divine will yields not assistance thereto, the party will reap no fruit, nor will he see such gainful results from the antecedents of beauty and wisdom and perfection. And a Prince wrote this proposition on the gate of the city of Nuṣṭúr, and there is a beautiful story and sweet tale connected with this.' The King asked, 'How was that?'

STORY I.

The Bráhman said, 'They have related that in certain countries of Rúm there was a prosperous king and mighty sovereign.

COUPLET.

Of mighty wisdom with high spirit blent,   His arm was strong, his heart intelligent.

He had two sons adorned with a variety of accomplishments, and graced with a multitude of eminent qualities.

COUPLET.

That by his mercy hearts did captivate,   This by his justice souls reänimate.

When the king accepted, with the phrase 'Here I am!', the invitation of his Creator, the elder brother appropriated, with the hand of predominant power, the treasury of his father; and having secured the hearts of the Pillars

---

[1] Or *bi-ghalaṭ* may mean with the rest of the sentence, 'Through error, they do not give a place to the wise even at the threshold.'

of the State, and of the ministers of the late king with the lasso of courtesy
and winning demeanour, and captured them with his perfect humanity and
mildness, seated himself in his father's place.

COUPLET.

A prince of happy fortune, in a yet more happy hour,
His father's rules obeying, assumed the reins of power.

The younger brother, when he saw that the Humá of empire overshadowed
the star-reaching head of his elder brother, and that the leader, Fortune, had
given the reins of the courser of the age to the grasp of his authority and
option; through fear that he might act perfidiously towards him, placed the
equipage of travel on the back of the dromedary of flight; and voluntarily
submitting to the affliction of exile and the perils of travel, and taking along
with him supplies of grief and lamentation, set out on his journey.

COUPLET.

I am weary of my fatherland, on my travels I will go,
But no provisions for my journey, save my grief for thee, I know.

The Prince set out alone on a long and distant expedition, and, as day
closed, reached a halting-place; and there grieving and lamenting over his
solitary and wretched state, he exclaimed,

COUPLET.

'Since each two steps have made my eyes of bloody tears a gushing spring,
And such my earliest march; say, how my journey to a close I'll bring?'

In short he passed that night solitarily. Next day when the fair-faced beauty
of the sun showed her comeliness from the curtain of the horizon, and the
sweetheart of day's luminary displayed from behind the veil of blue her
bright cheeks and radiant countenance,

COUPLET.

Heaven's wheel the sun's gate open threw meanwhile,
And decked earth's surface with a sunny smile,

the Prince prepared to set off, and a youth of fair countenance and
curling hair, of excessive sprightliness and infinite grace met him. The
Prince looked and beheld a lovely stripling, such that thou wouldst say they
had sewed the garment[1] of perfection on his person, and had consumed the
heart of the moon with the heat of envy at his beauty. His down was like a
fresh violet budding close to a green rose-leaf, or a ring of moist ambergris on
the surface of a tulip loaded with dew.

---

[1] The kabá is a long gown with flaps in the skirt, the skirt and breast open, and sometimes slits in the arm-pits: Kánún-i Islám: appendix, Dress, x.

VERSE.

With beard like ants near a rose fresh blowing,[1]
Which from the hyacinth scents gathering stray;
Its light down o'er the moon soft fetters throwing,
Led reason's self, adoring, blind, away.

When the royal youth beheld that captivating down and glowing cheek,

COUPLET.

That down of rarest beauty with those bright cheeks seemed to blend,
Like the wondrous grass that sprang up from the furnace of God's friend,[2]

he said to himself, 'Perhaps I could bear the burthen of the woes of travel with the support of the society of this stripling, and obtain security under the shadow of this cypress with cheeks like the rose, from the heat of this fire-raining desert.

HEMISTICH.

'T is sweet for him to wander who a comrade has like thee.'

Then those two jasmins of youth's garden, and those two tender trees by the rivulet of life, being pleased with each other's society, regarded the distressful wilderness as the rose-garden of Iram, and fancied the thorny brakes of toil to be the joy-augmenting flower-parterres of Paradise.

QUATRAIN.

Were nought but woes and cruel wounds from thy tresses all my gain,
On th' inhabitants of Eden, I still with scorn should look:
And to Paradise without thee they might me call in vain,
For Eden's self without thee, my soul, this heart could never brook.)

At the next stage, a merchant's son, (a youth intelligent and experienced, of just counsels, far-seeing, and of perfect understanding, such that by his perfect wisdom, when good sense was required, he could bind the cord of night on the neck of day, and at the time of dealing, could, by his sharpness and cleverness, obtain the sterling gold of the sun from the four-streeted market of the sky.

COUPLET.

Acute, sharp-witted, and of honeyed speech,   By long experience skilled his ends to reach;)

joined company with them; and thus was brought about the felicitous appearance of that trine.[3] On the third day a robust and lusty young peasant, (who possessed universal intelligence on agricultural matters and perfect skill in all the varieties of farming occupations, the felicity of whose operations was such in planting,[4] that every dry stick which he set in the

---

[1] His black moustachios near his red lips looked like ants near a rose.
[2] When Namrúd, or Nimrod as we call him, cast Abraham, 'God's friend,' into a furnace, the fire turned into a verdant meadow. See Ḳur'án, Sale's Trans., p. 247, note a.
[3] There is doubtless an allusion to astrology here. These three handsome youths formed, as it were, a trine, or conjunction of three fortunate stars.
[4] The editions have dihkání repeated three times in this sentence, which is altogether opposed to the spirit of Persian authors, who delight to exhibit their 'copia verborum.' I would, therefore, with one of my MSS. read bághbání for one of this dihkání group.

earth, coming to perfection like a young shoot, produced fresh fruits in abundance ; and the auspiciousness of whose proceedings in husbandry went to that point, that every clod upon which he set his foot, yielded corn without his requiring to sow seed ;

COUPLET.

> For him, the orchard freshening showers made wet,
> And, self-prepared, the field his wishes met ;)

became their comrade ; and by those four pillars thus united, the edifice of companionship received its completion and the maxim, ' *The best company is four*,' was elucidated. So the attached friends having forgotten—through the pleasure of intercourse—their regrets for their kin and country, were traveling on divers stages and journeys, and continued cheerful and content with the sight of one another.

DISTICHS.

> To those who sit with friends and loved ones near,
> A furnace will a field of flowers appear.
> Our wishes' fabric must through friendship stand,
> Without it, useless are thy tongue and hand ;
> Each comrade helps the craving heart to fill,
> And each acquaintance makes it purer still.
> Each meeting will some new advantage bring,
> From each conjunction some new blessings spring.
> When with one star another 's joined—behold !
> What blest results their blended beams unfold !

After traversing a vast distance, they arrived at the city of Nuṣṭúr, and selected a good lodging in a corner of the town to repose and rest in. Not one of them had any provisions or supplies left, nor had they a single diram or dínár. One of the party said, ' Our advisable course at present is, that we should each display our skill and ability, and secure by our labor the good things we want, that we may pass some days in this city in comfort.' The Prince said, ' Affairs are dependent on the decrees of God, and no difference is effected in them by the exertions or toil of man. Wherefore, those who are the wisest among mankind will assuredly take no steps in pursuit of such a thing, nor devote their precious life for carrion, which in spite of its perishable nature, is surrounded by many enemies.

STANZA.

> This world is to a carrion-carcase like,
> Round which a myriad vultures without pause
> A contest wage. These with their talons strike
> Those who, in turn, wound them with beak and claws.
> At length they spread their wings ; and, soaring, quit
> Their evil prey, nor can they taste or come near it.

The daily subsistence, which has been apportioned in the fabric, ' *We distributed their necessary provision among them in this present life,*[1] is not to be augmented by the aid of greediness and avidity, and all that the covetous man obtains is disaster and disgrace.

DISTICHS.

> What though we gather many a morsel—still
> More than fate grants will ne'er our stomach fill.
> Why, then, this trouble and anxiety
> For that which is withheld by destiny?
> Submissive bow to fate, contented grow,
> Put greed aside; live peaceful, happy, so.'

The handsome youth said, 'Beauty is a qualification which can be relied on for obtaining good things, and comeliness is a sure source of acquiring property and opulence. Whenever the *J* of *Jamál* (beauty) displays itself, it will be followed by *Mál* (wealth); and at all times that the *Z* of *Zaráfat* (gracefulness) appears, *Ráfat* (tenderness) and kindness will be sure to be joined to it.

COUPLET.

> The man of handsome face, do what he will,
> Has in his path all eyes fixed on him still.'

The merchant's son also read off an inscription from the page of his condition, and said, 'The capital of beauty is a coin of short endurance in the bázár of affairs, and in a short time nothing is left either of principal or interest. Right judgment and the advantages of judicious counsel, and experience and skill in transacting business, have the precedence of all other goods; and whenever the foot of subsistence stumbles against the stone of want, the results of good sense alone can afford a remedy; and whoever has nought left to support himself, can alleviate his wants only by the assistance of expertness in his dealings.

COUPLET.

> If thou dost all thy acts on prudence base,
> Thou mayest then thy goods securely place.'

The young peasant delivered himself as follows, 'Good sense and prudence do not succeed everywhere, nor does advantage always result therefrom. For if wisdom had much to do with the acquisition of fortune, it must needs follow, that whoever surpassed all others in knowledge and was before the rest of mankind in judgment and prudence, would set up the flag of his success in the plain of empire, and that the young tree of his felicity would be planted beside the rivulet of sovereign power. Yet we have seen wise men enough incarcerated in the prison of want, and have watched many who

---

[1] Kur'án, Ch. xliii., 31; Sale, p. 362, l. 32: 'We distribute their necessary provision among them in this present life, and we raise some of them several degrees above the others, that the one of them may take the other to serve him: and the mercy of thy Lord is more valuable than the riches which they gather together.'

had not the slightest scent from the rose-garden of ability and expertness,
yet walking at free-will and enjoying themselves among the parterres of
wealth and opulence. Hence they have said,

COUPLET.

' Heaven on the worthless fool bestows the reins of earthly bliss :
Wisdom and virtue hast thou both ?   See, then, thy crime in this !'

Wherefore the blessings of application, and the happy influences of toil,
bring men to a position of success and enjoyment; and it is by the means of
skill in their profession, and the advantage of knowledge of their craft, that
they are decked with the ornaments of delight and felicity.

VERSE.

Wouldst thou have gold, then labor on ;
  By knowledge only thou 'lt in nought succeed.
The king himself, spite of his crown and throne,
  Stands of the coin of laboring men in need.'

When it came to the Prince's turn again to speak, they requested him,
saying, ' Do you, too, be pleased to address us once more in elucidation of
this subject, and throw some light on this question which we are discussing.'
The Prince responded,

COUPLET.

' By me content and poverty shall ne'er disparaged be ;
  Go tell the king, ' Thy daily food is portioned e'en to thee ! '

I adhere to the same opinion, of the particulars of which I have already
given a notion. I do not, indeed, deny the justness of what you, comrades,
say, that something may be gained by the ornament of beauty and the
capital of good sense and toil. But what I assert is this, that if the comeliness
of fate's decree does not display itself from behind the curtain, the radiant
star of beauty cannot ascend from the horizon of success; and that until the
Curator, Providence, opens the door of the shop of the Divine will, the goods
of knowledge and ability cannot obtain any currency in the market of
acceptance. The advantage of the table of labor is a morsel which it is in
the discretion of Providence to apportion or not to the skilful; and the gain
of trade and agriculture is the ear of corn of a provision which accrues to
the husbandmen of the field of craft only from the stock of the will of the
Eternal One. And, without the Divine decree, every writing that versicolor
Fancy draws on the tablet of thought, in the end receives the impression of
decay, and every spell that the incantation-reader of the counsel employs, at
last assumes the semblance of an idle dream.

COUPLET.

What arts I used, what arts without avail !
  The spells I breathed passed idly down the gale.

Wherefore it is clearly established that if the Most High God wills it the wish of every person will be attained without toil or trouble. But if the Eternal Purpose is not linked with its accomplishment, labor and struggles are altogether unavailing. Consequently we ought to bow our necks to God's commandment, and place the head of resignation on the line of destiny.

HEMISTICH.

Our cure for fate is t' acquiesce—enough !

And just in this way that aged Farmer committed his affairs to God's grace, and in a short time, having acquired his wish, was liberated from the prison of trouble.' The Prince's comrades inquired, ' How was that?'

STORY II.

The Prince said, ' They have related that in the city of Andalús [1] there was a Farmer with an open hand and heart, who was successful in his agricultural occupations. Once on a time his receipts exceeded his disbursements, and he got together three hundred gold dínárs, and was very much delighted with that amount of money, and took care not to lay out a particle of it in his expenses. Every day he took out his well-stuffed purse, and counted the pieces, and made the lip of enjoyment smile with that mirth-augmenting saffron-colored coin.

COUPLET.

Showers from that yellow fruit came down unceasing,
Which, saffron-like,[2] were still his joy increasing.

One day in his wonted manner, having counted his gold, he had put it back in the purse, and was about to deposit it in a secure place, when an intimate friend came to the door and called to him. The Farmer, through fear lest he should come in and become acquainted with that glittering-faced bride, (which, in accordance with the direction, ' *Hide thy gold !* ' ought to be kept under the veil of concealment,) did not wait to secure it, but took it up and flung it into a pitcher, and set out with his friend to the village on account of a matter of importance, strictly charging his wife as he started to get ready a meal for them. As soon as the Farmer had gone, his wife wanted to cook some broth. Seeing the pitcher empty she took it up and went to the door and stood looking out for an acquaintance to pass by. It happened that the village butcher going to the city to buy a cow passed that spot. The Farmer's wife recognised him, and asked him civilly if

---

[1] Andalús, (that is, Spain,) so called by the Arabians, from Andalusia, the province which was first conquered in the year of the Hijrah 92 (A.D. 710), by Tárik bin Ziyád, under the Khaláfat of Al Walíd, the 13th successor to Muḥammad.

[2] Orientals use saffron in many drinks and pleasant beverages. Thus the Amírs of Sindh, who quaffed bowls of milk daily, colored the milk with saffron.

he would undertake the trouble of bringing a little water for her, by which he would, at the same time, oblige an old friend, and secure the merit of assisting one in a difficulty. The villager agreed, and the farmer's wife gave him the pitcher in which was the purse of gold. The butcher put it on his back, and went to fetch the water. On the way he perceived something move in the pitcher, and on examining it, saw the purse. Forthwith, drawing it delightedly into the sleeve of possession, he exclaimed,

COUPLET.

'Faith! that is luck which, without effort, to our fond embraces yields;
If toil alone can win them, I'll not value Eden's sparkling fields.

Thanks, grateful thanks to God (may His glory be magnified!) that without the annoyance of trouble, and the calamity of hardship and suffering, an abundant blessing and complete opulence have been bestowed on me. I must now think it right to show my sense of this unexpected good-fortune, and not abandon my profession, but store up this gold for a day of emergency.' Then, through delight at getting the gold, he forgot all about the water and the pitcher, and having purchased a fat young heifer with the money that he had of his own, he set out home. As soon as he had got out of the city, he thought to himself, 'If I keep this purse about me, I cannot be secure from the dread of thieves; and if I bury it anywhere in this city I shall never be able to breathe at ease, from anxiety of mind and troublous thoughts; and I have not sufficient confidence in any one to be able to confide this to him as a deposit.

HEMISTICH.

Seek not in this age for good faith, for it exists nowhere.

My best course is to put the purse in the Cow's throat and manage to make it swallow it, and after I have slaughtered it I will take out safely my purse of gold.' He then put the unfortunate cow to that torture, and made it like Sámiríy's[1] calf, full of golden treasure, and turned his face homeward. It befell that the son met him on the road, and told him some other things which had occurred in the village, and which the butcher was to

---

[1] See Sale's Translation of the Kur'án, p. 6, note *k* : 'The person who cast this calf (the same which is spoken of in Exodus) the Mohammedans say was not Aaron, but Al Sâmeri, one of the principal men among the children of Israel, some of whose descendants, it is pretended, still inhabit an island of that name in the Arabian Gulf. It was made of the rings and bracelets of gold and silver, and other materials, which the Israelites had borrowed of the Egyptians; for Aaron, who commanded in his brother's absence, having ordered Al Sâmeri to collect those ornaments from the people, who carried on a wicked commerce with them, and, to keep them together till the return of Moses, Al Sâmeri, understanding the founder's art, put them together into a furnace, to melt them down into one mass, which came out in the form of a calf. The Israelites, accustomed to the Egyptian idolatry, paying a religious worship to this image, Al Sâmeri went further, and took some dust from the footsteps of the horse of the angel Gabriel, who marched at the head of the people, and threw it into the mouth of the calf, which immediately began to low, and became animated; for such was the virtue of that dust. One writer says that all the Israelites adored this calf, except only 12,000.'

settle. The latter, in order to make some arrangements, returned to the city, and handed over charge of the cow to his son. Meanwhile the Farmer had returned with his friend from the village. Now a long time back, he had made a vow to sacrifice a fat heifer. When he saw one in such good case he was inclined to purchase it, and giving a little more profit to the butcher's son than he expected, he bought it; and bringing it home, made the necessary preparations for the sacrifice. Meanwhile the matter of the gold returned to his memory, and he went to remove the money from that place and to deposit it in a safe spot. The more he searched for the pitcher, the less he found it. He then asked his wife where it was? She in reply told him the circumstances. Hereupon sighs arose from the Farmer's heart, and the eye of his covetousness was weeping with poignant regret, and far-sighted prudence was laughing at his forlorn and ignominious plight.

COUPLET.

Folks that can weep for property and pelf;
Be sure, they do but each deride himself.

For some time the farmer was immersed in the whirlpool of care in a state of unconsciousness; and for an interval tormented himself in the vortex of dismay. At last he adopted feelings of resignation and submission, and said,

HEMISTICH.
'We leave it to His bounty what to do.'

He then commanded them to sacrifice the cow, and when the knife was used to open the intestines his eyes lighted on the purse of gold. At this sight he lost his senses with joy, and when he recovered himself, he took up the purse, and having cleared it of filth, he took out the pieces and kept constantly lifting up one after another, kissing them, rubbing them upon his eyes, and restoring them to their places, while he said,

HEMISTICH.
'May ill luck never thy existence mar;'

He then reflected, 'This time by the fortunate and accidental occurrence of such a strange affair—an extraordinary and mysterious coincidence that no eye has ever seen nor ear heard—this gold has been recovered. Hereafter this purse of money shall go nowhere but round my waist, and to be without it for a moment is a thing never again to be thought of.

COUPLET.

From thee to part! I cannot frame the thought,
From his own soul can one be torn by aught?'

Thenceforward the Farmer always used to keep the purse about his own person, and his wife used to reproach him saying, 'This conduct is alien from reliance on God, for to hoard implies distrust of the Giver of our daily subsistence. And since—in accordance with the saying, ' *Seek therefore your provision from God*,'[1] we ought to seek our daily bread from the treasury of His bounty,—the perfectly wise is he who does not display greediness in amassing money, but opens the eye of reliance to the overflowing beneficence of God, from a share of the table of whose benefits not a single creature is excluded; and feels sure that it is impossible to increase or diminish the allowance which has been predestined to him from eternity without beginning, and which the command of the Eternal One has fixed.

HEMISTICH.

The cup of fate nor more nor less contains.'

The Farmer replied, 'Wife! there is no alternative in this world of causes but to attend to means. In our outward behaviour we must be governed by the rule of cause and effect, and spiritually we must quaff the wine of resignation from the goblet of reliance on God.

COUPLET.

Sit not supine! Since cause does all things leaven,
Neglect it not; and leave the rest to Heaven.'

The wife held her tongue, and the Farmer tied the purse round his waist, and went about his avocations. One day, he was bathing in a spring of water, and undoing the purse from his girdle, put it down by the side of the pool. When he had finished, he put on his dress, and forgetting the money, left it there and went[2] his way. After him a shepherd came to the same spot to water his flock, and saw the purse of gold on the margin of the spring. He immediately snatched it up, and, in excessive rapture, retraced his steps, and going to his own abode, counted the money, and found it three hundred dínárs. He then said to himself, 'This is a round sum; were I to take anything out of it, it would impair the excellence of the number, and perhaps I could never make it up again to the same amount. I must be patient in unavoidable hardships, and store up this amount for a day of want.' Whereupon, the simple fellow, fixing his heart upon the gold; and fastening it under his armpit, and rubbing the clay of silence on his lips, went on, as before, with his duties as a shepherd. Meantime, however, when the Farmer remembered his money, he began, with his heart full of anguish,[3] to shower from his eyes the rain of regret,

---

[1] Kur'án, Fl. xxix., 16; Mar. 17; Sale, p. 298, l. 21: 'We also sent Abraham, when he said unto his people, Serve God and fear him: this will be better for you, if ye understand. Ye only worship idols besides God, and forge a lie. Verily those which ye worship besides God are not able to make any provision for you: seek, therefore, your provision from God; and serve him and give thanks unto him: unto him shall ye return.'

[2] By a typographical error the printed edition omits *rúi* before *bi-ráh dvard*.

[3] Lit., 'blood.'

and, with a hundred pangs and pains, ran searching about on the right hand and on the left.

HEMISTICH.

Much did he search, and yet not reach his wish.

At length, baffled and sad, he returned home, and told his family what had occured. His wife's heart was brimful of choler against her spouse. When she heard the state of the case, she loosed the tongue of reproach and said, ' O good-for-nothing fellow! thou didst display all these excessive precautions in taking care of the gold, and choosing to be stingy in thy daily expenses, kept thy family on short allowance. Now cry away and lament for the loss of it !' The Farmer replied, 'Thou sayest the truth,

COUPLET.

If we are panged with absence now, we cannot murmur at our lot,
For in the day of union we the tribute of our thanks forgot.

It was a downright blunder, a blunder downright, that I took such trouble to store up the cash, and withholding it from my wife and family, kept a watch over it with such prodigious care. No sensible man acts in this way, to tie a purse of gold round his waist, and suffer day and night, and undergo ready-money vexation for credit indulgences. And all of a sudden, a turn of fortune, which could never have been traced on the tablet of thought, makes its appearance from destiny's workshop; and, like me, he tumbles into a whirlpool of dismay, and is left a long way off from the shore of escape.

VERSE.

They that have gems and still at mining slave,
  Their lives in toil for other men bestow.
And since our cares augment, the more we crave ;
  Have we but milk and wine, why labor so ?
How long wilt suffer in pursuit of more ?
Contentment seek, and let thy woes be o'er.'

Then the Farmer employed himself in protestations of repentance and contrition, and vowed that he would never hoard up wealth again, and would expend without delay all that came to hand. So, seeking the divine favor by reliance on God, he committed his affairs to the Creator; and, acquiescing in the decrees of Providence, he placed the head of submission on the line of resignation.

HEMISTICH.

Sit down, and on the Almighty's bounty rest.

In the other direction, the shepherd, with the bag of gold under his arm, was feeding his flock. One day he was employed in the same business close by a well. Suddenly, a party of horsemen showed themselves in the distance. The shepherd, in dread lest they should take the gold from him, dropped the purse into the well, and as day was closing, he drove his sheep homewards. Just after he had gone away, the Farmer was going along, and a strong wind began to blow. It carried off his turban and threw it into that very well. The Farmer jumped down in a moment, and was looking for his turban, when all of a sudden he got hold of the purse of gold.

HEMISTICH.

He sought a pearl, and lo! a ruby found.

Having returned thanks to God, he went back, and told his family the story of finding the money, and when he counted it, there were the three hundred dínárs as before. At this the Farmer exclaimed, 'Behold! God Most High has from an invisible quarter conveyed to me the same amount which had disappeared.' He then fulfilled the vows he had made, and began to expend the money. Some he disbursed for his family, and a small portion he devoted to religious purposes, until two hundred dínárs were gone. However, after the Farmer had departed, the shepherd, having satisfied himself about his sheep, went in the night to the well, and found not his bright-faced Joseph therein. Jacob-like, he raised outcries, and called out, 'Ah! Joseph!' and said, 'After this loss, of what use is life to me; and in my regret for that beloved mistress, what happiness or enjoyment can I derive from existence?

COUPLET.

I wish not that the boon of sight be longer to me left,
When I shall be for ever of his blessed sight bereft.'

Thus the shepherd was wandering about night and day, grieving and distracted. After a considerable time, having gone back to the city, he chanced to pass by the Farmer's hut. The latter, in accordance with his generous habits, gave the shepherd a meal. After they had finished eating, they began to discourse of various matters. The shepherd was telling a story, but the signs of the most complete grief were evident in his manner of talking; and from time to time he was involuntarily shedding tears of regret. The Farmer inquired the cause of his weeping, and of the pre-occupation of his mind. The shepherd replied, 'How should I not be broken-hearted and distracted?

COUPLET.

If Sulaimán had had the loss that I, unhappy, rue,
Fairies for Sulaimán had wept, fairies and devils too.

Know that I possessed three hundred gold dínárs, and my heart's strength and soul's happiness, and light of my eyes, and joy of my breast sprang from that. On a certain day, from dread of some cruel fellows, I threw this money into a certain well, and I never found any trace of it again.' The Farmer, amazed at hearing this story, got up and went to his wife and said, 'This money, which we thought was our lawful property, and to which we extended the hand of expenditure and disbursement, making unrestrained use of it, belonged to our guest. And we, owing to our incautiousness, have fallen into the labyrinth of crime and disastrous error. Now what little is left, we must hand over to him by way of present, and take care not to divulge this secret, otherwise he will come upon us for all the amount, and we shall be unable to pay.' His wife agreed with him in this, and said, 'The rightful owner must have his rights restored to him; and we must have recourse to contentment and reliance on God, until God Most High gives us something in return for it.

COUPLET.

He who, with truth, on God relies,   His wishes' face soon meets his eyes.'

Hereupon the Farmer placed the hundred dínárs that were left, before the shepherd by way of offering. The latter, deeply obliged, took up the money and counted it. There were exactly a hundred dínárs. He said to himself, 'This is the first instalment, and I am in hopes that the remainder, too, will come to hand. Now I must take good care of this, that I do not fall into the same trouble a second time.' He then hollowed part of a thick stick which he had, and with which he used to drive his flock to pasture, and deposited in it the pieces of gold, so that no one should know it. One day he was standing on the shore of a large stream, and his stick fell out of his hand into the river. Though he tried to get hold of it again, he could not. Now the river flowed by the city's gates, and as the Farmer was making his ablutions beside the stream, he saw a staff which the water was bringing towards him. He took it up and carried it home. His dame was cooking, and there were no sticks left. The Farmer began to break the staff that the cooking might be finished. All of a sudden his lap, like the platter of the firmament, was filled with gold sparkling like fire. He took up the pieces and counted them, and there were just a hundred dínárs. Down he fell and prostrated himself in thanksgiving, and opened the hand of liberality and expenditure once more. Two or three days passed and the shepherd came again to the Farmer's house, and more disconsolate than before, recounted the story of the stick and the hundred dínárs. The Farmer asked, 'Speak the truth! whence didst thou get those pieces that thou didst lose the first time, and how didst thou amass them?' The shepherd told the truth, saying, 'On a certain date I found a purse at such a spring of water, and in the purse were three hundred pieces of gold, and those were the very same that I threw into the well; and these hundred dínárs thou thyself gavest to me.' The Farmer smiled and said, 'Thanks and praise be to the Lord! who has kept the right fixed in its own circle. Know that it was I who forgot the purse and left it at the fountain's side, and I too found it in the well, and the hundred dínárs that I gave to thee were the residue thereof, and the staff has come back into my hands, and these are the hundred dínárs which we are expending.' The shepherd remained astonished and said, 'From the marvelous incidents of this story we may learn that none can appropriate the predestined portion of another.'

And the object of adducing this tale is, that my companions too should not surrender the station of contentment, nor step beyond the circle of reliance on God, nor be blind to the wonders of fortune which result from destiny and Providence, but duly valuing the opportunity of life, cease to confide in wealth and beauty, since the reality of future events is concealed and hidden behind the curtain of fate.

HEMISTICH.

None know in what affairs may terminate.'

In short they brought that day to an end in such discourse.   The next day when the husbandman of Omnipotence displayed the rose of hundred leaves, the sun, in the parterre of the horizon with a hundred shining hues ; and the fragrant hyacinth of dark night drew over its countenance the curtain of concealment in the violet bed of the sky,

COUPLET.

Like tulip in the sky, the sun shone bright,
And the stars' blossoms were concealed from sight;

the farmer's son arose and said, 'Take your ease here till I bring for your inspection a share of the fruits of my labors; and to-morrow, when you have rested, each of you work for his livelihood as he may advise with himself.' The friends agreed to this, and the young peasant went to the gate of the city and asked, 'What is the best thing to do in this city?' They replied, 'Wood for fuel is now very valuable, and they are buying it at an exorbitant price.' The youth immediately went to the hills, and having tied up a heavy bundle, as much as he could carry on his back, carried it to the city, and sold it for ten dirams.   He then bought some nice food, and turned his face towards his comrades, and when he had come out of the city he wrote on the door, ' The fruit of one day's labour is ten dirams.'   In short, that day the companions eat a refreshing morsel from the table of the young peasant; and on the morrow, when the beauty of the world-adorning, brightly-shining sun illuminated the universe with the glitter of its perfect loveliness,

COUPLET.

The lustrous sun, with smiles and blushes red,
From out day's upper chamber showed his head;

they said to the handsome youth, 'To-day contrive with thy beauty that there may be something to make thy friends comfortable and happy.' The youth arose, and walked, deep in thought, towards the city, saying to himself, ' I cannot do anything, and yet without succeeding in my object I cannot go back; and I am in a strangely-embarrassing position, such that I have no face to conceal it, nor courage to tell it.

COUPLET.

Thy looks that ruin my affairs inflict this hardship, too, as well,
I cannot, dare not, for my life, my hardships to another tell.'

In this cogitation he entered the city and sate down ill at ease and out of spirits, at the top of a street. Suddenly, a pretty woman with curling ringlets, who possessed much wealth and property, passed by him, and beholding that captivating face and the enchanting downy hair upon it; gave the goods of patience and endurance to the winds of love.

VERSE.

Such ebullitions then her heart assailed,
Each several hair seemed vocal with love's lay.
She clapped her hands, her moon-like face unveiled,[1]
And cast her lasso-ringlets in his way.

She said to her maid, 'Look at this beautiful face, which is such that the rose-leaf, from shame at its freshness, droops like the yellow jasmine; and survey this graceful figure, from mortification at whose delicacy and elegance, the straight cypress has its hand on its head and its foot in the clay.

COUPLET.

My cypress from the garden comes of spirit and the heart,
Think not those clay and water trees can be its counterpart.

If I were to attempt the description of that lip, I should say it is a ruby blent with sugar, and should I read the writing of that soft down, I should call it a mischief-exciting calamity.

COUPLET.

Blessed God! what lineaments are here, and down in sunny line!
Thus, into one, God's mercy does the rose and grass combine.[2]

And we cannot but suppose, '*This is not a mortal, he is no other than an angel deserving the highest respect.*[3]

HEMISTICH.

This beauty goes beyond the bound of human race.

O damsel! bethink thee of a device, that this noble bird may fall ,into the snare, and employ some artifice that I may possess this beautiful Adonis.' The slave-girl assenting, approached the youth, and said,

---

[1] The late Mr. Swinton considered these lines to be among the most difficult in the book. I take *ḳasab* to mean here 'fine linen,' an unusual sense. As she unveiled, her locks *kamand-i dil shikan*, fell loose.

[2] Persian writers frequently compare a young man's beard to grass. To us the comparison seems inapt enough.

[3] Ḳur'án, Fl. xxviii. 31; Mar. 32; Sale, p. 177, l. 10: 'And when she heard of this subtle behaviour she sent unto them, and prepared a banquet for them, and she gave to each of them a knife; and she said unto Joseph, come forth unto them. And when they saw

VERSE.

'Light of my eyes! whose soul's beloved art thou?
　　Whose honey-lip and sugar-grove?
Thy lip makes uproar wild enough, I trow,
　　In the world's mart.　Come, tell me, love!
Upon whose table blest the salt art thou?

O my beauty! my lady has sent her devotion to thee and says, 'Thou appearest to be a stranger in this city, and[1] strangers are generally sad, and we possess a pleasant, agreeable residence and a delightful place. If thou wouldst condescend to come there, and entertain us for a short time with thy beauty, we shall gain immortal life and thou wilt suffer no loss.' He replied, 'I obey thy commands, and I have no excuse for declining.' He then went to the lady's entertainment and stopped with her till close of day.

VERSE.

Headlong desire seized his passions' rein,
　　And patience, shaft-like, from his bosom shot.
He, from so fair a bride, could not refrain
　　His love; but when he saw the oven hot
　　He shut his bread within, and blessed his lot.

At a late hour he thought of joining his companions. The lady placed a hundred dirams before him and offered thanks. And the youth, having provided supplies for his companions, wrote upon the gate of the city, 'The price of a day's worth of beauty is a hundred dirams.'

The next day, when the merchant of divine wisdom opened the door of the office of the azure sky, and gave to view the gold-worked brocade of the sun from the shop of high heaven to the traffickers of the market of the world,

COUPLET.

Heaven's jeweler poured down a golden sum;
From the sky's mart arose a busy hum;

they said to the merchant's son, 'To-day we will be the guests of thy sagacity and quickness.' The young merchant assented, and came to the city-gate. Just then a vessel laden with a variety of precious things, came by water to the gate, and the citizens delayed, that the goods might become cheaper. The merchant's son bought them at a proper value, and selling them the same day for ready money, made a thousand dínárs profit. He then prepared things to entertain his friends, and wrote upon the gate of the city, 'The gain of one day's judgment and good sense is a thousand dínárs.'

---

him, they praised him greatly; and they cut their own hands, and said, 'O God! this is not a mortal; he is no other than an angel, deserving the highest respect.' The above passage refers to Zulaikhá, Potiphar's wife, and some Egyptian ladies who had accused her of immodesty.

[1] I would certainly insert *ra* before *gharíbán* here, as is done by the best MSS.

The next day, when the sovereign of the stars mounted the throne of the fourth heaven,[1] and set up his banner in the metropolis of the sky,

COUPLET.

The morn with golden crown and silver vest,
Wearing that crown a throne of ivory pressed ;

they said to the Prince, 'Thou always boastest of reliance upon God, and extollest acquiescence in the Divine Will, and resignation. Now if thou art to derive any fruit from these qualities, thou must provide for us.' The Prince met their request with acceptance, and with a lofty spirit and a purpose void of the scruple of hesitation, turned his face towards the city. Fate had decreed that death should reach the king of that city that day, and the inhabitants were engaged in mourning for him. The Prince went as spectator to the deceased monarch's palace, and seating himself on one side, kept quiet. The warder observed that while all others were occupied with mourning and lamentation, one person, seated silent in a corner, did not join them in their demonstrations of grief. He formed the idea that it was a spy, and treated him with indignity. The Prince having quenched the fire of wrath with the water of forbearance, was exclaiming,

VERSE.

' When a proud fool intemperance displays,
I will with gentleness his roughness meet.
And though, displeased, a hundred cries he raise ;
To my pleased ear that brawling shall seem sweet.'

When they carried out the bier, and the palace became empty, the Prince remained in the same spot, and was looking about on all sides of the palace. The warder again waxed more intemperate, and confined him in prison. Night came on, and no tidings or intelligence of the Prince reached the companions. They said to one another, ' This hapless youth, basing his reliance on God, and finding no advantage therefrom, has turned his face from our society. Would that we had not imposed this task upon him, nor distressed his noble heart.' Thus they in this quarter were reproaching themselves, and in the other the Prince, overtaken with bonds and imprisonment, was sending, with the hand of thought, messages to his companions.

COUPLET.

' Ah ! swift convey my tidings to the birds of the parterre,
For their sweet voices, too, have reached the cage of my despair.'

The next day the nobles and ministers of the city, and Roots and Pillars of the State, having assembled ; were desirous of committing to some one the

---

[1] The fourth heaven is, according to the Muḥammadans, the heaven of the Sun and of Jesus Christ.

business of the government—for their king had no heir. Having entered
upon this deliberation, they were offering a great variety of opinions. The
warder said to them, 'Keep this matter close, for I have apprehended a
spy, and it is probable, too, that he has a companion. Heaven forfend that
they should obtain intelligence of your dissensions, and hence mischief arise!'
He then told them of the Prince and of his appearance there and of his own
rigorous treatment of him. They thought it best to send for him and to
inquire into his proceedings. Some one went and brought the Prince from
the prison to the assembly. When their eyes fell upon his realm-adorning
beauty, they perceived that that silver countenance had nothing of the spy in
it, and that from such a gracious person and noble nature, such proceedings
could not arise. Having treated him with all due respect, they asked, 'What
is the cause of thy coming? and what city is thy birth-place and native
land?

COUPLET.

Whence with this youth and grace dost thou appear?
Sit, if to glad our bosoms thou art here.'

The Prince answered them courteously, and informed them of his birth and
lineage, and detailed to them the death of his sire and his brother's taking
possession of the throne. It happened that a number of the nobles had
formerly waited on his father and had seen that pearl of a royal shell at a
corner of the imperial throne. They immediately recognised him, and
related to all the Pillars of the State, the condition of the dominions of his
ancestors and the extent of their territories. So the whole body of the
grandees of that country were pleased at seeing him and overjoyed at his
fortunate arrival, and unanimously agreed that he was worthy to govern
that realm, as possessing a generous nature and pure descent. They thought,
too, that he would indubitably follow the steps of his noble progenitors, in
setting wide the gates of justice and liberality to the people; and would
imitate their amiable qualities and praiseworthy practices, and combine with
hereditary excellencies acquired virtues, and preserve his people in tranquillity under the shade of his fostering care. Thus they regarded the flash of
divine glory which shone forth from his countenance, as a convincing proof
and lucid testimony to his capabilities for reigning and his qualifications for
sovereignty, and felt persuaded that the tokens of his worthiness to reign, and
the signs of his future renown could not but be apparent to every man of
penetration.

COUPLET.

Such glory shone in Sulaimán, whoe'er could doubt of it,
Both bird and fish would laughingly deride his sense and wit.

Wherefore, they forthwith inaugurated him, and the kingdom, with this
facility, passed into his possession; and through the blessed influences of

reliance on God, he obtained this excellent fruit. And whosoever chooses to plant his foot firmly on the ground of trust in the Divine aid, and continues to tread there with sincerity of purpose and purity of disposition, will obtain the results thereof in faith and in worldly matters, and will be felicitous in both states of existence.

STANZA.

> Canst thou secure the key of faith ? with that,
> Thou may'st the door of fortune's hoards undo;
> And with sincere dependance as a bat,
> May'st in this court success's ball win, too.

And it was an established custom in that city to seat the king on the first day, on a white elephant, and carry him round the city. This same rite they observed in the Prince's case, and when the latter came to the city-gates, and saw the words which his companions had written, he commanded them to write underneath, ' Labor and beauty, and good sense and perfect skill: these bear fruit when the Divine decree is consentaneous with them ; and the adventures of a person, who, the first day was fettered in the prison of suffering, and the next day seated in the imperial palace on the throne adorned with gold, are sufficient to warn us of this.' He then returned to the royal palace, and seated himself on the throne, and the kingdom was settled under his sway.

STANZA.

> When Fortune saw him on the throne, it raised applauding shouts and said,
> ' O thou who knowest how to sit upon the throne of regal sway!
> Gird now thy waist like mighty kings, and o'er the world triumphant tread,
> The time has come to act, the days of idleness have passed away.'

He then sent for his former companions, and made the possessor of good sense and ability share office with the minister of state, and the merchant's son he appointed over the crown lands and possessions. But as for the beautiful youth he bestowed on him a magnificent robe of honor and unbounded wealth, and said, ' Though it is painful to part with a dear friend, yet thy stay in this country is not advisable, that women be not tempted by thy fascinating beauty, and that become a source of immorality and mischief.' He then turned to the grandees of the assembly and said, ' There are many amongst you who are superior to me in understanding, and valor, and skill, and ability, but kingdoms are obtainable only by the Divine favor, and the aid of the Eternal One, as may be understood from the purport of the saying, ' *Thou givest the kingdom unto whom thou wilt.*' [1]

---

[1] Kur'án, Fl. iii. 25, Mar. 26 ; Sale, p. 35, l. 3 : ' Say, O God, who possessest the kingdom ; thou givest the kingdom unto whom thou wilt, and thou takest away the kingdom from whom thou wilt ! Thou exaltest whom thou wilt, and thou humblest whom thou wilt. In thy hand is good, for thou art Almighty.'

VERSE.

O object of the musings of the wise !
    Desire of the hearts of all in prayerful posture bowing !
The slave's, the monarch's, destinies
    Are willed by Thee.   Fortune's gifts are nought save thy endowing :
Unless Thy wisdom and Thy guidance lead,
Who can this road by reason's light proceed ?

My companions were laboriously exerting themselves to earn, and each
secured a trifle.   But I did not rely on my own wisdom and strength, nor did
I seek aid from any one's support or protection.   But I based my proceedings
on reliance on God, and I acquiesced in the Divine decree and the Supreme
predestination, and said,

COUPLET.

' The head must be submissive bent, the neck inclined obediently,
    For all the Righteous Judge ordains is justice, peace, and equity.

[After the Prince had thus spoken,] a man of eloquence among those
present arose and said, ' Everything that the King pronounces is a gem perforated by the diamond of wisdom, and gold tried on the touchstone of
knowledge : and there is no qualification for governing like understanding and
judgment, and the high merits and worthiness of the king are by this token
as clear as the sun, to all his subjects : and the Creator Himself knows what
are the qualifications of each, and what promotion and advancement each
accordingly deserves [as it is said], ' God best knoweth whom He will appoint
for a messenger.' [1]

COUPLET.

From the table of His bounties, by no limiting confined,
Each his due share in proportion to his worth is sure to find.

The good-fortune of the people of this country brought thee to this station,
and the vigorous auspices of the inhabitants of this land spread the felicitous
shade of a Humá over thee like the heads of the drooping-pinioned
subjects.

COUPLET.

Most blest the spot where moons, like thee, make choice of their alighting-place !
Happy the region where such kings with favor turn, like thee, their face !'

Another then rose and adorned his tongue with praise of the king of youthful
fortune, and throne lofty as the sky, and having placed the jewels of these
couplets on the tray of representation, he showered them, applaudingly, on
the royal head ;

----

[1] Ḳur'án, vi. 124 ; Sale, p. 103, l. 21 : ' And when a sign cometh unto them, they say, 'We
will, by no means, believe, until a revelation be brought unto us, likewise that which hath
been delivered unto the messengers of God.   God best knoweth whom he will appoint for
His messenger.'

STANZA.

'Monarch! whose happy, gold-bestowing hand,
    Successful casts a lasso on the sky;
As heaven itself, secure, the peaceful land
    Which sleeps beneath thy kingly canopy.'

Similarly each of the nobles delivered his sentiments suitably to his
position, and recited a select portion of the pages of the imperial virtues.
At last, a pure-minded, fair-spoken old man rose on his feet, and after
offering the fitting praises and eulogies, said, 'O king! On the subject of fate
and predestination, somewhat of which has been explained to the hearts of
the assembly by the gem-scattering tongue of the sovereign, this slave has a
story, and if the implicitly-obeyed command is condescendingly issued, I will
recite it and set it forth.' The king said, 'Bring what thou hast, and say
how that was.'

STORY III.

The old man said, 'I used once to be in the service of a great personage.
As, however, I knew the fickleness of the world, and was on my guard
against the wiles of that fraudful hag, and knew that that husband-killing
bride—the world—has, by disappointing many of those enamoured of her,
reduced them to despair; and that that perfidious mistress of evil deeds, has
overthrown, headlong, many a lover; I said to myself, 'O simple one! thou
art fixing thy heart on the friendship of one who has struck the hand of
rejection on the breasts of a hundred thousand prosperous kings, and given
to the winds of annihilation the stacks of the peace of mind of innumerable
renowned princes. Abandon this pursuit and build not thy house at a place
of passage, whence every moment thou must be prepared to set out.

QUATRAIN.

Who the world's customs well appreciate,
    Build not therein that they may dwell in it.
This ruined inn why should we renovate,
    When we so soon to others must it quit?

Awake from the slumber of supineness, for the time is short, and the steed of
action lame; and carry with thee a provision for thy journey from thy brief
existence here, for the way is long and protracted, and the heat of the fire of
the desert such as to melt life.

VERSE.

In every corner make good search to-day,
    That for the morrow thou mayst have supplies.
Distant thy halting-place and long the way,
    Then in providing for them both be wise.

At last, by using these reflections my refractory passions were rebuked, and with the utmost delight and real eagerness, I turned my face from the affairs of the world and the society of worldlings. One day I saw in the bázár that a fowler was offering for sale two hoopoes; and they expressed to one another by the language of their behaviour, the grief of heart which they experienced, and drooping at their imprisonment, supplicated God for the good tidings of release. I felt pity for them, and wished to buy them with a view to my own final salvation, and that by releasing them from their bonds, I might look for the blessing of liberation from the prison of the Divine wrath. The price the fowler set on them was two dirams—and that was all I had in my possession. I felt irresolute, therefore, and my mind would not permit me to expend those two dirams, and yet my inclination, was to liberate the birds. At last I placed my reliance on God, and having bought the two, I carried them outside the city, and let them go. They came and settled on a wall, and called out to me, and, as is the custom of the grateful, returned me thanks, and said, 'At present our hands fall short of requiting and recompensing thee. However, beneath this wall is a casket full of jewels of great value. Break down to it and take it up.' I was amazed at their words, and said, 'It is a wondrous thing that ye see a little box of jewels under the ground, and fail to observe the gem which is on the surface.'[1] They replied, 'When fate issues its decree, the eye of reason is darkened, and the day of understanding, which descries the minutest things, becomes obscured. The demands of destiny are in no wise to be set aside; and when they take place, neither has the prudent man any vision left, nor does the sight of the sagacious avail. And all this has taken place because the execution of the Divine decree was involved in it.

And this story bears just testimony to the speech of the king which he delivered on the subject of fate and predestination. Moreover, in corroboration of these sentiments, sages have said,

QUATRAIN.

'If thy affairs go ill, thou 'rt not to blame;
  If well, it is not owing to thy skill.
Have faith, and live on happy through the same,
  Since nought that happens, happens by thy will.'

The old man added, 'O king! I dug under that wall and secured the box, and I make it known in order that the king may issue his august commands for it to be conveyed to the public treasury.' The Prince responded, 'Thou hast sown the seed and hast reaped the fruit. It is not right that any should share in this with thee; and these jewels of wisdom, which in this assembly thou hast arranged on the string of recitation, are for

---

[1] *Dar zír-i khdk*, 'under the clods,' or 'under the dirt of the surface.'

me sufficient. For no gem can be more beautiful than good words, and by the philosopher's stone of language, the copper of bad money may be transmuted into sterling gold.

VERSE.

Say! language! whence is given thy wondrous magic power?
And who the alchymist that turns thee into gold?
Whence spring thy countless images? while, to this hour,
None can thy full resources ever hope t' unfold.
What bird art thou of so much beauty? We,
Our sole memorial leave behind in thee.'

Those present applauded the genius of the Prince, and at once bound their hearts in fealty to him; and having placed their heads on the line of his command, committed the reins of authority to the grasp of his option, and passed their lives in the shade of his munificence.

HEMISTICH.

Until the time when their turn, too, went by.'

This is the story of the advantages of reliance on God, and of resignation; and of the results of destiny and fate. And no wise man can dispense with knowing thus much, that if he delivers the reins of choice to the hand of destiny he will obtain all good things, and no event of importance will take place contrary to his wish; and the fact is,

COUPLET.

Fortune, in all her changes, shewed me nought
Such as I pictured in the glass of thought.

And how well is it said in the beginning of this ode,

COUPLET.

' If fate turns not affairs, why, always, then
Do they run counter to the wills of men?'

When the Bráhman had finished this discourse, and by the recital of this story had fully concluded the explanation of the precepts of Húshang, King Dábishlím performed the usual respectful salutation, and said, 'By the auspicious influence of the spirit of the sublime sage the veil of concealment has fallen from the face of my wish, and the desire I felt has been attained by the blessing of the society of my exalted teacher.

HEMISTICH.

Thanks be to God! my toil has proved not vain.

I now respectfully request that the Sage of luminous mind would accept an offering from me, and not reject the tribute which, through pure affection, I have brought.' The Bráhman replied, 'O King! I have contentedly withdrawn from the world's mansion to a corner and a morsel, and have washed the skirt of my heart from the pollution of worldly superfluities. It is impossible that I should ever again be stained with the filthiness of its appurtenances.

COUPLET.

> While I can slumber in the world unpained,
> 'Twere shame, by mixing with it, to be stained.

And if the king wishes to do me a service, and to put the chain of obligation round my neck, my wish is that he would draw on the string of compilation these words, blended with wisdom; and regard them as the guide of the way to salvation, and the leader in the path of perfection, and by this means, always keeping me in his gracious mind, not withhold from me the blessing of his prayers. For in accordance with the saying, ' *The prayer of the just man is not rejected,*' the request of the prayer of just kings is marked with the honor of acceptance.' The king assented to this, and having bid farewell to the Bráhman, returned to his own capital, and arranged on the string of compilation the jewels of wisdom which he had secured, and used always to refer to those admonitions in the occurrence of events; and in great emergencies, used to seek aid from their counsels.

STANZA.

> He who pursues what those more sage advise,
>   At last the station of his hopes will gain.
> But he who leaves the pathway of the wise
>   Is lost, nor finds the wished-for path again.'

When Khujistah Ráí had recounted from beginning to end this heart-enchanting story and incomparable tale, Humáyún Fál began, like a freshly-irrigated rose, to bloom on the bed of delight; and the young tree of his condition raised its head in the parterre of good-fortune. He made the vazír hopeful of his imperial bounties, and enlightened the eye of his heart with the acquisition of his wishes, and said,

COUPLET.

> ' Hail! to thy heart-delighting words, the spirits' entertainment-place,
> Thy clear discourse adds pleasure to the spirits of the human race.

By the full recital of this delightful story thou hast bestowed sweetness on the palate of my soul, and by the exposition of these words of wise conclusion, thou hast sown in the ground of my heart the seed of perpetual happiness. And henceforward, nought save these perfect admonitions shall be the guide of my government, and I will regard nought as the rule of the fabric of my practice but these salutary counsels. And these words have made a wonderful impression on my heart, and this is entirely owing to thy abundant sincere affection and truth; for although words may be essentially good; yet, by reason of the polluted nature of the speaker, they may yield no wholesome result; and advice, though springing from the purest wisdom, oftentimes, from the wickedness of the rehearser, produces no impression.

STANZA.

One stained with crime, though all he says be wise,
Makes no one better by his eloquence.
While in the pure of heart such doctrine lies,
That though maintaining silence, all men thence
Learn to be good by tacit inference.'

The vazír extolled the king, and said, ' That which has passed the wisdom-impressed tongue of the king is essentially true and purely wholesome; for the words of the fraudulent and the hypocritical have but a false lustre, and expire in a short time, like a fire made of wormwood. But the language of truth and purity, like the streaks of morning light, increase in brightness every instant; and, like the torch of the sun, appear more brilliant every hour.

COUPLET.

The words of passion ne'er can reach the spirit's inmost cell,
But, coming from the heart, they in the soul itself will dwell.'

Again Humáyún Fál addressed the vazír with flattering encouragement, and raised the flag of his good-fortune to the pinnacle of high heaven; and the vazír, beholding the tokens of the amiable qualities of the king, and the light of his praiseworthy virtues; arrayed the substructure of praise and benediction in the following manner,

VERSE.

' O king! thou, by thy virtue's excellence,
The worth of former monarchs hast surpassed.
Praised be thy faith and wisdom, justice, sense*;
Fortune, and realm, may they perpetual last!'

With these words the conversation closed, and Humáyún Fál, too, in the same way as Dábishlím, impressed on the pages of his own actions the graces of these tales, and fulfilled all the requirements of justice in building up the edifices of good administration, and left, as a memorial on the leaves of time, a good name and fair renown.

VERSE.

Two things life offers—fame, the virtuous deed :
Save these, ' <i>All things are subject to decay.</i>'[1]
Injure not others, help men to succeed,
Thus shalt thou reap a blessing for to-day;
And the next world, when this has passed away.

---

[1] Ḳu'rán, Ch. lv., 26; Sale, p. 392, l. 22 : 'Every creature which liveth on the earth is subject to decay : but the glorious and honorable countenance of thy Lord shall remain for ever.' The first couplet of this stanza is quoted somewhat differently in the life of Faridu 'd-dín 'Aṭṭár, in Daulat Sháh's Taẕkirah.

These are the few words which, on the call of the moment, the tongue of
the pen has aided in inscribing, and which, in the manner that the nature of
the subject[1] required, have been written down by the reed of exposition. And
my hope in the virtuous excellencies of the most eminent of mankind, and in
the good qualities of the lofty noble,[2] is, that he will conceal with the skirt of
indulgence the unweighed expressions and unsatisfactory style of this his
humble servant; and that, by way of cherishing the insignificant, and
condescending to the poor,

HEMISTICH.
Though it from end to end be all one fault,

will survey it with the eye of favor.

VERSE.

The pearls I in this bosom hidden had,
I 've one by one from heart to tongue conveyed.
And be the offering deemed or good or bad,
May it in thy indulgence be arrayed.
And since thus far I've breathed my story's spell,
Better to finish here, and say farewell.

THE BOOK IS HERE ENDED BY THE AID OF THE KING OF ALL GIFTS.

---

[1] For the ما یده *máidah* (better written ما ئده) of the printed edition, the lithographed
edition and the MSS. I have consulted, read *khámah*, 'pen.' Neither of these words is
very intelligible here.

[2] Shekh Ahmad: see p. 10 of this translation.

STEPHAN AUSTIN, PRINTER, HERTFORD.

LIST OF BOOKS

IN THE

ORIENTAL LANGUAGES,

ETC.,

PRINTED AND PUBLISHED BY

STEPHEN AUSTIN, HERTFORD;

AND WHICH MAY BE OBTAINED OF

Mr. J. MADDEN, 8, Leadenhall Street, London.

Messrs. LONGMAN and Co., Paternoster Row, London.

Messrs. WILLIAMS and NORGATE, Henrietta Street, Covent Garden.

Mr. W. ALLAN, Aldine Chambers, Paternoster Row, London.

Mr. DAVID NUTT, Strand, London.

Messrs. TRUBNER and Co., 12, Paternoster Row, London.

Messrs. R. C. LEPAGE & Co., 1, Whitefriars Street, Fleet Street, London; and
British Library, Calcutta.

Messrs. THACKER & Co., 87, Newgate Street; and at Calcutta and Bombay.

Messrs. HOLDER and Co., Bombay.

ANVÁR-I SUHAILÍ,

A NEW Edition of the PERSIAN TEXT. Edited by Lieut.-Col. J. W. J.
OUESLEY, Professor of Arabic and Persian in the East India College, Herts. 4to.

DUNCAN FORBES, LL.D.,

Professor of the Oriental Languages at King's College, London.

"Your edition of the Anvár-i Suhelí beats hollow all that have hitherto appeared. The
correctness of the text reflects the highest credit on Colonel Ouseley's care, as the neatness
of the typography does to your press. It is really a luxury to read such a book."

ANVÁR-I SUHELÍ.

THE FIRST BOOK. The PERSIAN TEXT. Edited by the Rev. H.
G. KEENE, late Arabic and Persian Professor at the East India College, Haileybury
Herts. Octavo.

ANVÁR-I SUHELÍ.

THE FIRST BOOK, literally Translated into English. By the Rev. H.
G. KEENE. Octavo.

ŚAKUNTALÁ;

OR, ŚAKUNTALÁ RECOGNIZED BY THE RING; a Sanskrit
Drama, by Kálidása; the Devanágarí Recension of the Text, now for the first time
edited in England, with literal English Translations of all the Metrical passages, schemes
of the Metres, and copious Critical and Explanatory Notes, By MONIER WILLIAMS,
M.A., Professor of Sanskrit in the East India College; formerly Boden Sanskrit Scholar
in the University of Oxford.

ATHENÆUM.

. . . " It was not till 1835 that he (Sir William Jones) was discovered to have used
one of the MSS. which the meddlesome pundits of Bengal have grievously injured by
their interpolations and fancied emendations. The text of the present edition, on the
contrary, is based on MSS. of a more ancient date, and the copyists of which were less
disposed to tamper with its integrity. The editor has also freely availed himself of Dr.
Boehtlingk's edition of the same recension. He has done everything in his power to meet
the wants of the students by supplying him with useful translations and explanatory notes,
as well as by adopting excellent typographical arrangements. The manner in which the
work is got up does great credit both to editor and publisher. If English scholars do not
now attain to a more correct appreciation of this great dramatist, it will be their own fault."

WESTMINSTER REVIEW.

" An important contribution to the study of Sanskrit literature is furnished by Professor Williams,—the first English edition of the masterpiece of the great Indian dramatist.
Kálidása's Sakuntalá led Sir W. Jones to his great discovery of the very existence, and
of the pre-eminent beauty of the Indian drama. His translation, which has captivated
many who could not read the original, is the only form in which it is known in this
country. There is an excellent German edition by Böhtlingk; but Professor Williams,
being able to profit by this profound scholar's labours, and, moreover, to collate a
greater number of MSS., appears to have produced a still more reliable text. The notes
are in English, and contain the matter of the Indian Scholia, besides frequent translations
and explanations. There are also short metrical notes. In the Prákrit passages the
Sanskrit is interlined, the Prákrit being distinguished by red ink. The complete
separation of the words (except where combined by crasis, as in Greek κἄν for καὶ ἄν), we
regard as a rational step, which we are glad to see taken by so high an authority as the
Haileybury professor. The accuracy and style of the typography, and quality of the
paper, reflect great credit on the publisher."

M. GARCIN DE TASSY,

Membre de l'Institut, in the "Journal Asiatique."

" M. Austin continue d'enrichir la littérature orientale d'ouvrages utiles qui sont en
même temps des chef-d'œuvres d'imprimerie. J'ai déjà eu l'occasion d'en signaler
plusieurs aux lecteurs du *Journal Asiatique.* J'ai à leur parler aujourd'hui d'un nouveau
volume, qui se distingue encore par la recherche de la composition typographique.
. . . . Dans cette édition nouvelle, M. Williams, l'habile professeur d'Haileybury,
a suivi, comme le Dr. Boehtlingk, la rédaction dévanagari, qui est la plus ancienne et
la meilleure. Il a eu à sa disposition non-seulement plusieurs bons manuscrits de l'East
India House et d'Oxford, mais trois différents commentaires. Son travail est exécuté
avec un soin parfait ; les passages pracrits sont distingués par l'emploi de l'encre rouge
et ils sont traduit interlinéairement en Sanscrit. Dans le texte Sanscrit, les mots sont

séparés au moyen du *viram*, toutes les fois qu'il n'en résulte pas d'inconvénient grammatical, ce qui diminue beaucoup pour les lecteurs européens la difficulté de la langue sacrée de l'Inde."

DR. ALBRECHT WEBER,
In the "Zeitschrift fur die Kunde des Morgenlandes."

"Mr. Monier Williams, whose previous works (mainly intended for the practical teaching of Sanscrit in the East India College) deserve the highest praise, takes a higher position by his remarkably pains-taking edition of the 'Sakuntalá.' The arrangement of the book is eminently useful—the notes and the translation of the metrical passages stand at the foot of the text—the Prákrit is interlineated with its Sanskrit rendering, so that it is especially fitted for practical teaching by lecture, or for private study. . . . The getting up of the book is 'splendid.' . . . And we may congratulate Mr. Austin, who displays so much taste, skill, and care in his publications, upon this last production of his press."

PROFESSOR CHRISTIAN LASSEN.

"Bonn, 12th April, 1854.

"Dear Sir,—I have had the pleasure of receiving the copy of your edition of the 'Sakuntalá,' which you have had the kindness to present me with, and should have offered you my sincerest thanks for this fresh token of your regard and friendship earlier, if I had not wished before to convince myself of the merits of your edition of *the most excellent of all Sanscrit dramas.* I am now happy to assure you that *you have improved in many passages the reading of Dr. Boehtlingk, and thereby rendered a signal service to the students of Sanscrit literature.*—Believe me, Dear Sir, Your truly devoted and obliged, CHRISTIAN LASSEN."—*To Professor Williams.*

IN THE PRESS,

Printed in the highest style of Art, with Polychromatic characteristic Borders, copied from Hindú and other Manuscripts; and Woodcut Illustrations, etc.,

A FREE TRANSLATION, IN PROSE AND VERSE, OF KÁLIDÁSA'S DRAMA,

ŚAKOONTALÁ,

BY MONIER WILLIAMS, M.A.

NEARLY READY,

Handsomely printed in Imp. 16mo.

BHAGAVAD-GÍTÁ;

OR, DISCOURSES ON DIVINE MATTERS of KRISHNA and ARJUNA: a philosophical Poem. The SANSKRIT TEXT with a VOCABULARY.

Also, a New Translation in Prose, of the

BHAGAVAD-GÍTÁ;

WITH very copious Critical, Philosophical, and Explanatory Notes; and Introductory Chapters on the Hindú System of Philosophy, a Critical Examination of the book, and an Index of Proper Names, by J. COCKBURN THOMSON, Member of the Asiatic Society of France.

SELECTIONS FROM THE

MAHÁBHÁRATA.

WITH a VOCABULARY. By FRANCIS JOHNSON, Professor of Sanskrit at the East India College. Royal 8vo.

LATELY PUBLISHED,
Roy. 8vo. 230 pp.

PRÁKRITA-PRAKÁSA;

OR, THE PRÁKRIT GRAMMAR OF VARARUCHI, with the COMMENTARY (Manoramá) of Bhámaha. By EDWARD BYLES COWELL, of Magdalen Hall, Oxford. The first complete Edition of the Original Text, with various readings from a collation of six MSS. in the Bodleian Library at Oxford, and the Libraries of the Royal Asiatic Society and the East India House. With copious Notes, an English Translation, and an Index of Prákrit Words; to which is prefixed an easy Introduction to Prákrit Grammar.

M. GARCIN DE TASSY,
Membre de l'Institut, in the "Journal Asiatique."

"Il était donc important de publier en entier le texte original de son ouvrage, et M. Cowell, jeune et digne élève de M. Wilson, et déjà connu par son *Vikramorvasi*, dont nous avons parlé en temps opportun, a voulu rendre service aux indianistes; et non seulement il a publié les sûtras de Vararuchi, d'après six manuscrits, mas il les a accompagnés du commentaire de Bhâmaha, de nombreuses notes, d'une traduction, d'appendices importants, et d'un index des mots pracrits, qui est de la plus grande utilité pour l'usage de ce volume. De plus, M. Cowell a placé en tête de cet ouvrage une *introduction à la grammaire pracrit*, qui se distingue par la clarté et la précision."—*Feb.* 1854.

ATHENÆUM.

"No one can acquire a thorough mastery over the modern dialects of Hindústan who has not first studied Sanscrit. . . The Prákrit, of which the volume before us treats, is a dialect—or rather collection of dialects—of the Sanscrit, forming a connecting link between that ancient language and the modern tongues of India. Vararuchi, the grammarian whose work is now for the first time presented to the English public in a complete form, is the oldest authority we have on the Prákrit dialects. Unlike Pánini, the other great Indian grammarian, he has been unfortunate in the treatment he has received from copyists and editors. Hence, Mr. Cowell has been called upon to expend much labour in the examination of manuscripts and other grammarians in order to prepare his text."

WESTMINSTER REVIEW.

"Mr. Cowell gives us not merely a standard native Prákrit grammar from a collation of several MSS., but a short grammar of his own more conformable to European system, and a translation of the former, which may serve as an excellent introduction to the grammatical system and phraseology of the Hindús. The accuracy and style of the typography and quality of the paper reflect great credit on the publisher."—*March* 1854.

PROFESSOR CHRISTIAN LASSEN.

"Bonn, 12th April, 1854.

"SIR,—I have had the honor to receive the copy of Vararuchi's 'Prákrita Prakása,' with which you have had the kindness to present me, and beg to offer you my sincerest thanks for this mark of your attention. I hope you will excuse the lateness of my acknowledging this present, by the consideration that I wished to examine this important work, and feel great pleasure in assuring you, that in my opinion, Mr. Cowell's edition cannot fail to receive the approbation of all Sanscrit scholars. He has for the first time made one of the most important Sanscrit works available for their use.—I have the honor to remain, Sir, with great respect, your truly obliged servant, CHRISTIAN LASSEN."
To Mr. Stephen Austin.

GULISTÁN;

A NEW Edition of the PERSIAN TEXT, with a VOCABULARY. By E. B. EASTWICK, F.R.S., F.S.A., M.R.A.S., etc. 8vo.

DUNCAN FORBES, LL.D.,
Professor of Oriental Languages at King's College, London.

"I consider it *everything to be desired.* Three grand requisites for beginners you have supplied—1st, *a good Vocabulary;* 2nd, the division of the work into sentences, by means of a simple punctuation. This part particularly pleases and flatters me, for I was myself the first that had the courage to introduce into this country this very rational and palpable improvement."

Beautifully printed with Coloured Border, and head and tail-pieces, and with Illuminated fac-simile Illustrations (in gold and colours), from a valuable MS. copy of the Gulistán, in the Library of the Royal Asiatic Society. Demy 8vo. elegantly bound.

GULISTÁN;

OR, ROSE GARDEN of SÁDÍ OF SHÍRÁZ, Translated for the first time into Prose and Verse, By EDWARD B. EASTWICK, F.R.S., F.S.A., M.R.A.S., etc.

The Publisher has the high satisfaction of referring to the following expressions in a note from the Hon. C. B. Phipps, Keeper of the Privy Purse to Her Majesty, dated "Windsor Castle, January 3, 1853," acknowledging the receipt of a copy of "The Gulistán," forwarded by the Publisher for presentation to Her Most Gracious Majesty the Queen:—

"*I have presented the beautiful copy of ' Gulistán' to the Queen. Her Majesty has accepted the book, and it was very much admired.*"

DR. MAX MULLER,

Professor of Modern Languages in the University of Oxford: in the " Zeitschrift fur die Kunde des Morgenlandes."

"The translation is careful, and executed with great skill, as might be expected from one who has edited the text of the 'Gulistán.'. . . . The exterior of the book is quite in Oriental style. Many pictures in illuminated colour-printing—faithful copies of Persian MSS.—vignettes,—and the binding ornamented with arabesques in gold—exhibit the skill and taste of the Publisher."

M. GARCIN DE TASSY,

Membre de l'Institut, in the " Journal Asiatique."

" Our readers will doubtless recollect that we made mention, in the *Journal Asiatique* of June, 1850, of the new edition of the Persian text of the 'Gulistán,' by Mr. Eastwick, taking occasion to recommend, in a merited eulogium, that useful publication. And now this truly indefatigable *savant*, who, in the space of a few years, has published many volumes of Oriental texts and translations, remarkable, the former for their correctness, and the latter for their fidelity, has just crowned his earlier performance—the 'Gulistán'— by adding to it a new translation. . . This translation has, to begin with, over former ones, an external advantage, if we may so speak—an advantage which it owes to the enlightened care and attention of the Publisher."

LITERARY GAZETTE.

" The richness of a Persian MS. has been in some measure simulated by the printer. The work contains several illuminations which will bear comparison with the best Eastern illuminations executed by hand. The typography is faultless, and a rich Persian arabesque in gold upon the cover completes the harmony of this most attractive volume."

ATHENÆUM.

" We like the translation before us, and it is, we think, a valuable contribution to our small stock of Oriental productions. . . . We cannot dismiss this book without a word of praise on the style of ornamentation and typography in which it has been got up. It does great credit to the country-press of Mr. Stephen Austin. We never saw colours, gold, and Oriental design more charmingly combined for the production of a beautiful volume."

EXAMINER.

"We must name here among gift-books, for the beauty of its typography and its illumina- tions, as well as for the richness of its matter, treated only as an Eastern story-book, Professor Eastwick's excellent translation of the 'Gulistán.' It is a delightful substitute for the old Books of Beauty, the very thing for a boudoir, and very fit for any study also. And London publishers will find it necessary to look sharply about them when a publisher in the small provincial town of Hertford can issue such a volume as this."

SPECTATOR.

" It is evident that Mr. Eastwick acts on principles of conscientious literality in translation. His verse is smooth, his prose fluent, his annotation critical. . . . This edition of Sadi claims attention on one other ground besides its literary merits. It is printed, bound, and published with a chaste richness that would do credit to any London publisher of ornamental volumes. The decoration, in coloured borders and headings, has an Eastern character; to which are added four fac-simile reproductions of illuminations contained in a MS. copy of the 'Gulistán' in the possession of the Royal Asiatic Society."

DICKENS' HOUSEHOLD NARRATIVE.

"Professor Eastwick has translated the famous 'Gulistán, or Rose-Garden,' of the immortal Sadi, by far the most popular of all the writers of the East. And the book deserves notice, even apart from its intrinsic literary value, for the elegant form and rich illustration which it owes to the spirit of a publisher in a small provincial town, Mr. Stephen Austin, of Hertford."

THE NATIONAL MAGAZINE.

"It is only just to remark, in passing, that, over and above the excellence of the translation, it is got up, to use a technical term, in an elegant Persian style, with Oriental embellishments, and does the highest credit to Mr. Austin, of Hertford, from whose press it issued last year. . . . . My readers will perceive, I think, that Sadi is no common writer; the Rose-Garden no every-day book. . . . . I hesitate not to say, that the reader will find in its pages abundant proofs that Sadi, judged not merely by the standard of his own country, but by a much higher one, was a man not only of great good sense, but of an enlarged and truly liberal mind."

VIKRAMORVASÍ;

A DRAMA, by Kálidása. The Sanskrit Text. Edited by MONIER WILLIAMS, M.A. 8vo.

This edition of the 'Vikramorvasí' has been favourably noticed in an article in the *Foreign Quarterly Review*, October, 1850.

VIKRAMORVASÍ;

TRANSLATED into English. By E. B. COWELL, of Magdalen Hall, Oxford. 8vo.

M. GARCIN DE TASSY,
Membre de l' Institut, in the "Journal Asiatique."

"Il y a déjà longtemps que le célèbre Wilson a dans son Théâtre Hindou, fait connaitre ce drame que la tradition attribue à l'auteur de Sakuntalá. Mais M. Cowell a voulu en donner une traduction littérale, en prose, en faveur des élèves du Collége civil de la Compagnie des Indes à Haileybury et pour accompagner le texte récemment publié par M. Monier Williams, Professeur de Sanscrit au même établissement. Ce dernier texte est la repro- duction de celui de Calcutta, si ce n'est que le savant éditeur a, dans l'intérêt de ses élèves, remplacé les passages Prácrits par leur traduction en Sanscrit: et qu'il a admis, en outre, quelques corrections de l'édition de Lenz. Quant à la traduction de M. Cowell, elle est très-propre à l'intelligence du texte; elle est de plus, enrichie de quelques notes d'érudition et d'un tableau raisonné de métres employées dans le drame."

BÁGH O BAHÁR;

AN entirely new English version, with Notes. By E. B. EASTWICK, F.R.S., F.S.A., M.R.A.S., etc. Royal 8vo.

ATHENÆUM.

"The 'Bágh o Bahár' is unquestionably a work of more value and importance than Solwân: and we are not surprised that Mr. Eastwick, who is Professor of Urdu at Haileybury, undertook its translation. *Urdu,* some of readers may like to know, is the Hindú word for a camp; but the Urdu language means the colloquial and ordinary tongue spoken by all classes—Hindús, Mussulmans, grown people and children—of our Eastern possessions. Hence its value to every person about to become a resident in India, and the reason why the Company reequire all candidates for office, civil or military, to be, to a certain extent, proficient in it. The 'Bágh o Bahár' is one of the works in which they are examined; and Mr. Eastwick's main reason for publishing this very literal and accurate version is, that it may be of use to all learners of Urdu. In this point of view it is valuable; and although we may not agree entirely with the translator as to the positive merit and interest of the work, we are quite ready to admit that the version was wanted, and that it must from its style and accuracy (as far as we are able to form a judgment on the point) supersede Mr. L. F. Smith's version, to the second edition of which Professor Forbes lent his name."

PREM SÁGAR;

A NEW Edition of the Hindī Text, with Notes and a complete Vocabulary. By E. B. EASTWICK, F.R.S., F.S.A., M.R.A.S., etc. 4to.

M. THEODORE PAVIE.

"En 1851, M. Edward B. Eastwick, professeur d'Ourdoo à l'East-India College, d'Haileybury, donna une excellente édition du *Prem Ságar*, à laquelle il joignit une traduction remarquable par sa scrupuleuse fidélité et par l'élégance du style. Ce travail du professeur d'Haileybury a prouvé une fois de plus que la langue anglaise, maniée avec habilité, s'adapte admirablement aux inversions modérées et au mouvement général d'un récit poétique. Entre le texte introuvable de Tchatourbhoudj-Misr et la version du *Prem Ságar* traduite de manière a n'y plus revenir, se plaçait le manuscrit de Lâlatch, moins ancien que le premier de ces deux ouvrages et supérieur au second comme monument littéraire (puisque le *Prem Ságar*, a été rédigé en prose par Cri-lallou-dji-Lâl en 1804)."—*Extract from the Preface to a French Translation of the Tenth Chapter of the Bhagavat Purâna.*

PREM SÁGAR;

TRANSLATED into English. By E. B. EASTWICK, F.R.S., F.S.A., M.R.A.S. 4to.

WESTMINSTER REVIEW.

"At a time," says the translator, "when the translation of the Vedas is unfolding to the world the religion of the Hindús as it existed in the dim ages of antiquity, a translation of the 'Prem Ságar' may be thought opportune, displaying, as it does, the religion of that great nation at the present day. . . . . The 'Prem Ságar' is a Hindī version of the Braj Bhákah translation of the tenth chapter of the 'Bhágavat Purána.' . . . We must not omit to mention the highly creditable way in which the original text is printed; the type is very clear, and great care seems to have been taken to render the work accurate, and the edition, indeed, in all respects, will bear a most favourable comparison with any published."

HITOPADEŚA;

THE Sanskrit Text, with a Grammatical Analysis, alphabetically arranged, and an English Index of Words, serving the purpose of a reversed Dictionary. By FRANCIS JOHNSON, Professor of Sanskrit at the East India College. Imp. 8vo.

PROFESSOR WILSON, M.A.,
Professor of Sanskrit in the University of Oxford.

"The Hitopadesa is the original of the celebrated 'Pilpay's Fables.' The great merits of this work as a CLASS BOOK, long since led to its introduction into the East-India College at Haileybury, near Hertford, but the first London edition contained many errors, which impaired its usefulness. The new edition has been prepared under more favourable auspices. A more perfect acquaintance with the language, greater facilities for collating the work with other editions, and with the Manuscript copies in the East-India Company's Library, *the increased means of typographical accuracy*, a copious Glossary, and a *new and more distinct type than any heretofore employed*, have combined to render the present edition superior to all that have preceded it.

"The Glossary, Sanskrit and English, which Professor Johnson has added, comprises between five and six thousand words, and it might with propriety be called a minor Lexicon, but the indefatigable editor has not been contented with this important addition,—he has subjoined a list of nearly five thousand English words with references to the passages in which their Sanscrit equivalents are to be found, and has thus supplied a want for which until lately no provision had been made,—a reversed Dictionary, English and Sanscrit. With these additions, this new edition of the Hitopadesa cannot fail to afford the most essential facility to the early study of the Sanscrit, the difficulties of which have been greatly lightened by the recent publications of Professor Johnson, and by none more than by his present edition of the Hitopadesa."

2 r

HITOPADEŚA;

TRANSLATED literally into English. By FRANCIS JOHNSON. Imperial 8vo.

AKHLÁK-I MUHSINÍ;

TO which are prefixed a few easy Stories for Beginners. Edited by Lieut.- Colonel OUSELEY. 8vo.

M. GARCIN DE TASSY,
Membre de l'Institut in the "Journal Asiatique."

"Il ne s'agit pas ici, comme on le pense bien, d'une édition complète de *l'Akhlák-Muhsiní*, mais seulement d'une partie de cet ouvrage renommé, partie dont M. Ouseley, Professeur de Persan à Haileybury, a publié le texte à l'usage du Collége. En tête de l'ouvrage, il y a dix historiettes d'un style facile et de sujets connus, destinées à préparer l'élève à lire les morceaux qui suivent. Viennent ensuite vingt chapitres, c'est à-dire environ la moitié de l'ouvrage ; car il se compose de quarante chapitres. On voit par là que cette édition est plus étendue que celle qui fut gravée en 1823, d'après un manuscrit, pour les élèves du même collége, puisque cette derniére impression s'arrête aux deux tiers du quinzième chapitre. C'est de cette première édition que M. Keene a fait une traduction qui vient aussi d'être publiée à Hertford et où il manque ainsi cinque chapitres et un tiers de l'édition de M. Ouseley, ainsi que les historettes du commencement. Au surplus, l'édition de M. Ouseley est très-correcte, qualité essentielle surtout, dans un texte publié pour des étudiants ; et la traduction de M. Keene est littérale et fidèle, comme celle qu'il a donnée du permier chapitre de l' *Anvdr-i Suhaili*. Les publications queje viens de mentionner, ainsi que le *Prem Ságar* et le *Gulistán* dont j'ai parlé dernièrement, l'*Hitopadeśa* du savant M. F. Johnson et tous les ouvrages orientaux qui ont paru à Hertford, pendant ces dernières années, ont été édités par M. Stephen Austin, imprimeur du Collége d'Haileybury. Les savants doivent savoir gré à cet habile typographe du soin avec lequel il a exécuté ces publications, qui se distinguent par la beauté des types orientaux et latins qui y sont employés."

AKHLÁK-I MUHSINÍ;

TRANSLATED literally into English. By the Rev. H. G. KEENE, sometime Professor at the East India College. 2nd edition. 8vo.

SANSKRIT VOCABULARY.

ENGLISH and SANSKRIT VOCABULARY. By E. A. PRINSEP, of the Hon. East-India Company's Civil Service. Royal 8vo.

INDIAN PENAL CODE.

Copy of a Penal Code prepared by the Indian Law Commissioners. roy. 8vo.

JUST PUBLISHED, August, 1854, *(300 pp., Imperial* 16mo.)
By JAMES MADDEN. 8, LEADENHALL STREET, LONDON,

TURKISH READING BOOK,

WITH GRAMMAR and VOCABULARY, and a selection of Original Tales, literally translated, with copious Critical, Explanatory, and Idiomatical Notes, and accompanied by Grammatical References : the pronunciation of each word being given as now used in Constantinople, by WILLIAM BURCKHARDT BARKER, M.R.A.S., Oriental Interpreter, and Professor of the Arabic, Turkish, Persian and Hindústáni Languages at Eton ; Author of "Lares and Penates ;" "Turkish Tales in English," etc. etc.

HERTFORD MERCURY.

"One of the peculiar features of the present times is an increasing tendency to the study of the Asiatic languages, arising out of the more intimate communication into which we have been brought with Asiatic people, by the railway and the steamship ; and the day is, perhaps, not far distant when the Oriental tongues will be considered as necessary a part of the education of a gentleman —certainly of a scholar—as Greek or Latin are, or have been.

* * * * * *

"The Turkish language has, besides the literary interest which it possesses in common with other Asiatic tongues, the additional attraction of being the spoken language of millions of people with whom we are in close alliance, and with whom we shall probably, in future, maintain a nearer intercourse than has before existed between any European and Asiatic nation. The study of Turkish therefore becomes a necessity of the times, and will long continue so when the war which has given the impetus to it has terminated, and the Ottoman nation is definitively introduced into the European family under the protection of the great Powers of the West. Projects for establishing colonies on rich but neglected tracts of the Turkish territory are already entertained, and if these should be carried out, the Turkish language will become as necessary a part of the education of an Englishman as French is now considered. But without speculating on future probabilities, there can be no doubt that greater facilities for acquiring Turkish than have hitherto existed are required; and these facilities are afforded in the work which Mr. Burckhardt Barker has presented to the public.

"Mr. Barker tells us in his preface that—'for a person who aspires to read and write a language with any degree of accuracy, something more is necessary than a superficial knowledge of grammatical rules;' and this 'something else' his grammar helps the student to. 'Simple but necessary forms and rules' are given as a 'foundation for observations of a more critical nature; and are followed by a grammatical analysis of every difficult word,' by which the rules are rendered more familiar; while constant repetition fixes them upon the memory. The book opens with a table showing the power and position of each letter in the alphabet. This is followed by an explanation of the vowel points and signs supplementary to the alphabet, in use among Arab writers. The parts of speech are then treated of, with great fullness and clearness, the table of verbs being extremely complete, and so arranged as to show the conjugations at one view. The chapters on 'Derivation' and 'Syntax' will also greatly facilitate the study of the language. Then we have, further to assist the student, a literal interlinear translation of the first chapter of the Gospel according to St. John, and of the 'Pleasing Tales of Khoja Nasr-il-deen Effendi,' and a vocabulary of nearly 4000 words. . . . . .

"The notes, critical, explanatory, and idiomatical, at the foot of each page contain copious references to the rules of Grammar and Syntax, so that, at every step he takes, the memory of the student is refreshed, and the rules which he has learnt by heart so applied, as to fix them indelibly on his memory. Great advantage will also be derived from the plan which the author has adopted of representing all the oriental characters by Roman letters. . . . We have said enough to show that the Grammar before us has merits which are peculiarly its own; and that it offers such facilities for acquiring the Turkish language, that there is no gentleman who may not in a few months make himself as well acquainted with it, as with any language of Modern Europe."—*August*, 1854.

Lately Published,

By JAMES MADDEN, 8, LEADENHALL STREET, LONDON,

THE AMÍRS OF SINDH;

DRY LEAVES FROM YOUNG EGYPT; with 12 Plates, and a Portrait in Chromo-lithography of Mír Muhammad. By an EX-POLITICAL. Third Edition. Demy 8vo.

DAILY NEWS.

"The volume before us is one of those rare productions; and apart from its literary merits, which are considerable, the quantity of information it contains, makes the publication one of great value to all who take any interest in Indian affairs. The author has a keen sense both of the picturesque and the ludicrous, and there is a raciness and *degagé* air about some of his sketches which put us in mind of 'Eöthen'"

MORNING CHRONICLE.

"A very entertaining and instructive narrative it is."

MORNING HERALD.

"The work is exceedingly well written."

ECONOMIST.

"His descriptions are graphic, and many of the adventures recorded of startling interest."

CRITIC.

"It presents the most graphic description of our lately conquered provinces in the East which has yet come to us."

SPECTATOR.

"A pleasant, lively, and informing volume of travelling observation."

FOUR VIEWS OF THE EAST INDIA COLLEGE,
HAILEYBURY, HERTS.

Drawn on Stone by W. L. WALTON. Imperial 4to.

LARGE VIEW OF THE EAST INDIA COLLEGE
Drawn on Stone by F. W. L. STOCKDALE. Imp. folio.

THE HAILEYBURY OBSERVER:

A MISCELLANY by the STUDENTS of the East India College, from the commencement in 1839 to the end of the first term, 1854, with the Lists of Authors and Editorial Committees. Seven vols. 8vo. (bound in four).

EPISTOLÆ ET EVANGELIA PER TOTUM ANNUM USURPANDA.

Post 8vo. interleaved and bound in purple morocco.

EXCERPTA EX ARRIANO,
With a Translation into English. Post 8vo.

EXCERPTA EX HERODOTO,
With a Translation into English. Post 8vo.

CICERONIS TUSCULANARUM DISPUTATIONUM.
Lib. I. Post 8vo.

EXCERPTA E QUINTO CURTIO,
With a Translation into English. Post 8vo.

FLORA HERTFORDIENSIS:

BEING a CATALOGUE of PLANTS known or reported to GROW WILD in the COUNTY OF HERTFORD, with the Stations of the rarer species. By the Rev. R. H. WEBB, Rector of Essendon; and the Rev. W. H. COLEMAN; assisted by various Correspondents. Demy, 12mo.

STEPHEN AUSTIN, PRINTER, HERTFORD.

41627